The Art of Plato

THE ART OF PLATO

Ten Essays in Platonic Interpretation

R. B. Rutherford

Harvard University Press

Cambridge, Massachusetts

1995

Printed in Great Britain

Library of Congress Cataloging-in-Publication Data

Rutherford, R. B.
  The art of Plato : ten essays in Platonic interpretation / R. B. Rutherford.
    p. cm.
  Includes bibliographical references and index.
  ISBN 0-674-04811-3
  1. Plato. I. Title.
B399.R6R88 1995
184–dc20   94-41991
                                                        CIP

Chapter 5 is reprinted (modified and expanded) with
permission from Andrew Barker and Martin Warner (eds.)
The Language of the Cave (Edmonton, AB: Academic
Printing and Publishing 1992).

To the memory of
David M. Lewis

All the conversations of Socrates have an exceptional quality, and they have the virtues of subtlety, inventiveness, and enthusiasm for enquiry. But perhaps it is not possible to do everything well ...

Aristotle, *Politics* ii. 6

While at Athens, I read the *Gorgias*, and in that work I above all marvelled at Plato because in the very act of mocking the orators he showed himself the supreme orator.

L. Crassus in Cicero's dialogue *On the orator* i. 47

I have felt ever since that the title of Platonist belongs by far better right to those who have been nourished in, and have endeavoured to practise Plato's mode of investigation, than to those who are distinguished only by the adoption of certain dogmatical conclusions, drawn mostly from the least intelligible of his works, and which the character of his mind and writings makes it uncertain whether he himself regarded as anything more than poetic fancies, or philosophic conjectures.

John Stuart Mill, *Autobiography* ch. 1

Contents

Preface

This volume, like my earlier book *The Meditations of Marcus Aurelius: a study* (Oxford 1989), is an attempt to advance the literary understanding of a philosophic writer, without losing sight either of his historical context or of the ethical, religious and other themes which are central to his work. In other words, it tries to say something about both the form and the content of Plato's works, and about the relationship between form and meaning. I am concerned with Plato's portrayal of his master Socrates, with his engagement with the sophists, with the different ways in which his ideas are presented in different dialogues, but also with more strictly literary issues such as his use of rhetoric, irony, poetic style and imagery, as well as with the significance of introductory episodes or passages of description, or the question why an argument should be given to a particular character in one of the dialogues. Anyone who thinks the answers to such questions obvious, or irrelevant to the study of Plato, is advised to close this book and leave it alone.

When I wrote my earlier study of Marcus Aurelius, I had at least the clear justification that no proper study of the *Meditations* existed. With Plato the problem is quite different. The amount of writing which appears every year on his doctrines and dialogues is enormous and shows no sign of abating. The production of yet another book aimed at both academics and the general public can be partially justified by the argument that most books on Plato, even now, are by professional philosophers, and that there is room for more to be said about him as a writer or dramatist. Books which do attempt to tackle that side of his work are often written without much attention to the literary traditions on which Plato was able to draw, or the social and cultural setting in which he grew up (both of these being areas in which classical scholarship has made great progress in the last twenty or thirty years). Nevertheless, I freely admit that not all of what I shall be saying is new, and that amongst the many books and articles which I have not read some of what I say may be said better; but Plato's work is a large enough corpus, and his stature as a writer and a thinker great enough, for a further attempt to illuminate his greatness to need little more apology. My aim throughout the book is to enhance some readers' enjoyment and understanding of at least some of Plato's work.

This book is deliberately subtitled 'essays': it is definitely not intended to be an encyclopaedic or magisterial survey of Plato as a whole. Some of his works, as will swiftly become clear, are barely mentioned. Others, particularly the *Republic*, could only be considered from a limited number of viewpoints. I have deliberately tried to restrict myself to works where I felt I had something to say; moreover, it was not my wish to make this a lifelong work or an unreadable *magnum opus*. Even if I had wished to work on the book for many years longer, I still could not have read anything like all that could be considered relevant. Naturally, I regret not having been able to consider the work of many who are labouring in the same vineyard, but I have begun to feel that more time spent on this book would not necessarily improve it greatly, and it seemed preferable to call a halt and to let others take these questions further. I apologise to those who feel that their contributions to the subject have been unjustly neglected.

In its methodology this book may seem old-fashioned, but if so it is not naively so. I have read a fair amount of modern literary theory, and have sometimes found it helpful; but I admit that the traditional procedures of comparison and analysis, combined with aspects of narratology, seem to me the most fruitful tools. Otherwise I have been eclectic, and there seemed no point in cluttering the footnotes with the names of fashionable pundits. In addition, I know that many who approach Plato from a primarily philosophic point of view feel automatic suspicion when any purely or mainly literary method is employed, and I should prefer not to put them off my work more than they already may be. In particular, I take this opportunity to dissociate myself from the approach to Plato adopted by the late Leo Strauss and his followers, which has had extraordinary influence, especially in America. I have read only one of Strauss's works (*The City and Man*), and have been unable to finish any of the books by his epigoni.

In a book of this size it is inevitable that some things must be omitted. One point which will surprise many, and over which I have long hesitated, is the exclusion of a general summary of Plato's philosophic standpoint. I do not deny that a synthetic picture can be useful, and that some parts of it may be generally agreed; but the trend of my argument is to suggest that Plato's thought was more flexible, his 'doctrines' more fluid, his positive statements through Socrates and others more rhetorically motivated and tied more closely to context, than is normally supposed. Hence a summary of his philosophy would either falsify a complex picture or be so simplistic and qualified as to be entirely banal. For related reasons I have done next to nothing by way of comparison between Plato and other ancient and modern philosophers. Even supposing that I were competent to draw such comparisons, they would inevitably be taken to imply that Plato was a writer in the same tradition and trying to do the same things as later thinkers, whereas I am concerned to stress his links with other genres and styles of writing. Again, the reader will find this gap amply filled by other works, many of which are listed in the bibliography. I have felt much more compunction about the selection of Platonic works treated at length, and particularly regret that space did not allow for a chapter on the *Phaedo*; fortunately Christopher Rowe's recent commentary in the Cambridge Greek and Latin Classics series has made that great work more accessible.

Some may still think the book too long. The chapters are intended as independent essays, though the first chapter attempts to lay the ground, and those which follow naturally pursue a common approach. Some general issues are discussed in connection with a single dialogue (e.g. eschatological myth in the chapter on the *Gorgias*), and I have done my best to minimise repetition of arguments and examples between chapters. Readers wishing to follow up a particular topic such as irony or imagery are advised to make full use of the thematic index. Translations of ancient authors are my own, unless otherwise indicated; in the final chapter I have gratefully made some use of existing translations by Cornford and Saunders for certain passages in the late works.

Although Oxford is full of philosophers, many of whom have an expert knowledge of the text and arguments of Plato's major works, it is not so easy to find other people who are interested in him from the viewpoint I have adopted in this book. I am all the more grateful to Edward Hussey, who did much to get me started through inviting me to collaborate with him in a seminar on 'Philosophy and Literature in the age of the sophists' in 1985, and to Donald Russell, who has always been insistent that the greatest of Greek prose writers must not be left entirely to philosophers. Much of the material in the chapters on the *Protagoras, Gorgias, Symposium* and *Phaedrus* has been tried out in lectures over the last decade, and versions of several chapters have been presented in seminars in Oxford, London, and St Andrews. In 1987 Martha Nussbaum and I organised a joint seminar on the *Phaedrus* in Oxford, which provided further impetus and ideas. A slightly shorter version of the chapter on the *Protagoras* was delivered at the University of Warwick in January 1992, and published in a collection entitled *The Language of the Cave* (= *Apeiron* 25.4 (December 1992)), edited by Andrew Barker and Martin Warner. I am grateful to the editors and publishers for permission to re-use this material here, and to the audiences on all these occasions for their comments.

Nearly fifteen years after his untimely death, it may seem no more than a pupil's piety if I mention my gratitude to Colin Macleod, who first helped me to understand something about Plato's methods and style; but those who also attended his lectures on the *Gorgias* will recognise that I have to a considerable extent been filling in detail in a sketch which he had begun. He read and wrote detailed comments on a very early draft of mine (1980) on the *Phaedrus*, and I have often turned back to those notes with profit. In more recent years, conversation with Stephen Halliwell and Doreen Innes has always been stimulating. I have been helped on many specific points, and encouraged at difficult stages, by Simon Hornblower, Niall Livingstone, Robert Parker and Catherine Whistler. I must also thank two graduate students whose work I have read, David Gribble and Lucinda

Coventry: since the latter's monograph regrettably remains unpublished as I write, it is all the more important that I should make clear that I have benefited from reading her work and from many exchanges. Discussion and argument with another former graduate, Owen White, have helped me to clarify my own position. On the production side, Madeline Littlewood of the Classics Office in Oxford deserves a special word of thanks for retyping several chapters which had been originally prepared in an outmoded word-processing format.

Finally, I should like to thank several colleagues at Christ Church. Hugh Lloyd-Jones originally recommended the book to Colin Haycraft at Duck-worth's, with a readiness which was much appreciated by a young scholar who had at the time still not submitted his doctorate. I hope that he will find some interest in it after so long a wait. Lindsay Judson has read and commented generously on drafts of several chapters, and I have been greatly encouraged to find that such an expert ancient philosopher sees some value in this very different project. Peter Parsons has not only given scholarly advice and allowed me to borrow books and offprints for quite outrageous lengths of time, but has been a tower of strength and benevolent support from my first day in the college. But the last word must be reserved for David Lewis, who died in July 1994, when this book was already with the publisher. Since cancer had been detected nine months earlier, he had faced his illness with a stoical detachment which deeply impressed his friends and colleagues. His death robs ancient history of one of its most distinguished scholars. His scrupulous attention to every type of evidence, and the skill and lucidity with which all the implications, large and small, were explored, are familiar to anyone who has given his work the careful scrutiny which it demands; equally obvious was his concern to see classical Greece as a complex whole, without subdividing the subject between faculties and specialisms. Those who knew him personally will also recall with affection his dry and sometimes quirky sense of humour, his passion for accurate recollection of detail, and the unselfish pleasure with which he listened to others' half-formed ideas and contributed his own penetrating suggestions. Although he did not see any of this book, there are many places where I have drawn on his profound knowledge of classical Athens, and I owe him a more particular debt for much enlightenment over matters concerning Plato, Dionysius and Sicily. He gave his permission for the book to be dedicated to him at a time when we both knew he was unlikely to see the finished product. I only wish it were worthier of him.

R.B.R.

Abbreviations and Short Titles

Names of classical authors are abbreviated according to accepted conventions (see e.g. LSJ xvi-xxxviii). Note esp. that 'Ar.' = Aristophanes, 'Arist.' = Aristotle. Titles of works have been anglicised wherever possible: hence e.g. Plato's *Statesman* (not *Politicus*).

Abbreviated titles for works of Plato

IAlc. = *Alcibiades* I (also called *Greater Alcibiades*)
Ap. = *Apology*
Charm. = *Charmides*
Clit. = *Clitopho*
Crat. = *Cratylus*
Crit. = *Critias* (*Crito* is given in full)
Grg. = *Gorgias*
Hipp. Mai., *Hipp. Min.* = *Greater Hippias, Lesser Hippias*
Lach. = *Laches*
Mnx. = *Menexenus*
Parm. = *Parmenides*
Phdr. = *Phaedrus*
Phil. = *Philebus*
Prt. = *Protagoras*
Rep. = *Republic*
Smp. = *Symposium*
Soph. = *Sophist*
Tht. = *Theaetetus*
Tim. = *Timaeus*

Other titles are given in full.

Other shortened titles

AJP = *American Journal of Philology*
Anc. Philos. = *Ancient Philosophy*
APF = J.K. Davies, *Athenian Propertied Families 600-300 B.C.* (Oxford 1971)
BICS = *Bulletin of the Institute of Classical Studies* (London)

C&M = *Classica et Medievalia*

CAH v² and vi² = *Cambridge Ancient History* (new 2nd edn.), vol. v (ed. D.M. Lewis, J. Boardman, J.K. Davies, M. Ostwald, 1992) and vol. vi (ed. D.M. Lewis, J. Boardman, S. Hornblower, M. Ostwald, 1994)

CAntiq = *Classical Antiquity* (formerly *California Studies in Classical Antiquity*)

CPh = *Classical Philology*

CQ = *Classical Quarterly*

CR = *Classical Review*

Diels-Kranz or D-K = H. Diels and W. Kranz, *Die Fragmente der Vorsokratiker*, 6th edn., Berlin 1951-4)

Dover, *GPM* = K. J. Dover, *Greek Popular Morality in the Time of Plato and Aristotle* (Oxford 1974)

F or fr. = fragment no.

FGH = F. Jacoby, *Die Fragmente der griechischen Historiker* (Berlin and Leipzig 1992-)

Friedlaender = P. Friedlaender, *Plato* (Eng. tr. by H. Meyerhoff) (New York 1958-69)

G&R = *Greece and Rome*

GRBS = *Greek Roman and Byzantine Studies*

Guthrie = W.K.C. Guthrie, *History of Greek Philosophy* i-vi (Cambridge 1962-81)

HCT = A.W. Gomme, A. Andrewes, K.J. Dover, *Historical Commentary on Thucydides* (5 vols., Oxford 1945-81)

HSCP = *Harvard Studies in Classical Philology*

ICS = *Illinois Classical Studies*

JHI = *Journal of the History of Ideas*

JHPhil = *Journal of the History of Philosophy*

JHS = *Journal of Hellenic Studies*

K-A = R. Kassel and C. Austin, *Poetae Comici Graeci* (Berlin and New York 1983-)

KRS = G.S. Kirk, J.E. Raven, M. Schofield, *The Presocratic Philosophers* (2nd edn., Cambridge 1983)

Laborderie = J. Laborderie, *Le dialogue platonicien de la maturité* (Paris 1978)

LSJ = H.G. Liddell, R. Scott, H.S. Jones, *A Greek-English Lexicon* (9th edn., Oxford 1940; with Supplement 1968)

OCD = *Oxford Classical Dictionary* 2nd edn., ed. N.G.L. Hammond and H.H. Scullard (Oxford 1970). A complete revision is imminent, ed. by S. Hornblower and A.J. Spawforth.

OCT = Oxford Classical Text

OSAP = *Oxford Studies in Ancient Philosophy*

PACA = *Proceedings of the African Classical Associations*

PBA = *Proceedings of the British Academy*

POxy. = *The Oxyrhynchus Papyri* (ed. B.P. Grenfell and others, London 1898-)

PCPS = *Proceedings of the Cambridge Philological Society*

PMG = D.L. Page, *Poetae Melici Graeci* (Oxford 1962)

Radermacher = L. Radermacher, *Artium Scriptores (Reste der voraristotelischen Rhetorik), Österreichische Akademie der Wissenschaften, Phil.-hist. Klasse*, 227. 3 (Vienna 1951)

RE = Pauly, Wissowa, Kroll and others, *Real-Encyclopädie der klassischen Altertumswissenschaft* (Stuttgart 1893-).

REG = *Revue des Etudes Grecques*

RhM = *Rheinisches Museum*

Riginos = A.S. Riginos, *Platonica: The Anecdotes Concerning the Life and Writings of Plato* (Leiden 1976)

SO = *Symbolae Osloenses*

TAPA = *Transactions of the American Philological Association*

WS = *Wiener Studien*

YCS = *Yale Classical Studies*

Zeller = E. Zeller, *Plato and the Older Academy* (Eng. tr. by S.F. Alleyne and A. Goodwin) (London 1888)

ZPE = *Zeitschrift für Papyrologie und Epigraphik*

Style of reference to Platonic texts

It is a long-established convention to refer to the Platonic works by page, section and line of the edition published by Henri Estienne (Latinised as 'Stephanus') in 1578. This has disadvantages, but any attempt to change practice now would cause chaos. Each page is divided into five sections (a-e), and each section runs to about 12 lines. It is important to realise that these divisions are purely of length, and have nothing to do with the sequence of thought. Modern translations usually give at least the page numbers, and the much-used compendium by Hamilton and Cairns includes section divisions too; for the exact reference to a particular line the reader has to turn to the Greek text.

1

Problems and Approaches

In the seventh, longest and most important of the letters which survive from antiquity under Plato's name, the author presents a fairly full account of how he came to be disillusioned with the politics of his time and turned to philosophy, under the influence of Socrates. He also gives a detailed narrative of the failure of his efforts to turn Dionysius II of Syracuse into a philosopher-king. At the heart of the letter he passes caustic judgement on a written handbook which has been produced by Dionysius on the subjects of Plato's instruction, and extends his criticism to others who have tried to summarise his teaching. The emphasis and eloquence with which he dismisses any such attempts have made this one of the best-known, but also most puzzling, passages in the Platonic corpus.

> I can say this much, at any rate, about all those who have written or intend to write, claiming knowledge of the subjects which are my concern, whether they maintain they have heard it from me or others, or that they have discovered it themselves: it is impossible, in my opinion at least, that these men know anything about the subject. No writing of mine exists on these subjects nor ever could exist; for this is not something that can be put into words like other teachings, but only when there has been long association and involvement with the subject, living together, then, as light is kindled from a fire as it blazes up, so it is born in the soul and at once nourishes itself there. Yet I know this much, that these matters, whether written down or spoken, would be best coming from me. I am injured not least because they are written down ill. But if I thought it was possible for them to be written down adequately for the multitude and voiced in words, what nobler task could I have spent my life upon than to write down what would bring great benefit to mankind, and to bring to light the nature of the world for all to see? (*Letter vii* 341b-d)

It must at once be admitted that some at least of the 'Platonic' letters are certainly spurious, and that the authenticity of the seventh too has been doubted on serious grounds, both historical and philosophical; nor have these doubts been treated as seriously as they deserve in some recent accounts of Plato, which naturally draw heavily on the letter for biographical data.[1] But what still needs to be said is that whether or not these words

---

[1] See esp. L. Edelstein, *Plato's Seventh Letter* (Leiden 1966), with F. Solmsen's review in *Gnomon* 41 (1969) 29-34. See also the papers by Gulley and Aalders in *Pseudepigrapha*, Fond. Hardt Entr. 18 (1972), and P.A. Brunt, *Studies in Greek History and Thought* (Oxford 1994) 282-342, esp. 313-32.

were written by Plato, they are an extraordinary statement by or about
the author of the dialogues, and they pose a serious question to any reader
of Plato's work: if, as the Seventh Letter declares, there is no written
statement of Plato's doctrines and theories, no philosophical manual of
Platonism, then how are we supposed to regard the dialogues and their
conclusions about justice and self-restraint, art and poetry, politics and
society, law and nature, life and after-life?

Nor is this question dependent solely on a brief passage in a possibly
spurious letter: for that passage is paralleled and at greater length in the
final scenes of the *Phaedrus*, unquestionably a genuine work of Plato and
one of his richest and most ornate dialogues. There Socrates, true to his
own historical personality (for as far as we know he wrote nothing), is
shown as rejecting and criticising the written word. He disparages the
medium which preserves a permanent written record of any kind of wisdom, on the grounds that only the living word, the process of verbal
dialectic, can offer the opportunity of further questioning and true learning
(*Phdr.* 275c-8b).[2] If this is so, what becomes of the richly-wrought, highly
sophisticated written work which we have almost finished reading, and
what insight or understanding remains after this skilled undercutting?
Obviously, the dialogue form is intended to mimic Socratic conversation,
to recapture something of the freshness and openness of oral discussion;
but the *Phaedrus* and the other dialogues remain books: they cannot be or
duplicate dialectic. In this passage and others like it Plato presents the
interpreter with a paradox and a challenge. Readers of Plato have an
obligation to respond to this challenge: since the author clearly wrote and
thought so much about the methodology of his philosophic teaching, we too
must make an effort to learn how to read him appropriately.

The rest of this chapter will consider a number of approaches to Plato,
and will outline the approach adopted in this book. It is not intended to rule
out other ways of reading so rich and complex an author, or to deny the
value of approaches not even discussed here. But I hope that some of the
problems raised may shed light on what Plato is, and is not, trying to do in
the dialogues, and that the more positive suggestions may lay a foundation
for the readings offered in later chapters. The *Apology* of Socrates, Plato's
version of his teacher's speech in self-defence, is the one work which is not
a dialogue, and presents rather different problems; it is discussed in the
last section of this chapter.

Corpus and chronology

We must begin from the writings of Plato himself, the body of work which
fills five volumes of the standard Oxford text. We are fortunate in that,
such was his fame and literary influence, all his known writings seem to

---

[2] It can be argued, however, that the *Phaedrus* does not go quite as far as the Letter: see e.g.
Kraut, *Companion* 20-2, and cf. ch. 9, below. The paradox is diminished but not expelled.

have come down to us: no evidence attests other works published but lost in the period of transmission.[3] But two problems immediately arise, the question of authenticity (is everything we have really by Plato?) and the question of relative chronology. Both may have serious repercussions for our view of Plato. On the former, widely varying views have been held, and most of the dialogues have been questioned at one time or another (the *Letters*, as already indicated, are a very different matter and form a special category of their own). But scholars are now more prudent in their judgements, and none of the major dialogues has been suspected for many years, though there is general agreement that a group of short works, some of which show clear influence from later schools of philosophy, are unPlatonic: these are segregated at the end of most editions and boldly but probably rightly designated 'Spuria'. They will not be considered in this book. Arguments concerning authenticity are often conducted on a highly technical level, but such analysis is rarely clear-cut; ultimately, whatever the details of style and verbal usage, the decision that a given author simply could not have written a specific work rests on the critic's sense of the author's range, aims and merits. Of the dialogues discussed at any length in this book only the *Clitopho* is a serious candidate for expulsion from the canon; of those referred to more briefly, doubts can reasonably be expressed about the two dialogues named *Alcibiades* and the *Theages*. But no conclusion reached here would be seriously affected if these works were proved spurious.

The problem of chronology is a more serious one, as it affects all the surviving works, authentic or otherwise. It is argued below that the best approach to Plato is to treat each dialogue as essentially self-contained, an independent literary artefact which does not build on its predecessors or form part of a larger structure or 'course' in philosophy. If this is correct, the importance of chronology is diminished but not removed: quite apart from the philosopher's interest in pursuing the development of a given topic in different places, the literary critic too may well find it helpful to trace the development of a particular technique or stylistic feature from 'early' Plato onwards, and such comparison is inhibited if we lack a basic chronological framework. In the end agnosticism may be the safest approach, but here a moderate form of the 'standard' chronology is adopted, and some explanation of its basis is necessary.[4]

[3] Cf. e.g. Zeller 45-9, Guthrie iv. 39-41. The fact that the *Critias* is unfinished is generally taken to mean that the project was abandoned; there is no evidence that more of it was ever known. Publication of unfinished works is readily paralleled in ancient times (e.g. Thucydides' *History*, Lucan's *de bello civili*, or in a different way Virgil's *Aeneid*). I set aside consideration of the so-called 'unwritten doctrines'; see Appendix B.

[4] Cf. Appendix A. For fuller discussion of chronological issues see Guthrie iv, ch. 2; H. Thesleff, *Studies in Platonic Chronology* (Helsinki 1982), with addenda in *Phronesis* 34 (1989) 1-26; L. Brandwood, *The Chronology of Plato's Dialogues* (Cambridge 1990) and more briefly in Kraut, *Cambridge Companion to Plato* (1992) 90-120; Ledger, *Recounting Plato* (Oxford 1989), esp. 224-5 (table of conclusions). For more specific studies see C. Kahn, *OSAP* 6 (1988) 69-102 (on *Protagoras* and *Gorgias*); M.L. McPherran, *OSAP* 8 (1990) 211-36; J.D. Moore,

A fundamental distinction must be made between absolute chronology and relative chronology. The former concerns the actual date of composition or publication (we have no way of determining whether these were always identical), the latter concerns the chronological relationship of individual dialogues. Clearly, if we had absolute dates for all Plato's works we would be completely apprised also of the relative chronology; but as things are, relative chronology (and often only a guess at this) may be the best we can do. Plato had a lengthy career: he was born in 428/7 BC and died in 348/7. It seems unlikely that he wrote anything before Socrates' death in 399, and some of the dialogues normally taken to be early concern his teacher's trial and death or have some relation to that event, or some apologetic purpose. This applies especially to the *Euthyphro*, *Apology* and *Crito*.

Internal evidence places some works: anachronistic references in the *Menexenus* fix its date of composition after 386, and an anachronism in the *Symposium* (193a) fixes that dialogue after 385. The *Meno* seems to be post-395 in view of a historical reference in 90a (though most critics would put it a good deal later on other grounds). If the fighting referred to in the opening pages of the *Theaetetus* is correctly identified as having taken place in 369, then we have a clear *terminus post quem* for that work as well. The *Laws* includes a reference to the conquest of Locri by Syracuse, usually taken to be a reference to 356 or even 352 (i. 638b). This fits well with the ancient tradition that the *Laws* was the last work of Plato, composed when he was already an old man.[5]

In a different category come cross-references from one dialogue to another. There is an amusing passage in the *Phaedo* where Socrates' friend Cebes mentions 'the theory you're always putting forward, that our learning is actually nothing but recollection; according to that too, if it's true, what we are now reminded of we must have learned at some former time.' Simmias intervenes with a request for a recapitulation of the proofs of this theory, 'as I don't recall them very well at the moment' – apparently a sly joke on the theme of recollection! (*Phaedo* 72e-73a) This seems to be a reference to the Meno, since Cebes goes on to remind him how people can be shown to 'know' the answer to problems involving diagrams and calculations if they are asked questions in the right way – a good generalised description of the experiment conducted with the slave in that dialogue. A rather similar though less obvious cross-reference can be found at *Phaedrus*

GRBS 15 (1974) 421-39 (on *Ion*), and in *Patterns in Plato's Thought* ed. J.M.E. Moravcsik (Dordrecht 1973) 52-71 (on *Symposium* and *Phaedrus*); E. Kapp, *Ausgewählte Schriften* (Berlin 1968), esp. 60-1, 90, 115 (arguing for the priority of *Phaedo* to *Symposium*). An ultra-sceptical approach to these matters is adopted by J. Howland, *Phoenix* 45 (1981) 189-214.

[5] W. Oldfather, *AJP* 44 (1923) 275-6 on the date. For the ancient testimonies see e.g. Arist. *Pol.* 1264b26 (later than the *Republic*), Plut. *Is. Os.* 370F (later than the *Timaeus*), Diog. Laert. iii. 37 (who says the work was unfinished at Plato's death). See further L. Tarán, *Academica* (Leiden 1972) 116, 128ff.

260e, where Socrates says that he seems to hear certain arguments in the offing, which will convince them that rhetoric is not an art: although he goes on to paraphrase them, the language and the emphasis perhaps suggests that this is an allusion to the fuller argument of this case in the *Gorgias* (cf. 260e5 with *Grg.* 463b, 501a). Less certain still, perhaps, is a passage in the tenth book of the *Republic* which *may* allude to the arguments for immortality in the *Phaedo* (x. 611b: 'that the soul is immortal our recent argument and *our other proofs* would constrain us to admit.').[6] More explicitly, notable passages in the *Theaetetus* and the *Sophist* seem to refer back to the *Parmenides* (*Tht.* 183e sq.; *Soph.* 217c). The *Theaetetus* also includes what may be a reference to the *Cratylus* (155d4 with *Crat.* 398d, 408b). The *Timaeus* opens with a curiously selective and slanted yet unmistakable backward reference to the discussion in the *Republic*. The *Sophist*, the *Statesman* and the unwritten *Philosopher* were intended to form a 'trilogy' (see *Soph.* 217a3), just as the *Timaeus* and *Critias* were planned as the first two of a sequence to be completed by the unwritten *Hermocrates*. There are also a number of passages in the *Laws* which refer to the constitution laid out there as a second-best (e.g. 739 throughout; 807b). It is natural to ask 'second-best to what', and indeed the Athenian tells us enough of what that better society would look like for us to recognise the state of the *Republic*. As we have seen, there were other reasons to suppose the *Laws* a later work than the *Republic*.[7]

Much of this can hardly be digested at first sight, but it will be apparent that there are still many dialogues unaccounted-for. We cannot easily say, for example, whether *Symposium* is earlier than *Phaedrus* or vice versa (the former seems more likely); we do not know how either relates to the *Phaedo* or the *Republic*; and a whole string of dialogues conventionally labelled early must float in a kind of chronological limbo in the broad range of 399-375 or so. Although there are also some indications of the relationship of certain dialogues to the works of other fourth-century writers, this is less helpful than we might hope because their writings too are often hard to pin down. Thus the *Menexenus* probably postdates Thucydides' *History*, but we have no other evidence for that great work's appearance before 386 anyway;[8] Plato's *Laws* 694c is evidently a dig at Xenophon's *Education of Cyrus*, but that too tells us nothing very helpful. Clearly, a rigorous chronology of Plato cannot be achieved by the scrutiny of particular allu-

[6] See S. Halliwell's commentary ad loc., who, however, also cites passages from the *Meno* and the *Phaedrus*.

[7] See further Zeller 96, 138. The *Laws* (iv. 713c sq.) also seems to allude to the *Statesman* (271d sq.): Zeller, 68, 70.

[8] The date of Lysias 2, which does make use of Thucydides' first book, is far from certain: 392 is a popular date, but any time in the Corinthian War (392-86 BC) is possible; and see K.J. Dover, *Lysias and the Corpus Lysiacum* (Berkeley 1968), 194, for agnosticism on the authorship of this speech. The Sicilian historian Philistus certainly imitated Thucydides, but may not have begun his history until his period of exile (386-367) (*FGH* 556 T5a, 13a).

sions; nor would the more rigorous sceptic accept even so modest a list of cross-references as this.

Other approaches have been adopted to reinforce the loose structure described above. One approach which has often been followed is to examine the development of Plato's 'philosophy' and chart the chronology of his work in terms of his progress. This method is fraught with uncertainties: how do we know how straight a line Plato's development followed? Why should we assume that he has abandoned a theory because it is not mentioned in a given dialogue? More will be said of this in connection with the debate about the unity or development of Plato's thought; but here, from the chronological point of view, it will be enough to single out one case, perhaps the most certain. In the *Phaedo*, *Republic* and elsewhere Plato makes Socrates attach very great importance to the so-called Theory of Forms; but in the *Parmenides* this theory, expounded again by Socrates (a youthful Socrates, however) is subjected to very severe criticisms from Parmenides of a kind not aired in those other dialogues. It seems hard to believe that the critique came first, the confident statement of the theory afterwards. Consequently, most scholars put the *Parmenides* after the dialogues in which the Theory of Forms is presented without serious reservations. The argument seems persuasive, though again the sceptic could find fault with its premises.

The other important approach is known as stylometry. By this is meant the analysis of trends in the author's style and use of words, particularly at the very small-scale level of 'routine' phrases, grammatical constructions, use of particles and conjunctions, and so forth – choices frequent enough to give a significant statistical sample and trivial enough to be (probably) almost unconscious. Pioneered by devoted editors with the aid of lexica and repeated reading, the method has naturally gained in momentum and efficiency with the advent of the computer age. The difficulty is, of course, that different critics may disagree on the significance of a given test; also, it is hardly possible to define the relationship between conscious choices by the author, motivated by the particular needs of a given scene or a specific work, and unconscious development of stylistic trends. It is a further assumption that these developing trends follow a clear and measurable linear development, as opposed to fluctuating in a less easily charted manner. However, some interesting results have been reached by this method, in particular as regards the 'late' works of Plato. Accepting the tradition that the *Laws* is the product of his final years, analysts have measured the degree to which other works resemble the *Laws* in vocabulary and other stylistic traits. There is considerable agreement that the *Sophist*, *Statesman*, *Timaeus*, *Critias* and *Philebus* come late in Plato's career, and it is encouraging that this conclusion accords well with arguments on independent grounds of literary form and subject matter. But considerable agreement is not the same as universal agreement, and where various tests or methods differ in their results it seems unwise to rest too much on stylometric techniques alone. Here if anywhere the warning allegedly inscribed above the entrance to the original Academy may be invoked: 'let no one who is unversed in mathematics enter here.'[9]

The dialogue as a critical problem

To some degree the problems of authenticity and chronology resemble questions which we face everywhere in the study of Greek literature, or indeed other literatures. Thus many critics have questioned the ascription of the *Rhesus*, a relatively undistinguished work, to Euripides, and more controversially the *Prometheus Bound* has recently been denied to Aeschylus. Again, stylistic analysis of Euripides' metrical technique has shed some light on chronology (here we are helped by the fact that a good many of his plays are firmly dated by other means, and so provide an unambiguous framework for further enquiry).[10] But the works of Plato also offer special problems of their own, many of which arise from the choice of dramatic dialogue form. We cannot simply say that Plato is a philosopher or a theorist when his writings owe so much to literature. Is he the first serious academic philosopher or a new kind of dramatist? We may contrast the practice of Aristotle or Cicero, Berkeley or Hume, all of whom wrote treatises as well as dialogues. Plato wrote *only* dialogues (the *Letters* apart): the only real exception is the *Apology*, a version of Socrates' defence speech at the trial in 399 (and even there, Socrates does his best to convert part of the proceedings into a dialogue with his accuser Meletus).

The *Apology* shares one central feature with the dialogues: the invisibility of the author. Plato himself never appears as a participant in his own works:[11] he is mentioned in them only twice, as present in the court at Socrates' trial and as absent, unwell, at the time of his master's death (*Ap.* 34a, *Phaedo* 59b). It is hard to suppose that this is to be explained solely by modesty, still less by chronological conscientiousness.[12] Plato, it is true, was born too late to know Socrates in his prime, but although he could not have been present at an encounter with Protagoras in the 430s, and was probably still too young to have attended Agathon's sympotic party in 416, he could easily have narrated, or presented himself playing a part in, some conversation of Socrates' final years. Instead he prefers to remain behind the scenes, a dramatist rather than a character or even a commentator. Socrates is the central figure for most of the dialogues, though in some

---

[9] For ancient references to this alleged warning see Zeller 21-2 n. 41.

[10] W. Ritchie, *The Authenticity of the Rhesus of Euripides* (Cambridge 1964), M. Griffith, *The Authenticity of the Prometheus Bound* (Cambridge 1977); M. Cropp and G. Fick, *Resolutions and Chronology in Euripides* (*BICS* Suppl. 43, London 1985) with earlier bibliography.

[11] L. Edelstein, *AJP* 83 (1962) 1-22. It is intriguing to find that Aristotle's practice in his lost dialogues was different: see Cic. *Att.* xiii. 19. 3-4, *QF* iii. 5. 1.

[12] As we have already had reason to observe, Plato is not averse to anachronism. See E. Zeller, *Abhandlungen der Berliner Akad., Phil.-hist. Kl.* (1873) 79-99.

probably late works (such as the *Timaeus*) the lead and the central expository role is taken by others, or he is shown as a young man and subordinated
to other thinkers. Thus in the *Parmenides* the younger Socrates, as
already mentioned, is discomfited by Parmenides' powerful arguments;
in the *Sophist* and *Statesman* Socrates is present but plays only a minor
role, the lead being taken by a 'stranger' or 'foreigner', described as
coming from Elea and belonging to the school of Parmenides and Zeno.
Clearly it would be implausible to see this visitor as representing the
Athenian Plato. Finally, in the *Laws*, there is no place for Socrates at
all: the dialogue is conducted by an 'Athenian stranger', who is never
named, a Cretan and a Spartan (the last two are named). It is naturally
tempting to identify this last stranger with Plato, but the equation
should not be taken for granted. Even if it is allowed, we can see that
there are considerable difficulties, given this range of different dialogue
techniques, in determining 'Plato's theory' or defining Plato's position
on the points discussed. Certainly we must not assume too hastily, as is
often done, that Plato simply uses Socrates as his mouthpiece, or even
that Plato endorses everything that Socrates says (a position which
leads to considerable difficulties in the interpretation of the *Protagoras*,
to name only one case).

Inevitably the reader must ask why Plato chose to write in dialogue form
at all. Such questions can never be answered with certainty, but we can at
least observe some of the opportunities which such a form offered. One
obvious advantage is the vividness and sense of immediacy that the form
allows: it enables him to recapture the atmosphere and intellectual pleasure of Socrates' company, and also to preserve the memory of the kind of
man Socrates was: eccentric, amusing, ingenious, playful, maddening,
physically grotesque – an extraordinary individual. In lesser degree this
also applies to the other friends and notable figures of the Socratic circle,
such as Alcibiades in various dialogues, Nicias and Laches in the *Laches*,
Theaetetus in the dialogue of that name – not all of them known personally
to Plato, however. Closely related to this reason is another, broader and
perhaps more significant: the dialogue form makes the discussion more
entertaining, more amusing, and lures the reader on. Philosophy presented
in this way is more accessible, more enticing, than formally presented
system-building or *ex cathedra* exposition. Many of the Pre-Socratic writers
had adopted a tone of authority, dispensing their wisdom to lesser mortals
in memorable but often oracular style (Heraclitus), or as the insight of an
inspired being (Empedocles); others had presented tight but teasing arguments (Zeno), but without much human warmth. Plato took a different
route to wisdom. Some of the dialogues end with the problem raised but
unresolved – that is, they conclude in *aporia*, perplexity, with no way out
found. Hence they are often referred to as aporetic dialogues (e.g. *Euthyphro*, *Laches*, *Charmides*, *Lysis*). These exploratory and inconclusive but
intriguing discussions may be seen as more an invitation or 'protreptic'

(exhortation) to philosophy, rather than philosophy itself.[13] Thirdly, the dialogue form enables Plato to avoid the appearance of dogmatism and to encourage independent thinking. This is surely central: the dialogues present different people expressing different views, and often these views clash and conflict. Since Plato does not intervene in person to arbitrate or sum up, at the very least the reader needs to assess the advances made in the course of the dialogue. Sometimes, when both or all the participants are baffled or dissatisfied, there is a strong implication that more work needs to be done. At other times, the reader's participation may be invited at an interim stage: we may have to consider the path not taken, or reconsider the answer too readily discarded. The situation may differ from dialogue to dialogue: in a work such as the *Hippias Minor* or the *Ion*, the conversation is informal and the arguments clearly lightweight, whereas it is difficult to suppose that the *Theaetetus*, even if it ends in *aporia*, does not represent a good deal of Plato's hardest thinking about knowledge – here, if anywhere, the reader must learn from and build upon the actual discussion.[14] 'Dialectic', a term based on the Greek word for 'conversation', 'discussion', is of the essence. Socrates in Plato extends and exalts oral exchange into a method, *the* method: it is by argument and mutual criticism that one must arrive at the truth.

In adopting this practice in his writings, Plato is in all likelihood faithful to the historical Socrates' own example. Socrates, as far as we know, never wrote anything; it was Plato and other disciples (Xenophon is the most notable; there were others, e.g. Aeschines of Sphettus, Glaucon etc.) who wrote down records of his conversations. In several passages of Plato, as we have seen, Socrates expresses reservations about the written word: books, he complains, cannot answer questions or clarify difficulties felt by their readers. Socrates' characteristic mode of activity is *oral* discussion. In the *Apology*, Plato has him tell the jury that he spends his days questioning and conversing with men in all walks of life: politicians, poets, craftsmen, 'young or old, foreigner or fellow-citizen' (21-2, 30a). Moreover, it is typical of him in Plato's dialogues to concentrate on individual inter-locutors, with whom he can carry on a dialectical discussion. He often claims, in fact, to be ill-equipped for any more ambitious form of debate. Indeed, attention to the individual opponent or dialectical partner is an important part of Socrates' method: the other characters in the dialogues have their own personalities, their personal axes to grind (professional pride, social standing, seniority of age). Hence the characterisation of the

---

[13] See further K. Gaiser, *Protreptik und Paränese bei Platon* (Stuttgart 1959). Even in a complex dialogue like the *Statesman*, it is remarked that the discussion is at least as much intended to make the participants 'more skilled at discussion' (*dialektikoterois*) as to reach a conclusion about the particular issue under consideration (285cd, cf. 286de).

[14] See further M. Burnyeat's introductory essay in Levett's translation of the *Theaetetus* (Hackett, Indianapolis 1990).

participants, above all the eccentric and infuriating personality of Socrates himself, are not mere additional icing on the cake, sugar on the philosophic pill.[15] Character is relevant to ethics: more precisely, to the kind of argument a participant puts forward and also to how well he stands up under Socratic questioning.

The dialogue form, then, is central to Platonic interpretation. But what exactly was this form, and how was it developed by Plato? Here literary history can make some contribution, in particular by showing that Plato's chief affinities as a writer are not with philosophic predecessors such as Anaxagoras or Cratylus, but with the incomparably richer and more stylistically brilliant world of Attic drama; other lively and entertaining genres such as anecdotal biography also make a contribution. No reading of Plato can be complete if it neglects the artistry and versatility with which he uses a relatively novel, and still developing, literary form.

The literary origins of Platonic dialogue

It is rare for the modern reader to be able to study a classical genre from its origins: for the most part, whether through the selection process of ancient librarians and critics or as a result of the accidents of time and chance, we normally have before us the central works which form the crowning achievement of a given tradition. This is most obviously the case with Greek tragedy and historiography, or Roman epic and elegy. The same reservations apply to the dialogue tradition.[16] The background to the Platonic dialogues as we have them can be considered from two directions: one, which has on the whole rather little to offer because of the gaps in our evidence, is to scrutinise references in the ancient sources to possible early authors of dialogue; the other is to consider what literary traditions may have contributed to the form as we see it in Xenophon and Plato. We have to accept that exact quantification of the debt to particular authors or sub-genres will remain impracticable. A further refinement is to enquire which writer first composed *Socratic* dialogues – Plato, Xenophon or other Socratic pupils? The evidence is hardly sufficient to answer this last question even tentatively: some points relating to the lesser Socratics will be discussed in the next chapter, but here we are considering the origins of dialogue generally.

One passage which has been prominent in discussions that pursue the first approach is a brief statement in Diogenes Laertius, referring to earlier authorities. 'People say that Zeno of Elea was the first to write dialogues. But Aristotle in book 1 of his "On Poets" says it was Alexamenos of Styros or Teos, and the same is said by Favorinus in his "Reminiscences". But

[15] For this image cf. Lucr. i. 933ff., Hor. *Sat.* i.1. 25ff.
[16] See generally R. Hirzel, *Der Dialog* (Leipzig 1895); more recent discussions include Laborderie, *Le dialogue platonicien de la maturité* (1978) ch. 1 and Thesleff, *Studies in Platonic Chronology* 53-64.

Plato, who brought the form to perfection, seems to me justly to carry away the prize for its invention as well as for its beauty.' (Diog. Laert. iii. 48= Arist. fr. 72 Rose). Alexamenos is a ghostly figure, about whom we know literally nothing else;[17] Zeno is a far more substantial thinker, but testimony about his work does not yield any more substantial statement about his writing in *dialogue* (he is elsewhere shown to have been interested in question-and-answer or 'dialectic', but that surely is a matter of argumentative method, not of literary form).[18] The admiring verdict awarding primacy to Plato clearly rests on no independent information, and expresses an evaluation rather than a serious argument. Modern scholars have often followed Diogenes' lead, but it should be obvious that we do not diminish Plato's genius by allowing that he may have had predecessors: the same might be said of Homer and Shakespeare.[19]

Three areas in earlier literature merit more sustained attention: the 'dialectical' dialogues of a more intellectual or exploratory nature in Athenian drama (naturally tragedy is most prominent here);[20] the antithetical and antagonistic forms developed by the sophists, and more particularly the use of mythical dialogue by Hippias and Prodicus for moral instruction; and, finally, the more anecdotal and informal writings of Stesimbrotus of Thasos and especially Ion of Chios, both writing in the mid-to-late fifth century.

Drama, particularly Athenian drama, involves dialogue – of an often highly emotional but also often acutely intelligent and precise kind. It is not accidental that in popular opinion, as reflected in comedy, Socrates was associated with Euripides: they shared a concern for verbal analysis, sceptical enquiry, and fast-moving question and answer. The 'agon' or contest-scene in tragedy (not only in Euripides) presents the antagonists criticising and attacking each other's position, often in highly abstract terms, in long rhetorical speeches of a kind deplored by Socrates in Plato but sometimes adopted by his opponents. More relevant to Socrates' own preferred practice is the shorter exchange, often in 'stichomythia' (usually one-line cut-and-thrust between two speakers). Although occasionally developed to a degree which we find artificial, this device brilliantly captures both the delicacy of tactful exploration of another's painful thoughts or experiences, and the rapidity of an interrogator's reactions when seeking

[17] POxy xlv. 3219, ed. M. Haslam (cf. Haslam, *BICS* 19 (1972) 17-38), gives us some further scrappy evidence for the controversy concerning him in antiquity: the anonymous author accuses Aristotle of malice in ascribing priority to Alexamenos, and attributes Plato's dramatic gifts to imitation of Sophron (see below).
[18] Cf. Kirk-Raven-Schofield, *The Presocratic Philosophers* (Cambridge 1983), 264-5, 278-9.
[19] Dialogue seen as Platonic creation by W. Jaeger, *Paideia* (Eng. tr. Oxford 1939-45) ii. 19, Wilamowitz, *Platon* (2nd edn., 1920) ii. 20-31; necessary distinctions drawn e.g. by A. Lesky, *Hist. of Greek Literature* (Eng. tr. London 1966) 513 (cf. Zeller 155).
[20] On comedy see esp. R. Brock, in *Owls to Athens* (Fest. Sir Kenneth Dover), ed. E.W. Craik (Oxford 1990) 39-49, an admirably concise and meaty paper. Some general remarks by Irwin in Kraut, *Companion*, 73ff.

out weakness, pursuing guilt, or hunting down error.[21] Good examples in Euripides are the so-called 'psychotherapy'-scene in the *Bacchae* (1259-1301), the dialogue between Theseus and Heracles in the play named after the latter (1109-45, 1229-49), and the interchange between Creusa and her unrecognised son in the *Ion* (255-368), in which the two take turns as questioners, and gradually learn about each other, sensing an affinity they cannot yet explain. We shall see that the biographical anecdotes which tell us of Plato's youthful efforts at tragedy are unlikely to preserve authentic tradition, but that does not mean that he was unaware of or unable to learn from tragic drama; indeed, he constantly refers to the tragic poets throughout his career, and shows a deep knowledge of their art and concern for its social impact.[22] In some passages he goes beyond quotation and allusion to larger imitation, especially in the agonistic core of the *Gorgias* (p. 167 below).

Already in the third century a historian could assert that Plato had a particular affection for Sophron, a Syracusan writer of dramatic mimes, seemingly in prose.[23] Here we must be more cautious, as we know little of the genre and the anecdote itself is, like other such stories,[24] suspect; but we can see that while tragedy could give something to Plato's presentation of high moral issues, mime might offer as a counterweight a more realistic, jocular and down-to-earth note which would be in keeping with the cheerful good humour of Socrates, particularly in puncturing pretension.

As we shall see in more detail in ch. 4, the eminent and expensive teachers known as sophists, innovators in their literary art as in their professional role and educative aims, developed many new forms of writing through which to advertise their instruction and to communicate skill in argument and style. Some of these were clearly influenced by and in turn influenced poetry: it is plain that, for instance, Gorgias' highly-wrought rhyming and rhythmical style adapts many poetic techniques, and he in turn was mimicked by Euripides and Agathon. Hence the influences of drama and sophistic writing upon Plato are sometimes hard to disentangle: Herodotus and Euripides both include in their work set-piece debates on the right constitution, a subject they may have derived from Protagoras' works, and the discussion of this subject in abstract terms but illustrated by colourful vignettes is prominent in Plato's *Republic* (esp. books 8 and 9).

---

[21] For discussion and bibliography see esp. C. Collard, *LCM* 5 (1980) 77-85; also M. Heath, *The Poetics of Greek Tragedy* (London 1987) 128-30.

[22] Cf. D. Tarrant, *JHS* 75 (1955) 82-9. For an attempt to go beyond the obvious, see the articles by H. Kuhn, *HSCP* 52 (1941) 1-40 and 53 (1942) 37-88.

[23] Duris, *FGH* 76 F 72 (Athenaeus). Cf. Diog. Laert. iii. 18, Riginos no. 128, and for further bibl., *Kl. Pauly* s.v.; Guthrie iii. 332f. There may be an allusion to an ancient categorisation of Sophron's mimes at Pl. *Rep.* v. 451c: see Adam and Halliwell ad loc.

[24] For example, the story that Plato sent a copy of Aristophanes' dramas to Dionysius in order to teach him about Athens (Riginos no. 129). The text of the Life of Aristophanes says that Plato sent the *Clouds* in particular (not mentioned by Riginos), but this phrase does look like an interpolation, and is bracketed by Kassel and Austin.

Antilogy, agon, eristic debate, dialectic, are hard to distinguish and each influences or contaminates the others. But as far as dialogue form is concerned, we can identify two works of the period (late fifth century) which are clearly prior to any experimentation by Plato himself, namely those by Prodicus and Hippias.

Both sophists seem to have dressed relatively straightforward moral didacticism in colourful mythical dress. Prodicus in his work entitled (somewhat mysteriously) *Horai* ('Seasons') included an elaborate scene in which the young Heracles was faced with a choice between the lascivious personification of Vice and the more dignified, less seductive, figure of Virtue: needless to say, the hero chose the latter. The passage is paraphrased at length by Xenophon's Socrates, with an admission, obviously ironic, that he has not done justice to the elegance of the original (*Mem.* ii. 1. 21ff. = Prod. B2). If despite that disclaimer Xenophon's adaptation is reasonably faithful, then the passage was rich in ornamental detail but not profound in its morality or its analysis of reasons to be moral. Heracles, as often in later literature, seems to have been used as an example to inspire others; but whether the lesson was spelt out in any kind of conclusion or protreptic to the reader we do not know. The relevant work by Hippias, his *Trojan Discourse*, is also known chiefly through one reference in a dialogue of the next generation, Plato's *Hippias Major* (286). It appears to have taken the form of the young Neoptolemus asking the wise old Nestor for advice on good conduct, but we do not know how lively an exchange followed, and how far Neoptolemus was shown as a willing or able student. No doubt Hippias saw himself in something like the role of Nestor. The line from the poetic tradition of older man advising younger or inferior (Hesiod and Perses, Theognis and Cyrnus (where the homosexual element enters)) down to works such as Plato's *Alcibiades* or *Charmides* may pass through the epideictic *Trojan Discourse*.[25]

A rather more promising line of development is our third influence, that of the early biographical or autobiographical tradition, and especially the work of Ion of Chios, tragedian, thinker and littérateur, an attractive figure who flourished in the mid-century (he was dead by the late 420s). He knew Cimon, Pericles, Sophocles and others, and preserved his recollections of them in a work entitled *Epidemiai* (apparently 'Visits'), of which we have some entertaining samples in later quotations.[26] Vivid visual description (Cimon was a big man, with a fine crop of hair), erotic flirtation and humorous banter (Sophocles liked pretty boys), political reminiscences (Cimon's account of his cleverest stratagem), comment on Pericles' proud

---

[25] Cf. further Gaiser, *Protreptik und Paränese* 61-4, R. Hirzel, *Der Dialog* 59-63, D. Gera, *Xenophon's Cyropaedia* (Oxford 1993) 50-4.

[26] On Ion see *FGH* 392; F. Jacoby, *CQ* 41 (1947) 1ff. = Jacoby, *Abhandlungen zur griechischen Geschichtsschreibung* (Leiden 1956), 144-68, with corrections by M.L. West, *BICS* 32 (1985) 71-8, and esp. Dover, *The Greeks and their Legacy* (1988), 1-12.

manner in society, literary quotation and discussion, often at the dinner-table[27] – we see here some of the ingredients which make the texture of Plato's writings so rich; and the interest in prominent figures matches the tendency in the early dialogues for Socrates to converse with notable politicians, sophists or generals (see esp. the *Laches*). What we do not see in Ion is any sign of moral discussion (though he certainly touched on matters philosophical elsewhere); but the scene-setting, the interest in personality and literary culture, and the lightness of touch in his work must have made a contribution not only to the emerging tradition of biography, but also to that related but distinct form, the Socratic dialogue, which commemorates an exceptional individual in a non-biographical mode.[28]

Stesimbrotus of Thasos, who wrote a pamphlet or essay on Themistocles, Cimon and Pericles some time after 429 BC, is often bracketed with Ion, but seems a less appealing figure and is probably less relevant to the present discussion.[29] His seems to have been much more a work of political polemic, and merges easily with a mass of other material, especially in oratory, which is only very vaguely comparable with Plato: for instance, the 'defence-speech' in the *Apology* can be compared with the tendency in forensic rhetoric to defend, and therefore narrate, the past career of the person on trial. Although the whole purpose of the *Memorabilia* of Xeno-phon is to vindicate Socrates' memory (see esp. i. 1-2, iv. 8), Plato usually has other aims, and certainly he does not achieve these by the crude invective of the courts.[30]

Dialogue is above all appropriate to Socrates' modus operandi, and it is safe to assume that Socrates' own practice is the primary stimulus behind all the works by his followers. Even in the caricature of the *Clouds* (p. 40 below), we see a man who teaches not through books or a fixed course of instruction, but by suiting his approach to the student's capacity and needs,

[27] The tradition of 'sympotic literature', which may antedate Plato (see esp. *PSI* 9. 1093), is specifically relevant to one of his works, the *Symposium*, and will be mentioned further in a later chapter. Cf. *Kl. Pauly* s.v. Deipnonliteratur; J. Martin, *Symposion* (Paderborn 1931); Gera, *Xenophon's Cyropaedia* 132-54.

[28] See further A. Momigliano, *The Development of Greek Biography* (Cambridge Mass. 1971) ch. 2, with ample bibliography. (A. Dihle, *Studien zur griechischen Biographie* (Göttingen 1956) argued that Socrates was the key stimulus in the emergence of biography, but Momigliano offers some qualifications of this view.) Cultivated Athenians at symposia seem to have recounted 'Aesopic logoi' and tales about other notables such as Simonides, often involving some witty interchange (cf. Ar. *Wasps* 1174-5, 1258-9); but this falls far short of written dialogue.

[29] *FGH* 107; F. Schachermeyr, *SB Wien* 247. 5, 1965 = *Forschungen und Betrachtungen zur griechischen und römischen Geschichte* (1974), 151ff.; K. Meister, *Historia* 27 (1978) 274ff.; C. B. R. Pelling, in *Characterization and Individuality in Greek Literature*, ed. Pelling (Oxford 1990), 215.

[30] Works by the other Socratic authors may have come closer to pamphlet warfare and to the forensic style: in particular, the written invective of Antisthenes against Alcibiades probably drew on the same topoi as Antiphon's forensic attack (frr. 66-7 Blass), or the attack preserved in the corpus of Andocides' speeches.

and by pressing him, through question and answer, to examine himself and produce his own suggestions (esp. 478ff., 694ff., 737, 740-2). As already emphasised, the interaction of personalities is crucial in Plato's earlier work (we shall see that there is a change, though not as sharp as sometimes claimed, in his later period). Dialogue, more than any other form, makes it possible to recreate the living exchange of ideas and the ingenious workings of Socrates' inquisitive mind. Plato not only surpassed all the other Socratic writers in his mastery of the form, but seems to have had a special fascination with it. Our evidence, though pitifully fragmentary, is sufficient to show that other disciples of Socrates (Antisthenes, Aristippus, and the rest) wrote in other genres as well; Plato wrote *only* dialogues.[31]

The Platonic dialogue is too familiar, too central to the classical tradition, for us to realise how remarkable it must have seemed at first. This is interestingly reflected in some comments by ancient critics, who, although they cannot of course serve as authorities to guide our own reading, do form a particularly important part of the 'reception' of Plato. Aristotle, in the same part of the work *On Poets* mentioned earlier, said that the form of the Platonic dialogue fell between poetry and prose (fr. 73); he also seems to have compared, or at least associated, the dialogues with the mimes of Sophron as a mimetic genre (fr. 72; cf. *Poetics* 1. 1447b10ff.).[32] Cicero (*Orator* 67) refers to a view which held that Plato's work deserved the title of poetry more than that of the comic poets. These comments refer in part to style, but also to the mimetic and quasi-fictional status of the works: they purport to record authentic conversations, but from an early date readers have detected implausibilities and anachronisms. In many cases Plato seems to challenge the reader with the elaborate frame-dialogues, references to distance in time, and comments on a narrator's inadequate memory or selectivity. Neither the origins nor the generic status of the dialogue form can be firmly established: in the one case this is a matter of lost evidence, in the other it reflects the genuine complexity of Plato's literary enterprise.

The continuing problem

We can see, then, that Plato in the dialogues is doing more than simply present his own ideas; more, even, than commemorating and defending his master (though an apologetic element and an implicit or near-explicit criticism of contemporary attitudes to the intellectual are present in a

[31] Friedlaender i, 157, who also asserts, on perhaps inadequate evidence, that not all the Socratics included Socrates in all their dialogues. The material is gathered by G. Giannantoni, *Socraticorum Reliquiae* (4 vols., Rome 1983-5) (though he puzzlingly omits Aeschines of Sphettus).
[32] See further Quintil. x. 1. 81, and other passages discussed by Laborderie, esp. 53-68.

number of dialogues).[33] Nevertheless, readers new to Plato or accustomed to reading him in a particular way will be likely to question the importance of the points made so far. Granted that Plato has his literary techniques and his additional motives, granted too that he has effaced himself from the foreground of his dramatic dialogues, surely it is still possible to define his intellectual position and to present a coherent account of Platonic philosophy? Does not the literary approach to Plato risk imposing on his work a fluidity and complexity which is not in fact present?

These objections are not without force. Before developing my own argument further, therefore, I shall survey a number of other approaches to these works which in different ways seek to gain more direct access to the mind of Plato.

Biography

The first and most traditional approach is the biographical. Biography is, however, always limited by its sources. If the seventh letter is authentic, we have one primary source of the first importance; if others among the letters are genuine, we are that much better off. But if doubt is justified concerning all the letters, we are thrown back on secondary and tertiary sources, some of them very late and very untrustworthy.[34] Ancient 'lives' of Plato survive from no earlier than the second century AD, though they undoubtedly draw on earlier material. We have an essay by the novelist-Platonist Apuleius, an interesting mélange of anecdotes and quotations in Diogenes Laertius' *Lives of the Philosophers*, and a number of brief lives by Platonist scholars such as Olympiodorus, intended as prefatory matter to commentaries on the works themselves.[35] Scrutiny of these accounts does not inspire much confidence. Not only do they differ amongst themselves, they are often trivial and anecdotal, they clearly draw on gossipy or prejudiced sources or introduce their own biasses, and they show a number of tendencies visible in ancient literary biography in general:[36] for instance, assuming that authorities praised in the writer's works have been important teachers of the writer, and introducing often improbable anecdotes to illustrate the early promise of the young author. Few will attach much credence to the tale that bees came and placed their honey on the lips of

[33] See esp. *Meno* 89e-95a (Socrates' encounter with Anytus); *Smp.* (the Alcibiades episode); cf. also *Rep.* vi. 487b-98c, and much else in that dialogue.

[34] Readers may expect some reference to the love-epigrams ascribed to Plato, one of which names Dion. They are almost certainly spurious, as shown by W. Ludwig, *GRBS* 4 (1963) 59-82, and D.L. Page, *Further Greek Epigrams* (Cambridge 1981) 125-7, 161-81; nor, if authentic, could they prove as much about his life and emotions as has sometimes been maintained – e.g. recently by M. Nussbaum, *The Fragility of Goodness* (Cambridge 1986) 228-32, who seems unaware of the discussions cited.

[35] See further Zeller, ch. 1; H. Leisegang, *RE* xi. 2342-7; Guthrie iv ch. 1; K. Gaiser, *Platons Ungeschriebene Lehre* (Stuttgart 1963), appendix of 'Testimonia Platonica'; Riginos.

[36] J. Fairweather, *Anc. Soc.* 5 (1974) 234-55; M.R. Lefkowitz, *The Lives of the Greek Poets* (London 1981), with useful translations; Fairweather, *PLLS* ed. F. Cairns, 4 (1983) 315-69.

the infant Plato (Riginos no. 3), a miracle-story also attached to the infant Homer, Hesiod and Pindar; but other equally symbolic tales are often quoted with much less caution: for example, that Plato in his early years wrote poetry, or more specifically tragedy, but burnt these miguided efforts once he had fallen under the influence of Socratic philosophy (Diog. Laert. iii. 5, etc.; Riginos no. 14). This is a clear case of a 'conversion-to-philosophy' narrative, and also functions as a partial explanation for the poetic richness of Plato's philosophic style, and perhaps his hostility to poetry: it thus seeks to explain a stylistic and literary phenomenon through biography. Anecdotes of this kind can be used only as suggestive illustrations; it is unsafe to quarry them for historical facts.

If we subtract the obviously fantastic or probably fictional, we can perhaps find more solid ground in a few rather general statements (though even these depend to some degree on accepting the Seventh Letter): Plato was born of a distinguished Athenian family, aristocratic and politically prominent; he might well have embarked on politics like his relations Critias and Charmides, but followed another path; he fell under the influence of Socrates at an early age, and was devoted to his memory throughout his life; he went abroad and studied with other teachers, who may have included Pythagoreans, in the years following Socrates' death;[37] thereafter he returned to Athens, and pursued a life of study and teaching, devoting himself to philosophy. At some date possibly in the 380s he founded an establishment or 'school' known as the Academy,[38] in an area of Athens where there was a shrine to the hero Hekademos. It appears that he and his friends (whether we should say pupils, disciples or fellow-thinkers is far from clear) met there regularly in a gymnasium and talked philosophy. How frequently they met, what the subjects of discussion were, how formal the arrangements were, how far Plato took the lead, whether they discussed the content of the dialogues (or of other authors' works?) is impossible to say; but the institution, if that is the right word, was established, and the circle came to include other notable thinkers such as Xenocrates, Speusippus (later Plato's successor as 'head' of the Academy – at least by then it had some semi-formal structure), and of course the young Aristotle. Some idea of popular perception of the school can be gleaned from a fragment of the comic writer Epicrates, preserved by a later anthologist.[39]

---

[37] Riginos, ch. 6. The best-attested of these journeys is to Magna Graecia (S. Italy). It must be emphasised that the determined sceptic can easily disbelieve any of them; there is no contemporary evidence to confirm the late accounts.

[38] Riginos, ch. 10; H. Cherniss, *The Riddle of the Early Academy* (Berkeley 1945); G.F. Field, *Plato and his Contemporaries* (London 1930), ch. 3; J. Glucker, *Antiochus and the Late Academy* (Göttingen 1978), esp. ch. 5; M. Ostwald and J. Lynch, *CAH* vi^2 ch. 12(a).

[39] Fr. 10 Kassel-Austin = 11 Kock (from an unknown play) ap. Athen. ii. 59c. I use G.C. Field's tr., op. cit. 38f.(except that I have made clear the crudity of the doctor's response, which Field bowdlerises). Cherniss, *Riddle of the Early Academy* 62-3, is sceptical. For further comic references to Plato see Diog. Laert. iii. 26-8. Many of his brief snatches might, however, allude to the published works rather than to the teaching of the school.

Obviously this is humorous distortion, but it is at least contemporary evidence.

> First speaker: Tell me about Plato and Speusippus and Menedemus. What are they working at now? What deep idea and what great argument is being examined by them? For the land's sake tell me truly, if you know anything about it.
>
> Second speaker: I know all about it and will tell you plainly. At the Panathenaea I saw a group of boys in the gymnasia of the Academy. And there I heard strange and indescribable things. They were defining and dividing up the world of nature, and were distinguishing the habits of animals and the natures of trees and the species of vegetables. And there in the middle of them they had a pumpkin and were inquiring of what species it was.
>
> A: And what did they decide that plant to be, and of what species is it? Tell me, if you know.
>
> B: Well, at first they all stood silent and bent over it for some time considering. Then suddenly, while they were still bending over it and examining it, one of the boys said that it was a round vegetable, and another said that it was grass, and another that it was a tree. On hearing this a Sicilian doctor who was there let go a fart at the nonsense they were talking.
>
> A: I should think they must have been very angry at that and shouted him down as a scoffer. For it was a rude thing to do in the middle of such talk.
>
> B: It didn't worry the boys. But Plato, who was there, told them very kindly, without being in the least disturbed, to try again from the beginning to define the species. And they went on with their definitions.

At first sight this looks rather like the travesty of Socratic conversation in the *Clouds*, but there may perhaps be more fidelity in this portrait. If so, there are a few points which can be extracted: the youthfulness of some of the members of the Academy; the openness of discussion (even an unsympathetic outsider may be within earshot); the interest in division into categories (something prominent in the *Sophist* and other works), and the presence of Plato as a kindly guide and encouraging figure, not a guru. Here too, however, we must be careful not to generalise too readily from a single piece of evidence. Finally, the biography by Diogenes Laertius preserves the philosopher's will (iii. 41-3).

So far we have not considered the episode of Sicily, which bulks so large in most accounts of Plato's life.[40] In what follows it is assumed that the seventh letter may be drawn on for facts, even if it does not give us Plato's authentic judgements on these. Although the precise dates are uncertain, it seems that Plato first visited Sicily in the 380s, during the reign of the strong tyrant Dionysius I (died 367), and at this stage also encountered the Syracusan Dion, a notable aristocrat and intellectual of the court. After the ruler's death, Dion and others entreated Plato to return to Sicily and take

---

[40] Besides the works already cited, see K. von Fritz, *Platon in Sizilien und das Problem der Philosophenherrschaft* (Berlin 1968). Mary Renault's *The Mask of Apollo*, probably her best historical novel, is a splendid fictional presentation of the whole affair.

the golden opportunity which the succession of the young and possibly malleable Dionysius II offered for the creation of a new ideal monarchy. This was in the mid-360s, when Plato was already a distinguished teacher and writer. The attempt was a failure, and Dion's own position was soon in jeopardy. Dionysius banished Dion, and Plato returned with some difficulty to Athens. Later he was forced by heavy pressure from Dion's friends to return and try to improve relations between his old friend and the tyrant: as was perhaps predictable, this visit was entirely fruitless. Dionysius confiscated Dion's property and kept Plato virtually a prisoner until the Tarentine philosopher Archytas secured his release. Dion's later career as an adventurer, seizing power in Syracuse by force in 357, does him little credit as a philosopher. Dion was later assassinated in mysterious circumstances. The Seventh Letter, which if genuine was composed in 353, is addressed to Dion's party following his death: it sets out Plato's role in the whole unhappy sequence of events, and counsels moderation.

Whoever wrote the letter, it is a fascinating and moving document; and the whole episode is part of history, not a concoction by later hagiographers.[41] But although it must have been a painful and difficult experience for Plato, it is not so obvious that it helps us interpret his dialogues, whether before or after the second and most significant visit to Sicily. Modern scholars have often seen the Sicilian episode as a crucial test for Plato's theories, after which his optimism and idealism (supposedly represented by the hopes for an ideal state in the *Republic*) were transformed into a harsher and more pessimistic outlook (represented by the more realistic and stricter regimes of the *Statesman* and especially the *Laws*). There are other ways in which Sicily is invoked to 'explain' aspects of Plato's life and work: more trivially, it is suggested that references to the pleasures of the Sicilian cuisine in the *Gorgias* can best be explained by placing that dialogue after the first visit to Sicily.[42] More significantly, the whole institution of the Academy has been seen as a training-ground for political advisers, men who were intended to mould rulers of the day, to transform them into philosopher-kings as Plato tried and failed to do with Dionysius.[43] It will be obvious that here the Sicilian episode and the Seventh Letter are being used as evidence in support of a particular interpretation of Plato's writings on politics: in the simplest terms, it is being taken for granted that the proposals made in the *Republic* and elsewhere are intended as realistic proposals which could be put into effect, *mutatis mutandis*, in the real communities of the contemporary Greek world. This is a hypothesis, and

---

[41] The view of M.I. Finley, that all later references to Plato's involvement are dependent on the Seventh Letter, is briskly rebutted by Guthrie iv 10n. See further H.D. Westlake, 'Dion', in his *Essays on the Greek Historians and Greek History* (Manchester 1969) 251-64.

[42] So e.g. E.R. Dodds, in his commentary, p. 26f. Admittedly the argument is not dependent on this point alone.

[43] See e.g. Guthrie iv 22f., Field, 43-5. A more cautious line is taken by Ostwald and Lynch (n. 38), and a powerful assault on this argument is launched by Brunt, *Studies* (1994), 282-342.

one which, it will be argued later in this book, probably pushes the dialogues and historical events too closely together. It must also be emphasised how different the picture would look, and how limited our evidence would be, if the Seventh Letter were rejected as a forgery. Certainly even with its evidence we cannot plot a continuous chart of Plato's moods or trace the growth of a pessimistic streak without extensive conjecture.

Another strand of the biographical approach to Plato is psychological speculation, especially as regards homosexuality. Here too the temptation, as in all literary biography, is to close the gap between life and art. The world of the dialogues is a male world: Socrates' wife is sent away at the end of the *Phaedo* because she is too upset, and the philosopher dies with his friends, not his family; no woman participates in the conversations presented in the dialogues;[44] and above all, the *Symposium* and the *Phaedrus* sublimely celebrate the erotic relationship between men (though not its physical consummation). It is a natural assumption, and may well be true, that the author was himself thus inclined, perhaps even beyond the normal pattern of his day.[45] But does this actually add much to our understanding of the dialogues? Some may feel that Plato's sexual nature adds a special quality to certain passages, and some thought-provoking comments have been made on his association of creativity with sexual passion;[46] but speculation on the possible motivations, sociological or psychological, which give rise to these pronouncements, take us into a region where little certainty can be found.

It is not being suggested that we study the dialogues without reference to their historical context and origins: indeed, the approach which is advocated in this book will depend heavily on knowledge of the literary and intellectual background of the dialogues. But we may distinguish between biographical information (of which we have very little that is dependable),[47] and historical information, about the late fifth and fourth century back-

---

[44] Diotima in the *Symposium*, though certainly an anomalous figure, is not strictly an exception: she does not participate in the dialogue, but only figures in the speech made by Socrates. The practice of other Socratic writers was different: witness Aeschines' lost *Aspasia*, and some passages of Xenophon (e.g. *Mem.* iii.11, the courtesan Theodote).

[45] See further Dover, *Greek Homosexuality* (London 1978), esp. 11-13, 153-70; D. Halperin, *One Hundred Years of Homosexuality* (London 1990), 118 with n. 27 (cf. n. 21 for bibl. on Plato's attitude to women).

[46] M. Burnyeat, *BICS* 24 (1977) 7-16, especially the conclusion.

[47] I reserve for a footnote a further variant on biographical interpretation, which might be called the genetic approach. This explains a thinker's development in terms of the influence of his teachers: in Plato's case, by citing a well-known passage of Aristotle which describes him as studying with Cratylus and being impressed by the problems of flux and change as set out by the Pre-Socratic thinker Heraclitus (*Met.* 987a32-b7). The influence of Socrates diverted him to ethics, but the Heraclitean-Cratylan problems re-emerged in his later period and shaped his later development. For an account along these lines see Irwin in Kraut, *Companion*, 51ff., 69 (Vlastos, *PBA* 74 (1988) 102-4 is visibly uneasy with the scenario). The mismatch between the alleged sequence of teachers and Plato's progress as a writer and thinker only goes to show that the ingredients cannot adequately explain the compound.

ground in general and Athenian society in particular (about which we know a great deal from a wide variety of sources).[48] It is clear that broader historical trends outside Plato's works can help us understand some of the most prominent themes within the dialogues: for instance, the decline of Athens' empire, the sophistic movement, the increased prestige of monarchy in Greece, with the concomitant disillusionment with democracy, the prevalence of internal discord (*stasis*) in the Greek states, and so forth. These may provide only a rather vague and approximate context, but they rest on firmer and more abundant evidence than the biographical tradition about Plato, which will be largely excluded in what follows.

Socrates and Plato

The second approach which has been adopted in most studies of Plato is to consider him in relation to Socrates. As already explained, Socrates is prominent in most of Plato's vast *oeuvre*, but is this Socrates as he really was, the 'historical' Socrates, or is he a Platonic creation? More precisely, does Plato advance beyond or diverge from Socrates in the half-century or more after his master's death? Put in these terms, the answer may seem self-evident: of course Plato must have developed, rather than stagnating. If this is accepted, the question becomes one of the nature and stages of this development. A model adopted by many distinguished scholars involves a division of Plato's writings into periods: in the early period, Socrates is portrayed as he was, and no fresh Platonic doctrine is introduced in those dialogues; in the middle period, Socrates becomes more authoritative, voices more positive doctrine, and goes beyond what it seems reasonable to suppose that Socrates really said – that is, while still preserving his authentic personality, he is used more as a spokesman for Plato, lending Platonic doctrine authority. In the latest period Socrates is more impersonal, and the doctrine is undisguisedly Plato's own.[49]

To accept this approach is to accept the need to choose one of three options: either Plato's work is communicating wholly Socratic teaching (a freakish view, but not one which has been entirely without its advocates);[50] or Plato's work communicates Platonic doctrine from the beginning, and the character of Socrates is in some sense a fiction from the start; or some kind of compromise position is the solution, with Plato at first going no

---

[48] In general see the standard histories of the period by J.K. Davies, *Democracy and Classical Greece* (Glasgow 1978, revised 1993), S. Hornblower, *The Greek World 479-323 B.C.* (London 1983, revised 1991) and others; also *CAH* vi[2] (1994). On *stasis* see esp. A.W. Lintott, *Violence, Civil Strife and Revolution in the Classical City* (London 1982).

[49] For a masterly account along these lines, and very full bibliography of earlier studies, see G. Vlastos, *Socrates, Ironist and Moral Philosopher* (Cambridge 1991), esp. chs. 2-3, supplemented by his *Socratic Studies* (Cambridge 1994).

[50] The view is associated especially with J. Burnet and A.E. Taylor. For decisive criticisms see W.D. Ross, *Proceedings of the Classical Association* 30 (1933) 7-24 = A. Patzer (ed.), *Der historische Sokrates* (Darmstadt 1987) 225-39; Guthrie iii. 351-5.

further than Socrates but gradually developing his ideas and then going on with fresh ideas of his own. The last is probably the most popular view (it appeals to lovers of compromise, and has obvious *prima facie* biographical plausibility), but the second view has been pressed from time to time, usually by scholars with literary interests rather than philosophers. Thus it has been emphasised that from the beginning, in the *Euthyphro, Laches* and even the *Apology*, Plato is already using his literary artifice to enhance Socrates' status, to suggest more than is explicitly stated, and to introduce certain patterns of argument which may be intended to train the reader or guide him to further thought.[51]

The 'Socratic question', as it is usually known (that is, the question how to recover the historical Socrates from the sources which preserve such different pictures of him), will be more fully discussed in the next chapter. It will there be argued that both Plato and Xenophon make Socrates in their own image, and that there is no reason to doubt that this process is at work, perhaps even unconsciously, from the earliest stages of their Socratic writing. In distinguishing Plato from Socrates we have no surer guide than a handful of passages in Aristotle, from which we learn that (in particular) Socrates interested himself in universal definitions, worked deductively, and did not 'separate off' the forms or ideas as independently-existing entities (as he is presented as doing in Plato's *Phaedo, Republic* and elsewhere). Here we have sound evidence from a reliable source of what we might ourselves have suspected: that Socrates concerned himself with the human, ethical side of philosophy,[52] and that it is Plato who carries the enquiry on to the metaphysical plane.

This much we may allow, but some have wished to go further, and even to distinguish the specific stage in a given dialogue at which Socrates departs from his original teaching. Thus Guthrie, for example, takes the transition at *Meno* 81a, where Socrates begins to quote the sayings of 'men and women who understand the truths of religion' about the soul and its afterlife, as effectively a signal that Socrates is here giving voice to Plato's teaching.[53] In a similar manner, Dodds tentatively endorses the view that

[51] See the radical analysis by M. Montuori, *Socrates, Physiology of a Myth* (Amsterdam 1981); also e.g. C. Kahn, *CQ* 31 (1981) 305-20 (repr. in H.H. Benson (ed.), *Essays on the Philosophy of Socrates* (Oxford 1992) 35-52). M.C. Stokes, in *Socratic Questions* ed. Gower and Stokes (London 1992) 26-81, argues for substantial invention in the *Apology*. See also C. Gill, *CQ* 23 (1973) 25-9, arguing for a 'softening' in the *Phaedo* of the actual effects of hemlock poisoning. The reductio ad absurdum of this approach is to be found in E. Dupréel, *La légende Socratique et les sources de Platon* (1922), for whom all events of Socrates' life, including his condemnation and death, are Platonic fictions.

[52] Cf. the famous remark of Cicero, *Tusc.* v. 10 that Socrates (unlike the Pre-Socratic writers) 'first called philosophy down from the skies, set it in the cities and even introduced it into men's homes, compelling it to consider life and morals, good and evil'. (See already Arist. *Part. An.* 642a25-31; more references in Zeller, *Socrates* 92f.)

[53] Guthrie iv. 241; cf. his introd. to the Penguin tr. of the *Meno*. So too Kraut, in *Companion* 6; cf. Vlastos, *Socratic Studies* 79.

Socrates' unaccustomed *makrologia* ('long-windedness') at *Grg.* 465e and 519e (in both of these passages Socrates apologises) is 'an indication that Plato's Socrates is "breaking out of the historical mould" (Rudberg) and becoming the mouthpiece for Plato's passionately held positive convictions'.[54] Or again, many have claimed that the first book of the *Republic*, which ends in *aporia*, is as far as the 'historical' Socrates can get by his authentic methods, and that book 2 is Plato's fresh start (a view often combined with the suggestion that the first book was composed at an earlier date and was originally independent).[55] Although none of these suggestions is intrinsically absurd or obviously false, it seems disturbing (and improbable) that Plato would have allowed the scissors-and-paste stage of his composition and thinking to show through quite so plainly. Rather, if there are changes of tone and direction, they should surely be explained in terms of the effect they have within the dialogue, as indicators that something important is being said, or something unusual happening. Rather than looking outside the work and appealing for an explanation to Plato's gradual detachment from his master (another 'psychologising' approach), it would seem more profitable to assume that the work is as the author would wish it and can be considered as a coherent whole.

In short, the view taken here is that the relation between Plato and Socrates, while undoubtedly an important issue, is not one which can be clearly mapped out as a linear development; that except in a few very broad generalisations derived from Aristotle, we cannot go through any dialogue and insist that this part is Socratic and this Plato; and that the probability is that the dialogues (including even the *Apology*) from the beginning bear Plato's stamp and should be considered as Plato's artistic creation. There is, doubtless, a difference between Plato and Socrates, and it is natural to suppose that the gap between them increased; but without more independent evidence about the historical Socrates there are severe limits on how far we can go.[56]

Plato's thought: unity or development?

A third mode of enquiry into Plato concerns the question of the coherence and consistency of his philosophical system: is it a unified set of doctrines which remain steadily unchanged throughout his work, or do his views develop? Though clearly related to the Socratic question, this issue may be kept distinct from it, since on some views of the Socrates-Plato relationship

---

[54] n. on *Grg.* 455e1-6a2 (p. 232); for a different view, see ch. 6, pp. 146, 168 below.

[55] See e.g. J. Annas, *An Introduction to Plato's Republic* (Oxford 1981), ch 2, esp. 16-18, 56-7. Cf. Vlastos, *Socrates* 248-51. Differently, L. Tarán, in *Platonic Investigations* ed. D.J. O'Meara (Washington 1985) 85-110. See now C.H. Kahn, *CQ* 43 (1993) 131-42.

[56] It is argued in ch. 2 that Xenophon does not provide adequate independent evidence, partly because he can be shown to have known and utilised Plato's works, and partly because he himself misunderstands, distorts or modifies Socrates' personality and ideas.

it remains a separate problem. For instance, if we take it that Socrates is Plato's mouthpiece from the start, is he mouthing the same words throughout, or does Plato change his views and consequently modify the views he gives to Socrates? Some interpreters have taken Platonism as a homogeneous doctrine, implicit or explicit from the earliest dialogues onwards, consistent though more fully expounded in the later, more ambitious works. Others see Plato as developing and correcting his views all through his lifetime (although most would see a core of central concerns, even if not a set of fundamental principles like Epicurus' *Kuriai Doxai*). A 'unitary' view is held or adopted in a very slightly modified form by many philosophers, partly because it makes it easier to consider together the evidence of a range of different dialogues concerning a particular concept (for instance the Theory of Forms). Thus Gosling's book on Plato is divided not by dialogue or period but by topic: chapter-headings include 'Pleasure', 'Knowledge and Perception', 'Wanting the Good'.[57] The unitarian approach even allows readers to import doctrines into dialogues which seem hardly to need them, on the basis of relatively small hints in the text, whereas the evolutionary view might postulate that Plato had still not worked out a conception fully, and that in a given passage we see only the germ of the idea. Thus in the *Euthyphro* is the theory of forms in its infancy, or fully-developed behind the scenes?[58] If the other view is adopted, that Plato's thought did gradually develop and evolve, then chronology becomes crucial and the procedure of arguing from one dialogue to another, even when they deal with the same topic, becomes more risky. Can we safely argue from the *Symposium* to fill in the gaps in the account of love in the *Phaedrus*? On the whole, despite such rare indications as the cross-reference in the *Phaedo* to the *Meno* (p. 4 above), it seems safer to assume that Plato's ideas did not stand still, that his philosophy did not spring fully-formed from his youthful mind, and that each dialogue must first be considered independently, as a self-contained work. Except in the special cases where trilogy-structure seems to have been part of Plato's design, we have no warrant for viewing any series of dialogues as a 'course' or connected group of works.[59] Literary considerations must also be given due weight. If a doctrine is not explained or not fully set out in a particular dialogue, that does not mean that it is presupposed, nor necessarily that it is superseded: it may be a question of the needs and priorities of the dialogue in question, or the particular concerns of the participants. For example, the eschatological myth of the *Gorgias*, unlike those of the *Phaedo*, *Republic* and *Phaedrus*, makes almost no reference to the concept of reincarnation. Does this indicate that Plato

[57] J. Gosling, *Plato* (in the series 'Arguments of the Philosophers', London 1973).

[58] This arises esp. from *Euthyphro* 5d, 6d; for discussion, see R.E. Allen, *Plato's Euthyphro and the Earlier Theory of Forms* (London 1970).

[59] *Pace* C.H. Kahn, who has argued for something like this position in a series of papers on the earlier dialogues: e.g. *CQ* 31 (1981) 305-20, *Journ. of Philosophy* 85 (1988) 541-9.

had not yet become interested in or convinced by that doctrine, or does it rather reflect the nature of the conflict presented in the dialogue? The starkness of the contrast between Socrates and Callicles would be blurred, the anticipation of Socrates' trial and unjust condemnation less tragic, if a longer perspective were allowed and the prospect of future lives admitted into consideration. In the *Gorgias* what counts is one's moral choices in this life, and failure to realise the importance of such choices will lead to eternal suffering. It would be excessive to rule out any form of comparison of dialogues and juxtaposition of passages in our study of Plato, but we must be cautious in deciding how much these comparisons prove.[60]

Plato the eternal questioner

At this point it will be appropriate to turn to another form of Platonic interpretation, one which has more in common with the approach adopted in this book, but which also seems to suffer from serious disadvantages. Recent studies have paid more attention to the kind of questions raised here: why has Plato constructed his dialogues in the way he has? Why is dialogue so important to him? Where does he stand himself? What is the point of the seemingly absurd or fallacious arguments which are often accepted by the participants? Some of the answers offered have laid particular emphasis on the 'play' element in Plato, and cast doubt on the possibility of extracting any conclusion, any message, any doctrine at all from the dialogues, preferring to see Plato as the ultimate questioner, constantly raising questions without offering final answers. In such interpretation irony and self-mockery play an important role. Plato is seen as the maker of paradoxes: he condemns writing but composes written works of supreme sophistication and suggestiveness; he condemns art and rhetoric, yet he himself is a supreme artist and the ultimate rhetorician; he expounds the plan for an ideal state, yet admits it can never be brought into practice; he declares that the soul, or the maker of the universe, are inaccessible to the human mind, and can only be described in similes or images, and yet his images are so compelling and memorable as to have influenced generations of subsequent thinkers. How can we hope to extract from his works any simple or summarisable principles of philosophy? Rather, the overriding imperative of the dialogues is to question everything, including their conclusions. Philosophy is a search, not a solution.

Obviously, there is much in this approach which is sympathetic and suggestive. The acknowledgement of the crucial importance of irony and 'play' in Plato is an essential insight without which, it can safely be said, a large number of the dialogues cannot possibly be understood: the

---

[60] For a full account of the debate between advocates of 'unity' and separatists, see E.N. Tigerstedt, *Interpreting Plato* (Uppsala 1977), valuable despite its aporetic conclusion.

Menexenus, Ion, Symposium and *Phaedrus*, to name only the most obvious examples.[61] It is also welcome to see the patronising assumption that Plato constantly committed foolish philosophic blunders without realising it replaced by a more positive approach, which allows that these fallacies may have some role to play in the context of the dialogue: even if the arguments are invalid, they may suggest truths or hint at a line of argument which if systematically pursued might lead to more satisfactory results. The latter approach helps considerably with a dialogue such as the *Euthydemus*, as has increasingly been recognised.[62] But the argument that Plato is perpetually a questioner, that he always undercuts what is said, that in all his works he frames answers with qualifications and questions, that he systematically deconstructs himself, seems to go too far. It ignores or at least neglects the frequency with which certain themes recur, and the commitment with which they seem to be expressed; it also fails to do justice to the differences in tone and seriousness amongst the dialogues; and it leaves us with a disturbingly diminished picture of Plato. If the only lesson to take away from his writings is the need to go on questioning, it hardly needs over thirty dialogues, a total of well over a thousand pages, to put that message across; and if Plato is, when all is said and done, above all a 'ludic' artist, then he must indeed fall victim to his own persistent criticisms of the frivolity and emptiness of the artists' creations. In short, as E.N. Tigerstedt has put it, 'the "panaporetic" interpretation of Plato [according to which he never offers any conclusions about anything] is as one-sided as the "pan-ironical" [according to which he can never be taken as saying anything straightforwardly or without reservation]'.[63]

It will by now be obvious that the process of interpreting Plato is anything but simple. Much of what was written in the past now seems lacking in subtlety or awareness of the difficulties such interpretation poses; much that is written today may be thought undisciplined, fanciful, or at best unprovable.[64] I do not expect the present work to escape such criticism. Nevertheless, without claiming that the other approaches discussed above are either foolish or unproductive of insights, I naturally prefer to pursue the critical method which I myself have found most

[61] See in general the collection of essays ed. by C. L. Griswold, *Platonic Writings, Platonic Readings* (London 1988), which suffers, however, from a persistent tendency among the contributors to proclaim the need for subtler interpretation without going ahead to put their principles into practice. On the *Menexenus* see esp. L.J. Coventry, *JHS* 109 (1989) 1-15. On irony see further below, ch. 3, pp. 77-8.

[62] Cf. R.K. Sprague, *Plato's Use of Fallacy* (New York 1962); R. Hawtrey, *Commentary on Plato's Euthydemus* (Philadelphia 1981).

[63] Tigerstedt, *Interpreting Plato* 103.

[64] Cf. my review of Ferrari, *Listening to the Cicadas* (1987), in *Phronesis* 33 (1988) 216-24; also C.C.W. Taylor's reaction to recent works dealing with the *Protagoras*, in his review of Goldberg (*CR* 35 [1985] 67-8) and in the introd. to his revised commentary on that dialogue (Oxford 1991). Also e.g. C. Gill on Scodel (*CR* 38 [1988] 225-6), C.J. Rowe on Coby (*JHS* 110 [1990] 225-6).

rewarding. Some statement of general principles may be of use at this stage as an indication to the reader of what to expect in subsequent chapters.

First, the dialogue form and other artistic forms need to be examined and as far as possible explained. The choice of the appropriate form is an essential part of any writer's task, and is all the more significant for Plato, writing as an innovator in a genre still in its infancy.[65] Formal considerations go beyond the general distinction between narrated and dramatic dialogues (p. 71), to matters such as the length of speeches, the use of myth or fable, notable changes in tone or stylistic register, elaborate framing constructions, similes and recurrent imagery, and many other stylistic or rhetorical devices which automatically receive attention from the critic of poetry, but are even now often neglected in the study of Platonic prose.[66] Formal structures in prose were developed in particular by the sophists and their pupils, and in many of the dialogues it is valuable to compare what we know of sophistic literature with the transformation and adaptation of their techniques by Plato.[67] Close reading and sustained critical commentary on the individual Platonic texts have already yielded rewards and advanced our understanding of the author's aims and methods.[68] Although inevitably selective and partial in its treatment, the present work is intended as a further contribution to the study of Plato's literary forms and the relation of these to his subject matter.

Secondly, the dialogues take place in a particular setting and involve particular characters. As for setting, this is obviously prominent and arguably significant in dialogues such as the *Symposium*, the *Charmides* and the *Phaedrus*. But perhaps particularly clear is the aptness of the location of the *Phaedo*, in the Athenian prison where Socrates is to meet his end; it can be no coincidence that the dialogue lays such emphasis on

---

[65] On the dialogue form see further pp. 10-15 above.

[66] A pioneering work which should here be mentioned as a major exception to this tendency is Friedlaender, *Plato* (Eng. tr. 1958-69). See esp. the general essays in vol. i. More recently see esp. J. Laborderie, *Le dialogue platonicien de la maturité* (Paris 1978). On imagery see P. Louis, *Les métaphores de Platon* (Paris 1945). On style per se the most substantial recent work is H. Thesleff, *Studies in the Styles of Plato* (Helsinki 1967), which suffers from methodological defects but remains a suggestive starting-point (Dover's review in *Greek and the Greeks* 73ff. is unduly harsh).

[67] Thus the *Euthydemus* presents or parodies the argumentative technique of *sophisticus elenchus*, later systematised by Aristotle; the *Menexenus* the formal funeral speech; the *Symposium* the encomium, and so forth.

[68] See e.g. S.R. Slings's 1981 commentary on the *Clitopho*; M.C. Stokes, *Plato's Socratic Conversations* (London 1986), introd., and the studies of the *Laches* and *Protagoras* (the chapter on the *Symposium* seems to me less rewarding); T. Baxter, *The Cratylus: Plato's Critique of Naming* (Leiden 1992). M. Nussbaum, *The Fragility of Goodness* (Cambridge 1986) includes a number of stimulating passages on the need for dramatic interpretation of Plato's dialogues (pp. 87-8, 122-35), but with the exception of her chapter on the *Symposium* the readings of particular works seem to be too firmly related to her book's overall philosophic theme to give an adequate account of the dialogues in question. There is a helpful though rather general essay by M. Frede, in *OSAP* Suppl. vol. 1992, 201-19, a volume which is devoted to the problems of Platonic interpretation.

death as an escape from imprisonment – the soul's captivity within the
physical body is ended by the purging, releasing process of death (esp.
Phaedo 65-8b, 81-2). Other examples will be discussed in later chapters.[69]
Where characterisation is concerned, as has already been said, the personality of Socrates is of special importance: interaction between Socrates and
others may shed light not only on the personalities of all concerned, but on
the nature of the problem under discussion and on the deficiencies of the
answers proposed. A Phaedrus or an Adeimantus would not behave like,
or argue like, a Thrasymachus. This may seem disturbing to those who
expect philosophy to be concerned with abstract and permanent truths, not
contingent upon the individual disputants' personalities. But Plato characteristically presents arguments in context, arguments between individuals and conducted in an individual way; and although these exchanges may
aim at establishing results valid for others, it is acknowledged that each
investigator must pursue the question further, in discussion with other
friends or independently (see e.g. *Phaedo* 107ab). Nor is it obvious that
Socrates himself is to be regarded as infallible or authoritative: he himself
emphasises his own ignorance, and if we accept that Plato has built on his
teaching or example, advanced or diverged from the positions held by
Socrates, then it is reasonable to allow that some criticism of Socrates may
be implicit or explicit in the dialogues. At the very least, those who respond
most eloquently and emphatically to Socrates' challenges (Callicles,
Thrasymachus, Alcibiades, for example) deserve a hearing.

Thirdly, there is the question of tone, and in particular the problems
raised by Plato's 'serious play'. As already suggested, the 'pan-ironic'
interpretation of Plato's works is surely too easy and insufficiently discriminating.[70] It is necessary to find an approach which, without total subjectivity, takes account of the humour, the comedy, the parody and the whimsy
which gives Plato's work so much of its enduring fascination. Here too
literary criticism has something to contribute. Platonic dialogue obviously
functions in different ways and presents different problems from (say) *Don
Quixote* or *Tristram Shandy*, but we should not suppose that the riddles
Plato has set are insoluble. Alcibiades' description of Plato's Socrates can
be applied to the enigma of the Platonic dialogue itself – outwardly
bantering and ironic, inwardly profound:

> For if anyone were to listen to Socrates' talk, it would seem utterly ludicrous
> at first – it's all wrapped up in such words and phrases, a veritable skin for
> an outrageous satyr. You see, he goes on about pack-asses and blacksmiths
> and cobblers and tanners, and he always seems to be saying the same things

---

[69] See also Friedlaender i, 158-61.

[70] Thus the short book by J.A. Arieti, *Interpreting Plato: The Dialogues as Drama* (Savage,
Maryland 1991), which sets out to demonstrate the banal thesis that Plato's philosophy is
actually *subordinate* to dramatic motivations, treats all dialogues in the same way and with
equal brevity (and in a sequence which has no obvious justification).

in the same ways, so that any foolish or inexperienced person would just laugh at his words. But anyone who has seen them opened up and dwelt inside them will first find that they are the only kind of conversation that has any sense in it, and then that they are the most divine, having within them the best images of virtue, and that they are the most far-reaching, the most utterly essential for anyone who is trying to be a good or honourable man to examine. (*Smp.* 221e-222a)

The *Apology*[71]

The speech of Socrates in self-defence at his trial is in some sense recreated in the work we call Plato's *Apology*; but that statement already suggests how hard a task it may be to distinguish the master and the author even here. Indeed, most of the methodological dilemmas described above with reference to the dialogues already present themselves in this work. Few works of classical Greek prose have been admired more: like the Funeral Speech of Pericles, it seems to preserve the ideas and commitment of an extraordinary man living in Athens' most distinguished days; but whereas Pericles praises and idealises the democratic community of Athens, Socrates earns still more admiration for his willingness to oppose the weaknesses or defects of his native city and to persist in that opposition to the point (effectively) of martyrdom. As with Thucydides' Pericles, we would like to feel that we are hearing the authentic voice of such a famous and influential personality.[72]

There are difficulties in adopting that view. Other versions of Socrates' speech were current in antiquity: we have one from Xenophon's pen which is probably later than Plato's and certainly does not rest on first-hand authorial knowledge (pp. 47-8, 55 below), and Xenophon himself refers to 'all the others' who have recorded Socrates' self-defence. Even if we grant that Socratic self-defences established themselves as a literary genre at an early date, we might still maintain that Plato's is the most faithful, the most authentic. After all, he himself was present at the trial, as the speech itself mentions (though scepticism may intrude even here: the *Apology* is, after all, our only evidence for Plato's presence, so that the argument becomes circular). What gives rise to more nagging doubt is the sheer artistry and rhetorical subtlety of the speech. Granted that Socrates may well have been acquainted with the tricks of the trade, is it not asking too much of him to produce extempore so polished and dazzling a performance? If it is accepted that the speech adapts and inverts not only rhetorical

---

[71] There are book-length studies of the work by C.D.C. Reeve, *Socrates in the Apology* (Indianapolis 1989), and by T.C. Brickhouse and N.D. Smith, *Socrates on Trial* (Oxford 1989). A commentary by M.C. Stokes is expected; meanwhile, see the valuable essay cited in n. 51 above.
[72] Burnet in his commentary (esp. pp. 63-6), R.S. Hackforth, *The Composition of Plato's Apology* (Cambridge 1933), and Guthrie iv. 71ff all argue for authenticity.

techniques in general but particular features of a specific sophistic text, Gorgias' *Palamedes*, then the case for Plato's having shaped the speech with an eye on his bookshelves seems all the stronger.[73] Other arguments concern the passage in which Socrates engages in dialogue with the accuser Meletus; granted, this was a practical possibility in Attic law, but surely Meletus answers too conveniently, lays himself open too frequently to Socrates' refutations (see esp. 26d)? As in the dialogues, literary artifice aids and accelerates the argumentative process. Although these arguments are not conclusive, we may be on safer ground if we treat the *Apology* as a Platonic creation, enhancing and building upon Socrates' actual words. If that is so, some arguments based on comparison are ruled out, namely those which assume that the *Apology* presents the 'true' portrait of Socrates and that later works introduce Plato's distortions. In fact, as we shall see, there are implicit in the speech some of the same contradictions which loom larger in the dialogues: in particular, the conflict between Socrates' humility and his amazing self-confidence, between his protests of ignorance and his fervent commitment to certain principles or firm beliefs.

The speech (or trio of speeches)[74] powerfully insists that Socrates has done nothing wrong, that the prejudices which his enemies are exploiting are the result of ill-informed or malicious misrepresentation, and that the chief source of enmity to him is the indignation which others feel when they are subjected to his questioning and their ignorance is exposed. Socrates goes on to describe the reason for his following this practice of questioning: it all stems from his effort to understand (and at first misguidedly to disprove) the Delphic oracle's declaration that he is the wisest of men. In the end, after initial bafflement and incredulity, he has come to the conclusion that he is 'wisest' in the sense that he, unlike other men, is aware of his own yawning ignorance; and he has continued in his efforts to reveal their own ignorance to them through repeated questioning and exhortation to 'care for their souls' or 'for themselves', rather than dissipating their energies in money-making or political jobbery. In a memorable passage, he presents himself as a gadfly constantly goading and bothering the Athenian state. Nor, he declares, would it be right for him to abandon this way of life, even to save his skin; that would be to disobey the (implicit) command of the god's oracle.

Some of the other striking aspects of the speech can be dealt with by more detailed consideration of a point already mentioned: that Socrates, though he insists on his inexperience in public speaking, in fact employs many of the devices of formal forensic rhetoric while at the same time

[73] On the parallels see J. Coulter, *HSCP* 68 (1964) 269-303, and K. Seeskin, *Dialogue and Discovery: A Study in Socratic Method* (Albany, N.Y. 1987), ch. 3; Guthrie iv. 76f. uneasily plays down their significance.
[74] The main speech precedes the vote; the second one follows after he has been found guilty and includes a counter-proposal of a lesser penalty; the third is a final address after the majority of the jury has voted to accept the sentence of death.

adapting or subverting them.[75] The opening of the first speech sets the keynote.

> I don't know what your experience was, gentlemen of Athens, as you listened to my accusers, but I nearly forgot myself under their influence, so persuasive were their speeches. On the other hand, they said virtually nothing that was true. And I was particularly amazed at one of the many lies they told, namely when they said that you must be on the lookout so as not to be tricked by me, as I am a clever speaker. This seemed to me to be the most shameless feature of their case: fancy them not being ashamed at being immediately refuted by my actual performance, when I am exposed as being not at all a clever speaker – unless, that is, they call somebody clever when he speaks the truth. For if that's what they mean, then I would agree that I am an orator, though not after their pattern.[76] So these men, as I say, have said little or nothing truthful, but from me you will hear the entire truth – certainly not expressed in finely poised phrases like theirs, gentlemen, nor decked out with the correct words and phrases; no, you'll hear my case put in no special order, in the words that come to mind – for I believe that what I am saying is right. Let none of you expect anything different. For it would surely not be proper, gentlemen, for me at my age to appear before you making speeches like a young man. And moreover, gentlemen, I do ask this favour of you, quite emphatically, and beg your permission: if you hear me making my defence in the same terms that I'm accustomed to use in the market, by the money-changers, where many of you have heard me speak, and in other places too, don't be surprised or make a fuss on that account. You see, it's like this. This is the first time I have entered a court-house, and I'm seventy years old. I'm altogether unfamiliar with the idiom of this place. So just as, if I happened to be a genuine foreigner, you'd be sympathetic, I'm sure, if I spoke with the same accent and in the same style as I'd been brought up in, just so now, it's a fair enough request, I think, that I'm making of you, to allow me to talk in my own way – perhaps it's an inferior way, perhaps not – but to give your attention to one thing, and scrutinise that – whether what I say is right or not. That's the proper role of a juryman, whereas a speaker's role is to tell the truth. (17a-18a6)

In this passage a number of themes already make their appearance: the contrast between the *persuasiveness* of his accusers and the *truth* of Socrates' own words (a contrast that lives on throughout Plato's subsequent writings on rhetoric); the insistence that Socrates must use his own natural manner of speech, even if it is not what the jurors are used to in court;[77] and his willingness to upbraid and correct his audience ('don't be surprised or make a fuss on that account'). The first theme is not contradicted but reinforced by the use Socrates makes of forensic commonplaces. Speakers in the Athenian courts regularly declare themselves 'unaccustomed to public speaking', and insist that whereas they are simple, plain-speaking

---

[75] See further Seeskin, 58-61.

[76] For the type of contrast drawn here, cf. *Symp.* 198b-9b, esp. 199b.

[77] Cf. the contrasts regularly drawn between the informal, conversational style of Socrates and the set-piece orations of sophists such as Protagoras: e.g. *Prt.* 334c-8e; p. 133 below.

men, their opponents are devious manipulators of arguments, too clever by half, even sophist-trained.[78] But this argument, however frequently used (and it is clearly a cliché), gains much more force in the mouth of Socrates, who makes much play with his ignorance of politics and public life, who has never been able to afford the education which might be bought from a sophist, and who here and subsequently dismisses the tricks of the rhetorical trade as prettifying (17b9) – at best undignified, at worst corrupt and shameful. Moreover, the theme of cleverness is related to that of wisdom. Athenian prejudice against intellectuals often leads defendants to play down their actual skill at argument; Socrates, as we see, does this as far as clever speaking is concerned, but goes on later to lay claim to *sophia*, wisdom, though of an unconventional kind: he knows that he knows nothing.

Forensic commonplaces are both reshaped and dismissed later in the speech. At 36d and elsewhere Socrates claims that he has been a benefactor of the city.[79] Defendants regularly made such claims, but in terms of their public service through campaigns, service in official posts, and 'liturgies' (financial contributions to public occasions or the like). Thus the speaker of Lysias 25 declares: 'I have been trierarch five times, fought in four sea-battles, contributed to many war-levies and performed my other liturgies more diligently than any other citizen' (12-13).[80] Socrates did not have the kind of wealth that would enable him to pay for a trireme; but he did play a part in Athens' military campaigns, at Potidaea and Delium, a part which he briefly mentions but does not exploit (28e; contrast the praise of his deeds by Laches and Alcibiades elsewhere in Plato). Instead he describes himself as a moral benefactor of his fellow-citizens – a provocative and irksome claim to those who did not feel they needed Socrates as a gadfly or nursemaid.

As for the rejection of standard forensic moves, the crucial example is his failure to appeal to pity. Again this is provocatively put. 'Perhaps some of you may be irritated, remembering their own behaviour, if in the past any of you was on trial in some less serious case, and begged and entreated the jurors with floods of tears, putting his own children up in the stand so that he might win as much sympathy as possible, whereas now I am going to do none of these things, even though I am (as it may appear) in the worst of dangers.'[81] '... It does not seem to me to bring any credit on myself, or on

---

[78] E.g. Antiph. 3 g 3, Dem. 22. 4, 23. 95-9, 35. 38-43, Aeschin. 3. 228, Dem. 18. 276; Dover, *GPM* 25-6.

[79] The point is put provocatively: Socrates declares that he has a better claim to be feted and fed at public expense in the prytaneum than any victors in the Olympic games (36e). For honours paid to athletes at state expense see e.g. *IG* i³ 131. 11ff. Intellectuals commonly criticised the exaggerated tributes paid to physical achievement: see Xenoph. B2, Eur. fr. 282, and C.M. Bowra, *Problems in Greek Poetry* (Oxford 1953) 15-37.

[80] For more examples see Lysias 25. 12-3, Dem. 25. 76; Davies, *APF*, xviii; cf. Eur. *Hipp.* 993ff.

[81] For this motif in extant oratory see Dem. 53. 29; 57. 70; 38. 27; 45. 88, Hyperides 4. 41, etc.; Dover, *GPM* 195. For parody, see Ar. *Wasps* 975-8.

you, or on the city as a whole, to do any of these things at my age and having the reputation that I have – it may be true or false, but still it has been felt that Socrates is in some way superior to the general run of men.' (34c-35a).[82]

Socrates' self-defence also requires comment at the level of form and style. As we have seen, he warns the jurors to expect no more than his normal style of disquisition, whether it is good or bad. This might lead us to expect a fairly chatty, unpretentious informality; and indeed Socrates does quote casual conversation (with Callias, 20a ff.), in which he makes use of his familiar low-key examples (cf. 25b); he describes his own bafflement on hearing the oracular verdict, quoting his own internal musing; and when he recounts his courageous actions at the time of the Arginusae trial and under the Thirty (32b-e), he introduces this apologetically, as a commonplace too much reminiscent of the courts (32a8: a reference to the practice, already cited, of recounting one's past services to the state). Still more strikingly, he imagines questions addressed to him by the jury and presents his answers (20c, 28b, 29c, 37e); and in dealing with the prosecutor Meletus, he insists on adopting his characteristic question-and-answer technique, thus turning his defence oration partly into a form of dialectic (24c ff.). Several features of this exchange recall motifs familiar in the dialogues: for example, Socrates mockingly accuses his opponent of teasing or making a game of him (27e; cf. e.g. *Grg.* 499bc); the silence of Meletus, which in fact indicates baffled indignation, is taken to show his assent (27c; cf. *Grg.* 505d sqq.); and Socrates' main tactic consists of showing contradictions in Meletus' ill-considered propositions (esp. 27a and e).

These are not the only remarkable aspects of the speech's style and manner. Another strand which runs through it is the presentation of Socrates as a heroic figure, one who merits comparison with the great men of epic myth.[83] Although this appears only gradually, it is surely present in his reference to his 'wanderings' and his 'labours' in service to the god's command: the language here must recall the wanderings and hardships of Odysseus and Heracles (22c). Clearer still is the quotation of Homer at 28c-d: challenged by his hypothetical critic to justify his pursuit of a way of life which leads to his own death, Socrates replies: 'You are wrong, sir, if you think a man of any merit, however little, ought to take account of risks of life and death, and not rather scrutinise in his every action whether he is acting justly or unjustly, whether his actions are those of a good man or a bad one.' Again, later in the trial, in his final speech, he makes a prophecy, 'for I am now at that point where the gift of prophecy comes most readily to men – when they are at the point of death' (39c). This is a common

---

[82] Note further 38d: he has not been condemned because he lacks verbal resources, but rather because of 'a lack of boldness and shamelessness, and because I am not prepared to say to you such things as would give you most pleasure to hear – you would have liked to hear me moaning and wailing and doing and saying many other things unworthy of me, so I claim, such things as you have been used to hearing from other people.' Cf. Ar. *Wasps* 552-8, 560-75.

[83] Cf. T. Irwin, in *Language and the Tragic Hero*, ed. P. Pucci (Atlanta 1988), 55-83.

theme in literature, but especially prominent in epic: both Patroclus and Hector in the *Iliad* prophesy in their dying moments.[84] The last such passage is in lighter vein, and shows a typically Socratic humour: if there is a life after death in Hades, he looks forward to the opportunity to question and converse with the great figures of myth, such as Agamemnon and Odysseus, and other men like himself who have suffered from an unjust condemnation (Ajax and Palamedes, for example) (41ab). In Socrates' eyes, Hades, instead of being a monstrous or threatening world of monsters and hellfire, is a delightful setting for prolonged ethical conversations: there, he explains, his interlocutors will never be able to get away from him, and they will not be able to execute him in order to escape his questioning! (41c) As in other Platonic works, traditional myth is reshaped and given a philosophic flavouring.

Socrates, then, is shown in the *Apology* as well able to beat the rhetoricians at their own game: as well as mastering their often trite commonplaces, he is able to claim the moral high ground by asserting his higher motives and nobler purpose, even hinting at a degree of heroism which finds its closest analogies in epic poetry. In these respects the *Apology* resembles the dialogues, in which Socrates often takes on the experts and argues them to a standstill, and in which his criticisms of rhetoric and poetry are often couched in richly poetic or highly imaginative language. The style and conception of the *Apology* goes well beyond anything we might expect in a 'normal' defence speech, let alone one delivered by an unpractised speaker. Instead of the strident pleas of contemporary oratory, self-righteous and scurrilous by turns, we meet here a much more versatile and mischievous speaker: challenging yet also humorous, severe but ironic, his tone changing from light and impertinent banter when dealing with his accusers, to vivid eloquence and passionate intensity when he describes his mission or alludes to his religious faith. The extraordinary mixture of humility and arrogance is perhaps best captured in the famous gadfly passage:

> So now, Athenians, I am very far from pleading in my own defence, as some might suppose; rather, I am pleading on your behalf, in the hope that you may not commit a crime with regard to the god's gift to you, by voting for my condemnation. For if you kill me, you will not find it easy to get another like me, one who has been firmly attached to the city by the god – if I may put it in a rather humorous way, just as if the city were a great and well-bred horse, which is rather sluggish on account of its great size, and needs to be woken up by some gadfly; it is in this way that the god seems to have attached me, being a man of that sort, to the city, and all day long I never stop settling here and there, waking you up and persuading and criticising each and every one of you. (30d-31a)

Whence does Socrates derive his amazingly firm conviction of his divine

---

[84] Cf. A.S. Pease on Cic. *On divination* i. 63-4. Reminiscence of an epic motif also figures in the *Crito* (see 44ab, recalling the language of *Iliad* 9. 363).

mission? How is it that he has concluded that his persuasion and exhortation of the Athenians must be so aggressive and provocative? We are not told, but Plato has brilliantly succeeded in making us both admire and value the dedication of Socrates to this task, and at the same time see very clearly exactly why the Athenians wanted to be rid of him.

For Plato, however, the execution of Socrates was a travesty of justice and an appalling indictment of the political and educational system which made such a misunderstanding or misrepresentation of a good man and a philosopher possible (cf. *Phaedo* 118a15-17; *Letter vii* 324d-5c). Much of the animosity which Plato's works show towards the rhetorical teaching of his time doubtless springs from the misuse of words in that fateful trial. But the *Apology*, as this account has tried to bring out, does not paint a purely idealistic picture. This is not to say that there is any point at which we are intended to doubt or criticise or disapprove of Socrates' sentiments, nor even of his way of putting them across. Plato does, however, do more than simply show us Socrates the philosophic martyr: he also makes clear just how demanding his ideal of life was, how different from everyday Greek values, how much he expected from his interlocutors, from the assembled jurors, from Athens as a whole. That he was condemned is shocking and wrong, but is it, even on the evidence of the *Apology*, altogether surprising?[85] In part at least, the *Apology*, like some of the dialogues, shows that Socrates *failed*. It was for Plato to explore why.

Appendix A. Chronological Table

The first column indicates dates of literary works which are well-established; the second presents less certain or vaguer dates; the third lists a number of relevant historical events. All dates are BC. This list represents a fairly conservative position, but it must be emphasised that some of the dates in col. 2 are controversial. For fuller discussion and bibliography see above, pp. 2-7. For a broad discussion of how ancient chronology is established see E.J. Bickerman, *Chronology of the Ancient World* (2nd edn. London 1980).

		c. 427 Birth of Plato
416 Agathon's first tragic victory		
		404 Defeat of Athens; government of 30 Tyrants
		399 Execution of Socrates
	390s? *Apology*, *Crito*, aporetic dialogues?	

---

[85] This is not to deny that there are other possible reasons unmentioned or understressed in the *Apology*: in particular, the association of Socrates with suspect political figures such as Alcibiades and Critias. See ch. 2, p. 43; and cf. Dover, *The Greeks and their Legacy* (1988) 135-58, esp. 154-7, 158.

c. 392 Aristoph. *Women at the Assembly*	post-395 *Meno* (probably a good deal later, in 380s)	
		??389/8 Plato visits Sicily
	380s *Gorgias, Protagoras?*	386 King's Peace
	post-386 *Menexenus*	
	post-385 Pl. *Symposium*	
380 Isocrates *Panegyricus*		
	post-378 Xen. *Symposium*	
	? 370s *Republic* ?	
	? 370s or 360s? *Phaedrus, Parmenides*	
	post-369 *Theaetetus*	
	(followed by *Sophist, Statesman*)	367 Dionysius II succeeds his father. Plato visits Syracuse at Dion's request.
		367 Aristotle joins Academy
		361 Plato's final visit to Syracuse
		357/6 Dion seizes power in Syracuse
		354 Dion murdered
	?? *Philebus, Timaeus, Critias*	
353 Isocrates *Antidosis*		
	post-352 *Laws*	
		347 Death of Plato. Aristotle leaves Athens
		338 Battle of Chaeronea (Philip of Macedon conquers Greece)
		338 Death of Isocrates
		323 Death of Aristotle

All dates concerning Plato in Sicily depend heavily on acceptance of the Seventh Letter as, if not authentic, at least based on sound knowledge. For a recent defence of this position see Brunt, *Studies in Greek History and Thought* 313-32.

Appendix B. The 'unwritten' or 'oral' doctrines of Plato

In a passage of his *Physics* in which he is discussing the nature of space, Aristotle makes the following cryptic remarks. 'This is why Plato in the *Timaeus* says that matter and space are the same; for the participant and space are identical. It is true, indeed, that the account he gives there of the "participant" is different from what he says in *the so-called unwritten doctrines*. Nevertheless, he did identify place and space' (*Phys.* 209b13). This tantalising reference has been linked by modern scholars with (in particular) a famous anecdote which comes down in various versions but which also seems to be Aristotelian in origin. Aristotle, according to one version, used to quote it to illustrate the need to preface a lecture with an account of the subject matter and the method to be followed. The story was that Plato announced that he would give a lecture 'On the Good', and a large audience assembled, anticipating much enlightenment on whether the good was (for instance) health or wealth. Instead they were treated to a complex mathematical argument, which concluded that 'Good is One', and left the audience bewildered.[86]

The debate arising from these passages and others concerns the nature of Plato's teaching, and indeed the workings of the Academy as a whole. Aristotle's reference has been taken to imply that Plato gave instruction on a whole range of subjects along quite different lines from the 'doctrines' of the dialogues; that, indeed, the dialogues are secondary and his oral teaching was the real tradition of Platonism (did not Plato himself disparage writing in the *Phaedrus* and elsewhere?). Some passages of Aristotle, and also many passages in later writers in the Platonic tradition, have been taken to reflect this oral teaching.[87]

The task of reconstructing and seeking to define Plato's real, oral, doctrines has been undertaken with particular zeal by a number of scholars in Germany, especially the so-called Tübingen school. Major figures are Krämer, Gaiser and Szlezak, some of whose work is now available in English.[88] Before the emergence of this new school theories of this kind were already current, if less fully developed. On the whole Anglo-American reception of these arguments has been cool and sceptical.[89] Cherniss in a work which is something of a tour de force, *The Riddle of the Early Academy* (1945), tried to refute the whole notion of Plato 'teaching' in the Academy (he made the important point that the anecdote in Aristoxenus refers only to *one* lecture and does not offer ground for supposing that this was a regular event, let alone a course). He argued that all the passages in Aristotle in which he might be thought to be dealing with Plato's unwritten teachings were in fact Aristotle discussing the dialogues, though often expanding or rephrasing the terms used in them. He did his best to play down even the reference in the *Physics*. Later, a long review by Vlastos of Krämer's book poured cold water on the whole enterprise: the arguments often depend on late sources, they involve major speculative leaps, they sometimes misinterpret crucial texts.[90] A non-philosopher may venture the comment that the emerging 'doctrine', a strange form of mathematical mysticism based on the ideas as numbers, may not appeal to all readers.

Cherniss almost certainly went too far. It is reasonable to suppose that Plato did

---

[86] Aristoxenus *Harm.* 30-1 and other versions; Riginos, *Platonica* no. 79. For very different views on the significance of this anecdote see Cherniss, *Riddle of the Early Academy* 1-13; K. Gaiser, *Phronesis* 25 (1980) 5-37 (in English).

[87] For a helpful brief summary, see J. Dillon, *The Middle Platonists* (London 1977) 1-11.

[88] H.J. Krämer, *Der Ursprung der Geistesmetaphysik: Untersuchungen zur Geschichte des Platonismus zwischen Platon und Plotin* (Amsterdam 1964; Eng. tr. as *Plato and the Foundations of Metaphysics* (Albany, N.Y. 1990)); K. Gaiser, *Platons ungeschriebene Lehre* (Stuttgart 1963; 2nd edn. 1968); T. Szlezak, *Platon und die Schriftlichkeit der Philosophie* (1985; Italian tr. 1989); J. Wippern (ed.) *Das Problem der Ungeschriebenen Lehre Platons* (Darmstadt 1972). For further bibliography see Guthrie v. ch. 8; Kraut, *Companion* 524-5; Tigerstedt, *Interpreting Plato* ch. 6. See also Kraut 526-7, for bibl. on Platonism after Plato.

[89] An exception is the eccentric book by J.H. Findlay, *Plato: The Written and Unwritten Doctrines* (N.Y. 1974), which includes a reply to Cherniss, but seems unaware of Vlastos. It is useful for the appendix translating many of the texts cited by Gaiser and others in support of their arguments.

[90] Vlastos, *Gnomon* 41 (1963) 641-55, repr. with a further appendix in *Platonic Studies* 379-403.

teach and discuss many subjects with his pupils or companions, whether or not he regularly lectured; we can hardly think that he preserved a total silence on the subject he clearly cared so much about, or that he would refuse on principle to clarify anything said in the dialogues. There may have been unwritten teachings in this loose sense, matters discussed at the Academy, on which Plato offered his ideas, perhaps even expounded his latest thoughts at some length. But what there clearly was not is an orthodox Platonic doctrine or dogma, still less a secret body of knowledge preserved with Pythagorean fidelity by all his disciples.[91] Any such conception not only runs counter to the open-mindedness which an unbiassed reader must constantly see in the dialogues, but also conflicts with the known facts about Plato's followers, who clearly argued amongst themselves, disagreed about the interpretation of the philosophy found in the dialogues, and pursued their own lines of thought, developing and diverging from 'Platonism'.[92] We know, for example, that different members of the Academy disagreed on whether there were 'forms' of artefacts or of evils or of negative terms.[93] Again, there was from an early stage disagreement as to how the *Timaeus* should be interpreted: was the cosmos literally created at some distant point in the past, or was this only a mode of presentation, a didactic symbol, to show the nature of something actually ungenerable?[94] Speusippus, who rejected the Ideas, nevertheless became Plato's successor as head of the Academy.

Moreover, if there were unwritten teachings, it is wildly unlikely that our fragmentary reports can enable us to recover them; and to many interpreters it may seem equally unlikely that a reconstruction of these teachings would shed much light on the dialogues. Whatever may be the case with exceptional works such as the *Parmenides*, the great majority of the dialogues were surely aimed at a wider audience than philosophers and theoreticians. A work of literary criticism need not apologise for concentrating on literary texts which survive in entirety, rather than pursuing a difficult and perhaps ultimately fruitless quest which seems to have the regrettable consequence of diminishing the interest of the surviving works of Plato.[95]

[91] On the tradition of secret doctrines among the Pythagoreans see e.g. Guthrie i. 148-53.

[92] Important points on this score are made by Cherniss, *Riddle* ch. 3; see also J. Lynch, *Aristotle's School* (1972) 54-63 on the Academy, 75-96 on differences between the Academy and Aristotle's Lyceum; M. Ostwald and J.P. Lynch, *CAH* vi[2]. 604-5, 622-33.

[93] Cherniss op. cit. 78, referring to his *Aristotle's Criticism of Plato* i 256-60, 265-72.

[94] Cf. Arist. *de caelo* 279b32, Speusippus fr. 54 Lang, Xenocrates frr. 33, 54 Heinze; R. Sorabji, *Time, Creation and the Continuum* (Ithaca, N.Y. and London 1983) 268-76.

[95] The reader who senses that my position is somewhat *parti pris* may like to contrast C.J. Rowe's comments on some recent work in this area: see his review-article in *Phronesis* 38 (1993) 214-16.

2

Socratic Literature and the Socratic Question

It will be clear already from the first chapter that the study of Plato is dominated to an almost unhealthy extent by a preoccupation with his relation to Socrates. In the greater part of this book Socrates will be considered simply as a character in Plato, and the so-called Socratic question – the enquiry into the character and opinions of the original, historical Socrates – will be largely set aside. But in the present chapter an attempt will be made to set out the other evidence which modern scholarship has thought relevant to the study of Socrates; although no final solution to the Socratic question will be offered (if indeed that question is soluble in the present state of our evidence), some ground needs to be cleared, and the investigation, though of limited literary relevance, has its own considerable interest, both as a historical issue and as a historiographical problem. As with two equally influential figures, Alexander the Great and Jesus Christ, the abiding interest and importance of Socrates' achievement is matched by the complex contradictions and uncertainties of the traditions which inform us of that achievement. The parallel may be reinforced by the observation that even those sources closest to the original in date may not have been the best equipped to assess their subject or to inform us about him.[1]

To put the Platonic portrait of Socrates in perspective, we shall be considering three sources of information about Socrates, each utterly

[1] The bibliography on this subject is immense. Guthrie iii provides most of the material and much sound good sense, though to my mind his approach is insufficiently rigorous. G. Vlastos's two essays, 'The paradox of Socrates' (in the collection *The Philosophy of Socrates*, 1971) and 'Socrates' (*PBA* 74, 1988, 89-111) are good for orientation; the latter is expanded in his book, *Socrates, Ironist and Moral Philosopher* (1991). A post-Vlastos study, of which I have not been able to take full account, is by Brickhouse and Smith, *Plato's Socrates* (Oxford 1994).

An anthology of contributions to the discussion, with full bibl., is A. Patzer, *Der historische Sokrates* (Darmstadt 1987) which includes Ross's 1933 paper. Much less valuable is the curious compilation by Mario Montuori, *The Socratic Problem: The History, the Solutions from the 18th Century to the Present Time* (Amsterdam 1992), which presents 61 extracts from 54 authors 'in their historical context'. Field, *Plato and his Contemporaries* 133-74 and Humbert, *Socrate et les petits socratiques* 213-87 are helpful on the lost figures such as Aeschines and Antisthenes. See further Laborderie, *Le dialogue platonicien* 507-13; more specific studies are mentioned below.

different in approach and aims from the others: Aristophanes, Xenophon and Aristotle. It will also be necessary to say something about the writers of Socratic dialogues which have not survived intact, but of which we know something through secondary sources – works by other pupils or friends of Socrates, such as Aeschines of Sphettos and Phaedo of Elis. Since the relationship of these works to Plato's literary career is unclear, source-criticism here merges into literary history: these little-known figures may have had some role in the development of the Socratic dialogue as a literary form. On the whole, however, our concern will be more with works which survive for our study.[2]

The earliest testimony about Socrates is also the most unreliable and notorious, the *Clouds* of Aristophanes. This play, originally produced in 423, was a failure, to its author's chagrin, but our judgement of why it failed is hampered, since we have a version which the poet appears to have partially revised but probably never produced.[3] Its main theme is the dangerous and corrupting teaching of intellectuals, represented by Socrates, who at first, in his dealings with the naive anti-hero Strepsiades, seems to be a preposterous figure absorbed in trivial experiments and verbal games, but who subsequently introduces the young man Pheidippides, smarter son of Strepsiades, to the teachings of the two personified Arguments, Right and Wrong. Convinced by the amoral and self-interested teachings of 'Wrong', Pheidippides abandons both morality and traditional religion, beats up his father, and scorns conventional values: such, it seems, is the effect of philosophy on its pupils. The play as we have it ends with a repentant Strepsiades venting his rage on the sophists' 'Thinking-Shop', which he burns to the ground, to the discomfiture of Socrates and his followers. There is some reason to suppose that this disturbing conclusion was added in the revised version, perhaps to satisfy popular demand for the punishment of the corrupters of the young.[4]

Socrates in this play seems to resemble the figure of Plato and Xenophon's dialogues only in his poverty and some of his physical attributes. His intellectual interests and views are an amalgam of the opinions of various thinkers, and he seems to be used as a typical example of the genus sophist, probably because he was himself an Athenian resident. Moreover, we know that he was a regular butt of old comedy, which seems frequently

---

[2] There are innumerable translations of Plato's dialogues on Socrates' last days, and often the *Clouds* is included in selections of this kind (e.g. T.G. and G.S. West's volume of 1984, containing *Euthyphro*, *Apol.*, *Crito* and *Clouds*). A sourcebook with a wider range is J. Ferguson, *Socrates* (London, Macmillan 1970) which collects much inaccessible material, but the reader must be on guard: his annotation is sparse and his translations often unreliable.

[3] On all matters concerning *Clouds* see Dover's indispensable commentary (Oxford 1968); on some points the shorter edition by A. Sommerstein also deserves attention. On the question of changes in the second version see Dover lxxx-xcviii; Guthrie iii. 376-7.

[4] For discussion of evidence for conflict between the older and younger generation during the later fifth century see M. Ostwald, *From Popular Sovereignty to the Sovereignty of Law* (Berkeley and L.A. 1986) 229-38; B. Strauss, *Fathers and Sons in Athens* (London 1993).

to adopt a traditionalist stance in opposition to new ideas, pretentious cleverness or would-be 'reformers'.[5] Other intellectuals were also guyed in comedy;[6] it is instructive to compare the treatment of Euripides, whose work Aristophanes clearly knew well and in part admired, but whom he repeatedly mocks for his modernity and his interest in ideas. It is significant that one recurrent joke is to accuse Socrates of helping Euripides write his plays.[7]

The interpretation of *Clouds* is a problem, just as the assessment of the political and social impact of Old Comedy generally is difficult. Although many critics have supposed that Aristophanes used his plays to comment on contemporary events in the strong sense of propounding his own views and attempting to shape public opinion,[8] it is now recognised that a more cautious approach is necessary, that the topicality of this type of comedy is mingled with fantasy and obvious absurdity, and that, in short, we must acknowledge a wide gap between drama and real-life events. The outrageous treatment of the demagogue Cleon (esp. in *Knights*) not only involved extreme distortion of his background and political competence, but also seems to have had no effect on his successful career: at any rate, the audience which awarded the first prize to *Knights* in 424 went on to elect Cleon to the generalship for the following year. The distortion of Socrates' behaviour and morals may have been equally conscious, and similarly devoid of effect. In his *Symposium*, Plato presents Aristophanes as present at the same dinner party as Socrates,[9] and even has Alcibiades quote a passage from the *Clouds* which describes Socrates' gait and his way of swivelling his eyes: although Aristophanes is treated humorously by both Socrates and the narrator, there is no hint of antagonism between them. These and other arguments make it implausible to see the *Clouds* as a deliberately conceived indictment of Socrates.[10] Its value to the student of Plato is not as evidence concerning Socrates, nor even necessarily for Aristophanes' misconceptions about Socrates, but rather for the comic

---

[5] For Socrates elsewhere in Old Comedy see e.g. Ameipsias' *Connos* (which came second over *Clouds* in 423); Eupolis, fr. 352 K = 386 KA; Diog. Laert. ii. 18, 27-8; Dover, *GPM* 10-13. Some of the other fragments could well be earlier than the first *Clouds*.

[6] V. Ehrenberg, *The People of Aristophanes* (2nd edn., Oxford 1951) 279f.

[7] *Clouds* (first edn.) fr. 376 K =392KA; Teleclides fr. 39-40 K = 41-2 KA; Callias fr. 12 K =15 KA; perhaps implied at *Frogs* 1491f. See also Dover's comm. on *Clouds*, pp. 209-10, for parallels between the *agones* in *Clouds* and *Frogs*.

[8] This view, ubiquitous in older studies, does not require detailed documentation, but see more recently G. de Ste. Croix, *Origins of the Peloponnesian War* 355-71, esp. 370-1, cf. 232-6. A different approach which also sees Aristophanes as offering a serious critique of Socratic teaching is to be found in the thought-provoking paper by M. Nussbaum, *YCS* 26 (1981) 43-97, but her attribution of her own reservations to the comic poet seems dubious.

[9] There is nothing implausible in this: on Aristophanes' social position cf. S. Dow, *AJA* 73 (1969) 234-5; *SEG* 33. 161.

[10] See further a series of articles by S. Halliwell, esp. *JHS* 111 (1991) 48-70, and in *Tragedy, Comedy and the Polis*, ed. A. Sommerstein, S. Halliwell, J. Henderson and B. Zimmermann (Bari 1993) 321-40.

image (and so to some extent the public perception) of the intellectual and his activities.

This argument may need qualification if we take seriously a claim made by Plato's Socrates in the *Apology*. There Socrates claims that the case brought against him by Anytus and others is all the more dangerous because so many of the jury have heard stories about him over many years, and how he has theories about the heavens and knows how to make the weaker case defeat the stronger. Consequently, the jurors have all sorts of prejudices against him which strengthen the force of the prosecutors' case, even though these statements about him are false. 'And the most incredible thing of all is that it is impossible for me even to know and tell you their names – unless one of them happens to be a comic poet' (18cd). A little later he makes this point more specific with a reference to Aristophanes, in whose play 'Socrates goes whirling around, proclaiming that he is walking on air, and uttering a great deal of nonsense about things of which I know nothing whatsoever' (19c). This passage, however, says nothing about Aristophanes' intentions, real or supposed, but only suggests that the satirical treatment of Socrates, in the *Clouds* and other plays like it, created a climate of opinion which the prosecutors can exploit. It would be artifical to suggest that Old Comedy never influenced any spectator's opinions on anything,[11] but it must be made clear that in satirising Socrates, however grotesquely, Aristophanes was doing nothing unusual in his genre and nothing which he might have expected to have unpleasant consequences for a man with whom he may already have been on very friendly terms.

That the satire is grotesque is generally agreed. Socrates in the *Clouds* is shown voicing various physical doctrines which can be associated with particular intellectuals of the period, whereas the Socrates of Plato and Xenophon has no interest in physical enquiry.[12] The Aristophanic Socrates takes fees (and indeed steals clothes), whereas the Socrates of the later writers insists that he has never done so, and has indeed no teaching he could charge for. The Aristophanic Socrates invites Pheidippides to learn the amoralism of the 'Unjust Argument', and expresses no anxiety about the moral corruption involved; whereas if we do not believe Xenophon and Plato when they describe Socrates' concerns as essentially moral, and particularly associated with the upbringing and education of the young, then we may as well admit that we know nothing of Socrates beyond a few details of his physical appearance. In short, the incoherence and implausibility of Aristophanes' portrait of Socrates are such that only the most

---

[11] M. Heath, *Political Comedy in Aristophanes* (Göttingen 1987), esp. 9-12, and Halliwell 1993 (see last n.), esp. 335-40, come near to suggesting this, though the latter's position is more carefully expressed.

[12] This is true even if the intellectual autobiography of *Phaedo* 96e-9d is attributed to the historical Socrates rather than seen as mirroring Plato's own disillusionment with thinkers such as Anaxagoras. The latter view is preferred e.g. by Vlastos *PBA* 1988, 90n.11; see also Rowe on *Phaedo* 96a2, who thinks the account a fiction shaped to make a didactic point.

paradoxical argument would maintain that it tells us anything independent and authentic about the real Socrates.[13]

Other passing references to Socrates in comedy are less controversial. A passage in Aristophanes' *Birds* (1281-3) can be read as associating him with enthusiasts for Spartan ways, and a fuller comment in the *Frogs* (1491ff.) describes him as talking with people in a modern and time-wasting way (as elsewhere, he is here connected with Euripides): 'So what is elegant is not to sit chattering next to Socrates, abandoning culture and leaving aside what matters most in the tragic art ...'. Ion of Chios, who has already been mentioned in ch. 1, seems to have mentioned Socrates in his autobiographical *Visits* (F 9), and the philosopher will have gained some fame or notoriety for his hardiness on campaign at Potidaea and Delium (mentioned in the *Laches* and the *Symposium*), as later for his strong stand at the debate on the fate of the generals after Arginusae and his resistance to the Thirty. But apart from these passages it is hard to find much unambiguous evidence for Socrates' actions or for Athenian opinion about him until the trial of 399. Much remains unstated in the terms of the indictment at that trial:

> Socrates is guilty of refusing to recognise the gods recognised by the state, and of introducing other, new divinities. He is also guilty of corrupting the young. The penalty demanded is death.[14]

Underlying this we can detect at least three strands of hostile opinion: the political, arising from Socrates' connections with oligarchic figures such as Alcibiades and Critias; the educational, reflecting suspicion of his involvement with the young and indignation at the readiness with which they learned to question and challenge their elders in dialectical fashion; and the religious, in the suspicion which more conventional Athenians felt at Socrates' alleged private divinity, the divine voice or *daimonion* (cf. *Euthyphro* 3bc). But Plato's claim in the *Apology* that Meletus and the others also exploited general antagonism towards intellectuals is only too plausible. It is artificial to rank these points in order of importance as explanations for Socrates' condemnation: different members of the jury will have been influenced by each to a different extent, and anger at Socrates' bearing at the actual trial will certainly have fanned potential hostility further.

After Socrates' execution, controversy about him ran high, and we can

---

[13] This is not to deny that a few features of the real Socrates may be recognisable, in a watered-down or parodic form, in the play: e.g. the question-and-answer method, or the insistence on introspection by the pupil (W. Schmid, *Philologus* 97 (1948) 209-28, R. Philippson, *RhM* 81 (1932) 30ff.; Dover xlii-iv seems hypersceptical here). But these are not *independent* characteristics, that is they are not identifiable as Socratic features without appealing to the other sources.

[14] The wording varies in our different sources: see Guthrie iii. 382. The variations do not seem significant.

sense the passion with which his defenders idealised and his critics pillo-
ried his memory. Socratic literature had its origin in apologetic writing. In
the *Apology* (39cd), Plato makes Socrates prophesy that there will be other
critics who will follow his example and continue to persecute the Athenians,
'critics whom up till now I have restrained, though you knew it not; and
being younger they will be harsher to you and will cause you more annoy-
ance' (cf. Xen. *Ap.* 26). It is usually supposed that this is a prophecy after
the event, that Plato here foretells his own work and that of others. This
would imply that the *Apology* was not the first example of Socratic literature, that indeed Plato himself was not alone or even the first. Our
information on the Socratic followers and writers on Socrates depends
largely on two passages in Plato, namely *Apology* 33d-4a, the list of those
present at the trial, and *Phaedo* 59b-c, those present at Socrates' death. We
can compare these lists with a passage of Xenophon (*Mem.* i. 2. 47-8), in
which Xenophon writes that although people criticise Socrates for being
the teacher of Critias and Alcibiades, they ought to remember how many
of Socrates' disciples were *good* men; a list follows. Many of those named
are also known to have written about the master: Aeschines, Antisthenes,
Crito, Phaedo, Eucleides, Glaucon (Plato's brother), Simmias and Cebes.
Who first participated in this literary movement was already disputed in
antiquity,[15] and probably does not matter very much. More important is
the nature of this literature – its scale and scope, its style, and above all
its status as fact or fiction or a subtle blend of the two.[16] By the time of
Aristotle it was established as a literary genre, the *Sokratikoi logoi*, which
he saw as mid-way between prose and poetry (*Poet.* 1447b11, *Rh.* 1417a21,
fr. 72-3). Our evidence suggests that most of these writings were fairly short
– more like the Platonic *Euthyphro* and *Ion*, or the individual chapters of
Xenophon's *Memorabilia*, than the more ambitious dialogues of Plato's
maturity. A single volume, we are told, could contain nine dialogues by
Glaucon, and another held 23 by Simmias (Diog. Laert. ii. 124).[17] Their style
appears to have been lucid and simple, quite unlike the elaborate extrava-
gances and vivid characterisation by style in works like Plato's *Sympo-*

---

[15] Cf. the related debate about the invention of dialogue (ch. 1, pp. 10-15). Besides texts
already cited there, see Diog. Laert. ii. 61, Aeschines imitated or drew upon dialogues by
Antisthenes and others; ii. 123, Simon the cobbler the first to write down Socrates' conversations. It is far from clear how ancient scholars could be certain of the priority of these various
figures, so close in date and each reading or making use of one another's work.
  Vlastos, *Socrates* 52 is incautious in citing Theopompus *FGH* 115 F 259 as evidence that
Plato plagiarised earlier dialogues by Aristippus, Antisthenes and Bryson. This kind of
accusation is common in ancient polemic about philosophers, and Theopompus, in general a
malicious writer, is an enthusiast for Antisthenes and antagonistic to Plato (cf. F. 275, 295,
359; M.A. Flower, *Theopompus of Chios* (Oxford 1994) 53-5, 93-6).
[16] Momigliano, *Development of Greek Biography* 46-8 has good general remarks on this.
[17] Cf. C.W. Müller, *Die Kurzdialoge der Appendix Platonica* (Munich 1975); Slings, *Clitopho*
24ff. The extant spuria probably give a reasonable idea of the scale and quality of much of this
work.

sium.[18] For that very reason, Aeschines' Socrates in particular was later thought to be a more accurate portrait than Plato's. There was room for scene-setting: Aeschines is quoted for a sentence (perhaps the opening of a work) 'We sat upon the benches in the Lyceum, where the stewards of the games order the contests' (F 15 Krauss). The authentic examples of the genre were much imitated, and later critics were unsure how many genuinely went back to the disciples of Socrates (e.g. Diog. Laert. ii. 64 [Panaetius], and many other passages).

Aeschines is the only one of these figures of whom we have substantial fragments.[19] Ancient criticism accepted seven dialogues as genuinely his, of which the best-known to us are his *Alcibiades* and *Aspasia*. There are clear analogies with Platonic dialogues in each case, though it would be rash to assert a direct influence either way. The *Alcibiades* seems to have been narrated to a companion by Socrates, who described how he gave advice to Alcibiades and sought to quell his arrogance by making him acknowledge his inferiority to the great statesman Themistocles. The result was to convince Alcibiades of his need for further education: so dismayed at his deficiencies was he that he was reduced to tears, resting his head upon his knees (vestig. ii-iii, pp. 38-9 Krauss). Socrates then commented to his friend on his own love for Alcibiades, a divine gift which enabled him to improve the young man. Compared with Plato's *Symposium*, the picture seems more idealistic: Socrates' powers are instantly and decisively effective, and Alcibiades is more deeply humbled. The effect of making Socrates himself the narrator is to make him seem a little self-satisfied. But the parallel with the apologetic purposes of Xenophon and Plato regarding Alcibiades is striking; interesting too is the device of making Socrates the narrator, a step which Xenophon never takes, but which becomes a regular procedure in Plato (*Charmides, Lysis, Protagoras, Euthydemus, Republic*). It automatically involves an element of fiction.

Aeschines' *Aspasia* is another work of which we know something and would like to know more. Here Socrates apparently discussed with Callias the education of the latter's children, recounting some of the achievements of great women of history, and advising him to entrust his sons to Aspasia. This remarkable woman, a beautiful and intelligent courtesan, mistress of Pericles,[20] seems to have made regular appearances in the Socratic litera-

---

[18] Key testimonia are Demetr. *On Style* 296-8, D.H. *Dem.* 2, 5-7, 23. See further W. Christ-W. Schmid, *Gr. Litteraturgeschichte* (6th edn. Munich 1912) i. 710; E. Norden, *Antike Kunstprosa* (3rd edn. 1915) 104ff.; F. Walsdorff, *Die antiken Urteile über Platons Stil* (Leipzig 1927); Humbert (n. 1 above).

[19] The fragments are edited by H. Krauss (Leipzig 1911) and more fully discussed by H. Dittmar, *Aischines von Sphettos* (Berlin 1912); new frr. in POxy. 13. 1608 (*Alcibiades*) and 39.2889-90 (*Miltiades*). Useful account incl. translations in Field (n. 1) 146-52. The *Aspasia* is the subject of a detailed study by B. Ehlers, *Eine vorplatonische Deutung des sokratischen Eros* (Zetemata 41, Munich 1966).

[20] Otherwise the major texts are passages of comedy, and the general account in Plut. *Pericles* 24 (see P. Stadter's commentary). The scholia to Pl. *Mnx.* 235e add a little.

ture: she is mentioned in Xenophon (*Mem.* ii. 6. 36) as a source for Socrates' knowledge about matchmaking (cf. *Smp.* 4. 56ff.), and is cited by Socrates in Plato's *Menexenus* as the source of Pericles' eloquence and his own. Aeschines made Socrates cite a conversation in which she sought to reconcile Xenophon and his wife with a little good-humoured moralising. Though the gaps in our evidence are tantalising, it seems safe to conclude that Socrates and Aspasia were genuinely acquainted, and that these passages are related. The *Menexenus* extends the range of Aspasia's expertise (though Aeschines seems also to have mentioned her rhetorical powers): she can even teach the great Pericles a thing or two about how to compose a speech! Plato is also exploiting the notion commonly found in comedy, that Pericles was dependent on her or under her thumb (cf. Ar. *Ach.* 526-34). It is tempting to suppose that the courtesan Theodote, with whom Socrates talks in Xenophon's *Memorabilia* (iii. 11), owes something to Aspasia. The same question may be asked about the authoritative figure of Diotima in Plato's *Symposium* – also an expert on love, but a priestess and wise woman rather than a lady of dubious virtue.

Light of quite a different kind is cast on both Aeschines and Socrates by a tantalising fragment from a speech composed by the orator Lysias in which the defendant attacks Aeschines for exploiting his and others' financial hardships. Though technically undatable, it is probably from the early decades of the fourth century, when Lysias was most active. The line taken in the surviving passage of the speech is a familiar one: philosophers are not necessarily morally upright people. The interest of the speech for us is not so much that Aeschines should be prosecuting a little-known citizen of Athens for an unpaid debt, but rather that it includes a reference to him as a pupil of Socrates. The speaker claims that he assumed Aeschines, being a philosopher and a pupil of Socrates, would deal fairly with him; but how wrong he was! '(I was) persuaded by him when he made these assurances, and besides, I thought that this man, being a student of Socrates, and one who uttered so many fine sayings about justice and virtue, could never possibly attempt or dare to do what the most depraved and immoral of men attempt.'[21] By this date Socrates' name could at least be used positively, with the implication that he was a man of principle and could be expected to instruct his followers in morality, rather than corrupting them.

It is time to turn back to extant authors, and to consider the Socratic writings of Xenophon. Well-born Athenian gentleman of conservative opinions, connoisseur of military techniques, comfortably married with sons who followed in their father's footsteps, horseman, dog-fancier and man of leisure, Xenophon has always attracted admirers for his fluent Greek and

---

[21] Lysias fr. 38 Gernet-Bizos ap. Athenaeus xiii. 611-12, cf. Diog. Laert. ii. 63. For an expert discussion of the social and financial side of the case see P. Millett, *Lending and Borrowing in Ancient Athens* (Cambridge 1991) 1-4.

solid good sense; recent criticism has begun to acknowledge that his works are more sophisticated and less transparently honest than they seem.[22] He participated in the last years of the Peloponnesian war as a cavalryman, and thereafter served under the would-be usurper of the Persian throne, Cyrus the Younger, in the expedition which collapsed with Cyrus' death at the Battle of Cunaxa (401). This expedition, and the prolonged journey of the army back to Greece, are chronicled in his *Anabasis*. In Asia Minor he fell under the influence of the Spartan Agesilaus, and when exiled from Athens for giving aid to the hated Persia, he found a home in the Peloponnese, at first in Sparta and later at an estate at Scillus near Olympia (394 BC). It is hard to ascertain anything about his career thereafter: his *Hellenika* ('History of Greece') takes the story of Greek politics down to 362, but he certainly lived as late as 355 and retained a keen interest in both Spartan and Athenian affairs. The chronology of his Socratic writings, as of his works more generally, is opaque, and their relation to Plato's writings seems tangled. Although some chronological suggestions are offered here, the comparison between his portrayal of Socrates and that of Plato does not depend on establishing these relationships. (Although it is arguable that Socratic influence extends to other portions of his large oeuvre, we should note that Xenophon did not confine his writing to the subject of Socrates; no more, indeed, did Antisthenes or Aristippus. The fascination which the figure of Socrates held for Plato may have been something special, perhaps even unique.)

The simplest and shortest of Xenophon's Socratica is his *Apology*, like Plato's an attempt to render Socrates' speech at his trial, but unlike his in that it does not offer the whole speech, but only parts, and is framed by editorial comment from Xenophon.[23] At the start, he remarks that others have written about Socrates' deliberations before his death, 'and that they have all reproduced the majesty (*megalegoria*) of his words, ... but they did not show clearly that he had now concluded that death was more desirable than life' (1). Clearly, then, there were earlier versions known to Xenophon; and in section 22 he comments that his is a selective version. He does not limit himself to the trial, but relates various connected apophthegms of Socrates before and after, and adds comments of his own, especially at the end. Socrates in his version prefers death to possible senile decay, a respectable enough reason with some parallels in other thinkers (Lucr. iii.

---

[22] For facts about Xenophon, and shrewd guidance amid speculations, see H.R. Breitenbach, *RE* ixA.2 (1967) 1569-1928, P. Cartledge, *Agesilaus* (London 1987) 55-66; G.L. Cawkwell's introductions to the Penguin Classics *Anabasis* and *Hellenica* are valuable but heavily anti-Xenophontic. J.K. Anderson, *Xenophon* (London 1974) is more 'popular', but an attractive survey. For reconsideration and partial rehabilitation of the *Hellenica* see C.J. Tuplin, *The Failings of Empire* (Stuttgart 1993), for the *Cyropaedia* see D. Gera, *Xenophon's Cyropaedia* (Oxford 1993). For Xen. *Oeconom.* see S. Pomeroy's commentary (Oxford 1994). The Socratic works are conveniently available in a recent Penguin volume by R. Waterfield (1990).

[23] For further discussions see e.g. H. Thesleff, *BICS* 25 (1978) 157-70, P.A. van der Waerdt, *OSAP* 11 (1993) 1-48. Xenophon's *Apology* has not infrequently been branded spurious: e.g. K. von Fritz, *RhM* 80 (1931) 36-68.

1039ff. on Democritus; Sen. *Ep.* 58. 36), but one that is not hinted at in Plato. In Xenophon, Socrates' tone is more aggressive, even arrogant: several passages illustrate this tendency, e.g. 13, 16 ('Who is there in your acquaintance who is less a slave to his bodily appetites than I am? Who in the world is more free ...?'), 21 ('I, because I am judged by some people supreme in that which is man's greatest blessing, education ...'), and the virtual encomium of himself at 17-18.

A similar effect can be seen in Xen. *Ap.* 14. Here, we find the anecdote about Chaerephon consulting the oracle at Delphi about Socrates: in Plato, as is well known, he asked Apollo whether there was any man wiser than Socrates (cf. Pl. *Ap.* 20e sq.). but the divine message here is transformed, expanded in a crudely panegyrical way: the god is said to have replied that there was no man 'either more free or more just or more self-disciplined than Socrates'. The crucial point in Plato, that Socrates is *wise* because he acknowledges his own ignorance, is lost in this amplification. Arrogance replaces the Platonic Socrates' humility. Wisdom is actually omitted in Apollo's reply here, but the quality appears at the end of section 16 as though it had already been mentioned. This does seem to indicate that Xenophon had Plato's account (or just possibly a parallel version) in his mind.[24]

In Xenophon's section 29f., Socrates makes a prophecy as in Plato, and with a similar reference to the power of men to foretell the future when on the point of death (cf. Pl. *Ap.* 39c). But whereas in Plato the prophecy is that the Athenians will not be free of critics, here it is something cruder and more personal, almost an ill-wishing of the accuser Anytus, whose son, Socrates declares, will go to the bad. Xenophon, editorialising, goes on to say that this did indeed happen, and so 'Anytus, even though dead, still enjoys an evil reputation for his son's wicked upbringing and his own cruelty' (31). We observe here how the 'framing' of Socrates' words by an over-eager advocate diminishes the authority and isolated dignity that Socrates possessed in Plato's version. The morality too is on a lower level: 'that paid Anytus out all right!'; Xenophon is practically gloating.[25]

---

[24] For other probable correspondences see (a) Xen. 26-Pl. *Ap.* 41b, the reference to Palamedes. In Xenophon the reference is more incidental, whereas Palamedes in Plato is integrated in a longer passage anticipating Socrates' posthumous career in Hades; moreover, Plato's *Apology* as a whole makes extensive use of Gorgias' *Palamedes* (ch. 1, p. 30 above). (b) Xen. 28 (Socrates strokes Apollodorus' hair) seems to echo Pl. *Phaedo* 89b (Socrates strokes Phaedo's hair); the latter passage seems more likely to be the model, as the situation is more natural: in the *Phaedo*, the characters are seated and conversing, whereas in Xenophon's scene they are on the move, having left the courthouse (27).

[25] On the contrast between Plato and Xenophon on retaliation see Vlastos, *Socrates* 297-300. It has been thought that this reference to Anytus as already dead is useful for dating Xenophon's *Apology*, especially since an Anytus is still alive in c. 388-387 to be attacked in a speech of Lysias (22. 8-9); but there is no necessity for Lysias' opponent to be either the accuser of Socrates or his son: cf. Davies, *APF* 40ff. Kirchner, *Prosopographia Attica* in fact lists 6 Anyti. But if the above argument is correct and Xenophon in the *Apology* is indeed imitating the *Phaedo*, then on the most plausible Platonic chronologies that would push Xenophon's *Apology* into at least the mid-380s and perhaps even later.

Much more substantial than the *Apology* is the collection of 'Reminiscences of Socrates', usually referred to by the Latin title *Memorabilia*, a work in four books. The chronology of the work is obscure: the only plausible anchoring-point is *Mem.* iii. 5, where the ambitions of Thebes and talk of her potential enmity with Athens are thought by many to imply that this passage was composed after the re-emergence of Thebes and in particular the Battle of Leuctra (371 BC). This is hardly decisive, for fear of Thebes' recovery might be a possible attitude much earlier; but there seems to be nothing more specific. Nor are many of the parallels that have been seen between the *Memorabilia* and passages of Plato's work particularly convincing in themselves or conclusive as indications that one is imitating the other.[26] The *Memorabilia*, like the defence-speech, have an apologetic aim: Xenophon is trying to show how wise, virtuous and just Socrates really was, and in the first two chapters of the work (a substantial portion which may have been published separately) he repeatedly refers to criticisms of Socrates which he attributes to 'the accuser' (i. 2, sections 9, 12, 49, 51, 56, 58). This section has generally been seen as a response to the pamphlet attacking Socrates by the sophist Polycrates, but there are difficulties with this view,[27] and it may be better to suppose that this is a hypothetical opponent to whom Xenophon ascribes all the various complaints he has encountered against Socrates.

Already in these chapters Xenophon has begun to dramatise and quote from Socrates' conversations. The rest of the *Memorabilia* consists of individual episodes involving Socrates in converse with a wide range of interlocutors, some of them named, others anonymous, some familiar from Plato, others unknown. The length of these exchanges varies, but they are never more than four or five modern pages, and usually much less. It now seems fairly well established that the *Memorabilia* do have a sort of structure or plan, however loose.[28] After the two chapters of prefatory response to 'the accuser', Xenophon proceeds to reply in detail to specific criticisms by demonstrating that Socrates *did* benefit his friends (i. 3-ii. 1: note the recurrent refs. to this theme, often at the beginning and end of chapters, e.g. i. 4. 19, i. 5. 1, i. 7. 1 and 5, ii. 1. 1). The next portion of the work is concerned with family relationships (ii. 2-3); ii. 4-10 deal with friendship, theoretical and practical, and with Socrates as friend and lover. Book iii. 1-5 is concerned with aspects of strategy and generalship. iii. 6-7 are a complementary pair on politics: in ch. 6 Socrates deflates the ambi-

---

[26] For a list of such 'correspondences' see A.H. Chroust, *Socrates: Man and Myth* (London 1957) 230n.39, but many of these seem quite illusory.

[27] Expounded in detail by N.R. Livingstone, unpublished thesis on Isocrates' *Busiris*. Objections to the traditional view are also raised by M.H. Hansen, in a forthcoming conference volume entitled *Athenian Democracy and Culture* ed. by M. Sakellariou.

[28] The pioneer work here was by H. Erbse, *Hermes* 89 (1961) 257-87; see also O. Gigon's commentaries on books i and ii, and Breitenbach, *RE* ixA, 1777ff. Waterfield 1990, 53ff. remains sceptical.

tions of Glaucon, who aspires to become an orator-statesman, whereas in
ch. 7 Charmides modestly proposes to abstain from public life, but Socrates
encourages him to embark on it! The remainder of book iii presents Socrates
in conversation with a range of individuals, although ch. 9 is more abstract
(definitions under headings; no interlocutors named), and ch. 13 and 14 are
composed of miscellaneous anecdotes or dicta. It is as though Xenophon is
rounding up various points that he is reluctant to leave out. The fourth
book does seem to be a unity, introduced by a kind of second preface, or at
the least a transitional prologue, and concluding (iv. 8) with Socrates'
death, with a kind of résumé of book iv and a peroration to that book and
perhaps the whole work. Xenophon returns to the topic of Socrates' useful-
ness to his companions, and illustrates this through a series of conversations which are, on the whole, longer and more Platonic than those of the
earlier books. I would hypothesise that book iv, whether or not it was
planned along with the rest, is a later composition, influenced by knowledge
of some of the Platonic dialogues.[29] Most substantial is the evidence of *Mem.*
iv. 7, clearly one of the most important chapters for determining the
character of Xenophon's Socrates. Here we are told that 'anything he
himself knew, he would teach most readily – all the things, at least, that
it befits a gentleman to know. Whenever he was less well qualified for any
kind of instruction, he would send them off to those who knew about the
area. And he also taught up to what point the properly educated man ought
to be experienced in each art.' (iv. 7. 1) Xenophon then proceeds to give
examples, all of which indicate that Socrates deplored futile and abstract
speculation. He approved the study of geometry as far as is required to
measure out land accurately, the study of astronomy as far as is required
to navigate by sea or land and the like; 'with regard to the heavenly bodies,
he would dissuade anybody from investigating how the deity contrives each
of them. For he considered that these subjects were too difficult for man,
nor did he suppose that the gods would smile upon one who sought out what
they had not wished to reveal' (6). And similarly on arithmetic.

It is of course possible that the original Socrates held something like
these views; and we can see some similarity to the account that Plato makes
Socrates give in the *Phaedo* of his early encounters with scientific speculation; Anaxagoras is criticised both there and in *Mem.* iv. 7. But it is very

[29] The following points seem to me to indicate this: (a) specific parallels with expressions or
remarks in *Gorgias* and *Republic*: compare iv. 4. 7 with Thrasymachus' attack on Socrates in
Rep i. 336cd; compare the complaint 'you are always saying the same things, Socrates' and
the reply 'yes, and *about* the same things too', which is found at *Mem.* iv. 4. 6 (Hippias) and
at *Grg.* 490e (Callicles); Socratic questioning convinces Euthydemus he is no better than a
slave in iv. 2. 39; cf. *Symp.* 173d, 215e; *Mem.* iv. 2. 17 is paralleled in *Rep.* i. 331c. (b) Xenophon
in book iv, especially ch. 6, seems more interested in Socratic *method* than before: note esp.,
in that chapter, his lucid account of Socrates' procedure of pursuing definitions of fundamental
terms. This may well go back to the real Socrates, but Xenophon's account certainly fits in
with the way he conducts arguments in early Plato, and may indicate reflection by Xenophon
on these works.

hard to believe that Socrates could have been quite so much the plain man, the advocate of traditional decent values, as Xenophon paints him here. This passage of Xenophon can hardly be independent of Plato's *Republic*, in which the preliminary intellectual pursuits of the Guardians are to consist of arithmetic, plane and solid geometry, astronomy and harmonics, and in which the purely practical benefits of these studies are explicitly disparaged (vii. 521c sq.; see esp. 525d2-3, 526d and 527de). Most scholars would agree that by this point in the *Republic* Plato has gone far beyond anything Socrates would have conceived or accepted. Perhaps we should see Xenophon's chapter as a counter-attack, tacitly dismissing Plato's more aetherial and impractical vision; but in emphasising the practical relevance of Socratic ethics, he loses something of the intensity and unconventionality of the 'authentic' Socrates.

The third of Xenophon's works presenting Socrates, the *Oikonomikos* or 'Estate-Manager', need not occupy us for long.[30] This is a dialogue in which Socrates first gives advice in his own right to Critobulus on how best to manage one's property (1-6), then narrates at greater length the conversation he has had in the past with Ischomachus, a prosperous and honourable gentleman (to modern eyes, an unbearably sententious and self-satisfied prig) on the same subject (7-21). Rich in information on social attitudes and agricultural practicalities, it has little to tell us about Socrates as a moralist, though there is the occasional touch of humour and self-deprecation (esp. 11. 1ff.). In this work it is universally agreed that Xenophon is using Socrates (and still more Ischomachus) as a vehicle for his own interests. Certainly the philosophic content of the work is negligible.[31] There is some interest, however, in the way in which Ischomachus tries to make Socrates see solutions for himself, and Socrates repeatedly comments with surprise that he turns out to know much more about agriculture than he had ever supposed. There are analogies here with the didactic method employed by Socrates in Plato, and more remotely with the theory of knowledge as recollection, found in the *Meno* and elsewhere. This may suggest Platonic influence.

Much more interesting and attractive is Xenophon's *Symposium*, the most ambitious of his attempts at dialogue.[32] The situation is conventional: besides Plato's work of the same name (of which Xenophon is probably aware),[33] we know of other dialogues with this title by the lesser Socratics.[34]

[30] Breitenbach 1967, 1837-71; Guthrie iii. 335-8; Pomeroy (n. 22 above), esp. 21-31 on Xenophon and Socrates.

[31] See however Waterfield's comments in the Penguin tr., 277-82.

[32] Commentary in Dutch by G. J. Woldinga (Amsterdam 1938); see further Breitenbach 1967, 1872-88; Guthrie iii. 340-4.

[33] A notable anachronism fixes the date of the Platonic work after 384, and the reference to the Theban Sacred Band in Xen. 8. 34 puts this work after the formation of that body in 378. Cf. Dover, *Phronesis* 10 (1965) 2-20 = *The Greeks and their Legacy* 86-101.

[34] In general on the symposium as a literary scene-type and the sympotic dialogue as a genre see *RE* 4a. 1273ff.; J. Martin, *Symposion* (Paderborn 1931).

The occasion of the dinner-party is the triumph of the young wrestler Autolycus in 422, and the party is being given by his lover the wealthy Callias (cf. Agathon's celebratory party in Plato's work). Xenophon introduces the work by saying that he thinks it beneficial to know how men of good character conduct themselves in their leisure activities as well as their serious concerns; this may indicate that the latter have been covered for Socrates already, in all or part of the *Memorabilia*. The ideas of leisure and light-heartedness recur throughout: good-humoured badinage, teasing and mockery punctuate a discussion of a type familiar in sympotic gatherings. The prescriptions for the organisation of the party are made by Socrates (2. 2ff.), rather more indulgently than we would expect from his more critical remarks at *Protagoras* 347c-e. He even at first *dismisses* the opening offered for a philosophic discussion, at 2. 7: 'Well, since the word is ambiguous, let's put it aside for another time. Now let's attend to what we have in hand, for I can see this dancer standing ready and somebody else holding hoops for her to jump through'! It is difficult to imagine Plato's Socrates, even in his most relaxed and convivial mood, speaking like this.

In the first half of the dialogue, each of the company has to say what he takes most pride in and then explain his choice. The conversation is conducted in a pleasant but hardly a profound manner, with no serious philosophy to speak of, until the subject of love is explicitly introduced by Socrates (the subject has of course been much in the air before this; the occasion itself, Callias' party for his boyfriend, makes this inevitable). Socrates gives an eloquent disquisition on celestial and earthly love, love of the soul or character as opposed to love of the body: we recognise motifs present in, and perhaps derived from, Plato's *Symposium*, notably Socrates' insistence that it is better to abstain from actual lovemaking.[35] Here, however, this seems to be directed ad hominem, a lesson for Callias in particular (cf. 8. 12), whereas in Plato it is laid down as a general principle and illustrated by Socrates' own self-control. But although this speech occupies a prominent place, it does not dominate the dialogue or move the discussion on to another plane as does the main speech of Socrates in the Platonic *Symposium*. Socrates in Xenophon's work is much less mystical and religious in his approach to beauty; indeed, although plenty of fun is made of his physical appearance, in general he is less weird, less strange, more of an Attic gentleman. It is in keeping with this that although he finds fault with the Syracusan entertainer's idea of a show, he welcomes the alternative entertainment, an erotic mime or dance involving a boy and a girl playing Dionysus and Ariadne, and the dialogue ends on a more worldly plane, with Socrates joining his friends in enthusiastic enjoyment. The contrast with Plato's dialogue, where the rumbustious arrival of Alcibiades

---

[35] The ethical advice does not, however, stray far from the norms of unphilosophic Athenian society, as can be seen from the orator Aeschines' description of the proper way to behave (1. 135-9).

serves to put Socrates' austere idealism in sharp relief, is very marked, and can hardly be accidental. Xenophon, in other words, shows us a Socrates more at home in this world, a moralist who can nevertheless share the pleasures and tastes of his less philosophic friends.

One of the founding fathers of Platonic interpretation, F.D.E. Schleier-macher, wrote: 'If Socrates had done nothing but discourse in a purer and loftier strain on subjects within those limits which are never passed in the *Memorabilia* of Xenophon, it would be impossible to understand how the charm of his speech could have emptied the market-place and the work-shops, the public walks and the schools, for so many years; how he could have satisfied so long Alcibiades and Critias, Plato and Euclid; how he could have played the part assigned to him in the dialogues of Plato; in short, how he could have been the founder and type of the philosophy of Athens.'[36] In more recent years a similar note has been sounded by an Italian critic, Montuori, in his radical study of the Socratic question: 'the field being thus limited to Plato and Xenophon, the former tending to idealise the figure of Socrates beyond all human measure, and the latter to drag it down to the level of his own mediocrity.'[37] These judgements are over-harsh: in Xeno-phon we sense something of the charm and moral earnestness of Socrates, but his arguments lack subtlety and his morality seems to be devoid of depth. Critics who are not prepared to dismiss Xenophon often try to reconcile him with Plato, on the assumption that elements common to both writers are probably authentic. This eirenic approach seems misguided, for although Xenophon's Socrates shares a certain amount with the Socrates of Plato's early work, the discrepancies are at least as important. A brief résumé of both should bring this out.

In both writers, Socrates converses with all kinds of people, including artisans, poets and so forth.[38] In both, he questions and criticises the beliefs of others. In both, he places a high value on virtue and wisdom. In both, he proceeds by seeking definitions (Pl. *Euthyphro, Laches, Charmides* etc.; Xen. *Mem.* iii. 9, iv. 6). In both, he receives supernatural guidance from his divine sign.[39] In both he is pious, attaches great importance to friendship, has extraordinary self-discipline and powers of endurance, is poor and fairly shabby. He uses constantly the analogy between moral activity and crafts or *technai*, as well as other comparisons and similar devices (in Xenophon animal parables are more prominent).[40] He makes fun of himself and of others in both authors, though we may want to distinguish the rather laboured humour and teasing in Xenophon (e.g. *Mem.* iv. 2. 3-5) from the

---

[36] *Platon: Werke* (Berlin 1804-1828), iii. 2. 295, cited by Zeller, *Socrates* 152. Cf. Vlastos, 'The paradox of Socrates' (see n.1) 1-3.
[37] *Socrates: Physiology of a Myth* (Eng. tr. 1982) 31.
[38] Pl. *Apol.* 21-2, 30a, Xen. *Mem.* i. 1. 10, iii. 10, iii. 11 etc.
[39] It is mentioned in the *Apology, Euthyphro, Euthydemus* and *Phaedrus* of Plato, and in Xenophon's *Apology* and *Memorabilia*; see below, and Guthrie iii. 402-5.
[40] For such parables see *Mem.* ii. 7. 13f.

developed irony which we find in Plato. Both Xenophon and Plato use the serious-comic antithesis in describing Socrates' manner of talking, though again Plato's deployment of it is more thoughtful.[41] Finally, both authors make Socrates claim special understanding of love, and present him as treating the friend-lover relationship playfully.[42]

In Xenophon, however, Socrates is both more knowledgable than in early Plato and knows about different things. He is interested (like Xenophon) in generalship, strategy, home economics. In Xenophon, he is not portrayed as constantly criticising rhetoric and poetry, nor is he opposed to political life: indeed, he encourages some of his friends to take part in public life (*Mem.* ii. 7; cf. i. 6. 15, Socrates as an educator of statesmen). Xenophon has much less about him encountering sophists. Nor is his Socrates so concerned with the form of disputation and discussion: the theory of argument and dialectical method seems to be a Platonic preoccupation. Another striking difference in style of talking is that, although he cites poetry readily enough, Xenophon's Socrates rarely uses mythological allusions and never enquires into their truth or deeper meaning. Predictably, he never uses a large-scale myth: the only apparent exception, the parable of Heracles, is morally straightforward, and in any case is explicitly drawn from Prodicus.[43] It goes with this that in Xenophon Socrates uses a lecturing style, whereas in Plato fundamental importance is attached to the individual contact with a single mind, a particular interlocutor. In the *Memorabilia* Socrates sometimes 'speaks' *in vacuo*, with no addressees named (i. 7. 1, ii. 4. 1ff.), at least once addresses mankind in the abstract (i. 5. 1); or his victims may be anonymous (iii. 2, 3). The larger gatherings do not materialise as participants in true dialogue; only in the *Symposium* does he attempt a more elaborate scene-setting involving a range of interacting personalities.

The content of Socratic morality is also crucially different in certain respects. Socrates in Xenophon is interested in practical ends. On the one hand, he cites the traditional ethical principle 'help your friends and harm your enemies' without disapproval (ii. 6. 35, cf. ii. 3. 14, more reserved), whereas Plato's Socrates speaks out firmly against this principle (*Crito* 49a; *Rep.* i. 335e). On the other hand, while generosity to friends is advocated, we look in vain for the moral premiss which Plato sets at the core of Socrates' beliefs, that 'it is better to suffer wrong than to do it' (*Grg.* 469ff., etc.).

It must be emphasised that there is little evidence of any special closeness between Xenophon and Socrates. Of course, Xenophon does

---

[41] See *Grg.* 481b, *Symp.* 216e, in contrast with X. *Smp.* 1. 1, 4. 28, etc.; *Mem.* i. 3. 8.

[42] Pl. *Lysis* 204b, 211e, *Symp.* 177de; X. *Mem.* ii. 6. 28ff., iii. 11, *Symp.* 8.

[43] *Mem.* ii. 1. 21ff. But see Julian, *Or.* 7. 209a, 215c, 216d-17a, on myths in Xenophon, Antisthenes and others. The last passage refers to the Prodicean myth. Briefer and more conventional uses of myth in *Mem.* ii. 6. 31, iii. 5. 8ff. (Athenian prehistory), iv. 2. 33. Diog. Laert. iii. 80 remarks that 'some' thought Plato over-fond of myths.

explain how he asked Socrates' advice before embarking on the expedition he describes in the *Anabasis*, and followed it in consulting the oracle of Delphi. But he also admits that he did ask the oracle a leading question and that Socrates was displeased by the way he had followed his advice (*Anabasis* iii. 1. 4-7). In general, Xenophon praises Socrates for more ordinary and conventionally admirable qualities than we see given prominence in Plato (witness, e.g., Xen. *Ap.* 25, and the general emphasis on his courage, civic virtue and service to the state, in *Ap.* 16-18). Xenophon's attitude to Socrates was probably not so far removed from that of Laches in Plato's dialogue of that name: the general, the practical military man, admires a moralist whose *actions* are a fitting image of his fine words and high principles (see esp. *Laches* 188c-9a: p. 84 below).

In assessing Xenophon's portrait of Socrates and comparing it with Plato's, it is essential to remember that he was not in Athens at the time of the trial. In the two portions of his work in which he treats the subject (the *Apology* and the final chapter of the *Memorabilia*, iv. 8), he explains that he has derived his information from Hermogenes (a real figure, who also appears in Plato's *Cratylus*). Furthermore, he probably left Athens shortly after Socrates' death (the date of his exile is disputed, but may fall as early as 398-7).[44] In that case it may have been some time before he could communicate with the more intimate companions of Socrates or acquire further knowledge of the dead man to supplement his own memory. It seems plain enough that he was not among the inner circle of Socrates' disciples. Plato never once mentions Xenophon as either present or absent, though it is usually thought that a passage in the *Laws* (694c) is a dig at the fictional hagiography of Xenophon's *Cyropaedia*. In the *Laws*, the Athenian says that Cyrus, 'although he was doubtless a good commander and a loyal patriot, ... never considered, even superficially, the problem of correct education; and as for running a household, I'd say he never paid any attention to it at all.' (These are Cyrus' constant concerns in Xenophon's biography.)[45] Likewise, Xenophon only once mentions Plato, and that is in a completely casual context (*Mem.* iii. 6. 1). Furthermore, we can see from the titles in Diogenes Laertius' account of the Socratics that they constantly wrote about one another. Thus Phaedo wrote a *Simon*, Euclides wrote an *Aeschines* and a *Crito*, Glaucon wrote a *Menexenus*, even an *Aristophanes* and a *Cephalus*, but nobody seems to have thought of writing a *Xenophon*. We know of only one work by a pupil of Socrates in which Xenophon (and his wife) did figure, Aeschines' *Aspasia*, referred to above.

Xenophon does indeed claim to have been present at the occasion of his own *Symposium*, but he takes no part in the conversation, and other

---

[44] For a recent discussion with older references see C.J. Tuplin in *Homo Viator: Essays ... J. Bramble*, ed. M. Whitby and others (Bristol 1987) 59-68. He opts for late 395/4 or early 394/3.

[45] The allusion to Xenophon was observed by Diog. Laert. iii. 34. For fuller discussion see S.W. Hirsch, *The Friendship of the Barbarian* (Hanover and London 1985) 96-100. Gera, *Xenophon's Cyropaedia* ch. 2 paints a more Socratic picture of the *Cyropaedia*.

evidence enables us to place the dramatic date of the work in 422.[46]
Xenophon would have been a mere child at this time, and this should make
us cautious of accepting his authority for the other scenes at which he
supposedly heard Socrates (see *Mem.* ii. 4. 1, ii. 5. 1, iv. 3. 2, *Oec.* i. 1, for 'I
once heard Socrates say ...' or similar openings).[47] He himself participates
in discussion only in *Mem.* i. 3. 8ff. Many scenes in the *Memorabilia* are
unlocalised, most are timeless. Often the situation is such that the presence
of other auditors is highly unlikely (e.g. ii. 2, in which Socrates rebukes his
eldest son for his behaviour to his mother).

None of these considerations finally establishes that the real Socrates
was not like the Socrates of Xenophon's portrait, but they all, I would
suggest, make it necessary to treat Xenophon's evidence with considerable
reserve. The simpler structure, style and thought of Xenophon do not make
him a more truthful witness; they mean rather that he is using different
literary forms and methods, and offering us a Socrates who is a simpler,
more respectable figure, close to his own interests and opinions, virtually
a *kalos k'agathos*. This is not of course to say that, on balance, Plato offers
the reader a more authentic picture. The besetting sin of Socratic scholarship has been to set these two writers against one another, and at one date
Plato has been in favour, at another Xenophon. But when confronted with
the choice between Plato and Xenophon, our answer must be that in fact
we cannot make a choice and say that one is 'true'. Both authors from the
beginning shape and select their memories, enhance and amplify the
original Socrates, interweaving his words and opinions with their own
preoccupations.[48]

The evidence of Aristotle is of a quite different kind. Although he too
wrote dialogues, we have no evidence suggesting that any of them used
Socrates as a character; in any case they survive only in fragments. He
refers to Socrates in his philosophic works at many points: sometimes he
means Socrates in Plato (as is often made explicit), but in certain passages,
particularly when he is dealing with the history of metaphysics or morals
in general or of specific doctrines, he gives us precious information about
the historical Socrates; in a very few places he explicitly distinguishes
him from Plato. Although Aristotle only joined the Academy in 368/7,
over thirty years after Socrates' death, we can hardly doubt that he had
questioned Plato about Socrates and heard about him from others.[49] It

---

[46] The key point being Eupolis' play *Autolycus*, produced in 421: this drama mocked the
victory of Autolycus to which Xenophon refers at the opening of his *Symposium*.

[47] Cf. Slings, *Comm. on the Platonic Clitopho* 27 with n. 20.

[48] By far the most persuasive and subtle attempt to weigh up the sources is that of Vlastos,
Socrates chs. 2-3, which is constantly enlightening even if one disagrees with his approach.

[49] See further W.D. Ross, *Aristotle's Metaphysics* (Oxford 1924) intr., xxxiii-xlv; T. Deman,
Le témoignage d'Aristote sur Socrate (Paris 1942); Guthrie iii. 355-9; Lacey in Vlastos (ed.)
The Philosophy of Socrates (1971), 44-8; Vlastos, *Socrates* 92-8. Others, however, persist in
the view that Aristotle's judgements are based solely on uncritical reading of Plato (e.g. C.H.
Kahn, *CQ* 31 (1981) 310n. 13, 314f.).

would be the height of scepticism to suppose that all Aristotle's comments on Socrates are elaborations upon or deductions from the dialogues of Plato and others. In Aristotle's terse assessments we cannot expect to find any fresh testimony on Socrates the man and the personality; but he offers us a philosopher's judgement on Socrates' place in the history of philosophy.[49a]

The most important passages come from the *Metaphysics*, and are brief enough to be quoted in full.

> (a) *Met.* 987b1-8: 'Socrates, however [unlike the Heraclitean school], was busying himself about ethical matters and neglecting the world of nature as a whole, but seeking the universal in these ethical matters, and fixed thought for the first time on definitions; Plato accepted his teaching, but held that the problem applied not to any sensible thing but to entities of another kind – for this reason, that the common definition could not be a definition of any sensible thing, as they were always changing. Things of this other sort, then, he called Ideas ...' (tr. W.D. Ross)
> (b) ibid 1086a37-b5: 'They [i.e. the followers of Plato] thought that the sensible particulars were in a state of flux and none of them remained, but that the universal was apart from these and different. And Socrates gave the impulse to this theory, as we said before, by means of his definitions, but he did not separate them from the particulars, and in this he thought rightly, in not separating them.'
> (c) 1078b17-31 (in part): 'Socrates occupied himself with the excellences of character, and in connection with them became the first to raise the problem of universal definitions ... He was seeking to deduce, and the essence is the starting-point of deductions ... Two things may be fairly ascribed to Socrates – inductive arguments and universal definition, both of which are concerned with the starting point of science. But Socrates did not make the universals or the definitions exist apart ...'

A further passage, in *On parts of animals* 642a24-31, also refers to Socrates' making a closer approach to definition of essences, but seems to imply that his method still fell short.

Many other passages would be valuable if we could feel sure that Aristotle had evidence independent of Plato and the Socratic writers for what he says, but such confidence is probably misplaced. Good examples are *Soph. El.* 183b6-8, which refers to Socrates' always wanting to ask questions rather than answer them, because he used to confess he did not know the answers, and *Nic. Ethics* 1127b22ff., which briefly alludes to Socrates' irony (in the sense of mock-modesty, in that he disclaimed qualities which he in fact possessed). Both of these could easily have

---

[49a] In general on the problems of using Aristotle as a source for the history of philosophy see Guthrie, *JHS* 77 (1957) 35-41, repr. in *Studies in Pre-Socratic Philosophy* ed. D. Furley and R.E. Allen, i (London 1970) 239-54; J.G. Stevenson, *JHS* 94 (1974) 138-43; also G.E.L. Owen, in *Aristote et les problèmes de méthode*, ed. S. Mansion (Louvain 1961) 83-101 = Owen, *Logic, Science and Dialectic* (London 1986) 239-51.

been written with no more than the Platonic portrait of Socrates in his mind.[50]

What, then, can we believe? Taking the Aristotelian testimony as our firmest and most unambiguous evidence, we can accept that Socrates was first and foremost, perhaps only, a moralist; that he sought definitions of moral abstractions, but without regarding them as separately existing entities, and that he was a pioneer of a certain type of argument, involving question and answer, and induction. We can also accept, as almost unanimously asserted, that Socrates did not write anything down;[51] it goes with this, and is confirmed by all authorities except Aristophanes, that he did not set himself up as a professional teacher, and did not charge fees. His poverty, ugliness and other striking physical facts (e.g. his toughness in hard weather) also seem likely to rest on authentic tradition;[52] likewise, perhaps, the professions of love for attractive young men, which seemed paradoxical and comic in one so plain. Beyond that it is hard to go, and we should reflect that Plato and Xenophon themselves may have found it hard to sum up exactly what the man they so admired actually believed, and to decide whether the many suggestive questions and ideas thrown off in different conversations hung together in any coherent way.

If we accept that Socrates only engaged in conversation, not formal exposition, and that he proceeded mainly or exclusively by questioning, then it is not surprising that his pupils had to build on and add to their memories, filling in the mystery of what was actually in Socrates' mind. Had they not done so, their portraits would have had no intellectual substance. It can be assumed that Socrates adapted his conversational approach according to his interlocutor: he would not speak in the same way, nor about the same subjects, to the practical Xenophon, the sophist Hippias, and the young intellectual Plato. Even if he did sometimes produce a deeply held principle of his own (perhaps 'virtue is knowledge' may be one such pronouncement), these may have been isolated, enigmatic utterances which different listeners might have interpreted in different ways. The disciples of Socrates each took away with them memories of an extraordinarily impressive man, a personality or a tone of voice, recollections of favourite lines of questioning, types of analogies – not quite a method, but

---

[50] I do not accept 'Fitzgerald's canon', according to which Aristotle used the definite article with Socrates' name when he was referring to the Platonic Socrates and omitted it when he was not. Aristotle, *NE* 1145b23-4 is a clear counter-example (cf. Pl. *Prt.* 352b); and in *NE* 1116b4 and *EE* 1230a7 we find the same doctrine ascribed to Socrates, his name being used with the article in the one case and without in the other. At most Fitzgerald described a general tendency.

[51] A few late texts which assert otherwise merit no credence: some are cited by Chroust, *Socrates: Man and Myth* 279 n.791.

[52] For a collection of texts on his physical appearance, and extant busts, see G. Richter, rev. by R.R.R. Smith, *The Portraits of the Greeks* (Phaidon, Oxford 1984) 198-204.

perhaps hints on the basis of which a more methodical procedure could be built. Socratic questioning may not have been a fully-fledged dialectical elenchus, for a systematic method seems more appropriate for a self-conscious teacher making use of writing; nor, perhaps, would Socrates' *eironeia* have been so complex and manifold, so highly *literary*, as Platonic irony.

Two features of Socrates which have so far been only briefly mentioned may serve to illustrate the uncertainties created by the nature of our source material. The first is what he refers to as his *daimonion* – literally, 'supernatural thing', seemingly a sensation or perhaps a voice which Socrates claimed he heard at moments when he was faced with an important choice. This was surely an authentic feature, and according to the *Apology*, characterised Socrates all through his life (31d), but it is represented in different ways by different authors.[53] According to Plato, it only acted negatively, warning Socrates not to do something because it would turn out badly: it dissuaded him from embarking on a political career (*Ap.* 31cd, *Rep.* 496c), or prevented him from leaving a discussion which seemed to be going on an unsatisfactory path (*Euthyd.* 272e, *Phdr.* 242b). In the *Theaetetus* another aspect is mentioned: the sign might warn Socrates not to take back a pupil who had left him in the past (151a). Xenophon, as we might expect, plays down the divine sign, trying to argue that it was on a par with the kind of divination which all men employ: this was one of the means, like dreams or omens or oracles, by which the gods communicated with mortals, and it was the conventional gods who guided Socrates in this way (*Mem.* i. 1. 2ff., cf. *Ap.* 12-13). But at the same time he broadens the scope of the sign, making it give positive advice as well as negative ('what to do and what not to do', iv. 3. 12). A further stage is reached in the curious work called the *Theages*, which is probably an imitation of Plato's early manner.[54] This work turns Socrates into a prophet: his insight (explicitly a voice here, 128d) can benefit others as well, if they will only listen. He describes several cases in which he has warned his friends not to do something, and they have either come to grief when they failed to heed him, or learned later how grateful they should be. Moreover, he has issued warnings at times of crisis for Athens: when the Athenians were setting off to Sicily, Socrates was there, a veritable Cassandra, to pass on the unease of his divine voice. In the *Theages* Socrates' physical presence and contact with his followers is seen in more portentous, even magical terms. The fascination of later readers of Plato with this mysterious side of Socrates is plain: the Stoic Antipater collected apocryphal tales of his prophetic powers, and there is a long history of attempts to explain the nature of his 'sign'.[55]

---

[53] See Friedlaender i. 32-6, Guthrie iii. 398ff., 402-5.
[54] See Thesleff, *Stud. in Plat. Chronology* 217f., with older bibl.
[55] A.S. Pease on Cicero, *On divination* 1. 123; E.R. Dodds, *The Ancient Concept of Progress* (1973) 192-3. Plutarch, *On Socrates' Sign* (*Moralia* 575ff.) is a dialogue which includes extensive discussion of the topic (tr. in D.A. Russell, *Plutarch, Selected Essays and Dialogues* (Oxford 1993) 82-119).

Whatever the biographical realities, the pattern seen here is typical: Plato presents Socrates strikingly and intriguingly; Xenophon waters down his oddities while at the same time making larger claims for his gifts; later writers expand and exaggerate the hints found in the classic texts. As usual, Aristophanes stands apart: in the *Clouds*, Socrates denies the existence of the traditional gods, but the new deities whom he invokes, and to whom he introduces Strepsiades, are wholly external, and are clearly derived from a medley of cosmological sources (247f., 264ff., 424, 627, etc.). Apart from the Clouds, who represent the fuzzy wooliness of intellectual thought, he swears 'by Respiration, by Void, by Air' (627), and invokes Air and Aether (264-5): this is the standard picture of the godless thinker, mirrored in the Euripides of the *Frogs* (892-3).

The other issue which requires some discussion is Socrates' political stance, and especially his attitude to the Athenian democracy. Many who are happy to make Socrates more of a mystic than a rationalist may still wish to see him as a keen democrat; but the pictures painted by Plato and Xenophon offer limited support for that view. As has been shown, he did not pursue an active political career, though he served in office when the lot fell to him, and opposed the illegal action of his fellow-citizens at the Arginusae trial; similarly, he served as a soldier and showed himself courageous and loyal. But his reluctance to take more of a role in politics places him among those whom the Thucydidean Pericles classed as *apragmones*, 'inactive', and of whom Pericles spoke with disdain: 'we Athenians are the only people who regard the man who has no share in these affairs not as one who minds his own business, but as one who has no business at all' (Thuc. ii. 40. 2).[56] Quietism is less offensive to modern eyes, disillusioned with political corruption;[57] but how sure are we that Socrates did not go beyond quietism? 'The accuser', as quoted by Xenophon, complained that he taught his companions to despise Athenian institutions, especially the allocation of office by lot; also that he was associated with oligarchic, anti-democratic types such as Critias (*Mem.* i. 2. 9ff.). Both Xenophon and Plato show him, in numerous passages, criticising not only the theory of democratic government but also the supposed 'experts', even the great figures of Athens' past – Themistocles, Cimon, even Pericles. If all this is true, then the case against Socrates might not seem negligible to the average juror, and the question may indeed become 'why did they wait until he was seventy?'[58]

---

[56] See further V. Ehrenberg, *JHS* 67 (1947) 46-67 (= his *Polis und Imperium* (Zürich-Stuttgart 1965) 466-501); J.B. Carter, *The Quiet Athenian* (Oxford 1985).

[57] But see Vlastos, *Socratic Studies* 127-33, for a powerful plea that Socrates owed it to his society to play a more active role, to speak out and use his eloquence and influence at a crisis such as the debate on Mytilene in 427.

[58] Chapter title in I.F. Stone's vigorously argued work *The Trial of Socrates* (London 1988). For an effective critique of Stone (though partly dependent on conventional premises about the development from 'Socrates' to 'Plato' in the dialogues), see T. Irwin, *Philosophy and Public*

The counter-argument[59] might be that both Plato and Xenophon are aristocratic in birth and anti-democratic in inclination; perhaps it is they who impose these opinions on the democrat Socrates? A compromise is possible: Socrates might be hostile to the misguided actions of a democratic government, as he was to the excesses of the Thirty; he opposed injustice and folly wherever they were found, and democracy has no monopoly on these qualities. Athens, for all its faults, was a remarkably tolerant and relatively 'open' society by ancient standards, and in particular prided itself on its *parrhesia* (freedom of speech).[60] Although wartime hardship and suspicion may have lessened this great benefit, Athenian democracy was still the society in which Socrates had grown up, been educated, and had the opportunity to talk freely and abundantly with friends and acquaintances all his life.[61] His known *actions* offer no support for ascribing to him anti-Athenian views.

It is widely accepted that the *Crito*, the short dialogue in which Socrates defends his insistence that it would be wrong to escape from prison by subterfuge at the eleventh hour, is a key text for assessing Socrates' attitude to Athens (once again, it must be objected, we fall into the vicious circle of deducing the non-Platonic Socrates out of Plato). In this work Socrates declares that he owes loyalty to the laws of Athens, even if he is suffering on account of the laws as administered, because he has in effect entered a contract with them: since he has never shown any wish to live elsewhere, he has implicitly accepted the terms under which he and his family have been reared and educated in Athens – that is, he must abide by the constitution under which he has chosen to live. Many complexities have been detected in this argument, and it is a difficult question how far it should be generalised. Socrates is an unusual citizen in that he has stayed so firmly at home throughout his life, rarely straying beyond the bounds of the city. Can the same arguments apply to other Athenians, or to citizens of other cities?[62] Plato may intend the reader to ponder the implications

---

Affairs 18 (1989) 184-205. For an interesting essay which bears on both political and religious hostility to Socrates, see W.R. Connor in *Georgika* (*BICS* Suppl. 58, 1991) 49-56 (but his argument that Socrates separated sacrifice from prayer has little foundation).

[59] Advanced recently by Vlastos, *Socratic Studies* ch. 4, though foreshadowed in earlier authors such as Popper, *The Open Society and its Enemies*, who sees Plato as Socrates' Judas (see below, p. 221).

[60] Eur. *Hipp.* 422, *Ion* 672, Pl. *Grg.* 461e, Dem. 21. 124, Aeschin. 3. 6; sourer version, Pl. *Rep.* 557b. See further G. Scarpat, *Parrhesia* (Brescia 1964); S. Halliwell, *JHS* 111 (1991) 48n. 3, and the whole of that paper.

[61] A point made below, at the opening of ch. 3, is important here: Plato and Xenophon, but especially the former, show us only part of Socrates' conversational life-style; he was happy to converse with poor men and artisans as well. The population of Platonic dialogue is socially biassed in favour of the propertied class.

[62] These and many other questions are discussed by R. Kraut, *Socrates and the State* (Princeton 1984), a penetrating and rewarding study. See also S. Panagiotou, 'Socrates and civil disobedience', in *Socratic Questions*, ed. B.S. Gower and M.C. Stokes (London 1992) 93-121.

further; as in other dialogues, it is not self-evident that what is right for Socrates can be exemplary for all men.

Perhaps Socrates never uttered these arguments, but if he did, he is at least expressing some gratitude to Athens, and he would surely allow that he had had his opportunity to convince the jury. As a matter of historical fact Socrates chose to live and die in Athens, and Plato was doubtless right to suggest in the *Apology* that his irritating ways would not be tolerated as readily, or for as long, in other states (37cd). Athens was the best society for Socrates, and he knew it. It need not follow that he endorsed all aspects of its constitution, let alone its policies. Much depends on how far we suppose that the historical Socrates pursued *political* questions in his discussions, as opposed to seeking definitions and exploring moral terms. If, however, he was seeking wisdom and expertise amongst all walks of life, he can hardly have avoided confronting some politicians (as both the *Apology* and the encounter with Anytus in the *Meno* present him as doing). In that case it would only be a matter of time before he would be showing their inadequate qualifications for their work. Socrates could swiftly discern that not everybody displayed equal intelligence and political or moral wisdom; whether he believed that all had the capacity to develop such wisdom is unclear, but the Athenian man-in-the-street would not necessarily draw these fine distinctions. Whether he merely exposed others' ignorance, to the delight and amusement of his young friends, or went further to criticise the premises of a democracy that gave power to the ignorant or the unqualified, as Plato represents him as doing (already in *Prt.* 319b-20c), it is impossible to say. It is too dogmatic to claim that 'the anti-democratic trend of his teaching is obvious',[63] but it may be a fair assessment if we emphasise the word 'trend' – this is a tendency, a direction in which both Plato and Xenophon were ready, by temperament and background, to move a long way further.

The Socratic question, like some other well-known 'Questions' in classical studies, will remain insoluble unless fresh evidence emerges; and even when new evidence does appear, as can be seen with the new papyri of Aeschines or the anonymous piece on the origins of dialogue (p. 11, n. 17), the problems still remain, and the jigsaw only becomes more complicated. If we are to go further, it can only be through the study of the images of Socrates in literature, and that is why literary analysis of the dialogue form, and presentation of personalities within it, is so important. The concern of this book is above all with the character of Socrates *in Plato*, and all these external and chronological considerations, however necessary and however fascinating in themselves, are essentially prolegomena.

---

[63] E. Barker, *The Political Thought of Plato and Aristotle* (N.Y. and London 1959) 51, endorsed by Guthrie iii. 416.

Appendix: Isocrates and Thucydides

Two other major literary figures can also be brought into relation with Plato, their near-contemporary, namely the rhetorical teacher Isocrates and, more doubtfully and tantalisingly, the historian Thucydides. What can be said with any certainty concerning exchange of ideas or direct influence between these writers has been said often, but on issues of this kind, so wide in their implications beyond the question of purely historical connection, each reader will no doubt continue to draw the comparison and will remain fascinated by the confrontation.

Isocrates is the clearer case, and our knowledge of the chronology of his writings is greater.[64] Plato mentions him, with ironic and two-edged praise, in the final pages of the *Phaedrus* (278e-9c), and it is all but certain that an anonymous critic, whose complaints about the sophists and Socrates Crito reports in the *Euthydemus*, is to be identified with Isocrates (p. 112 below). Isocrates never actually mentions Plato, but among the many passages in which he attacks his rival educators, there are a number where Plato is clearly meant, and a great many more in which he may be included, or in which Isocrates pronounces on matters where we can contrast Plato's very different views.

In his early career, from c. 403-c. 390, Isocrates was a professional composer of forensic speeches, a *logographos* in the manner of Lysias (with whom Plato mischievously compares him in the *Phaedrus*). His forensic speeches must all date from that period, and some of these datings are confirmed by internal evidence. He later did his best to disown his unworthy past.[65] In the late 390s he seems to have established his school for eloquence: his *Against the Sophists* (*Or.* xiii, an early work, as he tells us in *Antid.* 193) is a polemical pamphlet advertising his own teaching and attacking the methods and doctrines of others, namely the teachers of 'eristic' arguments, the composers of rhetorical handbooks and the metaphysicians or speculative thinkers. Among these rivals Plato and the Academy do not seem to be included, and it may be that they had not yet come to Isocrates' notice. The polemic of the *Helen*, however, does allude to the Platonic theory of the unity of the virtues (1 [cf. e.g. *Prt.* Dodds on *Grg.* 507a remarks that the doctrine is already implicit in earlier works such as the *Laches*]). We may therefore see a gap between Isocrates' *Against the Sophists* and his *Helen* (c. 380?), with at least some of the aporetic dialogues of Plato, and perhaps the *Protagoras*, appearing, or coming to Isocrates' attention, in the intervening years. The *Gorgias* perhaps picks up a phrase in the *Against the Sophists*, reusing it in a very different context.[66] A defence of rhetoric against its critics is offered by Isocrates in his *Nicocles* (*Or.* 3, esp. 5-10, uncertainly dated between 372-365 BC). This defence bears some resemblance to Gorgias' self-defence in Plato's dialogue, and here again we may suspect a direct link; other chronological considerations make it likelier that Isocrates is criticising Plato's over-hasty dismissal of the rhetorician's case.

Other links or parallels between the two writers are considerably later. It seems certain that the doctrine of Socrates that it is better to suffer wrong or injustice

---

[64] See further M. Ostwald and J.P. Lynch, *CAH* vi[2] ch. 12(a), with fuller refs. and bibliography; also C. Eucken, *Isokrates* (Berlin and N.Y. 1983), the fullest modern study, raising many issues which cannot be treated here.

[65] Cf. G. Kennedy, *The Art of Persuasion in Greece* 176, citing esp. *Antid.* 36ff. and Dion. Hal. *Isoc.* 18 (Isocrates' son claimed that his father's forensic speeches were forgeries!)

[66] *Against the Sophists* 17 and *Gorgias* 463a. In his commentary on the *Grg.*, however, Dodds questions the connection, and N.R. Livingstone suggests to me the hypothesis that it is a Gorgianic formulation.

than to do it (the theme which animates both the *Gorgias* and the *Republic*), is rejected by Isocrates in his speech the *Panathenaicus* (c. 342 BC). There Isocrates espouses the more 'realistic' view, cynically adding that there are some clever people (*sophoi*) who pretend not to accept this (*Panath.* 117f.). The reference in the *Philip* of 346 BC to the writing-up of laws and constitutions by certain sophists (*Philip* 12f.) naturally reminds us of the *Republic* and *Laws*, and it is by no means impossible that they are alluded to here. We must, however, remember that the composition of imaginary constitutions and the discussion of constitutional theory in general was another legacy that Plato had inherited from the sophists: Protagoras and Antisthenes both wrote on such themes, and there must have been much more of this type of writing of which we now know nothing.[67] A Platonic reference is not certain, though it is likely enough that he is included in Isocrates' critique.

Isocrates and Plato were at odds in their attitude to Athens' political and imperialist past, in their views on the status of knowledge and of the nature of education, and in their conception of 'philosophy'. Isocrates appropriated the word 'philosophia': denying the title to natural philosophy, eristics and to the ethical 'science' of the Academy. Believing that no true *techne* or science of moral education could exist (*Antid.* 274), he demanded and offered a more practical, empirical project, although he still sought to attribute to his own system the moral integrity and civic responsibility that critics such as Plato had generally found to be lacking in earlier sophistic methods of education. His rhetorical course was intended to make his pupils not only gifted speakers but ideal statesmen.[68] His view of prose literature was hierarchic: as we have seen, he dismissed forensic oratory and claimed himself to teach a more prestigious genre, that of symbouleutic (deliberative) oratory, with an added element of epideictic expansiveness. Isocrates himself did teach statesmen and generals, including Timotheus, and took greater pride in their deeds, he claims, than in their oratory. Clearly, he saw himself as deserving at least some credit for both (see *Panath.* 87, cf. *Antid.* 101-39).

Basing his defence on the naive assumption that the study and practice of speaking on high and noble themes inculcates a corresponding greatness and nobility of character, Isocrates attempted to bypass the Platonic objections to rhetoric. Through his readability, stylistic distinction and the use of high-minded commonplaces such as the value of general culture, the uniqueness of human reason, and the civilising power of oratory since the dawn of history, Isocrates, whose ideas were transmitted to western Europe through Cicero, became the ultimate ancestor of the modern liberal education.[69]

Plato's opposition rested not only on doubts about the moral status of rhetoric, but still more upon the way that Isocrates, in this a true heir of his master Gorgias, denied the possibility of absolute knowledge. Few principles are more vital to Platonic thought than the inferiority of *doxa* (opinion) to *episteme* (knowledge).[70]

---

[67] Cf. Hdt. iii. 80-2, Eur. *Supp.* (the agon); Diog. Laert. iii. 37, ix. 55 (Protagoras), vi. 1. 6 (Antisthenes). Note also Pl. *Politicus* 301e.

[68] Cf. Kennedy, op. cit. 177-9, 182-5; G. Norlin, intr. to the Loeb Isocrates, vol. i, xvi-xxx.

[69] See further H. Marrou, *Hist. of Education in Antiquity* (Eng. tr. London 1956) 87-91, 194-205; H.M. Hubbell, *The Influence of Isocrates on Cicero, Dionysius and Aristides* (Yale 1913), esp. 1-40; M.I. Finley, *The Use and Abuse of History* (London 1975) ch. 12, 'The Heritage of Isocrates', a challenging essay, if not altogether fair. For a much more detailed study of part of the tradition, see A. Grafton and L. Jardine, *From Humanism to the Humanities: Education and the Liberal Arts in 15th- and 16th-century Europe* (London 1986).

[70] See esp. *Meno* 97-9, *Rep.* v. 476 sqq., *Tht.* 170b sq., etc.

Yet Isocrates declared that 'since it is not in the nature of man to attain a science by the possession of which we can know positively what we should do or what we should say, in the next resort I hold that man to be wise who is able by his powers of *conjecture (doxais)* to arrive generally at the best course, and I hold that man to be a philosopher who occupies himself with those studies from which he will most quickly gain that sort of insight' (*Antid.* 271; cf. *Against the Sophists* 2, 7-11).[71] On the same principle Isocrates, though he does advocate the study of mathematics and astronomy, does so only for their practical or didactic value (*Antid.* 265-6), not because such studies offer access to reality or prepare the mind for such an ascent as is eloquently set out in the educational programme of the *Republic*. Isocrates' *paideia* is less demanding, perhaps even more real-istic, but we can see how radically opposed it was to the methods and ideals of Plato.

Nevertheless, the debate may not have been solely polemical. The two schools can hardly have failed to have some influence on each other. Although the early association of Isocrates with Socrates rests on no good evidence (anon. *vita Isoc.*, in Budé edition, line 8), Isocrates implicitly defends Socrates in his reply to the attack by the sophist Polycrates (*Busiris* 1-6); he argues with and criticises himself in a fashion hardly dialectical, but perhaps influenced by such methods, in the *Panathenaicus* (200ff.); and in the *Antidosis*, his defence of his life's work, he clearly takes Socrates and the Platonic *Apology* as models.[72] It is not impossible that Plato himself may have been stimulated by the example of Isocrates into forming his own philosophic educational principles and putting them into practice; above all, the philosophic orator-statesman, the *vir bonus dicendi peritus*, is an Isocratean conception.[73]

Certainly Plato did consider Isocrates a significant figure at the time of writing the *Euthydemus*. There, he is described as being on the border-line between politics and philosophy, and this ambiguity, though flawed, does seem more respectable than the debased dialectic of Euthydemus and Dionysodorus, whom the Isocratean figure has rightly criticised (*Euthyd.* 306a-c and context. See further p. 119 below). The *Phaedrus*, probably composed at least a decade later, is perhaps more patron-ising and may have vexed Isocrates more. In this dialogue many Gorgianic and Isocratean techniques of rhetoric are parodied, discussed and put to new uses, but the compliment paid to the young Isocrates at the end of the dialogue is a very back-handed one: he is a promising lad, who could do even better than Lysias (this after Phaedrus' admiration for Lysias and his oration has been shown to be ill-founded!); and he might one day rise to 'more divine pursuits' (*theiotera*); 'for there is a certain philosophy in him' (279a). *Tis* ('a certain, a kind of') must be emphatic here: there is a feline allusion to Isocrates' redefinition of philosophy (*Antid.* 268-70, 285, etc., with parallels in earlier works). The gap between the date of the dramatic setting and that of the publication of the dialogue may also be important: the reader naturally wonders, has Socrates' prediction really been fulfilled? Even if Isocrates unquestionably *is* a greater man than Lysias and his followers, has he really risen as high, achieved as much, as he might have had he

---

[71] Cf. the polemic against *doxa* and *philodoxoi* in Pl. *Rep.* v. 479e-80a with Isoc. xiii. 8. For further possible echoes between the *Republic* and Isocrates, see Adam's commentary on the *Rep.*, s.v. Isocrates (though, as he says, in many passages Isocrates need not be the only target.)

[72] For details, see Norlin, Loeb Isoc. i, intr., xvii; Kennedy, op. cit. 181.

[73] Esp. *Antid.* 276ff.; Radermacher, *Artium Scriptores* 164 (though see further below for the parallel of the Thucydidean Pericles).

followed some of the principles laid down in the *Phaedrus*?[74] It is hard to be sure of the tone here, but we cannot suppose that Plato's Socrates is wholeheartedly endorsing Isocrates present or past (as for instance Cicero assumed, e.g. *Orator* 42). Nevertheless, we need not suppose that Plato and Isocrates were on permanently hostile terms: we know that the Peripatetic Praxiphanes, in his dialogue *On the poets*, presented the two writers conversing on Plato's country estate (Diog. Laert. iii. 8 = fr. 11 Wehrli). The evidence is probably insufficient to go further; but the study of Plato's educational theory, above all in the *Republic*, can be fruitfully set in relief by sustained comparison with the work of Isocrates.[75]

Still more is this true of the contrast between the two greatest Greek prose writers, Plato and Thucydides.[76] It is at first sight astounding that more has not been done to examine their relationship. On closer investigation, it appears that much has been said, but very little has gained any kind of general acceptance. Plato never mentions Thucydides; it is indeed a notorious and peculiar fact that no fourth-century writer does.[77] The date at which Thucydides died and the date at which his history was made public are equally unknown. We know only that it was accepted as sufficiently authoritative for Xenophon (in the *Hellenica*), Theopompus and probably the Oxyrhynchus Historian to commence their histories in 411, at the point where Thucydides, no doubt involuntarily, left off.[78] Thucydides certainly survived the end of the war (ii. 65, v. 23, vi. 15), but no passage actually demands a date much later. A recently-published Thasian inscription commemorating a man named Lichas, son of Arkesilas, has been connected with the man of that name in Thucydides, who refers to his death in viii. 84. 5; this has been used to argue that Thucydides was still alive and writing in the late 390s, but the identification is dubious, and the deduction therefore unsafe.[79]

More detailed comparisons between Thucydides and Plato were attempted above all by Max Pohlenz in his early work *Aus Platos Werdezeit* (1913) 247ff. In particular he saw connections between Plato's pitiless and satirical analyses of democracy in the *Republic* and the Thucydidean Funeral speech (with which he also compared the *Menexenus*). The account of early history in the third book of the *Laws* also invited comparison with Thucydides' *archaiologia* (cf. also Pl. *Rep.* ii. 369-74). To these might be added the presentation of demagogues in both authors, the charac-

---

[74] I discuss the place of this passage in the dialogue as a whole in a later chapter (pp. 250ff. below). See further Thompson's commentary, appendix ii on Isocrates; for further hints and implications in the passage, and for an attempt to relate it to other polemical writings of the period, see J.A. Coulter, *GRBS* 8 (1967) 225-36.

[75] I regret that I have not been able to consider S. Usener, *Isokrates, Platon und ihr Publikum: Hörer und Leser von Literatur im 4. Jahrhundert v. Chr.* (ScriptOralia 14, Tübingen 1994), which appeared when my own work was in its final stages.

[76] I am indebted here to discussions with Simon Hornblower; there is some overlap below with his discussion in *Thucydides* (London 1987) ch. 5, though I do not follow him in the speculation that Thucydides actually knew Socrates.

[77] Except *Hell. Oxy.* fr. Flor. ii (p. 2 Bartoletti), in a fragmentary context. See further G. de Ste. Croix, in *The Ancient Historian and his Materials*, Fest. C.E. Stevens, ed. B. Levick (1976) 45-58, arguing that Aristotle did know Thuc.'s work and that *Poet.* 9 'what Alcibiades did and suffered' may allude to it.

[78] On these writers see further G.T. Griffiths in *Fifty Years of Classical Scholarship* ed. M. Platnauer (Blackwell, Oxford 1954, revised with addenda 1968); K. Meister, *La storiografia greca* (Rome and Bari 1992) 71-5, 78ff.; and on the composition of Thucydides' History, Andrewes and Dover, *HCT* v. 361ff., 437ff. See also p. 5, n. 8 above.

[79] For the inscription see J. Pouilloux and F. Salviat, *Comptes-rendus de l'Acad. des inscriptions et belles lettres* (1983) 376-403 (*SEG* 33. 702). Contra, see P. Cartledge, *Liverpool Classical Monthly* 9 (1984) 98-102; Hornblower, *Thucydides* 151-3.

terisation, eloquence and ambition of Alcibiades, the analysis of imperial expansion and political-moral decline, and the ideology of power as expressed by Callicles and Thrasymachus in Plato and by the Athenians at Sparta and Melos in Thucydides. But none of these comparisons is likely to be clinching, as these themes, however richly and inventively developed by these two authors, are nevertheless familiar material in fifth- and early fourth-century debate (e.g. the *agon* of Euripides' *Phoenissae* raises the issues of moderation versus ruthless ambition in politics, familiar to us from the *Gorgias*).[80] Consequently, response to the arguments of Pohlenz and others has been somewhat sceptical and negative.[81] There is, however, a remarkable parallel between the language and thought of Thucydides' *stasis* chapters (iii. 82-3), in which the historian discusses the changing meanings of evaluative words, and a passage in the eighth book of Plato's *Republic* (560-1). These passages can be said to have analogies of a sort in Isocrates;[82] but neither of the Isocratean parallels offered seems as sustained or as close, and this probably remains the best candidate for actual imitation of the historian by Plato.

The most obvious point of disagreement between these two authors is in their assessment of Pericles' leadership: for Thucydides, he was Athens' greatest leader and most prudent strategist, for Plato's Socrates, another in a long string of pseudo-politicians who pandered to the whims of the popular assembly without seeking to correct the deeper ills of Athenian society (*Grg.* 519a).[83] But the analysis of the actions and methods of Pericles' successors in Thucydides will be found to bear a much closer resemblance to Plato's critique of politicians in general and post-Periclean demagogues in particular.[84] Both Thucydides and Plato emphasise the *intellectual* element of statesmanship. Both demand that the statesman be a man of authority and integrity, one who controls and disciplines the emotions of his subjects rather than pandering to them or flattering them. The analogies are clear and firm between the rhetoric of Pericles, founded on psychological insight and political wisdom, and the power of the ideal rhetorical art which is sought in vain in the *Gorgias* and presented as a possibility, however fleeting or fanciful, in the *Phaedrus*.[85]

Thus in ii. 65. 8-9 the historian depicts Pericles' control of the people's emotions, his ability to strengthen their resolve or moderate their overconfidence. In the *Phaedrus*, Socrates alludes to the sophistic text-book of Thrasymachus on rhetoric, the *Eleoi* ('Lamentations'). He remarks: 'to pass to the application of pathetic language to the poor and aged, the master in that style seems to me to be the mighty

---

[80] E.g. cf. *Pho.* 498-502 with *Grg.* 481c5ff.; 535-48 with 483c and esp. 507e-8a.

[81] A.W. Gomme, *More Essays on Greek History and Literature* (1962) 128ff.; J. de Romilly, *Thucydides and Athenian Imperialism*, Eng. tr. (1963) 362-8; O. Luschnat, *RE* Supp. xii. 1276-84.

[82] Thus Adam on *Rep.* loc. cit., citing Isoc. *Areop.* 20, *Panath.* 131.

[83] There is a contrasting assessment in the *Phaedrus*, in which Pericles is praised for a philosophic loftiness of thought supposedly learned from Anaxagoras (270a); but that passage is not free of irony, though it was taken at face value by many ancient readers (e.g. Plut. *Per.* 4-6).

[84] See Thuc. ii. 65, etc.; in Plato, e.g. *Grg.* 503c-e, 514-19; cf. Irwin on 502e for parallels and contrasts in oratory of the fourth century.

[85] Thuc. ii. 13; ii. 59. 3 and 65. 8-9 on the rhetoric of Pericles; ii. 60. 5-6 for Pericles' statement of the necessary qualities of the ideal statesman. Compare on 'purified rhetoric' *Grg.* 480b-d, 503ab, 527c; *Phdr.* 269-72. Cf. G.F. Bender, *Der Begriff des Staatsmannes bei Thukydides* (Berlin 1938), esp. 5-26.

man of Chalcedon [i.e. Thrasymachus], who was also expert at *rousing* a crowd to *anger* and then *soothing* them down again with his *spells*, to quote his own saying.' (*Phdr.* 267d) These antitheses are part of the rhetorician's stock-in-trade ('making the small seem great, the great small', etc.), but the conception and imagery deserve attention: Thrasymachus saw himself as a spell-binder, a hypnotist or a magician manipulating the emotions of his entranced victims. The language of incantation and seductive magic recalls Gorgias' *Helen*, that central text of fifth-century rhetorical theory, in which the great sophist described the power of the word in terms ranging from tyrannical force to potent medicines.[86] Further, the arousal of *anger* (*indignatio* in later rhetorical theory) is a goal that resembles more that of Cleon in the Mytilene debate (or Antony in *Julius Caesar*) than the *rational* instilling of confidence by Pericles.[87] Indiscriminate appeal to the irrational, playing on the audience's weaknesses and encouraging their baser passions – these are the 'spells' refined and systematised by Gorgias and Thrasymachus, but they are suspect to Thucydides, as later to Plato. In the Funeral Speech, he made Pericles call for an ideal balance between *thrasos* (confidence) and *logismos* (reasoning) (ii. 40, esp. 2).[88]

What is lacking in Thrasymachus' formulation, as Plato makes clear in the *Phaedrus* itself, is a rational analysis of the emotions and indeed of the soul itself; and in a later passage of the dialogue, when Socrates insists that 'Thrasymachus, or *anyone else* who seriously proffers a scientific rhetoric, will ... describe the soul precisely, and let us see whether it is simple and uniform in nature, or like the body, complex' (271a), the allusion to Socrates' own enquiry in the opening scene of the work (230), and to his exposition of the answers, in the myth, is unmistakable. Both Plato and Thucydides, then, adapt and deepen the sophistic concept of the rhetorical virtuoso; in both writers, the true statesman needs judgement and wisdom, not just forensic tricks. That their verdict on Pericles differs should not obscure the essential similarity of criteria.[89] Here again both authors fall heir to and develop the central debates of late fifth-century thought: the status and limitations of rhetoric, the search for the 'best' constitution, the relationship of knowledge and morality, and the capacity of human reason to bind and discipline human nature.[90]

[86] The *Helen* (Grg. B11 D-K) is edited and translated by D.M. MacDowell (Bristol 1982). For discussion see esp. C.P. Segal, *HSCP* 66 (1962) 99-155, and J. de Romilly, *Magic and Rhetoric in Ancient Greece* (1974), chs. 1-2. The ground is retraced by G. Walsh, *The Varieties of Enchantment* (Chapel Hill 1984).

[87] See further Dem. 54. 42, Lycurg. 1. 134.

[88] Cf. C.W. Macleod, *Collected Essays* (1983) 86, 93, 97f.

[89] It is in any case open to dispute whether Pericles himself is not subject to some criticism, at least implicitly, by Thucydides: see H. Strasburger, in *Thukydides* ed. H. Herter (Wege der Forschung 98, Darmstadt 1968) 516; Macleod, op. cit. 153; E. Hussey, in *Crux*, Fest. G. de Ste. Croix (1985) 123-5.

[90] I return to the subject of Plato's debt to sophistic thought in ch. 4 i. On the timelessness of the issues they debated, see e.g. the fine remarks by Guthrie iii. 3-26, and Dodds, *The Ancient Concept of Progress* (1973) ch. 6.

3

Socrates at Work: his manners and methods

In the *Apology* Plato has Socrates tell the jury that he spends his days questioning and conversing with men in all walks of life: politicians, poets, craftsmen (*Ap.* 21-2), 'young or old, foreigner or fellow-citizen' (30a), but he makes plain that the young especially were attracted by his way of talking and by the challenging questions he raised. It may well be true that the historical Socrates wandered among all ranks of men: one of his disciples, Simon the cobbler, is said to have made notes of what he could remember of his conversation whenever Socrates came into his workshop (Diog. Laert. ii. 122, cf. Xen. *Mem.* iv. 2. 1, Plut. *Mor.* 776b).[1] In Plato's works, however, we see him as Plato himself must have encountered him, in his exchanges with the wealthy, leisured aristocrats of late fifth-century Athens, not just important but distinctly upper-class members of a society which was certainly a democracy, but was very far from being devoid of class consciousness and snobbery of birth.[2] The salon of the extravagant littérateur Callias, the household of the wealthy businessman Cephalus, protégé of Pericles, or the palaestra where the rather self-consciously well-bred young men exercise and read poetry to one another – these and not Simon's shoe-shop are the settings through which the Platonic Socrates wanders.

The characters of the dialogues are real historical personalities. This is often obvious, as with Aristophanes or Alcibiades, but it is true of all those who participate in the discussion, and we can often use the evidence of comedy, oratory or historians (especially Thucydides) to fill in some of the background to these figures. It is clear that in at least some cases the 'cast' of a dialogue are chosen to suit the subject matter (though this can also be seen in other terms, as Socrates in Plato, and perhaps in historical fact, tends to go along with the discussion and pursue the interests of his interlocutors). In the *Phaedo*, however, this deliberate choice of cast can be

---

[1] Modern scholars have sometimes maintained that Simon is a fiction, perhaps created by Phaedo for the dialogue which bears his name: see e.g. Zeller, *Socrates* 210. But the cobbler's shop has now been identified in excavation of the agora: see J.M. Camp, *The Athenian Agora: Excavations in the Heart of Classical Athens* (London 1986) 145-7, with pl. 125.

[2] See the important studies by J.K. Davies, *Wealth and the Power of Wealth in Classical Athens* (Arno Press 1981); also e.g. P.J. Rhodes, *JHS* 106 (1986) 132-44, B.S. Strauss, *Athens after the Peloponnesian War* (London 1987) ch. 2.

seen more clearly in the framing dialogue: the two who are engaged in recreating Socrates' final hours are Phaedo himself and Echecrates, a Pythagorean; Simmias and Cebes, pupils of the Pythagorean Philolaus, are prominent in the dialogue proper. It is not accidental that the content of the dialogue, with its central theme of the body as a prison-house for the soul, is strongly Pythagorean in inspiration.[3] Similarly in the *Euthyphro*, a dialogue which discusses piety, we can see significance in both the choice of setting, near the court of the archon basileus, and the character of the interlocutor – self-styled expert on piety, who is nevertheless undertaking the shocking task of prosecuting his own father. The connection and contrast with Socrates' own imminent prosecution is obvious.[4]

In the later dialogues too, most of the characters are real people, though there seems to be a tendency away from realistic situations and famous names: the anonymity of the Elean visitor and of the Athenian in the *Laws* are extreme cases of this tendency.[5] An increase in anachronism accompanies the decline in historical and circumstantial detail: ancient readers already felt some unease at Plato's bringing Parmenides and Socrates together (Athenaeus 505f.). In the last work of Plato's old age, the *Laws*, Socrates has vanished, and the lengthy discussion is conducted by an anonymous Athenian, Cleinias the Cretan and Megillos the Spartan. Of these figures nothing is known but what we learn from the *Laws* itself. The study of Plato's dramatic art must begin, then, from the earliest dialogues, in which the background is richly and suggestively sketched, the characters vividly presented, and above all Socrates is portrayed in all his loveable eccentricity, as a fascinating conversationalist and mischievous humorist rather than as an innovative thinker.

A number of the dialogues here presumed to be early (that is, from the first fifteen or twenty years of the fourth century) can be seen as sufficiently similar in method, subject-matter and length to be usefully compared. From this comparison we can build up a rough outline of the 'typical' early Platonic dialogue. Here the *Apology*, which is not a dialogue, and the *Crito*, which is tied very closely to the special circumstances of Socrates' impris-

---

[3] A rather different point is made in passing by Vlastos, in *The Philosophy of Socrates* (1971), 13, concerning the choice of characters' names: he writes of 'this complacent fanatic whom Plato ironically calls *Euthyphro*, 'straight-thinker'. *Noms parlants*, if frequently found in Plato, might point to invented characters, but we might question whether Plato meant us to take Euthyphro's name in this way. Friedlaender ii (see index s.v. 'names, significant'), etymologises several other names along similar lines. Play on names is certainly common in Greek literature (and life): witness the quip by a contemporary on the aptness of Thrasymachus' name (Arist. *Rh.* ii. 23. 1400b19-21). See further T. Baxter, *Plato's Critique of Naming* (Leiden 1992), on the *Cratylus* and the whole background of names and etymology in Greek culture.

[4] Cf. W.D. Furley, *Phronesis* 30 (1985) 201-8.

[5] Note e.g. the shadowy figure of Protarchus and still more that of Philebus, in the dialogue named after the latter. Some think Philebus a wholly imaginary figure: see Guthrie v. 198. Note also the absence of politicians or public figures from the later dialogues; Socrates deals more with academics, mathematicians, theorists.

onment (and so does not show him in a 'typical' situation), will be set aside; though probably early works, they are less relevant to the current enquiry (the *Apology* was in any case treated in ch. 1). The works under consideration are, for most purposes, the following: *Euthyphro, Laches, Charmides, Lysis, Ion, Hippias Major* and *Minor* (the authenticity of the last is questionable). The *Protagoras* and the *Gorgias*, though obviously works of greater length and complexity, are also comparable in certain ways. The first book of the *Republic* displays a number of the same characteristics and forms of discussion: this has often been taken to imply that the book was originally an independent and early work, and some scholars have even gone so far as to refer to book i as the *Thrasymachus*. Obviously this does not follow. We may reasonably expect to find some continuities in Plato's *oeuvre*, dramatic and formal continuities as well as doctrinal and thematic. The question of the structure of the *Republic* and the place of book i in that structure has not always been handled with sufficient literary finesse. At all events, the dialogues listed above do have marked similarities. These do not go so far as to enable us to define a fixed structure or establish a 'generic' typology, but they do permit some generalisations about Plato's methods in these early works; thereafter, we turn to the examination of some individual dialogues.[6]

The dialogues are either narrated by Socrates, or by a friend and disciple, or they are presented in purely dramatic, mimetic form without introduction.[7] For example, the *Charmides* and the *Republic* fall into the first category, the *Phaedo* and the *Symposium* into the second, and the great majority into the third (e.g. *Euthyphro, Crito, Laches, Gorgias*). *Euthydemus* and *Protagoras* strictly belong to the third group, but are almost entirely narrated to a single interlocutor by Socrates, so that the effect is rather closer to the first (particularly in the *Prt.*, in which we never return to the 'frame' scene). The combination of dramatic frame and narrative report can provide opportunities for interludes and comments by the listener (especially notable in the *Euthydemus* and the *Phaedo*). When Socrates is narrating, the frame dialogue normally follows the events narrated very closely: thus in the *Euthydemus* and the *Republic* he describes events of 'yesterday', and in the *Protagoras* the discussion has only just ended. By contrast, the episodes narrated by others are often set far in the past, usually in order to place the framing scene after Socrates' death, so providing the opportunity for pathos and recollection on the part of the narrator, and ironic foreshadowing in the narrated dialogue. The first device is most obvious in the *Phaedo*, in which an eye-witness describes Socrates' last hours and concludes with a narrative of his actual death. Comparable is the later *Theaetetus*, in which the frame dialogue is set in

---

[6] In general cf. D. Tarrant, 'Plato as dramatist,' *JHS* 75 (1955) 82-9.
[7] Cf. Diog. Laert. iii. 50 for distinctions of this kind drawn in antiquity. This and other passages are discussed in Lucinda Coventry's unpublished thesis.

369, at the time of Theaetetus' death, and the speakers warmly recall how accurately Socrates once predicted the dying man's merits, how he saw his potential while Theaetetus was still only a boy. Again an allusion is made to Socrates' forthcoming trial: the sad fact is that he did not live to see his prediction fulfilled.

The *Symposium* has a particularly intricate 'layered' structure. In the frame dialogue a friend asks Apollodorus to describe the episode, and Apollodorus explains that he did so to another friend only the previous day (part of their conversation is quoted), but he himself knows it only from Aristodemus. He goes on to narrate what Aristodemus told him (174a 'for he said that ...', and constant repetitions of such formulae). The point seems to be to emphasise the 'past-ness' of the events: the speakers depend on tradition. Also, the distancing of the narrative may be a warning that we should not take the dialogue either as a total account (note esp. 180c) or as literally true in every detail (cf. 223c-d). Within the narrative there are many other extensive speeches which often include further dialogue: in particular, Socrates' own speech includes a reproduction of a dialectical discussion between himself and Diotima. This is an extreme example of Plato's fondness for intricacy of structure, digression and 'play-within-a-play' effects. The opening of the *Theaetetus* suggests that he became rather more cautious in later years about this sort of 'layering' and in particular about the constant repetitions of 'he said that ...' (*Tht.* 143b-c). In that work, Eucleides explains that in recording the discussion he has used direct speech alone, in order to avoid such clumsy phrases; we thus have a dramatic frame enclosing a further drama.

The *number* of characters participating in a dialogue also deserves some attention. This varies widely: Socrates and one other in (e.g.) *Crito, Euthyphro, Hippias*'s, *Alcibiades*'s, *Ion, Menexenus, Clitopho, Phaedrus*; Socrates together with a whole circle of disciples in the *Phaedo* and a large company of friends in the *Symposium*; Socrates and a smaller number of interlocutors with whom he converses one at a time (*Tht., Crat.*), or with a large audience in a more 'naturally' or realistically presented conversation, in which all those present participate and there is no fixed order of speakers (thus *Laches, Lysis, Charmides, Euthydemus, Protagoras*), though often the 'realism' is calculated and not entirely random).

Different again is the *Gorgias*, in which Socrates deals with each of the main interlocutors in turn, passing from Gorgias to Polus to Callicles (compare *Rep.* i: Cephalus, Polemarchus, Thrasymachus). Here the sequence is cumulative: each exchange is longer and more vehement, and each new speaker draws Socrates out more, challenging him further. The progression from Gorgias to Polus to Callicles reflects three generations in the history of rhetoric and its influence on society and politics. Each speaker has gone further with rhetoric and further in the rejection of conventional morality as a criterion for its use.

Multiplicity of characters obviously provides variety – different outlooks and (as in the *Symposium*) different styles. But Plato uses the larger cast to make ethical as well as dramatic points. In the *Laches*, as we shall see, Laches' and Nicias' answers to Socrates' questions are both inadequate, and it seems that their methods and their approaches need to be combined, in dialectic as in life. In the *Protagoras* and *Euthydemus*, the picture is more negative. Whereas Callias is delighted to spend money on entertaining sophists and tries to have as many as possible under his roof, Plato shows how 'too many cooks spoil the broth': the large assemblage of sophistic teachers makes for a confused hubbub (314e sqq., esp. 315e-6a on Prodicus), and later for competition and conflict (317c, 318e).

It is typical of the Platonic Socrates to concentrate on a single interlocutor, with whom he can carry on a dialectical discussion. Whenever he is in a larger gathering, he attempts to turn the conversation into that form.[8] Contrasts between Socratic *conversation* or *dialectic* and sophistic rhetoric, especially epideictic or 'display' speeches, run through all of Plato's work (e.g. *Grg.* 448d-9d, 471d-8d, *Meno* 75cd, *Tht.* 172c-7c, etc.). Even in the *Apology*, where it might seem inevitable that Socrates must have recourse to continuous *oratory*, Plato has him transform his speech as far as possible into dialectic by having him question the prosecutor and supply his answers (*Ap.* 24c sqq.; cf. also such phrases as 28b 'perhaps someone may say ...', 37e); and in general the speech is deliberately anti-rhetorical in manner (17a-18a, 27b, 30e sq., 32a8, 39e5) and content (especially in its rejection of conventional *topoi* such as the appeals to pity, 34b sqq.). So too in the *Symposium*, Socrates' speech is not entirely, or even primarily, *in propria persona*, but a narrative of a dialectical discussion with Diotima (201e sqq.).

The setting and circumstances of a dialogue can also be significant. It is true that some have no particular location in time and place, while in others the place is mentioned but then ignored. But the scene is carefully set and sustained in the *Phaedo* and *Symposium*, repeatedly referred to in the *Phaedrus*. These details, while of no strictly philosophical import, do sometimes reinforce characterisation or suit the personalities or occasion. The shifting positions and relationships in the *Symposium*, at a dinner at which, according to convention, much importance attaches to one's place at table, reflect the changing course of the conversation (see esp. 222d-3a). The prison forms a grim backdrop in the *Crito* and the *Phaedo*: in the former Socrates is offered an opportunity to escape from it, which he declines, while in the latter death brings a truer escape, a 'cure' for the ills of life. The *Laws*, a work on a vaster scale than any of the other dialogues, offers a complete contrast in setting too, being the only work not set in Attica and among Athenians. Instead the three speakers are journeying through Crete, on their way to the sacred cave of Zeus. As the Athenian remarks,

---

[8] Contrast Xenophon's Socrates who, like the sophists, seems happy to address a larger crowd in a more expository, didactic way: also *Clitopho* 407a sq., one of many oddities about that very puzzling work: see p. 100 below.

Crete is famous for its mythical lawgivers, Minos and Rhadamanthus, sons of Zeus. The formulation of the legal code for a new city is thus begun under notable auspices.[9]

Turning back to the early group of dialogues, we find that they normally commence with an encounter between Socrates and one or more others. If there are several others, they are usually involved in conversation or some other pastime (such as gymnastics) when Socrates arrives on the scene. Thus in the *Gorgias* Callicles and the rest have just finished listening to a display by Gorgias. Sometimes a question is being hotly discussed, and the disputants seek Socrates' advice and views (*Lach.* 180bc: 'I'm surprised you're not calling in Socrates', cf. *Crat.* 383a). Similarly Meno consults Socrates about a question which is generally in the air, the relative importance of natural ability, teaching and practice (*Meno init.*). In the early dialogues there is often a figure of authority, an expert in a particular field, who is contrasted, both implicitly and explicitly, with Socrates the inquisitive amateur: thus Ion the rhapsode claims to know all about Homer and all the subjects dealt with in his poems; Euthyphro is in his own eyes an expert on piety and often lectures the Athenians on the topic; Laches and Nicias are respected men who have served their country on campaign, and so it is proper that they should be called in to advise on the education of young men, and that they should know how to define courage. The dialogues thus explore not just any old subject, but one which is relevant to the participants: either one of them is regarded as an expert or else he possesses or represents the quality, as in the *Charmides*, where the aim is to define the *sophrosyne* ('modesty') which all those present are sure that Charmides possesses. In the more complex dialogues the approach is developed. In the *Protagoras*, there are a whole string of experts who can disagree and get in each other's way (cf. the two brothers in the *Euthydemus*, especially at 297a, 303e). In the *Gorgias* we find a different twist: there, the initial question is to define just what – or who – Gorgias *is*, to identify his profession and explore his claim to practise an art.

Socrates is always interested in talking with people like this. He comes prepared to learn, frequently professing ignorance of what they would like to know (or claim already to know); the only thing he really knows about, he occasionally admits, is love (*Theages* 128b, *Lysis* 204b, *Gorgias* 481d, *Smp.* 177d, etc.).[10] Not only is he ignorant, he is no expert, he claims, in formal debate (*Ap.* 17b-d, *Phdr.* 262d), he cannot follow or remember long speeches such as the sophists favour (*Prt.* 334c sq., *Hipp. Min.* 373a, *Grg.*

---

[9] Sometimes, it must be admitted, the details of the initial setting are enigmatic. I can discern no reason for the preliminary reference to the festival of Bendis and the Thracian horseback riders in the first book of the *Republic*, though the transition from Socrates' reluctance to linger for further spectacle to Socrates the keen pursuer of philosophic enquiry obviously has moral implications (cf. *Charm.* 153d for similar concern to get down to business).

[10] On Socrates' ignorance see Vlastos, *Philosophical Quarterly* 35 (1985) 1-31, reworked as *Socratic Studies* 39-66; contrast M.M. Mackenzie, *CQ* 38 (1988) 331-50.

461d sqq., etc.), and he is overwhelmed, stunned, thrown into confusion by their rhetorical fluency or argumentative ingenuity (*Prt.* 328d, 339d sq., *Smp.* 198bc). But despite his alleged ignorance and inexperience, he seems to have an uncanny eye for the weak point in an argument or definition once it is proposed; and his typical practice is not to swallow a definition or a rhetorical speech whole, but to pick at it and examine its implications, its consistency, its underlying assumptions.

There are certain typical responses which Socrates' companions make to the kind of questions raised in the early dialogues, questions like 'what is piety?' (or courage, modesty, etc.). One common reaction, usually the first attempt at definition, is an *ostensive* one – the interlocutor cheerfully rattles off a number of things that involve or represent piety (etc.) and says that they are what piety actually *is*.[11] Socrates then points out the difference between enumerating *examples* and defining the *essence* of a quality, between actual objects or actions and the abstraction of which they are instances. (As we saw, this was one of the points which Aristotle singled out as a distinctively Socratic contribution, his search for definitions.)

Another characteristic move is the appeal to authority, either to a common or proverbial definition or to poetry, and especially to Homer. Thus in the *Republic* Socrates is talking to Cephalus, and reaches the tentative conclusion that we cannot say that justice is simply 'to tell the truth and return what one has received', at which point Polemarchus interrupts, saying 'oh, but it is, Socrates, if we're to believe Simonides' (i. 331d). This paves the way for an investigation of Simonides' dictum; it also indicates the automatic respect that the Greeks had for the poets, and prepares the reader for the all-out attack on poetic authority in books ii and iii. (Cf. further *Lysis* 213e-4a, *Charm.* 161a, 163b, *Theages* 125b sqq.) In the *Hippias Minor* Socrates enters a mild objection to this procedure: 'Let us leave Homer alone, since it is impossible to ask him what he had in mind when he composed these lines. But since you seem to be taking on the responsibility, and you are in agreement with what Homer is saying, give a joint reply on your own behalf and on Homer's' (365cd).[12] The irrecoverability of a poet's meaning is illustrated at greater length in the *Protagoras*.

The *Meno*, though a later work, well illustrates another aspect of the quest for definitions. Not all definitions are alike, in Meno's view. Some are naive and unhelpful, others are intellectually respectable and sound good. There is some gentle satire here, as Meno's stylistic tastes are shown to deflect him from the task of clear and economical definition. Socrates, in an attempt to define shape, suggests that it is the only thing which always accompanies colour (75bc). When Meno protests that this is a 'naive' sort

[11] See *Euthyphro* 5d-6e, *Meno* 71e, with Thompson's n., *Hipp. Mai.* 287e sqq., *Lach.* 191d, *Tht.* 146c. For a full discussion, see R.W. Puster, *Zur Argumentations-struktur Platonischer Dialoge* (Freiburg-Munich 1983). For other aspects of the quest for definitions, see M. Burnyeat, *Philosophy* 52 (1977) 381-98.

[12] See further M. Whitlock Blundell in *OSAP* Suppl. (1992),esp. 151, 167-8.

of definition, Socrates plays along and suggests a definition of colour in terms of Empedoclean theories of effluence: 'colour is an effluence from shapes commensurate with sight and perceptible by it' (76d). Meno is enthusiastic, and Socrates drily replies, 'yes, it's a high-flown (*tragike*) response, so you like it better'.[13] The point here seems to be that Meno's admiration for Gorgias and his teacher Empedocles makes him appreciate a definition in terms of their theories, irrespective of whether those are valid, whereas Socrates is aiming at a definition that will be true of necessity, almost a logical truth (though whether he has succeeded in finding one is another matter). The passage is a good example of something that is often true in Plato – that the tastes and personalities of the participants affect their arguments (cf. e.g. the speech of the doctor Eryximachus in the *Symposium* and see pp. 83, 94 below on the *Laches* and *Charmides*). Professionals can also, of course, be questioned in terms suited to their skills, and teased about them.[14]

Socrates' argumentative tactics defy full enumeration and classificaton, and can more easily be dealt with in discussion of specific scenes. But a few general tendencies can be noted here. His questioning usually focusses on *generalisations*: he suggests exceptions (e.g. *Lach.* 191a sq., *Rep.* i. 331c), he points out the need to define the terms in which an answer or solution has been couched (e.g. *Grg.* 448c-9a, *Meno* 79d, *Phdr.* 237b-d), and he constantly tries to relate an answer to other beliefs held by his interlocutor, enquiring whether they can be consistently held.[15] Socrates' dialectic has as its principal tool the so-called elenchus, which means 'interrogation' of a kind which leads to refutation.[16] The Socratic elenchus characteristically exposes contradictions between different beliefs: a simple example is Socrates' interrogation of Agathon in *Symp.* 199-201, in which Socrates shows him that he cannot hold *both* that Love is a god and benefactor of mankind and that Love lacks and longs for what is beautiful and good.[17]

Normally the interlocutor has not fully articulated the contradictory beliefs, even in his own mind, and so the Socratic questioning both clarifies his own opinions and exposes problems, so leading to greater self-knowledge (typically knowledge of his own confusion and ignorance). The elenchus may thus seem to be a negative process, but it has positive moral implications: error is better recognised, for then the effort to find the right path can begin.

Though the elenchus is by far the most significant weapon in Socrates'

[13] Cf. *Phdr.* 275bc.

[14] E.g. *Hipp. Min.* 369a, a joke about Hippias' mnemonic technique.

[15] See esp. R. Robinson, *Plato's Earlier Dialectic* (1953) chs. 2-3; also G.E.R. Lloyd, *Magic, Reason and Experience* (1979) 98-102.

[16] Vlastos, in *OSAP* 1 (1983) 27-58 with comments by Kraut, ibid. 59-70; id., *Socrates* (1991) ch. 4 and elsewhere; *Socratic Studies* (1994) 1-37, 135-6.

[17] Cf. T.H. Irwin, *Plato, Gorgias* pp. 1-2 for an example from the *Laches* and further comments; or e.g. *Rep.* i. 339a-e.

armoury, there are other characteristic features of his own dialectic which we learn to recognise as they are produced. Socrates is also fond of analogies and similes, in particular the so-called 'craft analogy' by which he compares intellectual or moral activity with proficiency at a particular craft or profession: a favourite and significant example is that of the doctor.[18] He also often illustrates intellectual or moral qualities by drawing comparisons with a physical sense (usually sight or hearing); and he compares moral or mental *processes* with physical or natural processes (e.g. *Smp.* 175d). These analogies, which probably originate in popular usage, are a natural didactic tool, for they make abstract discussion more concrete and easier to follow. But there is also a danger that the analogy may be imperfect or incomplete, a point which Socrates' companions sometimes make, but perhaps not as frequently as they should. Socrates' fondness for analogies is treated as something of a joke (see esp. *Rep.* vi. 487e-8a), and it is perhaps true that not all of them are intended to be taken seriously or as absolutely exact; but there is some danger of repeated usage giving them a status that has not been adequately established by argument.[19] The importance of analogy in Plato's thought can be seen at once when we remember that the comparison between society and the soul, between the organisation and structure of the city-state and of the human *psyche*, plays a fundamental role throughout the *Republic*.

Even more fundamental to Socrates' manner than his fondness for comparisons is his *irony*, and few ancient concepts have been so influential or given rise to such varied theories, ethical and critical.[20] Socrates' irony, surely a characteristic of the original man, is in Plato something extraordinarily rich and many-faceted. It cannot be summed up in a few sentences. It begins from his protestations of ignorance and incompetence at everything, which seem so obviously refuted by his skill at argument; hence he is accused of being a hypocrite by his more aggressive opponents (especially Thrasymachus). The Greek word *eironeia*, indeed, often refers to a kind of sneaky deceptive behaviour (e.g. Ar. *Wasps* 174, *Birds* 1211). The practical upshot of this is that because he insists that he cannot follow the clever

---

[18] For a detailed discussion of this see T. Irwin, *Plato's Moral Theory* (Oxford 1977) ch. 3, esp. 71-7. It will be obvious that I would be more cautious in ascribing as systematic a 'theory' to Socrates or Plato as is assumed in Irwin's discussion.

[19] In general see G.E.R. Lloyd, *Polarity and Analogy* (Cambridge 1966): on Plato, 289-303.

[20] Friedlaender i, ch. 7 is helpful if a little mystical. See also W. Boder, *Die Sokratische Ironie in den Platonischen Frühdialogen* (Amsterdam 1973), including an extensive bibliography on the topic; Vlastos, *Socrates* ch. 1 with Endnote 1; C.J. Rowe, *Nova Tellus* 5 (1987) 83-101. I have been helped by reading an unpublished paper by Edward Hussey on Irony. Greek ideas of the concept in its non-Socratic context may be gathered by considering Aristotle, *Nic. Eth.* iv. 7 and Theophrastus, *Characters* 1 (with commentaries by Ussher and Steinmetz); they are also discussed by O. Ribbeck, *RhM* 31 (1876) 381ff.; W. Büchner, *Hermes* 76 (1941) 339ff.; F. Amory, *C&M* 33 (1981-2) 49-80. See further D.C. Muecke, *The Compass of Irony* (London 1969), Wayne Booth, *A Rhetoric of Irony* (Chicago 1974), D.J. Enright, *The Alluring Problem: An Essay on Irony* (Oxford 1986), and many others.

arguments of others, the interlocutor is forced to explain things more fully, and frequently finds that he was not as clear about certain things as he himself supposed. Socrates' regular companions are accustomed to his playful manner, and some of them respond in kind.[21] But Socrates' irony concerns others besides himself, as when he praises men like the sophists and claims to admire or envy them: here too, we feel, he must be speaking with his tongue in cheek some of the time, though we may grant that at first he has genuinely high hopes about, say, Protagoras or Hippias. It is more puzzling that he should sustain the admiring tone after the wisdom of the charlatans in the *Euthydemus* has been exposed as a sham. Part of the explanation may be that it would be foreign to Socrates' personality to make emphatic or polemical comments about the inadequacy of others' ideas or arguments. This would, after all, imply that he knew better, whereas he is insistent that he does not have all, or any, of the answers.

But Plato's use of the concept goes further than this. He seems to see Socrates' ironic manner as the central feature of his character, the key to his life and thought. This tone of mild humour, at first so gentle that the impercipient do not notice it, is not confined to contexts where knowledge and ignorance are in question, but pervades the dialogues. Alcibiades' words are appropriate: Socrates hides his treasures within him, and 'playing his ironic game he passes his whole life among men' (*Smp.* 216e). Perhaps one reason for his adopting this tone is to ease the discomfort which others feel at being refuted, but that can only be a limited aspect of it, since in some ways he wants them to be shocked and dismayed: his role is that of a gadfly. The irony itself infuriates some of his interlocutors.

For Plato, we may suspect, the irony of Socrates made certain literary effects possible which he could not have achieved in other ways: in particular, the wonderful eloquence and grandeur of some of Socrates' most memorable speeches are all the more impressive because he has briefly dropped the ironic mask and revealed some of the 'treasures within'. Moreover, the half-serious, half-playful manner of Socrates makes it hard to feel sure, even when he himself is narrator of a dialogue, how firmly he is committing himself to a particular hypothesis or conclusion. A complex series of arguments can be dismissed with a smile; a whole dialogue can be put in a different perspective and described as 'play'. Just as Socrates' irony was surely developed and extended by Plato (who of course also introduced numerous instances of *dramatic* irony, a simpler concept), so too the questing, unceasing nature of Socrates' activity, which does not expect to reach a conclusion, is echoed and enriched in the often paradoxical and bewildering conversations of the dialogues. Irony, the dialogue form and Socrates are connected: in the non-Socratic *Laws* Plato uses other techniques to modify the tone and suggest inadequacies, but the magical quality is gone.

[21] E.g. *Rep.* 449c-51b, *Smp.* 175e, *Phdr.* 235b-e, 236c, and many other cases.

We return to the general characterisation of the early dialogues. Discussions in Plato do not usually follow a straightforward path. Besides false starts and digressions, there are often interludes, which may develop or illuminate themes of the dialogue in a non-argumentative form. One common type of interlude is the discussion of *methodology*, which recurs throughout Plato's work. Plato is concerned not only to follow through a philosophic argument, but also to discuss the proper form and manner of doing so. Pauses in the discussion are often punctuated by Socrates' remarks about the way they should deal with each other and conduct the argument henceforth. The proper length of speeches is sometimes discussed: this was a topic which had already been treated in rhetorical terms by the sophists.[22] Socrates insists that their primary concern should be to find the truth, not to score points off one another, nor to win applause and impress an audience as if they were competing or advertising their cleverness.[23] Nor should the participants hold back or hoard their knowledge (*Rep.* i. 344e): the search for wisdom is a common enterprise. They must speak freely, voicing their own true feelings and beliefs, without inhibitions or shamefacedness. Cheating or changing one's ground is unfair and illegitimate (*Charm.* 174b, *Grg.* 499bc). If men work together, they have a better chance of success (*Prt.* 348d); if a partner stumbles and makes a mistake, we should not guffaw or mock his error as if we ourselves were perfect. Abuse, invective or laughter do not constitute refutation (*Lach.* 195a7, *Euthyd.* 276d, 278d, *Grg.* 473de). But although the discussion should be between friends, and honest cooperation is the ideal, that does not mean that we should flatter one another or smooth over any differences: it is necessary, and right, that errors should be made clear, and above all in the all-important matters of morality and the proper way to live. The importance of the philosophic enquiry is frequently emphasised (*Lach.* 185a, *Grg.* 481bc, 500c, *Rep.* i. 352d, ii. 358d7f.). Moreover, we should seek wisdom wherever we may find it, and not be too proud or superior to listen to any possible helper, even if the advice may seem naive and unoriginal (note the references to 'old wives' tales' in *Grg.* 527a, cf. 512e; compare also *Phdr.* 275bc). Laches voices the proper attitude when he declares: 'that the teacher is rather young, or not as yet in repute – anything of that sort is of no account with me' (*Laches* 189a).

Such passages represent the ideal, not always achieved in practice. As the discussion progresses, tempers may become hotter; what begins as courteous and cultivated chat among friends can turn into embarrassment, indignation and even hostility as Socrates' interrogation punctures pretensions and exposes illusory claims to knowledge. Indignation at this treat-

---

[22] See *Prt.* 328e-9b, 334c-8e, *Grg.* 449c with Dodds's n.; *Rep.* i. 348ab; Prodicus ap. *Phdr.* 267b. Further, H. Hudson-Williams, *AJP* 71 (1950) 156ff.; C.W. Macleod, *Coll. Essays* (1983) 54.
[23] For criticism of *philonikia*, see esp. *Grg.* 457c sqq., *Phaedo* 91a. For the moral approach to discussion see further G.E.R. Lloyd, *Magic, Reason and Experience* (Cambridge 1979) 100-1.

ment is fiercest in the case of Callicles in the *Gorgias*, but we find other heated responses elsewhere: Critias in the *Charmides* (esp. 162d, cf. 169c), Thrasymachus in the first book of the *Republic*, Anytus in the *Meno*, and to some extent Laches in the dialogue of that name (though he is more concerned that Nicias should not do better than himself, 197a sq., 200a-c; he feels no resentment towards Socrates). The Socratic method challenges and alarms his victims: their vanity and their security seem threatened, as he makes them realise that they did not know what they thought they knew (*Ap.* 23c), that they cannot define or isolate qualities they feel sure they possess (*Lach.* 194ab, *Charm.* 176ab; cf. *Lysis* 223b, where, however, it is Socrates speaking). The younger listeners may be excited and stimulated by this procedure (*Ap.* 23c, *Theages* 121d, *Rep.* vii. 539b, *Tht.* 150d, *Phileb.* 15d sq.), as in the case of Cleinias in the *Euthydemus*. But the older and more conservative spirits such as Anytus are angry with Socrates, suspecting him of making fun of them and, more seriously, accusing him of undermining traditional morality through his questioning of accepted values (*Meno* 92e, 94e). In this they associate him with the professional teachers of novel ideas, the sophists, and as we shall see in the next chapter, they were not entirely wrong.[24]

Socrates' listeners protest against his way of arguing, his nit-picking, the way he swoops on slight inconsistencies or verbal slips. It is ill-mannered, they complain, and hardly the action of a gentleman, to catch people out in this fashion. Polus accuses him of boorishness (*Grg.* 461c, *polle agroikia*); more politely, Hippias complains of his manipulation of arguments so as to create difficulties (*Hipp. Min.* 369bc). Thrasymachus calls him a pettifogger or quibbler (*Rep.* i. 340d1, and what follows), Callicles describes him as a 'mob-orator' (*Grg.* 482c, cf. 494d). These criticisms are understandable, but not altogether fair. Insofar as casual or careless use of words does lead to confusion, ambiguity and error in both speech and action, Socrates' corrections and 'quibbles' are important both logically and morally. But it must have been difficult to accept that he was doing this unselfishly and without any kind of malicious pleasure; indeed, the most sympathetic of Plato's readers must occasionally feel that Socrates' teasing criticisms and comments in dealing, say, with Ion or Hippias, are faintly patronising and even downright irritating.[25] Interlocutors (and readers) find fault with his style of talking, with his constant mention of cobblers, farmers, tanners and so forth – what has all this to do with the large ethical and political issues which are under discussion?[26] Here again the reader needs to look more closely at the apparently naive and clumsy style of Socrates, to see the effectiveness of this style as an instrument to deflate

[24] For Socrates described as a 'sophist' see Aeschin. 1. 173, Androtion *FGH* 324 F 69.

[25] Cf. further *Apol.* 22c-3a; *Rep.* i. 337a; Kraut, *Socrates and the State* 246.

[26] For this criticism see esp. Callicles in *Grg.* 491a, cf. 497b, *Hipp. Mai.* 288d; also Alcibiades in *Smp.* 221e, protesting against such superficial complaints.

and cut down to size the high-flown rhetoric of the sophistic orator or the self-styled authority.[27] It is to some extent snobbery that makes Callicles so disdainful of Socrates' talk;[28] another ambitious aristocrat, the future tyrant Critias, reacts in much the same way, though less outspokenly (see *Charm.* 163b sq., where Critias specifically denies that anyone who manufactures shoes or sells dried fish can be said to be doing real work). If it is true that Socrates himself was the son of a stonemason,[29] then there is additional bite in the superior jibes of these aristocrats. But whatever the truth of Socrates' origins and profession, the main point remains one of principle: that class consciousness and social values are irrelevant to philosophic argument. Thrasymachus and others may accuse Socrates of 'small-mindedness', Hippias may complain that dialectic fumbles around in short, trivial questions and answers and fails to tackle the grand, important issues (*Hipp. Mai.* 301bc, 304ab), but the truth is that these minutiae *do* matter: only if Callicles and the rest consider the basis on which their ambitious claims rest can their grand declarations have any validity.

Not all conversations with Socrates end in resentment and displeasure, however: Anytus in the *Meno* and Callicles in the *Gorgias* are extreme cases. In the early dialogues a common conclusion is the realisation that none of the answers offered so far is adequate: the participants are in *aporia*, that is, they do not know what to try next (the situation at the end of *Euthyphro, Laches, Lysis, Charmides, Hipp. Min.* and *Mai., Protagoras* [see 361c] and *Republic* i; for the term itself, see e.g. *Laches* 200e, *Hipp. Mai* 304c).[30] This can be related to the original mission of Socrates as described in the *Apology*: praised by the god as the wisest of men, he concluded that he could only be so called because he was aware of his own ignorance, and so set about questioning others, at first hoping to find out their wisdom, later in order to reveal to them their own ignorance. As he explains to Theaetetus, it is better to be disabused of your erroneous belief that you know something than to go on supposing this, remaining uncorrected and unenlightened for the whole of your life (*Tht.* 210bc, the concluding speech of the work).[31] With the slate cleared, the erroneous beliefs removed, there is every prospect of setting out in search of real knowledge.

Not all of Socrates' interlocutors appreciated this process of correction,

---

[27] There is an analogy here with the 'plain-man' stance of later moralists and especially Roman satire. Cf. J.F. Kindstrand, *Bion of Borysthenes* (Uppsala 1979) 42-4, 47-9 and Horace, *Satires* (perhaps still more Lucilius: cf. N. Rudd, *The Satires of Horace* (Cambridge 1966) ch.4).

[28] See *Grg.* 490a, 491ab and esp. 489c, '(do you think I'm talking about) a rabble of slaves and nondescripts who are of no earthly use? ...'; cf. 512c on Callicles' snobbery.

[29] For the evidence see Burnet on *Euthyphro* 11b9; he is very sceptical.

[30] Cf. Slings, *Comm. on ... Clitopho* 196-7.

[31] The *Theaetetus*, however, cannot be regarded as simply aporetic in the manner of the shorter works cited: see below, p. 281, and e.g. D. Frede, *PCPS* 35 (1989) 20-49.

as we have already seen. Several passages attest the discomfort some of them felt at being reduced to helpless *aporia*. Even if they did not come to resent and dislike Socrates, they found the experience of talking with him painful and numbing: Meno uses the memorable comparison of Socrates to an electric fish or stingray to describe the effect his questions have (*Meno* 79e-80b; cf. *Euthyphro* 11b-e, *IAlc.* 116e, *Tht.* 149a9, 151c, *Soph.* 230b-d, and esp. *Rep.* vi. 487b-d). In the *Meno* in particular, Plato tries to answer this criticism, and to show that Socratic teaching could also pave the way for genuine self-improvement and lead on to knowledge. This is one function of the scene with the slave-boy, in which Socrates shows Meno the possibility of discovering truth even after being shown the falsity of one's previous opinions: the numbing process is a necessary prelude and does the slave no harm. Inspired by this example, Meno endorses Socrates' emphatic declaration that he is convinced of the need to search for what one does not know (86bc). Some of Socrates' friends do indeed accept the *aporia* in the same spirit as himself: they respond with humility and hope to go on to learn more. (Nicias in the *Laches* is a fine spokesman for these: see 187e-8b.) Others, however, make haste to get away from Socrates or end the discussion even though he is eager to continue (*Euthyphro*, *Prt.*), and the uncomfortable and difficult questions he has raised are generally postponed, much to his chagrin, 'to another occasion' (*eis authis* or similar phrases: *Euthyphro* 15e-16a, *Prt.* 361e; cf. the interruption at the end of *Lysis* by the boys' slaves). Sometimes it is suggested that they meet again the next day (as in the *Laches*);[32] on other occasions the time for resuming the discussion is fixed more vaguely and less sincerely. The *Euthyphro* strikingly brings out the reluctance of Socrates' victims to repeat the procedure. There Socrates is keen to carry on but Euthyphro hurriedly says: 'another time, please, Socrates; for at the moment I'm in a hurry somewhere [deliberately vague?] and it's time for me to be off ' (15e). But with Socrates' trial imminent, there may never have been another chance.[33]

This much, then, in general outline of the typical structure and movement of Plato's earlier works: these are the bare bones which he clothes with the flesh of historical personalities, humour, parody, paradoxes and sustained philosophic argument.[34] I turn now to a more detailed examination of particular works.[35] Here it makes sense to begin with dialogues in which Socrates deals with ordinary men, his fellow-Athenians, before

---

[32] Cf. the supposed temporal relationship of the 'trilogies' *Soph.* (on the day after the *Tht.*), *Statesman, Philosopher* (never written); *Tim., Crit.*, and the unwritten *Hermocrates*.

[33] A similar point is made more explicitly (and more poignantly) by Cebes in the *Phaedo*, 107a.

[34] Contrast the different slant given to this metaphor by G. Vlastos, in *Times Literary Supplement* 24 Feb. 1978, 230-1, for whom the arguments are the 'flesh and bone' of the dialogues, covered by a 'skin of graceful chatter and badinage'.

[35] For model analyses of two dialogues not considered in this book, see L.J. Coventry, *JHS* 109 (1989) 1-15, on *Menexenus*; M. Whitlock Blundell, in *OSAP* Suppl. 1992, 131-72, on *Hippias Minor*.

proceeding in the next chapter to discuss his more ambitious encounters with the professional sophists. The *Laches*, in which he talks with older men, and the *Charmides*, in which he converses with the young, present Socrates at his most charming, witty and ironical. Together, they offer a splendid introduction to Plato's work. It does not, of course, follow that they are actually among the earliest dialogues, but other considerations, including stylometry, do make this likely.

The *Laches*[36]

The *Laches* has a relatively firm dramatic date which is consistently maintained. The battle of Delium of 424 BC, in which Socrates did himself credit,[37] is in the recent past, while the death of Laches in 418 is obviously still in the future; likewise the Sicilian expedition and the downfall of Nicias. The two generals are at leisure in Athens, probably during the Peace of Nicias. Lysimachus and Melesias consult these eminent men on the question of proper training for their sons: how can they guarantee that they will grow up worthy of their distinguished ancestry? As the dialogue opens they have been watching a display of fighting in armour, and the merits of this form of combat are discussed inconclusively. Not until over half-way through the dialogue is the 'subject' of the work identified, namely 'courage' (190d5) – what is it, how can the boys attain it, can it be taught? Clearly, brave men and commanders such as Nicias and Laches must know the nature of courage, but under Socrates' questioning, deficiencies appear in both of Laches' attempts at a definition ('standing firm and not running away'; 'resolution of the soul'), and also in the more thoughtful attempt by Nicias ('knowledge which inspires fear or confidence in war or elsewhere', reformulated as 'knowledge of the grounds for hope and fear'). The dialogue ends in *aporia*.

It is obvious that the *Laches* is not composed solely, or even primarily, for the sake of the brief and flimsy 'philosophic' arguments used to support and refute these definitions. To say that the work is also intended to give a portrait of Socrates and of his interlocutors is no doubt true, but still does not take us very far; in greater or lesser degree, this could be said of any of the early dialogues. The following comments on structure, and on some specific passages, may help towards a unified view of both the dramatic and the philosophic aspects of the *Laches*.

It is a curious fact that so much time is spent discussing the merits and demerits of armoured combat. The initial speech of Lysimachus sets the scene and thrusts the 'man fighting in full armour' on our attention; later,

---

[36] This section was originally drafted in 1985. Since then M. C. Stokes has provided a detailed account of the *Laches* in *Plato's Socratic Conversations* (London 1986) 36-113.

[37] See *La.* 181ab; *Smp.* 221a sqq. For a historical account of the campaign, see Thuc. iv. 89-101; for a modern treatment, see D.M. Lewis, in *CAH* v² 425-7.

Nicias and Laches argue for and against the pursuit of expertise of this kind (181d-84c), with a wealth of vivid detail in Laches' speech in particular. Since the two experts disagree, decision is difficult, and so Lysimachus turns to Socrates asking him to arbitrate. His remark that 'if they were both in agreement, there wouldn't be so much need for an arbitrator' gives rise to a veiled rebuke from Socrates: does he judge by head-counting only, or by knowledge? (184d) From this we move to an enquiry into the credentials of those present: what is the knowledge they possess, who were their teachers, whom have they improved by their teaching? The discussion is moved from a more detached, superficially 'objective' debate on to a more intimate plane, on which self-revelation and mutual criticism will be necessary accompaniments to enquiry. Further, the subject of the debate moves from the concrete (the merits and drawbacks of a specific form of fighting) to the abstract (the definition and delimiting of a part of virtue). To emphasise this shift, Plato uses two principal devices: first, the two parts of the dialogue are divided by an interlude in which Nicias describes and praises Socrates' method of enquiry (187d-88c) and Laches endorses his praise; second, the form of the dialogue changes with its subject-matter, and whereas in the first half Socrates was in the background while Nicias and Laches debated in an *agon* (a sequence of two set speeches on a theme), in the second half Socrates takes the lead, but through the medium which is characteristic of him, dialectic, short questions and answers involving one person at a time (first Nicias, then Laches).

The dialogue is so structured to make a methodological point. In the earlier part Laches and Nicias were appealed to as authoritative figures, experts, and in their set speeches they take that role for granted, though they achieve different results. Lysimachus tries to get Socrates to play the same game, but he is dissatisfied with both the question they are treating and the way they are approaching it. Socrates' dislike of set speeches is mentioned in a number of the dialogues and most fully explained in the *Protagoras* (328e-9b; cf. *Rep.* i. 348ab): a wealth of points can be made without the listener having any real chance to stop the speaker and ask questions. Furthermore, Socrates does not come with the answers, but hopes to make some progress in finding them, through acknowledgement of ignorance (ironically presented as simply the result of his poverty, 186b sq.) and through a common enquiry.[38]

Admiration of Socrates as a person and approval of his proposed method of enquiry do not guarantee patient and self-critical performance in dialectical discussion. Plato often contrasts the initial readiness of a character to undergo questioning with the gradual irritation, unease or outright anger which the questioning provokes. In the *Laches*, the discussion is not prolonged and feelings do not run high, but there is certainly a contrast

---

[38] *Koinos*, 'common', and its cognates are frequent in such contexts: cf. *Laches* 196c10, 197e, and e.g. *Grg.* 498e, 506a, *Prt.* 330b.

between the more hot-tempered Laches and the more philosophically-minded Nicias, who has had more experience of conversation with Socrates (188a, cf. 180c, 200d). At the beginning of the questioning Laches is somewhat complacent: 'and so, Socrates, I invite you to instruct and interrogate (*elenchein*) me as much as you like, and also to learn from me whatever I know' (189b). He clearly does not foresee any difficulty. His reaction when his suggestions are shown to be inadequate is one of bafflement (194a6ff.). When Nicias offers his, taking a hint from previous exchanges with Socrates (194d), Laches scoffs at him (195a2 'what peculiar statements he's making'; a6 'that's just where he's talking nonsense'). At this point Socrates offers a mild rebuke: 'suppose we instruct him rather than abusing him' (ibid. 7), and Nicias accurately remarks that Laches doesn't want anyone else to do better than he did. The moral point here is perhaps obvious enough, lacking the subtlety of development that we find in, for instance, the *Gorgias*, with its sustained contrast between the arts of dialectic and rhetoric; nevertheless, the characterisation effectively points to potential defects in Laches.

The remainder of the debate develops this point, as Laches becomes more openly abusive (196a sq.), calls Nicias a sophist and a twister of words (ibid. and 197d), takes delight in seeing him on the run (197a), and finally makes sarcastic comments on his refutation (200a). Nicias' reply points the moral: 'Oh, well done, Laches. You think nothing of having just been exposed as ignorant about the nature of courage, but you look only to see whether I am going to cut the same sort of figure ... You certainly seem to me to be behaving in an all-too-human fashion, looking at your neighbour and not yourself' (200a). Plato puts this in the mouth of Nicias, Laches' equal, in order to avoid giving Socrates too sanctimonious a speech. Both Laches and Nicias in fact defer to Socrates, recommending that Lysimachus and Melesias make him a 'tutor' for their sons; but Socrates disclaims any ability to act as a teacher, and quietly reminds them that they all, Socrates included, have shown themselves in need of teachers: 'I say, gentlemen (and this can be kept between ourselves), that each one of us should seek out the best teacher he can find, first and foremost for ourselves, who are greatly in need of one, and then for the boys, disregarding either the cost or any other expense' (201a). The conclusion of the dialogue thus restates the point made by Nicias in his praise of Socrates: a man who is guided to self-scrutiny by Socrates' words will 'want and demand to go on learning, as Solon has it, as long as he lives, free of the delusion that old age brings wisdom in its train' (188b). These words are echoed by Lysimachus' conclusion on the last page of the dialogue: 'as I am the eldest, so I am the most eager to learn along with the boys' (201b).

The *Laches* thus illustrates the principle that behaviour in dialectical discussion has a moral significance that may be as important as the conclusions which are actually reached. The response of an interlocutor to Socratic questioning will reflect his moral character. This is made plain by the kind of definitions that Laches and Nicias produce: Laches admires a straightforward, uncomplicated and perhaps unthinking kind of courage, standing firm in the face of the enemy. This goes well with his admiration of the Spartans, revealed by his earlier speech (182e sq., 188d), to which Socrates teasingly alludes later (191b8, 193d11).[39] Nicias's definition is a more prudent and cautious formulation, invoking knowledge and the need for foresight about causes for hope and fear. There seems no doubt that Plato is here alluding to the careers of the speakers, glancing at events prior to and following the dramatic date of the dialogue.[40] Laches' praise of standing one's ground should be related to his failure to do so at Delium (*Smp.* 221ab) and later at Mantinea, where he met his death (Thuc. v. 72. 4 and 74. 3 ['the generals' include Laches, see 61. 1]). Nicias' definition is knowledge of what is fearful and safe; but his very prudence is his undoing at Syracuse some years later.[41] It can hardly be coincidence that Socrates emphasises the need for a general to be the master of his soothsayer, not dependent on him (199a, though Nicias has not actually said anything that rules this out, cf. 195e sqq.). Nicias' disastrous delay in withdrawing from Syracuse was partly on account of his reluctance to move without clearly favourable omens as interpreted by his seers (Thuc. vii. 50. 4, cf. 48).[42] In short, neither concept of courage is adequate, nor does either general fully live up to his claims and reputation in the end. It is indeed Socrates himself whose words and deeds are, in Laches' phrase, 'in harmony' (188c-9b), a sustained musical image that foreshadows much else in Plato (see esp. *Grg.* 482bc) and later writers.[43] His courage at Delium, which Laches praises, is mirrored in the dialectical sphere, in his resolution and readiness to continue the enquiry. This point is made, albeit light-heartedly, at 193e-4a, just after another reference to the need for words and deeds to correspond:

S: And is it respectable to be in this state?
L: Far from it.
S: Suppose then that we pay attention to the principle of which we are talking, to a certain extent?
L: What principle is that which you mean, and to what extent?

---

[39] Note also 193d1. Laches was in favour of peace with Sparta in 423 (Thuc. iv. 118. 11) and assisted in the Peace of Nicias of 421 (Thuc. v. 43. 2). On the diplomatic details, see A. Andrewes and D.M. Lewis, *JHS* 77 (1957) 177-80.

[40] For the technique, see the obvious foreshadowing of Socrates' trial in *Grg.* and *Tht.*; on the case of Callicles see p. 168; also, and especially, the Alcibiades-scene in the *Smp.*: see p. 181. Meno may be another case, if Xenophon's negative judgement on his subsequent career is believed: see Xen. *Anab.* ii. 6. 21-9, cf. i. 5. 10; R.W. Sharples's comm. (Warminster 1985) 18.

[41] Essentially I follow here the observations of M.J. O'Brien, *YCS* 18 (1963) 131-47 (repr. in J.P. Anton-G.L. Kustas (ed.), *Essays in Ancient Greek Philosophy* i (Albany, N.Y. 1972) 303-15), esp. 143: see Thuc. v. 16, vi. 25, vii. 50, 86; Ar. *Birds* 640.

[42] See further K.J. Dover, *JHS* 93 (1973) 63-4 (= *Greek and the Greeks* 142-3). On the character of Nicias see *HCT* iv, index s.v.; H.A. Murray, *BICS* 8 (1961) 33-46; H.D. Westlake, *Individuals in Thucydides* (Cambridge 1968) chs. 6 and 11.

[43] See e.g. Sen. *Ep.* 75.4 'concordet sermo cum vita'; 88.7, with Stuckelberger's note.

S: The principle that bids us endure. If you agree, we too should endure and be strong in our enquiry, so that courage herself may not laugh at our cowardliness in searching for courage ...

In other words, the moral qualities a man displays in life are also relevant in dialectic. The change of mood and method in the second half of the discussion meant that the enquiry would no longer be lifeless theorising or self-important pronouncements: as Nicias remarked in the interlude, 'in the end (anyone who talks with Socrates) finds that he has to give an account of his present and past life ... I was pretty sure, that with Socrates here, the subject of our discussion would soon be not our sons, but our selves' (187e, 188b).

The *Charmides*

In the *Laches* the sons of Lysimachus and Melesias were mere auditors, *kopha prosopa* ('mutes') like so many of the children in Greek tragedy. By contrast, in the *Charmides* (as in the *Lysis* and much of the *Euthydemus*) it is the young men who are at the centre of Socrates' attention and enquiries, and here above all the beautiful Charmides. The two dialogues *Laches* and *Charmides* may be fruitfully juxtaposed for various reasons: they are of roughly the same length, of similar dramatic date, they are both 'aporetic' definitional dialogues, they both illustrate Plato's skilful deployment of dramatic setting and personal detail; and the *Charmides* too, as argued below, includes significant details that foreshadow the future historical experiences and actions of the participants. One obvious difference is that whereas *Laches* is in dramatic form, *Charmides* is narrated by Socrates. The chief reason for this is that it enables Plato to give the reader direct access to Socrates' thoughts, and especially his powerful emotional reaction to the presence of Charmides (155b sqq.).

The setting of the *Charmides* in the wrestling school, the palaestra, is deliberate and significant. These schools, very much the environment of the wealthy youth,[44] were also the scene of homosexual romance and seduction.[45] It is appropriate, then, that the subject of the dialogue should be *sophrosyne* – modesty, self-control, virtuous self-restraint.[46] The setting also highlights the quasi-erotic quality of Socrates' relationship with young men, a theme developed more fully in the *Symposium* and *Phaedrus*. His admiration and affection for the young rests only partly, and superficially, on their physical beauty; what he really longs to see and loves is the beauty of a young man's soul, such beauty being defined, for Socrates, as know-

---

[44] Cf. K.J. Dover, *Greek Homosexuality* 41f., 54f.; Becker, *Charicles*, 4th edn. (1874) sc. 5; O. Murray, *Early Greece* (Glasgow 1980, revised edn. 1993) ch. 12 on the aristocratic life style.
[45] Dover, passim, and esp. Aeschin. 1. 132, 135.
[46] Cf. H. North, *Sophrosyne* (Ithaca N.Y. 1966); Dover, *GPM*, see index; Kindstrand on Bion fr. 13.

ledge and virtue. This is already hinted at early in the dialogue, when
Socrates, newly returned from the campaign at Potidaea, has satisfied his
friends' enquiries, and gets down to business: 'I now proceeded to ask them
about events in Athens, what the present state of philosophy was, and also
about the young men, whether there were any of their number specially
excelling in wisdom or beauty or both' (153d). Critias replies that it will not
be hard to answer his question as regards *beauty* once Charmides appears:
the form of this reply makes us suspect that he does not give *sophia* so much
attention. The erotic analogy is developed when Critias says how lovely
Charmides will look once he has stripped off; Socrates agrees that he will
be a gorgeous sight, but 'before we see his body, should we not undress him
with regard to his soul?' (154de).[47] There are other elements in the scene
which reinforce moral points. Decorum is observed by Critias' remaining
with Charmides, his relative and ward, as a kind of chaperon.[48] Nevertheless, Critias is prepared to pave the way for Socrates' conversational
encounter with the boy and even suggests a deception that will attract
Charmides' interest (155b). Charmides has had a headache, Critias explains: why doesn't Socrates tell him he knows a cure? This device is
adopted by Socrates, but deepened, as often when he accepts the suggestions of others; for Critias is only offering an initial move to get a conversation started, whereas Socrates extends both the idea of a cure and the
medical metaphor to present himself as a physician of the soul (156d sqq.;
note especially the combination of *epodai* ['spells' or 'incantations'], a word
elsewhere applied to Socrates' eloquence, and *kaloi logoi* [good or healthy
words]). His medicine is in fact dialectic, and it cannot be applied to an
unsuitable recipient, as he is at pains to explain.[49]

Before Socrates' actual exchange with Charmides begins, he describes
his feelings on seeing the boy and particularly on getting a quick glimpse
inside his tunic. The violence of Socrates' reaction is remarkable: 'and at
that moment, my good friend, I caught sight of what was inside his
garment, and caught flame, and then I could no longer control myself. It
struck me that Cydias was well-versed in matters of love when, alluding to
a beautiful youth, he warns someone "to beware that the fawn in the sight
of the lion may not be devoured by him". For it was just that kind of wild
beast which seemed suddenly to have got a grip on me. But still, when he
asked me if I knew the cure for the headache, I somehow answered, though
with difficulty, that I did know ...' (155d-e. Further comments by Socrates
on Charmides' beauty at 154c, 158c.)

Plato's Socrates is not simply an embodiment of reason. His philosophic

---

[47] The verb is *apodunai*; for the image, cf. *IAlc.* 132a, *Tht.* 162b, 169ab (the same idea is
implicit at *Prt.* 352a); below, p. 149f. on shame and self-exposure in the *Gorgias*.

[48] Cf. X. *Smp.* 1. 2 with 8.11; Dover, *GH* 53.

[49] We may compare the (probably spurious) *Theages* on Socrates' failures with some unsuitable pupils; the divine sign warns him that they are better sent away (this presumably derives
from *Tht.* 150d-51d, quoted below, pp. 281-2).

religion has its irrational side also (his inexplicable 'divine voice'), and here we see that for all his self-discipline he is a man of strong passions. His conversation often alludes to his love of the young and beautiful, especially Alcibiades (*Grg.* 481d; cf. *Meno* 76bc; *Smp.* for his relations with Alcibiades and Agathon), and his friends take this for granted in him, not looking beyond the deceptive and often frivolous exterior (*Prt.* 309a-c). It is clear though from the *Charmides* and from the later, fuller account of his behaviour by Alcibiades in the *Symposium*, that his passion was contained and controlled. There is a memorable anecdote in one of Cicero's dialogues, which may be derived from a dialogue by Phaedo, the *Zopyrus*, in which a physiognomic expert declared that Socrates' features showed him to have a lustful and violent nature. Those present laughed at the diagnosis, but Socrates insisted that the man was right: 'Socrates came to his aid, commenting that these qualities were indeed rooted in him, but he had expelled them by reason.'[50] It was through the power of reason that Socrates had dominated his passionate satyr-like nature. Part of the purpose of the *Charmides* is to demonstrate this aspect of Socrates' character, for throughout the rest of the dialogue he speaks freely and unembarrassedly to Charmides, showing no sign of desiring him or wanting to seduce him. Like Alcibiades, the boy finds Socrates all the more fascinating and exciting a companion for this reason (176b, where the language of enchantment recurs). In short, just as in the *Laches* Socrates can be seen as the embodiment of true courage, and in the *Euthyphro* of true piety (in contrast with Euthyphro's spurious version), so also in the *Charmides* his conduct exmplifies the ideal of *sophrosyne*, modesty and self-restraint. This procedure on Plato's part could easily have become repetitive and over-idealistic, and he does seem to realise this danger and abandon it after the dialogues mentioned. Two major works offer a more elaborate and thought-provoking version: the *Gorgias*, in which Socrates at one point describes himself as 'the one true practitioner of the political art' (521d), and the *Symposium*, in which multiple resemblances associate Socrates (as described by Alcibiades and the narrator) with the daimon Eros (as described in Socrates' own speech). Both of these cases, however, are more intricate and two-edged, less purely encomiastic.[51]

In 155d-8c Socrates describes the 'charm' or medicine with which he can cure Charmides' headache. As already noted, he moves swiftly from bodily healing to therapy of the soul, from 'a kind of leaf accompanied by a charm' to charm alone, embodied in words (157a; cf. *Phdr.* 270b). One further point that strikes the reader at once is the fluency with which Socrates attributes this (purely fictional) cure to a source: 'I learned it while serving with the army, from one of the physicians of the Thracian king Zalmoxis, who are

---

[50] 'Ab ipso autem Socrate sublevatus, cum illa sibi insita sed ratione a se deiecta diceret' (*Tusc.* iv. 80). Cf. *de fato* iv. 10; Guthrie iii. 390-402.
[51] See below, pp. 156-7, 199-200.

said to be able even to bestow immortality' (156d). As Socrates remarks and Herodotus confirms,[52] this king was a mythical figure, also regarded as a god. The provenance of Socrates' cure is therefore not only foreign and exotic but also religious. This is lively circumstantial detail which helps to stress the importance and value of Socrates' offer (a spiritual version, perhaps, of the gifts that a lover showers on his *eromenos*?).[53] Furthermore, it is quite common in Plato for Socrates to attribute his knowledge or insights to an authority, often a figure with religious associations. Thus in the *Symposium* the mysteries of Eros are imparted to him by Diotima, a priestess with a religious name; in the *Meno*, the doctrine of Recollection is ascribed to 'men and women who are knowledgeable about religion ... priests and priestesses who make it their business to be able to give an account of the functions they perform' (*Meno* 81a).[54] This device is one of the ways in which Plato tries to reconcile Socratic *ignorance* with his actually instructing people or voicing new doctrines.

The attempted definitions of *sophrosyne* have often been analysed from the point of view of Greek values and in more philosophical study of the dialogue's arguments.[55] This ground need not be retraced here, but a few points can be offered, as with the *Laches*, to suggest ways in which the dramatic and philosophic developments of the dialogue are related.

Six definitions are suggested. Of these the first three are offered by Charmides (though the third is one which he has learned from Critias, see 161b, 162c sq., etc.); the second trio belongs to Critias himself. They are as follows:

1-3: Charmides (158c-62d)
1. Calmness, or doing everything in an orderly and calm fashion.
2. *Aidos* (shame, modesty).
3. Attending to one's own business.

4-6: Critias (164c-75a)
4. Self-knowledge
5. Knowledge which knows other knowledges and itself.
6. Knowledge of what one knows and does not know.

As the page-references alone indicate, the exchange with Charmides is very brief, and there is little attempt to deal seriously with his suggestions. The

[52] iv. 94-6; cf. A.D. Nock, *CR* 40 (1926) 18ff.

[53] Ar. *Wealth* 157, etc.; Dover, *GH* 92f and 146.

[54] For further examples see *Grg.* 507e with Dodds's n. (the *sophoi* there may well be Pythagorean thinkers); *Phdr.* 262d, 274c sq. The occasional attribution of his own views to Prodicus' teaching or that of another named contemporary falls into a different, more frivolous category (e.g. *Charm.* 163d), and the rhetorical instruction he has received from Aspasia in the *Menexenus* is still more patently a joke.

[55] See esp. T.G. Tuckey, *Plato's Charmides* (Cambridge 1951); G. Santas, in *Exegesis and Argument*, ed. E.N. Lee et al. (Assen 1973) 105-32; N. van der Ben, *The Charmides of Plato: Problems and Interpretation* (Amsterdam 1985).

first of these serves to characterise him further: the self-conscious ideal he describes reflects his personality, his sense of what is 'proper', without delving beneath external appearances.[56] The second definition moves from outer modesty to the inner quality that should give rise to it, and this indicates progress, but the suggestion is dealt with in a trivial way by Socrates, who merely confutes it by appeal to a line from Homer, and Charmides himself seems eager to move on and try out 'another definition ... which I have just remembered that I heard from someone' (161ab, namely (3) above). This in turn is inadequately defended by him, and then first revived but hastily dropped by Critias. The more promising suggestion of self-knowledge is absorbed into the fifth definition, and it is really only the last two that receive discussion at any length or involving conventionally 'philosophic' analysis. Since all the suggested definitions are abandoned, with an almost gleeful review of their deficiencies by Socrates (175a-d), the reader is bound to ask what, if anything, Charmides is supposed to take away, how he is any better off at the end of the dialogue.

Indeed, few aspects of Platonic dialogue are harder to come to terms with than the persistent way that Socrates abandons lines of thought, treats arguments cavalierly, dismisses possible alternatives and asks what often seem flagrantly leading questions. Whatever may be thought about the later dilemmas of metaphysics and epistemology, it is impossible to believe that Plato did not see through most or all of the fallacies and dialectical sleights-of-hand which Socrates is presented as using here and elsewhere, any more than he was deceived by the virtuoso trick-arguments of Euthydemus and Dionysodorus in the *Euthydemus*. It is not a satisfactory solution to say that Plato was determined to make Socrates 'win' at any price; for in the *Charmides* at least he has given him foe-men wholly unworthy of his steel. The concept of 'winning' may be more relevant, for example, to the *Gorgias*, in which Socrates' emotions are more violently engaged and in which the agonistic structure (with its echoes from a famous Euripidean tragedy) presents the conflict of views between Socrates and Callicles with unusual intensity. There, Plato clearly does try to give Socrates as strong and persuasive a case as he can, but it can still be argued that he also shows us, through the dramatic form of the work, the tragic weaknesses of Socrates' idealism (see pp. 157, 171). In the *Charmides* and other works of lighter and more amicable tone, we need to find a rather different explanation for what seem to us inadequate or unexplored arguments. Two possible explanations, admittedly speculative and not necessarily exhaustive, may assist understanding of Plato's intentions.

One has already been used concerning the *Laches*, that the dialogues are illustrations of methodology and of the ethics of debate, as much as treatments of specific philosophic problems. This certainly applies with

---

[56] For the ideal of polite or correct behaviour, compare the speech of Right in Ar. *Nu.* 963f., with Dover ad loc. and *GH* 84-5.

equal force to the *Charmides*, in which a number of the same points are made. The personalities of the characters affect their performance: in particular, Critias' impatience and vanity (162bc), his anger (ibid.cd), his snobbishness (163b sqq.), result in his being willing to shift his ground and, through a quibbling 'distinction' (*diairesis*), to cheat slightly in the discussion (163 sq., esp. 163d6 sqq.). Similarly later, Socrates is moved to accuse him of concealing his true opinion (174b11f.; cf. *Grg.* 499bc). Critias wants to impress and show himself in a good light before the others (169c), whereas Socrates stresses that he should not be ashamed of being proved wrong: 'would you not say that the discovery of things as they truly are is a good common to all mankind? ... then be cheerful, sweet sir, and give your opinion in answer to the question, never minding whether Critias or Socrates is the person refuted' (166cd, cf. 161c5-6, 165b5 sqq., and *Grg.* 457c sqq., etc.). Here, as on a larger scale in the *Euthydemus*, there are moral lessons to be learned about the proper conduct of debate, irrespective of the conclusions reached.

Nevertheless, the reader remains puzzled by the inconclusiveness of Plato's 'conclusions'. The example of Socrates' original manner of conversation must be important here, though precisely how far and in what ways we shall never know. It seems likely, however, that Socrates himself did not normally put forward positive doctrines, that in his conversation there were recurrent themes (such as education, the acquisition of knowledge, the craft analogy and so on) which seemed to *imply* certain positions that were not usually spelt out, and in particular that he tended to ask questions rather than discourse and provide answers. In reproducing or reshaping the conversations of Socrates in literary form, Plato, it seems, either wanted or felt he ought to reproduce this elusiveness and inconclusiveness. Like his teacher, Plato does not see it as his task to do all the work for us. Often the dialogues suggest more than they assert, and leave it to the reader to develop some of these suggestions and explore the implications of what often seem perverse and paradoxical arguments. This is not, however, to say that the reader is given *carte blanche* to exercise the free play of his imagination with complete autonomy. There are often hints or strong suggestions as to which way one should be looking. These suggestions regularly arise from the so-called Socratic Paradoxes (that all virtues are related, or in fact one; that virtue is (or is inseparable from) knowledge; that no one willingly does wrong; that virtue is sufficient for happiness, etc.). Again we cannot, of course, be completely sure that Socrates formulated these sayings in precisely these terms, but the way that they recur in Plato and are developed or restated in different terms does support the hypothesis that Plato's philosophy is the product of extended meditation on certain unconnected and only partly explained sayings of his teacher.

How then are these remarks to be applied to the *Charmides*? It is noteworthy that the earlier definitions are to do with actions (external behaviour [1, perhaps 2] and following of precepts [3]), whereas the later involve knowledge. The typically Socratic principle, that all virtues are in some way bound up with knowledge, is not made explicit here, but is allowed to shine through the discussion, as if sign-posting the way for further consideration. In particular, Critias at a late stage answers the question 'what kind of knowledge will make a man happy?' with 'knowledge of what is good and evil' (174b); the significance of this point is stressed by Socrates' vigorous reaction. The point hinted at here and elsewhere in the work seems to be that neither conventionally 'right' or decorous behaviour (such as was involved in Charmides' first definition), nor knowledge *per se*, either of other knowledge or of itself, can be an adequate account of *sophrosyne*. What is needed is a self-conscious morality, which understands not only itself but its aims and *telos*. True 'self-consciousness' or self-knowledge would not be merely narcissistic, and knowledge by itself, without a moral dimension, could only enable a state (as in Socrates' 'dream', 173) to be run efficiently and correctly, not happily.

At the end of the dialogue Socrates speaks again to Charmides of his 'cure' and of Charmides' own *sophrosyne*. He expresses his disappointment at failing to find what they sought: now Charmides, if he does possess this virtue, cannot even be sure whether it is beneficial (175d-6a). Charmides' response should be compared with his original reaction in 158d, when Socrates asked him if he did indeed possess *sophrosyne*. There, he had blushed prettily, and gracefully avoided self-praise: 'for if I declare that I am not temperate, it would be a strange thing to say against myself, and also I should be accusing Critias of lying, and many others too who, according to him, think that I am. But on the other hand, if I say I am, singing my own praises, that will perhaps appear tiresome; consequently I do not know how to answer you.' The perfect decorum of his speech is in keeping with his first attempt at a definition (see above). By contrast, his response at the end of the dialogue shows a more chastened attitude and genuine uncertainty: 'Heavens, Socrates, I don't know whether I have or haven't got this quality. For how could I know what you yourselves (as you claim) are unable even to find a definition for?' (176a). The *kaloi logoi* of Socratic dialectic seem to have inculcated some degree of humility.

It remains to consider the significance of the dialogue's conclusion, and, as in the *Laches*, the future careers of the participants. No Athenian reader for generations to come could have failed to recognise in the charming and beautiful young man and his rather more bad-tempered guardian two of the most hated names of the last years of the fifth century. Critias we know from Xenophon to have been one of the leaders of the Thirty Tyrants, the pro-Spartan aristocratic junta which, with Spartan military support, controlled Athens from its defeat in 404 until the successful revolution of the democratic party. The restoration of the democracy was complete by summer 403, and Critias was dead much earlier, but not before he had been responsible for much bloodshed.[57] Charmides was a less notorious figure, not a member of the Thirty, but one of the ten appointed by them to control the Piraeus (Xen. *Hell.* ii. 4. 19, where we also learn that he fell in the same battle as Critias). These men were members of Plato's own family; if the Seventh Letter is genuine, he condemned and was sickened by their political actions (*Ep.* vii. 324b-5a) and compared their conduct unfavourably with the magnanimity of the restored democracy. Furthermore, it is clear that Socrates' association with such men, as with the equally notorious Alcibiades, must have played a part in his prosecution in 399, even if these issues were not openly discussed in court. The accusation that Socrates was responsible for the actions of Critias and perhaps Charmides evidently figured in subsequent attacks on Socrates, perhaps including the essay by Polycrates.[58] Xenophon strangely represents Socrates as urging Charmides into public life, a most un-Platonic scene (contrast e.g. the finale of the *Gorgias*). This chapter (*Mem.* iii. 7) cannot be dated, but it presumably means that at whatever date it was composed some people, including Xenophon, had given up any hostility to Charmides, however long Critias' name was remembered with hatred.

Where does Plato's *Charmides* fit into this picture, and is the author in any way referring to the political events in which, thirty years later, his two uncles were to meet their deaths? It is certainly hard to deny that Critias makes a less attractive impression on the reader than Charmides, and it is plain that his speech at 163bc, sneering at 'low' professions which cannot truly be called work, betrays all the contempt of an aristocrat for his supposed inferiors (Callicles' view of the *demos* may be compared, *Grg.* 489c, etc.).[59] We know also that Critias himself composed an elegiac poem in praise of Spartan *sophrosyne* (88B6-8 D-K):[60] in the extant verses there is little that can be connected with the definitions he offers in the *Charmides*, but the existence of the poem suggests that Plato may be obliquely contrasting Socrates' ideal of *sophrosyne* with a more partisan, politically slanted conception held by Critias and expounded in this poem. *Sophrosyne* was also, it may be added, an oligarchic catch-word: the *sophrones*, the 'decent types' were the 'better class' of people in the state, those with sober political judgement; here again there are Spartan overtones.[61] If the somewhat muddled statement by a late commentator on Aristotle (88A22 D-K.) is correct in saying that Critias wrote *politeias emmetrous* ('poetry on constitutions'), it is tempting to connect this both with the praise of Sparta

[57] Xen. *Hell.* ii, esp. 3-4; 'Arist.' *Ath. Pol.* 34-41; Davies, *APF* 322ff., with stemma in Table 1. For detailed narrative of the Thirty's rule, and bibliography, see Lewis, *CAH* vi[2] (1994) ch. 2.
[58] p. 49 above; cf. Xen. *Mem.* i. 2. 12ff.; Aeschin. i. 173; also Libanius, *Apol.* 136ff., esp. 148ff.
[59] The phrase at 163b7-8, 'or sitting in a house', is explained by Dover, *GH* 108, comparing Aeschin. i. 74: it means plying one's trade as a male prostitute. Coarseness is thus added to Critias' snobbery.
[60] These and other fragments of Critias' writings are translated in Sprague, *The Older Sophists* 241ff. On Critias as an intellectual see Guthrie iii. 298-304; Ostwald, *From Popular Sovereignty to the Sovereignty of Law* 462-5.
[61] Cf. esp. Thuc. i. 84. 2-4; also iii. 82. 8, vi. 89. 6, viii. 53. 3, 64. 5.

and with the imaginary well-organised state postulated by Socrates in the dialogue. Socrates stresses its *sophrosyne* and its foundation on the principle of 'each doing what he knows', but (as we have seen) expresses doubts about the happiness of its inhabitants (171d sq., 173a-d).[62] These fragmented observations may not cohere into a firm argument, but I would speculate that Plato is hinting that the discussion in the *Charmides* has wider *political* implications which are relevant particularly to Critias but perhaps also to his companion and ward.

The final exchange between Critias, Charmides and Socrates (176b-d) is another passage in which we may suspect, without being able to prove, that more is implied than the surface meaning of the characters' words. Charmides is eager to continue listening to Socrates, and Critias gladly endorses this and bids him stay by Socrates' side. The speeches which follow lay curious emphasis both on Charmides' obedience to his older cousin and Socrates' reluctance to resist them:

> 'Well then, Charmides', said Critias, 'if you do this, it will be proof of your modesty, if you allow Socrates to use his charm upon you, and never desert him in matters great or small.'
>
> 'You can be sure of my following and not deserting him', Charmides replied. 'For I would be behaving shockingly, if I did not heed you, my guardian, and failed to do as you bid me.'
>
> 'Well, this is what I do tell you', he said.
>
> 'I shall obey, then,' he replied, 'starting this very day.'
>
> 'Hey you there,' said I [Socrates]. 'What are you taking counsel about?'
>
> 'Nothing,' said Charmides. 'Our counsels are ended.'
>
> 'Then will you force me to do your will, and not give me a hearing?'
>
> 'You can assume that I will use force,' he answered, 'since Critias here so commands. You had better lay plans as to what your response will be.'
>
> 'But no plan is available,' I said. 'For nobody in the world will be able to oppose you when you seek to do something and use force to achieve it.'
>
> 'Then don't you oppose me,' he said.
>
> 'Indeed I shall not do so', I replied.

If this is teasing, it is curiously laboured. It is difficult not to suspect some significant anticipation in the reference to Charmides' obedience to his guardian, in the repeated mention of violence (the activities of the Thirty?), and above all in the way that the possibility of Socrates' resistance to them is dwelt upon – Socrates, who defied the attempts of the Thirty to silence him or implicate him in their actions.[63] In that case, problems remain: why is Charmides presented as so promising and admirable a boy, and why does Socrates specifically say he will *not* resist them? We must not, however, force a one-to-one correspondence on what may be a more elusive piece of

---

[62] It is intriguing to consider these passages as forerunners of Plato's own creation of an ideal state which, as is well known, does owe much to Spartan political and social structure. See further ch. 8.

[63] Pl. *Ap.* 32c, Xen. *Mem.* i. 2. 31-9 (Critias and Charicles), iv. 4. 3; Guthrie iii. 380f.

foreshadowing, a disturbing hint of darker things in store (such as is found at the end of a number of Greek tragedies).[64] The beautiful and intelligent Charmides embodies the promise of youth, its potential for goodness, but he still has to choose which mentor to follow, Critias or Socrates. At the moment the wishes and interests of all three are in accord, but the emphasis with which he protests his allegiance to Critias gives a clear indication of his future choice. The graceful banter of cultivated Athenian upper-class friendships is thus presented as a fragile surface which conceals potential conflict and the prospect of future violence.

The *Clitopho* and other criticisms of Socrates

The most sympathetic reader of Plato's dialogues can scarcely fail to experience some impatience and irritation at Socrates. His humorous teasing may sometimes appear heavy-handed, his irony transparent and mocking, his idealism naive simplicity.[65] His interlocutors are sometimes unable to contain their indignation: 'will the man never stop drivelling?' asks Callicles in the *Gorgias* (489b); and 'tell me, Socrates, have you a nurse?' demands Thrasymachus (*Rep.* i. 343a).[66] In *Republic* i Thrasymachus' accusations are directed especially at Socrates' notorious irony (337a) and his protestations of ignorance: he always asks questions and picks holes in other people's answers, never actually comes out and says what *he* thinks. It is easy enough to criticise others' ideas when you never put forward your own views to be criticised. To Thrasymachus, Socrates' 'ignorance' is a tactical move to lure his opponents on; his 'irony' is really hypocrisy.

Thrasymachus is an unattractive figure, but his criticisms have some force, not as regards Socrates' *motives* (for we can hardly doubt that Socrates is sincere enough), but as a critique of his methods. In the rest of book i of the *Republic*, Thrasymachus is 'refuted' in the standard fashion: inconsistencies or oddities in his position are exposed, weaknesses in his formulation exploited, until he is eventually driven into a corner and forced to admit (against his true belief) that he was wrong and talking nonsense.[67] The discussion is apparently over, but is then resumed, with Thrasy-

---

[64] I think particularly of Sophocles' *Philoctetes*, where it is generally agreed that the final scene hints at the future atrocities committed by the Greeks in the sack of Troy, in which the young Neoptolemus, so admirable a character in the play itself, will play a significant role. Yet although there is a small black cloud on the horizon, it should not be allowed to turn the interpretation of the *Philoctetes* on its head. The richly suggestive paper by T.C.W. Stinton, 'The scope and limits of allusion in Greek tragedy' (in his *Collected Papers on Greek Tragedy*, ed. H. Lloyd-Jones (Oxford 1990) 454-92), is highly relevant.

[65] Cf. *Rep.* i. 336c1, 348c12 for his *euetheia*, his naive simplicity; for the word, cf. esp. Thuc. iii. 83. 1.

[66] See also *Hipparchus* 228a; Hippias in Xen. *Mem.* iv. 4. 9-10 (a complaint not borne out by Socrates as portrayed in the rest of the *Mem.*).

[67] 354a10f., and many of his previous responses, show the insincerity of his submission.

machus' case restated in a more powerful and well-considered form, by Glaucon and Adeimantus; the remainder of the *Republic*, at least to the close of book ix, is a sustained reply by Socrates which includes much detailed exposition of positive doctrine. Socrates in the succeeding discussion becomes less and less like the vivid personality we know from the earlier dialogues and from book i; in particular, the account of the ideal state and the metaphysical teachings of the central books, although presented tentatively, are scarcely compatible with the conventional Socratic 'ignorance'. It seems that Plato is here extending the image of Socrates (and indeed expanding the dialogue form on a scale unprecedented in his own and others' work),[68] and that to some extent he is responding to Thrasymachus' criticisms, or rather the type of criticisms of Socratic method which, in exaggerated form, Thrasymachus represents. There are in fact other indications in the first book of the *Republic* that the methodology of Socratic dialogue was at this point an issue on which Plato was reflecting further (see esp. 340a, 341a sq., 345b, 349ab). In particular, Thrasymachus' behaviour shows up some of the weaknesses of Socratic dialectic, for towards the end of the book he makes only token responses, giving up the debate too soon (cf. Callicles). Thrasymachus, though radical, is not sufficiently *involved* (as indicated especially by 344de, 352d5 sqq.); he should be more concerned about the coherence of his position than he is.[69] Since Thrasymachus is not prepared to sustain the argument, Socrates wins a victory that is too easy, without his having been challenged sufficiently to defend or justify his beliefs. The movement from book i to the later part of the *Republic*, then, shows Plato seeking a new and more suitable argumentative form to convey the positive aspects or implications of Socratic teaching.

It is far from blasphemous to suppose that Plato sometimes saw the need to amend or criticise the Socratic method, just as he must clearly have developed and modified, even transformed, Socrates' actual teaching. If we know anything at all about Socrates, it is that the impact he had on Plato was as an enquirer, a seeker after knowledge rather than a dogmatist. To enquire further, to question and explore beyond Socrates' teaching, was to continue Socrates' own quest. To suggest that Plato criticised or at least reconsidered Socrates' method need not for a moment imply that he betrayed his master or that his devotion to his memory diminished. In the *Gorgias*, Plato seems to accept that, to some extent, Socrates failed – failed to reform or convert Callicles, as he failed to persuade or improve his fellow-Athenians.[70] In the *Symposium*, it has been suggested that Plato

---

[68] Cf. Slings, *Comm. on ... Clitopho* 24 with n. 4.

[69] C.W. Macleod, marg. on 349b1 *ouden*: Socrates means 'non *mei* interest sed *tui*'.

[70] Socrates' critique of Miltiades, Pericles and co. also ironically foreshadows his own failure as 'the one true statesman'. Neither the true nor the false practitioners of the political art can hope for success in a corrupt society; both Socrates and Callicles may have come to grief in the end: p. 168 below.

deliberately follows up Socrates' magnificent speech with the drunken, love-sick outpourings of Alcibiades in order to confront us with two incompatible ways of life, but without demanding that we choose Socrates' path wholeheartedly.[71] If there is any substance to these arguments, then there is a difference between Socrates and Plato (as also argued on the philosophic plane by most interpreters), and it seems probable that the gulf between the two thinkers increased, but this is a *creative* tension, resolved and masked by the medium of the dialogue, in which we find not only a sympathetic and affectionate, even a loving, portrait of Socrates, but also criticism and questioning of him and his work, both explicit criticism by the other participants and implicit criticism by juxtaposition, foreshadowing and other dramatic techniques.

One of the most interesting dramatic presentations of criticism of Socrates is the brief dialogue *Clitopho*, which has often been judged spurious or incomplete, partly because readers have found it so hard to accept that Plato would allow so vigorous an attack on Socrates as is put in Clitopho's mouth to go unanswered.[72] The *Clitopho* begins with Socrates asking Clitopho whether it is true that he, Clitopho, has been abusing him behind his back and praising Thrasymachus' teaching. Clitopho explains that this is only partially so: there is much about Socrates he has praised, but there are also things he would criticise. Socrates replies that he is ready to learn how he is going wrong. The rest of the work (some five pages in total length) consists of Clitopho's elaboration of his critique. It runs roughly as follows: Socrates is a marvellous protreptic orator, who can move and inspire Clitopho and others to the realisation that virtue must be sought and that we must care for our souls; all of this Clitopho accepts, but what is the next step? Is exhortation the only end? He has tried to question Socrates' other disciples in search of the positive teaching of the school (his questioning as described bears a marked resemblance to Socratic *elenchus*),[73] but their answers were confused and easily refuted; even Socrates himself has given him a demonstrably wrong definition of justice. Clitopho concludes by exhorting Socrates once more to divulge the knowledge that he surely possesses but is unwilling to impart; if Socrates still refuses, then he must have recourse to Thrasymachus. The final words restate his dilemma: 'for I shall tell others, Socrates, that you are worth all the world to one who has not been impelled to action (*protetrammenoi*, literally 'exhorted'), but to one who has been impelled, you are practically an obstacle on the road to reaching the goal of virtue and so becoming a happy man.' (410e)[74]

This curious little work is clearly related to the first book of the *Republic*. In the *Clitopho*, a student of that name is preparing to abandon Socrates

---

[71] Cf. M. Nussbaum, *The Fragility of Goodness* (Cambridge 1986) ch. 8.

[72] See e.g. G. Grote, *Plato* iii. 21; A.E. Taylor, *Plato* 12, and other works cited by Slings, 16ff.

[73] Slings 59.

[74] For a more detailed summary, see Slings 11-14.

and seek instruction from the sophist Thrasymachus, and in the *Republic*, he appears as the latter's companion and supporter (esp. 328b, 340a). There are also a number of verbal correspondences, which have been discussed in detail in the authoritative commentary on the *Clitopho* by Dr. S.R. Slings,[75] who concludes that the *Clitopho*, whether or not it is by Plato (he thinks not though he reaches this conclusion 'hesitantly and with some reluctance' (p. 257)), is later than *Republic* i and presupposes it. Here again, then, we have a case of deliberate foreshadowing, though intertextual rather than historical: the reader of the *Clitopho* knows that, however disappointed Clitopho may be with Socrates, he will surely not find wisdom or happiness in the teaching of the Thrasymachus who is portrayed in the pages of the *Republic*.[76]

As regards the content and interpretation of the work, a number of readings are possible. Is this a non-Platonic critique of Socrates as presented in Plato, or as he truly was?[77] Are Clitopho's comments justified, or is his view partial or deluded? He is (we presume) wrong to suppose that Thrasymachus has 'the truth'; is he right about Socrates lacking or hoarding it? Why is Socrates presented as orating to crowds (407a)? Is Clitopho's account of his own enthusiastic reaction to such speeches genuine or ironic, given that it bears some similarity to Socrates' ironic descriptions of his reactions to sophistic oratory?[78]

Slings in his commentary has offered a most ingenious and subtle interpretation, which I can only mar in a simplifying summary: his full argument must be consulted by any future student of this perplexing work. He holds that it is not really the *Platonic* Socrates who is being criticised by Clitopho, but the Socrates of other Socratic writings, who *did* indulge in rhetorical protreptic. The *Clitopho* contrasts Socratic dialectic or elenchus (as practised by Clitopho) with the more unsatisfactory and less enlightening didactic method of protreptic. In the contrast of different styles of teaching the dialogue resembles the *Euthydemus* (which is drawn upon at various points), although there Socrates does seem to adapt protreptic in an acceptable fashion.[79] Explicit protreptic achieves little, whereas implicit protreptic, as represented by Socratic elenchus and Platonic dialogue, can prepare the mind and lead the way to further enlightenment.

Slings is well aware of the difficulties in this interpretation, which are

---

[75] *A Commentary on the Platonic Clitopho* (Amsterdam 1981) 62ff. I take this opportunity of acknowledging my debt to this extremely useful and stimulating work, which deserves to be better known than it appears to be (it makes no appearance in the bibliography to Kraut's *Companion to Plato*).

[76] For Clitopho's historical career and other references to him, see Ar. *Frogs* 967, 'Arist.' *Ath. Pol.* 29. 3, 34. 3 with Rhodes's n.

[77] Xen. *Mem.* i. 4. 1 says that 'some' criticised Socrates along the same lines as Clitopho does here. Xenophon may of course be alluding to the *Clitopho*: see Slings 89-92, 245n.2.

[78] Cf. 407a6, e3-4, with *Euthyd.* 276d, 306e, *Smp.* 198b, *Rep.* i. 336d; also (less close) *Prt.* 339e.

[79] See esp. Slings 144, 233-9.

candidly set out in his book.[80] Chief among these is the way that Socrates
must on his reading stand for two quite different things: the flawed
protreptic and the ideal elenchus, Socrates in other writings and Socrates
in Plato. The situation in the *Euthydemus* is far clearer, with the two eristic
brothers plainly cast from the beginning as Socrates' opponents and the
representatives of an inferior form of education. If I find Slings's conclusion
impossible to accept, that does not mean that I do not admire his work,
which has shed a flood of light on a very difficult dialogue.

In the preceding pages it has been argued that Socrates can be criticised
in Plato, by characters in the dialogues and more rarely and elusively by
the author. The *Clitopho*, in my view, presents a possible line of criticism,
but Clitopho's position is not to be taken as the author's own. Clitopho
seems to have a distorted, exaggerated impression of one part of Socrates'
approach to teaching, namely the protreptic harangue.[81] Further, it is
indisputable that Clitopho *has* learned enough from Socrates about the
procedures of dialectic to confute the other anonymous followers by that
method; his eagerness to go further also indicates his positive response to
Socrates' exhortations. But he seems not to appreciate how much he has in
fact gained from the experience of being with Socrates.[82] He is eager for
more, and specifically for *answers* – the definition of justice and so forth.
He tries to extract these answers from Socrates, but remains repeatedly
(410b3f.) dissatisfied with the replies that Socrates provides. In short, like
so many of Socrates' companions (or Plato's readers!), he wants a solution,
an answer, 'Truth' on a plate. But this is what Socratic method of its nature
cannot provide; for Socrates genuinely lacks and himself is seeking the
truth; at most, as in the *Gorgias*, he has it as far as he himself is concerned,
a deeply felt and firmly held assurance of what is right and wrong for *him*
(the irrational or supernatural support of his mysterious voice perhaps
plays a part here). But others must continue to seek it for themselves, not
gather round listening to Socrates as if to a guru.[83] This interpretation
allows Socrates throughout the *Clitopho* to be the Platonic Socrates, but
viewed through Clitopho's impatient and dissatisfied eyes. The criticisms

[80] Esp. pp. 231, 235.
[81] Slings 148, 163ff., admits that this is present in the *Apology*, esp. 29d sqq., 36b sqq., and
indeed causes some conflict with the Socratic protest of ignorance; it therefore cannot be
wholly un-Platonic, and the co-existence of protreptic with elenchus to some degree must be
admitted. Cf. Slings 52.
[82] Cf. *Theaetetus* 150e, *Theages* 130, esp. ab, for such cases.
[83] Notice here that Socrates' practice, which Clitopho deplores, could be viewed in more
laudatory terms: see Cic. *de or.* i. 204 (mentioned but rather underplayed by Slings 91): 'ut
Socratem illum solitum aiunt dicere perfectum sibi opus esse, si qui satis esset concitatus
cohortatione sua ad studium cognoscendae percipiendaeque virtutis' ('as they say that the
famous Socrates used to remark that his work was complete, if anyone had been sufficiently
stirred by his encouragement to pursue the task of discovering and apprehending virtue'). My
interpretation here converges with general points made by M. Frede, *OSAP* Suppl. 1992, 210,
without reference to the *Clitopho*.

of Clitopho may point to weaknesses in Socrates' method, and he himself is certainly an example of a pupil lost *because* of the peculiar character of his teaching; but this account, I suggest, allows the *Clitopho* to convey a serious and recognisably Platonic moral, one which stimulates the reader to consider and evaluate Socrates' method in the dialogues. The *Clitopho*, then, is relevant to the study and criticism of Plato's dialogues, even if it is not itself to be numbered among them.

4

Socrates and the Sophists

Preliminaries

It would be impossible to summarise in the opening pages of a single chapter the significance of the sophists in the years between 450 and 400 BC, or the full impact of their teaching on Athenian culture and politics. Fortunately much good work on the sophists is readily available.[1] Here, after the briefest of introductory remarks, it will be sufficient to consider two essential questions: how hostile and how distorted is Plato's presentation of the sophists? and, was Socrates himself a sophist?

Modern understanding of the sophists is hampered by two main factors: first, the animosity of Plato (and to a lesser extent Aristotle)[2] toward many aspects of the sophistic movement; and secondly, the almost total loss of the sophists' own writings. Apart from fragmentary quotations and the occasional surviving short essay or oration (such as Gorgias' *Helen* and *Palamedes* or the anonymous *Dissoi Logoi*), we are dependent on anecdotal biography (as in Diogenes Laertius' *Lives of the Philosophers*) or on passing allusions in other writers, many of whom, even if well disposed to the sophists, may be unconsciously influenced by the Platonic critique. Nevertheless, we know enough to see that they were an intellectual and social phenomenon of the first importance.

The word *sophistes* does not at first denote the figures that we associate with it. At one time *sophos* ('wise' or 'skilled') and *sophistes* ('wise man' or

---

[1] See esp. W.K.C. Guthrie, *History of Greek Philosophy* iii (1969), reproduced in two separate paperback volumes entitled *The Sophists* and *Socrates* (1972); G.B. Kerferd, *The Sophistic Movement* (1981); E.R. Dodds, *The Ancient Concept of Progress and Other Essays* (1973) ch. 6; E.L. Hussey, *The Presocratics* (1972) ch. 6. Useful essays are collected in G.B. Kerferd (ed.) *The Sophists and their Legacy* (Wiesbaden 1981) and in C.J. Classen, *Sophistik* ('Wege der Forschung', no. 187, Darmstadt 1976), with very full bibliography. Many of the topics surveyed in this section are also treated by M. Ostwald, *From Popular Sovereignty to the Sovereignty of Law* (1986) ch. 2, and more briefly by the same author in *CAH* v^2 306-69 ('Athens as a cultural centre'). J. de Romilly, *The Great Sophists of Periclean Athens* (Oxford 1992) is an elegant synthesis. On rhetoric see Kennedy, *Art of Persuasion*; I. Worthington (ed.) *Persuasion* (London 1994). The heretical argument of T. Cole, *The Origins of Rhetoric in Ancient Greece* (Baltimore and London 1991), that the concept of rhetoric as a discipline is the invention of Plato and Aristotle, is challenging but untenable: cf. D.A. Russell's review in *JHS* 112 (1992) 185-6.

[2] For Aristotle's comments see Classen's essay in Kerferd's collection, cited in the last note.

'teacher of wisdom') were synonymous. In Pindar the latter is used of poets, in Herodotus of the law-giver Solon and (perhaps more critically) of the sage or proto-philosopher Pythagoras. Even authors of a period later than the sophistic age could use the term more broadly, meaning an expert, intellectual, scientist or pundit. Nor did the word at first, or even later, *necessarily* possess the pejorative implications ('trickster', 'cheat' or 'clever-clever') which it acquired in the later fifth century.[3] In the rest of this chapter, however, the word 'sophist' will be used in its strictest sense, meaning an itinerant professional practitioner of a wide range of intellectual skills, including rhetorical techniques, which he taught for pay and which he advertised as guaranteeing advancement in public life. The term thus refers in particular to Protagoras, Gorgias, Hippias, Prodicus and Thrasymachus in the pages of Plato (also to Euthydemus and Dionysodorus in the *Euthydemus*); it does not extend to disciples and pupils who sought to master these techniques for use in the political arena, without desiring to become sophists themselves. It thus includes Polus but not Callicles.

Sophistic thought and discussion undoubtedly had some background in pre-Socratic philosophy, notably the Eleatic school with their fondness for intellectual paradoxes and seemingly insoluble puzzles. Sophistic teaching was not solely practical: some at least taught astronomy, mathematics, even physics and metaphysics,[4] as well as the less rarefied arts of literary criticism, argumentation and rhetoric. Nevertheless, their claim to teach *arete* – an ambiguous term that could mean virtue, excellence, or simply political rather than moral preeminence – and their willingness to teach it to all comers for a fee, distinguished them as a new type, and also won them considerable distrust and disapproval. In Plato's *Meno*, the angry reaction of Anytus shows the 'typical' Athenian conservative's resentment at these new-fangled, trouble-making thinkers who dared to take education out of the hands of a boy's family (*Meno* 91c sq.). Protagoras refers to similar distrust and even to possible danger for men like himself (*Prt.* 316c sq., cf. 312a; Callicles in *Grg.* 520a; Xen. *Cyn.* 13, etc.). This attitude, and the pejorative sense of the word sophist, is certainly not merely Plato's invention;[5] it is prominent in Aristophanes, and not only in the *Clouds*: in a famous fragment of a lost play a character declares 'either a book, or else Prodicus or one of the babblers has corrupted the man' (Ar. fr. 490K. = 506K-A).[6]

---

[3] Synonyms: Diog. Laert. i. 12. Early uses: Pind. *Isthm.* 5. 28, Hdt. i. 29. 1, iv. 95. 2. More slighting uses: Aesch. *Prom.* 62, Ar. *Clouds* 331ff., 1309, Eur. *Rh.* 924, Dem. 18. 276. Cf. Kerferd, *CR* 64 (1950) 8-10.

[4] Kerferd, *Sophistic Movement* 37-41, esp. 39.

[5] Contra G. Grote, *History of Greece* ch. 67, a classic defence of the sophists which, despite some points that now need to be qualified because of new evidence, is still well worth reading.

[6] Note also Eupolis fr. 353K = 388 K-A, perhaps from the *Flatterers* of 421, which mocked Callias' devotion to the sophists.

The period of the sophists' greatest fame is also the age of Periclean Athens and of the Peloponnesian war.[7] Protagoras was a friend of Pericles and visited Athens more than once in the 430s or earlier. (Plato's *Protagoras* represents him and other prominent teachers being entertained by the wealthy Callias; the dramatic date is about 433.) Gorgias came rather later, with an embassy from his native Leontini in 427 (Thuc. iii. 86. 3, Diod. xii. 53. 1f.; perhaps alluded to in Ar. *Ach.* 634f.). Their influence or their writings must have preceded them to Athens: at any rate, the earliest extant plays of Euripides, the *Alcestis* of 438 and the *Medea* of 431 already display the strongly rhetorical traits that we associate with sophistic argumentation; and Antiphon's *Tetralogies*, opposed speeches deploying ingenious arguments on fictional but typical themes, may be earlier still, a product of the 440s.[8] Pericles' name is associated with a number of intellectuals by our sources (notably Plutarch): besides Protagoras, he may have known and patronised Anaxagoras, Damon, Sophocles and Herodotus.[9] Various prosecutions, notably those of Anaxagoras and Protagoras, have been interpreted as politically motivated and aimed at damaging Pericles himself. It may be to these that Plato makes Protagoras anachronistically allude in his dialogue, when the sophist speaks of the danger involved in his profession.[10] Although some of the evidence concerning these trials (and the motivations behind them) is questionable, we should at any rate accept that war-time Athens was not a wholly 'open' society in the sense of tolerating every expression of controversial opinions.[11]

What exactly did the rich young Athenians want from the sophists? Again Plato's *Protagoras*, in which the most distinguished of the profession is treated kindly though with some irony, provides the best evidence. When asked by Socrates what he thinks Protagoras will be able to teach him, the young Hippocrates thinks that he could be defined as 'a master of the art of making clever speakers' (*Prt.* 312d), and although Socrates is not satis-

[7] In general on Periclean Athens as a cultural centre see R. Meiggs, *The Athenian Empire* (1972) ch. 15, and Ostwald, *CAH* v[2] loc. cit. (n. 1).
[8] Cf. J.H. Finley, *Three Essays on Thucydides* (Cambridge Mass. 1967) esp. 68ff.; K.J. Dover, *CQ* 44 (1950), esp. 56-60 (= *The Greeks and their Legacy* 29-34).
[9] P. Stadter, *ICS* 16 (1991) 111-24, questions the whole tradition of Pericles as an intellectual patron; but his scepticism seems to go too far as regards Protagoras. It is not certain, but at least probable, that the anecdote which tells of the two men discussing a problem of responsibility (Plut. *Per.* 36) goes back to Stesimbrotus, a contemporary source; and the Platonic or pseudo-Platonic references in *Phdr.* 269ab, and *I Alc.* 104b, 118bc, despite their irony, reinforce the picture.
[10] See further G. Hill, *Sources for Greek History*, 2nd ed. (1951) 353; Dodds, *The Greeks and the Irrational* 189ff.; for a very sceptical discussion of the prosecutions see Dover, *Talanta* 7 (1976) 24-54 = *The Greeks and their Legacy* 135-58 (endorsed for different reasons by I.F. Stone, *The Trial of Socrates* (1988) 231-47). The evidence has been carefully reassessed by Ostwald, *Popular Sovereignty* 195-8, 528-36, and elsewhere.
[11] In general on tensions in the world of fifth-century Athens see Davies, *CAH* v[2] 27-33, a fascinating sketch.

fied, this certainly reflects one of the principal claims of these men. Later, Protagoras himself offers an account of his profession. 'From me,' he explains, 'he will learn (not arithmetic and astronomy and geometry and music but ...) sound judgement concerning his own household affairs, how he may best manage his home, and concerning the affairs of the city, how he may be the most able [or "powerful"] in word and deed on public affairs' (318e). Socrates, with some slyness, takes this pronouncement to mean that Protagoras is 'promising to make men good citizens' (319a), that is, to teach civic *virtue*, not political success. Speech and persuasion naturally play a vital role in a political career under the Athenian radical democracy, in which any major decision has to be ratified through discussion in the popular assembly. No less important is the role of forensic rhetoric, in order to defend and prosecute in the law-courts. The two spheres overlap, since many legal indictments were politically motivated: prominent in trials of this kind was the *graphe paranomon*, the prosecution for making an unconstitutional proposal. Hence, whatever else the sophists might offer (and in the speech quoted Protagoras seems to be sniping at the curriculum of his rival Hippias), they all seem to have taught rhetoric, and most of them wrote text-books on the subject or specimen speeches for study.[12] It is the power of persuasive and deceptive speech which is the real subject of Gorgias' *Helen*, and it is this same power of words which, in the *Clouds* of Aristophanes, Strepsiades covets as a way to avoid paying his debts. These are the men, he tells his son, who know how to make the worse, the unjust cause defeat the better (*Clouds* 99, 111ff, 883f.). The phrase became a cliché, a common jibe against the sophists, who were thus implicated in deception and dishonesty (cf. Prt. A21; Pl. *Ap.* 19b, *Euthyd.* 272a; Arist. *Rh.* iii. 1402a 3-28, Diog. Laert. ix. 55).

Speech and argument have to be about something, and the sophists did not teach simply the divisions of speeches or forensic tricks. Their students were taught how to expatiate on moral, social, political and religious generalities, the so-called *topoi* or *loci communes* (commonplaces), illustrated by particular examples from myth or history. Doubtless the depth of study devoted to such themes varied according to the teacher (and the pupil), but many of the most distinguished sophists had serious interests in subjects such as the development of human history (Protagoras' speech in Plato's dialogue),[13] constitutional theory (Prt. ap. Diog. Laert. iii. 37, ix.

[12] The evidence for these writings is collected in the valuable work of L. Radermacher, *Artium Scriptores* (Vienna 1951), which performs a similar service for early rhetoric to that which Diels-Kranz provides for pre-Socratic philosophy.

[13] Cf. Guthrie iii.79-84; also his *In the Beginning* (London 1957); the title essay in Dodds, *Anc. Concept of Progress*; Collard on Eur. *Supp.* 201-13.

[14] Cf. Hdt. iii. 80f., the *agon* of Euripides' *Suppliants*, etc. For discussion see Kerferd ch. 12. See also C. Farrar, *The Origins of Democratic Thinking* (Cambridge 1988).

55),[14] the origins of religion,[15] the nature of law,[16] and more metaphysical speculations about the possibility of knowledge and its relation to opinion – the theme of Gorgias' paradoxical work *On what is not*. This work unfortunately survives only through summaries.[17] In it Gorgias appears to have argued (1) that nothing exists, (2) that if anything existed, we could not know that it did or apprehend it, (3) that even if we could, we could not communicate the knowledge to anyone. Here the legacy of the Milesian pre-Socratics and the Eleatic school of Parmenides and Zeno is clear.

Another important theme, prominent in tragedy and Thucydides as well as in philosophy, was the relation of man-made law to the 'laws' of human nature.[18] 'Nature' versus 'law', *phusis* versus *nomos*, was as productive an intellectual opposition as nature and culture in our own time; indeed, the two debates have many points in common. What kind of validity did human law have, and was there such a thing as absolute law? These questions, exciting and stimulating to the young, would seem at best perplexing and pointless, at worst dangerously subversive, to older and more traditional minds. Doctrines such as 'the natural right of the stronger to rule' had serious and alarming political implications both within Athens and in her empire, as the students of the sophists were not slow to observe. Speakers in Thucydides, particularly the Athenians, employ such argument to justify their rule over others – or indeed to demonstrate that it needs no justification (Thuc. i. 76, v. 89, 105. 2, vi. 18. 3). Parallels in other writers show that this is not the invention or elaboration of Thucydides, but the common coin of political debate.[19] The intellectual revolution gives birth to political revolution in the year 411, when Antiphon, Peisander, Theramenes and others play leading roles in the attempted oligarchic coup at Athens; although other sources suggest that this revolution had an ideological dimension, Thucydides analysed it in terms of ambition and the exercise of sheer power. Not all the charges against the sophists can stand, and it seems clear that Protagoras, Gorgias and the other first-generation teachers were men of principle; but their students, men such as Alcibiades and Callicles in Plato, preparing themselves for the political arena in time of war, absorbed the new ideas without accepting the traditional restraints of orthodox morality.

---

[15] See esp. Critias (or Euripides?) B25 (for the dispute over authorship see A. Dihle, *Hermes* 105 (1977) 28-42); Kerferd ch. 13; J. Barnes, *The Presocratic Philosophers* (London 1979) ii 149-59. On the revolution in religious thought see esp. Burkert, *Greek Religion* (1985) ch. 7. F. Solmsen's book *Plato's Theology* (Cornell 1942) is still the best single authority on Plato's varied responses to these developments.

[16] Guthrie iii, chs. 4-7 passim; Kerferd ch. 10.

[17] See Grg. B1-3 D-K, with Guthrie iii. 192-200, Kerferd ch. 9.

[18] The guiding thread in M. Ostwald's valuable work: see *Nomos and the Beginnings of Athenian Democracy* (Oxford 1969); *From Popular Sovereignty ...* (1986); ΑΝΑΓΚΗ *in Thucydides* (Atlanta 1988).

[19] Guthrie iii. 84-116; Grg. *Helen* 5; ps.-Xen. i. 14; Antiph. B44; Democ. B267.

Plato, born in 427, grew up during the Peloponnesian war, and in a period when the sophists were becoming an established class in Greece, with their disciples becoming teachers in their turn. Although there is common ground among the sophists, as we have seen,[20] Grote was right to insist that we must not lump them all together as identical figures, and attach the doctrines or vices of one to them all. This applies equally to our study of Plato's attitude to them. Here there is room for disagreement,[21] but most readers would agree that the older sophists, particularly Protagoras and to some degree Gorgias, are presented with some sympathy and respect. They are not pawns on Plato's chess-board, but voice opinions which have considerable interest and validity, and which can plausibly be seen as echoing views expressed in their published works. But Plato does not show the same respect for various lesser figures, notably Hippias, who is treated with considerable satire; and although Prodicus' technique of distinguishing the meanings of words is seen as important, and Socrates sometimes defers to him, Prodicus himself is shown as having no real idea of how to apply it intelligently. Here we can hardly acquit Plato of some satirical exaggeration, but it is noteworthy that when Socrates' opponents *are* minor figures with clearly inadequate positions, the disputes are kept brief.[22] Although Plato disagrees with much that Protagoras and the others say, he still recognises them as figures of intellectual stature and treats them as such. His most violent attacks are reserved for the second generation of sophists or the sophists' pupils, men of lower intellectual pretensions and with more of an eye on the main chance, proponents of dangerous doctrines in morals, politics and theology. It is men like Thrasymachus and Callicles, those who question the very foundations of morality, whom Plato does his utmost to refute and discredit. As late as the *Laws*, the word sophist is associated in his mind with atheism and profligacy (x. 908d). In short, we can accept that Plato associates sophistic teaching in general, and certain sophists in particular, with dangerously mistaken ideas, and that he frequently mocked and satirised these opinions and their proponents. This does not mean that Plato's portrayal of the sophists and his presentation of their views bear *no* relation to reality, though it obviously means that we need to handle his evidence with care. But for the purposes of this book, the historical question of the sophists' beliefs and attitudes can be at least partially separated from the study of what Plato does with them, how these men are presented in the dialogues. The *Gorgias* and *Protagoras* can and should be read as dramatic works, not simply as polemical pamphlets; and a crucial part of Plato's dramatic technique is the contrast between Socrates and the professional sophists, a contrast that is brought out in

[20] See further Guthrie iii. 44-8.
[21] Thus, for example, G. Vlastos in his intr. to Plato's *Protagoras* in the 'Library of Liberal Arts' series, xxiv, finds the treatment of Protagoras in that dialogue 'merciless, if not cruel'.
[22] Both *Hippias*'s, Polus in *Grg*. For the same practice with non-sophistic opponents, cf. *Euthyphro* and *Ion*.

their methods of arguing, their style, their way of life, their mode of dress, and above all their philosophic principles and priorities.

This brings us to the second question posed in the opening paragraph: was Socrates a sophist, or how much did he have in common with them? In the indictment at the trial, Socrates' enemies tried to blacken him as a novel and dangerous thinker, implicating him with the physical doctrines of Anaxagoras (not a sophist himself, but another controversial intellectual); and in years to come, Aeschines could speak openly of 'Socrates the sophist' (1.173). In the dialogues, Socrates speaks openly and easily with the professional teachers; he is acquainted with their writings – Polus' text-book (*Grg.* 462b), or the rhetorical works discussed in the *Phaedrus*, or Protagoras' *On the truth*, quoted in the *Theaetetus*. He attends their discussions when invited (*Grg.*, *Euthyd.*, etc.) or when he can afford it (*Crat.* 384b). Clearly he and the sophists would have much in common in the eyes of an outsider. Socrates and the sophists both question traditional wisdom and seek to establish firmer criteria through reasoning; both place a high value on education and intellectual pursuits; both combine questioning and curiosity with scepticism and doubt; both discuss, criticise and find fault with the poets, often regarded as the fount of all knowledge.[23]

Even Socrates' characteristic question-and-answer procedure, which Plato refines and calls dialectic, may well have had parallels in sophistic techniques of discussion, for Plato presents both Protagoras and Gorgias as able to deal with issues in a brief, 'tutorial' manner as well as in a more expansive rhetorical style.[24] Consequently, even an acquaintance with considerable intellectual bent, such as Aristophanes, might not have been able, or sufficiently interested, to perceive the difference between Socratic elenchus and sophistic cross-questioning or 'eristic'.[25]

Nevertheless, important differences remain, many of which go beyond their philosophic preoccupations, and some of which can be confirmed by non-Platonic evidence. If we take men like Protagoras, Gorgias, Hippias and Prodicus as the chief examples of the genus 'sophist', then there is enough common ground in their way of life, their *modus operandi*, to bring out the contrast with Socrates without becoming involved as yet in their differences of doctrine and interests.

One immediately striking difference between Socrates and the rest lies in their *nationality*. Although Athens was a major centre, perhaps the chief centre, of sophistic influence, none of the major figures of that movement was Athenian-born; rather, they were drawn to Athens by her prominence

[23] Cf. esp. R. Pfeiffer, *Hist. of Classical Scholarship* i (1968) ch. 2; also F. Buffière, *Les mythes d'Homère et la pensée grecque* (1956).

[24] See esp. *Prt.* 329b3-5, 334d-5b; Kerferd 33. Cf. ch. 3, p. 73.

[25] See the remarks of K.J. Dover, *Aristophanes: Clouds*, pp. l-liv. (The alternative, perhaps preferable, is to allow that Aristophanes himself did understand the difference, but for purposes of comedy subscribed to the *communis opinio* in mocking intellectuals).

and prosperity as the supreme democracy and the centre of empire. Protagoras came from Abdera in Thrace, Gorgias from Leontini in Sicily, Prodicus from Ceos, Hippias from Elis, Thrasymachus from Chalcedon. They travelled widely, whereas Socrates notoriously never left his native Athens except when required to travel on campaign. Indeed, for him even to wander outside the city limits as he does in the *Phaedrus* is a matter for comment (230c-d). Very few Athenians could really be called 'sophists', though there is perhaps Antiphon, if the sophist who appears in the *Memorabilia* of Xenophon (i. 6), the author of the papyrus fragments *On truth* (87B44 Diels-Kranz), and the orator whose forensic speeches on homicide survive are one and the same man.[26] Here as before, we need to distinguish between the sophists themselves, the travelling professionals, and their young, well-born Athenian pupils such as Hippocrates in the *Protagoras*, Cleinias and others in the *Euthydemus*, and Callicles in the *Gorgias* (who has certainly learned much from the sophists, even though he abuses them).

Secondly, we should bear in mind the social status and eminence of the great sophists. They were distinguished and aristocratic figures, and it was aristocrats with whom they stayed in Athens: witness above all the *Protagoras*, in which the sophists (and their followers?) are being hosted by Callias (447b). Gorgias and Hippias had served on embassies from their cities to Athens; it was on such a mission that Gorgias had stunned the assembly with his brilliant style (Diod. xii. 53 = Grg. A4). Protagoras was an intimate of Pericles and discussed intellectual puzzles with him (Plut. *Per.* 36); Pericles is said to have paid him the high compliment of choosing him to frame the constitution for the Athenian colony at Thurii, founded in 444-443 BC.[27] Again contrast Socrates: allegedly the son of a stone-mason, he was never ambitious to hold any sort of public office and indeed claims to have made a fool of himself when the lot fell to him to serve once on the Council.[28] His interest was in individuals, not assemblies or audiences; in conversation, not rhetoric. So far from attaining public esteem or advancement, he remained poor to the end of his life (esp. *Ap.* 38b).

The last point reminds us of that notorious and lasting stigma on the sophists, that they took fees for their teaching. This does not seem so

[26] On this unresolved question see the excellent note of Andrewes in *HCT* v on Thuc. viii. 68. Other discussions are cited by Ostwald, *Popular Sovereignty* 360-4.

[27] But see Stadter (n. 9 above), whose scepticism here has some justification: Protagoras is not mentioned by Diod. xii. 10, only by Diog. Laert. ix. 50 (citing Heraclides Ponticus). On the colony at Thurii see V. Ehrenberg, *AJP* 69 (1948) 149-70 = *Polis und Imperium* (Zurich-Stuttgart 1965) 298-315.

[28] *Grg.* 473e, with Dodds's n. This is disingenuous on Socrates' part, however; see *Ap.* 32b (also Xen. *Mem.* i. 1. 18, iv. 4. 2) for the episode to which he was referring – the trial of the generals after Arginusae, at which it was the Athenian people, led by a hotheaded majority on the Council, who were acting not foolishly but outrageously, in demanding the execution of all the generals on a single vote. Socrates was the one member of the presiding body who persistently declared that this was illegal (cf. Xen. *Hell.* i. 7. 15, Diod. xiii. 101).

appalling to us, but it seems to have been novel in Greece at the time: Protagoras is said to have been the first to do so (*Prt.* 349a, cf. *Hipp. Mai.* 282cd). The sums in question were indeed colossal: Protagoras is said to have earned more money than Pheidias together with any ten other sculptors (*Meno* 91d), and Prodicus commonly charged half a mina for a single lecture (*Crat.* 384b).[29] Callias was notorious for squandering a great deal of his enormous fortune on Protagoras, Hippias and Prodicus (*Ap.* 20a, *Crat.* 391c, Xen. *Smp.* 1. 5). There can be no doubt that the sophists were extremely wealthy: we may recall Protagoras's boast that he would allow any pupil who was prepared to swear on oath that he did not think he had got his money's worth to pay whatever sum he thought it actually was worth (*Prt.* 328b). This is hardly the boast of a man who is badly off.[30] Again we should contrast this with Socrates, who always went around shoeless and shabby,[31] and seems to have had no particular means of support beyond the generosity of his friends. He claims, of course, to be unable to pay any substantial fine as an alternative to the death penalty (*Ap.* 38ab). It is sometimes asserted that Socrates was always perfectly well off in reality, as Alcibiades and the others would host him, fête him and help him out of any difficulties; from this it is deduced that he (or Plato) had no right to criticise the sophists for taking money. This is an absurd and unfair argument: there is a world of difference between the hand-to-mouth, perambulating life that Socrates led, in which it was a matter for remark if he was ever spruced up or had a bath (*Smp.* 174a, cf. 220b; Ar. *Birds* 1554), and the national acclamation and renown, the wealth and luxurious life-style, the continuous prosperity of the successful sophist.

It has already been said that the Socratic question-and-answer method may have some background in sophistic teaching procedure. But although this brief, dialectical form of instruction may have had a place in their courses, their more typical, and much more popular, form of exposition was the sophistic *epideixis* or display-speech. Here again, non-Platonic evidence for the practice of the sophists supports the picture in the dialogues. The occasions for the delivery of such speeches might be of considerable formality, and the sophists even performed and competed at Olympic festivals.[32] Otherwise their performances were in public places: Prodicus at the Lyceum (B8), Hippias in the 'school of Pheidostratus' (Pl. *Hipp. Mai.* 286ab). Gorgias would offer to speak on any subject whatsoever in the theatre at Athens (Philostr. *VS* i.1, p. 482 = Grg. A1a D-K). He spoke also at Olympia and at the Pythian games at Delphi (Grg. B7-9). Hippias likewise offered

---

[29] For a collection of testimonia in Plato concerning the sophists' fees, see E.L. Harrison, *Phoenix* 18 (1964) 191n. 44; for discussion of what can be believed and deduced, see Kerferd 25-8.

[30] Contrast the use of this anecdote by Grote, *History* ch. 67, Everyman ed. viii, 325f.

[31] 'His coat was a stock comic joke', Guthrie iii. 389.

[32] Grg. A1, B5-6, cf. 8; Pl. *Hipp. Min.* 364a; Guthrie iii. 42f.

to speak on any one of a prepared list of subjects, and to answer any question his audience might care to put (*Hipp. Min.* 363c7-d4).[33]

A sophistic *epideixis* was often the recitation of *prepared* written works, not improvisation or invention. Hippias explains that he has delivered his ethical dialogue, the *Trojan Discourse*, in Sparta and is preparing to do so again in Athens (*Hipp. Mai.* 286b-c). The same literary status may be assumed for other sophistic orations.[34] Although for some purposes improvisation remained important, it is clear that written books played a central role in sophistic teaching, both for self-advertisement (as with Gorgias' *Helen*, an encomium of his own art as much as of Helen) and for their pupils to take away and study (cf. Arist. *Soph. El.* 183b36ff.). Once more the contrast with Socrates, who himself wrote nothing and in Plato criticises writing, is inescapable.

Gorgias has just finished such an epideixis when Socrates arrives on the scene and Plato's *Gorgias* begins. He pompously declares that it is many years now since anyone asked him anything new.[35] Gorgias and Hippias are said also to have performed this sort of act in formal purple robes, in the tradition of the ancient poets and rhapsodes (Grg. A9; according to *Hipp. Min.* 368c, Hippias made his own! Polymathy again.) The ponderous formality of procedure is again quite alien to Socrates' chatty and unpretentious style of discussion, on which he is ready to embark with anybody he meets, on a street corner or at the dinner-table. Still more striking, and still more antithetical, is the self-assurance of the sophists in acting this way: as Dodds remarks, Gorgias sets himself up as 'a one-man brains trust'.[36] In such displays, both in historical fact and in Plato's brilliant recreations, the sophists are complacently sure that they have the *answers*, the whole truth. It is characteristic of Socrates in Plato that he constantly explores such claims, undermining their self-confidence and puncturing their pretensions with his incessant, sceptical, deceptively simple *questions*.

The *Euthydemus*[37]

The dialogue *Euthydemus* is formally 'dramatic': like the *Protagoras*, it opens with an exchange between Socrates and a friend, here Crito, which swiftly leads on to the philosopher's narration of a recent encounter: he describes how he met and sought instruction from two brothers, the

---

[33] Cf. *Meno* 70bc. On sophistic polymathy, see esp. *Hipp. Min.* 368, a central text; compare in abstract terms *Soph.* 232e. See further M. Whitlock Blundell, *OSAP* Suppl. 1992, 167n.148.
[34] Cf. Pfeiffer, *Hist. of Classical Scholarship* i (1968) 30ff.
[35] *Grg.* 448a; cf. Dodds ad loc.; Woodruff on *Hipp. Mai.* 282b.
[36] Commentary on *Grg.* 448a.
[37] Commentaries by Gifford and Hawtrey; for a book-length study see Thomas H. Chance, *Plato's Euthydemus: Analysis of What Is and Is Not Philosophy* (Berkeley and L.A., 1992).

sophists Euthydemus and Dionysodorus.[38] Also present on this occasion
were the sophists' followers and a number of interested young men, of
whom two lovers, Cleinias and Ctesippus, are particularly singled out. The
ensuing debate is unusual in Plato, in that there is no formal subject under
discussion. Although Socrates tries to get the sophists to show that wisdom
must be pursued by all, their actual performance involves questioning
those present on all manner of unconnected topics, and producing paradoxical results through clever word-play, deliberate misunderstandings,
and obvious logical fallacies. Formally the dialogue differs from the *Protagoras* in that we return to conversation between Socrates and Crito at
the end (cf. the *Menexenus*), and in that there is also an interlude two-thirds
of the way through, where Crito reacts to Socrates' narrative and a short
exchange between them ensues (cf. *Phaedo* 88c-9b). The comments of Crito
at the end partly express his own unease (he does not think that Socrates
should associate with such charlatans), and partly echo the criticisms of
both Socrates and the sophists which he has heard from an anonymous
figure who witnessed the occasion. This figure, who passes dismissive
judgements on both Socrates and philosophy, is usually identified with the
rhetorician and educational theorist Isocrates, though the reason for his
anonymity is far from clear (perhaps an effort to avoid anachronism).[39]

It is reasonably clear that the dialogue is more about method than about
a particular philosophic issue: many ideas and epistemological difficulties
are thrown up by the sophists' interrogations, but none is fully explored,
and although they sometimes reappear elsewhere in Plato's works, they
are evidently not the chief concern of this dialogue. Rather, the *Euthydemus* presents a contrast between different methods of teaching, between
Socratic questioning and sophistic browbeating, or, to use two quasi-tech-
nical terms, between dialectic and eristic ('disputation').[40] The narrated
section of the dialogue shows a series of exchanges. First there is a
question-answer sequence between the two sophists and the boy Cleinias,
who is reduced to bewilderment by their fast-moving paradoxes (275b-77c).
Then Socrates steps in and tries to restore Cleinias' confidence by a more
patient and consecutive series of questions, which he offers to the sophists
as a paradigm of how to question people in such a way as to encourage them
in the path of philosophy – a protreptic form of questioning (277d-82e).[41]

---

[38] There is little independent evidence on these men (though see Arist. *Rh.* 1401a28, *SE*
177b12), but there seems no reason to doubt that they are historical figures. For further
evidence and argument see Sprague, *The Older Sophists* 294-301, Hawtrey 13-14.

[39] On Isocrates see ch. 2, pp. 63-6; on this episode see Hawtrey 26-7, 30, 190ff.

[40] On eristic see further Thompson's comm. on *Meno* (1901), Excursus 5 (on 75c, 80e), 272-85;
Robinson, *Plato's Earlier Dialectic* 70, 84ff.; Ryle, *Plato's Progress* chs. 4 and 6; Lloyd, *Magic,
Reason and Experience* 62-5, 100-1; Kerferd ch. 6; A. Nehamas, *Hist. of Philosophy Quarterly*
7 (1990) 3-16; Vlastos, *Socratic Studies* 135-6.

[41] On the history of the form 'protreptic' see P. Hartlich, *de exhortationum a Graecis
Romanisque scriptarum historia et indole* (Leipzig 1889); I. Düring, *Aristotle's Protrepticus:
A Reconstruction* (Goteburg 1961) 19-24, 32-5; Slings, *Clitopho*, esp. 70-183.

But when the sophists take the lead again there is no attempt to follow Socrates' lead or to consider the subject on which he has embarked; instead we have more fireworks and ingenious logic-chopping. The sophists turn their main attention on Socrates, but a mischievous move on their part brings Ctesippus, Cleinias' lover, into the argument, hotly denying what they assert (that he really wants Cleinias 'not to be', because he would be different and changed if morally improved). At this stage the conversation becomes more heated, with Ctesippus sarcastic and aggressive, and the sophists mocking yet outrageous (283a-88b). Socrates, afraid that a real quarrel may ensue, steps in again to resume the questioning of Cleinias, taking up his questions from the point where he had left off before (288b-93a), and this time Cleinias responds more fully and thoughtfully (290b-d), so much so that Crito breaks in in surprise and admiration (290e-1a). Cleinias' progress is not, however, enough for them to resolve the question at issue, and Socrates appeals again to Euthydemus to help them. Another lively display of absurd arguments follows, and again Ctesippus plays a part, now showing himself an apt learner of the sophists' tricks, and (as Socrates comments) inclined to show off in front of his beloved (300c1), who in turn is worryingly ready to laugh at these futile games (300e). In the end Socrates is forced to a ridiculous and even blasphemous conclusion (that his household gods are 'his' in the same sense as animals and property, so that he can sell or dispose of them as he chooses). Socrates is shocked and dismayed, but Ctesippus is merely amused and seems to concede some grudging admiration of the sophists (303a).

The moral implications seem clear: the sophists' antics are a superficial pretence at philosophy, ingenious yet sterile, and all too easily picked up: they themselves have only recently acquired this 'wisdom', and Ctesippus is quick to catch on (300d7-9, 303e). By contrast Socrates' style of enquiry is less showy, more slow-moving, but more valuable, even if it does not reach a firm conclusion: he pursues a serious subject consistently, shares his difficulties with his companion, and (perhaps most important) draws out Cleinias, giving him the confidence to put forward his own ideas. Other aspects of the narrative reinforce these contrasts: for instance, the presence of an audience who react enthusiastically but superficially to the sophists' 'successes', who laugh and cheer at their ability to score trivial debating-points (276b, 303b). By contrast Socrates' genuine progress with Cleinias receives the more thoughtful approval of Crito, who also voices the reaction of the man-in-the-street to the sophists' perfomance: he is one of those who would be more ashamed to employ such methods of refutation than to be their victim (304d1-2, picking up Socrates' comment at 303d). Another feature which emphasises the weaknesses of the sophists' method is the combative imagery used to describe their procedures. Decribing them at the start of the dialogue, Socrates uses language which both amuses and disturbs the reader: having previously been experts at wrestling, fighting in armour, and so forth, the two brothers have now become experts in verbal competition (271c-2a). In part this is a joke about sophistic versatility (p. 111 above); it also suggests how shallow their acquaintance with philosophy must be. But the notion of wrestling also recurs later as a metaphor (esp. 277d 'and then Euthydemus was getting ready to give the young man his third fall, so to speak'; 288a 'the same old knock-down, fall-down').[42] This suggests that the two men have carried the same aggressive and combative spirit over into their argumentative style (as the very word 'eristic' implies). At one point they are even at odds with each other, when Dionysodorus allows Socrates to make a point which will undermine the sophistic paradox, and Euthydemus rebukes him (297a).

As in the *Laches* and *Charmides*, the characterisation of the participants is not only colourful and entertaining in itself, but also carries moral significance. Some aspects of this have already been outlined. The sophists are showmen, playing to their admiring audience; we see their indifference to the young pupil's confidence and well-being from the start, when Dionysodorus gleefully whispers to Socrates that whatever answer Cleinias makes, he will be refuted (275e). In a different way, Ctesippus is also showing off, trying to look good in front of Cleinias (283e, 300c1); and although direct and down-to-earth scepticism can sometimes be a virtue in dialectic, his ill-mannered attacks on the sophists do not advance the discussion, and do him little credit: in that part of the dialogue a distinction is drawn by Ctesippus himself between 'contradiction' and 'abuse' (285cd), but Socrates' account of the young man's tone and description of his own unease suggest that his behaviour, though understandable, is culpable (see esp. 285a, 288b3). The language of 'seriousness' versus 'play' or 'frivolity', common in Plato, is here used to characterise the different approaches of Socrates and the sophistic duo. To the sophists, the argument is itself a sport or game (like wrestling and the other sports in which they are expert); the smooth transition from one to the other as questioner is described by Socrates with a comparison to players catching a ball (277b), and he also compares these antics with the play and dancing which might precede the serious business of initiation (277de). But the sophists, as Socrates complains, are not prepared to drop the play and deal with them seriously (288bc, 293a) – that is, to stop shadow-boxing and conduct a continuous discussion on fair terms. When Ctesippus gets the hang of the sophists' tricks he pursues various unconnected lines of argument which are equally frivolous and futile: they bear no relation to truth or to Ctesippus' real interests, but only serve to discomfit the sophists (and only temporarily at

---

[42] The metaphor is used elsewhere in argumentative contexts: cf. *Tht.* 162b, Aesch. *Eum.* 589, 776f., Ar. *Knights* 490ff., *Frogs* 878, and esp. Protagoras' *Kataballontes Logoi* ('Knock-down arguments'). Plutarch, *Pericles* 8 is amusing in this context: it describes a remark by Pericles' political opponent, Thucydides son of Melesias (not the historian). When asked 'which is the better fighter, you or Pericles?', Thucydides, who was famous as a wrestler, replied that it was hard to tell, as when he had thrown Pericles, the latter would get up and make a speech that convinced the audience that he had worsted Thucydides!

that) (294b-d, 298b-e, 300d). Socrates' use of humour and teasing in this dialogue is in marked contrast: at 285a he is trying to defuse the situation, and prevent Ctesippus from exploding in rage: 'since they seemed to me to be getting too wild with one another, I tried to tease (*prosepaizon*) Ctesippus, saying ...' On the one hand we see an empty game of point-scoring which serves only to gratify the winner's vanity; on the other, a more tactful and thoughtful attempt to preserve or introduce a spirit of cooperation and common enquiry.[43]

The hardest of the characters to interpret is, strangely enough, Socrates himself. Although he himself narrates the episode, his evaluations and comments, particularly at the opening of the work, are the opposite of what we would expect: he expresses awe and wonder at the sophists' performance (272ab), blames himself for his own slowness, and is apparently eager to become their pupil – he even urges Crito to join him in attendance at their 'school' (304bc). Clearly we are dealing here with Socrates' notorious irony.[44] In this case, however, it is sustained in a peculiarly consistent fashion; although from the beginning we may be suspicious of the exaggerated praise he showers on the sophists, this does involve our bringing in our knowledge of Socrates' sceptical and questioning attitudes elsewhere.

Socrates' response here is *faux-naif*: he professes to admire the sophists, but reservations do make themselves felt. For example, at 273e5f. he addresses the sophists saying, 'Well, if you now truly have this knowledge, o be gracious! – for I humbly address you as gods ...' Both the extravagance of his prayer-like appeal and the eloquent 'if'-clause alert us to his possible doubts. Again, at 274de, he asks them if they can make a man a good man 'only if he is already convinced that he must learn from you, or can you do this also to one who is not yet convinced, through doubting that the thing, virtue, can be learned at all or that you two can teach it?' Although this entirely legitimate question is couched in general terms, it suggests to the reader that Socrates himself may not be so convinced.[45] Later passages in which Socrates comments on the sophists' attitudes, or on the reactions of the boys, give us further hints of his dissatisfaction. Examples are 276d4, the comment on Euthydemus' motive ('so that we might marvel at him still more'), the comparison of their verbal games with childish practical jokes such as snatching away stools as people sit down (278b), the reference to Dionysodorus' insincerity (286d11ff., cf. 302b3 on Euthydemus), the description of Ctesippus having become a *panourgos* (a thorough rascal, 300d7), and the comparisons of the sophists to dangerous mythical crea-

---

[43] For more 'play'-language see 283b. See generally G.J. de Vries, *Spel bij Plato* (Amsterdam 1949), and J. Huizinga, *Homo Ludens* (Eng. tr. 1949).

[44] Cf. Wayne Booth, *A Rhetoric of Irony* (1974), esp. chs. 3-4 on this particular type of text. For a still more sustained example of this kind of irony see Swift, *A Modest Proposal* ..., discussed by Booth 105-20.

[45] For comparable passages in the *Protagoras*, which employs similar ironies more intermittently, see 319a8ff., 328d3ff.

tures of ambiguous status: Proteus the shape-shifter and the many-headed Hydra, with Socrates cast in the more human, sympathetic roles of Menelaus and Heracles (288b, 297c).[46]

The unreasonable behaviour and self-satisfied manner of the sophists also helps guide our response to their eristic method.[47] Even a casual reading makes plain their insufferable conceit and the arbitrariness with which they switch from one set of assumptions, or one line of questioning, to another. Whereas Socrates' argument in the 'protreptic' sections is consecutive, coherent, and moves in a particular direction, the arguments of the sophists are fragmented, unconnected, opportunistic. They laugh at Socrates for bringing up things they said earlier, dismissing such points as irrelevant (287b; 295c10f.); they decline to establish any rules or conventions by which the discussion is to be directed (287cd); and they object to Socrates' adding qualifying phrases to his answers, or counter-questioning them, even when his question is only an attempt to clarify what was meant by that of Euthydemus (295b). 'You are avoiding the question, Socrates', snaps Dionysodorus (297b7) – outrageously, as he himself has deliberately deflected the discussion in order to evade *Socrates'* questioning.

This self-characterisation, combined with the continuing irony and the brevity of Socrates' own scattered comments, achieves the desired effect (making the reader condemn Euthydemus and Dionysodorus) without any heavy-handed editorial insistence on the point. Just as Socrates gives Crito an account of the events and leaves him to judge for himself the value of the sophists' teaching, so Plato leaves some of the work for the reader to do: neither Socrates nor Crito, nor the Isocratean figure at the end of the work, gives a final evaluation or adequate summing-up of the 'message' of the dialogue.

Neither constraints of space nor the concerns of this book will allow any detailed consideration of the arguments in the *Euthydemus*, arguments which modern readers have in any case treated with disdain. But two larger points deserve attention, both of which have implications for Platonic practice elsewhere. The first point is that at least with the sophists' arguments, the reader is meant to see that they are invalid, and presumably to consider the reasons why: that is, from one point of view the *Euthydemus* is a textbook on sophistic fallacies. Since Plato is clearly aware that these are fallacies, but uses them for dramatic or didactic purposes, it follows that the same may happen in other dialogues: speakers may put forward arguments which the author sees to be inadequate, but which serve either to characterise them, or to illustrate a type of error, or to challenge the reader. Just as an aporetic discussion is not a meaningless or unprof-

---

[46] See also the comparison of the sophists' 'education' with the magical but potentially lethal potions of Medea (285c). For a discussion of the Heracles-hydra parallel see R. Jackson, *CQ* 40 (1990) 378-95.

[47] See further L. Coventry, in Pelling (ed.) *Characterization and Individuality* 176-8.

itable one, so a fallacious argument, provided its fallacies are understood, can still be one from which a thinking person can learn. It would not of course follow that Plato is always aware of fallacy, or that he can never make the mistake of thinking an argument is valid when it is not; but the *Euthydemus* gives us good reason to hesitate before ascribing to Plato elementary failures in logic.[48] Questions still remain, which may require different answers in different cases: in particular, how much difference does it make when it is Socrates, not his interlocutors, who is guilty of the argumentative error? Is this also an object lesson for the aspiring logician to learn from?

The second broader comment on the arguments of the *Euthydemus* concerns their implications rather than their validity. Trivial and superficial though the sophists' argumentative moves almost always seem, they are not dealing with problems of no philosophic substance whatsoever. Euthydemus and Dionysodorus can plausibly be seen as heirs to some of the problems of ontology studied by the great thinker Parmenides, a figure for whom Plato retained a deep respect.[49] The questions that Parmenides raised, of how a thing can be or become something else, would preoccupy Plato in his later works: indeed, in the dialogue named after him he examines Parmenides' thought in depth. The formulations which the sophists use hint at greater things: it is not that they are, as Socrates ironically suggests, concealing their deeper wisdom, but that, having picked up only a few tricks of the trade, they have no interest in exploring the harder questions more rigorously. But the dialogue repeatedly suggests that there is more to the points they make than meets the eye. At 294e, for example, the argument that they know all things, that they knew them already when they were children, and that all others are in that happy state, bears a resemblance to the argument of Socrates in the *Meno*, that all knowledge is recollection of what we knew already: it needs only to be revived, for we have it within us from before our birth.[50] Again, the question 'how can anyone say something which "is not"?', raised in the second dialogue with the sophists, is considered more fully and fruitfully in later dialogues (e.g. *Tht.* 188d sqq., and *Soph.* 258-60). This procedure could be seen in two ways. On one argument, the aim is to remind an informed reader of Plato's arguments elsewhere, and so to indicate the superiority

---

[48] R. Robinson, *Essays in Greek Philosophy* 16-38, and esp. R.K. Sprague, *Plato's Use of Fallacy*, whose admirable book seems to be unduly neglected, perhaps because of its relatively modest claims and limited scope. Cf. Dodds, *Gorgias* pp. 249, 335-6, esp. 336 'it is not easy to suppose that Plato was unaware of what he was doing'. G. Klosko, *CQ* 33 (1983) 363-74 discusses the general problems involved in the identification of 'deliberate' or dramatically motivated fallacies in the dialogues.

[49] See *Tht.* 183e, and Sprague 13-14, 17f. etc. In general on Parmenides' thought see KRS 239-62.

[50] See esp. H. Keulen, *Untersuchungen zu Platons Euthydem* (Wiesbaden 1971); also Friedlaender ii 184-6, Hawtrey 21-2, Chance, passim.

of Platonic thought, as of Socratic method, to the triviality of the sophists. This would be a strongly unitarian argument, based on the assumption that readers are expected to make comparisons and cross-references between dialogues:[51] it might run into difficulties with chronology, since the *Euthydemus* is usually thought to be much earlier than the dialogues most concerned with being and not-being. Can Plato cross-refer to works which are still only at the stage of conception?[52] A more cautious approach might be to accept that Plato sees these problems as deserving more sustained and serious consideration than the sophists are willing (or able) to give them, but that his own ideas were still developing. As often, he allows other questions to appear on the fringes of the dialogue, or at the gaps in the argument, for the interested reader to pursue if he will. On this argument, the similarities to Platonic or other doctrines need not indicate specific cross-reference but continuing preoccupations. The phenomenon is found elsewhere in the shorter dialogues (e.g. in the *Ion*): where the interlocutor is not equal to the complexity of a theme, both he and Socrates are sometimes permitted to speak more truly than they know. It is as though the reader is being invited (not compelled) to join in the philosophic quest, instead of resting content with the entertaining inconclusiveness of the dialectical drama.[53]

We have already referred to the unusual formal features of the *Euthydemus*. The most striking of these is the ending, with its extended resumption of the frame dialogue between Crito and Socrates. This ending falls into three closely related parts: the transitional section containing Socrates' ironically enthusiastic conclusion to his narrative, which culminates in the invitation to join him in attending the sophists' school (is this a test for Crito?); Crito's negative response, which is combined with a report of the anonymous critic's objections to philosophy; and the closing exchange, in which Socrates comments on these objections and encourages Crito in his concern for his sons' education. It is natural to ask what these last few pages add to the dramatic section which forms the core of the dialogue, and how, if at all, they qualify the evaluation which we have so far made of the relative merits of Socrates and the sophistic pair.

The conclusion seems to serve a number of functions – possibly too many, for it is at least arguable that these last few pages introduce so many fresh ideas that they unbalance the dialogue in an unproductive way. First, the comments made by Socrates in his final address to the sophists make clearer than ever before that his admiration for them is ironic; for the points which he singles out for praise in their methods are all in fact clearly

---

[51] See ch. 1, pp. 23-5 on the problems raised here. Cf. e.g. Tigerstedt, *Interpreting Plato*, esp. ch. 5.

[52] Hawtrey 21ff., and in *Apeiron* 12 (1978) 14-18, argues that 290b-c allude in a comparable way to the curriculum laid down for the Guardians in *Republic* vii.

[53] Cf. e.g. T. Baxter, *The Cratylus: Plato's Critique of Naming* (Leiden 1992) 13 and passim.

deficiencies (shamelessness, internal contradiction and the amazing ease with which their tricks can be learned). Second, the conclusion, like the interlude at 290e sq., helps to characterise Crito: he is a plain man, an honest farmer and businessman (291e8, 304c4), not dismissive of philosophy but concerned that Socrates should not disgrace himself in public; while interested in learning and keen on getting a good education for his sons, he does not have a penetrating mind and is easily bemused by the superior attitude of the anonymous critic. He needs the encouragement and good sense which Socrates offers him in reply: like Cleinias in the dramatic part of the dialogue, Crito is reassured and impelled towards philosophy by Socrates' friendship and questioning.[54] Third, Plato uses this scene to show how hostile criticism of philosophy at Athens could embrace both Socrates' activities and those of men like Euthydemus and Dionysodorus. Philosophy could be attacked by intellectuals (for the anonymous figure, whether Isocrates or another, clearly represents this class) as well as by the man-in-the-street, or the comic poets who side with him. The dialogue has been partly directed at such critics, perhaps in order to help them to see the real differences between the different types of teaching illustrated in it.

It seems hard to deny that there is also a polemical aspect to the conclusion, which may be more relevant to Plato's time of writing than to the notional dramatic date of the discussion which Socrates narrates. The comments which Socrates makes about the critic and the group he represents, those 'mid-way between philosophy and politics', strike a new note in the dialogue, and seem to be given emphasis which is hard to justify on internal grounds alone. The critic complains that philosophy is an absurd waste of time, devoid of value, and that Socrates ought to be ashamed of himself for spending time in discussion with men like Euthydemus and Dionysodorus. As we have seen, it is not unknown for serious criticisms of Socrates' actions to be voiced in the dialogues, but the comments in this case seem self-satisfied and unreasonable: for one thing, they overlook the educative role which Socrates had briefly adopted, despite the unpropitious circumstances, in dealing with Cleinias. There is a parallel between the sophists in the dramatic part of the dialogue and the anonymous figure in the frame: both are aspiring to the title of wise men, both adopt a dismissive and superior attitude to the seemingly naive and ignorant Socrates, and both cause anxiety and uncertainty in those they encounter (Cleinias and Crito), rather than offering help or enlightenment. The anonymity of the rhetorical expert may, as suggested above, be an effort to avoid anachronism (for Isocrates was only a promising youth when Socrates was alive: see *Phdr.* 278e-9a); but it is probably more important that the figure represents a type: the type of the intellectual in public life, who has no time

---

[54] The analogies are reinforced by the echoes of the language of protreptic, which occurs in both scenes (compare 278c, 282d, with 307a and c).

for philosophy but bases his claims to special status on other skills.[55] Isocrates certainly belongs in this category, and it seems plausible to see a number of passages in his works as directed against Socrates and his followers, a fact which may have fuelled Plato's hostility. But whereas Isocrates polemicises (e.g. in his *Against the sophists*), Plato dramatises. As a result, the dialogue presents not only a contrast between methods of going about philosophy (and education), but also a contrast between assessments of those methods. Whereas Socrates is willing to speak with the sophists and try to learn from them (though detaching himself from their activities with his pervasive irony), the anonymous figure despises both the sophists' eristic and Socrates' efforts to find common ground with them. Crito is baffled by the conflict between his own conviction that philosophy is worthwhile and the other man's firm condemnation of it; the reader too has to make up his own mind, having witnessed the discussion and taken stock of the assessments.

The last section of the dialogue is in some ways the most straightforward. Irony and obliqueness give way to Crito's frank statement of his anxiety for his sons' proper education: is philosophy the right thing for them? Socrates here speaks plainly, and reminds Crito that there are good and bad teachers of every art, the important thing being to judge the value of the subject taught, not the merits of the teachers. 'Test it nobly and well, and if it seems to you to be a bad thing, then turn every man away from it; but if it seems to you as I myself think it to be, then pursue it in confidence and practise this art of which we speak, both yourself and your sons' (307c, the closing words of the dialogue). All men need philosophy – not just Crito's boys, but their father as well. Here again Socrates takes a protreptic role. Just as he has never spoken out explicitly in condemnation of the sophistic brothers, so he does not grandly offer himself as the man for the job, but leaves Crito to work towards his own conclusions (though Crito has also made clear that it is when he is in Socrates' presence that he feels most strongly the urgency of seeing to his sons' education).[56] The conclusion of the dialogue, like the rest, offers an ethical model: Socrates is a guide and an influence for Crito, not a figure of authority. The outcome remains in doubt.

[55] For the anonymous figure as a type see Wilamowitz, *Platon* i. 304, ii. 165-7, Friedlaender i. 194, Chance 199ff. A subordinate point may be that to bring Isocrates explicitly into the dialogue would create complications because of his appropriation of the term 'philosophy', in a different sense, for his own teachings (p. 251). On the other side, we should note the verbal jingle at 304e4-5: this does look like an allusion to the style of Isocrates, pupil of Gorgias. Cf. Norden, *Kunstprosa* i. 115-19. For a parallel to this ambiguous relationship between individual and type see Hor. *Epistles* ii. 2. 91-107, where the unnamed elegist resembles Propertius. See C.O. Brink's commentary on these lines.

[56] On the importance of Socrates' presence cf. *Smp.* 215c-6a, *Theages* 130d-e, etc.

The *Protagoras*

Whereas in the *Euthydemus* Socrates had encountered a pair of sophists acclaimed by their immediate hearers but dismissed as non-entities by the listening Crito and the figure of 'Isocrates', in the *Protagoras* he faces one of the most distinguished of the profession, and the level of debate is on an altogether different plane. It is also probably relevant to recall that later in his career Plato took Protagoras seriously enough to devote a great part of the *Theaetetus* to the examination and exploration of his most famous saying, 'man is the measure of all things' (fr. B1, *Tht.* 151-2, 161-79). It would be surprising, then, to find the sophist a straw man in the dialogue which bears his name. Moreover, it is longer and more intricate than the *Euthydemus*, and the issues raised do not depend on trivial wordplay or on obviously outrageous false reasoning.

Nevertheless, the dialogue has often puzzled and irritated students of Plato. Much of the uncertainty felt by readers concerns the unity of the work – not that anyone has ever seriously doubted that it is indeed entirely a work of Plato, and wholly characteristic of him, but there is undoubtedly room for discomfort on the level of conceptual unity: what is the *subject* of the *Protagoras*, what is it about? The main discussion seems to wander bewilderingly, some would say perversely – from the nature of Athenian democracy through the evolution of human society, the unity of the virtues, the analysis of a poem by Simonides, back to the virtues and particularly courage, and then on to a refutation of the popular view of the power of pleasure and emotion over reason. At the end, very little seems to have been settled. And what is the relevance of the introductory scenes, first between Socrates and an unnamed friend, then between Hippocrates and Socrates at the beginning of the narrated part of the dialogue, before the two of them arrive in the presence of the great sophist?

The other great area of uncertainty concerns the last phase of the dialogue, in which Socrates extraordinarily defends the principle often called the hedonic calculus: that is, he supports the argument that pleasure is the good, and that the function of the intellect is to weigh pleasures judiciously against one another, practising an art of measurement which will enable one to weigh up present discomfort or pain against future pleasure or profit. By this means, Socrates makes an ingenious transition to a doctrine found elsewhere in Plato, that no man does wrong voluntarily;

it is only that he has made the mistake of miscalculating the relative amounts of pleasure which he will derive from an action. Could Socrates ever really have held this 'hedonic' view of virtue, and if he did not, what does Plato mean by presenting it with Socrates as its advocate?

It may be helpful to approach these major issues indirectly, by looking at the dialogue as it unfolds, and considering, as in previous chapters, some of the more dramatic and verbal aspects of the *Protagoras*, including characterisation, interaction, tone, rhetorical style, and so forth.[1] One aspect which clearly merits attention is the personality of Protagoras himself, and in particular how conscious he is of his own status and prestige (not least in rivalry or opposition to the other sophists present). The narrative comments by Socrates regularly lay emphasis on his *amour-propre* and his reluctance to be proven wrong (333d, 335ab, 338e, 348b, cl, 360e). As elsewhere in Plato, the personalities and the reactions of the participants are relevant to the way the discussion progresses. We need only consider the way in which Socrates comments on Protagoras' unease and displeasure, and how often the inconclusiveness of an argument is due to Socrates' tactful restraint, to his willingness to refrain from driving his point home all the way (332a, 335a9ff., cf. 362a). There is a contrast to be drawn here with the *Gorgias*: in the latter dialogue, and especially in the conflict between Socrates and Callicles, there is no concession or compromise: antagonism is open, tempers are hot, and the polarisation of views is taken much further. Arguments and propositions in Plato cannot readily be divorced from their original setting: we must beware of ignoring the occasion, the personalities and the method, which lead a speaker to adopt a certain position.

We begin in a sense at the end. When the dialogue opens, Socrates has just come from the discussion which the dialogue contains, and narrates the whole episode to an eager friend. Part of the point of this 'framing' device seems to be to show that Socrates is not an out-and-out opponent and critic of Protagoras. We do not find him, now that he can speak openly, pouring forth an indictment of Protagoras' ignorance, the futility of his method and aims, or the like. Rather, Socrates is still admiring and interested by all that he has heard and seen of him– not without qualification, however, as is suggested by the following exchange:

> 'And the stranger really seemed so beautiful to you that he appeared more beautiful than the son of Cleinias?'
> 'How can what is supremely wise not be more beautiful, my dear fellow?'
> 'Then you've just been in the company of someone *wise*, Socrates?'
> 'The wisest of all those of our time, if Protagoras seems to you to be the wisest.'
> 'What's that you say? Protagoras is in town?' (309cd)

---

[1] Cf. in general Stokes, *Plato's Socratic Conversations* 32-3; also M. Schofield, in *Socratic Questions*, ed. B. Gower and M.C. Stokes (London 1992) 122-36, whose approach overlaps with mine at a number of points.

Protagoras' name has so far been held back: this is the moment at which Socrates reveals the name of his recent interlocutor, and we note at once the eloquent 'if' clause, which throws the evaluation open for discussion. It would be wrong, however, to assume that Socrates is being ironic in a crude way here (as if he were inwardly scoffing 'Ha ha, wisest of men today – *that's* a laugh!'), and that is certainly not how the unnamed friend interprets him. Rather, the friend is as excited as Hippocrates was when he learned that Protagoras was back in Athens. Socratic irony is richer and more complex than 'the customary conception of irony – i.e. the mere exchange of a yes for a no';[2] it does not convey outright dismissal or condemnation of its object, but raises doubts and questions, as Socrates is already doing here. So too his equation of beauty and supreme wisdom is put in the form of a question, one which his companion fails to meet. Instead he rushes on with a counter-question. Socrates' challenging equation of beauty and wisdom, which would be true only in an ideal world, is left hanging; as a result, Alcibiades' beauty and Protagoras' wisdom are both called into question.

Socrates' qualifications, then, are lost on the anonymous friend; he is another Hippocrates. Recent critics have already noted (and we can see this again in the *Gorgias* and the *Phaedrus*) how often Socrates' conversation and personality are ineffective, having no lasting influence on the listener.[3] In the present case, we never return to the frame and therefore do not know how the friend reacted at the end of Socrates' narration (contrast the *Euthydemus*); nor are we given any hint of Hippocrates' verdict on the dazzling exchange which he has actually witnessed. The reader is left to evaluate Protagoras' performance for himself.

It is notable that the opening dialogue concludes by stressing the enjoyment that the friend and Socrates will derive from the latter's reca-pitulation: the point is emphasised by the repeated use of the word *charis* (310a). This may be unimportant, but a possible explanation might be that it points forward to a recurrent theme of the dialogue as a whole: pleasure in the discussion and in Protagoras' rhetorical prowess; good and bad pleasures in the view of the common man and in the more sophisticated and paradoxical version of this view put forward by Socrates. It is common for Plato to introduce a dialogue with key words or word-play or half-serious ideas which gain in significance and seriousness as the argument advances. A very obvious example is the opening of the *Hippias Major* where Socrates remarks 'Ah, it's Hippias, the handsome and the wise' (281a): as in the initial exchange of the *Protagoras*, a question mark is raised about whether these two attrib-utes do go together, either generally or in the case of Hippias.[4]

Socrates' narrative begins at night, with himself sound asleep in bed,

---

[2] Friedlaender ii. 13. See further Vlastos, *Socrates* ch. 1, and my remarks in ch. 3, pp. 77-8 above.

[3] See ch. 6 below, on the *Gorgias*.

[4] Cf. P. Woodruff (ed.), *Plato, Hippias Major* 36.

when the youthful Hippocrates arrives to bring him the news of Protagoras'
arrival in Athens (which in fact is not news to Socrates), and to demand
that Socrates escort and introduce him to the great man. Humour and
implicit comment are at once apparent: Hippocrates heard about the
sophist's presence in Athens late the previous night, and nearly came
dashing to wake Socrates up at once; Socrates has known about it for longer,
and appears unmoved and disinclined to lose sleep over it. What emerges
clearly from the episode is Hippocrates' naiveté. He is scatter-brained in
general (310c 'I meant to tell you I was going after my slave, but something
else put it out of my mind …'). He is all-a-twitter (cf. 310d3) with the great
news, desperate to gain access to Protagoras, but he admits he has never
seen the man or heard him speak. In terms of Socratic dialectic this is a
warning sign: in the *Gorgias* Polus sarcastically asks Socrates if he would
say that Archelaus of Macedon, or the great king of Persia himself, was a
happy man or an unhappy one, and Socrates replies: 'How do I know? I've
never met the man' (470d). Similarly though more indirectly here, Socrates
is kindly but sceptical. The earliness of the hour gives him an excuse to chat
with the boy before they actually go to Callias' house, where Protagoras is
residing, and in that conversation Socrates takes the opportunity to sow some
doubts. These doubts focus on the central questions which Hippocrates in his
enthusiasm has failed to consider: just what kind of a man is Protagoras, what
is his teaching, what does he do to people? Similarly in the *Gorgias*, when
Gorgias agrees to converse with Socrates, the first question the latter puts to
him is deceptively simple, yet momentous: 'who he is' (447d).[5] The questions
of who Protagoras is and what he teaches remain important throughout the
dialogue and arguably unanswered by the end, because Protagoras does not
have a single, adequate, clearly formulated answer to give.

The exchange with Hippocrates also serves to show the contradiction in
his position, a contradiction which reflects the ambiguity of Athenian
attitudes to the sophists,[6] exemplified by Callicles' sneer in the *Gorgias*
(520a), Anytus' abuse in *Meno* (91c, 92ab), and of course the views of
conservative thinkers as echoed in Aristophanes' *Clouds*. Hippocrates is
eager to meet and learn from Protagoras, but when it is put to him that he
will become a sophist himself by so doing, he blushes violently ('for',
remarks Socrates, 'it was just then becoming light enough for his face to be
seen').[7] He admits that he would feel ashamed to turn himself into a sophist,

[5] Cf. Sophocles, *Oedipus the King* 413-15, Euripides, *Bacchae* 506f. All three passages play
on the apparent simplicity of the cornerstone precept of Greek morality, 'know thyself'.

[6] Cf. Guthrie iii. 32-4, 38ff., Kerferd, *The Sophistic Movement* 20-2, and ch. 4 i above.

[7] Friedlaender i. 159-60 suggests that this is a form of symbolism ('came the dawn …'). Plato's
young men blush often, and sometimes this is significant: see esp. *Charm.* 158c, *Lysis* 204bc
(to be contrasted with 213d, where the reaction indicates excited involvement with the
argument rather than simply pretty decorum). Quite differently, see *Rep.* i. 350d 'then I saw
something I had never before seen – Thrasymachus blushing …' (with embarrassment and
vexation now that his argument has been overturned). For a wide-ranging study of the literary
use of this phenomenon, see C. Ricks, *Keats and Embarrassment* (Oxford 1974).

and Socrates kindly suggests that perhaps what Protagoras teaches is not so much the trade of sophistry (a *techne* of such a kind that if you learn it you become such an artisan yourself – like someone learning carpentry); rather, perhaps it is something that you learn for the sake of general culture, as befits a private citizen and a free man (312b).[8] This calms Hippocrates' embarrassment for the time being; but it is also intended to suggest how vague and suspect Protagoras' claims are, when his aspiring pupils cannot be sure what benefit they will derive from their instruction. At this point Socrates takes the opportunity to give the young man a lecture on the danger of willingly and ignorantly submitting his soul, the most precious part of himself, to an unknown foreigner. How much more careful he would be with his body!

The naive and uncritical attitude of Hippocrates *is* blameworthy, and it would be wrong to label Socrates as priggish, or to suspect that he is carping at Protagoras out of jealousy or rivalry. His aim is rather to awaken Hippocrates to a properly questioning attitude: instead of accepting Protagoras' reputation on trust, he should consider for himself the significance of what he is doing, and judge whether Protagoras is the right teacher to choose (cf. *Laches* 180a-b). In other words, Socrates wants him to cut loose from Athenian fashion and think for himself.

One other passage in this introductory scene merits comment, again for its moral implications rather than for any strictly philosophic content. 'When we arrived at the forecourt', explains Socrates, 'we paused and went on talking about something which had occurred to us on the walk. In order that this might not be left unfinished, and so that we could go in having settled the topic, we stood there in the forecourt and talked on until we came to an agreement' (314c). This finds a close parallel in the *Symposium*, when Socrates gets left behind on the way to Agathon's, and falls into a trance, meditating on an unspecified subject until he has reached a conclusion (174d sq.): this practice, according to Aristodemus, is habitual with him (175b). In the *Gorgias*, Socrates more than once expresses anxiety that they should not leave the argument unfinished, or 'without a head', as he puts it in one speech (505c10f.).[9] These passages seem to contrast Socratic determination with the more relaxed or uncommitted discussion techniques of lesser men. In the *Protagoras*, the decision to conclude the subject which had occurred to them *en route* should be contrasted with the rambling inconclusiveness of the subsequent debate, and with the notable tendency for the discussion to change course or method. Once Socrates and Hippocrates are inside Callias' house, variety and disorder become the keynotes, and there is a disturbing readiness to give up half way. Socrates

---

[8] Compare Callicles' attitude to philosophy: all very well as part of one's education, certainly desirable for a free youth; but there should be no thought of pursuing it further in adult life (*Grg.* 485; cf. Dodds's commentary, pp. 272f., 275).

[9] Cf. Dodds ad loc., for parallels in four other dialogues.

expresses his anxiety about this more than once (347c1-2, 348a9); at the end of the dialogue he is still eager to go on further (361d), but it is Protagoras who is reluctant and would prefer to postpone (ibid. e, 'till another time').[10] Perhaps the setting too may contribute to this contrast. Socrates and Hippocrates conclude their discussion privately, just the two of them (the ideal dialectical situation) in the open air; contrast the indoor confusion and hubbub, the division of the company into a series of cliques within, as described in the entertaining passage which follows (314e-16a). Callias obviously regards it as a major coup to have as many sophists as possible under his roof (he is supposed to have spent more on sophists than all their other Athenian patrons put together; see *Apol.* 20a). As one would expect, however, the result is absurd and chaotic, with each of the sophists holding forth independently; it is, as Socrates remarks, impossible to hear them indoors in competition with one another, especially Prodicus with his booming, resonant tones (316a1). This initial impression is borne out by subsequent developments, for the sophists compete with one another in other, less likeable ways, to score points off one another or to show off: we see this at 317c and 318e, and again later, in the way in which Prodicus and Hippias back up Socrates against Protagoras. Socrates in his account of the scene quotes a number of phrases from book xi of the *Odyssey*, comparing the three great sophists with the three great sinners in Hades (315bc). This is jesting and relatively casual, it is clearly not portentous denunciation; nevertheless, it plays a part in guiding our expectations of and our reactions to what follows.

Once Socrates has presented Hippocrates to Protagoras, and offered him the choice of private or public discussion (a choice which may prove significant for the progress of their discussion), Protagoras gives a general account of himself, explaining that he is not, like some, ashamed of professing the sophistic art, nor does he regard dissimulation as the best defence against those who might disapprove of him. In the course of this speech he names various poets and priest-like figures, sages of the past, who have concealed their sophistic status behind other labels – *poiesis*, *mousike* and so on. He himself, however, is quite ready to proclaim himself a sophist and a teacher of *arete* (loosely, 'excellence') (316c-17c). The declaration is interesting, as it aligns the sophists, and especially Protagoras himself, with the poets. The analogies are clear: the poets too were considered figures of wisdom and authority; they were often seen as teachers of virtue and morality (Protagoras alludes to this use of poetry in schools later, 325e); and of course they gave pleasure through their performances. The sophists inherit something of their role as entertainers and myth-makers, as Protagoras' speech will show. The reference to Simonides also paves the way for the critique of his poetry later in the dialogue: at that stage, however, the sophist acts as critic, and therefore assumes a

[10] Cf. ch. 3, p. 82 above, on the end of the *Euthyphro*.

position of superiority to the poet (though ambiguously, since his own criticism is then challenged). Protagoras' speech thus sets his profession in a distinguished tradition, but also suggests that some of the uncertainties concerning the interpretation and evaluation of poetry may be applicable to his own teachings. In what sense poets *do* teach their audiences and listeners has never been a simple question, and was the subject of active debate in the late fifth and early fourth centuries,[11] by Plato and others; as will emerge, some of the same doubts can be raised about Protagoras' exposition of his principles.[12]

We turn now to the major speech of Protagoras, in which he most fully and most convincingly presents his view of human society and of his own role as a teacher.[13] I take it for granted that, although no doubt it bears *some* relation to the historical views of Protagoras, this speech is not straightforwardly lifted out of a published work of Protagoras, whether his *On the original state of things* or another,[14] any more than the speech ascribed to 'Lysias' in the *Phaedrus* is likely to be an authentic speech by Lysias. Even if these were authentic and un-Platonic, however, the important question would still be how they play their part in the Platonic context: in the present case, what place does the speech of Protagoras have in the dialogue *Protagoras*?

The speech is an epideixis or 'display-piece', of a particularly sophistic kind. It is very clearly signposted and structured: as in Gorgias' *Helen* or Agathon's speech in the *Symposium*, there are clear divisions when a new argument is introduced (323c, 324c5-d1, 326e 6f., and the final summary, 328c). In the preliminaries, Protagoras offered his audience a choice between a *muthos* ('story') and a *logos* ('argument'); when his audience leaves the choice to him, he says that perhaps a *muthos* will be 'more pleasurable' (320c). Again we observe the stress on pleasure as the aim, typical of epideictic rhetoric. Furthermore, the choice is not, as is customary with Socrates, a choice of the necessary and appropriate form, but seems arbitrary: either will do, the form is not integral to the message. And indeed Protagoras demonstrates his versatility (or his lack of consistency?) by switching to a *logos* or more 'modern' style of argument for the second part of his speech (324d).

The speech is intended to show why the Athenians are right to suppose that political intelligence is common to all citizens and also why, despite

---

[11] Cf. Aristophanes, *Frogs* 1030-6, etc.; M. Pohlenz, *Kleine Schriften* ii (Hildesheim 1965) 436ff.; H. Flashar, *Der Dialog Ion als Zeugnis platonischer Philosophie* (Berlin 1958); D.A. Russell, *Criticism in Antiquity* (London 1986) ch. 6.

[12] On this passage and its resonances later in the dialogue see also M. Trapp, in *Homo Viator, Essays ... J.C. Bramble* (Bristol 1987) 41-8.

[13] There are innumerable discussions both of the speech *per se* and of its value as a source for the genuine views of Protagoras. G.B. Kerferd's analysis in *JHS* 73 (1953) 42-5 retains its value; see also Guthrie iii. 63-7, and esp. C.C.W. Taylor's commentary.

[14] For discussion see Taylor's commentary 77-9.

that, it is teachable, and Protagoras is a suitable and indeed an exceptional teacher. That is, it combines social analysis and self-advertisement. The other point Socrates makes, that notable fathers appear unable to teach their sons to excel in politics, is essentially subsidiary, and perhaps does not deserve the space it receives in Protagoras' reply, for, once we grant that such skill is teachable, it is not surprising that (as Protagoras says at the end of his speech) some should be abler teachers than others. The speech needs to be seen as a response to a particular set of questions in a specific place: had Protagoras not been in democratic Athens but (say) in an oligarchy, he might have had an easier case to present, for he could have discounted the proposition that all men possess some degree of political *arete* and declared Athenian practice misguided.[15] As things are, he is presented with a challenging task and responds firmly and persuasively. Besides the main thrust of his argument, he enlivens his case with interesting and enlightening observations or 'talking points', for instance in his comments on the rationale of punishment (324ab). The impression we receive is of a clever, quick-witted and articulate man.

There are nevertheless problems in Protagoras' speech, not all of which can be treated here. Four of these difficulties can be isolated, and should suffice to establish that his case is flawed: some of the points made here will help to show how the rest of the dialogue builds on the effect of this major exposition by Protagoras.

(1) It is still far from clear at the end of the speech what exactly Protagoras is prepared to teach his pupils. This was only partially settled at 318e-9a:

> 'With me he will learn about only that which he has come to learn. The instruction I give is sound judgement concerning his own household affairs, how he may best manage his home, and concerning the affairs of the city, how he may be the most able [or "powerful"] in word and deed on public affairs.'
>
> 'Am I following what you say?' I said. 'For you seem to be talking about the art of politics (*ten politiken technen*), and to be promising to make men good citizens.'
>
> 'This is exactly the profession which I do profess, Socrates', he answered.

Even in this short exchange there are plenty of ambiguities: is Protagoras teaching good judgement, social skills, articulacy as a speaker, or 'how to win friends and influence people'? How important is the 'household' side, which drops out of the discussion? Is Socrates in his reply using 'good' in

---

[15] For such flexibility in different places cf. Pindar, *Pythian* i. 75ff; Hippias in Pl. *Hipp. Maj.* 285-6; G. Anderson, *Philostratus* (London, Sydney and New Hampshire 1986) 34f. (cf. St Paul, 'all things to all men'). This argument would be weakened if Protagoras is correctly seen as a champion of *democratic* theory first and foremost: see e.g. J.S. Morrison, *CQ* 35 (1941) 1-16, and C. Farrar, *The Origins of Democratic Theory* (Cambridge 1988); but the evidence for this seems somewhat limited. For the extreme sceptical position, which probably goes too far, see P. Stadter, *ICS* 16 (1991) 111-24.

the moral sense, and was that presupposed by what Protagoras said, or is it a significant new point?

If one pursues this question of definition through Protagoras' speech, one finds little further clarification. *Arete* continues to be the chief term used, with or without the adjective 'political', but in the myth Zeus makes Hermes pass on *aidos* ('shame') and *dike* ('justice') to men, and elsewhere *dikaiosyne* and *sophrosyne* ('justice' and 'self-restraint') are used as components of political *arete* (323a), *adikia* ('injustice') and *asebeia* ('impiety') as its opposites. In 324d the emphasis looks to be on success in politics (which might, but need not, entail moral authority), whereas in 325d and 326a-c the stress is on moral awareness. In 328b, in his final summing-up, Protagoras declares his talent to be 'in helping someone to become a fine gentleman' (*kalon kai agathon*), a phrase which notoriously suggests social and worldly status rather than moral preeminence.[16] In short, even the single term *arete* seems to mask confusion between at least three ideas: success (or the capacity for it) in a career, political skill and judgement, and moral awareness as required in public life. These ambiguities are crucial to Protagoras' whole self-presentation as a teacher.[17]

(2) The division of the speech into *muthos* and *logos*, already mentioned, raises problems. Although Protagoras, in the sophistic manner, modernises the mythology (introducing, for instance, the conception of primitive man as brutish, and referring to theories about natural competition and conflict between the species at 320e-1b), there remains a considerable mythical residue, and it seems hard, if not impossible, to carry out a full-scale rationalisation, converting the myth into a coherent non-mythical explanation.[18] For example, in the myth Zeus confers the precious gifts of shame and justice on mankind, and so ensures man's survival; but what does this mean in non-mythical terms? Where does man's innate potential for morality come from if not from a supernatural source? And if it was not supernaturally derived, what was the point of telling the mythical version in the first place? Or again, in the *logos* section, the reference to the laws, which guide the citizens to walk in the paths of virtue, as 'discoveries of the good and ancient lawgivers' (326d6) leaves unexplained where the lawgivers derived their 'goodness' from, and how they made their special discoveries.

(3) Protagoras' central argument in reply to Socrates' doubts is that everyone who is not merely bestial has some basic level of *arete*, for otherwise he could not exist in a community; nevertheless, he can still claim

---

[16] Cf. de Ste Croix, *Origins of the Peloponnesian War* (1972) 371-6.

[17] My colleague Lindsay Judson suggests to me that Protagoras' general philosophic position may be relevant here: can he, as a relativist, make such distinctions? In other words, what is excellence and success for one person may not be so for another. Cf. Vlastos' introd. to the *Protagoras* (1956) esp. liv.

[18] M.J. Edwards, *SO* 67 (1992) 89-102 makes valuable observations on the defects of Protagoras' myth, and on the contrast with myths narrated by Socrates elsewhere in Plato.

to be a teacher of *arete* at the more advanced level (he also asserts that work in schools, study of the poets and obedience to the laws instil it). But this argument seems again to slide between different conceptions of *arete* and very different degrees of it. Which is Protagoras offering to teach, moral and social virtue or political success, and do they have any necessary connection with each other?And does not his argument reduce the concept of political *arete* as possessed by an average Athenian to an unacceptably low level? Can such minimal adherence to social norms really be called *arete* in anything like the same sense as the preeminence in society which Protagoras claims to teach?[19] Further, even if we accept Protagoras' argument, he has reduced his own contribution. He never claims that he can teach *arete* where nothing was there before, only that he can enhance the basic potential which people already have. (In the *Gorgias* too, it turns out that the sophist's concern with the fundamentals of moral instruction is casual compared with his concern with worldly success.)

(4) Socrates' initial question concerned the democratic assumption of the Athenians that any citizen, not just the experts or the elders, was able and entitled to contribute to political debate in the assembly. Protagoras in his reply refers more than once to the beliefs of the Athenians and of men in general (322d, 323a, c, 324c, etc.). The form of argument is perhaps questionable, for it is not being asked simply what the Athenians can be shown to believe, but whether those beliefs are justified. But more significantly, Protagoras here accepts the argument from majority or universal opinion: the Athenians and everybody think or do X, therefore X must be at least probably right.[20] This suits his argument here, but is not his regular position: we may contrast a number of passages later which suggest a more dismissive and contemptuous attitude to 'the masses' (esp. 352e3-4, 353a 7-8).[21]

Socrates' reaction to Protagoras' speech provides another nest of significant words and imagery:

> After Protagoras had made a display of such length and of such matter, he concluded his speech. And I sat spellbound, and continued to gaze at him for quite some time expecting that he had more to say and eager to hear it. (328d)

There is a strong implication here that in Socrates' view something crucial has been left out – namely, a definition and coherent conception of *arete*, its sources and function, and the way in which it is to be taught. The word 'spellbound' picks up the initial description of Protagoras as he was when Socrates and Hippocrates arrived, enchanting his audience with his voice in the manner of Orpheus (315a: there, the same verb, *keleo*). Plato

---

[19] Cf. Taylor's comm., 82-3.
[20] On the history of the 'consensus-argument' see A.S. Pease's note on Cicero, *On divination* i. 1, D. Obbink, *OSAP* 10 (1992) 193-231.
[21] Compare further *Tht.* 162de, esp. e2; 172ab.

regularly uses such language to describe both the poetic prose of the sophists[22] and their concentration on the emotions, the pleasure-loving elements in their audiences. In both these respects, he has precedent and justification in Gorgias' *Helen*, with its memorable account of the psychology of *logos*.[23] Socrates' reaction to Protagoras, then, acknowledges the sophist's persuasive skill, but at the same time insinuates the suspicion that stylistic and intellectual glamour may mask basic confusion.

It is from this point on that dialectic, and the ethical and methodological issues which it involves, become more important in the dialogue and affect its formal structure. The rest of the dialogue considers the 'one little thing' which Socrates still wants to know after Protagoras' epideixis: namely, how are the virtues related? Are justice and moderation and holiness and courage and wisdom all parts of *arete*, and does a man who has one of them have them all? But this enquiry into the unity or diversity of virtue does not proceed straightforwardly. The following table shows the structure of the rest of the *Protagoras*:

328d-334c:	Following up Protagoras' speech, Socrates questions Protagoras about the virtues
334c-338e:	Methodological interlude. Long speeches vs. short, etc. Protagoras undertakes the task of questioning.
338e-347a:	Discussion of a poem by Simonides. Protagoras criticises it as inconsistent, Socrates defends and interprets it.
347a-348c:	Second methodological interlude, after which Socrates takes up the questioning.
348c-360e:	Resumption of enquiry into the relationship of the virtues, with special reference to courage.
360e-362a:	Socrates sums up; conclusion of the discussion at Protagoras' request; farewells.

Even this bare summary should make clear that formally the *Protagoras* is not simple. After the performance by Protagoras, we turn more to question-and-answer, Socrates' preferred form of discussion; first Socrates is the questioner, then Protagoras, then Socrates again. The main subject, the unity of virtue, is abandoned at 334c because of Protagoras' growing dissatisfaction, and not resumed until much later. In between, Socrates, Protagoras and others argue about the merits of long versus short speeches and other aspects of the discussion, and we have a chance to hear something from the other persons present in Callias' house. Eventually Protagoras agrees to continue in brief question-answer style, but only with himself as the questioner and on his chosen subject, poetry: the discussion of

---

[22] Cf. *Mnx.* 234c-5c, *Smp.* 198; J. de Romilly, *Magic and Rhetoric in Ancient Greece* (Cambridge Mass. 1975) chs. 1-2.

[23] For text and translation see MacDowell's 1981 edition, with bibliography.

Simonides' poem comes in, it seems, *à propos* of nothing, though the fact that its subject is *arete* gives it a certain specious connection with the rest of the dialogue. It is clear from Socrates' comments at the end of that section that the whole poetic discussion has been, for him, a pointless digression. Only after a further exchange on methods, and after the rest of the company have brought considerable pressure to bear on him, is Protagoras prepared to submit once again to Socrates' interrogation on the supposed main subject; and he makes some difficulties even at that stage.

In short, the structure of the dialogue is intimately related to the characters of those conducting it, and itself serves to illustrate, no less than the *Laches* or the *Euthydemus*, right and wrong ways of approaching a discussion of ethical or any other themes.[24] Like other eloquent or professional speakers in Plato (Callicles in the *Gorgias*, Thrasymachus in book i of the *Republic*), Protagoras has done his set piece, his epideictic combination of myth and argument, and wants to rest on his laurels, or at least remain in control of the discussion; he is much less happy to become the questioned party, the victim of Socratic elenchus, and to have the inconsistencies or oddities in his position exposed to view – above all in front of his fellow sophists, before whom he was previously happy to show off (cf. Socrates' plausible diagnosis at 317cd 'I suspected that he wanted to put on a performance in front of Prodicus and Hippias and show off because we had turned up to admire him ...'). This also takes us some way towards understanding the problem of the dialogue's unity; for it seems that a unified, unilinear development of the argument is not possible precisely because of the differing views and attitudes of those involved in it. Protagoras' concern for his own prestige prevents him from being as committed to the pursuit of truth as Socrates: he naturally does not want to admit that his original epideixis was radically flawed. Moreover, the dissension among the sophists and others present about how the argument should be conducted illustrates the difficulty of conducting a discussion at all with so many vociferous and self-important personalities present; as already mentioned, we can contrast this with the more intimate, one-to-one conversation between Socrates and Hippocrates while en route.

It would be tedious to consider all these episodes in detail. I shall comment selectively first on the methodological interlude at 334c-8e, and then on the discussion of Simonides, before proceeding to the most puzzling part of the dialogue, the final section on the 'hedonic calculus'.

The exchange on *makrologia* ('lengthy speech') and its opposite, *brachylogia* ('conciseness'), develops a theme found elsewhere in Plato, the concern for the appropriate form.[25] Protagoras wishes to continue with long and elaborate speeches, whereas Socrates complains that he cannot keep up

[24] On the ethics of dialectic see above, ch. 3 pp. 76, 79, and G.E.R. Lloyd, *Magic, Reason and Experience* (1979) 100-1.
[25] Cf. *Grg.* 449c and Dodds's n.

with these and would prefer short dialectical question and answer. The dispute is prompted by a long and largely irrelevant display-speech by Protagoras, which in its style and its generalisations has very much the flavour of a sophistic set-piece (334a-c; cf. e.g. *Grg.* 448c4ff., p. 145 below). When Socrates protests, Protagoras resists, and in the end makes clear his irritation by a refusal to compromise:

> 'Socrates, I have entered into contests of words with many people, and if I had regularly done as you ask, and conversed in the way my opponent told me to converse, then I would never have looked superior to anybody, nor would the name of Protagoras ever have been known among the Greeks.'
> I realised that he was displeased with the answers he had given previously, and that he would not be prepared willingly to converse under my questioning ... (335a)

Later, Socrates himself contrasts Protagoras' conception of how to conduct a discussion with his own: 'I thought that a conversation with people talking to one another was something distinct from a public oration' (336b). Protagoras' references to competition and superiority betray his anxiety to come out on top, just as his preference for elaborate set-speeches belongs more to the combative sphere of oratory than to dialectic.

Again, this is a significant contrast, not a polemical clash of methods or an instance of Socrates simply being difficult. Extended sophistic mono-logue is subject, for Plato, to both formal and moral objections: exposition in this style may lead to fine rhetoric, but it is harder to follow and allows the introduction of more questionable statements, doubtful transitions and grandiose periphrases (cf. *Rep.* i. 348ab). The comparison with political oratory, like the comparison later of poets and books, is hardly complimen-tary. Moreover, the sophists claimed to be able to give answers of any length, a point Socrates makes at *Protagoras* 334e (another instance of their carefree versatility);[26] hence Socrates' request is scarcely unfair, even though we can understand Protagoras' feeling that this restriction cramps his style.

The subsequent discussion, as Socrates gets up and threatens to leave, offers a chance for the others present to put their views and illustrate their styles. Callias' amiable intervention needs little comment: he simply tries to smooth things over, and emphasises how much they are all enjoying themselves – pleasure prevailing over instruction again. After him Alci-biades, supposedly the beloved of Socrates, intervenes in support of his friend (336b7). This is the first time Alcibiades has spoken, though he was mentioned as present at 316a (the scene-setting), as well as in the initial exchange between Socrates and his friend. His participation here and at 347b presumably represents the help Socrates there says he had from

---

[26] Cf. Prodicus ap. *Phdr.* 267b; ch. 3, n. 22 above.

Alcibiades. In both cases he directs the conversation back on to more Socratic dialectical lines. His is not a flawless diagnosis of the situation, for he too uses competitive language (esp. 336c2-4), rightly as regards Protagoras, wrongly concerning Socrates. He hints at Socratic method (336c6-7), and he sees through Socrates' pretence of forgetfulness, describing it as 'play' (336d3). The insight of Alcibiades into Socrates' character may not be so profound as in the *Symposium*, but as in that dialogue he sees more clearly than the others present.

Prodicus, with his subtle, indeed excessively recondite distinctions, is one of the most interesting of those intervening (337a-c). His speech, like many in Plato, is misguided without being merely absurd. His distinctions and his argument are inadequate to the occasion, but they suggest truths. Thus his advocacy of common participation but not equality (337a3) is picked up by Socrates in his speech a little later; his warning against eristic, that is, quarrelsome and point-scoring argument, resembles many remarks by Socrates elsewhere, for eristic can be regarded as a kind of parody or travesty of dialectic. That is what we find in the *Euthydemus*, in an argument where mutual goodwill and consistency are absent. Prodicus' final comment is also striking, in part because it takes up the 'pleasure/hedonism' theme.

> ... we who listen would derive in that way the most enjoyment, though not pleasure (*euphrainoimetha* as opposed to *hedoimestha*): for one derives enjoyment from learning or the exercise of purely mental intelligence, whereas one gains pleasure from eating or some other pleasant, purely physical experience. (337c, tr. Taylor, with slight modifications)

The fact that Prodicus' speech in no way corresponds with normal Greek usage points to the artificiality of any such antithesis; and indeed the speakers, including Socrates, are constantly speaking of their pleasure in the actual discussion (e.g. 335c6, 361d6), and enjoyment of epideictic literature in particular is often compared with or metaphorically expressed as enjoyment of food, drink and sensual experiences.[27] Prodicus' speech thus suggests the ways in which the discussion falls short of the ideal.[28]

Hippias' speech is much more elaborate and stylistically rich: ornate metaphors such as 'the council-chamber of wisdom' (337d6), inversions, pleonasm (e3, 338a8f.), and the unnecessarily florid sailing-metaphor in his finale. Again there is stress on the pleasure they are deriving from the discussion, and complacency too, in the self-satisfied description of the company as 'the wisest of the Greeks'. Hippias finally proposes 'that we select an umpire, chairman or president to see that each of you keeps to

---

[27] Cf. J.C. Bramble, *Persius and the Programmatic Satire* (Cambridge 1974) 50-1, and E. Gowers, *The Loaded Table* (Oxford 1992) 41-6.

[28] On Socrates' attitude to Prodicus see further M. Burnyeat in Benson (ed.), *Essays on the Philosophy of Socrates* 56 and 63 n.9.

the moderate length' – whatever that is! This bland advocacy of 'civilised' concessions to one another is accepted by everyone except Socrates, who replies with some sharpness that this will not serve, as there are differences among them in intelligence and judgement; but he preserves the decencies by putting the comment in the form of a compliment to Protagoras (338c 2-3). The difficulties of debate are suggested by the recurring question of how much the participants are *like* each other: Prodicus says that they should hear the speakers impartially but not equally; Hippias calls the rest his kinsmen or fellow-citizens in nature: 'by nature like is kin to like' (337d1). Socrates instead draws attention to the differences among them: 'the fact is that it would be impossible for you to choose anyone wiser than Protagoras, and if you choose someone inferior, pretending he is better, that would be to insult him ...' (338c). This objection is not merely putting Hippias down; it is necessary to remind the company of the crucial differences in the two approaches to debate, rather than having the whole procedure lumped together in a jumble of non-rules such as Callias and Hippias proposed. Socrates concludes that they should not have one single arbitrator, but all act as arbitrators together (338e2). This is a paradox, and perhaps a worrying one: certainly the combined judgement of the audience reaches no very substantial decisions or conclusions in what follows. But Socrates' suggestion differs from Hippias' in that it quietly points to a truth – that all the audience *do* need to judge the speeches, and the subject matter, for themselves, not just applauding unthinkingly or relying on the authority of a supposedly wiser judge. (A somewhat similar point is made more clearly at *Rep.* i. 348ab: the company must be their own advocates and judges alike.)

The discussion resumes with Protagoras asking the questions; he now embarks on the famous discussion of Simonides' poem on the good man.[29] The way he introduces this (338e) is revealing: 'Socrates, I consider that the supreme part of a man's education is cleverness about words' (*not* actions or realities). Thus the sophist shifts his ground on to territory in which Socrates has little interest, as emerges from his comments at the end of this section (347c-8a; cf. *Symp.* 176e).[30] Protagoras' change of tack is evidently due to his finding Socrates' style of discussion too uncomfortable. In this section he uses the poem as a kind of scapegoat: he has become the questioner, but instead of tackling Socrates directly, he pokes fun at and picks holes in the poem, which cannot answer back. This probably does

---

[29] See D.L. Page, *PMG* no. 542; transl. e.g. in R. Lattimore, *Greek Lyrics* (2nd edn., Chicago 1960) 55f.; discussed by C.M. Bowra, *Greek Lyric Poetry* (2nd edn., Oxford 1961) 326-36, and often since; see P.E. Easterling, *PCPS* 20 (1974) 41f.; M. Dickie, *HSCP* 82 (1978) 21-35.

[30] It is particularly notable that this form of discussion shifts the enquiry from a direct encounter with moral questions to an investigation of what a poet thought about moral questions – an investigation difficult in itself and unprofitable if we do not accept Simonides as an 'authority'. Cf. the critique of the poets as 'teachers' elsewhere in Plato: see e.g. Dodds on *Grg.* 501d1 sqq., pp. 320-2.

reflect sophistic methods of literary criticism accurately enough. We know that Protagoras and Prodicus were both much concerned with correct use of words, and that Protagoras found fault with the first line of the *Iliad*.[31] Here, however, the mode of criticism is given a sharper ethical point. Protagoras is not only sidetracking the main discussion, but trying to avoid being shown up further. Instead he accuses the poet of self-contradiction, the very fault which Socratic elenchus is designed to expose and resolve,[32] and the fault of which he himself seems guilty. As in other dialogues, when the sophists show the way, Socrates is prepared to follow; but characteristically he handles the task of interpretation differently.[33] Instead of denigrating the poet, he defends his consistency, and indeed makes Simonides into a somewhat Socratic figure, one who recognises human limitations and imperfections, and who shows a pessimistic but realistic humanity. One particularly clear analogy betwen poet and philosopher is 344b, where Socrates maintains that the whole of Simonides' poem is an actual elenchus of the saying by Pittacus from which the poem takes its starting point. In other words, according to Socrates, Simonides has been playing a Socratic role, conducting an interrogation of Pittacus, testing his wisdom and exposing his pretensions.[34] Similarly at 345de, Socrates glosses Simonides by attributing to him the characteristically Socratic principle that no one does wrong willingly. The point is not that Socrates' reading of Simonides is any more plausible than others' – indeed, it involves some clearly far-fetched moves. Rather, the difference lies in the kind of lesson he draws from it; whereas Protagoras patronises the poem, Socrates asks what truths it can be seen to contain or imply.[35]

Protagoras' unease and reluctance to continue once the discussion of the poem is over are very clear: at 348b he keeps a resentful silence, and refuses to be frank about his feelings (348b1-2, 5). Alcibiades again steps in, and shames him into rejoining the conversation (348c1ff.); then, after another digression on method by Socrates, in which he assures Protagoras that he is not trying to cheat or bamboozle him, the last phase of the main discussion, on the unity of the virtues, begins.

The argument which ensues must be seen in context, as an argument between Socrates and Protagoras, in the light of all that Protagoras has

---

[31] Prt. 80 A 29 D-K (= Arist. *Poetics* 19. 1456b15ff.), etc.; C. J. Classen, in *Sophistik* ed. Classen (Darmstadt 1976) 215-47 (= *PACA* 2 (1959) 33-49); R. Pfeiffer, *Hist. of Classical Scholarship* i (1968) 32-9. The approach is parodied in Aristophanes' *Clouds* (658ff., 681ff., 847ff.), and especially in the *Frogs* (1119-97); cf. C. Segal, *RhM* 113 (1970) 158-62. For a different side to Protagoras' criticism see A30 D-K = P.Oxy ii. 221 (tr. Guthrie iii. 269).

[32] See e.g. *Grg.* 482b-c, with Dodds's n.; Lloyd, *Magic* ... 101 nn. 233-4.

[33] For other discussions of the interlude on poetry see (from very different angles) D. Frede, *Rev. of Metaphysics* 39 (1986) 729-53, and R. Scodel, *Anc. Philos.* 6 (1986) 27-37.

[34] For a different view see M. Trapp, art. cit. (n. 12), who sees Protagoras as a modern Simonides, Socrates as the heir of Pittacus and the Seven Wise Men whose laconic profundities he praises at 343a-b.

[35] Cf. his attitude to myth at *Phdr.* 229c-30a (quoted below, pp. 173-4).

claimed or attempted to prove earlier. The central issue of the dialogue, as should now be clear, is what is the nature of the *arete* which Protagoras claims to teach? With that question come others: what is the relation between *arete* and knowledge or wisdom? How useful or powerful are they? How effectively can the wisdom (*sophia*) imparted by the sophist govern human nature, and the natural drives of pleasure and pain which, in popular opinion, are constantly dominating and overruling the power of reason?

An important strand in the argument is this theme of popular opinion, the views of the masses. As before with the poet Simonides, so here the general public are brought in as alternative subjects of interrogation, this time by Socrates. In part this is tactful, to ease Protagoras' position; in part it may enable him to achieve some sleight-of-hand with the argument.[36] But the main point is surely to call into question Protagoras' relation to popular ideas: is he above them and operating on a different plane entirely, or is he in fact accepting or entangled in them? Here as elsewhere in the dialogue Protagoras' attitude is ambiguous.[37] At times he claims to be above paying attention to popular ideas (333c1-3, 352c8-d3, 352e, 353a7-8), but earlier he appealed to universal opinion as evidence in support of his own case (323a5ff., etc.; see above, p. 130), and in 351b-d, after some wavering, he assents to the popular distinction between good and bad pleasures, being clearly uneasy about agreeing that pleasure in itself is always a good thing. By 359c he is again trying to appeal to – or shuffle off the question on to – 'what people say', but there Socrates insists on bringing the question home to 'you' (ibid. d1).[38]

Socrates has cited the view of the masses–that knowledge is a weak thing, unstable and easily overcome by pleasure. Naturally, as an exponent and salesman of knowledge, Protagoras resists this view emphatically (352c9-d3: 'it would be particularly disgraceful for me of all men not to maintain that wisdom and knowledge are the most powerful forces at work among men'). But he and the rest of the sophists are much readier to accept the modification of this view which Socrates, by a devious route, presents to them (358a): that men are overcome by pleasure because of ignorance: they simply have not appreciated correctly the relative pleasure-potential of immediate and more remote experiences, and so have made a mistaken choice. But although this meets with their approval, as giving a more

[36] It is hard to deny that Socrates, here and often, makes some illegitimate moves in his arguments, and it may be assumed that Plato was aware of this. But to point to the fallacies is not the end of the enquiry, but the beginning. See also Vlastos, *Socrates* ch. 5 (esp. 135-9 on the discussion of poetry in this dialogue). Some of the points he makes are persuasive, some passages might be read differently, but he poses important questions.

[37] Cf. Stokes (n. 1) 353f.

[38] Cf. the important passage in *Rep.* vi. 493a: ' Every one of those individual teachers, whom the people call sophists ... in fact teaches nothing but the beliefs of the people expressed by themselves in their assemblies. That is what he claims as his wisdom.'

prestigious role to knowledge, it is a degraded conception of knowledge, and leaves pleasure as the primary principle, the *telos* according to which choices are to be made – surely the most disturbing feature of the popular attitude.[39]

Socrates' use of the hedonic calculus should not, then, be over-literally interpreted as expressing his own view of the relationship of knowledge and pleasure.[40] Rather, this argument is employed to demonstrate once again the inadequacy of Protagoras' thinking about his profession and its intellectual basis. Protagoras is entrammelled at least partly because he lacks a critical or dialectical approach; that is, he does not analyse the terms which he and the populace use in common, for instance 'pleasure', 'knowledge' and above all *arete*. This deficiency is surely rooted in his relativism: whereas Socrates seeks absolute standards, Protagoras is on record as saying that one thing is sweet (or pleasurable, or good) for one individual, but the reverse for another (esp. B1). Throughout the *Protagoras* we lack a coherent rationale of what Protagoras teaches and how he goes about it. For Socrates, the core of his teaching is lacking; for a true morality will guide the choice of pleasures by reference to a *telos* beyond them, and it is that which Socrates is constantly asking for in his dialogue with the people Examples include 354b7f. '... or can you point to any result looking to which you call them good, apart from pleasures and pains? They would say no, I think'; 354d2, 8, 354e8ff., 'But even now you are free to withdraw, if you can give any other account of the good than pleasure, or of evil than pain. Or are you willing to say that good is a pleasant life without pains?', 355d6, 8: all of these passages leave the question open, but disturbingly imply the inadequacy of the answers being provided.[41]

Like the interpretation which Socrates offered of Simonides' poem, the 'hedonic calculus' theory does not answer every question raised so far, but only brings a particular phase of the discussion to a conclusion which neither Socrates nor Protagoras will find satisfactory. The speech of Socrates after he has brought the sophist to agree that courage is a form of

---

[39] I find attractive the view of M. Nussbaum, *Fragility of Goodness* (1986), esp. 106-17, that Socrates would endorse the need for an art of measurement with which to discriminate between different objectives, whereas he is not committing himself to the view that pleasure should be the quantifiable criterion measured by that art. Her additional suggestion (112, 450), that hedonism is in any case ethically respectable strikes me as historically ill-founded for ancient Greek culture in general and Plato in particular: see further Dover, *GPM* 124-6, 208-9.

[40] Cf. Stokes (n. 1), 358-70, and esp. D.J. Zeyl, *Phronesis* 25 (1980) 250-69; also R. Weiss, *Anc. Phil.* 10 (1990) 17-39. For the view that Socrates does accept this doctrine see esp. Taylor's comm., 208-10, and J.C.B. Gosling and C.C.W. Taylor, *The Greeks on Pleasure* (Oxford 1982) 45-68. (A variant is the position that Socrates or Plato or both really did go through a *phase* of believing this principle (cf. e.g. Dodds, *Grg.* p. 21; but see Guthrie iv. 231). If so, however, would the conception be restricted to one dialogue?)

[41] Vlastos's 1956 introduction, p. xl n. 50, seems to me to underplay the significance of these qualifications.

knowledge makes clear that Socrates is not content with this 'victory'; instead he emphasises the paradoxical aspects of their conclusion, and insists that the quest for a definition of *arete* has only begun (360e7-8). In this speech he picks up the mythical aspect of Protagoras' long epideixis earlier, perhaps as a compliment to Protagoras, but perhaps also as an indication of the kind of personal lessons or morals that can be drawn from the myths:

> For my part, Protagoras, when I see all our discussion here in such total disarray, I feel completely committed to getting it cleared up, and I would be ready for us to go through these matters thoroughly, and get to the stage of defining *arete*, and to reconsider whether it is teachable or not ... in that story of yours I preferred Prometheus to Epimetheus; taking him as model and taking forethought for my whole life I am busy considering all these subjects, and if you were prepared to join me, as I said back at the start, I would have the greatest pleasure in sharing the enquiry with you. (361cd)

Protagoras' reaction, however, is courteous but uncooperative. After complimenting Socrates on his zeal and his ability, he prefers to put off further discussion for another time. 'It is time now to turn to some other subject' (e6). Socrates' acceptance is equally polite, but we cannot help feeling that Protagoras has failed a test: he lacks the determination, and the concern for truth, which would enable him to ignore his own failures or false moves and concentrate on the enquiry at hand.[42] Socrates, on finding that Protagoras is not willing to pursue that enquiry, immediately remembers an engagement elsewhere and departs (362a2, cf. 335c5-6).

It will by now be clear that the *Protagoras* is well-named; that is, it could not simply be entitled (e.g.) *On political arete*.[43] The part played by Protagoras, with all his eloquence, prestige, vanity, dignity and tetchiness, is essential to the form and development of the argument; hardly less significant is the constant presence of an audience of patron, trade rivals and potential disciples. It is relevant too that Socrates is presented as still a relatively young man at the time of the conversation (esp. 317c – Protagoras is old enough to be the father of any of those present; 361e). Hence Socrates and Protagoras are not conversing as equals. Personalities influence the discussion; Protagoras at various points avoids interrogation, Socrates makes concessions or tactfully plays along. The consequence of all this is that the dialogue cannot be an ideal model of dialectical argument on *arete*; it is contaminated by other motives and methods, affected by the agonistic

---

[42] Dr A. Barker suggests that Protagoras here lacks *courage* to continue, and that this is apt in view of the special attention which the dialogue has paid so far to the place of courage in relation to the other parts of virtue. For a comparable, though more explicit, form of self-reference see *Grg.* 505c (see p. 156), and compare further *Laches* 194a, *Charm.* 162c3-4, *Phaedo* 73a, 92c5, *Rep.* i. 336e, iv. 442e1, *Phdr.* 277b4.

[43] Diog. Laert. iii. 59 mentions an alternative title 'The sophists' – more acceptable?

tendencies of the sophists, soured by *philonikia* ('desire to win')[44] on at least one side, and set against a background of spectators who want a good show rather than a philosophically correct solution. It is not surprising that the dialogue then ends inconclusively. I have suggested that the one conversation which we do not overhear, the private dialogue of Socrates and Hippocrates as they approach the house of Callias, provides an ideal model of the purely dialectical discussion, which does reach a resolution. Thereafter, we might say, things simply go downhill. When he begins to survey the scene within Callias' house, Socrates compares the vision of the three sophists with the vision Odysseus has of the great sinners in Hades; he thus evokes a descent into the underworld (315bd). Just so, the philosopher of the *Republic*, having seen the truth of the world above, must return to the cave to attempt to teach his former fellow-captives (vii. 514a-20d); and just as they resist his efforts to enlighten them, so the company in Callias' house in the end fall short of the dialectical ideals which Socrates offers and endeavours (imperfectly?) to exemplify in his own performance.

---

[44] On this important term see ch. 6 below, p. 148.

6

The *Gorgias*[1]

Introductory

The *Protagoras* and the *Gorgias* have much in common. Both present Socrates testing himself against one of the great sophists of the day, in the household of a wealthy Athenian host, and amid an audience of enthusiastic and involved listeners. Both, in the course of the discussion, also admit considerable methodological comment, indirectly shedding light on Socrates' dialectical method. Two major differences will help us see why Plato composed not one but two dialogues on this pattern. First, the *Gorgias* is in dramatic form throughout, with no narrator, whereas in the *Protagoras*, after only a page of introductory dialogue, Socrates takes over as narrator of the episode, and we never return to the 'framing' scene with the anonymous friend. The result is that in the *Protagoras* we see events unfolding very much through Socrates' eyes: it is his words which set the scene, comment on moods and reactions, and control our perspective; whereas in the *Gorgias* we are spectators without a guide, lacking an editorial authority to prompt our judgements. It is less natural for us to align ourselves with Socrates: he is not present as a friendly narrator inviting our sympathy. Secondly, the *Gorgias* differs from the *Protagoras* still more conspicuously in the limited role assigned to the figure after whom it is named. Whereas Protagoras was preeminent throughout his dialogue, Gorgias converses with Socrates only for a short time, before yielding the stage to the other antagonists, first Polus and then Callicles. After Polus' intervention at 461b Gorgias has little to say in the dialogue, beyond genial comment and efforts to keep the peace when the debate becomes more heated or threatens to break down (463d-4a, 497b, 506ab). The dialogue,

---

[1] The *Gorgias* is splendidly edited with wide-ranging commentary by E.R. Dodds (Oxford 1959), perhaps the finest modern commentary on any work of Plato. The Clarendon Plato translation by T. Irwin is also admirable, and although primarily philosophical, it does not neglect literary aspects. See further C.H. Kahn, 'Drama and dialectic in Plato's *Gorgias*', *Oxford Studies in Ancient Philosophy* 1 (1983) 75ff. For a powerful critique of Plato's whole approach to rhetoric in this dialogue see B. Vickers, *In Defence of Rhetoric* (Oxford 1988) ch. 2. What survives of Gorgias' own works is accessible in Diels-Kranz no. 82, and in Radermacher, *Artium scriptores* 42-66. The remnants are translated in R.K. Sprague, *The Older Sophists* 30-67, and the most important of these, the *Helen*, is edited with tr. and notes by D.M. MacDowell (Bristol 1982). For a recent discussion of the *Helen* with bibliography, see J.I. Porter, *CA* 12 (1993) 267-99.

then, falls into three sections of increasing length: Socrates and Gorgias; Socrates and Polus; Socrates and Callicles.

This unusual and (in view of the title) unexpected structure deserves more detailed attention. Why does Socrates face three successive interlocutors? Essentially, the sequence is of cumulative force: each exchange is longer and more intense, even vehement; each new speaker goes further, draws Socrates out more and challenges him more profoundly; in each case Socrates reacts by rising to greater rhetorical heights, by the end adopting a form of discourse more solemn and intense than is usual for him. Further, the Gorgias-Polus-Callicles sequence reflects three generations in the history of rhetoric and its influence on society and on politics. Gorgias is the grand old man of the subject – distinguished, urbane, a little vain and patronising. His way of life is long established and he is satisfied with it, even to the point of complacency: 'a well-meaning but somewhat muddle-headed old gentleman'.[2] Polus is a younger man (e.g. 461c, 463e), also a professional teacher of rhetoric[3] and from Sicily, like Gorgias and his predecessors. Polus is not himself a politician, but his horizons are broader than those of Gorgias, and he has more of an eye on the main chance: while he does not himself aim at political power or tyranny, he admires and envies those who do, and whereas Gorgias condemns those who use rhetoric for unjust ends, we may suspect that Polus thinks they are justified provided they can get away with it, though his moral position appears somewhat muddled, and he is by no means entirely free from conventional disapproval towards wrongdoers.[4] Callicles is the only Athenian of the three, and also a young man, probably younger than Polus; he is a wealthy, snobbish aristocrat about to embark upon a political career at Athens (484c sqq., 515a, and much of what follows). He is also a great deal more clear-headed about what he wants from the art of rhetoric, which he sees as an instrument of his devouring ambition. He is a long way further than Polus down the road of deliberate immorality, as his speeches from 480 onwards make very clear.

This outline already shows that the dialogue, like the *Republic*, moves from a smaller question (the definition of rhetoric and of Gorgias' profession) to much larger issues – indeed, at a relatively late stage Socrates defines their subject as 'who is the happy man and who is not' (472c8 sq.), and again as 'how a man should live' (500c3). Characteristically, the apparently academic discussion becomes of vital importance to all those involved, and especially to Socrates and Callicles. The whole dialogue, but especially their exchange, presents a clash of two ways of life, that of the philosopher and that of the orator-politician. Both Socrates and Callicles are passionately committed to defending their choice and to convincing the

---

[2] Dodds, p. 9.
[3] Fragments in Radermacher 112-14.
[4] Cf. C. Kahn, *OSAP* 1 (1983) 95.

other of the justice of their case. But the description of the dialogue's subject as 'philosophy versus rhetoric' or 'philosophy versus politics' is over-simple. Socrates is not retreating into a world of theory and shutting out all the hubbub of the assembly: rather, he is deeply engaged with and concerned for the Athenian state,[5] and even presents himself as the one true practitioner of the political art (521d). Nor is his rejection of rhetoric straightforward, for he himself waxes rhetorical within the dialogue (a fact on which he comments more than once; we can assume that Plato meant it to be noticed). Indeed, on another level, that of method, the dialogue subtly compares the techniques, the aims and the effects of rhetoric with those of Socratic dialectic: the methods and morality of argument are even more prominent in the *Gorgias* than in the *Protagoras* (where this subject was chiefly dealt with in the two interludes at 334c-8e and 347a-8c). Finally, because of the power and eloquence with which Socrates maintains his position and his way of life, it may be tempting to consider the dialogue as chiefly a defence or vindication of Socrates (like Xenophon's *Memorabilia*). Again, however, we shall find reason to qualify such a formula. An important feature of the *Gorgias* is Socrates' ultimate failure to convince: dialectic and Socratic rhetoric combined still do not persuade Callicles, and the end of the work is overshadowed by the prospect of Socrates' eventual trial and death. Here again, the dramatic form of the dialogue is of the greatest importance: we witness the conflict between the main speakers as it happens, without the distancing or reassuring effect of a frame-dialogue; and we end not with a placid 'summing-up' or polite conclusion, but with a powerful appeal by Socrates which remains unanswered.

Gorgias

As in other dialogues, the opening exchanges carry considerable significance. Callicles speaks first:

> Call.: This is the way they say you should arrive for a war and a battle, Socrates!
> Soc.: You mean we've really arrived just too late for a feast?
> Call.: Yes, and a very elegant feast too. Gorgias has just been displaying to us (*epedeixato*) a rich store of good things.

After a series of apologies and explanations, Callicles says that Gorgias will be prepared to give them another *epideixis* at his house, where the sophist is staying, to which Socrates replies 'Excellent news, Callicles; but would he be prepared to converse with us?' (447b9-c1). There is a paradoxical point here: most people would expect a sophistic epideixis to be an elaborate showpiece, a tour-de-force, both greatly preferable to and much more

---

[5] Though see Vlastos, *Socratic Studies* ch. 4 and Epilogue, for a powerful argument that Socrates' concern for Athens did not go far enough. Cf. ch. 2, p. 60.

difficult and demanding than conducting an everyday conversation. The contrast between Gorgianic rhetoric and Socratic dialectic is introduced right away. Socrates is not interested in the display oratory which Gorgias has been demonstrating: he wants to talk with him, not to be talked at.

Moreover, the proverbial reference to war and battle as opposed to feasting and food is a casual means of introducing imagery which becomes important later in the dialogue, in particular when Socrates compares the flattery and sweetness of sophistic rhetoric with the confectioner appealing to children's sweet teeth, though careless of their health. By contrast, dialectic, or conversation as Socrates practises it, is a less comfortable, less indulgent form of communication, which aims at exposing contradictions, rather than glossing over them. It can become aggressive and even openly hostile as rhetoric of Gorgias' display-type would rarely do; but that hostility is not of the vicious and destructive type which we meet in Greek forensic oratory. Even in his most violently critical speeches Socrates is trying to help his interlocutors see their error and turn to the right path. In short, the contrast drawn at the start is subsequently acted out in the dialogue itself: from a comfortable and superficial, even self-indulgent, performance by Gorgias, we pass to serious debate and conflict, in which real issues are at stake. As will emerge, this contrast of forms of discussion has its analogy on the level of politics, in the role of rhetoric in public life. The great political leaders (some of them pupils of the sophists) are the confectioners, pampering and flattering their all-too-willing audience (518b sqq., etc.); whereas in Socrates' view a true politician will fight against the unhealthy desires of his people (e.g. 521a).

Callicles goes on to describe Gorgias' recent performance: he has challenged those present to ask him questions, and answered everyone (447c). Socrates is delighted by this offer, and using Chaerephon as his intermediary, proceeds to ask Gorgias his question, namely 'who he is' (447d1). This deceptively simple enquiry, which nevertheless leaves Chaerephon momentarily thrown, encapsulates Socrates' practice of going straight to the nub of things: the form of the question embraces both Gorgias' moral character and his profession. The enquiry also introduces the ubiquitous Socratic craft-analogy: what *techne* is it of which Gorgias is a master? What is he and what exactly does he teach? As we shortly learn, Socrates has considerable doubts as to whether rhetoric is in fact entitled to be called a *techne* at all.

At 448a we have a pleasant illustration of Gorgias' complacency ('no one has asked me anything new for years'); the enquiry is then briefly deflected by the obstreperous Polus, who butts in and takes over the task of answering – ostensibly because Gorgias is tired, but really because Polus is keen to get his oar in. Here and later, Polus, is presented as something of a boor, or as Socrates punningly calls him, 'a colt' (463e). His intervention is chiefly characterised by its Gorgianic jingling style, which is hard to reproduce in English:

Chaerephon, many are the arts devised among men, invented skilfully from skills: for skill makes life proceed according to art, while lack of skill makes it proceed according to chance. Of each of these arts different men partake in different ways of different examples, and the best of men have a share in the best of arts; one of these is Gorgias here, and he partakes of the most excellent of the arts. (448c)

As Socrates delicately points out, Polus has given an encomium of rhetoric, not a definition (448e), and the term encomium evokes all the falsity and exaggeration of that genre of oratory (cf. esp. *Smp.* 198). It is perhaps also noteworthy that encomiastic praise of rhetoric is itself a motif of sophistic literature, most relevantly the praise of *logos* in Gorgias' own *Helen*, and this is also exemplified in Gorgias' own speech later (452d5ff.).[6] Polus' reaction to Socrates' question is to launch straight into part of the orator's stock-in-trade; but his elegant style is intended to impress rather than to instruct. He is short on dialectical ability, as is immediately shown by his failure to see what is wrong with his answer.

In this initial exchange one further instance of significant imagery requires comment: the medical metaphor, which runs all the way through the *Gorgias* and is indeed basic to Plato's thinking about both philosophy and statesmanship.[7] Already at 447b1, when it emerges that Socrates and Chaerephon have arrived late, Chaerephon promises to put things right, or rather to 'heal' or 'remedy' this lateness. This seems a relatively light-weight use of the image: Chaerephon is simply a well-meaning and placatory individual. More interesting is the reference to Gorgias' brother Herodicus, who was a doctor. Chaerephon clarifies Socrates' enquiry about the nature of Gorgias' *techne* through the analogy of the doctor (Socrates had used the example of a shoemaker, but Chaerephon tactfully upgrades this). Medicine can be seen as analogous to the rhetorical art, and Gorgias himself had used this comparison in the *Helen*:

The effect of speech upon the condition of the soul is comparable with the power of drugs over the nature of bodies. For just as different drugs dispel different secretions from the body, and some bring an end to disease and others to life, so also in the case of speeches, some distress, others delight, some cause fear, others make the hearer bold, and some drug or bewitch the soul with a kind of evil persuasion. (14)

Within the dialogue, Gorgias himself takes up this comparison when he describes the benefits rhetoric can bring; for he and his brother have often visited patients in need of treatment, and when Herodicus was unable to convince them to accept this treatment, Gorgias brought his powers of

---

[6] See further Isoc. 3. 6ff., 4. 48ff. (with G. Mathieu's n. in the Budé edn.), 15. 253ff.; Cicero, *de oratore* i. 31-2; Radermacher, *Artium scriptores* p. 167.

[7] Cf. H. Ruess, *Gesundheit, Krankheit, Arzt bei Plato* (diss. Tübingen 1957); V. Pöschl, *Bibliographie zur antiken Bildersprache* (Heidelberg 1964) 521.

persuasion to bear. Yet the imagery which Gorgias had used in the *Helen* helps us see what disturbed Plato about this procedure: for Gorgias there describes persuasion as a kind of drug (or poison – *pharmaka*), which brings about irrational and sometimes dangerous changes in the patient. This means that the doctor may be helpless to counter the false persuasion of the rhetorician, whom the ignorant may find more plausible and enticing. For Plato, medicine should be a reasoning process based on knowledge, which the patient either shares or consciously accepts and respects. In Plato the medical image is transferred to the philosopher, the surgeon of the soul: whereas the sophist feeds and sweetens, Socrates cuts deep and treats the sickness. Similarly, the true statesman must treat the illness of the body politic (464b sqq., developed at 518e-19a, 521d sq.). In 478a, Polus admits that the sick in body should be taken to the doctors, and by analogy that the unjust and intemperate soul should be brought to trial and made to suffer the just punishment. In the final section of the dialogue, the myth of the afterlife, the analogy reaches its grimmest phase: the morally sick soul is pictured as scarred and deformed, no longer able to conceal its corruption behind a fair facade, when it comes to the seat of judgement in Hades.

Another theme is that of the proper mode of discussion, and specifically the issue of short speeches versus long, *brachulogia* and *makrologia*. Socrates asks Gorgias to reply briefly and not to launch on set speeches (cf. *Prt.* 334c-5a). Gorgias replies that there are some questions which require longer answers, but accedes for the time being (449bc). Socrates, of course, very much prefers short, dialectical exchanges, and so opts for *brachulogia* though somewhat modifying its meaning: whereas the sophists meant rhetorical brevity, he means dialectic. Here, as often, formal and practical considerations shade into ethical. In Plato and others, long rhetorical orations are suspect because they cannot be questioned and tested at every stage. The listener is carried away and forgets the details. Socrates' qualms about *makrologia* also find some justification in the fact that several of the sophists seem to think that they have done their bit when they have delivered a striking and powerful set speech: indeed, in book i of the *Republic*, Thrasymachus, having delivered his forceful *rhesis* on the rights of the stronger, prepares to leave, and has to be held back by the others (344d). Similarly in the *Gorgias* both Gorgias and Callicles are happier declaring their principles in the grand manner, or summing them up with appropriate superlatives (451d7-8, 452d5-8), than actually submitting to point-by-point questioning about them from Socrates.

Some critics have been puzzled by the way that Socrates, after questioning the value of *makrologia*, should then be prepared to employ it himself later in the dialogue; and Socrates himself draws attention to this anomaly (465e, 519e). This is, however, a common feature of the dialogues, in that Socrates adapts his approach and even his form of discourse to the interlocutor (as in the *Symposium* with the encomium); his dialectic is *ad hominem*. This is not a straightforward process, however. It is important that Socrates does offer his long speeches for questioning and investigation, rather than expecting them to be swallowed whole; that is, his speeches are Socratic in spirit, whether or not the historical Socrates ever did play the role of an orator. But although Socrates adapts rhetorical techniques to a moral end, he is also, arguably, 'infected' by Callicles' oratory and responds with his own, which must still be vulnerable to some of the general criticisms of long speeches as a form of argument. Callicles accuses him of 'playing the mob-orator' and of 'showing off like a boy' (482c); the aggressiveness of these complaints is unattractive, but it may be true that, because of his environment and the character of his opponents, Socrates is forced to lapse from the ideal philosophic mode.

Gorgias' first substantial speech constitutes a defence of rhetoric (456-7c). He takes up a position which corresponds with what we know of his general attitude: in the *Meno* (95c) it is mentioned that Gorgias never claimed to teach *arete*, as some of the sophists did, but laughed at such claims: 'he thinks his job is to make people clever speakers.' His defence is comparable to that of Aristotle in the preface to the *Rhetoric*: certainly, rhetoric can be misused, but it is not in itself a bad thing, it is neutral. Everything can be misused and can do harm, with the exception of virtue itself. Hence it is unfair to blame the teachers. But this defence, and the example of good use of rhetoric which he gives (how he has persuaded his brother's patients to be treated) do not sit well with the grander and more sinister account of rhetoric which he gave in an earlier answer to Socrates, at 452d:

> (Rhetoric is) in truth the greatest good, and the source of freedom to men for themselves, and at the same time of power for each man over other men in his state.[8]

This passage introduces the political aspect of rhetoric, as an instrument to gain power in a state; moreover, it implies the possibility of absolute power, even tyranny, for the man who has the skill to win it, slavery for those who do not possess that skill. Gorgias has clearly no interest in power for himself; but tyranny is an enticing ideal for Polus and a potential goal for Callicles.

Moreover, the language which Gorgias uses in his defence serves to undermine his case, or at least to introduce disturbing elements. In 456c8 he admits that rhetoric is a part of the competitive art, and develops the idea with a series of analogies with the boxer, the wrestler and the man who fights in full armour, a man who has acquired these techniques in order to become superior to both friends and enemies. Such a man, Gorgias

---

[8] Cf. *Philebus* 58a = Grg. A 26 D-K, 'I often heard Gorgias say that the art of rhetoric differs from all other arts. Under its influence all things are willingly but not forcibly made slaves.'

explains, *ought* not to go and beat up his friends or his parents (we remember the behaviour of Pheidippides in the *Clouds*); but he fails to show any reason why he *would* abstain from doing so.[9] And although he begins by insisting that rhetoric has done work of value in the medical sphere, he admits in 457b what has been implicit in the argument from the start, that an orator could discredit the good doctor and take away his prestige as easily as he could enhance it. If justice and injustice are so closely tied up with rhetoric (are indeed its subject matter, 454b7), then Gorgias and his like cannot, in Socrates' view, afford to maintain a lofty moral neutrality: they must take the ethical questions raised by rhetoric more seriously, and they must include an ethical dimension in their teaching.[10] This is what Gorgias is subsequently led to admit that he will do (460a), but it is obvious that he says this only out of embarrassment or shame (see below). He clearly has no idea how he would go about such instruction. Even the way he puts his answer suggests his vagueness: 'well, Socrates, I suppose if he happens not to know [sc. about justice and injustice], he will learn this from me too' (by a process of passive absorption?).

Socrates' reaction to Gorgias (457c4ff.) takes an unusual form. He does not reply straight away, but embarks on a cautious and apologetic speech on method, on his view of how a dialectical discussion should be conducted, and what they should try to avoid (cf. already 453b-c). Here Socrates is anticipating what will in fact happen in the *Gorgias* itself: disagreement, bad temper, abuse and angry departure. He foresees that they are liable to get into deep waters, and that although the discussion is pleasant and urbane at the moment, to continue runs the risk of giving offence. *Philonikia*, fondness of winning (457d4), is a significant word in this kind of context (cf. *Prt.* 360e, *Phd.* 91a). In Socratic discussion one should not be fighting for victory, but for the revelation of truth; this sharply distinguishes dialectic from rhetoric in the law-courts, where of course victory is all-important and truth takes very much a second place to pragmatic distortions. Later in the dialogue, Callicles accuses Socrates himself of being 'keen on victory' but Socrates denies this: 'I do not ask these questions out of desire to win, but out of my genuine desire to know' (515b). At 505e, moreover, he twists the language of victory, saying 'I think we all ought to be eager to win the contest of knowing what is the truth and what is false'. As Socrates says in this passage, he is not attacking Gorgias as a person, or trying to humiliate him, but only to make the argument clear. He himself would as gladly be the refuted one as the refuter, and will be grateful if another can rid him of his false beliefs. Although, as we have seen (ch. 3, pp. 79-82), many of his interlocutors grow impatient with these declara-

---

[9] On the prevalence of such anxieties at this period, see Ostwald, *From Popular Sovereignty* 229-38.

[10] Cf. S. Halliwell's essay in I. Worthington (ed.), *Persuasion* (London 1994), 224-34, esp. 228-30.

tions, we do Socrates an injustice if we follow his critics and accusers in believing this to be a false pose or a cheap argumentative trick: this is what Socrates lived and died for (*Apol.* 38a).

At this stage the discussion is in suspense. Socrates allows Gorgias a chance to let it drop if he is not prepared to go the whole way in investigating the question raised. In fact, Gorgias' response is rather lukewarm. He suggests that, as he has already given quite a long *epideixis* to the company, they may be rather tired; perhaps he and Socrates should not keep them from other business. It seems probable that Gorgias is here trying to ease out of the discussion without losing face. But instead there is an enthusiastic reaction insisting that the discussion be continued (though Gorgias is shortly displaced by Polus). Callicles' contribution at this point is interesting: he remarks that he has been involved in many discussions and has never enjoyed himself as much as now (458d). Even if you go on for a full day, he says, you will give me pleasure. Obviously, this is in contrast with his indignation when he later becomes the object of Socrates' interrogation; also, the two verbs he uses seem deliberately chosen to highlight the pleasure-element in his reaction, and so perhaps prefigure his hedonism as expounded later.

Polus

We have already anticipated the further development of the argument with Gorgias, in which the sophist is driven to admit that he will include in his curriculum some moral instruction if necessary. It is at this stage that the second part of the dialogue begins, as Polus interrupts with characteristic rudeness at 461b. This second phase continues to 481b, where Callicles more politely intervenes with a murmured expression of incredulity addressed to Chaerephon. These two interventions are deliberately parallel. In particular, Polus accuses Gorgias of being ashamed, or too squeamish, to say that he wouldn't teach morality if his pupil were ignorant; and later Callicles observes that Polus has fallen into just the same trap. By admitting that doing wrong is more shameful than suffering it, Polus has, as Callicles sees it, become entangled in conventional values and has not said what he really thinks (482c sq.).

This conception of shame as a failure in frankness, a reluctance to reveal one's true beliefs, is another important motif in the dialogue. It is introduced casually at an early stage, at 455c8, when Socrates asks Gorgias to be frank and explain just what his profession is, because there may be many people present who are interested in becoming his pupils, but who would feel ashamed to ask him outright. In 460a1, pursuing the same enquiry, he begs Gorgias to 'unveil' the power of rhetoric, to take off the concealment. That image too is developed elsewhere in Plato; it is one reason that several dialogues are set at the palaestra and gymnasium, for the undressing and revelation, with all the delightful homosexual byplay and banter which accompany it, are mirrored on the metaphorical and moral level. In Socratic discourse, the interlocutor needs to come out and show himself, to bare his soul.[11] In all such passages, the aim is to get behind the vague or uninvolved response, to get the speaker to state his real beliefs, to bring out his most cherished opinions and have them tested. This is part of what is hinted at in Socrates' initial question early in the dialogue: who is Gorgias? In the myth at the end, too, the souls are to be judged naked, striped of conceal-ment and pretensions. Socrates, then, is on the side of Polus and Callicles to this extent, that he wants and insists on frankness, and does not want others to cover up their real opinions with a safe, orthodox morality. He criticises his interlocutors more than once for this kind of false shame (489a2, 494cd), and he praises Callicles not least for his candour (487 passim, esp. d; cf. 492d). In short, he wants his friends to have the courage of their convictions, to speak out as Callicles and Thrasymachus do; but that should not be the end of the matter. Their beliefs still have to be tested: are they compatible, do they stand up to scrutiny, or does the dialectical process expose contradictions in their beliefs which they did not suspect? Hence the impassioned rhetoric of a Callicles, with its poetic embroidery and its vivid image of the superman, is all very fine, but does not settle anything; what matters is how this concept, and Callicles himself, will stand up under dialectical questioning.

Returning to the Polus episode, we shall consider, however briefly, some of the stylistic and formal aspects which distinguish him as a character and as an interlocutor; for in the *Gorgias*, as elsewhere in Plato, the way that people react or respond to Socratic conversation mirrors their approach and attitude to life. Polus, as we have already seen, is something of a boor or a 'colt', as Socrates charitably puts it. He is entirely inexperienced in dialec-tic, and this is reflected in the rather wandering sequence of the conversa-tion while he plays the part of the questioner. He tends towards speechifying, a natural consequence of his profession; his questions are often not real enquiries but rhetorical exclamations and expressions of incredulity. He is slow to take points – in particular, it takes him quite a while to understand Socrates' distinction between 'what men want' and 'what seems best to them', i.e. what they *think* they want, explained gradually at 466d sqq.; even after that, he seems to forget it or fail to make use of it at 469c7. He does not listen closely, and misremembers: see 466a 'what are you saying, then? Rhetoric seems to you to be flattery, does it?' 'I said it was a part of flattery. Do you not remember that, Polus, at your age? How will you fare presently?' (that is, when you're older).[12]

---

[11] Cf. esp. *Charm.* 154de, *I Alc.* 132a, *Tht.* 162b with 169ab. See also *Prt.* 352a9-b1, ctr. 348b etc.

[12] This is perhaps a joke on the art of memorising, which was one aspect of rhetorical training and may well have figured in Polus' own *techne*: it is also needed by the philosopher, as Plato prescribes elsewhere (*Rep.* 487a), and even the Socrates of the *Clouds* insists on it, though he has a hard time with Strepsiades (Ar. *Clouds* 129, 414, 631).

Polus' exchanges with Socrates are also characterised by repeated exclamations of incredulity, e.g. 467b10 'what monstrous and extravagant statements you make, Socrates', to which Socrates replies, 'don't just utter abuse, Polus'; rather, if you have questions to ask me, go on and show that what I'm saying is false. In other words, neither rhetorical questions nor exclamations nor abuse constitute a refutation, however important they may be in oratory. But Polus seems unwilling or unable to learn anything from Socrates, for he repeats this kind of comment later (473a1, 473b8-9, 480e1), repeatedly dwelling on the oddity or strangeness of Socrates' attitudes. Despite their regular emphasis on the novelty of their arts, the sophists are seen to be less extreme in their paradoxes than the seemingly more conventional Socrates.

Polus' main contribution to the dialogue is his emphasis on the power which rhetoric, combined with a judicious amount of dishonesty or ruthlessness, can bring to its user. With this section of the *Gorgias* we begin to move further away from rhetoric pure and simple, and into the realm of what it represents, namely immoral ambition. Here there is a basic contradiction in Polus' attitudes, well analysed by Kahn.[13] He admires success, power and wealth, however they are obtained; but he also condemns and fears criminal actions or overt injustice when it comes close to home. Thus he envies and admires the tyrant Archelaus of Macedon, who seized power unjustly by a bloody series of treacherous acts;[14] but his reaction is one of dismay, and much more critical, when Socrates vividly brings the idea of killing to gain power down to a more personal level, with his picture of himself as a lunatic in the agora with a knife under his cloak (469c sqq.). Here (as later with Callicles' hedonism) we see Socrates giving real life precision to vague ideas or ideals: how would this work in practice, how would you feel if it were done to *you*?

Before pursuing this further, something should be said concerning the importance of the concept of tyranny in fifth- and fourth-century democratic Athens; for this is a concept that will be still more prominent in the Calliclean section of the dialogue. Tyranny fascinated the Athenians as an ideal of government diametrically opposed to democracy; and tyranny, along with oligarchy, were constant bogies just round the corner. In particular, Athenian democrats feared that an internal revolution might bring about a restoration of oligarchy, or tyranny, the more extreme form – as indeed happened, though only for short periods and under severe pressures, in 411 and 404.[15] This anxiety is mirrored and often satirised by

[13] Art. cit. in n. 1, at pp. 84-97. For criticism of Kahn's discussion see T.H. Irwin, *Rev. Internat. de Phil.* 40 (1986) 49-74. On the discussion with Polus see also C.N. Johnson, *Phoenix* 43 (1989) 196-216.

[14] Some see Plato's account of his accession as exaggeration or propaganda: see N.G.L. Hammond and G.T. Griffith, *History of Macedonia* ii (Oxford 1979) 133-7.

[15] See further Ostwald, *Popular Sovereignty*, for a detailed and authoritative account of both ideology and history.

Aristophanes (e.g. *Wasps* 345, 488ff.). It had a genuine basis in that Athenian aristocrats were by no means all content with the democracy, especially once the Peloponnesian war had crippled their finances and damaged their estates (Thuc. ii. 65. 2): we see something of their ambitions and secret contempt for the *demos* in Callicles. Alcibiades too was suspected of aiming at tyranny (Thuc. vi. 15. 4, 28), and Thucydides presents him, after his flight to Sparta, as brazenly dismissing democratic government as 'an acknowledged folly' (vi. 89. 6). In tragedy, we find many tyrants in the fullest and most hostile sense: Zeus in the *Prometheus Bound*, Lycus in Euripides' *Heracles*, Creon in the *Antigone*, Pentheus in the *Bacchae* (with some additional complexities or complexes). Various tragic charac- ters, especially in Euripides, praise tyranny as the supreme ambition and the source of greatest happiness: e.g. *Troades* 1169 'tyranny, which is equal to godhead',[16] a line sourly quoted and criticised by Socrates in his account of tyranny in the *Republic* (viii. 568b). Particularly close to the *Gorgias* in a number of ways is a scene in Euripides' *Phoenissae* (503ff.), in which the villainous Eteocles speaks with Calliclean fierceness and frankness (503 'I shall speak out, concealing nothing ...'): 'I would go to the rising-point of the sun and stars, to the depths of the earth, if I were capable, so as to possess that greatest of all the gods, Tyranny!'[17]

In general, what the Greeks seem to have found especially fascinating about tyranny was the idea of complete freedom: the tyrant is the one man who does not have to answer to anyone, who need obey no superior law or authority: he can give full rein to any desires or whims without fear of retribution.[18] The tyrant, for example the Persian king, commonly used as an example in such contexts, is accountable to no one. This unaccountabil- ity is the exact reverse of the principle of Athenian democracy, in which all magistrates have to render account at the end of their period of office. Thus in Aeschylus' *Persae* it is mentioned that Xerxes, even if he fails, is 'not accountable to the city' (213; cf. Hdt. iii. 80. 3 and 6), but later in the play, in Darius' majestic speech, there is a pointed echo when Zeus, the punisher of mortal arrogance, is described as *euthunos barus*, 'a harsh supervisor' (828): it is Zeus who has called the king to account. In the *Prometheus*, it is Zeus himself, the new tyrant of Olympus, who has this kind of unassail- able authority (324); and we find a comic version in the *Wasps*: the jurors,

---

[16] Cf. Ar. *Wasps* 619ff. for the tyrant as a god.

[17] Other parallels between this scene and the *Gorgias* may also be detected: the stress on shame, the insistence that it would be *anandria* (cowardice) not to pursue this end; and the interesting response of Jocasta, in praise of equality (*isotes*) – not just democracy, but a kind of cosmically based order and geometric justice. This last passage is quite similar to what Socrates says at *Grg.* 507e, an intriguing parallel which may suggest that Plato remembered the passage, or more probably that both writers are drawing on some earlier thinkers such as the Pythagoreans.

[18] See further K. Raaflaub, *Die Entdeckung der Freiheit* (Vestigia 37, Munich 1985) ch. 5; C. Tuplin, in *Crux* (Fest. G. de Ste. Croix), ed. P. Cartledge and F.D. Harvey (Exeter 1985) 348-75.

unlike the magistrates, are not called to render accounts, and this is what makes their power tyrannical and godlike (587-9; cf. *Knights* 1111ff. on Demos). Philocleon's comic picture of power as self-indulgence expresses vividly what is also Plato's concern in the *Republic*: the idea that the man who has complete freedom will surrender himself to the unrestrained pursuit of pleasure. Polus assumes this, Callicles asserts it; Socrates' intention in both the *Gorgias* and the *Republic* is to show that this ideal is misguided and that a man who pursues such a false ideal is not only wrong but sure to be unhappy. Thus the discussion of the tyrant in the *Republic* (books viii-ix) concludes by proving that he is not the happiest but the most evil and most wretched of men. Here as elsewhere the *Gorgias* seems to try out on a smaller scale themes which are further developed in the *Republic*. Both works, for instance, develop the idea – which is surely a true and important qualification – that the tyrant's power and freedom are flawed by his perpetual fear: Persian monarchs and Greek tyrants alike are subject to conspiracy and assassinations; and the tyrant, like Periander in Herodotus' story (v. 92η), is bound to fear and strike down his ablest allies and his closest advisors.[19] This is related to a point made in the *Republic*: if all men were utterly competitive and all sought to outdo each other, there would be no way to conduct human society; the solidarity and security of any company of human beings, even a gang of thieves, depend on qualities which are conventionally considered virtues: loyalty, keeping of promises, and so on (*Rep.* i. 351). Laws and a framework of *nomoi* are necessary for a society to exist. But Plato wants to go further: the cruel and self-centred behaviour which is thought typical of the tyrant not only harms those near him and society, it also harms *him*: even if his evil actions benefit him practically, they destroy him morally. But this is only hinted at or lightly sketched in the Polus episode; it is more fully developed in the later parts of the dialogue, and in the *Republic*.

Against this background, we may consider Polus' use of the tyrant theme in the *Gorgias* itself. The motif is first introduced at 466b10, where Polus remarks that the *rhetores* (a term which embraces politicians as well as instructors) can kill and rob and send into exile anyone they want, 'just like tyrants'. A little later he makes clear that he thinks this power enviable, whether or not it is employed justly (468e-9a). He several times appeals to Socrates himself: wouldn't *you* accept that kind of power, and envy the man who possesses it? (468e6, cf. 469b, c 'you mean you wouldn't accept the power of a tyrant?'). His incredulity brings out Socrates' apparent eccentricity and unconventional attitude. As already mentioned, Socrates counters with the image of himself as a lunatic with a knife – isn't that a position of power? Polus is thrown by this more freakish and uncomfortable picture,

---

[19] See *Grg.* 510b, *Rep.* viii. 567bc, ix. 578a; also Aesch. *Prom.* 224f., Eur. *Suppl.* 445ff., Arist. *Pol.* viii. 1311b23ff.; Cic. *Off.* ii. 23, iii. 84, Tac. *Ann.* vi. 6. See also D.M. Lewis, *CAH* vi² 153-5, on the tyrant Dionysius I.

and his reply reveals his crudely prudential outlook – a man like that is bound to be caught and punished. Whether this is true or not we may doubt, but it shows us that for Polus what matters is whether you can get away with crime. The wrongdoer on the grand scale has a better chance of doing so than the petty criminal in the Athenian agora: he is also more glamorous and exciting. Polus is too cynical to accept the Socratic view that there are some things which are right and wrong whatever the consequences and whatever your status. To Polus, the equation of 'just' with 'good', 'unjust' with 'bad' is quixotic naiveté:

> Oh, it's a difficult matter to refute you, Socrates. Don't you know that even a child could prove you wrong? (470c)

This image of Socrates as a naive child is one which is related to the metaphorical patterns of the dialogue as a whole: Socrates seems childish to his opponents, and Callicles will make much of this, urging him to give up the babyish pursuits of philosophy and 'be a man'; but in the image of the sweetmaker and the doctor, it is the Athenian people who are the children who want to be indulged, and who will not submit to justice and correction.

At 471 Polus invokes the up-to-date example[20] of the tyrant Archelaus, launching upon a full-blown sarcastic response to Socrates, a kind of crazy hymn to Archelaus' injustice, which recounts his crimes rather than demonstrating his happiness (Socrates has said that if he is unjust, Archelaus must be wretched, and Polus takes up the task of establishing his injustice rather than addressing the harder question of the state of his soul).There is a certain frenetic, jumbled quality about Polus' exposition, as he frantically piles on the details. Again the rushed and flustered style mirrors personality. Polus has a good deal of fun with Socrates' paradoxes: 'so then he was a slave, and happy by your account, but now how amazingly wretched he's become ...', and again, 'now that he's done these unjust acts, he hasn't realised that he's become utterly wretched'; 'he didn't want to become a happy man' (471a7ff., b6, c2). But these formulations, which seem preposterous to Polus, make perfect sense in Socrates' moral picture: whether he knows it or not, Archelaus *must* be a wretched man if he has committed all these crimes, and any apparent prosperity or well-being is only self-deception. Hence Polus' attack misses the target by a long way, for he only provides the ammunition for Socrates' unaltered judgement, while for the reader he reveals his own moral poverty by his admiration and envy of such a man.

One or two other passages in the dialogue with Polus require comment. In 473b12ff. he launches upon a grisly description of the punishment of the

[20] Sophists and other authors influenced by them favour novelty in their material: see Grg. *Helen* 5, Ar. *Clouds* 547, *Wasps* 1044, Thuc. i. 73. 2, ii. 36. 4, vii. 69. 2.

unjust man or tyrant who fails in his ambitious bid for power: thus the failed tyrant is juxtaposed with the successful one. The lurid detail of racking and mutilation is heightened by rhetorical technique (*enargeia*), and Polus' long rhetorical question implies that no man in his senses could be in doubt about the answer. But Socrates replies with typical firmness: 'you are trying to make my flesh creep, excellent Polus, and not questioning me; and a moment ago you were calling witnesses [i.e. the many Athenians who would misguidedly agree with Polus].' In other words, to call up these terrifying visions of torture and punishment makes good rhetoric, but is not a serious examination of Socrates' position.[21] Polus is trying to unsettle Socrates, and that is not a fair method of argument.

A similar point is made in the next exchange. Socrates states his position: the tyrant who *escapes* punishment is the more unhappy man. At this point he breaks off and asks Polus why he's laughing; is this a new kind of elenchus, which involves laughing at somebody when he says anything, instead of questioning him? The scholia here point out that Polus is following a Gorgianic precept: in the courts, said Gorgias, you should dissolve your opponent's seriousness with laughter, and disrupt his laughter with your seriousness (fr. 21 Rad., not in Diels-Kranz). Polus' use of this device, however, is fairly unsophisticated; it amounts to no more than incredulous scoffing. There is a contrast between this and the more subtle, flexible and varied form of humour which Socrates himself habitually employs; between laughter as a means to mock or denigrate, avoiding engagement with something you do not want to understand, and a kind of humour which is based on past intimacy and which creates a bond, rather than emphasising the gulf between opponents.[22] The latter is not the only kind of humour Socrates employs, but it is an important aspect of it, and it has its basis in the need for friendship and frankness between partners in dialectic. By contrast, the laughter of Socrates' opponents often signifies a failure to be frank, or a failure to understand and learn from what may seem absurd.

By the end of the exchange with Polus, Socrates has reached a typically paradoxical conclusion about the true function of rhetoric. Its real value, he maintains, is to ensure that one obtains punishment for oneself and anyone else one cares about: that is, the orator must use his powers to expose his own and others' crimes and win the appropriate penalty. Like Polus earlier, he piles on the detail in a series of parallel clauses: 'he should

---

[21] Cf. *Crito* 46c, where the same verb, *mormoluttomai* (rendered above as 'trying to make my flesh creep'), is used to describe the way the people 'conjures up a host of bogies to terrify our childish minds by subjecting us to chains, execution, confiscation of property'; these matters, for Socrates, are terrors for children; they do not and should not affect our assessment of the *principles* involved. It is only the child in us that is afraid (cf. *Phd.* 77e, death as a bogeyman).

[22] See further H.D. Rankin, *C&M* 28 (1969) 186-213; G.J. de Vries, *Mnem.* ser. 4, 38 (1985) 378-81. More generally relevant on background is S. Halliwell, 'The uses of laughter in Greek society', *CQ* 41 (1991) 279-96.

denounce most of all himself, then any of his household or his friends who may be committing wrong; he should not conceal his unjust action, but bring it into the open so that the guilty man may pay the penalty and become healthy; he should force himself and others not to flinch like a coward, but to close their eyes and offer themselves nobly and bravely, as if submitting to the surgeon's blade and burning; he should pursue what is good and honourable, taking no account of the pain, but offering himself for flogging, if his unjust action deserves flogging, for prison, if it deserves prison ...' (480cd). Socrates deliberately minimises the resemblances to the normal practice of orators, who often say and no doubt sometimes believe that they are bringing men to punishment because they deserve it. He might have stressed much more the orator's duty to pursue the guilty, but instead introduces a further paradox, concerning the use of oratory against one's enemies: if an enemy commits a crime, we should do everything in our power to prevent them from being punished for it, and to keep them alive as long as possible. The best thing of all would be to make the enemy immortal in his wickedness! (e5ff.) But this mischievous picture of avenging oneself on enemies by letting them get away with their injustices is not very seriously meant; it is introduced by the deceptively casual parenthesis 'if one really ought to do harm to anybody, an enemy or anybody else' (480e5). This is presented only as a hypothesis,[23] and one which we have good reason from elsewhere in Plato to suppose that Socrates does not accept (cf. esp. *Rep.* i. 335e-6a).

Perhaps the most striking thing about Socrates' paradoxical conclusion is the way that he redefines rhetoric so that it comes to resemble dialectic. In an ideal world, the philosophic orator would ensure the proper workings of justice and make certain that he himself, and all he cared for, received the treatment they needed, even if it must be painful and unpleasant. This is very much what Socrates tries to do in the *Gorgias* – to draw his interlocutors into a discussion that is justly and fairly argued, that will increase their mental and moral health, and that may be uncomfortable. He is ready to subject himself to questioning and treatment too: he wants to be put right, instructed and castigated. By contrast, Polus and Callicles are reluctant to put up with such treatment: in the case of Callicles, Socrates makes the point that he won't submit to being *punished* even in a discussion about that very subject, punishment (*kolazomenos ... kolazein,* 505c).

Socrates' transformation of rhetoric into a dialectical art of punishment and self-improvement is all the more surprising because rhetoric was often represented by the sophists and their pupils as the art of self-preservation par excellence; it is a means of protecting one's life and property, as Callicles emphasises in his main speech (484d, 486a sq.). Socrates later draws the

---

[23] Note the use of *ara* at 480e5, marking this as a false assumption: see J.D. Denniston, *The Greek Particles* (2nd edn., Oxford 1954) 38.

analogy between the rhetor-advocate and the pilot of a ship. Just as a pilot cannot know whether the people he has brought safely to shore were actually worth saving, so the rhetorician may win the case and rescue life and property, but what guarantee has he that the defendant would not be better punished, or dead? (511c sqq.)[24] In short, Plato uses paradox and humour to make, again, a serious point: that orators, and the Athenians in general, overvalue life *per se*, not taking account of its quality: preservation of self and property are put above moral well-being. A true rhetoric, that is an ideal form of that art, would not make this kind of misjudgement. The superficiality of contemporary rhetoric is thus exposed: it does not go below the surface, and does not seek to bring about moral improvement or enlightenment, as dialectic can.

Nevertheless, Socrates' paradoxical conception cuts both ways. Obviously, it provides a critique of the real world by contrasting it with an ideal; but the whole passage is disquieting just because it pays so little attention to the real potential of unjust rhetoric in the existing structure of society. Socrates alludes to this lightly at 480e7: one has to take care not to be treated unjustly by an enemy. But Socrates, as the dialogue repeatedly reminds us, eventually *is* condemned; and his ideal picture presupposes a wholly just society, which Athens is not. Later statements make clear that he is aware of this (e.g. 521cd), but we are perhaps meant to see him as, in a way, too good for this world; the intense bitterness of the *Gorgias* largely stems from the gulf between Socrates and the world as it, unfortunately, is. Plato makes us see with great clarity that such a man can neither bring his ideals to fulfilment nor stoop to compromise. The whole dialogue is about Socrates' choice of life and what it can lead to – a kind of martyrdom; and it leaves us with the problem memorably, even tragically stated, not with a bland or hagiographic solution.

Callicles

When Callicles re-enters the discussion he is still the urbane Athenian gentleman whom we saw behaving so courteously at the opening of the *Gorgias*; we have as yet no hint of the violence and antagonism to come. Instead of bursting in like Polus, he asks Chaerephon in polite but perplexed tones: is Socrates serious about this, or is he just fooling around? (481b) At once it should be obvious that the antithesis is too extreme; Callicles fails to see that you can jest and build up paradoxes and create fantasies while still being, on another level, very serious about what this kind of 'play' implies or serves to convey. However, Chaerephon too takes the line that Socrates must be one or the other, and having assured Callicles that Socrates is entirely serious, adds 'there's nothing like asking him'. This

---

[24] Cf. the parallel argument at *Hipp. Maj.* 304a sq., and further *Laws* iv. 707cd, Ar. *Knights* 1377, Soph. *Phil.* 108f., Tac. *Dial.* 5. 5ff.

phrase echoes the opening scene, where it was used with reference to Gorgias (481b9 ~ 447c5). This must be deliberate: Socrates has now moved to the centre-stage, showing himself a much more extraordinary man than Gorgias; and Callicles has moved from being the complacent patron to a state of astounded curiosity. He goes on to question Socrates direct: surely, if he really does mean what he says, the whole world would be turned upside down.

Socrates begins his reply with a reference to the possibility of communication, a key theme of the dialogue. 'If people had not certain feelings in common, some sharing one feeling, some another, but some of us had *unique* feelings, unshared by the others, it wouldn't be easy to reveal one's experience to one's neighbour' (481c). This is a counter-claim directed at theories such as Gorgias', that knowledge is incommunicable and all experience is dependent on *doxai* (opinions). It also points to the need to establish common ground if communication, including dialectic, is to exist. Socrates does not say – what would be untrue and unrealistic – that everyone is the same and has the same experiences. He does hold, however, that all men do share some feelings or experiences, the problem being to identify these and build on them. Dialectic needs to move from shared belief because it seeks a willing, conscious, rational response, unlike rhetoric which aims simply at victory, conviction by any means, including lying and manipulating prejudice, exploiting unexamined assumptions, and so forth.

The parallel experience which Socrates identifies as forming a bond between himself and Callicles is love; the comparison is a richly revealing one, with implications for the whole of the remaining discussion. They are both, he observes, not only in love but in love with two different beloveds: Socrates is in love with Alcibiades and with philosophy; Callicles is in love with the Athenian demos ('the people') and with Demos, son of Pyrilampes, a beautiful male aristocratic youth of the day (cf. Ar. *Wasps* 98).[25] This dual passion is a potential source of conflict: divided goals and conflicting desires are common topics in Plato, on both the everyday and the philosophic levels. But Socrates' true relation with Alcibiades, as is shown in the *Symposium*, is that of pursued to pursuer, contrary to all expectation and popular belief (see esp. 217c, 222b). His choice of love is firmly made; he is in truth the lover of philosophy, who always says the same thing. His passion is single-minded and consistent. By contrast, Callicles still woos both the Athenian people and the boy Demos; and both of them are capricious and inconsistent. What Socrates is saying here should be connected with Callicles' twin ambitions, as revealed in the subsequent discussion: to become a successful politician in democratic Athens, which involves 'court-

[25] See further *APF* p. 330. Callicles' other intimates mentioned by Socrates at 487c, especially Andron, may have oligarchic connections (see Dodds's n., and Ostwald, *Popular Sovereignty* 246).

ing' the demos;[26] and to fulfil his more sinister aims as an aristocrat who scorns the Athenian people as a rabble and aspires to supremacy, that is, tyranny.[27] This latter ambition goes with being a lover of the boy Demos, a member of one of Athens' most aristocratic families (related, indeed, to Plato's own). Thus although the joke starts from a pun,[28] it bites deeper: Socrates is already hinting at the conflict within Callicles which he eloquently stresses at the end of this speech and subsequently exposes.

A further aspect of Callicles' love-affairs is linked with the theme of frankness or openness. As Socrates hints here, his love leads him to conceal his beliefs and flatter his beloved, a practice which Socrates condemns in love as in all other walks of life (cf. esp. *Lysis* 204eff., 210e on the ethics of love; *Lovers* 132d, on pretence). This anticipates the exposure of Callicles' behaviour as *kolakeia*, base flattery which aims at pleasing the beloved rather than improving or instructing (502-3, 515ff., 521b, etc.). The man who is to win power with either a tyrant or the tyrannical demos must make himself as like his master as possible, flattering and appeasing him in every way: this is what Callicles' lauded 'political life' amounts to. Aristophanes helps us gloss Plato in this area, with his presentation of rival politicians abasing themselves before the grumpy figure of Demos, pampering him and flattering him in the most hypocritical and humiliating ways.[29]

Socrates' speech culminates in an appeal to Callicles not to dismiss what philosophy has to say to him out of hand, but to test and look seriously at her conclusions about doing wrong and being punished for it. The intensity of his concern (marked partly by the oath, partly by the elaborate structure of his peroration) characteristically results in more paradox: 'if you leave this issue unexamined, then by the dog, god of the Egyptians, Callicles will not be in agreement with you, Callicles, but he will be out of tune in the whole of your life. And for myself, I think, o best of men, that it would be better for me that my lyre were out of tune and discordant, or a chorus of which I was sponsor, or that the majority of men disagreed with me and contradicted me, than that I, a single individual, should be out of tune with and contradict myself' (482bc). For dialectic is not just an exchange or competition between different individuals, one correcting the other; it is concerned with the self as well. Here, the point is that Callicles owes it to himself to get clear on these issues. Socrates' teasing account of his dual

---

[26] For the image of the politician as 'lover of the *demos*' cf. Ar. *Knights* 732, 734, 1341 and Neil's n.; Demosthenes *proem* 53. 3; A. Burckhardt, *Spüren der athenischen Volksrede in der alten Komödie* (diss. Basel 1924) 40ff.; W.R. Connor, *The New Politicians of Fifth Century Athens* (Princeton 1971) 96ff. The scene in *I Alc.* 131e-2a is probably an imitation of the *Gorgias*.

[27] Contrast G.B. Kerferd, *PCPS* 20 (1974) 48-52, who emphasises the democratic aspects of Callicles.

[28] Oddly branded 'atrocious' by Vlastos, *Socratic Studies* 94.

[29] See the whole scene from *Knights* 763-973, e.g. 904-5 ('I tell you, Demos, I'll provide you with a bowl of state pay to slop down for just doing nothing!'), 910-11 ('Blow your nose, Demos, and then wipe your hand on my head!' – 'No, on mine!').

love affairs has already revealed some division in Callicles' aims, and he presses him here to reveal his grounds for disagreement with Socrates too – a disagreement which must, in his view, conflict with Callicles' own better self.[30]

Callicles' speech at 482c-86c, one of the longest in the dialogue, is also the most powerful challenge to Socrates' moral position. I select here only a few passages which convey something of its passion and power; but the following discussion will demand that the reader be familiar with the whole speech.

> My opinion is that those who make the laws are the weak and the majority. They pass laws convenient to themselves and to their own advantage, praising and blaming on the same principle. They terrify the stronger members of the race, those who are capable of taking more, telling them that acquisitiveness is shameful and wrong, and that this is what wrongdoing is, trying to have more than other people ... Nature itself demonstrates the truth that it is just for the better man to have more than his inferior, the stronger than the weaker. There is plenty of evidence to prove that amongst other animals and in entire cities and races of men, this has been judged right – that the stronger should dominate the weaker and have more possessions. By what 'right' did Xerxes launch his campaign against Greece, or his father against the Scythians? Or one could name innumerable other such cases. These men perform such actions according to the natural law of justice, indeed, yes by Zeus, the law of nature, even if not perhaps the conventional law that we lay down.
>
> What we do is mould the best and strongest among us, taking them from their early days, like lion-cubs, and by spellbinding and bewitching them, we make them slaves, telling them that men must have equal shares, and that this is honourable and right. But I believe that if a man should arise who had a strong enough character, he would shake off and break up and escape all those shackles, trampling beneath his feet our writings and spells and incantations and laws which all violate nature, and rising up the former slave is revealed as our master, and right away the justice of Nature blazes forth. Pindar too, in my opinion, demonstrates the points I am making in that poem in which he says ... that Heracles drove off Geryon's cattle without purchasing them or receiving them as a gift, since this is indeed what is naturally just, that cattle and other possessions of the inferior and the weak should all belong to the better, stronger man ...
>
> ... Yet my dear Socrates – don't be annoyed, for I'll say this out of friendship – doesn't it seem shameful to you to be as I think you are – you and the rest of those who pursue philosophy too far? For now, if anyone were to get hold of you or anyone else of your type and get him into prison, claiming that you'd committed a crime even though you were innocent, you know you wouldn't have any way of helping yourself; you'd be gasping and gaping with nothing to say, and when you got into court, if you happened to be up against a very base and villainous prosecutor, you'd be done for, if he wanted to set the

---

[30] For an attempt to elucidate this strange insistence that his opponent in reality agrees with him, see Vlastos, *Socratic Studies* ch. 1, esp. 17-29.

penalty as death. But how can this be wise, Socrates, this art which 'takes the well-born man and makes him worse' – makes him unable to defend himself or save himself or anybody else from the direst dangers, but instead allows him to be deprived of all his property by his enemies, and to live absolutely without honour in the state? To put it crudely, with a man like that, you can even shove his face in and get away with it. (483b4-484c3, with some omissions, 486a4-c3)

It has been argued, by no less distinguished a scholar than E.R. Dodds,[31] that Callicles is in some sense Plato's other self, Plato in politics, as he might have been had he not been disenchanted with Athens. Dodds quotes with approval the words of Alain: 'Plato paints *himself* here as he might have been, as he feared to be.' This seems a little overstated, and rests partly on the close connection Dodds makes between the *Gorgias* and the passage in the Seventh Letter in which Plato speaks of his intention to embark on a political career, like other members of his family, and his disillusionment with both the rule of the Thirty Tyrants and the restored democracy, which dissuaded him from any such enterprise. If, however, we reserve judgement as to the authenticity of the Seventh Letter, and remember also how flimsy the case is for dating the *Gorgias* anywhere near either Plato's decision to abandon any such hope of a political career, or the date of the letter itself, then we can perhaps look at Callicles with more objective eyes, and see him as a brilliant and memorable portrait, but surely not of the kind of politician Plato could ever have been or expected to be. This is not to deny that, at least in his earlier speeches, Callicles' words are eloquent and seductive; but his glorious ideal of the strong man has its inherent weaknesses, and under dialectic he crumbles, becomes shrilly abusive and indignant; in the end he is reduced to shouting and scoffing, and finally to sullen silence. There can be no doubt that Plato means us, by the end of the dialogue, to dislike him and to feel sure that he is dangerously wrong.[32]

The following discussion of the speech of Callicles will examine some of its principal arguments and weaknesses, while also looking ahead to see how these arguments are criticised or followed up in the later part of the dialogue. Much must inevitably be omitted or treated selectively.

(1) The *physis-nomos* argument. This debate (comparable in some aspects with equally famous modern debates concerning heredity vs. environment, nature vs. culture) had its origin in the Greek encounter with different cultures which possessed different *nomoi* (customs, laws). The Hippocratic writers, especially the author of the work *On airs, waters and places*, explain the difference between cultures by environmental determinism, and Herodotus follows this kind of scheme on a large scale, in his

---

[31] In his commentary, 267; cf. introd., pp. 14, 31. See also Friedlaender i. 167.
[32] Dodds's reading of Callicles as Plato's *alter ego* is also criticised by Guthrie *HGP* iii. 106-7, iv. 296.

study of the expansion and national character of different peoples.[33] Such
observation encouraged cultural relativism: extended to the moral and
religious sphere, this raises far-reaching questions about absolute values.
Have they any external validity, or are they made by man, potentially
unmade, destroyed or transformed by man? Sophistic writers took an
interest in anthropology, especially the origins of human society, how
nomoi came about, and whether they answer a need in *physis*.[34] The 'social
contract' theory is one such analysis: a rather abbreviated and prejudiced
version is given by Callicles here, and a fuller and more sympathetic one
by Glaucon and Adeimantus in *Republic* ii. The earlier sophists seem to
have simply observed the relativity of *nomoi*, producing theories about the
origins of society and its basic motivations without actually calling them
into question. In other words, there is no evidence that Protagoras or
Gorgias took the further step of sweeping away traditional moral standards
and sanctions, of asserting that because they were man-made, they were
meaningless. This is a further step taken by their pupils and juniors, men
like Callicles and Thrasymachus in *Rep.* i, as also by the Unjust Cause in
the *Clouds* and the intellectual Athenians for whom he perhaps speaks.[35]
Here again Plato must be seen as the heir to an important sophistic debate.
The *Republic* presents a theoretical construction of an ideal society based
on human needs (cf. ii. 369c sq.); more broadly, the project there is to
reinstate absolute values, to show that *nomos* is a force rooted in human
nature and cosmic law, without going back to a now irrecoverable pre-
sophistic, naive view of the world.

	Callicles introduces the *nomos-physis* debate because he thinks Socrates
is playing an illegitimate logical trick, using a double standard and moving
from one to the other – a tactic analysed and formalised by Aristotle (*Rhet.*
ii. 23. 1399a30 and *Soph. El.* 173a7ff., which alludes to the *Gorgias*).
Callicles means that Socrates misled Polus into replying with a concession
to *conventional* belief – that doing wrong is worse than suffering it – and
then proceeded to take this as truly the case in nature, rather than just
commonly held. *Nomos* in Callicles' view dictates things which have no
basis in *physis*. But if, as Plato does, we reject this assumption, then
Socrates' manoeuvre, while still subtle and disingenuous, is less vulnerable. As has often been said, Socrates and Callicles are alike in many
ways:[36] they are both discontented with much popular opinion and with the
unthinking acceptance of traditional beliefs; they both want to get at what
people *really* think and what is really the case; but Callicles' sweeping

[33] *AWP* 16. 10ff., 23. 30ff.; Hdt. ii. 35. 2, ix. 122; cf. iii. 38 on *nomos* as ruler of all things. See
further F. Heinimann, *Nomos und Physis* (Basel 1945); Guthrie *HGP* iii. ch. 4; Dodds, *Ancient
Concept of Progress* ch. 6.
[34] T. Cole, *Democritus and the Origins of Greek Anthropology* (Western Reserve Univ. Press
1967). Further refs. in ch. 4, n. 13.
[35] See *Clouds* 1039ff., 1071ff., esp. 1074, 1077ff. Cf. further Soph. *Phil.* 120, Thuc. v. 105, etc.
[36] E.g. J. Annas's review of Irwin's comm., in *Mind* 91 (1982) 126.

rejection of *nomos* as having no basis at all in reality and no roots in human nature is a naive and unrealistic view, and the way that he has taken over wholesale various clichés of contemporary debate suggests the confusion of his position, as indeed do his haste and indignation.

One weakness of his case is pointed out by Socrates immediately;[37] Callicles uses the language of 'might is right', the doctrine that the stronger naturally rules and has a right to rule wherever he can. In other words, he seems to be committing himself to a view that according to what is 'natural' the weak will always be dominated by the strong, by a law of necessity. Like Pheidippides in the *Clouds*, he uses analogies from the animal world to back this up (483d; *Clouds* 1427). But Socrates turns this argument against him with the suggestion that the *demos* is stronger in a democracy, so that it is natural law, and right, that it should rule; Callicles indignantly rejects this, his anti-democratic prejudices showing through clearly now (489bc). He attempts to restate his case: it is the *better* man, the wiser and superior, who should rule (489e). This is, as a moment's thought shows, a very different position, and Callicles' mind is still not altogether free of confusion then, but it is clear from the whole sequence of argument that his initial formulation was inadequate, high-sounding but muddled. It goes with this that his examples are in fact ill-suited to his case. He refers to the Persian campaigns: 'by what right did Xerxes make his expedition against Greece, or his father against the Scythians?' (483d) Both of these expeditions failed, so that they are hardly appropriate or encouraging examples for the superman who despises law and restraint. Similarly, Callicles misuses and misinterprets the Pindaric passage, as all modern scholars agree.[38] His quotations from the *Antiope* of Euripides are vulnerable to criticism, too (see (3) below).

Callicles' exaltation of the right of the stronger is summed up in the striking phrase 'according to the law of nature' (483e). That is, he brings together the conventional opposites, asserting that they are identical – the only real *nomos* is that of *physis*. Plato too believed that *nomos* vs. *physis* was ultimately a false antithesis: 'the social and the natural order are expressions of the same divine law';[39] but he believed, as 507-8 show most clearly, that the nature of the world is based on order, *kosmos*, not on chaos (*akosmia*). This is the point of his emphasis on 'equality' in that passage, which picks up and gives a deeper meaning to the democratic ideal of *isonomia* ('equality under law') which Callicles had spurned (483c). The chorus of Euripides' *Bacchae*, in a difficult but suggestive passage, also combine the two opposed principles: what is *truly nomos* lies in *physis* and is associated above all with the god Dionysus and with the divine forces in

---

[37] For a modern account of it see Kahn, art. cit. 98ff.
[38] For a survey see M. Ostwald, *HSCP* 69 (1965) 109-38, repr. in *Pindar und Bakchylides* ed. W.M. Calder III and J. Stern (Darmstadt 1970); also H. Lloyd-Jones *HSCP* 76 (1992) 45-56 = *Academic Papers* i (Oxford 1990) 154-66.
[39] Dodds, *Gorgias* p. 338.

life. The chorus humble themselves before the authority of divine law: 'that
which is sanctioned by custom over long ages and is also forever natural'
(*Ba.* 895-6). Plato was closer to the chorus here than to Callicles.[40]

(2) 'The right of the stronger.' Much of what has already been said under
nomos and *physis* is relevant here too; but it may help to focus attention on
what Callicles actually wants, and how he presents his aspirations. We
notice first the very frequent use of comparatives, rather freely and indiscriminately associated with one another: 483c1 'stronger men', c1-3 the idea
of 'having more', d1 'the better man', d2 'the more powerful', e4-5 'the best
and mightiest of men'. There is also heavy emphasis on 'being a man' or
'manly' – both in the sense of growing up and not messing about with
childish philosophic questions, and in the sense of *andreia*, courage and
resolution, which he builds into his picture of the great man shortly (esp.
491b). In 489e he agrees that the men he means are 'the better and superior,
who are also more intelligent'. It seems not to occur to him that you might
be stronger, or more courageous, without necessarily being wiser, or indeed,
in some senses, better; he simply combines all the qualities he admires, not
surprisingly as he obviously sees *himself* as the great man of the future.
But although he seems at first to idealise power per se, Socrates shows him
that it is not so easy to exclude moral criteria. If he wants to say that the
tyrannical man *ought* to rule over the people, he has to call on further
evaluative words such as 'better' or 'wiser'. Later still, we see in the
discussion of pleasure that his hedonism is in conflict with his ambition;
and in the discussion of flattery, the Calliclean 'superman' is still further
cut down to size; he must be a flatterer, even a catamite, if he is to succeed
(510, esp. cd).[41]

Socrates' dialectic, then, exposes the inconsistencies and the uncomfortable realities which underlie Callicles' grand generalities and fine words.
This also makes clear that it is not so easy to cut oneself away from the
beliefs, presuppositions and ways of thinking which one's upbringing and
social environment have made part of oneself. Thus for instance Callicles'
arrogant attitude towards the *demos* is based on snobbery and aristocratic
hauteur at least as much as on any clearly thought-out moral principles
about who should govern.[42]

The ideal of *andreia*, courage and manliness, is also developed and to
some extent turned against Callicles as the dialogue advances. Comparison
of the following passages brings this out:

(a) 483a-b: Callicles declares that no real man ought to allow himself to

[40] See further, *Laws* x. 890d.
[41] 521b2 sq. bring out Callicles' shame and discomfort at the prospect; see also 494de, for the
comparison with the catamite. See below, p. 170.
[42] For his snobbishness see Socrates' comment at 512cd: Callicles would never let his daughter
marry an engineer.

be wronged by another; that is the act of a slave, one who would be better dead than alive.

(b) 484c-5e (esp. 485d3-e2): the man = the politician, the boy or child = the philosopher, according to Callicles.

(c) 491b: Callicles' ideal is the *andreios* (the brave man).

(d) 494b: Socrates insists that Callicles ought to persevere under dialectic, 'for you're a brave fellow'. In other words, Callicles needs to show in his performance now the qualities he claims in the larger sphere of politics. In fact Callicles fails conspicuously: he becomes irritable and wants out, and so the discussion breaks down.

(e) 522e represents a reversal of this theme, as Socrates turns Callicles' warning back upon him. In Callicles' view rhetoric is a necessary form of self-preservation: without it, you can be unjustly accused and put to death. Socrates here replies that no one really fears death unless he is wholly 'unreasoning and cowardly' (*anandros*). He thus shows up Callicles' 'self-protection' as a low, prudential aim which puts too high a value on life for its own sake, on any terms.

At 483e6 Callicles drew a memorable comparison between the strong man and a lion. Society, according to Callicles' way of thinking, hypnotises and subdues the leonine man's violent nature from birth onwards, and usually succeeds; but if he has a nature sufficient to the task, he will shake off the chains of social training and man-made law and trample all restraint underfoot. The lion-cub, tamed in its youth but ultimately reverting to type, is a fable used as a parallel in a magnificent chorus of Aeschylus' *Agamemnon* (737ff.); but Plato's use of the parallel has added point in view of the animal imagery through which he often characterises the different aspects of the human soul, above all the passions and appetites (e.g. *Phdr.* 246a-d, 253c sqq.). In the *Gorgias*, as in the *Republic* when Thrasymachus is compared with a wild beast (i. 336b, cf. de), this descriptive technique has a moral element: Callicles condemns himself through the unthinking savagery with which, lion-like, he would rip and tear apart the society which has nurtured him.[43]

A final instance of Callicles 'undercutting' himself occurs at 484cd. Here he is saying that the man of noble spirit, if he dallies too long in philosophy, is sure to end up ignorant of all that should be familiar to 'the one who is going to be a gentleman (*kalon kagathon*) and a man of reputation', and rather surprisingly goes on to say that such a man has to know about the *nomoi* and other public affairs of the city. Clearly, this represents a more

---

[43] For further animal-images see *Phdr.* 230a (Typhon); *Rep.* ix. 588b sqq.; *Tim.* 70e; and see C. Segal, *Hermes* 106 (1978) 332, who draws attention to the mythical background of metamorphosis (as in the *Odyssey*, e.g. with Circe and her pigs), and ancient moral interpretations thereof. Note also Hes. *Works and days* 276ff., and my *Meditations of M. Aurelius: A Study* 149.

realistic attitude than his vaguely expressed hopes of dashing *nomoi* and the like underfoot (484a). Further, this brings out a weakness in Callicles' whole argument: rhetoric and politics presuppose an ordered society with laws and established ways of doing things, in which the shrewder and more cynical politician can operate and exploit conventional laws. Not even a Callicles could survive in a primitive chaos of anarchic violence, and if he himself were to become a tyrant, he too would wish to lay down laws, even if they were enforced by 'the right of the stronger'. Consequently, the news that *nomoi* are meaningless is not news he should be keen to spread around. Although he is happy to scoff at conventional morality, he is in fact dependent on it: he needs a civilised society, not a jungle inhabited entirely by *physis*-types like himself. Also, his hopes of excelling are set in traditional terms: he wants to be 'a gentleman and a man of reputation', that is, not far distant from the traditional Athenian aristocrat. Here again we see that he is not in fact the 'free' man he envisages, but entangled in his society and its values. And here again, it is the old-fashioned and naive Socrates, the hole-in-the-corner philosopher, who turns out to be more radical in modifying traditional values and terminology: see 512b-e, where Socrates points out that Callicles' snobbery has no status if he follows his principles through; 527d, where he urges that humiliation in the courts and physical violence will do Callicles no harm (in a deeper sense) 'if you are in truth a *kalos kagathos*'.[44] Despite his claim to cut through what is customary and conventional, Callicles is still very much concerned with dignity and appearances, whereas Socrates is indifferent to all but what he sees as reality.

(3) The use of the lines from the *agon* of Euripides' *Antiope*.[45] In his main speech Callicles used this play to indicate the different paths of life which he and Socrates follow: 'the saying in Euripides applies: "each man is eminent in this field, and exerts himself in it, passing the greatest portion of his day, where he himself is best" – but wherever he is inferior, he avoids that and abuses it ...' (484e). And again, more explicitly: 'I am a reasonably good friend of yours, Socrates. And my feeling at the moment about you is just what Zethus in Euripides felt about Amphion – I mentioned him just now. For this is just the sort of thing that I feel like saying to you, as he did to his brother: 'Socrates, you are neglecting what ought to be your concern, and you are distorting the nature of your soul, noble as it is, in a childish dress; you could not put forward a sound case in the deliberations of justice ... my good chap, listen to me. Stop your questioning, practise the harmony

---

[44] Cf. also 515a.

[45] See Dodds, pp. 275-6; D.L. Page, *Greek Literary Papyri* (Loeb edn.) no. 10; French edn. of the fragments with notes by J. Kambitsis (Athens 1972). For other sources see 'Apollodorus' *Bibl.* iii. 5. 5 with Frazer's notes. The adaptation of this scene in Plato has been discussed a good deal in recent times: see A. Wilson Nightingale, *CAntiq.* 11 (1992) 121ff.; S.R. Slings, in *Fragmenta Dramatica*, ed. A. Harder and H. Hoffmann (Göttingen 1991), 137-51, and J.A. Arieti, *Interpreting Plato: The Dialogues as Drama* (Savage, Maryland 1991) ch. 5.

of the world's affairs, practise an art which will give you the reputation for sense, and leave these subtleties to others – whether one ought to call them nonsense or just trivia – "because of them you will dwell in empty halls." Imitate not men who question others about these tiny issues, but those who enjoy a real life and reputation and many other good things' (485e-6a, 486cd). Later, Socrates himself alludes to the same play: 'Well, Gorgias, for myself I'd be pleased to continue the discussion with Callicles here, until I've paid him Amphion's speech in return for that of Zethus' (506b; cf. 489e).

The play is of more than incidental relevance to the *Gorgias*. Briefly, the plot was, it appears, roughly as follows. Zeus had wooed Antiope, a princess of Sicyon; she bore twin sons, whom she exposed in shame; with predictable efficiency they were rescued and raised by a herdsman, and were named Amphion and Zethus. Meanwhile the tyrant Lycus took over Sicyon and their mother was enslaved; she escaped and eventually was recognised by her sons, who then took revenge on the tyrant and his wife. Hermes in an epilogue set any remaining difficulties to rights. But the most famous part of the play was the *agon* or competing speeches, in which the practical brother Zethus, athlete and herdsman, argued against his musical brother, Amphion: in essentials, a debate on the active versus the contemplative ways of life. It is hard to suppose that this exchange had any very close contact with the rest of the play.

Plato adapts the debate, making the significance for the intellectual still stronger. Both debates plainly reflect their authors' interests: poetry and music in Euripides, philosophic argument in the *Gorgias*. But two important contrasts seem clear: the result of the *agon* in the *Antiope* was that Amphion yielded (as Horace attests in the *Epistles*, i. 18. 43), whereas of course Socrates does not; and the long fragment of Hermes' speech at the end of the play (fr. 48 Kambitsis) shows that, despite this, Amphion and his art were vindicated by the *deus ex machina*, as Hermes foretells the magical construction of Thebes, with the stones following the notes of the lyre: a miraculously practical justification for the arts. The same speech, indeed, names Amphion as king (fr. 48. 97). In other words, in Euripides we have a melodramatic tragi-comedy with a happy ending and a whimsical resolution to the brothers' dispute; in Plato, the picture is much darker. Socrates will not yield and will go to his death for it, with no divine intervention, no one to speak for philosophy's enduring value. Plato here can be regarded as outdoing the poets: his drama is more tragic, and bleaker; his confrontation of the two opposed ideals is more sustained, more seriously engaged, dominating the dialogue and integrated in a way in which Euripides' scene could hardly have been. In Euripides, Zethus' case is decisively refuted, by divine authority: poetry *does* have its value; in Plato, the picture is much more ambiguous.

That ambiguity is heightened if we accept the speculation of E.R. Dodds[46]

---

[46] Introd. to the *Gorgias* commentary, p. 13.

that Callicles himself, of whom we know nothing from any source outside the *Gorgias*, may have come to grief in his subsequent political career, which would be a part-explanation for the silence of the historical record.[47] More substantially, it would add further point to 519a7 'and perhaps they [the Athenian people, when angry] will seize on you, if you're not careful, and on my companion Alcibiades, when they lose both their more recent gains and what they had before, though you aren't wholly responsible for the evils, but perhaps partly responsible.' If this theory is right, then both Socrates and Callicles would be victims of the anger of the Athenian people, and it would be plain to the original readers of the dialogue that Gorgianic rhetoric failed to provide Callicles with the security and self-protection for which he commends it to Socrates. On the other hand, it is also common knowledge, and foreshadowed in the dialogue, that Socrates is condemned. The choice between philosophy and rhetoric must therefore be made on other criteria than their value for self-preservation.

The adaptation of the scene from the *Antiope*, then, goes a good deal further than the insertion of the odd enlivening quotation. Despite its antagonistic quality, however, the central exchange of speeches does not constitute a prose *agon*, for Socrates does not actually give a full reply to Callicles straight away. His own speech at 487-8b is not a response to the Calliclean arguments but a call upon him to enter upon the enquiry which might make a response possible. It is true that he makes a fair number of long speeches in the rest of the dialogue, and that they do pick up Callicles' arguments, phrases and examples in the manner of the Euripidean *agon*-style; but the difference is that this happens *throughout* the rest of the dialogue. No single speech by Socrates replies *en bloc* or point-by-point to the rhesis of Callicles. This is a further aspect of the rhetoric-dialectic contrast, and by this means Socrates remains faithful to his general principles of dialectical method. He distrusts the form of debate in which one speech answers another: too much gets lost on the way (cf. p. 132f. above). Nor does he have a 'Socratic position' ready-made, to present outright in reply to Callicles' position; he needs to explore the arguments of Callicles in order to evolve and articulate a response. Hence the worries which critics have felt about Socratic *makrologia* in the *Gorgias* may result from looking at the question too much in terms of length. What matters more is how the speeches, long or short, are used; and from this point of view Socrates' approach remains dialectical, despite the difficulties he encounters when Callicles resigns from the conversation (see esp. 505d-6b).

(4) Callicles as a friend. Although Callicles finds Socrates' views unconvincing and is impatient with him, he nevertheless protests his goodwill and friendship (485e, 486a). We are not dealing with a future enemy such

[47] D.M. MacDowell in his edition of Andocides' speech *On the mysteries* (Oxford 1964) introduces the name Callicles by emendation at 127, a suggestion now endorsed by M.J. Osborne and S.G. Bourne, *Lexicon of Greek Personal Names* ii (1994) 247.

as Anytus, who in the *Meno* departs with a thinly-veiled threat. Socrates' knowledge of Callicles' *amours* and past conversations with friends confirms their closeness; and in an important passage he refers to the bond between the two of them:

> I think that someone who is to test adequately the soul which lives aright and the soul which does not needs to have three qualities, all of which you have: knowledge, goodwill and willingness to speak freely. For I come across a lot of people incapable of testing me because they aren't wise like you. Others are wise, but unwilling to speak the truth because they don't care for me as you do. Again, our foreign visitors here, Gorgias and Polus, are wise and friends of mine, but short on free speaking, and more prone to shame than they should be ... If you agree with me about anything in this discussion, then this will have been adequately tested by me and you, and we will no longer need to take it to another touchstone. For you would never have agreed with me on anything either from lack of wisdom or from excess of shame, nor again would you concede it to deceive me; for you are my friend, as you say yourself. (486e-7b, 487e)

The motif recurs several times later in the discussion (e.g. Socrates' appeal to Callicles by Zeus 'God of friendship', *Philios*, 500b, 519e).

The relationship between Socrates and Callicles, and Callicles' character, are thus of great importance for the development of the dialogue. Socrates in Plato regularly converses with friends, and one reason for this is that being a friend imposes some responsibility to be open and frank about one's beliefs. Socrates does not want the kind of friend who will play along with him, agreeing and conceding the argument in order to keep him happy: he wants to engage on a real level, to be challenged and to pursue a common search. Ideal dialectic should be a mutual challenge and support, a testing of one another's knowledge (514d5). In short, Socrates wants a true friend, and such a one will be a critic, not a flatterer.

This is what Socrates hopes of each questioner in turn, but above all of Callicles. In fact, however, far from having 'the three things which are necessary', Callicles proves to have only second-best versions of each. The 'wisdom' he has amounts to little more than worldly wisdom, dressed up with a few modish ideas: we have seen already how vulnerable even his initial formulation of his doctrines are, and they are further exposed as he endeavours to defend and modify them.

Because of the 'friendship' between them, Socrates feels sure that Callicles will not try to deceive him (487e, above), but his hopes are in fact dashed when Callicles sidesteps and changes his ground in the argument:

> 'For quite a while now I've been listening to you and agreeing, Socrates, observing that even if someone concedes something to you as a joke, you latch onto it eagerly like a boy. As if you really think that I or anyone else doesn't think that there are some pleasures which are better and others worse.'

> 'Oh really, Callicles, what a scoundrel you are. You treat me like a child, now saying that things are this way, and next that they're another way, and deceiving me. I didn't think at first that you'd voluntarily deceive me, because I thought you were a friend.' (499bc, cf. 500b 'and for the sake of Zeus God of friendship, Callicles, don't think you can play games with me, and don't answer at random, contrary to your own opinion ...')

Callicles scoffed at Socrates' philosophic play, but he himself plays with Socrates in a more damaging way, deceiving him and falsifying his real beliefs; he thus fails to live up to his claim that he is Socrates' friend.

As for 'free speaking', frankness, here too Callicles falls down. The motif of shame is redeployed in the analysis of Callicles' hedonism. First he accuses Socrates of shameful behaviour in the way he plays around with the argument, hunting down inconsistencies: aren't you ashamed, asks Callicles, to carry on like this at your age? (489b). He also resents and objects to Socrates' trivial and even vulgar examples (esp. 494 cd); and when Socrates brings up the case of scratching, and the notion of the infinite pleasure of the male prostitute, Callicles too is driven into a position of embarrassment and shame, though he hits back at Socrates with a disgusted reproof: 'aren't you ashamed to bring the discussion into topics like that, Socrates?' (494e). From one point of view, Callicles' reaction here is inappropriate, a kind of false shame, in that he objects to Socrates' use of everyday examples, shoemakers and the like, etc., because they do not fit in with his high-flown picture of the man of destiny; they offend against rhetorical decorum (cf. 521b2-3). Socrates' tactics, then, are *ad hominem*, deflating pretensions and enquiring into just what, on the everyday, down-to-earth level, the Calliclean ideal would mean (the constant harping on the idea of the politician as a flatterer pursues the same tactic).[48] But from another point of view, Callicles' reaction is more than aesthetic; it is morally significant. His distress at the example of the catamite shows that he is not a consistently amoral hedonist, and that, whatever his intentions, he has not – and perhaps, in Plato's eyes, *cannot* – cut himself entirely free from conventional morality. This also raises the question whether anyone else could do so; whether the image of the free man, the leonine man, is in fact realisable.

As the dialogue moves into its final stages, Callicles' crossness and indignation become steadily more marked; he has to be induced to stay in the discussion at all by Gorgias' entreaty (497bc), and in the end his responses are monosyllabic, sullen and, importantly, insincere (e.g. 510a1 'let that be the case then, Socrates, so that you can get the argument over with'; 513e1 'it can be so for you if you like'; 516b 'yes, certainly – just to gratify you'). He has given up all attempt to engage with Socrates or learn from him; his attempts at longer interventions introduce no new arguments

---

[48] Cf. ch. 3, pp. 80-1.

but only reiterate points he already made in the central speeches.[49] Now that Callicles has closed his mind to persuasion, Socrates is thrown back on his own resources, and adopts the peculiar method of questioning and answering himself, playing the part of Callicles as well as his own. It seems that the dialectical process has broken down (cf. 500bc, 501c, 505c-6c, 519d). The discussion in the later parts of the *Gorgias* also suggests why, above all at 507, in the more metaphysical passage on cosmic harmony. The man who seeks only to satisfy insatiable desires is incapable of living a normal life; he is like a robber. 'For such a man could not be dear to any other man or to god. For he is incapable of communal life (*koinonein*; cf. 506a, 527d2 "in common"), and the man in whom there is no common feeling cannot possess friendship' (507e). Although the sentences that follow introduce a different strand of imagery (the Pythagorean ideas of geometric equality), the thought is fully integrated with the rest of the dialogue: tyranny and power, like self-centred hedonism, are goals which can only isolate the man who pursues them from his fellow-men; and so they are contradictory to the ideals of friendship and cooperative search for truth that are all-important to Socrates.

In the finale of the work, Socrates again tries to bridge the gap between himself and Callicles, with all the eloquence that he can muster, and perhaps that is one reason why he also introduces the myth, as a last resort. He trumps the speech of Callicles with multiple echoes of the latter's warnings, and again tries to draw the young man into agreement with him, for example through the use of 'sympathetic' plurals.[50] But the silence of Callicles at the end signifies not his consent but Socrates' failure; Socrates is talking in a void. It is no accident that the dialogue in which we hear perhaps most about dialectical method should be a work in which Socrates so conspicuously fails to persuade, in which dialectic, even refined against the counter-methodology of rhetoric, does not prevail. Thus Plato sets the moral optimism and conviction of Socrates in a pessimistic, indeed a deliberately tragic, setting.

The myth[51]

Listen now, as they say, to a very fine *logos*, which you will think is a *muthos*, I suppose, but I consider it a *logos*. And I shall tell you what I am about to tell you as what is true (523a; cf. 524a8-b1, 527a).

---

[49] See e.g. 511a5ff., 521b3, 521c3ff., with Socrates' replies in each case.

[50] 527de; see further Macleod on Hom. *Iliad* 24. 600. Note also the culminating vocative at 527e7, the last words of the dialogue.

[51] In general on Plato's major myths see L. Edelstein, *Journ. Hist. Ideas* 10 (1949) 463-81; Friedlaender i, ch. 9; J. Annas, *Phronesis* 27 (1982) 119-43; S. Halliwell's commentary on *Republic* 10 (1988) 17ff. Fuller, book-length studies include L. Brisson, *Platon, les mots et les mythes* (Paris 1982), with a chronological bibliography from 1835; W. Hirsch, *Platons Weg zum Mythos* (Berlin 1971) is more abstract. There is a helpful discussion of philosophic myth in a broader context in F. Graf, *Greek Mythology* (orig. 1987, Eng. tr. Johns Hopkins 1993) 178-91. Diog. Laert. iii. 80 implies that some authorities criticised Plato for excessive use of myths.

So begins the last speech by Socrates in the dialogue; we hear nothing more
from his interlocutors. This long speech is dominated by a lengthy narration
of the soul's destiny in the afterlife. This is the first dialogue we have dealt
with which ends with a myth, as opposed to using mythology on the way
or incidentally. In this respect the *Gorgias* is comparable to the *Republic*,
which concludes with the myth of Er, and more approximately with the
Phaedo, which also ends the formal discussion with a mythical speech by
Socrates, but then concludes with the actual death-scene. The *Phaedrus*
and the *Statesman* are radically different in two respects: the myth in the
Phaedrus is only partly, and in the *Statesman* not at all, concerned with
the afterlife; and in both those dialogues it occurs mid-way through, not as
the concluding set-piece. Although mythological allusions and comparisons
are common elsewhere in Plato, the three myths of judgement have always
posed a special problem for interpreters, and the *Gorgias*, with its firm
insistence on the validity of the tale, raises these worries in an acute form:
in what sense does Socrates take the myth to be true? And does Plato take
it as he does? How are we to understand this conclusion, and how, if at all,
is the earlier argument affected?

These questions have sometimes been treated too much in isolation from
Plato's use of other quasi-mythical utterances, fables and 'stories': the term
muthos is if possible even more wide-ranging than the English 'myth'. The
whole question of *muthos* versus *logos*,[52] a contrast emphasised in the
passage quoted above, is one aspect of the great question of Plato's own art:
what kind of a writer is he, a philosopher or a poet or both; and what does
this imply about his works and their intellectual status? Although the
following discussion will return to the myth of the *Gorgias*, it is intended
to be relevant to these wider questions, and to the treatment of myth in
other dialogues, especially the *Phaedrus*, in later chapters.

First, a few words about sophistic background, another of the leitmotifs
of the book. Moral questioning of myth had its roots earlier: we find attacks
on Homer for his immoral stories of the gods in Xenophanes and Heraclitus,
and there are revisionist versions of myths in Pindar which surely stem
from moral concern and not merely from a desire for novelty (see e.g. *Ol.*
i). Closely related, but slightly different in approach, is the consideration
of myth with a fresh and rather sophisticated eye – identifying logical
inconsistencies and improbabilities, and even correcting them; rationalisation and historicising of myth; bringing the old stories up to date and giving
them a modern, even an anachronistic sparkle. The sophists tried their
ingenious hands at all these approaches. Sophists used myth, but did not
feel bound to follow its original form and tone: thus Protagoras, if Plato's
dialogue is to be trusted, could have revised the story of Prometheus and

---

[52] On the antithesis cf. W. Burkert, *Structure and History in Greek Mythology and Ritual*
(Berkeley and L.A. 1979) 3 and n. 14; M. Detienne, *The Creation of Mythology* (Chicago 1986)
44ff.; also Arist. *Met.* 1000a9-22.

Epimetheus in order to make it form part of a general account of the evolution of human society which for the most part owes little to traditional myth.We also have evidence for a moralising myth by Prodicus, who presented Heracles' choice of life, between Virtue and Vice, in a vividly pictorial antithesis (Prodicus B2 D-K = Xen. *Mem.* ii. 1. 21-34, presumably originally an epideixis).[53] Hippias too used myth for moral ends, as he tells Socrates in the *Hippias Major*, describing a composition in which Nestor advised Neoptolemus on what sort of activities are honourable and will make him most famous. Again this was clearly an epideixis, and probably intended to advertise Hippias' curriculum as much as old Nestor's! Also, we have Gorgias' *paignia* ('play-things', *jeux d'esprit*) on Helen and Palamedes, revamping myth and putting it in modern forensic dress. In other genres, we can see the influence of sophistic revisionism in Euripides' innovative and extended myths (especially in the passages in which his characters criticise or pour scorn on conventional motifs and mythical *data*);[54] in prose, Herodotus provides many sophisticated examples of myth demythologised or re-organised (e.g. i. 122, ii. 55f., 112ff. esp. 120. 1-3; cf. Hecataeus *FGH* 1 F 19, 26, 27 etc.).

Returning to Plato, we can see that he is familiar with such rationalising expedients. He seems to have some kind of cosmic allegory in mind in the *Republic*, when he says that the story of Cronos castrating his father is unacceptable even if it is allegory (*huponoia*, literally 'sub-meaning'), because the young do not understand allegory for what it is, but simply remember the story (ii. 378de).[55] More suggestive is the marvellous passage in the opening scene of the *Phaedrus*. Here Phaedrus has mentioned the story of Boreas, god of the North Wind, abducting the Athenian maiden Oreithyia near where they are walking, and he asks Socrates if he believes this tale. Socrates answers as follows:

> I shouldn't be doing anything unusual if I did disbelieve it, in the fashion of the intellectuals; and then I could do a clever rationalisation and say that it was the North Wind that threw her down on the rocks nearby while she was playing with Pharmaceia, and that after she'd died in this way people said she had been 'carried away by Boreas' ... But in fact, Phaedrus, I think that accounts of this sort are very charming, but really they are the sort of task that suits an ingenious and laborious person, one who is not entirely enviable, for this reason – after this performance he next has to set to rights the form of the Hippocentaurs, and after that the Chimaera, and in come flocking a whole host of such Gorgons and Pegasuses and a multitude of other unman-

---

[53] And perhaps the same work as Plato mentions as a prose encomium of Heracles (*Smp.* 177b; cf. Guthrie iii. 277f.). Cf. ch. 1, p. 13 above.

[54] See esp. Eur. *Electra* 513-46; R.P. Winnington-Ingram, *Arethusa* 2 (1969) 127-42.

[55] For cosmic allegorising of e.g. the battles of the Gods in Homer, see Theagenes 8A 2 Diels-Kranz, and the Derveni papyrus, an allegorising commentary on an 'Orphic' theogony (*ZPE* 47 (1982) from p. 300); see further N.J. Richardson, *PCPS* 21 (1975) 65-81; D.C. Feeney, *The Gods in Epic* (Oxford 1991) ch. 2.

ageable creatures, strange and miraculous in their natures. If someone is to go ahead with his scepticism to expound each and every one of these by criteria of probability (*eikos*), using a rather backwoods ingenuity, he is going to need a great deal of leisure time. As for me, I simply don't have the leisure for that, and the reason, my friend, is this. I cannot yet, as the Delphic maxim has it, *know myself*. And it seems ludicrous to me to investigate matters which are beyond my scope while I remain in ignorance of this. So I let these questions alone, and follow conventional belief, while I examine not them, but myself, as I just said. I am trying to find out whether I am a beast of more parts than Typhon, and more inflated and puffed up, or whether I am a gentler and simpler creature, naturally possessed of a divine and less typhonic lot. (*Phdr.* 229c-3oa)

Socrates' humour here is, as usual, pointed and two-edged. The supposed sophistication of the allegorists and rationalists is in fact *agroikos* (bumptious, naive, clumsy); the uncritical attitude of Socrates is not as idle and old-fashioned as it might appear, for he is not ignorant of modern ideas, and can spin a rationalising interpretation as well as the next man. This means that we must take seriously his own pursuit and the rationale behind it. The intellectual antics of the so-called 'intellectuals' (*sophoi*) neglect what is closest to home, the apparently obvious and deceptively simple goal of self-knowledge and self-criticism. Moreover, the multiple word-play on Typhon the monster and the similar Greek words for humbug, vanity and smoke punningly conveys a serious point about human nature; Socrates is asking whether it is not as strange and monstrous a creature as the mythical beasts. This paves the way for the imagery of the divided soul and the charioteer and his horses later in the *Phaedrus*; it is also a range of imagery found elsewhere in Plato's accounts of the soul, notably in the composite of man, lion and many-headed beast which lurks in the soul according to the *Republic* (588cd). The 'many-ness' of the soul, the question whether Socrates is himself more manifold, more complex than Typhon, is another joke with a point, for singleness, unity is the aim of Socrates and the goal to which he also tries to guide his friends. In short, in the *Phaedrus* we see Socrates using the sophistic questions and paradoxes as a spring-board for his own ironic yet deeply serious moral exploration of his own and others' goals.

Socrates' criticism of the rationalisers, then, is not based on a conviction that all myths are true – indeed, he says he holds no opinion one way or the other on that. Rather, he regards this kind of interpretation as an endless and fruitless task. He is concerned to learn from the myths, as from all sources, what he can apply to himself. Moreover, it also suits his personality and general attitude to adopt a rather old-fashioned, *faux-naif* view of the myths and their modish interpreters. The novelty of Socrates is not blazoned to the world as are the brave new theories of the sophists; his true originality tends to emerge gradually and surprisingly, after his more up-to-date interlocutors have dismissed him as an old Cronos (i.e. a dotard, *Euthyd.* 287b). He does not assume that an exciting new method will produce the best results just because it is new. Although he is familiar with sophistic teachings, it is part of his style to go in the opposite direction, often appealing to older and simpler examples and authorities (527a, 512e; cf. Hor. *Sat.* ii. 6. 77f.). The point is not that he thinks that the old views are always best, but they merit consideration on their merits, not summary dismissal (cf. *Phdr.* 275bc).

Ethically the myths of the afterlife are extremely simple (especially that which ends the *Gorgias*); stylistically and rhetorically, however, they operate on a higher plane than Socrates normally achieves. In the *Phaedo* the myth is referred to as an *epode*, a kind of incantatory spell which the friends of Socrates should chant to themselves in order to reassure themselves against the fear of death; that is, it operates on the emotions and has less purely rational content than the dialectical parts of the dialogue. Here we see, perhaps, a kind of purer rhetoric, a persuasive use of myth in the service of philosophy; but it is neither conclusive nor argumentative, and the same passage of the *Phaedo* makes a clear qualification as regards its truth value:

> Now to insist that these things are exactly as I've described them would not be appropriate for a man of sense; but that either this or something like it is the case regarding our souls and their habitations, given that the soul evidently is immortal, this, I think, *is* fitting and worth risking, for one who believes that it is so – for the risk is a noble one – and one ought to repeat such things to oneself like a spell; that indeed is the reason I have so prolonged the story. (*Phaedo* 114d)

This is clearly a more qualified assertion than Socrates' more impassioned commitment to the truth of the myth he expounds in the *Gorgias*, and suggests that although a few generalisations are possible, the myths in Plato should not be lumped too readily together; they need to be viewed in their particular contexts in the dialogues. Perhaps the firmness and intensity with which Socrates maintains his position on the afterlife in the *Gorgias* suits the intensity of the discussion prior to this. By contrast, for example, in the *Phaedrus*, the atmosphere is much more relaxed, the relationship between the two friends more humorous, and even the majesty of the myth is deflated from time to time with incongruous touches, and is subsequently dismissed as 'play'.

This point is reinforced when we consider the way in which the myth is introduced in different dialogues. When Socrates proposes to give an account of the soul's journey in Hades, Callicles' response is ungracious and rude: 'well, since you've finished everything else off, finish that too' (522e). A far cry from the eager enthusiasm of Socrates' audiences elsewhere: in the *Republic*, at the equivalent point, Glaucon declares 'you could tell me nothing which it would give me greater pleasure to hear' (x. 614b1, cf. *Phaedo* 110b, *Phdr.* 243b).

The myth of the *Gorgias* is thematically connected with the preceding discussion, in that it concerns *judgement* in the afterlife. This suits the forensic-rhetorical theme of the dialogue. In contrast, in the *Phaedo* the judges are hardly mentioned; and the myth of the *Republic*, like the rest of that work, focuses on man's choice of life and its consequences: 'The one who chooses bears the responsibility; god is not responsible' (617e, cf. 619c4ff.). The *Gorgias* myth also picks up, echoes and sometimes reverses a wide range of motifs from the earlier part of the dialogue, some of which have already been mentioned. It responds to Callicles' accusations, with a wealth of verbal echoes, especially in 526e-7a, which answers Callicles' warning that as things are, Socrates will be incapable of defending himself in a lawcourt (486b). Callicles will be in the equivalent position in Hades:

> And I can find fault with you because you will be unable to protect yourself when the trial and the judgement of which I spoke just now takes place for you; no, when you come before the judge, the son of Aigina, and when he gets hold of you and carries you away, you will be gaping and gasping there in just the same way as I would be here, and maybe somebody will beat you and shove your face in disrespectfully, and altogether humiliate you.

Also, the theme of the souls' nakedness recalls Socrates' call for frankness and honesty rather than concealment of one's self and one's true feelings; the kings and tyrants who are condemned in Hades to everlasting punishment correspond to the ideals of Polus and Callicles (there is a specific reference to both the Great King and Archelaus of Macedon); the soul that is full of 'asymmetry' (525a5) reminds us of the praise of equality and cosmic order at 507e; the 'many witnesses' of 523c, who once testified for the rich but are now debarred from helping them, remind us of the exchange between Socrates and Polus at 471e sqq., where Polus insisted that everyone would agree with him; in reply, Socrates maintained that even if Polus could muster countless distinguished witnesses who took his view, that kind of refutation would be meaningless in dialectic. What counts is the one-to-one confrontation and comparison of beliefs (472b). Above all, the chief innovation which Plato has made in the old mythology, the image of the scars on the naked soul, which are visible signs of their evil-doing when they are arraigned before the judges, conveys Socrates' conviction that to do wrong is to harm yourself, your own soul, even while you are still alive. Even if there is no after-life, this still applies: these scars are not the consequence of posthumous punishment, but are inflicted on the soul by its owner during his lifetime. 'The worst of all evils is for the soul to journey to Hades full of many misdeeds' (522e).

Though this and perhaps other details may be Plato's own invention, the presentation of Hades in the *Gorgias* is the most traditional and straightforward of his large-scale myths. Its mythical background is broadly Homeric: Zeus and the other gods, Thersites, Minos as in book xi of the *Odyssey*, and again from that book the great sinners (525d, where Homer is cited). Contrast the more recherché cosmography of the *Phaedo*, with its extraordinarily complex picture of the earth's surface and interior; there, Homer's rivers are used (Styx, Cocytus, and so forth) but their setting becomes colourful fantasy. In the *Republic*, the Fates are traditional enough, but we find that they are the daughters of *Ananke*, Necessity, a more up-to-date principle;[56] contrast Hesiod's *Theogony*, where they were daughters of Night (217ff.). In general, the myth of the *Republic* treats traditional myth and cosmology very freely, especially in the picture of the distaff of Necessity. This clearly derives from the idea of the Fates as spinners, but Plato has made much more of the distaff, turning it into a central structure around which the universe revolves. Epic-tragic elements are blended with pseudo-science in the *Phaedo*, numerical and musical theory in the *Republic*. The *Gorgias* myth is more traditional because of the seriousness of Socrates' mood and the intensity of the confrontation. This climax, a last appeal as Socrates endeavours, in effect, to save Callicles' soul, leaves less room for irony and philosophic play than there is in the *Republic* and even the *Phaedo*, let alone the *Phaedrus*. It is Plato's starkest picture of justice beyond this world, but it is also put in terms which deliberately stress Socrates' traditionalism, his faith – in Callicles' eyes, his naiveté.

This is not in fact the first excursus into mythology in the *Gorgias*. Earlier, Socrates had tried to use a myth of a more sophistic and modern kind at 493a-494a, in which the old story of the water-carriers in Hades was interpreted allegorically, with an ingenious series of puns and plays on words reminiscent of Tiresias' lecture-style exposition in Euripides' *Bacchae* (272-97). These ideas were introduced as not Socrates' own: he has heard them second-hand, from the intellectuals, who were reporting the witty conception of 'some story-telling clever fellow, perhaps a Sicilian or an Italian' (493a). Perhaps at least part of the point there is that Callicles is expected to approve of such ingenious interpretations,[57] and of Sicilian thinkers generally: Gorgias and Polus, after all, come from Sicily. In that earlier myth, then, Socrates' tactics are directed *ad hominem*, whereas at the end of the dialogue, the distance between himself and Callicles having been fully revealed, he reverts to an older-style and more uncompromising faith. There, he had drawn on sophistic or speculative opinion in a way which Callicles might regard as intellectually respectable, but Callicles did not find this at all persuasive (494ab); *a fortiori*, then, how can he be swayed by the myth at the end, with its unsophisticated mythology and simple faith?

Indeed, Socrates no longer seems to expect to convince Callicles: at 527a5-6 he anticipates that 'perhaps this will seem old wives' tales to you and you will think little of it', and the qualification in 526e hints at his own

---

[56] Cf. Dover on Ar. *Clouds* 377, 1075.
[57] Rather as Meno approves of the high-flown Empedoclean definition of shape which Socrates teasingly offers (*Meno* 76d; cf. ch. 3, p. 76 above).

inadequacy to his self-appointed task: 'I exhort all other men, as far as I can.' In the end, the dialogue's effort at persuasion has failed: Socrates has persuaded only himself, and the final myth brings out both the strength and the loneliness of his convictions. The appeal which is meant to move and sway Callicles seems likely to distance him still further; and the *muthos-logos* passage at the opening of the speech may suggest that while the myth may be 'true' for Socrates, in that he has no doubt of it, its truth is incommunicable to a man like Callicles. Socrates needs the sympathetic response of a man who has not closed his mind, but who will join him in a cooperative search for the truth – as a true friend.

7

The *Symposium*

A summary cannot do justice to any Platonic dialogue, least of all Plato's dramatic masterpiece, the *Symposium*. The brilliance of the setting, the variety and vividness of the personalities, the corresponding shifts of style and tone, the eloquence of Socrates' central speech, and the delightful inconsequence (or so it appears) of Alcibiades' drunken reminiscences: all of these elements make the dialogue one of the easiest and most entertaining to read. The universal interest of its subject, love, also helps to account for its popularity, though here many modern readers must make an effort to come to terms with the homosexual ethos which is accepted as normal in Athenian upper-class society. Recent work has done much to remind us of the 'otherness' of ancient behaviour patterns and emotional life, and despite its immediate appeal, the *Symposium* is a text which makes clear that modern attitudes, whether heterosexual or homosexual, cannot be simply mapped on to a remote and radically different society. The strangeness of many of the arguments used in this dialogue is a healthy antidote to the assumption that ancient experience is readily accessible to the modern reader.[1] Finally, the dialogue offers us the most complete, detailed and entrancing portrait of Socrates in Plato's works, while also including the liveliest presentation of Alcibiades. Through Plato's dramatic art we know and can visualise this pair better than any other characters in fifth-century Greek history.

The *Symposium* is the only work of Plato in which we see Socrates at a drinking party. It seems, however, that this was not only a regular setting for Socratic dialogues, but also a genre in itself – 'sympotic literature'.[2] This is sufficiently clear even if we discount Xenophon's *Symposium* as probably a later work influenced by Plato. There was ample precedent in poetry: Homer's heroic feasts, the gatherings of comrades described in archaic lyric and elegy, and perhaps especially the prescriptive verses of Xenophanes,

---

[1] See the influential study by Foucault, *The History of Sexuality* (Eng tr. 1978-86), developed in classical studies esp. by J. Winkler, *The Constraints of Desire* (1990), and D.M. Halperin, *One Hundred Years of Homosexuality* (1990) (with e.g. Dover's review, *CR* 41 (1991) 161-2; J. Thorp, *Phoenix* 46 (1992) 54-61); cf. Halperin, Winkler and Zeitlin (edd.), *Before Sexuality: The Construction of Erotic Experience in the Ancient Greek World* (Princeton 1989).

[2] See further Hug, *RE* 4a. 1273ff.; J. Martin, *Symposion* (Paderborn 1931); D. Gera, *Xenophon's Cyropaedia* (Oxford 1993) 132-54.

in which he defines the proper topics for poetic performance at a party (fr. 1). Closer to Plato are the descriptions of parties in comedy (the drunken Philocleon lowers the tone of, and finally breaks up, a high-society occasion in the *Wasps*); closer still are some of the fragments of Ion of Chios, who described both Cimon and the poet Sophocles in sympotic contexts (F 6 and 13). The opening page of the *Symposium* itself refers to a figure otherwise unmentioned in Plato, Phoenix son of Philippos, who has given a rather different account of the occasion to Glaucon, although apparently his source is the same as our narrator's. This might be a reference to a different written version. Much later, Plutarch (*Mor.* 823d) refers to literary accounts of Socratic symposia with Callias or Alcibiades as hosts (the former fits Xenophon's work, but the latter must be a lost dialogue). In general terms, Xenophon implies that the material for such accounts existed when, in the *Memorabilia*, he says that 'whenever he accepted an invitation to dinner, he resisted without difficulty the common temptation to exceed the limits of satiety ...' (i. 3. 6; cf. iii. 14. 1-6).

Because of the gaps in our evidence and the enormous influence of Plato's work, it is hard to establish what features were already prominent in sympotic literature in the early fourth century, and what he himself contributed. It does seem likely that certain elements were standard, as literary motifs but also as regular procedure in real-life symposia.[3] It is clear that the drinkers normally appointed one of their number as symposiarch, and that he dictated the strength of the wine and other procedural matters: Eryximachus in the dialogue assumes this role, until Alcibiades ousts him. Regular entertainment involved music, dancing and girls; the diners could also entertain themselves, often with songs or verses which they would exchange or try to cap. The game of 'comparisons', which involved seeing unexpected likenesses and expressing them wittily, is well-known from the *Wasps* and plays a part in the speech of Alcibiades; it is used elsewhere in Plato, notably in the *Meno*.[4] When speeches are made in turn, as here, there is an obvious element of competition: rivalry seems to be common in the symposium (it can of course be aggravated by drink), and sometimes has erotic motivations. Love, in fact, seems to be another standard feature: often the participants may include lovers (as here with Agathon and Pausanias), and the conversation commonly turns upon love. Here the speeches are concerned with praising and defining Eros; elsewhere advice on wooing, teasing enquiry about the progress of an affair, or efforts at matchmaking are attested.[5] The atmosphere is light-hearted but

[3] Martin (see previous n.) 1ff., 33ff., 116ff., 149ff., 185ff.; G.J. Woldinga, *Xenophons Symposium* (Amsterdam 1938) 3-10. On the symposium as a central feature of Greek life see esp. O. Murray (ed.), *Sympotica* (Oxford 1990), with bibliography and illustrations (cf. already Murray, *Early Greece* (Glasgow 1981) 197-203).

[4] Ar. *Wasps* 1308ff.; *Meno* 80; see also Fraenkel on Aesch. *Ag.* 1629ff.

[5] On *erotikoi logoi* see Hug-Schöne's edition of the *Symp.*, x-xv; F. Lasserre, *MH* 1 (1944) 169-78.

not necessarily free of tensions: seriousness and comedy are combined in a setting in which many things can be said more openly, in jest and stimulated by wine, than they would be in the cold light of day. The potential of the genre was recognised by many later writers: the philosophic symposium (continued by Aristotle and Epicurus) was one species in a large range, and we can trace the development of the form through many centuries. Farcical and anarchic in Petronius, learned and literary in Athenaeus or Macrobius, elegantly allusive in Plutarch, devoutly Christian in Methodius (fourth century AD), it has had a fertile history.

The form of Plato's dialogue, though familiar, requires a brief résumé. The story of the convivial gathering in 416 BC is narrated some years later by Apollodorus to a friend: he admits that he was not himself an eye-witness, but derived his knowledge from Aristodemus. At the time of the events he narrates, he himself was only a child (173a), but he is now an ardent disciple and emulator of Socrates, a mirror-image of what the faithful Aristodemus was then (173b). The narrative which follows, then, looks back to a time of greater prosperity and hope, when Agathon was a beautiful and successful youth and had not yet emigrated from Athens (172c), when Alcibiades, though a noisy and disruptive figure, had not yet abandoned his country's cause, and when Athens' empire was still at its height. Yet the frame-dialogue seems to imply that Socrates is still alive (esp. 172c5). The effect of the distancing of the events in time is therefore complex, for the narrator, Apollodorus, can see some of the ironies and disappointed hopes implicit in his story;[6] but the reader, guided by Plato, can detect signs of further misfortune, with the death of Socrates, the supposed teacher and corrupter of Alcibiades, still in store. We have already considered the other effects of this layered narrative structure (ch. 3, p. 72): while reinforcing the sense of a tradition preserving the memory of Socrates, it also distances the narrative and casts some doubt on the authenticity and exactness of the account. These doubts must be reinforced by the explicit selectivity of the account given (178a, 180c) and by Aristodemus' drowsiness towards the end of the party (223c-d). The value of the dialogue lies deeper than as a literal historical record.

In its vivid scene-setting and continuing consciousness of the physical context of discussion, the dialogue which the *Symposium* resembles most closely is the *Protagoras*. In both Socrates proceeds to a communal gathering in the company of a friend, arrives when the occasion is well underway, and participates at first as a welcome new face, but gradually comes to dominate the conversation. In the *Protagoras* it is the great sophist who is at the centre of attention (though with plenty of competition from his

---

[6] Especially if Alcibiades is now dead, as suggested by Nussbaum, *Fragility of Goodness* 167-71 (hereafter cited by author's name); but I find it hard to believe that her elaborate argument there is truly necessary, or that even an informed contemporary would have made the deductions that she has.

fellow-teachers); here, the host himself, Agathon, is the celebrity. In both works Socrates' arrival is preceded by an odd episode in which his commitment to philosophy is stressed: there, he and Hippocrates remain outside to conclude their discussion (p. 125 above), while here, Socrates falls behind and stands alone in a state of trance-like contemplation, only later joining the drinkers, when he has resolved a problem to his satisfaction. That he pursues this thought alone, and without communicating it to the others when he arrives, suits the general impression we receive from this dialogue, in which Socrates is in some respects a more isolated and austere figure.

The occasion of the dinner-party is to celebrate Agathon's first victory in a tragic festival, at the Lenaea of 416. Much is made of the beauty and charm of the young man, who is admired and complimented by all; Socrates' comments alone administer first much-needed ironies (175de), and later correction (194, 198-201c). Furthermore, the notion and the imagery of drama are of some importance in the dialogue: besides the tragic poet Agathon, the comedian Aristophanes is present; Alcibiades' wild talk of satyrs and sileni leads Socrates to describe his speech as 'your satyric and silenic drama' (222d), and at the conclusion of the dialogue Socrates is seen trying to persuade the befuddled and sleepy dramatists that, contrary to the convention at Athens, the same man can compose both tragedy and comedy. (This is in part a characterisation of Socrates' practice and Plato's own art, as we shall see.) The speeches delivered by the individual diners are treated as 'performances' in a competition; Agathon's in particular is greeted with uncritical applause (198a) which seems to mirror his success in public on the previous day (175e, 194b). In the final stages of the dialogue Alcibiades crowns Agathon in celebration of his victory in the tragic contest (213ab), but when he realises that Socrates is present, begs Agathon to surrender some of the ribbons, 'so that I may crown Socrates' head as well, and what a wonderful head it is! I don't want him to be complaining that I made a garland for Agathon and none for him, when his words have conquered the whole world, not just yesterday, Agathon, as yours did, but all the time' (213e). These passages and others confirm that the dinner at Agathon's is a kind of dramatic contest in which Socrates wins the prize: the thinker triumphs over the poet. In part, no doubt, the analogy is a kind of festive fun, a jest sustained by the characters and also by the author behind them; but reflection on the further careers of both Socrates and Alcibiades should remind us that there is a tragic side to this drama.[7]

No less important is the more rhetorical or sophistic side of the contest. The proposal of Eryximachus is that each of those present should make a speech in praise of Love, as this good and generous god has been so unjustly neglected by poets and by writers of prose *encomia*, who none the less find time to write ridiculous works in praise of salt and the like (177ab).

---

[7] See further P.H. von Blanckenhagen, *GRBS* 33 (1992) 51-8; D.E. Anderson, *The Masks of Dionysus: A Commentary on Plato's Symposium* (State Univ. of N.Y., Albany 1993).

Eryximachus is referring to the paradoxical encomia commonly composed by sophists with tongue in cheek, to show how rhetorical brilliance could enliven the least promising of subjects or restore dignity and good reputation even to the most villainous characters. Gorgias' *Helen*, a paradoxical defence of the mythical adulteress, is a surviving instance. Many others were known in antiquity: Alcidamas *On Death*, Polycrates' works in praise of Clytemnestra and Busiris, and in later times Lucian's *Encomium of a fly*.[8] The characteristics of encomia were already well developed by Plato's time. Agathon's speech observes the rules closely, just as it is composed in a highly mannered Gorgianic style suited to the genre. Socrates' criticisms of that speech and of the untruthfulness of the whole genre also imply that its manner and methods are well known (198b-9b).[9] Socrates' critique, and his subsequent puncturing of Agathon, recall the contrast between rhetorical grandiloquence and dialectical precision familiar from earlier dialogues.

Both the real and the paradoxical version of the encomium are relevant to the *Symposium*. Love and Eros are natural subjects for a serious encomium, and such works were often composed in honour of deities: in essence, these prose works are the inheritors of the tradition of the lyric hymn.[10] But when Alcibiades appears and learns what the others are doing, he speaks instead an encomium not of Love the divinity, but of his own love, Socrates. This is a paradoxical subject, seemingly comic and preposterous. Accordingly, Alcibiades' speech is greeted by the company with unthinking and irreverent laughter (222c). But at the beginning of his speech he declared that, though he would praise Socrates by comparisons, he was doing so not just to make them laugh, but in the cause of truth (215a). Here then, as in their enthusiastic reaction to Agathon's speech, the audience is being insufficiently critical; for all his drunkenness and incoherence, Alcibiades has a more profound understanding of Socrates than they.

From the beginning of the dialogue proper, much emphasis is laid on the *strangeness* of Socrates. Already, when Aristodemus arrives at Agathon's house, he has had to leave Socrates behind, meditating in a nearby doorway. Though Agathon remarks on the oddity of his behaviour,[11] it emerges that this is a common habit of his (175b1-2; confirmed by Alcibiades later, 220cd). We note that it is not just any friend, but only an intimate, a disciple and lover (*erastes*, 173b), who can interpret Socrates'

---

[8] Also Libanius' *On Thersites* (in vol. viii of Forster's edn.). See further Menander Rhetor, ed. Russell and Wilson, intr.; A.S. Pease, *CP* 21 (1926) 27-42; V. Buchheit, *Untersuch. zur Theorie des Genos Epideiktikon* (Munich 1960). Erasmus' *In Praise of Folly* is in the same tradition.

[9] For the criticisms in 198e1-2 in particular, cf. *Mnx.* 234c, Isoc. *Busiris* 4, Radermacher, *Artium Scriptores* p. 174.

[10] Cf. Isoc. 9. 8-11, 15. 166; Men. Rh. iii. 333 sq. (Spengel), with Russell and Wilson ad loc.

[11] 175a10 *atopon legeis*, 'what a strange tale you bring'; *atopos* is a key word, cf. 215a, 221d.

actions: thus Agathon is perplexed, but Aristodemus is not.[12] These intimates, Aristodemus in the main narrative and Apollodorus in the frame,
are devoted followers of Socrates: they follow him, spend time with him
philosophising, and count all time wasted that is not spent in this pursuit
(172c4-3a3, 173b3-4, 173c2-d3). They are philosopher-lovers; their devotion
to their master is a healthy and contented version of the exaggerated
passion of Alcibiades, as a number of similarities make clear.[13]

   Other details of the introductory scenes also pave the way for the two
most important speeches, those of Socrates and Alcibiades. In the *Symposium*, one key word is *kalos*, 'beautiful' or 'fine'. There is a cluster of
instances at the beginning of Apollodorus' narrative (174a). Aristodemus
asks where Socrates is off to 'having become so beautiful', i.e. looking so
splendid; Socrates replies that he has beautified himself so that 'fair may
call on fair'. The idea of Socrates being beautiful is almost a paradox (it is
sufficient to refer to Alcibiades' description later in the dialogue of his
extraordinary appearance),[14] and this draws attention to the incongruity
of referring to Socrates and Agathon by the same adjective. While it may
be that each is *kalos*, they must be so in different senses. For Socrates,
beauty is present where there is wisdom, and the relationship of these two
qualities (whether they naturally co-exist, which is truly admirable, which
should be preferred) is a common theme in the dialogues.[15] But whereas
Socrates described Agathon as fair, Aristodemus in his reply is happy to
refer to him as 'wise' (174c7; note that *sophou*, 'wise', is his own addition;
it does not occur in the Homeric quotation which he adapts.)

   The theme is further developed in the exchanges between Socrates and
Agathon. When Socrates appears, his host welcomes him warmly and tells
him to sit by him so that, by clasping Socrates, he may draw off some of the
benefit of his reflections outside. Socrates takes his seat, remarking that it
would be a very fine thing if wisdom were so easily transmissible by contact,
'like water in cups running along a woollen thread from the fuller into the
emptier goblet' (175d). But what is his own wisdom in comparison with
Agathon's which stunned an audience of thousands yesterday? This ironic
exchange, with the characteristic use of a homely image, hints at a serious
point: how *is* knowledge or wisdom actually transmitted and how far is it
dependent on personal contact, whether physical or sharing a presence?
The case of Alcibiades is again foreshadowed: for him, Socrates' influence
and his own self-awareness are lessened when he is parted from the
philosopher (216bc). Similarly Apollodorus and Aristodemus, the 'true'
disciples, are constantly following Socrates around: *suneinai, sungignes-*

---

[12] For the use of *erastes* here see Dover, *Greek Homosexuality* (hereafter *GH*) 157: the word
can denote simply a 'fan' or acolyte, and in this early passage it is natural for the reader to
assume that it bears that sense; but the deeper implications of the term are explored later.

[13] Cf. e.g. 216a-c; A.D. Nock, *Conversion* (1933) 166; *Essays* ..., ed. Z. Stewart (1972) 470.

[14] See further Guthrie iii. 386-90; Vlastos, *Socrates* 251-3.

[15] See e.g. *Charm.* 153d; *Prt.* 309b-d (p. 122 above), with Dover, *GH* 158-9.

thai, sundiatribein, these words of co-existence are important in this dialogue and elsewhere for the philosophic search which Socrates' friends enjoy (cf. e.g. *Theages* 128b, 129e), and the closest analogy is with the constant association of lovers (cf. esp. 211d). Further variations on this theme of contact and companionship include Aristophanes' fantasy of the perpetual union of partners locked in sexual embrace (192d sq.), and the physical 'assault' of Alcibiades, throwing his arms around Socrates in an effort to seduce him: like Agathon's more delicate appeal, this is an attempt to draw on Socrates' wisdom and use it for his own ends (219b-d). But the most significant and contrasting use of the words for contact is in a very different context, when Socrates speaks of the soul 'grasping' ultimate beauty: no merely physical embrace this, but the passionate apprehension of what is truly real and beautiful (209c, 211b, 212a).

Just as from one point of view Aristodemus and Apollodorus prefigure Alcibiades and mirror his relationship with Socrates, so from another angle Socrates' behaviour towards Agathon includes features that are later exploited. Agathon, like Alcibiades, is a beautiful and successful young man, but probably more than a few years younger than Alcibiades (who was born c. 450). Agathon welcomes admiration and attention from all who will give it; Socrates offers a certain amount of flattery, the ironic edge of which largely escapes Agathon; and when Alcibiades arrives, there is much jesting and disingenuous comment from Socrates about Alcibiades' jealousy whenever he, Socrates, has anything to do with another man (213cd). Socrates even feigns alarm that Alcibiades will beat him up! (ibid. d; cf. Xen. *Smp.* 8. 4) The obvious interpretation of this sequence would be that Socrates is now transferring his affections to the younger Agathon; he is, it seems, playing the fickle lover. But in fact it is Socrates who fascinates, but eventually eludes, both 'beauties'.

The first five speeches

From these more general remarks it is time to turn to a closer examination of the speeches. One of the most attractive features of the *Symposium* is that so many other speakers besides Socrates are allowed their say, and that they offer such varied perfomances in appropriately characterised styles. Selective quotation and comment can show something of Plato's virtuoso range here, but for a full appreciation the reader must turn to the dialogue itself.

Phaedrus, the initiator of the contest, is the first speaker quoted: his is a poetic speech, laden with quotation and literary reference, with rather little to say about himself or his native Athens or the company's own emotional lives. The most striking passage is the 'utopian' wish in which he seems to anticipate the creation of a body such as the Theban 'Sacred band', founded in c. 378 BC.[16]

---

[16] Dover, *The Greeks and their Legacy* 94-5 documents this remarkable military innovation.

So if some means could be found to form a city or an army of lovers and their
loves, there is no way they could run their society better than by abstaining
from every shameful act and competing with one another in their pursuit of
honour; while as for fighting, such a force might be few in number but would
still prevail over virtually all mankind! For a lover, I think, if he were
abandoning the ranks or throwing away his weapons, would rather be
observed by anyone rather than his beloved, and indeed he would choose
death many times over sooner than that. As for abandoning his beloved or
not helping him when he's in danger – nobody is so base that Love himself
could not inspire him towards virtue, so as to be a match for the noblest of
men. And certainly what Homer describes, about god 'breathing might' into
some of the heroes, is something that Love does for lovers, a gift that comes
directly from him. (178e3-79b3)

Pausanias' speech is more concerned with the social ethos of homosexuality as practised at Athens: he remarks, with a sociologist's self-importance, that practices in other states are divergent. The distinctions he
draws between Heavenly and Earthly Aphrodite, between love which
incurs shame and love which is honourable, between heterosexual and
homosexual desire, are worthy of his master Prodicus (see *Prt.* 315d). The
map he draws of Athenian practice is well-observed, but the deductions he
draws seem self-interested, for he is himself the pursuer of Agathon.[17] One
passage may be singled out for its unconscious relevance to a later part of
the dialogue.

But this, I think, is the actual situation: love is not a simple thing, as I said
at the start. It is neither honourable nor disgraceful in itself, but honourable
if practised honourably, disgraceful if practised disgracefully. To gratify a
base lover or in a base way is disgraceful, but to grant his wish to a virtuous
lover honourably is honourable. The base lover is the one who is promiscuous,
loving the body more than the soul; he is not constant, because what he desires
is not constant. As soon as the body's bloom, which is what he loved, begins
to fade, 'he's off and away through the air', putting his many promises and
protestations to shame. But the lover who cares for a fine character remains
loyal throughout, being attached to something that endures. (183d3-e6)

As we shall see, Pausanias' easy generalisations are too simple to be applied
to the paradoxical relationship between Socrates and Alcibiades.[18]
The doctor Eryximachus, who takes Aristophanes' place while the comedian is troubled by the typically low-brow discomfort of hiccups, is a more
richly comical figure in his own right. Starting by dismissing the speeches
so far, he launches upon a pseudo-scientific exposition which declares Love
to be all-important for his own science of medicine, and for gymnastics,

[17] Cf. *Prt.* 315de, and Dover, *GH* 84. For a remorseless dissection of his rhetorical performance
see H. Neumann, *TAPA* 94 (1964) 261-7 (marred for modern taste by his repeated reference
to homosexuality as a 'vice').
[18] See further 184ab, 184c7-5c2, and cf. 218c-9d; Halperin (n.1) 116.

farming, poetry and music too. By assimilating love to related concepts such as harmony and health, he dilutes the term so far as to make it almost meaningless. His patronising manner extends not only to his fellow-diners but also to the poets and to Heraclitus ('though his mode of expression certainly leaves much to be desired', 187a4). The following extract gives the flavour:

> For medicine, to put it in a nutshell, is knowledge of the body's desires for repletion and evacuation, and the man who can distinguish between good and bad desires is the most skilled of physicians. He will be good at his job when he can make them change places, so that a patient comes to have one desire rather than another. He needs to know how to implant desire where it is not, but should be, and likewise to remove the desire which is there already. For he must be able to reconcile the most antagonistic elements in the body and make them long for one another. These antagonists are the extreme opposites – cold versus hot, bitter versus sweet, dry versus moist, and all that kind of thing. It was our master Asclepios, so the poets say (and I believe it) who established our profession, through his knowledge of how to instil love and harmony in these conflicting opposites. And so the art of medicine, as I say, is entirely governed by means of this god of love, and just the same goes for the arts of exercise and of agriculture ... (186c5-e4)

Yet even he has some things to say that hint at Socrates' later revelations– particularly the conception of love as something transcending the physical world; and when he brings in divination as a mediating process between men and gods we catch a glimpse of later developments, an anticipation of the prophetess Diotima (188b6ff). His self-satisfaction, however, disqualifies him from being a serious contributor.

Unexpectedly, Aristophanes' speech turns out to be not only highly amusing but imaginative and touching – or perhaps this surprises only because modern readers tend to assume that Plato can have had no time for the clownish denigrator of Socrates.[19] As he says himself, his oration is comical but not laughable (189b) – again, a small point with wider implications. His speech is in mythical form, explaining the sufferings of mankind from love through an aetiological tale which has captivated most readers: once we were whole creatures, but Zeus punished us by dividing each whole into two incomplete halves, and ever since we have been searching for our lost halves in a painful quest for completeness.

> Before that time we were one, as I said, but now, because of our wrongdoing, we have been divided up by god, just as the Arcadians were by the Spartans. So there is reason to fear that, unless we are well-behaved towards the gods, we may be split up still further, and then we would wander around looking like those people who have been sculpted in profile on stone, sawn apart at the nostrils, just like halved counters in a game. With that danger in mind, we must exhort every man to show the gods reverence, so that we may evade

[19] For qualifications of this view see ch. 2, pp. 41-2 above.

that punishment and gain the reward, with Love as our champion and leader.
Let no one act in opposition to love (and anyone who is hateful to the gods
opposes them), for if we are friends and make our peace with the god we may
yet find and chance upon our own beloveds – something which few of us
achieve as things are today. (193ab)

This is the one doctrine voiced by earlier speakers which Plato makes
Socrates/Diotima explicitly correct in his speech (205de) – as Aristophanes
is quick to spot (212c). We need not see this as aggressive polemic, however:
Diotima herself presents her own 'story' in opposition to the Aristophanic
'story', and although the versions clearly compete, they are allowed to
co-exist in the dialogue.

Agathon, the star of the tragic firmament, is the last to speak before
Socrates himself. His is the speech which comes closest to the rhetorical
structure of a conventional encomium:[20] according to him, Love is the
fairest, finest, most beautiful of beings, the supreme benefactor of mankind.
What gives a special quality to the speech is his extravagantly poetic style,
which can hardly be conveyed in translation:

And so, Phaedrus, Love seems to me to be the first of the gods, and being
fairest and best he is responsible for such qualities in others thereafter. And
I have a fancy to put a thought in verse, declaring that this is he who brings
about

peace among men, windless calm on the sea,
slumbering winds, and sleep from cares set free.

He is the god who rids us of alienation, fills us with affiliation, who brings to
pass all gatherings like this one tonight; in festivals, in choruses, at sacrifices
he is there and leads the way. He supplies mildness, exiles wildness; he is
dear giver of goodwill, no giver of ill will; propitious and kind, admired by the
wise, adored by the gods, envied by the unfortunate, treasured by the
fortunate; of luxury, delicacy, glamour, grace, desire and longing he is the
father. He cares for the good, cares not for the bad. In distress, despair, desire,
discourse he is helmsman, serviceman, ally and best protector, bringing order
to all gods and men, fairest and best champion, whom every man should follow
singing beautiful songs, partaking in the melody that he sings, as he beguiles
the thoughts of all the gods and all mankind. (197c-e)

In the scene which follows, Socrates waxes ironic in his criticism of the
style of Agathon's speech, and subjects him to a swift dialectical examination which questions the premises of his encomium. This critique, fallacious or not, points to deficiencies not in Agathon's own argument – for he
can hardly be said to have one – but in his conception of Eros. Socrates'
chief response is that Eros is a relative term, it must mean love of
something. Love needs an object, something outside itself, therefore love

[20] Cf. Dover's commentary, 11-12; also Buchheit (n. 8 above). On the style see Dover, *Lysias
and the Corpus Lysiacum* 90-1, Bury xxxv sq.

and desire imply a need or a lack. Agathon's Eros is an all-powerful divinity showering blessings on mankind (197de and *passim*).[21] Of course in other contexts Socrates may imply and say that the gods are generous and kind to men, that they give us all that we have, but it is a different point that needs to be made here. Agathon's panegyric has described the attributes of Eros in a vacuum, without relating his conception to human needs and deficiencies. For Socrates, man has to do much more of the work himself. He cannot just sit around as the passive recipient of divine generosity. Moreover, man is *always* seeking, striving, searching, always incomplete. It goes with this that Socrates in his speech widens the gulf between man and god: Eros, he argues, is a *daimon*, half-way between the two; he is an intermediary and man's best helper, but he helps the lover on the way to something that he, Eros, does not himself possess, just as Socrates helps his friends *towards* knowledge which he has not himself attained.[22]

One point that the first five speakers have in common is their competitive aim: their speeches are rival versions, and there is a good deal of correction and criticism of previous speakers (and of more remote figures, as when Phaedrus criticises Aeschylus or Eryximachus Heraclitus (180a, 187a)). This is prominent in the openings of most of the speeches: Pausanias begins by correcting Phaedrus (180cd), Eryximachus begins by criticising Pausanias (185e-6a), Aristophanes asserts that he will take a line different from Eryximachus or Pausanias, adding 'for indeed, mankind seems wholly to have failed to discern the true power of Eros' (189c); finally, Agathon criticises the methodology and structure of all the previous speeches (194e). This rhetorical opening also obliquely contributes a moral point: for the speakers are competing rather than cooperating, and in the manner of the sophists they place a high premium on novelty – new myths, new styles, new interpretations of myths, new cosmologies.[23] Socrates' theory of love is in many ways still more revolutionary, but he does not blazon its novelty so stridently. For one thing, he claims no credit for it himself, but attributes it to Diotima; for another, his opening gambit is not to scoff at his predecessors but to admit that he himself held mistaken views in the past until Diotima corrected them. He himself was once misguided and ignorant, like Agathon: this softens and makes more tactful Socrates' refutation of his

[21] Similar remarks in the earlier speeches at 188d, 193d.
[22] For more detailed study of the earlier speeches, see T. Gould, *Platonic Love* (London 1963) ch. 2; L. Edelstein, *TAPA* 76 (1945) 85-103 (on Eryximachus); K.J. Dover, *JHS* 86 (1966) 41-50 = *The Greeks and their Legacy* 102-14 (on Aristophanes). Aristophanes' speech is also thoughtfully discussed by Nussbaum, 171-6, and by C. Salman, *Interpretations* 18 (1990-1) 233-50. See also Bury's commentary, pp. xxiv-xxxvi, lvii-lx. This last work remains by far the most useful guide to the dialogue.
[23] Cf. Ar. *Clouds* 547, *Wasps* 1044, Grg. *Helen* 5, Thuc. ii. 36. 4, vii. 69. 2, etc. It is also true, of course, as one of the anonymous readers of this book points out, that Plato counters the claims of novelty in the orators 'by arguing that there are deep-seated truths which are the same for all, and permanent, not new'.

host. The earlier speakers, then, declared their own authoritative versions (Eryximachus is particularly self-satisfied in his conclusion, clearly supposing that the last word has been said, 188de); by contrast, Socrates speaks of what he has learned from another source.

The speeches vividly represent the personalities of the participants, and in particular each describes Eros in terms which suit his own tastes and interests. Phaedrus' speech is saturated with mythical allusions and quotations: his interest in myths is well attested in the *Phaedrus* (e.g. his enquiry about the story of Boreas, 229b) and helps explain the form of Socrates' main speech there. Pausanias' speech is a piece of pedantic social or sociological analysis (though with an underlying personal motive, since he is trying to advance his relationship with Agathon); Eryximachus' view of Eros is a medical and scientific one, and he presents the deity as a divine healer and peace-maker (compare Eryximachus' own pacifying role in the dialogue, 176c-e, 214a-c). He too has an ulterior purpose, though hardly a concealed one: he openly declares that he will begin by discussing the art of medicine, so as to pay honour to his own profession (186b). Aristophanes' speech also, in its fabulous situation, its free and irreverent use of the gods, its concentration on physical detail and on the lighter aspects of sexuality, and of course its lively humour, is suited to his profession.[24] Above all Agathon's speech, with its Gorgianic rhythms, its prose that continually seems about to turn into poetry, and its ornate but vacuous eulogy, is a brilliant Platonic parody which reveals the true poverty of Agathon's wisdom; but Agathon also attributes to Eros the qualities in which he himself takes pride: he is young, soft, gentle, beautiful and, most prominently, he is a poet, and one who soothes and beguiles his audience (196d sq., 197e4 *thelgon*). Agathon gladly praises his own profession as Eryximachus had his (196d7-8). Love, for Agathon, possesses all imaginable virtues and showers all possible blessings on mankind; but his mellifluous prose-poem of praise lacks any coherent intellectual foundation.

We have seen, then, that each of the speakers praises Eros in a manner suited to his own tastes, and that two of them, Eryximachus and especially Agathon, make him in their own image. Obviously, this has its function as characterisation, but it also paves the way for the more fully developed conception of Eros in Socrates' speech, in which Love, and the lover, becomes a seeker after wisdom, a philosopher, with characteristics very like Socrates' own. Alcibiades' speech tells the same story, but complements Socrates': whereas in Diotima's exposition Eros begins to look something like Socrates, in Alcibiades' encomium it becomes clear that Socrates has

---

[24] For detailed analogies with comedy, note the references to divine anxiety about missing out on sacrifices, 190c4-5: cf. Ar. *Birds*; the unkind reference to tragic or disturbing events of recent history, 193a (cf. e.g. Ar. *Birds* 186 on Melos, *Lys.* 1093-4 on the hermae affair); the reference to politicians as passive homosexuals in 192a (cf. Ar. *Knights* 878-80, Pl. Com. fr. 186.5K = 202 K-A, Dover *GH* 141-2).

many of the qualities of Eros; but Alcibiades, not having heard Socrates'/Diotima's account, does not fully grasp the significance of these qualities. For him, they are part of the uniqueness and wonder of the individual Socrates.

Socrates

Socrates' speech, which in a sense forms the climax of the dialogue, is preceded by a mischievous refutation of Agathon's position which paves the way for Socrates' own 'teaching'. It is surprising, however, that Socrates' previously vaunted 'knowledge' about love is derived from a source so far unmentioned (and not mentioned in any other Platonic text) – a woman, the prophetess Diotima of Mantineia. We have seen before that Socrates often attributes knowledge to other sources not present, and that these sources sometimes have religious associations – unnamed 'wise men', perhaps Pythagoreans, in the *Gorgias* (507e-8c), men and women who know about the afterlife in the *Meno* – but the attribution to Diotima, a named figure, is peculiar, and paralleled only partially by the much more jokey figure of Aspasia, Pericles' intellectual mistress, to whom Socrates ascribes his rhetorical skill in the *Menexenus*; in any case, Aspasia is not actually quoted verbatim.[25] Diotima is probably a fiction, but there remains a puzzle: why does Plato introduce her at all?[26] Granted that the Socratic knowledge must be given a source, why a woman, and why this particular choice of personality? Explanations can be offered on various levels: on a literary plane, as a possible adaptation and transformation of Aspasia, perhaps as presented in a lost dialogue of Aeschines; on the level of argumentative strategy, in order to avoid implying that Socrates has himself been involved in the past with a male erotic mentor; on the level of significant imagery, because a woman is a more appropriate voice for a doctrine that makes so much use of the metaphors of pregnancy and birth.[27] On another level, that of dramatic effect, the introduction of Diotima, a woman of authority and some asperity, into the exclusively masculine world of sympotic bonding, marks a decisive change of tone and seriousness, setting Socrates' speech apart: for this and many other reasons, it is not just another improvised effort to meet the challenge originally proposed by Eryximachus.

Diotima herself is employed by her creator in a number of ways. Formally, she makes it possible for Socrates to follow a dialectical procedure

---

[25] Aspasia seems to have figured in a number of works by the Socratic circle, though we do not know who used her first: see further Ehlers (cf. ch. 2 n. 19).

[26] The question is discussed with great vigour in an original and acute paper by Halperin, in his *One Hundred Years of Homosexuality* (1990) 113-51, marred only by his love of modern critical jargon.

[27] Arguments along these lines are considered and documented by Halperin (see last n.), 115-16, 122ff.

within his speech, as he describes her own instruction and cross-questioning of him on past occasions. Initially, she is used to soothe Agathon: the
poet, discomfited by Socrates, is to take comfort from the discovery that
Socrates himself once made these same foolish assumptions (201e), and
was rebuked – and by a woman at that! – in much sharper terms. For one
characteristic of Diotima which persists throughout her speech is her
imperious manner, her sharpness with Socrates. ' "That's obvious," she
said; "a child could tell you" ' (204b). 'I said again that I didn't know, and
she said, "How do you think you'll ever master the art of love, if you don't
even know that?" ' (207c). Again, at 209e-10a she wonders whether he will
ever be able to rise to the highest mysteries of love, but declares that she
will instruct him, 'and you must try to follow if you can'. At one point a slyly
humorous characterisation escapes the Platonic Socrates: 'she replied in a
properly professorial manner' – literally, like a sophist (208c).

These contrasts between the modest and good-humoured Socrates and
the sharp-tongued priestess, combined with the suggestion that Socrates
may not be capable of the ultimate mysteries, perhaps encourage us to
doubt whether Diotima's doctrine should be taken *tout court* as Plato's own.
Her scepticism about his ability also leaves open the question whether
Socrates is now at the pinnacle of the ascent or simply further up than all
his peers: in the terminology of the Stoics, is he *perfectus* or merely a more
advanced *proficiens*?

Her speeches have a good deal to say about art and literature, subjects
already prominent in the dialogue. Here again we should remember the
presence of the two dramatists. In essence, Diotima asserts that the
offspring of the body are inferior to the offspring of the mind, though the
desire for both arises from the human longing for immortality and lasting
renown. Those who are pregnant in the soul give birth to wisdom and
virtue: such men are poets and artists, but above all wise lawgivers such
as Solon and Lycurgus (209). Pregnancy of mind can lead a man to seek the
company of beauty, which will stimulate his mind to give birth to great
thoughts: 'and if he also has the luck to find a soul that is beautiful and
noble and well-formed, he is even more drawn to this combination; such a
man makes him instantly teem with ideas and arguments about virtue –
the qualities a virtuous man should have and the customary activities in
which he should engage; and so he tries to educate him' (209b). Does this
not remind us of Socrates' way of life? Already in the *Charmides* Plato
showed that Socrates, although a passionate man and one who delighted
in the company of attractive youths, was completely in control of his
passions. In Alcibiades' narrative of his fruitless attempt at seduction, we
see this self-command demonstrated once more, and in much more tempting circumstances. This is more than just a high-minded *exemplum*. Socrates' positive actions, the moral challenge that he lays down to those with
whom he talks and associates, are set in relief by the firmness with which
he refuses what seems irresistible. In his dealings with Agathon and

Alcibiades, he does not seek amorous dalliance, he does not want to exchange flattery and compliments, but to conduct a serious discussion; love and affection are, for Socrates, inseparable from dialectic.

At the climax of the speech is the doctrine to which Diotima refers with a note of doubt as to whether Socrates can rise to these heights (210a, already quoted). Whereas the earlier speeches saw love as a state of mind and a pattern of behaviour which existed within human society and was practised as an end in itself, Socrates' speech, in essence, assimilates the lover to the philosopher, one who aspires to beauty and goodness such as can only be found in what is divine and eternal, not in the world of change, imperfection and ignorance which most of us inhabit.[28]

> After this (the aspiring philosopher) must regard the beauty of men's souls as more valuable than the beauty of the body, so that even if someone has a decent soul but little physical beauty, that is enough for the lover to love and care for him, and to give birth to words, and seek out the arguments which will make young men better. As a result, the lover will be compelled next to regard the beauty in institutions and laws, and to see that this beauty is all akin; and after that he must be led up to types of knowledge, that he may behold their beauty too, and gazing now at a vast field of beauty he no longer plays the slave to the charms present in a single individual (as a household slave admires the beauty of a boy or a man or a single pursuit), being no base or mean-minded lover. Instead, turned now towards the great sea of beauty and contemplating that sight, he will give birth to many fair and marvellous words and thoughts in his unstinted love of wisdom, until, when he has gained in strength and vigour in that place, he can look upon one single form of knowledge, which is knowledge of beauty like this. (210b6-e1)

This radical redefinition of love seems to involve the abandonment of individual love and the gradual ascent to love of purity and virtue itself – the ascent, that is, from imperfect instances to the absolute world of the Forms. The philosopher will not rest content with the beauty of one particular boy, one particular law or custom or form of activity, but will press on always towards the ultimate goal.

> 'And in that condition of life, dear Socrates,' said the lady from Mantineia, 'there, if anywhere, life is worth living for a man, when he is contemplating beauty in itself. If ever you behold that sight, it will not appear comparable to gold or clothes or lovely boys or young men, whom now you see and are stunned by. At the moment you and many others are prepared to gaze upon your darlings and spend all your time with them, and, if it were only possible, not even to eat or drink, but only to look at them and be with them. How do

---

[28] F.C. White, *JHS* 109 (1989) 149-57 convincingly argues that the philosopher in the *Symposium* aspires to knowledge of the good, not the beautiful; beauty is the means, not the object of the ascent. To the earthbound the distinction may, however, be a fine one. For discussions of the doctrine of Diotima see further J. Stannard, *Phronesis* 4 (1959) 120-34, D.M. Halperin, *Anc. Phil.* 5 (1985) 161-204, C.H. Kahn, *Rev. of Met.* 44 (1987) 77-103.

we think it would be, then, if it were possible for any of you to look upon
Beauty itself, in its uncontaminated, untainted, undiluted form, not
stuffed full of human flesh and colouring and lots more mortal rubbish –
but what if any of you could look upon that divine and unitary essence of
Beauty?' (211de)

There are analogies here with the *Phaedo*, the most otherworldly of Plato's
dialogues, in which the opposition between body and soul, physical world
and metaphysical, is explored in a different way.[29] Closer still is the
principal speech of Socrates in the *Phaedrus*, which similarly proposes a
philosophic view of eros. Yet in both dialogues Socrates' account raises
doubts in modern minds as to whether Plato is by this stage really talking
about love in any sense which we can recognise.[30] Is this not rather a kind
of contemplative ecstasy, the enthusiasm of a mystic rather than a lover?[31]
In the *Symposium*, the speech certainly changes our perspective on love
and its effects: instead of being a self-contained activity, pursued for the
pleasure (of whatever kind) that it brings to one or both partners, it proves
to be the high road to salvation and purification. A continuing debate
among modern scholars concerns the degree to which Plato's concept of love
leaves room for the reciprocal feeling of individuals for each other.[32] It is
not merely that the activities of the partners in the individual relationship
occupies a fairly small part of Diotima's account. More important to this
argument is that the beloved is now beloved not for his own sake but for
the sake of the Forms, to which the philosophic lover will ascend. He loves
his beloved only as a useful instrument in the task of ascent: the philosopher as he climbs the 'ladder' to true beauty will discard its imperfect
imitations. In the words of the most distinguished exponent of this view,
in the *Symposium* and the *Phaedrus* Plato glorifies a spiritualised egocen-
tricism, which leaves no place for private experience, individual preference,
or love of whole persons. Plato, it is claimed, 'is scarcely aware of kindness,
tenderness, compassion, concern for the freedom, respect for the integrity
of the beloved ... (Plato's theory) does not provide for love of whole persons,
but only for love of that abstract version of persons which consists of the

[29] See esp. *Phaedo* 65de, 66c, 67a, and esp. 80a-83b; E. Rohde, *Psyche* (Eng. tr. London and
New York 1925) ch. 13 (one-sided, as is natural in a work focussing on this subject); Dodds,
The Greeks and the Irrational 212-14.

[30] E.g. Dover, *GH* 161-2; see also his edition of *Symposium* viii, 6-8, 138 etc.

[31] On the legacy of these and other Platonic passages to mystical tradition see A. Louth, *The
Origins of the Christian Mystical Tradition* (Oxford 1980).

[32] A. Nygren, *Agape and Eros* (Eng. tr. by P.S. Watson, Philadelphia 1953) was influential
here, but some of his points were refuted by R.A. Markus, *Downside Review* 233 (1955) 219-30
= Vlastos (ed.), *Plato, a Collection of Critical Essays* ii (N.Y. 1971) 132-43; cf. A.H. Armstrong,
Plotinian and Christian Studies (London 1979) ch. 9, and J.M. Rist, *Eros and Psyche* (Toronto
1964) part i ch. 2. The debate was placed on a much higher level with the stimulating paper
by G. Vlastos, 'The individual as an object of love in Plato', repr. in his *Platonic Studies*
(Princeton 1973) 1-34.

complex of their best qualities.'[33] However much we admire the beauty and imaginative grandeur of this vision, we should not close our eyes to the human cost.

So far-reaching a critique could not but be overstated. The challenge presented by Vlastos in particular has provoked some valuable counter-arguments.[34] It may be observed that even if the description of the philosopher's ascent makes the beloved seem a means to an end, that may be too clinical a view of what actually happens in the philosopher's experience; he does not necessarily see it that way or intend from the beginning (if at all) to reject the beloved. Moreover, love as presented in the *Phaedrus* is not simply self-centred passion; it involves a desire to increase goodness and beauty, to make another person better and more beautiful. The kindness that the lover shows to the beloved is amply described by Socrates:

> So it comes to pass that the lover's soul follows the beloved, reverent and awestricken. As for the beloved, since he is served in every way as if he were a god, and receives that service not from a feigning lover but from one who truly feels that experience, and he himself is by nature friendly to his admirer ... as time passes, age and inevitability draws him to admit the lover into his company: for never has it been fated that bad should be dear to bad, nor that good should not be dear to good. And when he has agreed to allow the lover to talk with him and accepted his company, the goodwill that emanates from the lover when close at hand stuns the beloved as he perceives it ...
>
> If the better parts of their minds prevail and guide them to an ordered life and philosophy, then blessed and harmonious is the life they pass here on earth, in command of themselves and orderly in their ways, enslaving that part by which evil appears in the soul, and liberating that by which goodness is introduced. When they die, they become winged and light of step; by that stage they have emerged victorious from one of the three truly Olympian challenges, and no greater good than that can be granted to man by human sobriety or divine madness ...
>
> [and as for the lovers who do yield to their bodily desire, though sparingly:] ... These two pass their life as friends, though less than the other two, dwelling together in love in the rest of their lives, believing that they have given and received the greatest of pledges, which it would be wrong ever to dissolve by becoming enemies. And at the time of death they are wingless, but they depart from the body eager to gain wings, so that it is no small prize that they bear away from their lovers' madness ... (*Phaedrus* 254e8-55b5 (part), 256a7-b7, c7-d6)

This does not read like the description of an exploitative or egocentric

[33] Vlastos, art. cit. 30, 31. On p. 20 Vlastos declares that he will be mainly concerned with the *Symposium* rather than the *Phaedrus*, but he is not wholly consistent in this; the present account is also relevant to both works. The paper also contains interesting criticisms (p. 15) of the conception of *philia* in the *Republic* – more justified?

[34] Besides works already cited note esp. A. Price, *Love and Friendship in Plato and Aristotle* (Oxford 1989) chs. 2-3 (see esp. pp. 102-5); also Nussbaum, 166-7, 173-9; Ferrari, *Listening to the Cicadas* (1987) 173f., 185ff., 224.

relationship, even though it is not very like what many moderns refer to as love, whether homosexual or heterosexual. It is obvious that the lover does care for the beloved, and vice versa, without this excluding the higher aspirations of their souls.[35] The same pages of the *Phaedrus* describe how, through associating with the lover, the younger boy also falls in love, though to a lesser degree (255b-e); this differentiates the palinode from the earlier speeches, in which the beloved's feelings were ignored. Thus it is not the case that the lover is due to fly to the world of the Forms and enjoy eternal beauty, leaving the discarded soul of his beloved behind. Both may hope for the joys and enlightenment of the life to come. (The dual and plural forms of 256b, c7, d-e also make this clear.)

The presentation of the lovers' relationship in the *Symposium* is closely parallel to this account. There, Diotima describes the creative urge of mankind as compelling some to beget children, others to aim at a more permanent memorial – poetry, laws or other forms of wisdom. It is with the aim of creating something beautiful in mind that the man of virtue seeks a beautiful soul in another:

> To a young man like this he at once finds it easy to talk freely about virtue and what a good man ought to be and to do, and so he seeks to educate him. For grasping the beauty in this youth and associating with it, and remembering it present or absent, the lover gives birth to and generates what he has long been nursing within, and sharing the task with that beautiful beloved he rears the offspring with him. Hence men like these have a much greater communion and a stronger bond of affection than the bond created by children, for they have shared in raising fairer and more eternal offspring. (209bc)

Although the emphasis in this passage is on the desire to gain an immortal name through creative achievement, it would seem paradoxical to deny that there is also a desire to benefit the individual friend and posterity in general.

It is necessary, however, to draw some distinctions between the *Symposium* and the *Phaedrus* in their treatment of philosophic love. The argument of Diotima in the *Symposium* is probably more vulnerable to criticisms of the kind raised by Vlastos. Although the relationship with an individual is important at the outset, and has (as the passage above shows) an educative element, there is little room for the beloved's personality or responding emotion; more important, the 'ladder' metaphor explicitly involves the abandonment of the lower rungs, as the lover scans beauty's wide and open sea, leaving behind the slavish and trivial desire of a single object (210d, cf. 211d).[36] Diotima's doctrine, which Socrates endorses, though perhaps without having yet journeyed all the way, is harsher and more

---

[35] See also 252d5ff., 253b3-c2, on the educative role of the lover. Cf. *Smp.* 209bc.

[36] Questioned, however, by e.g. Irwin, *Plato's Moral Theory* 169 with n. 58.

exclusive of the individual's role in love than the more indulgent and sympathetic picture of the lovers' relationship given by Socrates in the *Phaedrus*. Both may be thought lacking from a modern viewpoint, in that they pay small regard to the diversity of interests and pursuits which seem to us a natural feature of friendship and love. But there is a danger of seeing too much significance in such omissions: we need not suppose, in the *Symposium* any more than elsewhere, that Plato is giving us the complete picture.

Alcibiades

The companions of Socrates are given little time to react to the awesome climax of their friend's speech. In one of the liveliest scenes in Plato's work, a battering at the door heralds the arrival of Alcibiades, garlanded and intoxicated, cheerfully congratulating Agathon and insisting on joining (and accelerating) the symposium. At the beginning of the evening, the company had agreed to Eryximachus' proposal that they go easy on the drinking, send the flute-girl away and generally pass their time in a more cultivated, less self-indulgent way (176, esp. e). Alcibiades arrives accompanied by other revellers and a flute-girl, staggering in drunk (though not so drunk that he doesn't know what he is saying, 212e sq.); he expresses his displeasure at their all being sober (213e sq.), starts drinking from a mighty wine-cooler, mocks Eryximachus for his protests (214ab), but accepts the challenge to make an encomiastic speech. Somewhat later, another mob of drinkers crash the party, in an even more advanced state of intoxication than Alcibiades, whereupon deep drinking becomes the rule and a number of the original diners slip away. All of this is comic enough, and makes easy reading, but there are serious implications in the narrative. The proper conduct of drinking parties is a subject which occupied philosophers in antiquity:[37] it is one aspect of a more wide-ranging question, whether one should go through life regularly denying temptations, or whether moderate and sociable indulgence in pleasure is acceptable. Socrates in the *Symposium* is a living example of self-discipline and self-control: although he is no kill-joy, and the party is hardly complete without him (174e, 175c), it is well known that he can go on drinking without ever showing any sign of getting drunk (176c, cf. 220a). This is proven further at the end of the dialogue, where he drinks the two playwrights under the table, then departs to pass another day in his usual style. As with drink, so also when exposed to other bodily pleasures or hardships, Socrates cannot be affected or defeated, as Alcibiades' speech makes clear. By contrast, Alcibiades' own conduct shows his weakness and lack of self-control, which extends to the chaotic structure of his own speech. He is not,

[37] Xenoph. B1, *Prt.* 347c sq., *Laws* i-ii; C.W. Macleod, *Collected Essays* 264, 282.

he assures the company, so drunk as to be unable to speak the truth, and his speech contains important insights, but it is evident that he is only a step away from the unthinking and intrusive celebrations of the gate-crashers who arrive later on. Further, Alcibiades' frankness about his attempted seduction of Socrates, his lengthy complaints about his repulse, his account of his own confused emotions, offend against the standards of decorum and discretion which have so far been maintained at the party. It was thought improper for a lover to provide such intimate details or to refer to his love-making with anything more than vague allusion or euphemism.[38] Here again, Alcibiades' comic conduct reflects on his character, even though his frankness also provides much enlightenment ('not for laughs, but in the cause of *truth*', 215a; cf. 214e6).

Alcibiades, then, changes the subject and lowers the tone of the conversation. Having missed the earlier speeches and that of Socrates himself, he does not know or care about the slanted social commentary of Pausanias, the medical or cosmological double-talk of Eryximachus, or even the sublime mythological-mystical vision with which Socrates ended his speech. What concerns Alcibiades is not 'Love', capitalised and generalised, but his own love, his own undisciplined and unfulfilled passion for Socrates – a passion which, however, we should recognise as self-interested and based largely on his desire to draw on Socrates' supposed wisdom.[39] Here as elsewhere in the dialogues it is important not simply to classify Alcibiades as 'bad' or wrong, and Socrates as right: in their speeches Plato seems deliberately to oppose to one another two totally different, yet vividly imagined personalities, two incompatible ideals and ways of living, thinking and feeling. The positioning of Alcibiades' entrance is a vital part of the dialogue's structure. From one point of view he arrives too late, he has missed everything, including perhaps the 'truth' about love (199a, cf. 177d). But from another point of view, he supplies what was lacking, and puts the case for the other side. The dialogue does not end with the majestic vision of the soul's ascent upon the ladder of love to ultimate knowledge and fulfilment. To fade out with the eloquence of Socrates ringing in our ears, or with applause and acclamation from his audience, would be too easy. Instead Plato returns us to what is, for most of us, the real world – a world in which Aristophanes can get worked up about a minor point in Socrates' great speech where there was an allusion to his own (212c), and in which Socrates' metaphysical aspirations need to be qualified by Alcibiades' physical longings.

Enough has been said to indicate that the climactic speech of Socrates on Love and the eulogy of Socrates by Alcibiades complement one another

[38] See esp. Dover, *GH* 53-4.
[39] I am indebted here to discussion with David Gribble. It is too simple to see Alcibiades as a sympathetic, human figure whose devotion is rejected by the austerely inhuman Socrates. Equally, however, we must not be too cynical about Alcibiades' motives: that he feels genuine affection for Socrates seems clear e.g. from 216b, 218ab.

and must be studied together. Socrates' speech is at first dialectical and systematic, and in its later part, for all its verbal and rhetorical splendour, remains coherent, controlled, inspired by a passionate desire that is nevertheless guided by reason. The perfect command of style and syntax, especially in the final pages describing the revelation of beauty itself (210-11), mirrors the state of mind of the true philosophic lover. In contrast, the speech of Alcibiades is disorderly, chaotic, unstructured, full of exclamations, interjections (215b7, 216a2, 216e4, 217b, etc.) and reversals of direction (e.g. 221d, 'oh, and I left this out in my initial remarks ...'; cf. 215a, a preliminary apology for this practice). His intoxicated condition leads him to pour forth indiscretions, extravagant claims, boasts and self-pity. Both speeches narrate a dialogue between the speaker and his mentor, but whereas Socrates' studious submission to Diotima is complete, and he shows himself now an apt pupil, Alcibiades' exchange with Socrates ends with his incredulous defeat both in argument and in action, and his subsequent response to this failure is to waver between rebellion and shame-faced devotion. Whereas Socrates' speech was completely detached from his own emotions and described only the instruction he had received, Alcibiades is completely absorbed in his own feelings of shame, longing, resentment and so forth, which he pours forth without inhibition. It is difficult to deduce just what he has learned from Socrates, and what he wants or hopes for from him now. Whereas Socrates' speech says little of ordinary life and concentrates on the highest aspirations of human creativity (dismissing even physical child-bearing), Alcibiades' speech is composed of a flood of particulars: sileni, satyrs, dolls, physical comparisons of every kind; the narrative of attempted seduction; strings of names (218a, 221c, 222b); the incidents on campaign and the outcome of particular battles. Above all, his speech wonderfully evokes the physical presence, the idiosyncrasies and appearance of Socrates, his style of speech and his whole way of life. Socrates' speech describes an intellectual ascent to ideal beauty; Alcibiades', a series of increasingly shameless attempts to recall Socrates to the world of physical pleasure (217a sqq.).[40] In short, Socrates' speech and Diotima's teaching tend to the universal, whereas Alcibiades' speech, like his life, is gloriously sensual, and in praising Socrates he rejoices in the particular.

Any more detailed comparison of the two must begin from the crucial point, worked out most fully by Bury in his admirable commentary on the *Symposium*, that Eros in Diotima's account, and Socrates in Alcibiades' speech and elsewhere, are alike.[41] The mythical account, by Diotima of the birth and character of Eros is the clearest passage from which to demonstrate this similarity. Eros is always poor, he is far from being soft and beautiful, but rather rough-skinned and shoeless, he sleeps on the ground

---

[40] This contrast is shrewdly noted by Bury, p. lxiv.
[41] See Bury pp. lx-lxiv.

The Art of Plato

and without any covering, he dwells in doorways and on road-sides under the sky; he is always in need (203cd). So too Socrates' poverty is well known. He is wearing shoes, exceptionally, in this dialogue, because Agathon's party is a special occasion; his endurance of hardship in the open air while on campaign is described by Alcibiades in detail (220); he also mentions how Socrates walked through snow and ice without footwear; and earlier in the evening, as we have already seen, he spent some time in a doorway contemplating a problem (175a; cf. 220d). Eros is a deviser of cunning plots (203d4), as is Socrates (213c4-5). Still more explicitly, Eros is described as a philosopher throughout his life (203d-4a). Between mortality and immortality, between ignorance and knowledge, he seeks what he lacks. He is not a god but a daimon (202d sq.), just as Alcibiades calls Socrates *daimonios*, 'strange, wonderful, hardly human' (219b7-c1: 'that truly wonderful and almost divine man'). The association of Eros with the beautiful and the young (209b, etc.) and with the task of giving birth to dialectical 'fair words' further reinforces the analogy.[42]

In Diotima's exposition, the lover who ascends the ladder of reality will come to scorn the violent passions that he once felt for the beauty in an individual body (210e); similarly, much to Alcibiades' chagrin, Socrates 'has scorned and scoffed at my youthful bloom and treated me outrageously' (219c *hubrisen*). In more general terms he had remarked earlier: 'he doesn't really care a scrap about people's good looks; on the contrary, you can't think how much he actually feels contempt for them' (216d). Here we need to recall the conventions of courtship in Athenian homosexual affairs. As Pausanias explains in his speech, such relationships were not straightforward, nor were the roles of the participants interchangeable. The lover, the *erastes*, was the older man, pursuing and trying to please a beautiful young *eromenos*, a beloved boy. Popular opinion praised the *erastes* and encouraged him in his pursuit, but condemned the *eromenos* if he yielded too readily, 'cheapened' or worse still prostituted himself.[43] As the older and uglier man, it is apparently obvious that Socrates must be the pursuer, the *erastes* of Alcibiades and other beautiful boys, and he himself generally speaks as if this is so (*Prt.* 309a, *Grg.* 481d, etc.). But Alcibiades' possessive attitude, his anger and resentment at the way Socrates treats him, are more suitable to a pursuer, an *erastes*, one who has to cope with the caprices and indifference of a young man who can have his pick of lovers.[44] Our suspicions here are confirmed by Alcibiades' speech, in which he describes the reversal of roles in his relationship with Socrates: Socrates seemed to admire and pursue him, but in the end, finding that Socrates was never willing to declare himself, Alcibiades was reduced to taking the initiative

---

[42] 210a *gennan logous kalous*, 210d; cf. 218a, on the effect of Socrates' words on Alcibiades. See also 213e3 sq.

[43] See Pausanias in *Smp.* 182d-5b, with Dover, *GH* esp. 81-91.

[44] Cf. the description of the possessiveness of the *erastes* in *Phdr.* 232cd, 239ab.

himself, arranging suitable occasions, keeping Socrates with him late into the night, 'for all the world as though *I* were an *erastes* laying a trap for my beloved' (217c7-8). The inversion is made still more explicit in Alcibiades' peroration, which also brings out further the analogy between himself and Agathon:

> That, gentlemen, is the speech I am offering in praise of Socrates. And I have put in a bit about my complaints regarding his behaviour, explaining how outrageously he's treated me. But it's not only me he's done this to; the same thing has happened to Charmides Glaucon's son, and Euthydemus son of Diocles and a great crowd of others, all of whom he's hoodwinked by turning out to be the beloved instead of the lover he appeared to be. I tell you, Agathon, don't be deceived by him in the same way, but learn from our sufferings and beware – don't be like the fool in the proverb, the one who learns by bitter experience. (222ab)

The role-reversal is prepared for in a number of passages in earlier speeches, the significance of which becomes clearer in retrospect: 180a, the division of opinion among the poets as to which was the lover, Achilles or Patroclus; 204c, in Diotima's speech, 'you thought that Eros was the beloved, not the lover'.[45] Much of Pausanias' speech may also be applied to Alcibiades' position. Pausanias argues that it is acceptable to yield to a lover 'in order to improve one's moral state' (184ab, 185b); this suits his own interest, as he himself is a lover of Agathon. But while Alcibiades tries to follow this rule, Socrates does not accept it, and we are driven to suppose that Pausanias' statement of 'the rules of the game' is too simple. Like the image at 175d, this suggests that knowledge and virtue may not be so easy to communicate.

If these observations are correct, then it can hardly be an accident that Agathon in his first exchange with Socrates responds to his teasing in terms which are later echoed by Alcibiades. He laughs at Socrates, calling him a *hubristes*, a difficult word: metaphorically, as here, it means 'dreadful, outrageous'; in its literal sense, 'an outrager', one who commits an act of violence or assault. Alcibiades later takes up this term and also uses it to describe Socrates, combining it with his satyr-image.[46] This again indicates the similar roles of Agathon and Alcibiades. But the word also reinforces the paradoxes of the relationship between Alcibiades and Socrates. *Hubris* is commonly used to signify *sexual* assault and rape,[47] and would be naturally associated with the eager passion of the *erastes*, forcing himself upon his beloved. The comparison of Socrates with the notoriously lusty

---

[45] This gains further significance when we realise how similar Socrates himself is to Eros: see p. 200 above.

[46] Agathon: 175e; Alcibiades: 215b, 219c, 221e, 222a. On the term, see also Dover, *GH* 35. See further M. Gagarin, *Phoenix* 31 (1977) 22-37, with modifications by N.R.E. Fisher, *Hybris: A Study in the Values of Honour and Shame in Ancient Greece* (Warminster 1992) 458-66.

[47] Lys. 1. 2, Dem. 19. 209, etc.; LSJ s.v., II. 2; N. Fisher, *Hybris* 104-11.

satyrs also suits this picture of Socrates' *hubris*. But in fact it is here the younger man, Alcibiades, who tries to force himself on Socrates, and the latter's *hubris* is to spurn his advances – what most people would call modesty, *sophrosyne*![48] The outrageousness of Alcibiades' complaints, the topsy-turviness of his scheme of values, bring out more piquantly the absurdity of his position.

Alcibiades' reaction to the 'scorn' of his beloved is a witty variation on the normal pattern of *servitium amoris*, the willing servitude of the *erastes*, as described in Pausanias' speech. Here the reversal of roles and the exceptional attitude of Socrates both play a part. It is the presumed *erastes* (Socrates) who scorns the other partner; and the 'slavery' which Alcibiades finds thrust upon him (219e) is not simply *servitium amoris* (as in 183a, 184b), but a realisation, instilled by dialectical reproof, that for all his looks, wealth and prestige he is no better than a slave (215e). He even describes his flight from Socrates and disobedience to his precepts in terms appropriate to a runaway slave (216b; *drapeteuo* is the standard term for this).

Another important element in the analogy between Eros and Socrates may be discerned by tracing the imagery of religious initiation and the Mysteries, a metaphor which is important in other dialogues too. Diotima, a priestess, is initiating Socrates into the mysteries of Love (esp. 209e-210a), and uses religious language throughout (e.g. 201e). As in the mysteries of Eleusis, the final fulfilment of the initiation is to see some wonderful revelation which is hidden from all but the privileged few.[49] So too in Alcibiades' speech, mystery language recurs, irreverently but not altogether frivolously, as the drunken youth nears the climax of his narrative, and bids the profane, those who have not shared in the madness and the rites of philosophy, to close their ears (218b).[50] As Diotima introduces Socrates to the truth about Eros, so Alcibiades introduces his friends to the equally wondrous and awe-inspiring truths about Socrates, the true lover and the personification of Eros.

It is natural to ask just how important this delightful development of parallels actually is. How far is the equivalence between Socrates and Eros an elaborate joke, how far is it to be taken seriously? We cannot expect to be able to draw a straightforward line and say that one speech is true, the other false, one serious, and the other purely comic. Alcibiades' reference to the ironic play of Socrates, which masks a deep seriousness (216e), can be extended to the art of Plato himself. Several passages earlier in the dialogue have introduced the idea that something may be amusing without

[48] This word is commonly used as the opposite of *hubris*, cf. Pl. *Phdr.* 237e-8a, LSJ s.v.; Fisher op. cit. 13-18, 111-17; also Dover *GH* 97, on its absence from the world of the satyrs.

[49] W. Burkert, *Greek Religion*, Eng. tr. 1985, 276-8, 287-90, 323-5, and the same author's subsequent work, *Ancient Mystery Cults* (Cambridge Mass. and London 1987). See esp. 210e, 211e. For a fuller study see Chr. Riedweg, *Mysterienterminologie bei Platon, Philon, und Klemens von Alexandrien* (Berlin 1987).

[50] 217e sq. is analogous to Diotima's transition at 209e sq.; cf. also 215c6.

being trivial or meaningless (189b, 193b6 with d8, 197e6-8, 212e, developed at 214e, 221de). Both Socrates and Alcibiades declare that their speeches contain truths (199a; 214e, 215a): if Alcibiades' speech seems comic, we should allow that, like Socrates' speeches elsewhere, it may convey serious thought despite, or even through, its jests.[51] Since the two speeches complement one another so skilfully, Alcibiades too must be supposed to offer some insight not only into Socrates but into love.

Not all that Alcibiades says of his beloved is kind or complimentary. He sees him as a strange, inhuman, even monstrous being, a satyr or a silenus. The violence of his reaction to Socrates' words and admonitions should be noted: his soul leaps and is thrown into a turmoil (215e), as if inspired like a Corybantic dancer; he is filled with shame and misery, he is beaten and bitten by philosophic words, his wound is more painful than a viper's bite (217e-8a). Socrates, by contrast, is invulnerable, as strong as Ajax (219e); he is unique, there has never been anybody like him, nor will there be again (221cd). Often Alcibiades would gladly see him dead, but he knows if this happened he could never bear the pain (216c).

Alcibiades' speech has more to say to us than any simple encomium. It presents emphatically not only the resolution and uniqueness of Socrates' attitude to love, but his *strangeness*.[52] The result must be to complicate our attitude towards Socrates and his doctrine. His detachment, his amused reaction to Alcibiades at the end of the latter's speech (222c), and his effortless outwitting of Alcibiades, ensuring that he gets his own way about the seating arrangements (222e-3a),[53] all make clear his superiority, his immunity to Alcibiades' efforts and entreaties.

It is important not to exaggerate our response to this aspect of the scene: we do not or should not suddenly dislike or fear Socrates,[54] but we must realise just how special, how extraordinary, he and his way of life are. In a way we can warm much more readily to Alcibiades, whose antics and emotional outbursts we may criticise but can immediately understand, whereas much in the metaphysical splendour of Diotima's teaching is hard to accept or comprehend. But another factor which must affect our judgement of the two is, as mentioned before, the future career of Alcibiades, and its relevance to the condemnation of Socrates.[55] Through this foreshadowing Plato here, as in the *Gorgias*, may be casting some doubt on the

---

[51] Note also that there are lighter touches in Socrates', though not in Diotima's, speech: see esp. 208c1.

[52] Nussbaum 183-4, and throughout her discussion. For a sympathetic yet valuable critique of Nussbaum see A. Price, *Anc. Phil.* 11 (1991) 285-99.

[53] Here again we find an echo of Eros: 223a8, esp. *euporos* 'resourcefully', reminds us of Eros' father in the myth, Poros ('Resource').

[54] This position seems to me to be greatly overstated by Nussbaum, 198-9.

[55] Cf. ch. 2, p. 43. Nussbaum 166 makes a number of suggestions which add detail to the general anticipation of Alcibiades' part in events of the next year: e.g. the playful talk of novel mysteries quoted above may anticipate Alcibiades' profanation of the genuine Mystery-rites.

effectiveness of Socrates' teaching. Socrates would not compromise with
Alcibiades, any more than with Callicles; and Socrates died for his ideals,
that is, because he *is* the kind of man he is. But if there is truly no one like
him in the present or the past, can these ideals continue to convince or
persuade his weaker and more worldly followers?

The finale

Critics have always been fascinated by the final, captivating scene of the
Symposium, in which the faithful Aristodemus, unable to keep his eyes
open, drowsily watches Socrates arguing with the tragic poet Agathon and
the comic poet Aristophanes until they consent out of exhaustion to the
principle that the same man knows how to create tragedy and comedy, that
he who is a tragic poet will also be a comic one. The detail of the argument
is not reproduced, and speculation as to the form it took is pointless: what
matters is to see why the question is raised at all and why it stands where
it does, at the conclusion of the dialogue.[56] We may derive some help from
earlier passages in the dialogue, above all Alcibiades' description of Socrates' own serio-comic style and method: 'and practising his irony and frivolity
he conducts his entire life among men. But I do not know if anyone has
beheld the glorious riches within when he is serious and is opened to view.
But I saw those riches once ...' (216e). Again, Alcibiades describes how
many people would laugh and think nothing of the way Socrates talks: 'he
goes on about pack-asses and blacksmiths and shoemakers and tanners,
and he always seems to be saying the same old thing in the same old way,
so that anyone who wasn't used to his style would think it utter nonsense.'
Socrates' less discriminating critics, like those of Euripides, think his style
and manner unworthy of high subject-matter.[57] Yet this is the same
Socrates that surpasses the eloquence and the seriousness of all the other
speakers with his sublime peroration, truly a fitting hymn in honour of
Love. As Alcibiades goes on to say: 'but anyone who has seen them opened
up and dwelt inside them will first find that they are the only kind of
conversation that has any sense in it, and then that they are the most
divine, having within them the best images of virtue, and that they are the
most far-reaching, the most utterly essential for anyone who is trying to be
a good or honourable man to examine' (221e-2a).

Socrates is the supreme ironist, the greatest practitioner of serious
humour, sometimes called *spoudaiogeloion*. This passage and others confirm the importance already attached to this paradoxical mixture (attempted in various ways by most of the earlier speakers: above, p. 203).
Later the concept was watered down and made more commonplace, as in

---

[56] Besides Bury's interesting note here, I have learned most from D. Clay, *Arion* n.s. 2.2 (1975)
238-61, repr. in Anton-Preus (ed.), *Essays in Greek Philosophy* ii (Albany, N.Y. 1983) 186-202.
[57] Cf. Aristophanes on Euripides, *Frogs* 959, 1058-88, etc.

satire and philosophic sermonising, until it became little more than a jocular, chatty form of moralising, full of gnomic wit and lively examples.[58] In Plato's Socrates it remains a truly original artistic and philosophic medium, almost a method, not just a pose or a tone of voice. It is also an aspect of Plato's concern for unity of soul and self (*Rep.* iv. 443-4; *Phdr.* 230a, etc.): Socratic dialectic appeals to and should spring from the whole man, and the *philosopher* is the one who needs to be both tragedian and comedian. It is Socrates, with his deeper understanding of human desires and divine beauty, who seeks to leave a worthy memorial after him – not through art and writing, like the dramatists, but through his influence and teaching; and it is Plato who gives that teaching immortality through the drama of dialogue. The *Symposium* brilliantly and movingly combines the tragic and the comic – and indeed the satyr-play too. Here we must remember Socrates' two-edged comment on Alcibiades' performance, which he describes as 'this satyric and silenic drama of yours' (222d). This implies that Alcibiades' resolution of the two great genres, tragedy and comedy, is a shadow of Plato's, imperfect and approximate: satyric drama represents a mean between the two (as in Horace's *Ars Poetica*), and at this date may have lacked the prestige of either.[59] Hence this speech of Alcibiades', confused and disorderly in its composition, undisciplined in its emotional effects, is not a true fusion. Although Alcibiades gets some way there, just as he discerns truths about Socrates that go further than the rest of the company, his own version of the tragi-comic union collapses into a sort of buffoonery: he *himself* merits the Silenus-satyr comparisons that he paradoxically bestows on Socrates (yet another role-reversal).[60] The true and complete union belongs to Socrates, in his very way of life; to Plato, in the mirror-world of art.[61] Thus we, as readers or audience, witness in the *Symposium* the comedy of speechifying, parody and pretension, the satyric antics of the violent and passionate Alcibiades, and the tragic vision of the nobility and eloquence of Socrates, who despite all his unique qualities and fascination will at some point in the future, not far away from the time of the frame-dialogue, be forced to leave this company of friends once and for all.

[58] See further J.F. Kindstrand, *Bion of Borysthenes* (Uppsala 1979) 47ff.; N. Rudd, *The Satires of Horace* (Cambridge 1966) 96-7.
[59] Cf. R. Seaford's comm. on Eur. *Cyclops* (Oxford 1984) 16-18.
[60] Note the characteristic violence of satyrs: as Alcibiades says, they are *hubristai*. They are also creatures of Dionysus. This suits his antics both now and a year hence much better than Socrates' behaviour at any time.
[61] For a different approach, and some further bibliography, see Nussbaum 469n. 55, who sees Socrates as antagonistic to both tragedy and comedy, in contrast with Plato, the artist. But in this dialogue, at least, both Plato and his Socrates surely adopt an ambivalent or paradoxical stance towards art: Socrates' criticisms of Agathon are then followed by a speech which includes myth and poetic elaboration.

8

The *Republic*

The *Republic*, Plato's best known work, is also among his richest and most complex. It would be absurd to embark on a plodding summary of its 300-page discussion, and here even more than in other chapters I shall assume that the reader has some familiarity with the whole.[1] But it may be worth spending a little time on the reasons why the *Republic* has become, for most people, the central Platonic dialogue, in an effort to account for its colossal influence.

The most obvious point is that it is the longest of the works, apart from the *Laws*, which most readers find more difficult and less imaginatively exciting. Its length makes it natural to see it as a particularly significant and crowning achievement. Its range of subject matter also ensures its appeal to a wide readership: political theorists, psychologists, historians concerned with the ideology of the Greek state, educationalists, littérateurs, can all find something for them in the *Republic*. Its formal subject is 'Justice', but as often in Plato this fairly specific issue is set aside for long stretches of the dialogue, and the companions of Socrates follow him through many digressions and side-roads examining the right and wrong way to live, for both an individual and a society. The *Republic* is astonishingly inclusive: elaborate mathematical speculation co-exists with satirical comment on contemporary social types and clear-sighted criticism of political motives; scrutiny of the proper form and content of poetic and musical training plays a part in one section, while elsewhere Socrates finds a place for discussion of the rights of women to be treated as equals in his utopian state. The range of styles and shifting moods are equally remarkable: vigorous and aggressive argument (from Thrasymachus in book i) gives way to the insistent and sincerely puzzled concern of Glaucon and Adeimantus in their challenge to Socrates in book ii; later, we find the sublimity of the vision of the Guardians' ascent to pure wisdom, or of the myth of Er, and we also hear a more pessimistic and qualifying tone, perhaps a more realistic voice, as Socrates tells of the potential corruption

---

[1] For fuller discussion of the arguments of the *Republic* from a more philosophical viewpoint see N. White, *A Companion to Plato's Republic* (Indianapolis 1979), J. Annas, *An Introduction to Plato's Republic* (Oxford 1981); see also C.D.C. Reeve, *Philosopher-Kings: The Argument of Plato's Republic* (Princeton 1988). Guthrie iv gives a paraphrase with comment on selective points.

of the philosophic nature, and of the inevitable decline of the utopian state, should it ever come into being: 'Hard as it may be for a state so framed to be shaken, yet, since all that comes into being must decay, even a fabric like this will not endure for ever, but will suffer dissolution' (546a). There are sayings and images in the *Republic* which have become a part of western culture, even amongst those who have never perused the whole work: the challenge to liberal ideas posed by Thrasymachus' cynical 'justice is nothing but the interests of the stronger party', the concept of the social contract (book ii), the paradox of the philosopher becoming a king, the brilliantly satirical account of the democratic ship of state (vi. 487e-8e), and above all the moving image of the prisoners in the cave, the scene which represents the ignorance and helplessness of mankind before they are made to undertake the difficult and at first blinding ascent to the light of true knowledge (vii. 514a-21b).[2] Even when these are not the only, or even the earliest, Platonic treatment of such ideas (Thrasymachus, for example, is a close analogue to Callicles in the *Gorgias*), it is often the version in the *Republic* which has had most influence. Although other dialogues pursue the analogy between soul and society, it is the *Republic* which takes that comparison as its central theme; moreover, this is done through the perennially fascinating device of constructing a 'utopian' state, one which will show both society and individuals following the right path. Plato's was probably not the first such creation (there is some evidence, for instance, that Protagoras tried his hand at this form), but his is the first that survives from the ancient world, and this feature especially of the *Republic* has had innumerable imitators.

A final point, to which we shall return later, has made the *Republic* central to many controversies, both about Plato and about education, ancient and modern alike. It is in this dialogue that the Greek poets, especially Homer, are most extensively criticised, and the seemingly reckless way in which Socrates proposes to censor some of the greatest episodes of epic and tragedy has astonished those who admire Plato himself as a superbly gifted writer with clearly 'poetic' qualities. How could such a man compose such a severe, and yet such a strange, indictment of the arts? And how far are Socrates' criticisms here to be seen as normative throughout Plato's works? The distinction of Plato's name has meant that few later critics of poetry have been able to ignore his attack: and yet there remains a paradox, a dilemma for the critic of Plato himself.

What follows can hardly do justice to these questions, and there are many aspects of the *Republic* which will not be considered here. This chapter is divided into three parts, of which the first addresses the structure and design of this massive work, considering more fully some of the guiding themes which unite it; the second is concerned with the 'utopian'

---

[2] For its influence see Arist. fr. 12 Rose (from his *On philosophy*), and Pease on Cic. *ND* ii. 95-6, which is our source for that fragment.

state constructed in the central books, and with the charges brought against Plato by some of its modern critics; the third returns to the judgements of Plato on poetry and, after some consideration of the continuing strengths of his arguments, examines some of the features of language and imagery in the *Republic* itself which align Plato with the poets as much as against them.

Form and structure

Questions of structure and subject are intertwined. What is the subject of the *Republic*? Before taking this question further, it should be said here that the modern title is a misnomer. It derives from the Latin *res publica*, which in its turn translates the Greek title *Politeia*, meaning 'State' or 'Political constitution'. (This title for Plato's work was already used by Aristotle, notably in his critique of Plato's proposals in book ii of the *Politics*). These Greek and Latin terms do not imply any particular type of constitution, certainly not a liberal or quasi-democratic type of the kind which, especially since the French Revolution, the English word calls to mind today. We shall indeed see that many aspects of Plato's state are far from liberal. The title, however, is too firmly embedded in modern usage for an attempt to replace it to seem anything but pedantry.

We may also ask whether the construction of an ideal state and constitution is actually the main aim of the work. In ancient catalogues of the Platonic corpus, and in our manuscripts, an alternative title is 'On Justice'. In the early part of the work justice is sought in the individual, and the interlocutors' concern is with how each of them should behave to earn the title of a just man. The idea of examining the virtue 'writ large', in a society studied from its origins, is introduced almost unexpectedly by Socrates (ii. 368d), and launches the group on a new project which is formally a digression. It would of course be naive to suppose that what is formally secondary cannot be integral, even central to the work; but the relationship between these two sides of the enquiry, and between the 'digressive' sections and the whole, seems to call for further examination.

Book i, like the *Laches, Charmides* and other works, is an 'aporetic' discussion of various possible definitions of a moral quality, in this case justice, ending in bafflement. At the opening of book ii, Socrates remarks that he had thought that this was the end of the matter 'but it was actually, as it seems, only the "proem" ' (we might say 'overture'). Glaucon and Adeimantus express at some length their dissatisfaction with the way in which Thrasymachus was dismissed, and challenge Socrates to show that justice is valuable for its own sake, not simply because it pays better or leads to other favourable consequences. To this proposal Socrates' suggestion that they should contemplate justice in a whole society is a rather surprising response, but they are soon involved with the 'founding' of such a society. It is not until iv. 427d that, with the utopian state 'established', they begin to look for the cardinal virtues, including justice, in the activities of its citizens. That book offers an elaborate analogy between the functioning of a just community and that of a just soul;[3] but intriguing though this analysis is, we may feel a little disappointed in the actual definition provided of justice, which amounts to very little more than 'do your own job and mind your own business' (433).

Nevertheless, it appears that the enquiry is moving on to a different phase, as Socrates prepares to describe the defective forms of society, in which injustice is prevalent (v. 449ab). At this point, however, two of the company, Polemarchus and Adeimantus, insist that Socrates return to and explain a casual reference he made earlier (iv. 423e) to the citizens in their utopia having women and children in common: how would this work, and what would its consequences be? Socrates protests that they are making him embark on a further huge subject, which he hints will involve a swarm of difficult questions; but at their insistence he will undertake it. The next phase of the discussion deals with the regulations for marriage and child-birth among the Guardians, which will involve a kind of commune-system. Socrates begins to discuss other aspects of the utopia (beginning with its military practices), but is hauled up short once more, this time by Glaucon, who points out that he is leaving aside the crucial question whether such a society could ever come into being, and if so how (v. 471c, referring back to 458ab). It is here that Socrates comes out at last with the famous declaration that there can be no rest from troubles for states, nor can their ideal commonwealth appear, until philosophers become kings or kings philosophers. Then he delineates the true philosopher, contrasting this ideal picture with the superficial conception of him held by the common man, and also with the uselessness and vulnerability of the philosopher in the world as it is. Yet a philosophic ruler could come into being, if he were educated in the right way (vi. 502d re-introduces this theme); and much of book vii is a sketch of that education and its sublime results (the ideal society here takes second place to the development of the individual intellect: see above all 532-4).

It is not until viii. 543a that Socrates feels that their questions have received a sufficient answer for them to leave the topic of the philosopher-kings and return to the point from which they had 'digressed': namely, the bad constitutions which bring about unjust societies. Thus the central section of the *Republic*, including the images of Sun, Line and Cave, the concept of the Idea of the Good, and the educational programme of the philosopher, are all included in a 'digression'! Books viii and ix are mostly concerned with more familiar matters: the portraits, always penetrating and sometimes sharply satirical, of the different types of society and citizen (timocratic, oligarchic, democratic and tyrannical), draw on a much more

[3] On this theme see esp. T. Andersson, *Polis and Psyche* (Göteborg 1971); a brief conspectus of important passages in his pp. 244ff. See also Halliwell on x. 605b5.

realistic (though sometimes caricatured) body of material and have a completely different tone from the preceding books: we may compare the way in which, after the sublimity of the Socratic expositions in the *Symposium* and the *Phaedrus*, we return to more down-to-earth, or more accessible, though less inspiring topics. Having reached the moral nadir of the political and psychological sequence with the tyrant, the ultimately unjust man, Socrates draws the strands of discussion together, using the psychological analyses of book iv and other arguments to show that far from being the happiest of men, the tyrant is supremely wretched and pitiable. In this way he gives his response to the challenge put to him in book ii: because the unjust man allows the beast in him to be master, rather than making it subject to what he has within him that is divine, he perverts his nature and is in no way more fortunate than, or even to be compared with, the just man. The emotional power of the argument is impressive, though we may feel that Socrates builds in too many of his own assumptions for the conclusion to be wholly satisfying.

With the reply to Glaucon and Adeimantus seemingly complete, the main argument is at an end; the tenth book, accordingly, has often been seen as an appendage or epilogue. Yet it restates the argument against the arts in a more penetrating form, and extends the praise of the just man beyond this life, enabling Socrates to conclude the work, as in the *Gorgias* and (rather differently) the *Phaedo*, with a myth of the afterlife, continuing some of the themes of the dialogue through different images and on a different plane. It is notable that in book x, even more than in books viii and ix, the ideal state has faded in importance; and the myth of Er stresses the importance of the individual's choices with reference to all mankind, not only a privileged class.

The above outline is not intended as a résumé of the *Republic*, but as a means of clarifying some aspects of its structure.[4] In writing a dialogue of such length, Plato seems to have been concerned to sustain the conversational manner more easily preserved in smaller works; and one way of doing this was clearly to allow digressions and fresh starts, with Socrates reacting to objections or interruptions from his companions. Granted that Plato does not want to make them exponents of theories in their own right, this provides a way in which they can be shown as participants rather than merely admiring listeners. Thus books ii, v and the 'philosopher-king' section in vi all begin with a protest from his friends that Socrates is not doing full justice to a question, and each time new issues and ideas are raised, even though Plato makes clear that they cannot be exhaustively discussed even in so long a work.[5] As on a smaller scale in the *Gorgias*, it swiftly becomes clear not only that many other issues are related to the formal subject (here, the definition of justice), but also that that subject is

[4] See further the analysis at the end of this chapter.
[5] For examples of passages in which this point is emphasised see below, p. 235.

more complex and significant than might be thought at first. In some ways the *Republic* becomes more difficult and demanding as it progresses: book i recalls the manner of the simpler early dialogues, books ii and iii, with their easy style and leisured pace, give the impression that the enquiry will be more straightforward than it later proves, and the central books, especially books vi and vii, contain some of the densest and most difficult passages in the work. Books viii, ix and x are perhaps again easier to grasp, but presuppose the psychological and metaphysical arguments dealt with in books iv, vi and vii: hence the discussion of the tyrant in book ix has more depth than the superficial treatment in book i (or in the *Gorgias*); the account of the general education of the guardians in book iii is extended by the more detailed catalogue of the curriculum of the Guardians proper in book vii (as anticipated at 416b et al.); and the account of poetry in book x cuts deeper than the rather one-sided approach in books ii and iii, where little more is done than produce a sample anthology of unsatisfactory passages.

The structure of the *Republic* has often been considered from a rather different standpoint, one which has clear affinities with the study of the Homeric Question. The scholarly tradition which attributed different sections of the *Iliad* and the *Odyssey* to different bards, and which sought to identify the chronological layers of the works of Herodotus and Thucydides, has not left the *Republic* unscathed.[6] In an earlier chapter we have seen that it is common to separate the first book, often renamed the *Thrasymachus*, as an early dialogue later incorporated into a larger whole. It has also frequently been suggested that book x was a later addition, perhaps in response to criticism of the views on poetry expressed in the early books.[7] An even more drastic form of analysis has proposed that the whole of books v, vi and vii, the major 'digression' signalled at 543c, is a later insertion: according to one version of this view, book v in particular responds to the comic utopia of Aristophanes, the *Ecclesiazusae* ('Women at the Assembly'), produced in 392: Aristophanes is thought to have taken up and spoofed the idea briefly floated in book iv of women in power, whereupon Plato produced an expanded version of the *Republic* in which this idea was treated more seriously and at length.

It is easy to caricature such views, but they are useful if they encourage readers to seek alternative explanations for the surprising features or

[6] Most of the suggestions cited go back to K.F. Hermann, *Geschichte und System der platonischen Philosophie* i (Heidelberg 1839) and to A. Krohn, *Der platonische Staat* (Halle 1876); see also, in English, Jowett and Campbell's volume of Essays (Oxford 1894) 1-20 (in which Campbell gives an account of these theories and attempts a reply); E.L. Harrison, *Phoenix* 21 (1967) 37-9; Thesleff, *Studies in Platonic Chronology* (1982) 102ff., 137ff., 184ff.

[7] Thesleff, 184-6, with earlier bibl. A most ingenious version of this argument is offered by G.F. Else, *The Structure and Date of Book 10 of Plato's Republic* (Heidelberg 1972), who claims that the critic to whom Plato is here replying is none other than Aristotle in his *Poetics*! For contrary arguments see Halliwell, *Aristotle's Poetics* Appendix 1; on the broader issues, N. Rohatyn, *Gymn.* 82 (1975) 314-30.

difficulties in the *Republic* which they are intended to solve. As a general principle we should not be too ready to suppose that the author's scissors-and-paste work is so glaringly obvious, or that, in a work which is clearly his most ambitious to date, he would be content with clumsy and unmotivated insertions. We can surely assume that, even if the *Republic* does make use of earlier material, that material has been consciously integrated in the work, and the author is at least reasonably satisfied with its new place there. In other words, the critic's primary concern should be with the function of a given part as it stands, and not with its inevitably speculative genesis. With these points in mind, I shall say something about the place of book i and book x in the larger design of the *Republic*.[8]

Book i, as already indicated, shares much with the aporetic dialogues such as the *Laches* or the *Protagoras*: the vividly defined dramatic setting, the fast-moving interplay of characters, the consideration of conventional ideas which are found wanting. The elderly Cephalus yields place to his lively young son Polemarchus, who in turn is ousted by the boorishly aggressive Thrasymachus; each finds Socrates a willing and ingenious opponent. If we consider this book from the point of view of the *Republic* as a whole, we can see many points at which it sets ideas in motion, though without developing them in full. Thus the views of poets are already invoked and called into question: Cephalus quotes Sophocles and Pindar, Polemarchus Simonides; Socrates mischievously refers to Homer in a playful move to establish that justice is actually skill at cheating, and more soberly implies that the misguided saying of Simonides is really characteristic of the thinking of some cruel despot – Periander or Xerxes or his like (335e-6a).

As this last example shows, the first book also introduces the concept of the despot or tyrannical ruler. Cephalus recalls Sophocles' remark that in passing into old age he has escaped the tyranny of desire or lust: political imagery is applied to psychological forces, in a way that foreshadows later discussions. More significantly, Thrasymachus in a long speech declares that rulers rule for their own profit and care no more for the good of their subjects than shepherds feel concern for their sheep (343b sqq.). Throughout the *Republic*, a central theme is the question who should rule, and why, and on what principles. Already in book i Socrates argues that only those who do not wish to rule should be permitted to do so (347cd), a paradox which is given fuller meaning when we are told of the intellectual satisfactions which the philosophic ruler must temporarily abandon when he undertakes in his turn the task of government (in the famous comparison, descending from the sunlight into the cave). The ruler acts in the interest of his subjects, not his own.

---

[8] On the arguments concerning book v and Aristophanes I may refer to Halliwell's commentary on that book. See also Adam's edition, i. 345-55. On Plato and comedy see R. Brock, in *Owls to Athens*, ed. E.W. Craik (Oxford 1990) 39-49. On book i cf. p. 23 above.

Again, Socrates moves readily in the latter part of book i from state to individual, as he will do later. In particular, at 351a sqq., he argues that neither a state nor any other body of men, not even a gang of thieves, will be able to function effectively unless they cooperate and deal fairly with one another; if injustice and stasis prevail among them, the result will be self-destructive. He then draws the analogy of division and dissension in the individual: justice is the principle of internal order and unity, and the unjust man 'will have a divided mind and be incapable of action, for lack of singleness of purpose; and he will be at enmity with all who are just as well as with himself' (352a). The psychology here is not fully explained: it will be dealt with at greater length in book iv.

It will be agreed by separatist and unitarian alike that there is a marked difference of tone between book i and what follows, and that book ii marks a new beginning. But the explanation of this need not be independent composition. The point can be made most forcibly with reference to Thrasymachus. His powerful and impetuous attack on Socrates, his emotional language and sweeping eloquence, followed by bad-tempered retreat, mark him as a Calliclean figure. The parallel with the *Gorgias* is reinforced by the dialectical difficulties which ensue: Thrasymachus will not tolerate Socrates' style of conversation, refuses to answer as he really thinks, and makes clear that he is only cooperating in order to bring the dispute to an end (see esp. 350de). Clearly, Thrasymachus is anything but an ideal interlocutor; equally clearly, he is not convinced by Socrates' counter-arguments, though he cannot find a way around them. It is significant that he is replaced in book ii and afterwards by Glaucon and the rest: their common concern with defending justice makes possible a richer and more cooperative exchange. As in the *Theaetetus*, the *Timaeus* and other later works, Plato seems to abandon head-on opposition between Socrates and characters of totally different outlook, and allows a more productive interchange of ideas. The very length of the *Republic* brings this out: there is no thought of postponing or wavering in the enquiry, and Socrates' companions urge him on, or act as a sounding-board for his ideas, rather than obstructing or opposing him. At least twice in the later books the point is made that their support should encourage and aid Socrates (450d, 474a); moreover, other types of discussion, such as forensic clashes (348ab) or eristic debating (454a-c), are deliberately set aside or opposed to their own practice. This contrast of argumentative mode is often interpreted as showing the authentic Socrates being displaced by an improved Platonic figure with more doctrinal authority (cf. ch. 1, p. 23). It might be better to see this undoubted change of approach as an attempt to dramatise a more productive form of dialogue, in which criticism is not absent, but there is a joint concern to pursue the discussion to its end. Glaucon and the rest, as has already been mentioned, are prepared to insist on Socrates' examining a point passed over, or to make him explain himself more fully; nor are their other interventions confined to trivial agreements. Rather than seeing the *Re-*

public as thinly disguised Platonic preaching, and Socrates' companions as ineffectual yes-men, it may be preferable to regard this as a model of serious and committed dialectic, with the young men as 'model' interlocutors.[9] Even Thrasymachus, we note, is won over in the books which follow (whereas Plato could easily have represented him, had he wished, as leaving in disgust after his discomfiture in book i): his boorishness is toned down so that his support for Glaucon and the others is merely expressed in more colourful and jocular language (450ab); and Socrates is able to claim, in the course of the account of the true philosopher, that Thrasymachus will not disagree with him now: 'we have just become friends – not that we were enemies before' (498cd).

I turn now to the last book. In dealing with both transitions, from book i to ii and from book ix to x, the concept of 'false closure' may be valuable.[10] By this device we are led to suppose, by the structure of the argument and by certain formal features (e.g. the note of finality in Socrates' speech at 354a-c, and the parallels with similar speeches at the ends of other dialogues), that the discussion has reached its proper conclusion, only to discover that the last word has not yet been said. This device is employed in various ways elsewhere in Plato, and of course in other authors.[11] In Platonic dialogue, it sustains the mimicry of real conversations, where fresh starts and new notions are commonplace; more significantly, it reminds the reader that the discussion between Socrates and his companions is not the end of the story, that at any point the debate can be re-opened. This is made particularly plain in the *Phaedo*, where it is naturally important that Socrates himself will not be able to participate in any future conversations: hereafter, his friends are thrown upon their own resources.[12] In *Republic* x, the open-endedness of the discussion of poetry is highlighted by the challenge – admittedly a demanding and far-reaching one – to the defenders of poetry to rally to her aid and present a reasoned argument that she is beneficial to the state. To see this as directed at Aristotle or any other individual writer is to blunt the force, and the lasting seriousness, of the challenge.

Book x refers back to the earlier books of the *Republic*, and depends on them, in many ways.[13] That is of course as we would expect: even the most extreme separatists would not argue that book x was composed *inde-*

---

[9] Cf. L.J. Coventry, in Pelling (ed.), *Characterization and Individuality in Greek Literature* (Oxford 1990) 174ff.

[10] In general for bibliography and ideas concerning closure in classical studies see D.P. Fowler, *Materiali e discussioni* 22 (1989) 75-122.

[11] E.g. at the transition between books 23 and 24 of the *Iliad*, or at *Odyssey* 23. 299, a more tempting *telos* than 296, signalled as such by some ancient critics (has the scholium been displaced?); cf. Hor. *Epist.* 2. 2. 204. A forthcoming volume edited by D. Fowler and D. Roberts collects essays on this topic.

[12] See 106e-7b; for false endings in the *Phaedo* see 69e, 84b, 106e fin., 114c8, 115a3.

[13] References in Halliwell's commentary, 24n1.

pendently of the *Republic* proper, and simply attached as an afterthought. The point at issue is whether book x provides a more appropriate or satisfying ending, in literary or philosophic terms, than book ix; whether, in other words, the work is completed, or merely supplemented, by the concluding book. On a trivial level, it may be observed that as things stand, the ninth book ends with a memorable but brief comment by Socrates (quoted below, p. 225) answered by an anaemic 'Probably so', from Glaucon (592b); the conclusion of book x with the long mythical narration by Socrates is far more moving and impressive. (We should of course grant that an earlier version of book ix might have ended slightly differently.) It may also be observed that the *Gorgias* similarly ends with a myth, and that in a number of ways that work, which is also the longest of the certainly early dialogues, can be seen as 'trying out' ideas which are more fully explored in the *Republic*.[14]

More substantial arguments concern the reappearance of the theme of poetry and its place in education and society. Book x falls into three parts: the renewed critique of the arts, an argument for the soul's immortality, and the myth of judgement. The last two are connected: if the soul is immortal, then calculations concerning the consequences of justice and injustice cannot be confined to the span of one's life, but must embrace all time. Book ix brought the argument concerning this life to a conclusion, but book x caps this argument, looking beyond the political sphere to the universal. The punishment of Ardiaeus, the tyrant of Pamphylia, in the afterlife takes the description of the tyrant's misery to its final stage (615c-6a). But the account of poetry and the myth of Er are also linked, as will be argued further below: the myth, in a sense, represents the 'purified' or philosophic poetry which plays a more responsible educational role and avoids the folly or misstatements of the epic poets and the tragedians. It is appropriate for a writer, at the conclusion of his work, to reflect (however elliptically) on the nature of his art, as for example many of Pindar's odes contain comments on his poetic task in the closing lines.[15] The challenge to poetry, and the way in which Plato, as far as possible, meets that challenge himself, bring to an appropriate culmination the many allusions to artistic creation and composition which have appeared throughout the work.

Many other connections can be discerned, of which one of special significance is the portrayal of the soul as something crucially important and supremely precious. That it is more important than the body is assumed from a very early stage (353d, cf. 403d, 585d); it is declared that its function is to rule, and that it is the principle of life, akin to the Forms (585c, cf. x. 611e); although it is superior to the body, it is affected by the bodily

[14] T. Irwin, in his comm. on the *Grg.*, introd., p. 10.
[15] E.g. Pind. *Ol.* 1, *Py.* 1 and 3. Hom. *Od.* 24. 192-202 (Agamemnon on Penelope and Clytemnestra as examples for future poetry) may have been influential here. (Later, compare the tendency of the Augustan poets to end books with poems which reflect on their own poetic roles and choices: e.g. Virg. *Ecl.* 10, Hor. *Odes* 3. 30, *Epist.* i. 20.)

activities and can be influenced by its environment and 'made worse'. The central passage in book vi on the good as the highest form of knowledge shows the object to which the soul may aspire from an earthly, though mystical, perspective; in book x Socrates expresses the same conception in universal mythical terms: the soul is immortal, indivisible and capable of pursuing the good. The cosmic vision of the Universe in the Myth of Er gives a wider context for all the soul's aspirations, and also fills out a number of more incidental references to the Pythagorean ideas of the harmonious cosmic order (530d names the Pythagoreans, and that whole passage probably owes much to them; see also 546a-d, 583b, 587b ff.). A whimsical earlier reference to reincarnation (498d) also finds its eventual explanation in the myth (though such ideas are also present in the earlier Platonic dialogues).

In a different category are connections of language and imagery. As early as the opening pages of book i Cephalus referred to men's fears as death comes near: at that point they begin to wonder if the old stories of Hades which they mocked as young men may be true after all (330de). In the closing pages Plato shows us how those fears are and yet are not justified: the old wives' tales are transformed into a myth that is awesome and inspiring without being dismal or dispiriting.

A number of metaphors and images run through the *Republic*: while not sufficient in themselves to guarantee unity of conception, they do reinforce our sense that the work is a coherent one, with the same preoccupations running through it.[16] The image of the 'journey' being undertaken by those involved in the conversation is one example: the dialogue begins with Socrates describing how he 'went down to the Piraeus yesterday'; Socrates refers to the 'longer road' which they will have to abjure (435d, 504bc); later he sets up their own 'journey' in discussion as a parallel to the dialectical journey which the prisoner, or the human being, makes in emerging from the cave (532e3, cf. b4); and the image of journeying is especially prominent in the Myth of Er, reaching its climax in the closing words of the dialogue, 'and [so that] in that thousand-year journey which we have *gone through*, we may fare well' (621d).[17] The metaphor of ascent is another which is naturally prominent in the cave image, but occurs often elsewhere (e.g. 452c, 568c9f., 584d); again it reaches a climax in the myth, with the two shafts

---

[16] See the valuable paper by D. Tarrant, *CQ* 40 (1946) 27-34. For another strand of imagery, not treated here, see C.J. Classen on hunting, in a helpful dissertation, *Untersuchungen zu Platons Jagdbildern* (Berlin 1960).

[17] This passage, like 532e, is an example of the figure found often elsewhere in Plato and in ancient literature, whereby a writer (or here, a narrator and his interlocutors) is said to do what he is describing: see Macleod, *Collected Essays* 205, al.; F. Muecke, *CQ* 32 (1982) 52; G. Lieberg, *Poeta Creator* (Amsterdam 1982). See also Ov. *Tr.* ii. 439, Longinus 9. 11, 9. 14 (if *planos* is right), 15. 4.

leading upwards to the heavens – the route followed by the virtuous souls – and down into the earth (614c, and what follows).

One image which has stronger moral implications is that of man as a beast, or with the potential to become one. It is amusing, and perhaps no more, when Thrasymachus in book i is compared with a wild animal hurling himself on the terrified Socrates (336b, cf. d), though recollection of the 'leonine' man conceived by Callicles in the *Gorgias* may already give us pause (p. 160 above). But there is more depth given to the animal language when Plato comes to deal with the appetitive element of the soul (e.g. iv. 439b4), with the ungovernable desires of the 'great beast', the *demos* or mob (vi. 493bc), with the comparison of a tyrant with a man who, having tasted human flesh, becomes transformed into a wolf (565de, cf. 415d), and later with the contradictions in man himself: in book ix, we are told that a man has within him, as it were, a conflicting triad, man, lion and many-headed beast (588b sqq.).[18] Although analogies are often drawn between men and animals (the ruler should be a conscientious shepherd, i. 343a, 345c; the guardians are to be like keen watchdogs, 375-6; the procreation of children will be handled as one runs a flock of animals, 459de), it is important to remember that what is best in man, reason, transcends the animal state and must not be drawn back into it.[19] Here too book x seems to cap or at least provide a suitably memorable conclusion to this chain of images: the immortal soul, embedded in the body, is compared with the sea-god Glaucus: formerly a fisherman, he became a strange hybrid monster, and this passage adds the colourful details of his being encrusted with barnacles and seaweed which obscure his inner humanity (611c-12a). That man is not only like the animals but can become one of them, for good or ill, is a further dimension explored in the myth, with its account of transmigration.

Again, in the latter section of book x we find references to prizes which the just man wins from men and gods; it has been suggested that this, and the similar reference in the closing paragraph ('when, like victors in the games collecting gifts from our friends, we receive the prize of justice'), recalls and 'trumps' the more worldly concerns of the athletes engaged in the games at the festival of Bendis in book i – the companions of Socrates, it will be remembered, have passed up the spectacle of the torch race on horseback, becoming absorbed in the all-embracing disquisition of the philosopher.[20] Some may regard such 'connections' as illu-

---

[18] Compare *Phdr.* 229-30, a characteristically more whimsical and self-mocking passage (quoted on pp. 173-4 above).

[19] On the shepherd (a somewhat ambiguous comparison, as some parts of book i, and 422d, indicate!) see further *Statesman* 275 sq., *Laws* 713d sq., 735b sq. For further animal-analogies see P. Louis, *Les métaphores de Platon* (Paris 1945) 185-8; Halliwell, comm. on book 5, 34 n. 39, 140.

[20] See further 465d, 503a, 504a, 583b, 613bc; D. Tarrant, art. cit. (n. 16) 30.

sory, others as trivial; but it is at least clear that Plato gave special attention to the openings and conclusions of his dialogues.[21]

The ideal society

The *Republic*, as we saw, is the first extant 'Utopia'.[22] That term was coined by Sir Thomas More as the title of his Latin essay, published in 1516, which describes, in Platonic manner, an imaginary society.[23] The title means 'no place' (cf. Samuel Butler's *Erewhon* and William Morris's *News from Nowhere*), but because of the ambiguous use of the letter 'u' for the Greek negative 'ou', it can also be interpreted as 'good place' (Greek eu), so emphasising not the non-existence but the ideal qualities of the society so portrayed. Modern critics have coined the opposite 'dystopia', to describe a work portraying an imaginary state which conspicuously falls short of any ideal, where conditions are bad or unpleasant: the classic example is George Orwell's horrific *Nineteen Eighty-Four*. When an imaginary state is a prosperous one, enjoying an 'ideal' existence, it may seem a mere dream – hence 'utopian' comes to mean 'impractical'. In ancient times Plato's *Republic* was commonly viewed thus, as a fantastic never-never land (e.g. M. Aur. ix. 29).

But is the state of the *Republic* a 'utopia' or a 'dystopia'? It is contrasted with the world of contemporary Greece: unlike the city-states of Plato's time, it is ruled by the wisest and best-qualified, who have undergone a testing programme of studies to equip them for this task; it is stable and well-organised, resistant to external influences and well able to resist attack or invasion; it is free of internal discord, with each individual well-suited to his profession and each citizen content with his place in a specific class. The women too are to play their part in the society; if a woman is mentally equipped for high office, her abilities must not be wasted merely because of her sex. A community of well-balanced souls, leading healthy lives and guided by unselfish and self-sacrificing rulers, the imaginary

---

[21] Cf. the anecdote about the pains which Plato is said to have taken to find the best arrangement of the words in the opening sentence of the *Republic* (D.H. *On composition* 25 and elsewhere; Riginos, no. 137, is sceptical as usual). See generally *Beginnings in Classical Literature*, ed. F.M. Dunn and T. Cole (= *YCS* 29 (1992)), including an essay on the opening of the *Phaedrus* by D. Clay.

[22] See further H. Vretska, *Kl. Pauly* s.v. Utopie; J. Ferguson, *Utopias of the Ancient World* (London 1975); D. Dawson, *Cities of the Gods: Communist Utopias in Greek Thought* (Oxford 1992). For modern development of the form see J.A. Hertzler, *The History of Utopian Thought* (1923); F.E. and F.P. Manuel, *Utopian Thought in the Western World* (Cambridge Mass. 1979); Isaiah Berlin, *The Crooked Timber of Humanity* (London 1990) 20-48. According to Diog. Laert. iii. 37, a passage which includes other dubious assertions, Aristoxenus said that nearly all of the *Republic* was plagiarised from Protagoras' *Antilogika*. Riginos, 165f. and elsewhere, shows that this is a typical element in the anti-Platonic tradition, but given Protagoras' known interests in the development of society it is possible that some truth underlies it. (Cf. Diog. Laert. ix. 55, ascribing a work *Peri Politeias* to Protagoras.)

[23] See further H.R. Trevor-Roper, *Renaissance Essays* (London 1986) 24-58.

state seems to merit the title Socrates gives it at one point, 'Kallipolis' ('the fair city', vii. 527c).[24]

Further reflection may cause greater unease. We may set aside for later discussion the rigorous censorship which is to limit the artistic creativity in the city (at x. 607a it is said that in the field of poetry they will admit only 'hymns to the gods and encomia of good men'). More disquieting is the class structure (or 'castes', as some have called it) among the citizens: the higher class of guardians is to be divided into Guardians proper (the philosophic rulers) and a secondary class usually called 'Auxiliaries', who will be the military force of the city. Below these are the common citizens, especially artisans. Plato says little of slaves, but it should never have been doubted that in his state, as in all Greek communities, they will continue to perform their supporting role.[25] What is much less clear is whether individuals of ability can move between the classes: for the most part birth seems to determine social status through the generations, and although some concession is made at an early stage, it has been held that this is contradicted later (viii. 546-7a),[26] and in general Plato seems more concerned with the demotion of those who fall short of the standard than with the promotion of the talented.[27] Aristotle already complained about the way in which Plato concentrates on the ruling class and ignores both practical details regarding the lower classes and their overall well-being. In response to a question from Adeimantus, Socrates says that they are not founding a state with a view to the happiness of one particular class, but of the state as a whole (419-21c); but Aristotle comments that 'the whole cannot be happy unless most, or all, or some of the parts enjoy happiness', and that Plato seems to deny even the Guardians happiness (*Pol.* ii. 5.1264b).

Much more disturbing is the power and freedom of action which Plato allows the Guardians. They are, it seems, above the law, and cannot be accountable; although it is assumed that they will take office in turn, reluctantly doing their duty between periods of philosophising, it is hard to suppose that such a system could operate for long without some of them becoming ambitious for more lasting authority. The initial foundation of the state will involve drastic measures, including the deporting of all non-philosophic citizens above ten years old, so that their children can be reared and educated as has been prescribed, free from corrupting influences (540e sqq.);[28] and there is a disquieting reference to the need for the

[24] For a fuller survey of the Platonic state see e.g. Zeller, ch. 11, on the whole offering a very positive picture.
[25] G.R. Morrow, *Mind* 48 (1939) 186-201; Vlastos, *Platonic Studies* 140-6. The contrary arguments raised by B. Calvert, *CQ* 37 (1987) 367-72 have little positive force, and he himself concedes that Plato's position may have been inconsistent.
[26] Against Popper, *Open Society* 141 on this point see Robinson, *Essays in Greek Philosophy* (Oxford 1969) 76-7.
[27] Popper 49, 225 n.31, 272.
[28] Cf. Popper 165ff.

philosophic kings to 'clean their canvas' before they can begin their task, a phrase which may be read as giving them carte blanche to exile or otherwise dispose of dissenting elements (500d-1a).[29] Questioning and unorthodoxy will meet with severe punishment. In his concern to ensure the stability of the state, Socrates proscribes change or development: like God and the Forms, the ideal state would be inviolable and unaltered. Individual enterprise or originality are out of place in such a society: the individual exists for the sake of the state, and the state's obligations to even the obedient individual are few.[30] 'By persuasion or constraint [a combination to which we shall return] the law will unite the citizens in harmony, making them share whatever benefits each class can contribute to the common good; and its purpose in forming men of that spirit was not that each should be left to go his own way, but that they should be instrumental in binding the community into one' (519e-20a). Elsewhere the citizens are compared with the parts of the human body, an influential metaphor (462c).[31]

Quite obviously, modern admiration for and sympathy with the ideal state of the *Republic* will hardly be unqualified. In the present century the issues with which Plato was grappling have come very much alive, especially with the establishment of nations which in one way or another set the state's needs above the individual's, and which have placed their rulers *de facto* above the law. The criticism of ancient literature cannot and should not be purely aesthetic or value-free, and the way in which modern scholars have removed Plato from his pedestal and branded him a totalitarian has stimulated much fruitful debate which cannot be adequately covered here. One work in particular has earned its place on every syllabus of political philosophy, Sir Karl Popper's *The Open Society and its Enemies* (1945), of which volume 1 is sub-titled *The Spell of Plato*.[32] Fuelled by anger and dismay at the political events of the 1930s, powerfully written, vigorous in its polemic yet rich in detailed documentation, it is still, over 50 years on, an exciting and eye-opening work. Some of Popper's views have already been implied: he sees Plato as a determined opponent of democracy, an ideologue who greatly admired the conservative and militaristic Spartan system, and who in the *Republic* set out a blueprint for practical political solutions to the problems of his day, solutions which involved the arrest of

---

[29] Popper 166; cf. *Statesman* 293c-e.

[30] Cf. *Laws* 903c; Popper 80, 242 n. 35.

[31] See Rutherford, *Meditations of M. Aurelius* (1989) 150-1; de Ste. Croix, *The Class Struggle in the Ancient Greek World* (1981) 444-5.

[32] All references are to this first volume; the second is concerned with Hegel and Marx. I cite from the fifth edition of 1966. See also R.H. Crossman, *Plato Today* (1937), and other works cited in Popper 216 n. 31. R. Bambrough (ed.), *Plato, Popper and Politics* (Cambridge 1967) is a collection of contributions to the debate, of rather uneven value: those by Unger and Meyerhoff are helpful, but better than either is R. Robinson's review of Popper, repr. in his *Essays in Greek Philosophy* (Oxford 1969) 74-99. Tigerstedt, *Interpreting Plato* 32ff. discusses the Popper controversy. F.M. Turner, *The Greek Heritage in Victorian Britain* (1981) ch. 8 gathers much material illustrating earlier background to this kind of criticism of Plato.

all political change, the restoration of a primitive 'tribal' mentality, the suppression of the individual's private existence, and the imposition of government by a master class over a master race. Perhaps the most striking of his main arguments is the presentation of Plato as Socrates' Judas: Socrates was a free and independent thinker, the supreme defender of the right to freedom of thought and speech, the man who admitted his own ignorance and claimed this as his only wisdom. But Plato, whether deliberately or unconsciously, transformed and traduced him, making him the spokesman for an oppressive and anti-intellectual regime which would destroy freedom of thought and which would have dealt even more summarily with Socrates than did the Athenian democracy in 399.[33] By contrast, the Athens of the late fifth century, the era of Pericles, the sophists and the 'Great Generation', is praised for its humanitarianism, its liberal attitude to slaves and citizens alike; all of this reinforces the indictment of the *Republic*, since it shows that Plato was turning his back on more humane and generous doctrines of ethics and politics, looking instead to the fiercely restrictive ideals of Sparta (e.g. 228).

It is not difficult to criticise Popper's arguments on many points of detail.[34] His idealisation of Athenian society leads him to paint a quite unrealistic picture of the condition of slaves and the respect paid to them by citizens (43, 334-5); it is very unlikely that infanticide, permitted in Plato's state, was unknown in Athens;[35] the use of literary texts is often naive, as Popper attributes to Critias,[36] Sophocles, Euripides and Herodotus the sentiments of speakers in their works; similarly, the difficulty of using Thucydides' version of Pericles' speech as evidence for Pericles' own ideals is not properly faced (186; 255 n. 16 is not adequate); the evidence for animosity between Plato and his fellow Socratic Antisthenes is unreliable (194, painting Antisthenes as St Peter to Plato's Judas);[37] and so forth. On a different level of argument, Popper's concept of 'tribalism', as a supposedly child-like state of innocence in which men are content with their

---

[33] Popper chs. 6-8 are central; see also 306 n. 56, the long note explaining his position on the Socratic question. Note p. 132, the contrast between the Socratic and the Platonic ideal of the philosopher: 'a modest, rational individualist and ... a totalitarian demi-god'. On p. 153 (cf. 147-8) Popper argues that Plato saw himself in the role of philosophic god-king.

[34] For an exhaustive and somewhat indigestible attempt at a point-by-point reply see the 645-page work of R.B. Levinson, *In Defense of Plato* (Cambridge Mass. 1953); Popper's response to this, in the revised edn. of *The Open Society* (1962), 323ff., repr. in Bambrough 199-219, makes some effective points in his own defence.

[35] Note the implications of Pl. *Tht.* 160e-1a, and see further R. Sallares, *The Ecology of the Ancient Greek World* (London 1991) 151-7; Halliwell on *Rep.* 5. 460c3-5.

[36] The authorship of the passage in question is in any case disputed (though Popper perhaps would not have known this); it may well be by Euripides, see A. Dihle, *Hermes* 105 (1977) 28-42.

[37] Riginos, *Platonica* nos. 43-8, 103; see further the overall picture in G. Owen's essay on 'Philosophical invective', in *OSAP* 1 (1983) 1ff. (= Owen, *Logic, Science and Dialectic* (London 1986) 342-64).

complete dependence on their society, an 'organic' yet 'closed' society, is
open to serious criticism; he himself surprisingly admits that 'there is no
uniformity in tribalism' (172), and in general his broad-brush accounts of
historical evolution can seem strangely glib.[38] He is also worryingly prone
to psychological biography, both of Plato (esp. 195f., on his self-deception
and 'bad conscience' over his distortion of Socrates' true opinions), and of
his generation, who are said to have suffered from the 'strain of civilisation'
(176, cf. 188 'the perennial revolt against freedom'; 189).[39]

   These criticisms do not necessarily damage Popper's main theses. Other,
perhaps more substantial points may be added. First, Periclean Athens
was probably less admirably 'open', less generous in its humanitarianism,
than Popper would maintain; in particular, the idealistic contrast of Athenian imperialism with Rome's empire (181-3) will not stand up to scrutiny.[40] It was the Thucydidean Pericles, in the same Funeral Speech which
Popper so much admires, who extolled patriotic devotion and military glory
above the claims of individual grief (ii. 43-6); and in a later speech after the
plague had shattered Athenian morale he spoke more severely, and in
terms which elevate the good of the community above those of individual
citizens (ii. 60). The conception that the state has first claim on the
individual is not so remote from normal Athenian thinking as might be
supposed from Popper's denunciation of that principle in the *Republic*.[41]
Secondly, it is not clear that Socrates was quite so much 'a good democrat'
as Popper, contrasting him with the pro-Spartan Plato, makes out. At the
very least, he was associated with 'laconizers' in Athenian popular opinion;
and if we think any of his comments on democratic debate in the *Protagoras*
(319b-20c) and elsewhere are characteristic of the historical Socrates, then
his support for Athens' constitutional procedures cannot have been unqualified.[42] Thirdly, although it is obvious that Plato has drawn a good deal
on Spartan institutions for the utopian society (e.g. the restrictions on
coinage, or the common meals), there is much that is alien to Sparta, and
we know from the *Laws* that in his most austere old age he still found much
to fault in that form of government, and in the militaristic way of life

---

[38] P. 200 takes the prize, with the breathtaking parenthesis '(Only much later, in the dark
ages, was it [social change] arrested by the spell of the Platonic-Aristotelian essentialism.)'.
[39] See further pp. 14, 28f., 79f., 109, 155f., 171. Classical scholars will recognise the diagnosis
of late fifth century 'failure of nerve', as described by E.R. Dodds in his classic *The Greeks and
the Irrational*, chs. 7-8; Dodds is explicitly influenced by Popper on this point (255 n.1). On
the dangers of psychological biography see the entertaining paper by H. Lloyd-Jones, in *Freud
and the Humanities* ed. P. Horden (1985) 152-80, repr. in his *Academic Papers* (Oxford 1990)
ii 281-305.
[40] See e.g. P.J. Rhodes, *The Athenian Empire* (*G&R* New Surveys 17, 1985) esp. 36ff., and the
fuller account in *CAH* v[2]. See also M.I. Finley, in *Imperialism in the Ancient World*, ed. P.D.A.
Garnsey and C.R. Whittaker (Cambridge 1978) 103-26 = Finley, *Economy and Society in
Ancient Greece* (London 1981) 41-61.
[41] Dover, *GPM* 288ff.; S. Hornblower, *Thucydides* (1987) 122-6 (cf. his note on Thuc. ii. 60. 2).
[42] On the question of Socrates as 'democrat' see above, ch. 2, pp. 60-2.

there.[43] As he says repeatedly in the *Laws*, that way of life cultivates only one part of virtue (i.e. bravery), not the whole (e.g. 630d-31b, endorsed by Arist. *Pol.* 1271b1ff.). The military aspect of Plato's own state is important, and it is quickly recognised that wars will be necessary for the acquisition of property (373de, cf. 422e ff., 466e ff.); but it goes too far to paint the city as primarily an armed camp, a military or imperialistic power on the lines of Nazi Germany. The Greek states accepted that war would be a necessity at some stage for them all; it would be harder to find evidence for pacifism in the ancient world than for a movement for the abolition of slavery.[44] It should perhaps be added that there is no trace in the *Republic* of any suggestion that other races should be subjugated or exterminated, and no such inference should be drawn from Popper's use of the emotive terms 'master class', 'master race' and 'human cattle'.[45]

It is time to turn to a different kind of criticism which might be directed at Popper's analysis, one which draws more on the literary approach adopted so far in this book, and in the first part of this chapter. It must again be emphasised that the *Republic* is a dialogue, and one in which Socrates not only meets with considerable opposition and incredulity from his companions as he expounds his ideas, but also seems to falter and doubt himself, even to dismiss seemingly serious propositions as absurdities or near-impossibilities. It is of course possible to dismiss all such qualifying or self-deprecating phrases as artful devices whereby Plato masks his real purpose: thus Popper analyses some passages of badinage and jocular self-dramatising as a cynical means of deflecting the reader's eye from the sinister message which Socrates is putting across (esp. 140-4, 270-3), and even declares that 'his self-deprecating remarks are not based upon awareness of his limitations, but are rather an ironical way of asserting his superiority' (131).[46] But this hard-headed division of the text of the *Republic* into 'Plato's totalitarian message' and the stylistic or rhetorical ornament which lulls the reader into submission and makes that message palatable suggests an over-simplified view of the relation between form and content. It would go too far to defuse the *Republic* by denying it any practical relevance to events in the real Greek world, for the whole question of the practicality of the utopian proposals is repeatedly raised; but we must also recognise that these passages, and the framing of the utopian sections in

---

[43] See further Morrow, *Plato's Cretan City* 40-73; E.N. Tigerstedt, *The Legend of Sparta in Classical Antiquity* (Stockholm, Göteborg, Uppsala 1965-78) i 244-76; E. Rawson, *The Spartan Tradition in European Thought* (Oxford 1969) 65-72.
[44] Pl. *Phaedo* 66c, *Laws* 626a; cf. Dover, *GPM* 313-15.
[45] See his index s.v. racialism. The racialism he sees in the *Republic* is principally of an internal kind, regarding the subjection of the inferior classes, as prescribed by the notorious 'myth' or 'noble lie'.
[46] Popper's identification of Socrates with Plato is extreme here; yet it is striking how close this comes to the common criticisms of Socrates made by opponents such as Thrasymachus.

a broader discussion, distance them from practical politics:[47] to take only one point of contrast with the *Laws*, none of the party is in any position of responsibility regarding a new colony or foundation, as is the Cretan Cleinias in that later dialogue.

The 'unreal' character of the discussion is emphasised in a number of ways. One of these is the repeated use of the term *muthos*, 'story' or 'imaginary tale', to describe what the 'founders' are doing as they plan their ideal community. 'Let us take our time then, and spin our yarn as we educate our citizens in imagination', says Socrates in book ii (376d). Later the same sort of phrase recurs: 'the constitution which we are telling a tale about in our argument' (501e, with *muthos* and *logos* strikingly combined). Elsewhere he admits that their account may seem to be only a *euche* (a wish or aspiration, 450d1, cf. 499c, 540d). The proposition that the 'one change' needed would be the emergence of philosopher-kings is clearly marked as a paradox (473c-4a). It is also emphasised that what they are doing is only giving a mere sketch or outline (414a6f.) – artistic metaphors are applied to their imaginative construction throughout the dialogue.[48] Even the models of existing types of state in books viii and ix are to be regarded as only rough sketches; to give a total account would be a vast task (548cd).[49] Yet there is also a sense in which the work plays on the elaborate way in which they set out plans *in detail* for what may be an impossibility (458ab, 471c). Two other passages stand out: in one, after a powerful speech on the need to find worthy students of philosophy, such as Justice herself would approve, Socrates changes his tone, declaring that 'I seem to be inviting ridicule myself.'

> 'I was forgetting,' I said, 'that we are only playing, and I spoke with rather more intensity. For as I spoke I was looking at philosophy, and watching her undeserved humiliation. I think that in my distress and anger at those responsible I said what I did with undue seriousness.'
> 'No indeed', he said, 'not as far as I was concerned, as I was listening.'
> 'Still it seemed so to me as I declaimed,' said I. (536bc)

Here, as in the *Phaedrus*, Socrates seems to cut their grand speculations down to size: when all is said and done, they can still be seen as 'play'.

The other passage is the one which concludes book ix. There, having

---

[47] Cf. D. Clay, in Griswold (ed.) *Platonic Writings* 19-33, who helpfully argues that although the society hypothesised in the *Republic* would indeed be a 'closed' society, it is described in an 'open' dialogue: that is, further criticism, exploration and even rejection of Socrates' argument are possible.

[48] Below, pp. 235-6. Cf. e.g. Pindar, *Ol.* 6. 1ff.; Ar. *Thesmo.* 48-57.

[49] See also Cherniss, *The Riddle of the Early Academy* 66-8, who claims that part of the mathematical programme planned for the Guardians involves techniques or branches which had not yet been properly developed, and that Plato admits this as regards stereometry (528bc); cf. 530c, 531c (mathematical harmonics). If this is right, there is a further 'unreal' aspect to the discussion. For a different approach, see now D.H. Fowler, *The Mathematics of Plato's Academy: A New Reconstruction* (Oxford 1987), esp. 106-54.

completed the argument that the tyrant is the unhappiest of men, Socrates describes the proper way of life of the virtuous man, here detached from any political context: indeed, Glaucon adds that, as Socrates has portrayed him, such a man will have no wish to take part in politics.

> 'Yes, by the dog, he will,' I said, 'at least in the city which is his own, though perhaps not in his own homeland, unless some divine good fortune befalls.'
> 'I understand,' he said. 'You are speaking of the city of which we have now completed the foundation, the city which exists in our talk, since nowhere on earth, I suppose, does it lie.'
> 'But still perhaps it is laid up as a pattern in heaven, for one who wishes to look upon it and to found it in himself as he looks. It makes no difference, though, whether it exists or ever will exist. For such a man would involve himself in the politics of that city alone, and no other's.'
> 'Probably so.' (592ab)

This muted conclusion is almost the last we hear of the ideal state (as already indicated, the founding of the city becomes a less prominent concern after the close of book vii, and attention turns more to the individual soul). Enigmatic as it is, it does not suggest any great optimism regarding active political change, and the mood of retirement and inner practice of virtue seems more reminiscent of the sombre portrait of the philosopher at bay, in society as it is, which stands at the heart of book vi (496: below, p. 238).[50] The call for political reform in the *Republic* is neither univocal nor strident.

The *Republic*, then, is not an easy work to interpret. Socrates and his friends, while apparently engaged on an open and relatively light-hearted discussion, following the argument wherever it blows them (394d), develop a vision of an 'ideal' society which, whatever may be said about its practicality, combines a sublime concept of the soul's developed potential with regulations and restraints which seem calculated to limit human creativity and development at every stage and in every class – for although much is said about the happiness of the philosopher who can reach for the beauty of the Good, it is hard not to feel that the satisfactions which this pursuit of knowledge can bring will be counterbalanced by a denial of many other potential joys. As in the *Symposium*, Plato seems to place enormous emphasis on one part of the human psyche, the intellectual or spiritual part, while ruling out any but the slightest concession to the other elements. (The same of course applies to the class structure in the state, which is divided on precisely parallel lines: state and psyche are analogously conceived.) There are passages in the *Republic* which would move almost any reader to love goodness and beauty; but it is not so clear that the dialogue can persuade us that only in the life of the mind is goodness and beauty to be found.

---

[50] Cf. also the digression in the *Theaetetus*, esp. 173cd. Perhaps un-Socratic (cf. Dodds's *Gorgias* 275), but in a different sense from what Popper's argument requires?

This much we might allow readily enough, for it is natural that any philosophic insight should be partial; and it could be added that the 'framing' of the theoretical or doctrinal passages of the dialogue with so much incidental elaboration, questioning and uncertainty, interjection and undercutting, helps to make the work less dogmatic, less final in its definition of the good for man and society. 'Romantic' irony is not absent from the *Republic*, even if less frequently discernible than in (say) the *Phaedrus*.[51] But when all is said, Popper's book retains its value because it makes us see that along with much that is moving and admirable, there are also facets of Plato, and of the utopian state, which are repugnant, even hateful. Popper interpreted this in terms of a split between Socrates and Plato – the former a lover of open discussion, a committed democrat, a martyr for the right to question everything, the latter a determined legislator for others, sure of his own beliefs and prepared to use any ends, even violence, to impose them on others for their own good.[52] The picture may be overdrawn, but there is an important truth here. Of the five points which Popper stresses as crucial to his argument, the first is fundamental: in the utopia of Kallipolis Socrates would have been condemned unheard.[53] Whether we phrase it in psychologising terms or not, there is a gulf between Socrates and Plato which the *Republic* is perhaps the first work to bring clearly to light. We may clarify this gulf by focussing on the opposition of *peitho* and *bia* ('persuasion' and 'compulsion').[54]

The opening page of the dialogue seems to play with the two alternatives, as Polemarchus and his friends jokingly threaten to use force in order to make Socrates and Glaucon stay in Piraeus with them: they are more numerous, 'so unless you are more than a match for us, you must stay here.' Socrates replies that there is another possibility: 'we might convince you that you must let us go.' But Polemarchus replies, 'How will you convince us, if we refuse to listen?', and they concede that they cannot do so, whereupon Adeimantus intervenes with persuasive arguments of his own (327c-8a). Trivial and light-weight in itself, the exchange hints at important motifs of the dialogue: persuasion and violence come to the fore again in the argument with Thrasymachus, where we meet an opponent who 'refuses to listen' in earnest, making only resentful and formal assent (349a,

---

[51] For definitions see M.H. Abrams, *Glossary of Literary Terms* (5th edn., New York 1985) s.v. irony; cf. Muecke and others cited in ch. 3, n. 20; P. Conrad, *Shandyism: The Character of Romantic Irony* (Oxford 1978).

[52] It is important to recognise that Popper never doubts that Plato's belief that his reforms would be beneficial for others was wholly sincere (e.g. 170-1).

[53] The five points are listed in the 'Reply' to Levinson, pp. 330-1. Of the others, point 4, which concerns the 'Noble Lie' and Platonic eugenics, has been dealt with by Unger ap. Bambrough 94ff.

[54] The antithesis is traditional: see esp. R.G.A. Buxton, *Persuasion in Greek Tragedy* (Cambridge 1982).

350de, 351c6, d7, 352b3-4, 354a10f.).[55] Socratic dialectical persuasion seems inadequate with such an antagonist, and Glaucon at the opening of book ii voices his misgivings, asking Socrates if he wishes them merely to seem persuaded, or really to be so (357ab). Later passages where persuasion is placed in a less attractive light include the 'noble lie' or myth of races which is to be established as a 'charter myth' of the imaginary state (414b).[56] Where persuasion will be adequate, it seems that Plato will prefer willing acceptance of rules and training; but if there is resistance, if persuasion is not enough, his guardians will have the power to coerce and punish.[57] The wiser have a duty to educate and correct the ignorant; the worrying aspects of this doctrine emerge more clearly in the discussion of warfare, where we learn that the army of the good city will act 'as correctors and instructors through war, not as enemies' (471a). The ordinary man does not understand what is best for him, does not see what philosophy can give to mankind – look at how Socrates was condemned (496d hints at Socrates' death; cf. 517a). The account of the defective constitutions in books viii and ix reinforce these suggestions, by showing how indiscriminately and yet how destructively violent politics are at the moment. So much folly, so little understanding – if only it could be put right, by the intervention of one who knew what needed to be done. It is hard not to think here that Plato, disillusioned by the politics of his time and by the poor repute of intellectuals, is allowing himself the luxury of imagining what could be done if power were in the right hands – a very different thing, however, from planning a personal takeover bid.[58] It must have been hard for a man of Plato's gifts to avoid the occasional reflection on the path which he might have followed, had he emulated his relatives and entered political life. This tendency is taken much further in the *Laws*; in the *Republic*, however, if the above argument has any force, the dialectical and the authoritarian sides of Plato are held in a fascinating tension.

[55] Note also 345b, where Thrasymachus frustratedly exclaims: 'How am I to persuade you if you're not convinced by what I've said already? Am I to carry the argument into your soul and plant it there?' 'Zeus, no,' responds Socrates. Force-feeding is no good in dialectic: one has to make a conscious and willing choice.
[56] See further 461c (in the 'eugenics' passage); 515e (forcible removal of a prisoner from the cave); 547b (how strife first arises in the utopian state), 548b (ctr.536e); 606a, 607e (the need to suppress the longings aroused by and for poetry). In a different category are passages like 411d (on the *misologos*); 440d. On the *peitho-bia* vocabulary see Popper 271n.10; 316n.69; G.R. Morrow, 'Plato's concept of persuasion', *Phil. Rev.* 62 (1953) 234-50, and *Plato's Cretan City* 552-60 on the *Laws*. For more recent discussion see C. Bobonich, *CQ* 41 (1991) 365-88.
[57] Note e.g. 410a: physicians and judges will actually put to death those who are 'incurably corrupt of mind'. Cf. Slings, *Clitopho* 241n.5.
[58] Popper 153 seems, moreover, to go much too far in supposing that Plato envisaged himself, in his fantasies, as the philosopher king. (His use of the singular is curious; Plato always speaks of them as a class, and indeed of a group who will take it in *turns* to serve as rulers – a point which rarely if ever emerges in Popper's discussion.) See esp. 540ab, quoted at the end of this chapter.

The critique of art

In modern British society, where the arts are for the most part trivialised or marginalised, it is hard for many to understand the extraordinary importance which the Greeks attached to art and literature. Music, dance, word and song were combined above all in the dramatic festivals, themselves in some sense ritual or religious occasions, which had all the more impact for being exceptional opportunities, not available throughout the year. Behind the modern forms of tragedy, dithyramb and comedy, in which fashions changed and new poets might oust the old, there stood preeminent the awesome, almost divine figure of Homer, 'the poet', as he could be called without further specification. Homer was the life-blood of Greek education: schoolboys would learn him by heart, rhapsodes perform his works at the Panathenaic festival, and he was the source of material and spirit for much of Greek tragedy.[59] The Greeks (with the exception of a few small-scale sects such as the Orphics) had no bible, no sacred books; priests of an individual god did not pronounce on points of doctrine, even at Delphi, and there was no hierarchical clergy.[60] Hence the importance of the poets in education as well as in many aspects of social life, from the symposium to the marriage ceremony.

Artists of all kinds give pleasure, but poets, dealing with verbal concepts and directly or indirectly commenting on experience, are also expected to instruct.[61] A famous text which enshrines this view is Aristophanes' *Frogs*, in which the god of tragedy, Dionysus, descends to Hades in order to recover a dead poet who can revivify and inspire Athens in the dark years at the close of the Peloponnesian War. In the end he chooses Aeschylus, the stern, almost archaic figure of moral stature, rather than the modern, modish Euripides. The contest between these rivals tells us much about the perception of tragedy, and the critical standards applied to it, in the time of Plato's youth. At odds though the two dramatists are on almost every point of aesthetics, they are in agreement as regards the duty of a poet to be a teacher (1008-12, cf. 1054-5). We can see from more sober evidence that this was the common view in Greek society. Poets offer guidance to others in practical and moral problems; the characters of epic and drama can be seen as exemplary (see esp. Lycurgus 1. 100ff., quoting 55 lines of Euripides' *Erechtheus*). Protagoras in Plato's dialogue treats this as something well-known: 'the teachers ... set before them [their students] at their benches the works of good poets to read, and make them learn them by

[59] Cf. Rutherford, *JHS* 102 (1982) 145-60.

[60] Cf. W. Burkert, *Greek Religion* (Eng. tr. Oxford 1985) passim, esp. 119-31 on 'The spell of Homer'; shorter accounts by R. Parker, in *Oxford Hist. of the Cl. World* ed. Boardman, Griffin, Murray (1986) 254-74; L.B. Zaidman and P. Schmitt Pantel, *Religion in the Ancient Greek City* (Eng. tr. Cambridge 1992).

[61] See generally D.A. Russell, *Criticism in Antiquity* (London 1981) ch. 6.

heart; they contain a lot of exhortation, and many passages praising and eulogizing good men of the past, so that the child will be fired with enthusiasm to imitate them and filled with the desire to become a man like that' (325e). 'Laws are too brief to give instruction; they merely state the things that must be done;[62] but poets, depicting life itself, select the noblest actions and so through argument and demonstration convert men's hearts' (Lycurg. 1. 102, tr. Burtt: examples follow from Homer, Tyrtaeus, epigrams). It is notorious that such selection may pay little attention to the original context and meaning of a poetic tag.[63]

If poets were teachers, on what authority did they teach? The *Apology* suggests that the original Socrates had crossed swords with the poets and questioned their 'inspired' knowledge; the *Ion*, an amusing but inconclusive work, shows him puncturing the complacency of a rhapsode or professional reciter of Homer, who at first adopts the common idea that Homer is an expert on all the subjects which feature in his poetry (generalship, chariot-racing, medicine and so forth), and subsequently takes a naive pride in the 'inspired' wisdom which he acquires at second or third-hand, from the god via the poet.[64] As often in the aporetic dialogues, larger issues and questions are half-revealed but not explored: does the *poet* himself possess the knowledge Ion lacks? What is the status of the poet's knowledge, and can the audience learn anything from the rhapsode's performance, even if Ion is too self-satisfied to acknowledge his own ignorance? If poets do not 'know' what they describe, how can they do so well, and why should they be respected for what seems a mere sleight-of-hand?

A further point made in the *Ion* sheds much light on the emotional response of at any rate an Athenian audience to the performance of poetic works. Ion describes the enthusiastic state in which he renders particularly powerful episodes: 'when I recite a pathetic passage, my eyes fill with tears; when it is alarming or terrifying, my hair stands on end in terror and my heart jumps.' His audience reacts similarly: 'I can see them each time from up on the platform, weeping and looking fierce and marvelling at the tale' (535). The passionate involvement of audiences, especially in the theatre,[65] bears witness to the power of poetry and music, and helps explain Plato's unease.

Contrary and critical views of poetry were not lacking. Plato refers in *Republic* x to 'an ancient quarrel between poetry and philosophy' (607bc),[66]

[62] Cf. below, ch. 10, p. 298, on Plato's attempt to solve this with 'preambles'.
[63] See further M. Heath, *The Poetics of Greek Tragedy* (London 1987) 38-47, 71-89.
[64] H. Flashar, *Der Dialog Ion als Zeugnis Platonischer Philosophie* (Berlin 1958); G.M.A. Grube, *The Greek and Roman Critics* (London 1965) 48-9; Russell, *Criticism in Antiquity* 74-5.
[65] A.W. Pickard-Cambridge, *The Dramatic Festivals of Athens* (revised by Gould and Lewis, Oxford 1968 and 1988) 272f., 274; on music cf. 257ff., and the source-book by A. Barker, *Greek Musical Writings* (Cambridge 1984-89); M.L. West, *Ancient Greek Music* (Oxford 1992) esp. ch. 2.
[66] Cf. E.R. Curtius, *European Literature and the Latin Middle Ages* (1948: Eng. tr. 1953), ch. 11.

and long before any philosophic comment on the arts, the poets themselves had drawn analogies between poetry and lies.[67] 'Poets tell many a lie', said Solon (fr. 29 W.). Pindar doubts the tradition about Pelops' ivory shoulder ('for me it is impossible to call one of the blessed gods a glutton', *Ol.* 1. 52ff.), and questions the testimony of Homer concerning Odysseus' achievements (*Nem.* 7. 20ff.). Xenophanes complains that 'Homer and Hesiod attributed to the gods all the things that bring reproach and disgrace among men – theft, adultery, deceit' (B11). Heraclitus was more forthright: 'Homer deserves to be thrown out of the public contests and given a beating, and the same goes for Archilochus' (B 42). Allegorical interpretations of shocking episodes seem to have begun in the fifth century with scholar-critics such as Theagenes, who allegorised the Battle of the Gods as a conflict amongst the elements;[68] but for Plato this did not touch the real problem. We can see, then, that his attack on poetry in the *Republic*, foreshadowed in a milder form in his earlier works, stands in a tradition of moral criticism of particular aspects of epic and other verse, especially criticism of poetry which might seem to glorify or excuse outrageous behaviour amongst gods and men (cf. Ar. *Frogs* 1043ff., on Euripides' 'bad women'); but what is extraordinary about the *Republic* is that it extends this critique to poetry, and indeed to art, as a whole.

We should distinguish between the discussion in books ii and iii, and the later resumption of the theme in book x.[69] The former is an attack based on the impropriety or blasphemy of many passages, which must be censored if the guardians in the ideal state are to receive a sound education. In the course of this discussion Socrates lays down a number of general guidelines for making statements about the gods, and also shows his willingness to criticise the conduct of the heroes – the self-indulgent anger and grief of Achilles in the *Iliad* make him no proper role-model for the man of virtue. But despite a number of incidental remarks, this does not go much beyond a large-scale attempt at bowdlerisation of the texts, and one which seems increasingly grotesque (perhaps consciously so) as the philosopher whittles away at the classic authors, chopping out unacceptable portions. The discussion of musical modes which follows this makes clear that here too there are appropriate and inappropriate styles: the former will inculcate moderation and courage, the latter will tend toward degeneracy and emotional indiscipline. This line of criticism essentially continues the existing tradition of finding fault with specific passages.

In book x there are two further lines of argument, both more original

---

[67] See my commentary on *Od.* 19. 203; G.Walsh, *The Varieties of Enchantment* (Chapel Hill 1984); L.H. Pratt, *Lying and Poetry from Homer to Pindar* (Ann Arbor, Michigan 1993).

[68] Pfeiffer, *Hist of Cl. Schol.* i. 8-12, with modifications by Richardson, *PCPS* 21 (1975) 65-81.

[69] The bibliography on both is vast: see esp. P. Vicaire, *Platon, critique littéraire* (Paris 1960); Iris Murdoch, *The Fire and the Sun* (1977); *Plato on Beauty, Wisdom and the Arts*, ed. Moravcsik-Temko (1982); Halliwell's comm. on book x; G. Ferrari in *Cambr. Hist. of Lit. Crit.*, ed. G. Kennedy, i (1989) 92ff.

and more searching. The first is rooted in Plato's metaphysics, and especially in the theory of forms. Here the examination of the poetic arts is extended to include all art, and especially the visual. This approach involves the criticism of art on grounds of its unreality: it is merely an imitation of life. Moreover, in the light of the theory of forms, the artist merely imitates the transient and imperfect objects and actions of this world, which are themselves only imitative of the true reality that gives them a kind of existence. In other words, the artist is creating a copy of a copy; he is merely working on a still more imperfect and inferior imitation. The argument is sharpened by concentrating on the knowledge which the artist possesses or lacks: 'the painter will make a semblance of a cobbler, though he knows nothing about cobbling, and neither do his public – they judge only by colours and shapes' (600e). Similarly the poet creates an illusion of detailed and accurately observed reality – but the creation remains an illusion, shadows without substance. If the poet really could say anything, teach anything about virtue or any of the professions, he would not be content with illusions, but would turn to action, to life. 'Do you think,' asks Socrates, 'that if anyone could make *both* the object of imitation *and* the image, he would let himself take image-construction seriously and make it the guiding principle of his life, as though it were the best thing he had?' (599a).

The third argument is a development of the moral one, but this time concentrates more on the psychological effect on the individual, less on the unworthy presentation of the subject matter. The psychological analysis draws on the imagery of the divided soul which was developed in the intervening books. Here the emphasis is again primarily on literature, and tragedy and comedy are particularly prominent. Socrates argues that the emotional effect of poetry is not just agreeable though pointless, but actually harmful: it weakens the moral fibre and stimulates all the morally deplorable emotions. Tragedy encourages, even forces us to give way to grief and mourning in sympathy with the characters; it enhances emotions which we would gladly check and contain within ourselves. Comedy encourages us to indulge those low and buffoonish tastes which in everyday life and conversation we would despise in others and above all in ourselves. Socrates sums up as follows:

> Poetical imitation in fact produces the same effect with sex and anger and all the desires and pleasures and pains of the soul, which in our view accompany every action. For poetry waters and fosters those feelings when what we ought to do is to dry them up; it establishes them as our rulers, when they ought to be under control, so that we can be better and happier people rather than worse and more miserable … And so, Glaucon, whenever you meet people who extol Homer, claiming that this poet has educated Greece and merits study for education and for the conduct of all human activities, and so that one may live equipped for all one's life through this poet's teachings – you ought to be friendly to people like this and greet them warmly (for they are as good as

they are able to be), and you should agree that Homer is the supreme poet
and the first of the tragedians, but remember that the only kind of poetry that
must be admitted to our state consists of hymns to the gods and encomia of
virtuous men. But if the pleasurable Muse should be admitted in lyrics or
narrative poems, then pleasure and pain, I tell you, will reign in the state in
place of law united with reason, which we have always jointly agreed to be
the supreme authority. (606d-7a)

Poetry and the arts, then, are vulnerable on three counts: they include
morally objectionable or educationally undesirable material; they pretend
to a knowledge and authority which they do not possess, and so mislead
and deceive the ignorant; they gratify and degrade the emotions, rather
than enhancing one's moral and intellectual self-command. There are no
concessions here to 'art for art's sake', or 'purely aesthetic' values; Socrates'
position is uncompromising. If literature cannot speak from knowledge, if
it does not teach, then it does not deserve the exalted role in education
which it has so long enjoyed. There is no point in answering that poetry
gives pleasure; Socrates himself readily admits that (595bc, 607cd), and
describes its power in seductive terms which bring it close to the magical
deceits of rhetoric as defined in Gorgias' *Helen*.[70] Socrates' point is that
pleasure is not enough.

It is easy to mock Plato's criticisms, just as it is common to make fun of
philosophy in general. Censorship is suspect in modern democracies, and
it is understandable that the treatment of the arts has joined the indictments in the works of those who see Plato as a proto-totalitarian. The
second critique has been particularly subject to attack, since few if any of
Plato's modern readers have sympathy with any version of a theory of forms
(and indeed, Plato himself seems to have had grave reservations about that
theory later in his career, though that did not make him modify his
judgements on poetry).[71] But it is better to admit that there is an irrefra-
gable element in the Platonic onslaught.[72] There *is* a fundamental difference between life and art, and art must of necessity be a selection, a partial
and perhaps significant selection, from experience (even if it be the experience of imagination); in which case, whether we believe in Forms or not,
it enjoys a derivative, even a parasitic status in relation to reality. In
general, two strategies have been adopted to resist Plato's criticisms. On
the one hand, we find the formalist response, which in many different ways
insists on the independent status of works of art, in a world of their own

[70] In particular note the magical term *keleo*; see J. de Romilly, *Magic and Rhetoric in Ancient
Greece* (1975) chs. 1-2. Cf also *Mnx.* 235a-c, *Prt.* 328d (quoted above, p. 130), *Smp.* 198b-9b.

[71] See esp. *Parm.* 130b-6c on the Forms; for later comment on the arts, see esp. *Laws* 632-41,
643-50b, and other passages gathered by R.F. Stalley, *An Introduction to Plato's Laws* (1983)
ch. 12.

[72] See esp. Murdoch (n. 69 above); J. Gould, in *The Language of the Cave*, ed. A. Barker and
M. Warner (Edmonton, Alberta 1992) 13-25. More generally in defence of poetry see W.B.
Stanford, *Enemies of Poetry* (London 1980), an entertaining but rather light-weight survey.

with their own rules, codes and language:[73] such arguments widen the gap between art and life, and may be thought to reinforce one side of Plato's case, that art is an extravagant and rather self-indulgent luxury. The other approach, which has been adopted by most of those who have explicitly sought to answer Plato's critique on its own terms, is to accept that art must show itself to be morally responsible, that it must play a part in society, but to argue that in some sense art does have access to knowledge, even if this is not a straightfoward, factual or demonstrable kind of knowledge. Plato did not believe, it seems, that the artist could imitate the Forms themselves, bypassing physical reality, but some later thinkers in antiquity did try to develop this idea.[74] In modern terms, we might wish to say that the poet or artist has some insight, however partial, not shared by others, which enables him or her to comment significantly on some aspect of experience, and that the form or medium chosen by such a person will be such as to communicate that insight more sharply or memorably than others might be able to do.[75] Yet the questions remain – what kind of insight, how is the communication effected, how can misuse or misunderstanding not occur, if the artist cannot put his cards (that is, his knowledge) firmly on the table for inspection and assessment?

The psychological aspect of Plato's critique is the one which most readers today will find most forceful.[76] We cannot afford to ignore the influence of art – from the cinema screen to the explicitly erotic novel – on the individual's desires and drives. The Aristotelian solution – that exposure to such influences tends to purge or dissipate our emotions in a beneficial fashion – is at best unproven.[77] The criticisms which Plato directs against rhetoric and against poetry have much in common: both are performed in public, before mass audiences (Plato, like most intellectuals, fears and distrusts the combined emotions of a crowd – e.g. 604e);[78] both involve elaborate style and ornament which please the refined taste without clarifying the thought; both appeal directly and dangerously to the emotions; both seem to express important ideas or to give some special insight (the 'teaching' which, as we saw, many Greeks thought present in poetry),

---

[73] This summary is absurdly cavalier, but fuller discussion would be out of place here; see further e.g. M.H. Abrams, *Doing Things with Texts* (New York and London 1989) 3-30, a helpful general survey; J. Culler, *Structuralist Poetics* (London 1975).

[74] See the rather brief treatment in Russell, *Criticism* 104-6; M.H. Abrams, *The Mirror and the Lamp* (Oxford 1953) ch. 2.

[75] This combination of the moral and the formal analysis is ultimately traceable to Aristotle, justly understood (the concept of Aristotle's criticism as solely formal/aesthetic is mistaken; see Halliwell, *Aristotle's Poetics* 24-7).

[76] For a recent treatment see J. Lear, *Phronesis* 37 (1992) 184-215.

[77] Some such theory seems to underlie the enigmatic reference to 'catharsis' in the *Poetics* (cf. *Politics* 1341b32ff.), though the details are far from certain: see Halliwell, *Aristotle's Poetics* Appendix 5.

[78] See further *Grg.* 501e sqq.

yet when analysed in private, with a cool head,[79] both often seem at best vacuous, at worst dangerously remote from the truth of what can be known (given the proper philosophic ability and the willingness to apply it) about morality, politics, religion – and indeed art itself. Although the possibility that certain poets are indeed inspired is often raised (the possibility is never admitted, or only in jest, with orators), it is clear that this does not grant them a special rank above the rest of their profession (partly because such inspiration is not open to objective testing), and the inspired poet plays only a very minor role in Plato's thinking about the subject.[80]

Socrates himself begins the renewed criticism of poetry in book x in hesitant style: 'I must speak out; though a certain affectionate respect which has held me from childhood onwards inhibits me from speaking about Homer ...' (595b).[81] Similarly he appeals to Glaucon's own experience: 'are you too, my friend, not enchanted by poetry, and especially when it is through Homer that you behold her?' (607c; cf. 387b, 397d). At the close of the critique, he allows that some future poet or prose writer may take up the challenge and compose a defence of poetry: here, too, the *Republic* for all its moral fervour leaves an option open. It is also noteworthy that Plato, here and in many other parts of his oeuvre, employs poetic language and uses terms and imagery which invite comparison of his own writings with those of the poets.[82] To go through all the possible instances would be a laborious task: only a few will be mentioned here. As for dialogues other than the *Republic*, it may suffice to refer to the *Symposium*, in which, as we have seen, comic and tragic dramatists are both trumped by Socrates' 'performance' (p. 182); to the *Phaedrus*, where Socrates presents himself as an inspired poet, in a sense Stesichorus incarnate (p. 255 below), and to the *Phaedo*, where he is at first versifying Aesop, and shortly before he takes the hemlock, he playfully remarks, 'and now my destiny summons me – as a tragic figure might put it!' (115a), following this comment with the charming anti-climax, 'and the hour is all but come for me to take a bath'. In a context which might excuse or even demand grand phrases, Socrates prefers his faux-naif, humorous style; yet the evocation of tragedy not only sets up a tension and contrast between Socrates' confrontation of his death, and the characteristic behaviour of tragic characters, but also

---

[79] As is done, e.g., with the Simonides poem in the *Protagoras*, and with Lysias' speech in the *Phaedrus*.

[80] The obvious exception might seem to be the *Phaedrus*: see esp. 245a. But that dialogue is a very special case, partly because the inspired figure is Socrates himself. See further ch. 9 below, pp. 255-6. See Dodds, *The Greeks and the Irrational* ch. 3, and for a fuller study of this theme E.N. Tigerstedt, *Plato's Concept of Poetical Inspiration* (Helsinki 1969).

[81] The suggestion by Popper 53, 228n.39, that this is hypocritical should not be taken seriously. See rather Halliwell, *Republic* x, 3-13.

[82] Imagery from the other arts, notably sculpture, is also frequent (we may recall that Socrates himself was a stonemason). See e.g. ii. 361d (addressed to Glaucon); iv. 420c ('moulding'); vii. 529de, 540c. Further, P. Louis, *Les métaphores de Platon* (Paris 1945) 209-11.

illustrates Plato's own silent competition and love-hate relationship with the drama.[83]

We return to the *Republic*. When the catalogue of defective states has been completed, Socrates invites Glaucon to judge who will be the first in happiness, who second, and so forth; Glaucon replies in terms which confirm that the image of the dramatic festivals is intended ('as if they were choruses ...'); and Socrates takes up the idea, suggesting that he act as herald himself and proclaim the result of the contest (580a-c). In the same section, a mythological image is employed to help them define the divided nature of the human soul: '(we need) one of those natures that the ancient fables tell us of ... such as that of the Chimaera, or Scylla, or Cerberus ...' (588cd).[84] A rather different point is made when Socrates confesses his incapacity to describe the Form of the Good: neither philosophy nor words themselves, it seems, are equal to the task, although he will be prepared to undertake a description of the offspring of the good and what is most nearly made in its likeness (506de, with Adam's n.). When he warns that he is afraid that in his incapacity he may deceive them and present them only with a counterfeit likeness, the language used recalls Gorgianic ideas of rhetorical deception (507a). Again, a slightly earlier passage makes clear that for all its length and detail, the account of the soul and the Forms given in the *Republic* is imperfect, a shorter and simpler version of what the Guardians must study (504b-c, referring back to iv. 435d). The same point is made at 533a: Socrates would give a full account if only he could: 'then, Glaucon, I would show you no longer an image (*eikona*) of my meaning, but the truth itself, as it appears to me – though whether rightly or wrongly I shouldn't properly affirm' (533a). Here Socrates recognises the limitations of words, and also characteristically casts doubt on the certainty of what he seems to 'know' (cf. *Phaedo* 114d). Or take the passage which applies the simile of the prisoners in the cave: 'We must apply this image (*eikona* again) as a whole ... and if you assume that the ascent and contemplation of the things above is the soul's ascent to the intelligible region, you will not mistake my hope, since that is what you desire to hear. But God knows whether it is true' (517b). We may suppose that Plato is concerned to preserve, even in the vast exposition of the *Republic*, the original modesty and admissions of ignorance which were surely typical of Socrates; yet the preoccupation with the limits and imperfections of his methods and words seems to go deeper still. Abridgement, sketch, copy, half-articulable insight – the descriptive language is significant. It seems that the exposition in the *Republic* is partial and tentative; the gap between what Socrates has achieved and what the poets can do is not so vast as we at first anticipated. In 472cd Socrates speaks of their efforts to find the pattern of justice and injustice and expresses some doubt as to whether the reality can match it

---

[83] See further Halliwell, *PCPS* 30 (1984) 49-71.
[84] Cf. above p. 165 for other mythical beast-creatures in the *Republic*.

(the language here recalls passages in which he speaks of using the Forms as a model for action). Yet he also introduces the idea of painting, and paradoxically suggests that the painting might exceed the possible reality: 'Do you think that he would be any the less a good painter, if after portraying a pattern of the ideally beautiful man and omitting no touch required for the perfection of the picture, he should not be able to prove that it is actually possible for such a man to exist? ... Then were not we, as we say, trying to create in words the pattern of the just state?'[85] On the one hand, the philosopher outclasses the artist through his access to the realities of the Forms; on the other, the two professions are set in pointed combination. We may also see the same pattern in the use of rhetorical language and conceptions: when Glaucon and Adeimantus ask Socrates to undertake the main argument of the work, they pose their request in terms which invite him to undertake an *encomium* of virtue and a *psogos* (or 'denunciation') of wrongdoing (358a8, d1-2, 366e; cf. later 419a-20a).

Plato, according to the critic Longinus, was a follower and imitator of Homer: 'he could not have put such a brilliant finish on his philosophical doctrines or so often risen to poetical subjects and poetical language, if he had not tried, and tried wholeheartedly, to compete for the prize against Homer, like a young aspirant challenging an admired master' (13. 4).[86] Longinus is thinking primarily of style, but the comparison can be extended. The prologue to the myth in book x introduces this account of the after-life in terms which recall Homer's *Odyssey* ('I shall not be telling you an "Alcinoan" tale, but rather one of a brave man, Er the son of Armenios, a Pamphylian by descent', 614b). An 'Alcinoan' tale means a tale like that of Odysseus at the court of the Phaeacian king Alcinous, which included his narrative of experiences in the underworld. It thus evokes the world of myth and poetry (and perhaps of poetic lies),[87] as a foil to Plato's own myth-making.

The ambiguous relationship between philosophy and poetry is splendidly captured in an earlier passage of book x. Socrates, as we have already seen, asks Glaucon if he does not feel the enchantment of poetry, especially that of Homer, and Glaucon assents (607c). Shortly afterwards, however, he uses similar language about philosophy: 'as long as poetry is unable to vindicate herself, we shall, as we listen to her, repeat our present argument as a charm (*epōiden*) to protect ourselves, taking care not to slip back into the boyish love from which most people suffer ...' (608a).[88] Thus the magic

---

[85] See further 487e-8a; 500e, 501b (the philosopher-rulers as artists emulating a heavenly model).

[86] Cf. Proclus' commentary on the *Republic*, Essay 6, book 2 (ed. Kroll, i, pp. 163-70).

[87] The narratives of Odysseus were sometimes seen as fictitious (i.e. fabrications by the hero) in antiquity, though Homer gives us no warrant for this: see Juv. 15. 16, with Courtney's commentary.

[88] On the term *epōide* cf. P. Laín Entralgo, *The Therapy of the Word in Classical Antiquity* (1970); E. Belfiore, *Phoenix* 34 (1980) 128-37.

of philosophy – the counter-spell embodied in the eloquence, the *poetry* of the *Republic* itself – is needed in order to dispel the bewitchment of poetry and the false ideas which it brings.[89] Plato is the greatest critic of Homer and tragedy; but he also learns from them and seeks to rival them.[90] To put it in another way, Plato uses the arts of literature in the service of philosophy.[91]

The *Republic* is too many-sided a work to be easily summarised, still less evaluated in a few sentences of 'conclusion'. It absorbs many features of the earlier dialogues into a larger and more ambitious framework – the informality of conversation, the constant recourse to analogy, imagery and quotation, the synthesis of deep commitment with self-deflating humour in the person of Socrates –, while also advancing further in both methodology and theory, combining aspects of philosophy – political theory, social analysis, metaphysics, epistemology, theology, human psychology – which in the earlier works had previously been treated more as independent though related spheres of enquiry. The resulting union of many lines of thought and different preoccupations is dazzling, though perhaps not flawless: there are places where the argument seems over-long and where easier points are laboured (e.g. the 'censorship' passages in books ii and iii), while elsewhere more complex and more important principles are accepted with surprising ease.[92] Plato himself seems at times conscious, as has been suggested above, that even the vast structure of the *Republic* cannot contain and do full justice to all that is being drawn into the discussion. Other aspects of the work may puzzle or disturb us in other ways. The argument began (after the slighter preliminary skirmishes with Cephalus and Polemarchus) with an attempt to justify the conviction that justice is superior to, and should be chosen in preference to, injustice. The demonstration of this, though rich in emotional force and intuitively sympathetic, depends to a considerable extent on accepting the hierarchical view of the soul which Socrates expounds in book iv, and the arguments for this view of the soul, and of human psychology, have left many readers uneasy. The political dimension of the work has already been discussed: although the negative criticism of corrupt states and citizens is brilliantly written, and full of political acuteness, the positive recommendations for the reform of

---

[89] Cf. the (characteristically graver and less suggestive) parallel in *Laws* vii. 817, esp. b (quoted on p. 308 below).

[90] Russell, *Criticism* 104 is right that Plato never formally proposes the notion of a philosophic poet (and with all qualifications the dialogues remain prose – though see Arist. *On poets* fr. 72 Rose (=1(a) Janko)), but the implications of passages such as these point in that direction. For further comment on the 'poetic' quality of the *Republic* see C. Segal, *Hermes* 106 (1978) 315-36, a thoughtful if sometimes fanciful paper.

[91] Besides the concluding myth of the afterlife, other 'constructive' uses or adaptations of myths include e.g. *Rep.* 407c-8c on Asclepius (note the explicit countering of the poets in 408b).

[92] Cf. the typically Oxonian comment of Ryle ap. Bambrough, 87, 'No tutor would accept from a pupil the reasons given by Plato for the following quite important doctrines ...'

society would produce a repressive and rigidly structured regime, even if (as could scarcely be guaranteed) sufficient guardians could be recruited to run the state before the elaborate educational scheme could be set in motion for the induction of their successors. On another level, we see in the central discussions of philosophic study in book vii a further development of the tendency of the *Symposium*, where Socrates became the spokesman for a remote and other-worldly ideal of contemplation. Dialectic no longer denotes the lively yet constructive exchange between open-minded friends, but instead refers to an internalised intellectual process of hypothetical reasoning: the ascent to the Form of the Good is undertaken in solitary thought, inexpressible in words.[93]

Yet the *Republic* remains a work which will always stimulate debate and command attention. In answering the challenges of Thrasymachus, Glaucon and Adeimantus, Socrates challenges not only his companions but the reader to follow his lead and, if the answers found seem lacking, to go further. Above all, the dialogue emphasises in countless ways the significance of the individual's choice of life – the choices made by the souls in the myth are only the reflection in fabulous terms of a theme which runs through the work.[94] Perhaps nowhere in Plato are the contrasts between the philosopher (or man himself) as he might be, and as he is, so powerfully delineated. The juxtaposition of two characteristically eloquent passages may be the most effective way of bringing out that opposition between ideal and actuality. The first has already been mentioned as one of the darkest and most pessimistic passages in the dialogue, one which clearly foreshadows Socrates' own death; the second comes at the climax of the education of the philosopher-ruler, after he has attained the insight that the abstract sciences, crowned with dialectical reasoning, can give.

> Those who have joined this small company, and who have tasted how sweet and blessed a treasure is philosophy, recognise clearly enough the insanity of the multitude, and know that (to put it simply) nobody achieves a single good thing in politics, nor is there any ally with whom one might safely go to the aid of justice; instead, like a man falling amongst wild beasts, being unwilling to join in their crimes and unable, a lone individual, to resist their universal savagery, he would meet an untimely end, without benefiting his city or his friends, unable to help himself or others. Taking all this into account, preserving his tranquillity and minding his own business, he takes refuge as if sheltering behind a wall from the stormy blast of dust and hail when a wind is driving it along. Gazing at the rest of mankind, bloated as they are with unlawfulness, he thinks it enough if somehow he himself can live his life here on earth innocent of injustice and impious deeds, and if he can make his departure from this life with a fair hope, revering the gods and generous of heart. (vi. 496c-e)

[93] On the shifting sense of dialectic see R. Robinson, *Plato's Earlier Dialectic* 69-75.
[94] Note the striking way in which the myth is interrupted by direct protreptic by Socrates at x. 618b-19a.

And when those fifty years have elapsed, those who have survived the course and excelled in every respect at every stage, physically and intellectually, must be brought to the goal, and compelled to turn the light of their soul to look upon the actual source that grants light to all, and gazing at Goodness itself, using it as a pattern to follow, they must each in turn order the city and the citizens and themselves, for the rest of their lives. The great part of their lives they will spend in pursuit of wisdom, but when their turn comes, they will suffer for a time in political life, and each govern for the sake of the city, not doing it because it is something fine in itself, but as a necessity; and once each generation has trained others like themselves in the same fashion, leaving successors as guardians of the city, they will depart to the isles of the blessed and dwell there. The city must erect monuments and offer sacrifices to them at public expense, as divine beings, if the priestess of Delphi assents, but if not, as fortunate and god-like men. (vii. 540a-c)

Although the context in each case concerns the philosopher, the issue is a broader one – between committed altruism and self-protective withdrawal, between moral and political engagement and quietism. Whether we are prepared to make the leap from actual to ideal (or, to adopt the Platonic image, to undertake that laborious ascent) is another choice, which each reader of the *Republic* will have been forced to ponder.

Appendix: The plan of the *Republic*

As will be obvious, many discussions continue across book-divisions; only books i and x have a clearly 'separate' status, which may easily be exaggerated. It is most unlikely that these divisions go back to Plato: they are first referred to in the first century AD (Thrasyllus ap. Diog. Laert. iii. 57), and other divisions were current.

Book i. Introductory: false starts at the task of defining justice. Is injustice profitable? What is the value of justice?

ii. Restatement of the case for injustice by Glaucon and Adeimantus; challenge to Socrates. Beginning of the main enquiry; agreement that the individual-state analogy should be used. Construction of model society begins. Principle of one-man-to-one-job.
  Necessities and luxuries.
  The Guardians of the state; their character defined (376). Question of the education of the Guardians introduced.

iii. Education. Criticism of the poets and of dramatic recitation. Music and metre. Aims of education, physical and mental.
  Selection of the rulers from the larger class of citizens educated on these principles. Guardians contrasted with Auxiliaries.
  The 'Noble Lie' (414-15).

iv. Duties of the Guardians.
  Virtues in the state. 434d-441c: analysis of the tripartite soul on the analogy of the state's social structure. Virtues in the individual.

v. Other aspects of the model society. Equality of women; abolition of family structures; practices in wartime.

471c-7a: resumption of the larger question of the model state: could it ever come into being, and in what circumstances? Central paradox stated: only if philosophers can become kings or vice versa (473).

Definition of the philosopher. Doctrine of Forms. Knowledge versus belief, reality versus appearance.

vi. The philosopher a worthy ruler. Contrary opinions raised, explained and rejected. Philosophy only 'useless' because it is not understood, or corrupted, by contemporary society.

The philosophic ruler not an impossiblity (497a-502c).

The training of a philosophic ruler.

Knowledge of the Good. Images of Sun and Line (506e-11e).

vii. Image of the Cave (514a-21b). Higher education of those selected to be philosophers. Mathematics: arithmetic, geometry, solid geometry, astronomy, harmonics, dialectic (531c-5a). Programme of studies in terms of age-classes.

viii-ix. The decline of society, and the analogous corruption of the soul. How states decline from the perfect condition. Timocracy (548c ff.), oligarchy (550c ff.), democracy (555b ff.) and tyranny (562a ff.), with their corresponding characters. Concluding picture of the life of the unjust man.

Just and unjust lives compared (including much more on the tyrant) (576-88).

Justice, not injustice, is profitable (588b-592b). The enquiry concluded.

x. 595-608b: discussion of poetry resumed. Art and Reality. Art and emotion; the influence of art on character.

608c-612a: immortality of the soul; further rewards for the just soul. Rewards for virtue in this life.

613e-621: rewards and punishments in the afterlife; the myth of Er. Conclusion.

9

The *Phaedrus*[1]

Socrates and Phaedrus

The problems which confront readers of Plato in general are particularly acute in the interpretation of the *Phaedrus*. They may be summed up as problems of form, of content and of tone. Most readers find it hard to grasp the relationship between the first half of the dialogue and the second – granted that situation and characters remain unaltered, are they dealing with the same issues, and with the same seriousness? It is also difficult to define the subject matter under discussion – is it love, or a particular type of love, or rhetoric in general, or rhetoric as applied to love, or rhetoric as the antithesis of philosophy? What conclusions, if any, are reached, either in the dialogue as a whole or within Socrates' main speech, superficially the most explicit statement of positive doctrine in the work? Again, we face formidable difficulties in determining the tone of the dialogue: is it a serious analysis of the philosophic significance of love, and does this analysis relate to other aspects of Plato's thought (such as reincarnation and the immortality of the soul, both of which are prominent in Socrates' main speech)? Or are we to take seriously Socrates' later diminution of the seriousness of that speech, in the passage where he dismisses it as a mere approximation, and even as 'play'? Two other paradoxical aspects of the *Phaedrus* have led to perplexity or invited a negative, 'deconstructive' reading of the dialogue (and by extension of Plato in general). First, Plato makes Socrates lay heavy emphasis in this very dialogue on the need for unity and coherence in a work of art (264, 268), and yet most readers have felt that, compared with (for example) the *Phaedo* or the *Symposium*, the *Phaedrus* lacks unity, at least by some definitions. Secondly, the last section of the dialogue includes a critique of the written word as a vehicle for wisdom, as Socrates asserts that the philosopher will resort to writing only as a leisure activity, without attaching any importance to the results. It seems that here too we are forced to see the *Phaedrus* itself as somehow lacking, limited or deficient as a consequence of its own status as a work made up of written words.

---

[1] This chapter was already complete before I saw L. Rossetti (ed.) *Understanding the Phaedrus* (Proc. of the II Symposium Platonicum, Academia Verlag, Sankt Augustin 1992). Detailed reference to a volume containing thirteen longer articles and twenty-nine shorter contributions is naturally impossible here, but most of the topics covered in this chapter are also touched on there.

More pointedly than in the *Republic*, more whimsically than in the *Symposium*, Plato seems to be directing his irony, and that of Socrates, at his own work.[2]

It seems important, however, not to exaggerate this ironic, negativist reading. It was argued in the first chapter that the panironic approach to Plato is an oversimplifying and reductive method, in that it does not discriminate sufficiently amongst the shifting tones and voices of the dialogues. In the *Phaedrus* too there is surely some solid ground: few would doubt, for example, that the condemnation of contemporary rhetorical theory as terminologically rich but intellectually vacuous is to be taken seriously, however amusing the sarcasm with which the criticism is presented. More specifically, the same passage in which Socrates refers to his main speech as a form of play and as an approximation also includes a more positive note: '... we said that the madness of love was the best, and fashioning some sort of image for the erotic experience, in which perhaps *we grasped hold of some truth*, though it may be that in other respects we went astray, and by mixing together a *not wholly implausible* tale, we made play in measured and pious vein with a mythical hymn in praise of your master and mine, Phaedrus, namely Love, who watches over beautiful young men' (265b-c). The positive elements here need to be given due weight as well as the negative. Accordingly, it will be assumed in what follows that the *Phaedrus*, for all its humour and playfulness, does have something to say, and that it is the interpreter's task to elucidate a text, rather than to celebrate its impenetrability.

As with other dialogues, it may prove helpful to begin from the fundamental matters of character and setting – the more so here, since so much is made of the idyllic rural situation by the banks of the river Ilissus. The dialogue involves only two participants, Socrates and his young friend Phaedrus (that Phaedrus is the younger is mentioned at 257c8). This immediately differentiates it from dialogues with a large cast such as the *Protagoras* or the *Symposium*. The effect is to make the conversation more intimate and private. This is reinforced by the unusual setting in the countryside, where there is no chance, or very little, of another person stumbling on Socrates and Phaedrus and joining in their discussion, as Anytus appears and makes an aggressive third in the *Meno*. The country represents a healthier and purer place than the town, where Phaedrus has just attended an epideictic performance by the orator Lysias. He declares that his doctor has recommended country walks as healthy exercise: as

---

[2] Chronology might of course be relevant to this question: thus M. Nussbaum, *Fragility of Goodness* 200-33 argues that the *Phaedrus* is a recantation of the *Republic*'s austerity, and that it represents, indeed, a reinstatement of poetry. The dating and related matters are discussed by G. de Vries, in the introd. to his commentary, by Thesleff, *Studies in Platonic Chronology* 171-80, and by C.J. Rowe, *PCPS* 32 (1986) 120-1. I am inclined to accept a relatively late date, but do not feel that the debate is very relevant to the points I wish to make. J. Tomin, *Antichthon* 22 (1988) 26-41 argues for a very early date.

often in Plato, medical and moral health are treated as parallel. Other important features of the setting will emerge, but it is clear from the start that the antitheses between town and country, Lysias and Socrates, rhetoric and philosophy, are going to be significant. The opening words of the dialogue, Socrates' apparently innocent question 'Whence and whither away, my dear Phaedrus?', already introduce a central point about Phaedrus' situation: in literal terms, he is coming from Lysias (who represents rhetoric) and meets or comes to the presence of Socrates, the philosopher and critic of rhetoric. More broadly, it seems that Phaedrus is at a crossroads in life, a point at which he should choose between these two pursuits (see esp. 257b, quoted below).

It is now time to consider the nature of Lysias' speech, which has so excited and delighted Phaedrus. Its argument is paradoxical: that a young boy besieged by admirers should yield his favours to one who does not love him rather than to one who does; and its form is dramatic, with the speaker presenting the argument of the non-lover directly, in the first person ('You know my situation ...'). This is a typical sophistic *paignion* ('plaything'): like Gorgias' defence of a notorious adulteress, or Polycrates' encomium of Busiris, it exploits a wide range of rational arguments in order to convince the listener of a proposition which at first seems contrary to all common sense. The issue itself may seem a trivial fiction, but Plato uses this speech as a springboard for a number of more important themes. Most obviously, the speech itself is shown to be deficient in both stylistic and moral terms, and Phaedrus' initial enthusiasm is thus exposed as ill-founded. Socrates swiftly produces a speech on the same theme which is better argued and more skilfully composed than Lysias' effort, and subsequently reverses the argument, recanting his criticism of Love and the lover, in the magnificent main speech. Secondly, the speech of Lysias is treated as a paradigm of the defects of contemporary rhetoric. While this critique of orators and handbook-writers continues familiar themes found in the *Gorgias*, *Menexenus* and elsewhere, Socrates also introduces a less familiar positive note, in describing the more intellectually respectable rhetorical art of which the philosopher would be master. Thirdly, the status of Lysias' speech as a written text is emphasised: at first Phaedrus feigns to have memorised it, but the sharp-eyed Socrates observes a piece of paper sticking out from under Phaedrus' cloak, and makes him reveal and read aloud from the transcript which he has brought away with him: 'much as I love you, I am not going to let you practise on me when Lysias himself is present' (228e). This identification of Lysias with his book paves the way for the critique of written works at the end of the dialogue, for as Lysias is in fact not present, he cannot defend himself or reply to Socrates' questions and criticisms. Also, Phaedrus' unsureness of his ability to recall the speech word for word anticipates the objection that books make the memory lazy and the mind uncritical of what it has learned (275ab), an objection well illustrated by the carefree enthusiasm of Phaedrus, which is so easily deflated when he is made to look more attentively at Lysias' composition (263d-4e).

As we have seen in earlier chapters, it is characteristic of Plato's Socrates that he not only encounters and criticises sophistic arguments and forms, but also adapts and transforms them. Thus in the *Symposium* he both criticises and gives more profundity to the encomium, in the *Euthydemus* the protreptic (and to some extent the methods of the sophistic elenchus). In the *Phaedrus*, the main sophistic feature is the epideictic form of the paradoxical argument, which we have already seen to be prominent in Lysias' speech. Although Socrates eventually counters this argument and praises the lover, his own speech retains something of this paradoxical, counter-intuitive element, since he argues that the relationship will be purest and most beneficial if there is never any physical consummation of their love. But whereas Lysias' paradoxes were hardly more than an ingenious game, Socrates' speech is founded in a much more coherent and vividly imagined metaphysical theory.

Similarly, Plato adapts certain phrases and ideas from the sophistic essay by Alcidamas, 'On those who compose written speeches', in which the sophist argues for the superiority of improvised oral speeches over written texts.[3] Alcidamas represents one stage in a debate continued by Isocrates, who held similar views (5. 25-7, *Ep. Dionys.* 2-3). But Plato's treatment of the antithesis is far more profound: his questioning of the value of writing is not simply concerned with effective delivery and technique, but with the very possibility of distilling knowledge in books, which cannot be tested and questioned by the reader (274b-8b). Again, the way that Socrates takes Lysias' speech and his own as specimens, to examine and criticise, corresponds to a teaching procedure attested among the sophists.[4] Even the sophists might expect their pupils to take away their works and study or analyse them, but Phaedrus' idolisation of Lysias' speech means that he has made no effort to assess it, and needs to be goaded and guided by Socrates before he can see what a poor effort it is.

The dialogue, then, presents a confrontation between sophistic rhetoric and Socratic philosophy: in this it may be compared with the *Gorgias* and the *Euthydemus*. One important part of Socrates' critique of rhetoric is that it relies on verbal and argumentative trickery, without any more profound knowledge of the human soul. This theme – what is the soul like? is it simple or complex, divine or monstrous? – is introduced, with typical playfulness

---

[3] Radermacher, *Artium scriptores* B xxii. 15. For the verbal parallels see Friedlaender i, 111-12, and on Alcidamas generally N. O'Sullivan, *Alcidamas, Aristophanes and the Beginnings of Greek Stylistic Theory* (*Hermes* Einzelschr. 60, Stuttgart 1993). That Alcidamas precedes Plato is the usual view, but has been questioned: see refs. in Thesleff, 174n.43, and now T. Cole, *The Origins of Rhetoric* 118, 173. Tomin, *SO* 67 (1992) 80-8 naturally supports the view that the *Phaedrus* is the earlier text.

[4] Gorgias 82 B 14; cf. Plut. *Demos.* 8; *Mor.* 504c on Lysias and a client reading the speech he had commissioned; Kerferd, *The Sophistic Movement* 30ff. See ch. 4, p. 111 above.

and wit, in the initial exchange at 229e-30a: Socrates has no time to consider sophistic rationalising of myth because he does not yet *know himself*, which is what matters much more than clever interpretative games.[5] Similarly, the teasing exchanges between Socrates and Phaedrus, in which each tries to get the other to do what he wants, make reference to their intimate knowledge of one another: 'Ah, Phaedrus, if I don't know Phaedrus, I have even forgotten myself ...' (228a 5-6, echoed by Phaedrus at 236c). Later, the main speech of Socrates presents a brilliant mythical image of the human soul, the image of the charioteer and his horses; and in the second half of the dialogue he outlines a form of ideal rhetoric with a philosophic basis, which would depend upon a thorough knowledge of the soul of its addressee. The philosophic orator must be able to describe the nature of the soul, whether it is simple or complex (this echoes Socrates' own enquiry into himself at 230a); he will be able to analyse what it does and how it is affected or influenced; he will categorise the forms of speech appropriate to a given type of soul (270c9ff., 271c10-72b4, 273de, 277bc). All of this finds analogies in Socrates' *own* practice, in this dialogue and elsewhere. When Socrates declares that Thrasymachus, or *anyone else* who seriously offers a systematic rhetoric based on knowledge, must describe the soul with precision, the self-reference is hard to miss (271a; for similar allusions, see 258d, 278c1).[6]

The fact that so much stress is laid on the mutual understanding and friendship of Socrates and Phaedrus makes desirable a closer examination of their relationship. This examination will also help explain the choice of love as a major theme of the dialogue.

The conversation between the two is of a kind familiar elsewhere in Plato's work: Socrates encounters an enthusiastic but naive young man who is enamoured of something that is morally suspect or damaging to him. Socrates' task is to enlighten him, to guide him to higher concerns and to a better state of mind. Callicles in the *Gorgias* is a conspicuous example of such a problem case: there, of course, Socrates fails. Hippocrates' adulation of Protagoras in the dialogue of that name provides a closer parallel: there, Socrates seeks to calm Hippocrates down, and to make him see just what he is getting himself into, and how little he really knows about Protagoras and his teaching. In the *Phaedrus*, Phaedrus is infatuated with Lysias' ingenious and paradoxical rhetoric. Lysias in a sense *is* the non-lover, the detached and cynical wooer whose weapon is pragmatic argument rather than a lover's devotion. By contrast, Socrates is the lover, who cares for Phaedrus more deeply and intensely than Lysias. This argument needs careful phrasing: it is not being suggested that either Lysias or Socrates is attempting a genuine physical seduction of Phaedrus, still less that any-

---

[5] For a fuller account of this passage see p. 174. On self-knowledge see further C.L. Griswold, *Self-knowledge in Plato's Phaedrus* (Yale 1986).

[6] Cf. W.H. Thompson's comm. (1868) xvii ff.; C.J. Rowe, *PCPS* n.s. 32 (1986), esp. 108ff.

thing physical comes of it either in or outside the dialogue. Indeed, such a strict application of the analogy runs aground on the fact that Lysias appears to be younger than Phaedrus, and is described as his 'darling' or 'beloved'.[7] What *is* being suggested is that the rival attractions of Lysias and Socrates, rhetoric and philosophy, are analogous to the appeals launched by the non-lover and by the genuine lover, and, more firmly, that the relationship between Socrates and Phaedrus, as enacted in the dialogue, bears a resemblance to the relationship between the ideal lover and beloved as described in Socrates' main speech (esp. 252c-253c, 256a7-b7). The relationships are comparable, not identical: the main speech moves, as we shall see, on a different level intellectually and stylistically from the rest of the dialogue, and the analogy should not be forced too far.

What is certainly clear is that Lysias' speech seems enticing and attractive to Phaedrus: indeed, his response to it as he reads it aloud is practically ecstatic: he beams with delight as he reads, as Socrates banteringly comments. He remarks that he was able to model his own response on that of Phaedrus: 'thinking that you understand these matters much more than I do, I followed your cue, and went into ecstasies in your wake' (234d). *Erastes* ('lover') and synonyms were often used to describe the passion of a fan for his idol, and the sophists were particularly liable to such idolatry. Thus Phaedrus' emotional reaction combines literary ardour with quasi-erotic overtones, and also with the idea of inspiration, since Socrates' use of the language of bacchic ecstasy evokes the wild and wondrous loss of self-control familiar from Euripides' *Bacchae* and other texts. But Phaedrus' reaction is lavished on an unworthy object, whether we consider the speech per se or its author to be the chief recipient. By contrast, Socrates offers Phaedrus the more rewarding and profound affection of the older lover, 'a lover that is no pretender but loves in all sincerity' (255a: pretence and hypocrisy are naturally associated with rhetoric). It is with Phaedrus, and other young men like him, in mind that Socrates prays that he may never be deprived of 'the lover's art' (257a).

This reading is strongly supported by the striking passage following the recantation of Socrates, in the scene between his first and second speeches (241c-243e). At the start of his first speech Socrates, unlike Lysias, had given a little introduction, almost in a story-telling or fable style: once upon a time there was a boy with a lot of lovers ... one very cunning one pretended he wasn't really a lover, in order to gain advantage ... he made this speech ... (237b). This imagined situation is picked up in the later interlude, where Socrates asks urgently 'what has become of that boy I was just talking to? I want him to hear this too, to make sure he doesn't go off and grant his favours to the non-lover before we can stop him!' Surely this concern would

---

[7] 236b, cf. 257b, Phaedrus as Lysias' *erastes*; 237a10 is more ambiguous. The situation is complicated by the fact that Lysias' date of birth is disputed (C. Carey, *Lysias, Selected Speeches* (Cambridge 1990) 1-3). For Phaedrus see *APF* 201, an indecisive discussion.

be trivial and absurd if it were only on behalf of a fictional character. Moreover, Phaedrus replies: 'Here he is, very close all the time, whenever you want him' (243e). In other words, the boy is, or is assimilated to, Phaedrus.

A crucial passage for the interpretation of the dialogue in terms of a vital choice which Phaedrus must make, and as a choice which is bound up with love, is the closing passage of Socrates' main speech. 'Such, dear Love, is the recantation that has been offered and given in payment to you, as beautiful and good as was in our power, especially as I was obliged to put it into poetic language on account of Phaedrus. Grant your pardon for what was said before, and rejoicing in this offering, be gracious and kind. Do not take from me the art of loving which you have granted me, nor impair it in your anger, but allow me to be honoured even more than now amongst the fair. And if any part of the speeches Phaedrus and I spoke before offended you, blame Lysias, the father of the speech, and make him stop this kind of discourse. Turn him instead towards philosophy, as his brother Polemarchus has been turned, so that his admirer here may no longer waver as he does at present, but may turn the course of his life single-mindedly towards love, accompanied by philosophic discourse' (257a-b). In other words, the *Phaedrus* is in part a conversion-dialogue, presenting the process of Phaedrus' turning to philosophy.[8]

The point is followed up in the second half of the dialogue, at 260e-261a, where Socrates and Phaedrus are considering the claims of rhetoric to be a *techne*, a science, as opposed to a mere knack. Socrates says that he thinks he can hear certain arguments approaching which are solemnly protesting that rhetoric is no true science – clearly, philosophic arguments such as are advanced in the *Gorgias*. Phaedrus replies 'we need those arguments, Socrates; bring them hither, and ask them what they are saying', where-upon Socrates summons them in high-flown style: 'Attend on us now, ye noble beasts, and persuade Phaedrus ... that unless he is sufficiently devoted to philosophy, he will never be an adequate speaker on any subject.' That is, philosophic knowledge is in fact indispensable to rhetoric. (Rhetoric here is of course true rhetoric, a very different thing from the art of Lysias.)

This reading of the *Phaedrus*, considering Socrates as a lover wooing Phaedrus, helps make sense of the dramatic setting. This idyllic and secluded country scene is well-suited to erotic activity, especially seduction or abduction.[9] It is from a flowery meadow, while playing with the Nymphs, that Persephone is abducted by Hades.[10] Many of the rape-scenes in Ovid's

[8] On the whole conception of conversion in ancient times see above all the brilliant survey by A.D. Nock, *Conversion* (Oxford 1933), esp. ch. 11 on conversion to philosophy; also Nock, *Essays on Religion and the Ancient World*, ed. Z. Stewart (Oxford 1972), i. 469-80, an essay on 'Conversion and Adolescence'.

[9] On the setting see further H. Görgemanns, in *Philanthropia kai Eusebeia* (Fest. A. Dihle), ed. G.W. Most, H. Petersmann, A. M. Ritter (Göttingen 1993) 122-47.

[10] *hDem.* 1ff., with Richardson's nn.; likewise Creusa in Euripides' *Ion* (887ff.), or Europa in the charming poem by Moschus.

Metamorphoses are set in similarly delicious and unprotected spots.[11] Above all there is the story of Oreithyia, explicitly associated with the spot (229). Other verbal analogies support this connection: the spot is suitable, says Phaedrus, for young girls to play (229b8), and Socrates refers to Oreithyia playing with her sister Pharmakeia (229c8); compare the later references to what Socrates and Phaedrus have been doing as 'play' (265c1, 278b) Here, of course, there is no seduction: that would be out of keeping with Socrates' character, as we have seen before in the *Charmides* and still more in the *Symposium*; and it would be inconsistent with the principles espoused in the main speech, according to which the ideal love will be unphysical.

Thus Phaedrus, having first been an uncritical and unqualified devotee of Lysias, in danger of being 'seduced' into his world of dull style, corrupt values and false rhetoric, is gradually led by Socrates to see the defects of that world and to aspire to philosophy in the company of his loving friend. In the closing pages of the dialogue there is a light-hearted agreement that Phaedrus will tell the results of their discussion to his 'companion' Lysias, and that Socrates will do likewise to his friend, 'the fair Isocrates', previously unmentioned. Isocrates is here described as Socrates' *paidika* (that is, the beloved rather than the lover), and Lysias as the *paidika* of Phaedrus. In both cases this is metaphorical and symbolic, not literal. Phaedrus must attempt to guide and instruct Lysias, his *paidika*, just as Socrates hopes he can be a beneficial influence on Isocrates.[12] We should not see this as purely mischievous by-play: what was at first mere banter is given fuller moral content by the exposition of philosophic *eros* at the heart of the dialogue.

At the very end of the work Phaedrus joins readily in Socrates' prayer, saying 'Make the prayer for me too; for what friends have they share' (278c). Friendship ends the dialogue as it began it (the opening words, we recall, combined the motifs of Phaedrus' direction in life and of friendship: 'whence and *whither away*, my dear Phaedrus?', 227a1).

It would be pleasant to leave Phaedrus like this, firmly in the right camp, a firm and permanent convert to Socrates' way of life and philosophic priorities. But things are not that simple. The 'conversion' of Phaedrus, however whole-heartedly expressed, seems to have been only partial or temporary. It has long been noted that Phaedrus' name appears on the inscription recording the names of those whose property was confiscated after the mutilation of the Herms in 415 BC; that is, Phaedrus was convicted and exiled for playing a part in that mysterious affair, a strange mixture of vandalism and blasphemy which we may find hard to take seriously today, but which, occurring practically on the eve of departure of the Sicilian expedition, caused a tremendous furore and led to a large

---

[11] C. Segal, *Landscape in Ovid's Metamorphoses* (*Hermes* Einzelschr. 23, 1969).

[12] For the significance of this passage in assessing Plato's view of Isocrates see below, p. 251.

number of prosecutions.[13] We seem, therefore, to be dealing with a more
oblique instance of the device of foreshadowing used more openly in the
Symposium (where Alcibiades' riotous behaviour prefigures his involvement in the profanation of the Mysteries). Here, as also probably in the
Charmides with Critias and Charmides (later members of the Thirty
Tyrants), Socrates' influence upon his wayward friends is shown to be
powerful but not lasting: in the end, these characters go astray.[14] What does
this signify for the *Phaedrus*? In part, perhaps, it distances Socratic ideals
and ideas from reality, as in the *Republic* doubt is cast on the realism or
relevance to reality of the proposals for the ideal state: are these discussions
practical or serious proposals, or is it all a game, a grandiose fantasy or a castle
in the air?[15] In part, it exploits the time-lag between the dramatic date of the
dialogue and the actual date of composition: this is how it seemed in that
cheerful and optimistic period in Phaedrus' youth, but look how it all came out
in the end.[16] Perhaps Socratic optimism (to know the good is to follow it; virtue
is knowledge, etc.) is also contrasted with Platonic pessimism.

It has indeed been pointed out that there are in fact serious difficulties
in finding a date at which this dialogue can sensibly be supposed to have
taken place, given what we know about the periods of absence from Athens
of both Phaedrus and Lysias.[17] Is this merely a case of Plato's well-known
penchant for anachronism, or is it, as Martha Nussbaum suggests, a
further indication that 'this story isn't true', that Phaedrus' conversion to
and acknowledgement of the value of Socratic philosophy and Socratic eros
might have happened, should have happened, but in reality did not? If so,
this would be another way, in addition to the reflections on method and
myth, the critique of writing, and so forth, in which the dialogue is drawing
attention to its own status as a written and fictional work. But the case is
perhaps weakened not only because, as already mentioned, Plato has a
tendency to set the scene of his dialogues in a rather vague temporal
location,[18] but also because it is a premiss of this argument that Lysias'

[13] For the detailed narrative, see Thuc. vi. 27-9, 60-1; Andocides, *On the mysteries* (ed.
MacDowell); the inscription is in R. Meiggs and D. Lewis, *A Selection of Greek Historical
Inscriptions* ... (revised edn. Oxford 1988) no. 79B = C.W. Fornara, *Translated Documents* ...
Archaic Times to the End of the Peloponnesian War (Cambridge 1983) 147D: Phaedrus' name
occurs at line 112. For a full modern account see Ostwald, *From Popular Sovereignty* 322-33
with Appendix C; also C.A. Powell, *Historia* 28 (1979) 15-31.
[14] On the *Charmides* see ch. 3, pp. 93-6 above.
[15] See e.g. 536c (they are at play); 376d, 501e (talk of the state as a myth), and p. 224 above.
[16] At a seminar in St Andrews at which a part of this chapter was read, Sir Kenneth Dover
pointed out to me that Phaedrus might, after all, have been innocent of the charges, or Plato
might have believed him to be. In that case, obviously, the interpretation of his 'conversion'
would be different – perhaps even an attempt at exoneration? But the analogies with cases
where Plato cannot have believed the interlocutors innocent (Critias, Alcibiades, perhaps
Meno), and the other evidence for his interest in the corruption of philosophic potential (esp.
Rep. vi. 487b-97a), seem to me to support my reading.
[17] M. Nussbaum, *Fragility of Goodness* 212f., cf. 229; see also Rowe's introduction, pp. 13-14.
[18] Cf. Dodds's comm. on the *Gorgias*, pp. 17-18, on the contradictory indications in that
dialogue.

brother Polemarchus (died 404), referred to in 257b, is still alive, and it is far from clear that that passage must imply this.

The significance of Phaedrus' career can be doubted,[19] but it is obvious that when we come to the unexpected allusion to Isocrates at the end of the dialogue, this cannot be elucidated without reference to the historical career of that writer. Here the gap between dramatic date (undeterminable, as we have seen, but to be imagined as c. 420-415?), and its date of composition (hardly before 380, perhaps much later) becomes crucial. By this stage Socrates has won Phaedrus over with his lover's devotion, and now Isocrates seems to be an object of similar concern, again presented in erotic terms (Isocrates is described as Socrates' *hetairos*, 278e6ff.; and as his *paidika*, 279b2).[20] Isocrates, like Phaedrus, is a young man with potential for the philosophic life, and is therefore attractive to Socrates: the ambiguity between beauty of body and of soul is a regular feature of Socrates' relationships with handsome young men.

> 'Isocrates is still young, Phaedrus, but I'd like to tell you what I prophesy for him.'
> 'What sort of prophecy is that?'
> 'He seems to me to be superior in natural gifts, going beyond the oratory of Lysias and his like; there is a nobler character in his make-up. As a result, it would not surprise me if, as he advances in years, even in the rhetorical sphere at which he is currently trying his hand, he were to surpass all others who have turned their hands to that field just as men surpass boys. Moreover, if these themes do not satisfy him, perhaps a more divine impulse may carry him on to greater things. For there is a kind of philosophy innate in that man's intellect, my friend. This is the message that I am bearing from the gods of this place to my darling Isocrates, and you must take the other message back to Lysias, who is yours.' (279ab)

The talented Isocrates, at the time at which the conversion in the *Phaedrus* is to be imagined as taking place, is not yet a Lysias-type, but like Phaedrus he is tempted in that direction, towards the practice of rhetoric. Like Phaedrus, he still has a chance to take a different path; but like Phaedrus again, in the end he will disappoint his early promise. As we saw in an earlier chapter, at the time he wrote the *Euthydemus*, c. 392-385(?), Plato did consider Isocrates a significant figure. There, the anonymous critic, whose complaints about the sophists and Socrates Crito reports at the end of the work, is described as being on the borderline between politics and philosophy, and this ambiguous position, though clearly not satisfactory in Socrates' eyes, is at least more respectable than the debased dialectic of the

[19] E.g. by C.J. Rowe, commentary, p. 12: 'these facts have no obvious bearing on the argument of the *Phaedrus*.' It may be, however, that 'argument' is to be taken strictly here, whereas I am concerned at present with the overall effect of the work.
[20] On the vocabulary, see Dover, *Greek Homosexuality* 16f., 20.

two sophists in that dialogue, Euthydemus and Dionysodorus, whom the Isocrates-figure has rightly criticised (*Euthyd.* 306a-c and context).

The *Phaedrus*, probably composed at least a decade later, is perhaps more patronising, and no doubt irritated Isocrates more. In this dialogue many Gorgianic and Isocratean techniques of rhetoric are parodied, discussed, or put to novel use, but the compliment paid to the youthful Isocrates is a very back-handed one. He is a promising lad, who could in time do even better than Lysias (this after Phaedrus' admiration for Lysias and for his oration has been shown to be ill-founded!); and he might one day rise up, guided by a 'more divine impulse', for 'there is a kind of philosophy in him' (279a 9f.). *Tis* ('a certain, a kind of') must be emphatic here. Isocrates has got some sort of philosophy. There is surely a feline allusion (by Plato, not 'Socrates') to the way that Isocrates talks about his teachings as 'philosophy' and denies that title to natural philosophy, eristics, dialectics and the ethical science of the Academy.[21] The reader naturally asks, has Socrates' prediction about Isocrates really been fulfilled? Even if Isocrates unquestionably is a greater man than Lysias and his followers, has he really risen as high, achieved as much, as he might have done if he had followed some of the principles laid down for the philosophic orator by Socrates in the *Phaedrus* itself? It is hard to feel sure of the tone here, but we should not ignore our external evidence of how Isocrates did turn out; and therefore, I would argue, we cannot suppose that Plato is whole-heartedly endorsing Isocrates present or past (as for instance Cicero assumed, notably in *Orator* 42). As already suggested, the absent Isocrates and the present Phaedrus both stand at the crossroads between rhetoric and philosophy and share a potential for the latter: Phaedrus seems to make the right choice, but later backslides, while Isocrates manages to sit on the fence, to keep his ambiguous status, never wholly committing himself to philosophy in the fullest, most Socratic sense; he only has 'a kind of philosophy'.[22]

Love and desire in the *Phaedrus*

It is time to turn to the speeches on love, and especially to the longest and most eloquent, Socrates' main speech. Some paraphrase will be necessary in order to make certain points clear.

---

[21] See *Antid.* 268-70, 285, etc., with parallels in earlier works, e.g. *Evagoras* 77-8, *Against the sophists* 16, *Helen* 5, *Panath.* 28-30, 270. I have found it hard to avoid some repetition here from ch. 2.

[22] See further Thompson's commentary, Appendix 2; for further hints and implications in this passage, and for an attempt to relate it to other polemical writings of the period, see J.A. Coulter, *GRBS* 8 (1967) 225-36. The ironic tone of the passage is rightly reasserted by G.J. de Vries, *Mnem.* 24 (1971) 387-90, against groundless objections by Erbse.

The speech of Lysias[23] is naturally the simplest and most straightforward. Plain and lucid in style, its novelty and interest depend purely on its paradoxical starting-point – the argument that a boy with a wide choice of lovers will do better to favour a man who is not in love with him. Structurally it is uncomplicated, even naive, with no developing argument: as Socrates later complains, the points made could be rearranged in any order without this making any serious difference (264b). As the situation might lead us to expect, the argument is conducted in a highly rational, unemotive style, in the tone of a reasonable man pointing out advantages, disadvantages, options to be chosen and dangers to be avoided (this sustained rationality makes Phaedrus' ecstatic delivery of the work still more bizarrely inappropriate). There is much repetition of vocabulary and phraseology (notably transitional phrases such as 'and moreover', or 'furthermore'). Rhetorical questions are employed, arguments introduced to be knocked down (233c6, d5), and there are touches of the antithetical sentence-structure more familiar in Gorgias and his like (233b6ff., e5ff.), but for the most part the speech is fairly unadventurous in terms of style. Decorum is preserved carefully, with the use of a number of periphrases and euphemisms when the speaker refers to the favour he is asking from the boy (231c7, 232c1-2, e1, 234a1).[24]

More significant is the moral aspect of the speech, and the value-system which it seems to imply. The keynote is struck from the start: 'You know my situation, and you have heard that I consider it *advantageous* to us that this should happen.' The concepts of expediency and self-interest are used throughout the speech: it is assumed that no other principles should govern a rational man's actions. The boy should consider how to get most benefit, and how to avoid harm, but this seems to be seen in material terms, or at most in terms of his reputation. Athenian attitudes, familiar already from Pausanias' speech in the *Symposium*, are presupposed here: one section of the speech opens with a reference to 'established convention' (*nomos*) (231e3). It is assumed that the boy will not want people talking about his affair, and the non-lover promises discretion of a kind which (he claims) lovers would not be able to sustain (232a, 234a4-5, c2). Prudential and material motives come into the speaker's perspective a great deal: he emphasises that lovers commonly neglect their household and their financial interest, expending their substance (231a, cf. 234b). He takes a low view of human nature throughout: while in love a man may do anything for his beloved, but it is reasonable to expect that when he is involved with

---

[23] I assume that this is not simply an authentic work by the orator, but the evidence does not admit of proof. For agnostic discussion see Dover, *Lysias and the Corpus Lysiacum* 69-71, 90-3; also De Vries's commentary, 11-13. One argument for at least partial authenticity is that a purely Platonic creation would make 'Lysias' too much of a sitting duck for Socrates' criticisms; if this is granted, then the Lysianic speech may have some basis in a real text (cf. Demosthenes 61).

[24] On such phrases see Dover, *Greek Homosexuality* 44f., 83.

someone else, he will be prepared to do his former friend harm (231c); lovers will not be able to restrain their self-esteem and satisfaction enough to refrain from boasting of their conquests (232a); they will be jealous of others and prevent their beloved from associating with those of superior merit (232cd); they are flatterers, who will praise all the beloved's qualities and actions, without discriminating, and so the boy will learn nothing and gain no moral improvement from the affair (233a);[25] when the lover's passion is spent he will seek excuses to break off the relationship (234a7f.).

Although the emphasis in the speech is on expediency, other considerations are not entirely excluded. At 232c the lover's paranoia is directed at potential rivals of greater wealth and also of greater intelligence: 'fearing that those who possess wealth will outdo them with their money, and that the educated will come off better in terms of intellect' (though even here it is assumed that the boy will associate with the latter for selfish reasons). The language of *arete* (excellence) also figures, as a criterion for choosing a worthy non-lover. Indeed, the need for such a criterion becomes particularly plain at the end of the speech: 'You will perhaps ask me, then, if I advise you to grant favours to all who are not in love with you. I for my part think that not even the man who was in love with you would tell you to take this attitude to all those who were' (234b). But the speaker goes on merely to state the obvious pragmatic objections to such promiscuity (reduced gratitude from the beneficiaries; lack of secrecy). No principle is suggested by which the boy should discriminate amongst non-lovers. Moral evaluation, like philosophy, is conspicuous by its absence from the Lysianic speech. These deficiencies later earn it dismissal as a work full of 'urbane naïveté' (242e5) – an eloquent oxymoron.

Whereas Lysias' speech is treated as an artefact, self-contained and complete, Socrates' speeches are created *de novo* on the spot and are elaborately framed by preliminaries and qualifying commentary. The first of his speeches is deliberately introduced as a challenge to that of Lysias: although Socrates feigns reluctance, it is he who begins to tempt Phaedrus with the prospect of a further oration. His reservations about the nature of the argument he will be presenting are made clear, however, by his self-protective attitude: 'I shall speak with my head covered, so that I can rush through my speech as quickly as I can, and not lose my way through shame, from looking at you' (237a). Superficially this refers to Socrates' embarrassment at competing with so gifted an orator as Lysias (cf. 236d); but more fundamentally, it expresses his moral objections, which emerge

---

[25] This is one of the few hints of a moral or intellectual aspect in this speech, and one which is developed later. Cf. esp. the opening scenes of the *Lysis*, where Socrates is trying to help the love-sick Hippothales, who is foolishly flattering his beloved by composing poetry in his honour, praising his ancestry and generally swelling his head (205a-6a). Socrates takes a hand and tries to show Hippothales by his own example that 'this is the way you should converse with a beloved, humbling and restraining him, not puffing him up and indulging him as you do' (210e).

more explicitly in the subsequent interlude (esp. 242de, 243c). The frame-passage (p. 246 above), in which the speaker is described as a lover pretending to be a non-lover, partly alludes to the hypocrisy of Lysias' rhetorical art, which plays with fictions and imaginary situations; but it also distances Socrates himself from what he is saying; like the speaker, he is only pretending to adopt the views his speech proposes.

The speech pursues a similar line to that of Lysias, but few would dispute that it is a superior performance in style and expression. As for structure, most notably, it begins with an insistence on the need for a clear and agreed definition of love; thereafter, the argument is well-organised and vividly presented. The points made in the main part of the argument echo and put more pungently the argument of Lysias: the lover is less self-controlled than the non-lover, and so a less safe and sensible companion; he will be jealous of the boy's achievements, his other associates, even his family, and will prevent him from improving himself; he will eventually fall out of love, and then will fail to keep the promises he has made, but will abandon the boy. Socrates breaks off before voicing any contrasting praise of the non-lover's qualities. Perhaps the most striking difference from Lysias' speech is the intellectual quality of the argument. The insistence on definition is only one aspect of this: Socrates also takes pains to divide the forces which govern the mind into desires and judgements, and to distinguish between their effects (237d6ff.), a passage which anticipates the 'scientific' method of division and collection which he praises later in the dialogue (265a ff., cf. 253c7). The other passage which shows an interest in intellectual psychology is the conclusion of the speech, in which the change of heart in the lover when he has lost his passion for the boy is presented as a transformation into another person: 'he changes in himself and adopts a different ruler or master, sense and sanity in place of love and madness, and he has become a different person without his beloved realising it … His beloved demands a return for the favours he has done him … thinking that he is talking to the same man; while the other through shame cannot bring himself to say that he has become a different person …' (241a, cf. b).

The Socratic speech also gives pride of place to the harm which will be done to the beloved's mind by association with a lover (harm to the body and to his personal property come in second and third place). The jealous lover will deprive him of the advantages of associating with others, and in particular will prevent him from increasing his wisdom through divine philosophy (239a-b; as we saw, the word did not appear in the speech of Lysias). The speech returns to this point at its close, with emphatic eloquence: (if he submits to the lover) 'he is necessarily surrendering himself to someone untrustworthy, peevish, jealous, disagreeable, harmful to his property, harmful to his physical condition, but by far most harmful to the education of his soul, than which in truth there neither is nor ever will be anything more valuable in the eyes either of men or of gods' (241c). The references to the soul, as also to philosophy, expand the horizon of the speech and give a more profound meaning to the 'advantage' and 'harm' in terms of which Socrates, like Lysias, couches his argument; but these references are not fully explained: philosophy is taken as a term well understood, not in need of definition itself. More significantly, the nature of love as it affects the beloved is still not considered: it is the lover and his psychology who dominates, and the possibility of a fruitful emotional relationship, one which would involve reciprocal feeling, is not allowed to enter the picture. In short, Socrates' speech marks a distinct advance on Lysias', in that it is superior in structure and expression, more eloquent and sophisticated in style; but in terms of argument it is still not a satisfactory account of love's effects and defects; and the fact that Socrates himself voices misgivings about it, and abandons it unfinished, reinforces our sense that there must be more to be said.

We have still to consider Socrates' references to his 'inspired' state as he utters the speech. This motif runs through the first part of the dialogue, and is closely linked with the sacred aspects of the setting – Socrates and Phaedrus have settled down in a place with strongly religious associations. They are watched over by figurines of the Nymphs and by Achelous (230b etc.), and there are later references to the Muses (237a, 259b-d) and Pan (263d, 279b8). Phaedrus is described as being in ecstasy over Lysias' speech, and Socrates mockingly claims to be sharing in his manic frenzy (234d; cf. already 228b7). The motif gathers strength as Socrates embarks on his first speech: at 235c-d he feels his breast swelling and his mind inspired from some unknown source; at 238c-d his speech begins to fall into rhymes, and he describes it as dithyrambic; at 241e he fears he is in danger of possession by the Nymphs, and abandons his increasingly poetic speechi-fying to prevent this. Later, at 262d, he blames the gods of the place for the aptness with which both his speeches serve as illustrations of points he wishes to make. Similar is another late reference, 263d: 'aha, so by your account the Nymphs, daughters of Achelous, and Pan, son of Hermes, turn out to be more skilled in the art of words than Lysias, son of Cephalus.'

This last passage pointedly juxtaposes the sacred and the secular, divine inspiration and human knowledge. Lysias' speech was an obvious product of modern, rational and prudential morality, self-interested and pseudo-sophisticated. Socrates' first speech introduces nobler conceptions such as 'divine philosophy', but as yet they lack any clear metaphysical framework. The initial scene-setting placed strong emphasis on the sacred setting, and the exchange between Socrates and Phaedrus about the Boreas myth raised the question of the validity of such tales: do they have a historical origin, are they merely fictions to be exploded by the clever moderns, or can they be a source of wisdom in some non-literal sense? (cf. p. 174 above). It is not surprising, then, that the discussion in the dialogue should continue to have a religious aspect: first, in the 'inspired' speeches of Socrates; secondly and more seriously in the intervention of his divine sign, which protests at his attempted departure and impels him to put right the wrong he has done through his slanderous account of Love; and finally in the main speech, in which he relates the experience of lover and beloved to a religious and eschatological world-view, offering a vivid and highly poetic vision of the divine origins of love.[26] Further, whereas in his first speech he was uneasily resisting the inspirational influence of the Nymphs and therefore broke off before completing it, in the main speech he waxes poetic without reservation, and entrances Phaedrus with a prose-poem which far surpasses the Lysianic performance.

The reader naturally asks how seriously the idea of inspiration or possession by Nymphs should be taken. These ideas seem foreign to the normally clear-headed and unpoetical Socrates. It is certain that Socrates is treating Phaedrus and his enthusiasms with a good deal of irony, and plausible that this extends to his strangely lyrical description of the setting too (230bc, cf. the passage on the cicadas at 259a-d). Nor does it seem likely that the gods of the place would first give Socrates the inspired eloquence to utter a blasphemous account of Eros, and only then put him right. Moreover, it is not as though Socrates himself is unaware of the doubtful status of his speech in praise of the non-lover: as we saw, he is unhappy about the task from the start. It seems probable, therefore, that Socrates is playing up to the setting, deliberately reacting in ways which suit the traditional stories about poetic possession and the like, rather than experiencing an authentic religious experience. The genuineness of the divine sign, a well-established aspect of Socrates' mental life, should not be doubted, but it is clear that Socrates knew perfectly well that there were things wrong before he tried to leave and heard that inner warning. This is not, however, to dismiss the whole string of references to inspiration as a foolish pretence. Phaedrus had commented earlier on the oddity of Socrates' venturing into the country, and Socrates had remarked that country places and trees could not teach him things, whereas men could. In the course of the dialogue, however, he uses the fiction of inspiration by the gods of this spot as a means of learning from, and teaching through, the countryside. More substantially, the concepts of divine possession, correction and prophetic utterance focus attention still more firmly on the religious and mythic aspect of life, the side which the 'urbane naïveté' of Lysias' speech, and even of Socrates' first speech, had sadly neglected. The myth of the soul's flight and of the gods, the account of the cicadas, and the story of Thoth and Thamus, all have a religious dimension.

Turning to the central speech of Socrates, the 'palinode' in which he retracts his previous condemnation of love and its associated madness, we at once find ourselves in a different world. The longest speech in the dialogue, it is also the richest and most ornate – or, more precisely, most *poetical*; it is introduced with a host of poetic allusions as the speech of

---

[26] See also the references to saying what is pleasing to the gods, at 273e and 274bc.

Stesichorus of Himera,[27] and at the end Socrates describes it as poetically worded 'of necessity, for Phaedrus' benefit' – a hint that the poetic style is in part *ad hominem*, to suit Phaedrus' taste, or indeed his very soul.[28] The Palinode thus exemplifies the rhetorical and persuasive skills which Socrates requires of the true orator in the second half of the dialogue.

Beginning with a defence of certain categories of madness, including and concentrating on the madness of love (244a-5c), Socrates' speech passes to an argument for the immortality of the soul (245c-6a), then to a description in elaborate metaphor of the soul's composite nature (it is like a charioteer with two horses) and of its association, while in its incorporeal state, with the gods and acquaintance with the eternal Forms (246a-8d). It is the inevitable fate of the soul to forget the vision once clothed in earthly flesh, but the sight of beauty, as in the experience of seeing a youth and falling in love, can awaken that memory and give the soul its wings anew. But the physical side of that experience is painful and powerful, and there is often conflict within the soul (the metaphor of the charioteer and horses is developed), with one part revering the beauty of which it sees the image in its beloved, while another part is filled with a craving for crudely physical satisfaction. Yet the well-governed soul of a lover with self-control can deal with these baser impulses and make the relationship he shares with a beloved boy a fruitful one for them both (255), without succumbing to physical desire; in which case their life is one of joyous pursuit of wisdom and philosophising, and their fate will be a fortunate one in the afterlife. In short, it is love which offers the blessings of a life devoted to wisdom, and it is through love that the soul regains (in the imagery of the myth) its wings, and revives its memory of the divine Forms which give meaning and order to the universe and to human life. No crude and self-interested evasion of love can bring such blessings: 'the acquaintance with the non-lover, which is diluted with mortal sobriety, dispensing miserly advantages of a mortal kind, engenders in the beloved's soul a meanness which is praised by the multitude as virtue, and will cause it to wallow mindlessly around and under the earth for nine thousand years' (256e-7a). The speech ends with a prayer to Eros, part of which has already been quoted in connection with the hopes it expresses about Phaedrus (p. 247 above).

Much is mysterious and obscure about this speech, some things perhaps deliberately so. If we begin from what is obvious and reasonably certain, some of the difficulties may at least be more clearly identified.

It is self-evident that this is a speech which goes far beyond what Phaedrus might expect, and beyond what would be necessary to reply to Lysias, or to Socrates' earlier speech, on their own terms. Equally obvi-

---

[27] Presumably there is a pun on *himeros* ('desire'), as suggested e.g. by Nussbaum 211.
[28] See Phaedrus' speech in the *Symposium*, which is full of references to myths and the poets. It is Phaedrus who brings up the story of Boreas and Oreithyia earlier in this dialogue; and Socrates later describes him as *philomousos*, 'lover of the Muses' (259b).

ously, it introduces to the dialogue themes and ideas which are more prominent elsewhere in Plato's works: the relation between soul and body, the soul's immortality, the potential conflicts within the soul, the afterlife and the transmigration of souls, 'recollection', the Forms and their divine beauty, which transcends all earthly 'realities'. Much of this is familiar ground from the *Phaedo* and the *Republic* – though, as before, we may wish to reserve judgement as to whether precisely the *same* doctrines are being expounded, or comparable ideas explored in different images and in a different way.[29] The association of philosophic insight (here, recollection of the otherworldly life before birth) with the life of the lover brings the speech closer to the doctrine of Diotima in the *Symposium* than to the other analogous passages in the *Republic* and elsewhere. That speech in the *Symposium* also seems comparable in that there, too, the vision of the soul's ascent is presented in a single, supremely eloquent speech, rather than discussed at length or discovered through dialectic. In its structural position, also, the speech in the *Phaedrus* provides a parallel with the *Symposium*: in both dialogues, Socrates' account of the 'truth' about Love is placed not at the end but at the heart of the dialogue, and the remainder of the work passes on to other matters, with the grandeur and eloquence of the speeches of Socrates left behind – not forgotten, but qualified and set in perspective. In the *Symposium*, Alcibiades, who has missed Socrates' exposition, takes over the proceedings and the drinking gains momentum; in the *Phaedrus*, although Phaedrus' response is enthusiastic, it still appears to be principally aesthetic, and it is striking that he does not try to enquire further into the meaning and detail of the myth, or question Socrates about the conclusions he reached. Instead he still seems to see it as a further challenge for Lysias, who will now have to surpass Socrates' effort (257c, cf. 243d8-e1); he does at least concede that Lysias may have some difficulty in doing so!

But even if Phaedrus' reaction is somewhat disappointing, what can the more critical reader learn from or say about the speech? Throughout the dialogue, there is a contrast between divine insight and the more pedestrian world of human reason, between divinely-sent madness and the selfishly cautious good sense of ordinary mortals, between the wonders of the philosophic vision and the trivial technicalities of contemporary rhetoric. This contrast forms part of the larger contrast which is surely fundamental to Plato's work, between the world we normally inhabit, the sordid and transient world of everyday mortality, and the world of true reality and permanence, the divine world of the Forms. Throughout his life Plato returns to this theme in different ways. Here the speech of Socrates, which is later referred to by its author as a 'mythical hymn' (265c1), provides a means of describing the truly real world to which the human soul naturally belongs and to which it always longs to return. This is not a dialectically

[29] See e.g. Ferrari, *Listening to the Cicadas* 125-32, 200-3.

demonstrable vision, and so it is appropriate that it should be couched in mythical form, and that the idea of poetic inspiration should be used – poetry, elsewhere treated as the enemy of philosophy, is here employed in its service. It is admitted, not only in the later passage which plays down the significance of the speech, but within the speech itself, that this is an approximation, an imperfect account, not a statement of absolute truths: 'To say what kind of thing the soul is would require a long exposition, and one calling for utterly superhuman powers; but to say what it is *like* requires a shorter one, and within human capacity. So let us speak in the latter way' (246a). 'And as for the realm above the heavens, there is no poet who has ever yet hymned it as it deserves, nor will there ever be. But it is like this ...' (247c) Plato surely does not intend his readers to press the imagery and the detailed doctrine too hard.[30]

Something may be said, however, about the account of the lover, the ostensible subject of the speech. It is obvious that he is assimilated to the philosopher (cf. esp. 256a, 257b5-6), and there is a natural temptation to think that we have passed beyond all the concerns of the earlier speeches. In several respects, however, Socrates caps or responds to the points made against the lover. Whereas in his first speech Socrates had argued that the lover wants his beloved to be inferior to himself, the Palinode argues that the lover fosters and reveres the soul of the beloved, not inhibiting or suppressing it (239e ff., answered by 252d-3c). According to the Palinode, the real aim of the lover's relationship will no longer be bodily pleasure but finding fulfilment in the joint pursuit of philosophy (256a; cf. *Smp.* 210-11, esp. 210d). This contrasts sharply with the whole persuasive point of the earlier Socratic speech, where the appeals to wisdom, health and so on are merely bargaining counters, and the boy's physical submission remains the real objective. Further, the Palinode argues that the lover can also be a friend, and that their friendship will last beyond their passion, even if it is physically satisfied (256cd, countering 232e-4a, 240e sq.). On a metaphorical level, the description of love as a sickness, introduced in Lysias' speech (231d), is not so much contradicted as revalued in Socrates' account in the palinode of the lover's madness (244a sq.). Madness, it appears, can be beneficial, even a gift from the gods. Similarly the language of 'benefit' and 'harm' (e.g. 232c, 234c; 239b, 241c; 245b), as of government and restraint (e.g. 232a4f, 233c2, 250a), is employed in all three speeches, but with very different nuances. In the Palinode, Socrates stresses that in the divine dance there is no place for jealousy (247a7), and that the lover will have no feelings of jealousy or slave-like hostility (253b);[31] this reverses the references in the earlier speeches to competition between the lover and rivals, and to the grudging jealousy of the ex-lover (232c, 240a, c-e, 241c).

---

[30] For qualifying passages of this kind cf. *Phaedo* 114d; *Rep.* 414a, 533a, etc.

[31] For the language here cf. 243c8. On the jealousy-motif, see M. Dickie, in *Nomodeiktes* (Fest. M. Ostwald), ed. R.M. Rosen and J. Farrell (Ann Arbor, Michigan 1993) 379-96.

The speech of Socrates, then, transfers the theme of love from a rhetorical showpiece, grounded in a crudely reductive view of human morality and human potential, to a more ambitious philosophical exposition and a far more awesome stage. Love is set in its psychological and even its cosmic context. Love, poetic madness and philosophy are united – indeed, they are almost assimilated to one another. Philosophy as pursued with a likeminded partner in love will enable a mortal to aspire to divine wisdom and beauty, insofar as this is possible to man.[32]

We have already considered some aspects of the Socratic 'doctrine' of love in an earlier chapter, where it was argued that the view of it as self-centred and self-advancing was exaggerated. A reading of the *Phaedrus* tends to support that argument. Differences between the *Symposium* and the *Phaedrus* arise in part from their dramatic form and from the particular characters involved in each. Socrates in the *Symposium* is a strange and bewildering, even a disturbing figure: earthly desires and relationships mean far less to him than to any other member of the party. Despite his solid and colourful physical presence, he is almost an otherworldly figure. All of this reinforces the essential gulf between his ideals and the life-style of Alcibiades. In the *Phaedrus*, where Socrates is dealing one-to-one with a close friend and potential convert to philosophy, this remoteness and inaccessibility would be quite misplaced, and the different situation is reflected on the level of doctrine. It is appropriate, therefore, that the dialogue should be concerned with rhetoric as well as with love: for the essence of rhetoric is communication and persuasion, contact between individuals. The conventional rhetoric of Lysias and the sophists is indifferent to the truth of the arguments presented and to the well-being of the addressee; what matters is to convince, by whatever means, to win one's case or earn one's fee. By contrast, the philosophic rhetoric which Socrates proposes in the second half of the work, however utopian and whimsical the proposal may be, will be based on genuine insight *both* into the truth about the subject *and* into the character and needs of the interlocutor. In other words, within the *Phaedrus*, even if not in all of Plato's works, philosophic rhetoric merges into philosophic love: the two are both exemplified in Socrates.[33]

The unity of the *Phaedrus*

Unease and perplexity about the subject and coherence of the dialogue go back to antiquity. The ancient commentaries refer to different views on the

---

[32] The language and concepts here tend towards mysticism: see further *Theaetetus* 176b. A. Louth, *The Origins of the Christian Mystical Tradition* (Oxford 1981) ch. 1 gives a good account of this side of Plato's thought.

[33] See further pp. 245-7 above on the closeness and mutual understanding between Socrates and Phaedrus.

skopos ('goal' or 'theme') of the work: is it a dialogue on love, or on rhetoric? Or is its real subject 'the good'? The Neo-Platonist Hermias quotes and endorses the view of Iamblichus, that it is a work concerning 'that which is in every way beautiful'. Modern dissatisfaction can be more entertaining: we read of 'the contrast between the classic architecture of the *Symposium* and the Gothic art of the *Phaedrus*'![34] There is general agreement that there is a problem about the shape of the *Phaedrus*: roughly, it is felt that it falls too clearly into two halves, the break coming with the end of the Palinode.[35] The first half of the dialogue is dominated by the long speeches (though with conversational preliminaries and interludes); the second half is entirely conversation. Moreover, the conversation in the second half seems to wander, with digressions and false starts. The theme of rhetoric dominates, and specific criticisms of contemporary rhetoric (the *eikos*-argument, the handbook writers, the writing-down of speeches) loom large. The theme of love fades into the background, becoming once more merely a subject for speech-makers to treat well or ill, and the panoramic vision of the soul's progress from earth to heaven is forgotten. Although the speeches of the first half are sometimes taken up as examples for comment and criticism, this is done less often than we might have expected, and the comment is confined to structure and style; there is no attempt on either side to pursue the ideas of the speeches, especially the Palinode, in a dialectical fashion. The change of style and tone does seem sufficiently striking to rule out the easy responses that other dialogues have more than one subject,[36] or that the free movement of the discussion mimics the naturalism of authentic conversation. These explanations may be valid supporting points, but as solutions to the question of the dialogue's unity they do not convince.

Critics do not always make clear exactly what kind of unity they find wanting. If we think of the traditional post-Aristotelian triad, we can be in no doubt that the unities of time and place are satisfied, and indeed of characters as well – Socrates and Phaedrus both continuously present.[37] Action is always the hardest of the three to tie down, but it seems at least that the interlude in the country is a self-contained episode. The difficulty arises more from the inconsistency of style and tone,[38] the differing levels

---

[34] P. Shorey, *What Plato Said* 198. I owe these references to de Vries's introd., 22-4. See further W.C. Helmbold-W.B. Holther, *Univ. of California Publications in Class. Philol.* 14 (1952) 387-417, R.P. Winnington-Ingram, *Dialogos* (Hellenic Studies Review) 1 (1994) 7-20 (originally a lecture given in 1953), and the discussion between M. Heath and C.J. Rowe in *OSAP* 7 (1989).

[35] Some, however, dismiss such anxieties as non-problems (e.g. Guthrie iv. 130-1, 412; more elaborately, M. Heath, *OSAP* 7 (1989) 163 and context).

[36] See e.g. Heath 166-70, a thought-provoking section in its own right.

[37] We may also note various formal devices which create a balance between first and second halves: in particular, both halves end with a prayer by Socrates which Phaedrus endorses.

[38] Helmbold-Holther do indeed try to assert a unity of mood and tone (of an ironic kind) throughout, but this seems to oversimplify.

of seriousness and intensity, shifting so easily to humour and badinage. It is also hard to deny, as already indicated, that love fades out of the limelight with surprising finality after the first half of the work.

If, however, we see the lover's care for the beloved mirrored, however imperfectly, in the relationship between Socrates and Phaedrus, and if we take the themes of rhetoric and love to be united in the idealised philosophic love which employs 'fair words' – if, in short, we see the art of love and the art of purer, philosophic rhetoric as both embodied in Socrates, then the two halves of the dialogue are seen to be intimately bound together in subject. In earlier dialogues this technique was seen in a simpler form, with Socrates implicitly or explicitly providing a near-perfect example of the virtue under discussion (courage in the *Laches*, self-restraint in the *Charmides*, etc.). In the *Gorgias* he styled himself the one true statesman (521d). Similarly in the *Phaedrus*, he shows his mastery of the art of rhetoric in suiting his speech to the personality of Phaedrus, and it is his affection for Phaedrus, and for all young men of noble soul, which prompts him to reach such rhetorical heights.

Nor does this exhaust the ways in which Socrates enacts the theories he expounds in the Palinode. When he defines the different varieties of good madness, madness that is not harmful but beneficial, each in some way resembles Socrates' behaviour or attributes in the dialogue. These categories are: (i) the madness of the prophet: Socrates described himself as a *mantis*, 'though not a very good one', at 242c, after the intervention of his divine sign, and we see him 'prophesying' again in connection with Isocrates at the end; (ii) the purificatory or expiatory madness which purges sin (as exemplified in the case of Orestes): we can compare Socrates' acknowledgement of his blasphemy about Eros, which must be expiated by a further speech, the main speech being a recantation. (iii) Third comes the madness of the poet. Compare earlier Socrates' breaking into verse, his references to Anacreon, Sappho and the poets (235c), his invocation of the Muses (237a), and in the main speech his confessedly poetic discourse, a myth about heaven and the gods which he introduces as the speech of the lyric poet Stesichorus. In short, as far as the dialogue form will allow, he is himself a poet. (iv) As for the madness of Love, it is hardly necessary to say again that Socrates is an expert on love (a point of which we are reminded in the opening exchange, 227c3), and is in a sense wooing Phaedrus in the main speech: we recall the wording of his prayer to Eros at the end of that speech, 'Take not from me the lover's talent with which thou hast blessed me' (257a).

The quest for further unifying elements, particularly connections that will bridge the gap between first and second halves, has led many critics to explore the language and imagery of the dialogue, a method which has had much success in the criticism of Greek tragedy.[39] A great many motifs

---

[39] See above all A. Lebeck, *GRBS* 13 (1972) 267-90. It is no accident that this scholar was also a gifted interpreter of Aeschylean tragedy. See also Ferrari, *Listening to the Cicadas* passim, with my comments in *Phronesis* 33 (1988) 216-24. (K. Dorter, *JHPh* 9 (1971) 279-88 follows a similar approach, but without Lebeck's finesse.)

and phrases recur in the course of the dialogue, sometimes literally and sometimes metaphorically. A typical pattern is for the phrase or image to be used casually, literally or in an everyday manner in the early part of the work, then more imaginatively and daringly in the myth or the main speech; later the same idea may appear again, often brought back down to size with the lowering of tone in the second half. One example is the motif of food: Phaedrus has attended Lysias' epideixis in the house of Morychus, a notorious glutton.[40] Socrates takes this up: 'obviously Lysias has been giving you a feast of words' (227b6). As in the *Gorgias*, display-oratory is presented as a kind of rich food. At 236e8 rhetoric is again described in feast-terms, and in more comic vein in 230d6: Socrates pictures himself as a hungry animal who can be lured all over Attica if someone dangles a book in front of him! Very different is the use of the verb *hestiao* (feed upon) in the myth, at 247e, where the soul beholds and feasts upon 'what truly is'. Indeed, there is a whole range of food and nurture words in this context, at 246e1 ff., 247e4-6, 248b5.[41]

Another such small-scale motif is introduced at 228a4: Phaedrus would rather be able to do a Lysias from memory than to have 'much gold'. It is developed in the next interlude, where Phaedrus promises, if Socrates produces a better version of Lysias' argument, that he will erect a life-size golden statue of him at Delphi; Socrates replies fondly: 'You are a dear, and truly gold, Phaedrus' (235e2). This contrasts external, physical gold with a golden character, internal standards of value. The same ideas are in play at the end of the dialogue, in Socrates' final prayer to Pan: 'Dear Pan, and all you gods of this place, grant that I may become beautiful within; and that what is in my possession outside me may be in friendly accord with what is inside. And may I count the wise man as rich; and may my pile of gold be of a size that only a man of moderate desires could bear or carry' (279bc).[42] Again, internal moral wealth is preferred to extravagance and excess. The fact that Phaedrus joins in Socrates' final prayer shows something of the influence that the conversation has had upon him.

More substantial and far-reaching thematic echoes may be discerned in Socrates' reply at 228a-c, with its teasing opening: 'If I do not know Phaedrus, I have forgotten even myself.' This points to the intimacy of the pair, and also hints at the theme of self-knowledge, raised later in 230a and elsewhere. The theme of forgetting is also one that occurs throughout. Socrates has forgotten where he heard the finer accounts of love and the non-lover which he refers to at 235c; the soul sees the Forms but will always tend to forget them unless philosophic love sustains it and nurtures its

---

[40] 227b5, with Ar. *Ach.* 887, *Wasps* 506, *Peace* 1008 and scholia.

[41] The same technique is used with 'grasping' and other contact-terms in the *Symposium* (p. 185 above).

[42] Note also, tangentially connected with this passage and certainly linked with each other, 251a and 252d.

wings (249-50, 254, etc.). Those who have recourse to Thoth's invention of writing will find it a formula for reminding them, not a true stimulus to the memory (274e sq.). That passage is also prefigured in the initial exchange, in the way that Phaedrus has opted for a written text of Lysias' speech rather than really memorising it, as he at first claims to have done (228a-e).

One more starting-point for themes and motifs of this kind can be seen in the ironic account of the rationalising sceptics at 229c-30a (already quoted, p. 174 above). Perhaps the most important thematic aspect is the contrast between modern sophistication and apparently naive faith. Here again, we see modern sophistic thinking and Socratic philosophy on opposing sides. The chief tool of the demythologiser is *eikos*, probability, that catch-word of sophistic argumentation. This term is also prominent in the generalising arguments of Lysias (231c7, 232c2, 233a2), and naturally recurs in the discussion of rhetorical theory (267a, 272e). In the passage on Boreas the pseudo-sophistication of the rationalisers is shown up: their cleverness is in fact *agroikos*, countrified and bumbling. The critique of these 'wise men' can be extended to Lysias and his like, for the craze to demythologise stems from the same intellectual roots as the passion for paradoxical argument exemplified in the Lysianic thesis. The two are associated also through their neglect of the religious dimension. In the later parts of the dialogue, the same hostile irony is directed at the terminological complexities of the handbooks (266d-7e),[43] and at the self-importance of their authors. From a different angle, the wisdom which Pericles, in popular judgement the supreme statesman-orator, is said to have derived from Anaxagoras is a caricature of the insight which the philosophic orator might learn from his communion with reality (269e-70a).[44] Wisdom itself is indeed a recurring motif – who is truly wise, the clever sophist or the seemingly naive Socrates? Where is wisdom found – in the salons of Athenian sophisticates or in the old-style tales from Egypt which Phaedrus at first scorns (275b)?[45]

Criticism of this kind naturally runs the risk of lapsing into fanciful over-interpretation, and it is understandable that some recent accounts of the *Phaedrus* have had little truck with it.[46] This seems an unduly restricting approach: granted that some suggestions may have a firmer basis than others, the idea that similar wording or parallel imagery may indicate a significant connection between passages is not self-evidently wrong, and has yielded fruit in the study of other classical authors. Presumably most

[43] On this section see esp. G. Kennedy, *AJP* 80 (1959) 169ff.; *Art of Persuasion* 52ff.
[44] Neither 'talkativeness' nor 'lofty utterance' is devoid of irony. Cf. T.A. Szlezak, *Mus. Helv.* 35 (1978) 28. Yet Plutarch, *Pericles* 4-6 and others were prepared to read the passage straight.
[45] For other passages relating to this theme see 242e5, 245c2, 278d.
[46] Little of this kind in Rowe (who does not cite Lebeck's pioneering paper); brisk scepticism in Heath, *OSAP* 7 (1982) 160-1. Even Aeschylus has been denied the conscious deployment of this technique (M.L. West, *Gnomon* 59 (1987) 193-8).

critical methods are open to abuse or over-use, but it is hardly feasible to abandon all methods open to that danger. A more serious criticism might be that these elaborate patterns of imagery and motifs do not actually do enough to reassure the reader that the work is actually a unity. They produce connections without coherence; the experience of reading the dialogue is still one of perceiving startling changes of mood and style. In particular, the status of the Palinode, and the myth that it contains, remains puzzling.

It is preferable, then, to accept that there is something unusual about the *Phaedrus*, and in particular about the Palinode and its relationship to the whole. It would at first appear that this speech not only forms the climax but conveys the central doctrine of the work. Yet later it is almost ignored, and the comment made at 265b seems to undercut it considerably. Other aspects of the central speech may reinforce this sense of contradiction. It is a curious mixture of the profound and the bizarre. The argument for the immortality of the soul is absurdly brief and mock-technical (245c ff.), sitting very strangely in its context: almost a parody, perhaps, of text-book arguments.[47] Absurdities or humorous details are abundant, more so than in the myths of the *Gorgias* and the *Republic*, especially in the way in which the symbolic language of the myth (horses, wings, flight) is given concrete physical reality in passages like 248b, where the ascending soul is in danger of being bruised by the kicking hooves of the horses belonging to the soul immediately ahead of him (cf. also 251b sq.). There is repeated play with specious etymologies: admittedly, such things are taken fairly seriously (it appears) in the *Cratylus*, but here there seems almost a deliberate effort made to draw attention to their implausibility (244c sq., 251c, 252bc; cf. already 237a).

Through humour Socrates can also point to the weakness or imperfections of all that is being said, suggesting that much of it is merely tentative, foolish, 'playing around'. Socratic irony and Socratic ignorance come very close together here: Socrates regularly claims that he knows nothing about these subjects, and cannot claim any expert competence in discussing them, and so it is natural that he should laugh at his own feeble efforts to blunder through difficult philosophic territories. It goes with this that he rarely allows that much has actually been established by the end of the dialogue: the *Phaedrus* is one of those in which he most patently takes away with one hand what he seemed to be giving with the other (esp. at 265bc, but also in the discussion of writing: see below). This open-endedness and the admission that so far only part of the work has been done is also an encouragement to others to go further in their own discussions and thoughts.

The problem of the unity of the dialogue can be explored in the light of

---

[47] Compare e.g. Philolaus 44 B2 D-K (= KRS no. 425); Melissus 30 B 1-2 D-K (= KRS 525-6). For other 'text-book' passages, see 245c4, 246a3-4, b5-6.

this open-endedness. Here there is an analogy between the dialogue *in toto* and the Palinode: the latter like the former is a strange mixture, not clearly unified. Again 265b, Socrates' description of the main speech, is significant here: 'by fashioning *some sort of image* for the erotic experience ... and by *mixing* together our not wholly implausible speech ...' Socrates acknowledges that he has not in fact produced a perfect and uniform work such as he describes as the ideal in 264 and 268. The same is true of Plato's achievement (or deliberate under-achievement) in the *Phaedrus* as a whole. Unity is also, as we have seen, a theme on other levels besides the literary: Socrates' enquiry at the beginning of the dialogue is concerned with his own nature and whether it is simple or complex (230a), and Phaedrus is divided within himself, between rhetoric and philosophy (257b). The ideal is simplicity and singleness of nature, for both man and literary work;[48] but that remains an ideal, and the more realistic condition, in the everyday world where man forgets the Forms and has only dim recollections of pure Beauty, is bound to be complexity, and hence lack of unity.

There are, broadly speaking, three strategies one can adopt when unity of the kind that we would generally acknowledge seems to be lacking. The first is to revise our criteria of unity,[49] accepting that ancient readers enjoyed diversity and changes of tone and direction as well as intensity and uniformity: thus we can and should admire both the *Oedipus Rex* and the *Andromache*, both the *Aeneid* and the *Metamorphoses*. There is much truth in this argument, but to my mind it reduces the criteria for unity to an unacceptable degree. The second is to look for subtler or more varied kinds of unity, binding the work at a different level from the obvious level of action or plot, through the verbal texture and imagery. As will be clear from the discussion so far, I myself have much sympathy with this approach, and like Lebeck and others I have tried to show that connections of this kind, large and small, obvious or subtle, do exist. But there is also a third strategy, perhaps compatible in many instances with the second: to accept that the work in question is *not* unified in the conventional or expected way, and to argue that this is deliberate on the author's part: he is disrupting the norms of the genre (as Euripides surely does in the *Heracles*) or shattering and upsetting our expectations. There is, I think, something of this in the *Phaedrus*: that Plato praises unity in a work which seems to most readers bafflingly diverse and varied in matter and tone is neither coincidence nor incompetence, but deliberate; it points to the imperfections of the written word, to the unfinished nature of this, and every, treatment of philosophic themes. It also reflects the complex and non-simple natures of the participants. Whatever is the case with Socrates, the *Phaedrus* is

---

[48] Cf. generally *Rep.* 423b, 443c-e, 445c.

[49] This is essentially Heath's approach, in the article cited, and in relevant parts of his other works (*The Poetics of Greek Tragedy* (London 1987) 98-111; *Unity in Greek Poetics* (Oxford 1990), chs. 1-2).

complex in part because Phaedrus himself is complex and divided; and if the discussion in the second half seems rambling and peculiar, or if the second half as a whole seems to fail to live up to the promise of the Palinode, that may be related to the fact that Socrates eventually failed with Phaedrus.

Writing (in) the *Phaedrus*

Although the main lines of this chapter's argument should by now be clear, it is necessary to consider the famous passage on writing, and its place in the dialogue, at greater length.[50] The *Phaedrus* began with a speech by Lysias, the status of which was at first unclear: was it in Phaedrus' head, fully memorised, or not? In fact it turned out to be inside his cloak, and Socrates insisted on his reading the speech aloud rather than testing his friend's powers of recollection. After Socrates' Palinode, Phaedrus refers again to Lysias, expressing doubt about his ability to match the quality of Socrates' performance, 'if indeed he were willing to produce a further extended speech in response. For, my splendid friend, one of the politicians just the other day was abusing and reproaching him for that very thing: throughout his whole attack he kept calling him a 'speechwriter' (*logographos*). Perhaps therefore he may refrain from writing for us out of self-esteem' (257c).

The criticism to which Phaedrus refers can be paralleled in other fifth- and fourth-century texts. Despite the Athenian literary achievement and the enthusiasm of audiences for other literary forms, there seems to have been a long-standing prejudice against clever speakers, and against those who wrote speeches for others to deliver in court (a profession followed not only by Lysias but by Isocrates in his earlier career). The orators themselves exploit this prejudice.[51] Phaedrus' concern about this point brings us back with a jolt to the everyday realities of Athenian society. Socrates is quick to dismiss this fear that Lysias may cease writing, and makes amusing play with the fact that the politicians themselves take pride in 'writing' of another kind – the public inscriptions commemorating their decisions and naming the proposers (258a). The theme of writing runs through the rest of the dialogue, treated lightly here and in the mocking

---

[50] This section has been prominent in debates about the significance of the change from 'oral' to 'literate' culture in classical Greece (esp. in the work of E.A. Havelock and his followers). This topic will not be considered here, since it seems to me clear that more disciplined studies have shown that any simple talk of a magical or momentous transition is misguided. Books were familiar objects, though few other than intellectuals would own many (note esp. Pl. *Apol.* 26d, Xen. *Mem.* iv. 2. 1, Eupolis F 304K = 327 KA; Hdt. vi. 27, though concerning Chios c. 500, merits pondering). Cf. esp. F.D. Harvey, *REG* 79 (1966) 585-635; R. Thomas, *Oral Tradition and Written Record in Classical Athens* (Cambridge 1989) and the same author's *Literacy and Orality in Ancient Greece* (Cambridge 1992).

[51] See e.g. Antiphon fr. 1a col. 2 (p. 109 Thalheim); Aeschines 1. 94, 170, Demosthenes 35. 38-43; cf. Dover, *Lysias* 155-6.

account of the rhetorical handbooks, but more thoughtfully in the last section of the work, from 274a to 278b. There, Socrates narrates a story (he does not admit, though Phaedrus suspects, that it is his own invention) of how the Egyptian Thoth proudly presented his inventions, including 'letters' (*grammata*) to the king Thamus, but was told that this invention at least was a bad one, 'a formula not for memory but for reminding'. If the art of writing is spread abroad, people will come to depend on it, and will no longer retain knowledge in their own minds (274c-5b).

Socrates goes on to apply the moral of the story to the writer of speeches and in particular to the true rhetorician whom they have tried to define in the preceding discussion. It shows naïveté to suppose written words worth much, for they cannot defend themselves, nor can they choose to whom they speak. Whereas the true rhetorician will suit his discourse to the personality of the listener, the written speech is frozen and lifeless. It is the spoken word that has value, and that can 'write in the soul'. Writing things down may be a useful enough reminder (for old age brings forgetfulness), but no one should suppose that written books are to be taken seriously: the sensible man, the philosopher, will treat writing as a form of recreation, and one greatly preferable to the self-indulgent pleasure of drinking parties and the like. But his real work, and his real satisfaction, will be to sow the seeds of *logoi* (arguments, rather than speeches?) in the responsive soul, to see those seeds germinating, and to know that there will be further sowing and growth at a later date.

> (It is a far better thing than writing) when one employs the dialectical art, finding a suitable soul, and planting and sowing it with words that are grounded in knowledge, words which are able to help themselves and the farmer who planted them, which are not infertile but carry a seed, whence other words are born in other personalities, able to make that seed immortal and eternal, and causing their possessor to enjoy happiness, as far as ever a man can. (276e4ff.)

A moment later, he also uses the metaphor of father and offspring for the same process of propagation: speeches that are written in the soul are the legitimate offspring of the philosophic orator – his own soul, and those of others. All else, and especially the illusory 'wisdom' of written speeches, should be regarded as play: the noun *paidia* and its cognates is constantly repeated in this passage. Again we see a link with the early parts of the dialogue: Lysias' oration is a typical example of a sophistic *paignion* or plaything, and its triviality has been exposed; but in the eyes of Socrates it, and other works of far greater merit, are also trivial and 'play-things' in a deeper sense.

What are we to make of all this? Not surprisingly, a wide range of interpretations could be cited, ranging from those which minimise the implications and in particular try to save Plato's own writings from this condemnation, to those which allow the 'play' element full rein and see it as undermining everything that Plato wrote or might have written.[52] The extreme version of the former, 'defusing' approach seems hardly tenable: the passage must be intended to be startling and paradoxical. Plato does not mean simply to dramatise Socrates' own aversion to writing, without the reader being intended to notice that this condemnation occurs within a written work. Nor can the criticism of writing be confined to the works of Lysias, Isocrates and their kind: the message of the Nymphs is to be passed on not only to the orators, but to Homer and the poets, Solon and the lawgivers (278bc); and the words of Socrates leave no room for exceptions: the philosopher is one who 'considers it inevitable that in any written discourse on any subject there will be much frivolity, and that no utterance, metrical or otherwise, has ever been written down that deserves any serious notice ...' (277e5ff.; see also 277d8-9, denying any such work 'definitive status [*bebaioteta*] and lucidity').

The denigration of writing, then, extends within the drama of the dialogue to Lysias' speech first and foremost (and others like it), then to other speeches which are written down and circulated without their author being present to give them his voice; then to other works of literature, including the works of the poets, even Homer himself, and the performances of the rhapsodes, who, although they do deliver their works orally, do so without allowing for questioning and teaching (277e-8a). Thus far Socrates' position is intelligible and consistent with his attitudes elsewhere. It is the fact that this critique survives within a written work that complicates the picture: does the critique demolish itself? There is a paradox here which artfully echoes the slighter conflation of written work and oral performance earlier on, where Lysias' speech was both. Analogously, the *Phaedrus* in a sense *is* a conversation, and one which involves a true philosopher-orator at work 'sowing seeds'; but of course it is *also* a literary work, an artefact which survives its author and cannot explain itself. On the other hand, if it represents the 'recreation' of a philosopher, it does seem to fulfil the requirement that such recreational writing should not be conducted in too serious or self-important a spirit, but should be regarded as 'play': for even outside this passage the language of play has been prominent,[53] and the dialogue is, as we have seen, rich in humour of

[52] See e.g. H.L. Sinaiko, *Love, Knowledge and Discourse in Plato* (Chicago 1965) ch. 1 (rather general, and over-dependent on the Seventh Letter); R. Burger, *Plato's Phaedrus: A Defense of the Philosophic Art of Writing* (Univ. of Alabama Press 1980); C.L. Griswold, *The Monist* 63 (1980) 530-56; Rowe, 'Public and private speaking in Plato's later dialogues', in *Platon: los dialogos tardios* (Symposium Platonicum 1986, Mexico 1987) 125-37; Ferrari ch. 7, and in the *Cambr. Hist. of Literary Criticism* i (1989) 142-7. On paradox see M.M. Mackenzie, *PCPS* n.s. 28 (1982) 64-76. The 'deconstructive' end of the spectrum is represented most eminently by Derrida, 'La pharmacie de Platon', *Tel Quel* 32-3 (1968) repr. in *La Dissémination* (Paris 1972) 69-197 (= Eng. tr. *Dissemination* (Chicago 1981) 61-171), an essay which seems to me to have been vastly overpraised.

[53] It is important throughout Plato's work: see the survey by Guthrie iv. 56-66. Further, see P. Plass, *TAPA* 98 (1967) 343-64; De Vries's *Phaedrus* commentary, 18-22, and his fuller

many kinds – teasing personal jokes, word-play, etymologies and puns, bizarre images and engaging paradox. We should not press the deconstructive argument too far: Socrates does not say that there can be no relationship between the subject matter of oral discussion and the subject of a written work (indeed, the former is said to be an *eidolon*, a ghostly image or reflection, of the latter: 276a9), nor does he say that there is *no* place for anything but play in something which is written down. There is still, perhaps, room for some seriousness – even if that too must not be taken very seriously. We may suspect that Plato himself, in recreational mood, might have enjoyed our bafflement.[54]

The riddles of the *Phaedrus* will never be definitively solved: as Socrates has told Phaedrus, there is no certainty or lucidity in a written work (277d8, cf. 278a4-5). Much more could be said, plausible or less so. Some conclusions do seem unambiguous. There is no reason to suppose that Plato has become more favourable to contemporary rhetoric, or to the methods of the sophists, between the *Gorgias* and the *Phaedrus*.[55] Both take a severe attitude to the pseudo-science of rhetoric as practised by the experts, though the *Gorgias* deals more with the vital issue of political oratory, whereas the *Phaedrus* is concerned less with public speaking and more with epideictic. Whatever reservations may be felt about the quality or permanence of Phaedrus' 'conversion', the dialogue clearly does dramatise the process of philosophic love, exemplified in the subtle and generous rhetoric of Socrates, who delicately leads Phaedrus away from the corrupting world of Lysias and towards a higher set of values. The main speech of Socrates, a highly poetic and ornamented 'mythical hymn', is eminently well-suited to Phaedrus' tastes. It has been suggested above that neither that speech nor the dialogue as a whole is a completely satisfactory unity of the type required by Socrates in the dialogue itself. It may now be added, in the light of the section on writing, that such a unity would itself be a slight and trivial goal in a mere written work. Perhaps the imperfection of form mirrors the imperfection of the medium: no written speech, no written work, can be more than 'play', and perfection of unity and coherence would be an achievement of little substance.[56] Just as the sublimity of the myth (itself flawed by intermittent frivolities?) collapses into more prosaic discourse, so too the ideal organic unity is not actually attained by the dialogue itself.

---

account in *Spel bij Plato* (Amsterdam 1949); J. Huizinga, *Homo Ludens* (Eng. tr. 1949) ch. 9. Again we can detect some background in the sophistic texts: besides Gorgias' *Helen*, which he mischievously dismisses as a *paignion* in the closing sentence, see Alcidamas B xxii. 15. 34 Radermacher; Isoc. *Busiris* 9. Agathon in *Smp.* 197e uses the same concluding commonplace.

[54] After drafting this chapter I saw C.J. Rowe's thoughtful paper in *Nova Tellus* 5 (1987) 83-101, including a treatment of the 'writing' section with which I am happy to find myself in close agreement. I am grateful to the author for sending me a copy of this somewhat inaccessible article.

[55] The assertion that rhetoric is no true *techne* persists as late as the *Laws* (xi. 938a).

[56] Cf. Ferrari, 232.

So, again, Socrates insists that the dialectician who has access to truth but does not trust it to mere books is still not *sophos* but only *philosophos*:

> Phaedrus: What names would you give him, then?
> Socrates: The title of 'wise', Phaedrus, seems too mighty a name to me, worthy only of a god. But to call him either 'lover of wisdom' or some such name might be both more appropriate and in better taste. (278d)

Similarly, the interpreter need not and should not claim to have achieved the ultimate goal.

10

Further Perspectives

> It looks as though I need new tactics ... I must have weapons different from
> those of my previous arguments, though possibly some may be the same.
> (Socrates in Philebus 23b)

Introductory: the *Theaetetus*

This chapter will be concerned with the works of Plato's later period,
concluding with the *Laws*, seemingly unfinished at his death in 347. The
greater length and complexity of most of these works make it impossible,
in a book of this size, to offer the fairly detailed readings which have been
usual in earlier chapters; instead, I shall attempt a general characterisation of this later phase, before dealing in slightly more detail with the
most startling and in some ways the most influential of these texts, the
Timaeus, and finally, in a much more selective way, offering some comments on the *Laws*.

To discuss the later works in any general way requires some definition
of which dialogues fall into this category. Here we return to several of the
chronological and methodological issues considered in the first chapter;
some recapitulation is inevitable.[1] It is asserted by ancient authorities,
notably Diogenes Laertius, that the *Laws* is the last work of Plato. Other
dialogues which are almost universally regarded as late include the *Sophist, Statesman, Timaeus, Critias*, and *Philebus*.[2] The arguments rest partly
on cross-references and other such connections, partly on stylometric
arguments: these are the dialogues which approximate in style to the
manner of the *Laws*. In particular, in these works Plato observes certain
conventions of prose rhythm and avoids hiatus (i.e. the conjunction of a
vowel at the end of one word and one at the beginning of the word which

---

[1] For discussion of chronological questions see esp. Thesleff, *Studies in Platonic Chronology*
184ff.; Brandwood, in Kraut, *Companion* ch. 3.

[2] G.E.L. Owen in a famous paper argued that the *Timaeus* should be placed much earlier on
philosophical grounds, but after much illuminating debate the tide of opinion seems to have
turned against him: see Owen, *CQ* 3 (1953) 79-95 and the reply by H. Cherniss, *AJP* 78 (1957)
225-66, both repr. in R.E. Allen (ed.) *Studies in Plato's Metaphysics* (London 1963) and
elsewhere. Other criticisms of Owen are advanced by J.M. Rist, *Phoenix* 14 (1960) 207-21, and
by C. Gill, *Phronesis* 24 (1979) 148-67. More bibl. can be found in Thesleff (n. 1), 189-92, esp.
189n.18.

follows) to a far greater degree than in any other works. The *Sophist* and *Statesman* were clearly planned together, as part of an unfinished trilogy (the third would have been the *Philosopher*); similarly the *Timaeus* began a trilogy of which the truncated *Critias* is the only other part. The *Parmenides* and the *Theaetetus* are usually thought to belong with the *Sophist* and the *Statesman*, partly again because of cross-references, partly because of their related subject matter. It is likely, however, that they were composed somewhat earlier than the others cited: possibly *Parmenides* came before *Theaetetus*, in view of one passage in the latter where Socrates refers to an encounter in his youth with the aged Parmenides (*Tht.* 183e). We should of course remember that Plato may have been at work on more than one dialogue at one time, and may have planned several as a group (as indeed the novel trilogy-structures encourage us to suppose).

Some broad generalisations about these works are necessary to bring out the differing character of Plato's later oeuvre. Whereas the dialogues which we have so far considered in this book are concerned, on the whole, with moral, political and metaphysical questions (and often with the connections which unite these concerns), the later works are different, but in various ways. One group (the *Parmenides*, *Theaetetus*, *Sophist* and *Philebus*) is concerned with matters of epistemology and highly abstract psychology. By contrast, the *Timaeus* and parts of the *Laws* show a new fascination with the physical universe and with astronomy or cosmology as a study with moral import, especially relevant to belief in the gods. Thirdly, the political aspect of Plato's thought continues, in the *Statesman* and the *Laws*, but appears less idealistic and fantastic; there is more attention to constitutional forms (already prominent in books viii and ix of the *Republic*), to the particularities of legislation and administration, and to the everyday needs of individual citizens. Also evident is a growing interest in early history (albeit fictional or semi-mythical history): the myth of the *Statesman*, the narratives of Critias, and especially the third book of the *Laws*.[3] Negatively, we hear less of the more mystical and transcendent aspects of Plato's metaphysics: the concept of recollection and transmigration, the theory of Forms, and the psychological hierarchies mapped in the *Republic* and the *Phaedrus* are not completely abandoned, but they are distinctly less prominent. As for Plato's philosophic confrontations with his predecessors, we can discern a clear shift away from his concern with sophistic thinkers, and a greater preoccupation with the theories of the older Presocratics, especially Zeno, Parmenides and the Pythagoreans. Here as elsewhere the *Theaetetus* seems transitional – it tackles not only Protagoras' views but those of Heraclitus, which are seen as underlying or anticipating the sophist's doctrine.

Turning from content to form and dialectical medium, the most obvious

---

[3] See R. Weil, *L'Archéologie de Platon* (Paris 1959); Morrow, *Plato's Cretan City* (1960) 17-92; Guthrie v. 330-1.

point is that narrated dialogues come to an end with the *Parmenides*, which is in fact a curious hybrid. Its first part (126a-137c) is a typical opening in which a conversation involving Socrates is recalled by others (cf. the *Symposium*), and this early section involves a limited amount of scene-setting and narrator's comment (130a, 136e). The longer second part is entirely in dialogue, as if Plato had wearied of perpetually repeating 'he said' and preferred to focus on the argument.[4] The opening exchange in the *Theaetetus* seems to meet this difficulty, with the rather elaborate explanation which Euclides gives Terpsion of how the conversation was recorded by him from notes. 'You see how I wrote the conversation – not in narrative form, as I heard it from Socrates, but as a dialogue ... I wanted to avoid in the written account the tiresome effect of bits of narrative interrupting the dialogue, such as "and I said", or "and I remarked", whenever Socrates was referring to himself, and "he assented" or "he did not agree" where he reported the answer' (*Tht.* 143c). Since Terpsion remarks that this was a good idea, and no difficulty seems to arise in the dialogue because of it, we may reasonably suppose that this represents a change of policy by Plato. If this argument is accepted, no narrated dialogue should be placed later than the *Theaetetus*.

The most conspicuous change, however, is in the role of Socrates. In the *Parmenides* he is a young man encountering great thinkers, at first articulate and enthusiastic in putting forward a version of the theory of Forms, but then dismayed and deflated by Parmenides' criticisms.[5] He is told that he needs more exercise in philosophic argument if he is to fulfil his promise; in the remainder of the dialogue Parmenides, in a long and highly abstract exchange with a compliant youth named Aristoteles, gives an example of the kind of argumentation he has in mind. This second part of the *Parmenides* is probably the most difficult philosophic argument in all of Plato, and it is certainly the passage in which Plato comes closest to abandoning dialogue completely. At the end there is no recapitulation or resumption of the informal conversation. It is also startling that in the *Parmenides* Socrates does not behave or speak like Socrates; he is characterised only as an earnest enquirer. Was Plato unsure of how to portray his master in his youth? By contrast, in the *Theaetetus* he is his usual humorous and sympathetic self (though perhaps taking the initiative more than in the early dialogues – no more than in the *Republic*, however), dealing with the charming and intelligent young Theaetetus, and the older mathematician Theodorus. In the *Sophist* Socrates, Theaetetus and the others are still present, the scene is supposedly the next day, but a new figure, a stranger from Elea, has joined them and takes the lead, conversing in that dialogue

---

[4] G. Ryle, afterword to his 'Plato's Parmenides' in Allen, *Studies in Plato's Metaphysics* (1963) 145, felt that this could only be explained if the two parts were composed at separate dates.

[5] How seriously Plato himself took these counter-arguments is hotly disputed: for discussions see e.g. the essays in Allen (ed.) *Studies in Plato's Metaphysics*: Allen's brief introduction is an economical piece of scene-setting. See further Guthrie v. 32-61.

with Theaetetus and in the *Statesman* with another youth, confusingly called young Socrates.[6] In the *Timaeus* and *Critias* again Socrates is present and takes part in the opening exchanges, but yields the stage to the characters after whom the works are named (Critias also plays a part in the *Timaeus*). Dialogue is here abandoned: the bulk of the *Timaeus* consists of a lengthy exposition by Timaeus, in a rich and hieratic style, which reaches a majestic conclusion, again without returning to the original frame. In the *Philebus* Socrates is again more prominent (perhaps because the subject being discussed, pleasure and pain, is closer to his familiar moral concerns?), but the discussion, though it has moments of liveliness, is somewhat ponderous and ill-formed: it begins by referring to an earlier exchange (note also 19d-e), and ends very abruptly, so that one might even suspect this of being a further unfinished experiment. In the *Laws*, as is well known, Socrates does not appear and is never mentioned. Although Aristotle casually refers to it as a Socratic work (*Politics* 1265a11), it is obvious that the location in Crete would not suit the stay-at-home philosopher (see *Crito* 52a-c and *Phaedrus* 230cd), and this may be sufficient explanation.[7] But the absence of Socrates from the *Laws* seems symbolically appropriate, as the culmination of his changing role.

There is also a change in the cast of characters other than Socrates. Although these are still certainly or probably historical figures, they are no longer prominent in politics but in science and thought: Theaetetus, young Socrates and Theodorus in mathematics, Zeno and Parmenides in Eleatic philosophy, Timaeus in the Italian Pythagorean school;[8] of Philebus and Protarchus we know nothing for certain, but several passages seem to suggest authentic background to their controversies (e.g. 44b sq. on Philebus' enemies). The Spartan Megillus and the Cretan Cleinias are unknown elsewhere, and are probably 'stock' figures representing their societies: as we shall see, what characterisation there is of them mostly alludes to (e.g.) Laconian brevity. The Athenian in the *Laws* is anonymous, but not to be simply identified with Plato (an interpretation found already in the ancient scholia): to go no further, neither of the other characters refers to him as an eminent writer or thinker. The gap between author and character may be narrowed; there may be more of Plato in the visitor from Elea and in

---

[6] He was a real person: see Arist. *Metaph.* 1036b25ff.

[7] I mention only for amusement the theory of G. Ryle, *Plato's Progress* ch. 2. Working from the unprovable but not self-evidently absurd premiss that the dialogues were acted out in the Academy ('eristic moots'), Ryle moves with cheerful confidence to the assumption that Plato always played the role of Socrates, and that the latter's diminished role in certain dialogues is adequately explained by Plato's ill health (for no one else could be permitted to play the master).

[8] If Critias in the *Timaeus* and *Critias* is the tyrant (cf. p. 93 on the *Charmides*), this would be an example pointing the other way (and the Sicilian general Hermocrates would have been another); but although this is a notorious crux, I incline to prefer the view that the man in this dialogue is the oligarch's grandfather. For discussion see Guthrie v. 244; *APF* 322-6; Welliver (n. 41 below) 50-7.

276 The Art of Plato

Timaeus than in any earlier work, more still in the main speaker of the *Laws*, but there is still a difference. One final generalisation may be added: no obstructive or aggressive figures, no conceited sophists or self-interested professionals, appear in the later dialogues: Thrasymachus, himself 'educated' into good manners in the later books of the *Republic*, has no successors. It has been suggested that Plato is following his own prescriptions in the *Republic*, in refraining from dramatising figures whom his readers ought not to imitate.[9]

A popular view of Plato's literary development might be caricatured as follows: in the early dialogues he allows his dramatic and stylistic talents full scope, creating brilliant portraits and stunning parodies: this tendency reaches its height with the *Symposium*. In the *Republic* we see the apex and the turning-point: within that work Socrates is transformed from his endearing and amusing self into a Platonic mouthpiece, and thereafter becomes a colourless figure. With that change the dialogues lose their life and energy, become intellectually more rigid but also more difficult and long-winded, as Plato forgets Socrates, turns to weird speculations in the wake of the Pythagoreans, and loses his sense of humour in his gloomy old age. The *Laws* brings this regrettable tendency to its sterile conclusion.

It will already be clear that the truth is more complex, and in what follows I shall try to point to some of the merits and interest of the later works as well as their deficiencies. Obviously, the sketch given above neglects the fact that the *Phaedrus* and the *Theaetetus*, two of Plato's liveliest and most imaginative works, are probably later than the *Republic*. If we are right in seeing the delightful *Theaetetus* as composed shortly after the *Parmenides*, which comes nearest to abandoning the dialogue form, then it is obvious that we cannot graph Plato's 'decline' as a writer of dialogue on a simple curve. There are strong lines of continuity in Plato's writing, and we can see some of the later works developing in more detail themes and ideas which occasionally appeared in the earlier period. Thus the fascination with language and its relation to concepts, and the analysis of Heraclitus and Protagoras, which modern philosophers have found so absorbing in the *Theaetetus* and *Sophist*, can be paralleled in the earlier *Cratylus*;[10] the cosmic geography of the *Timaeus* is prefigured in the myths of the *Phaedo* and the *Republic*; the perennial Socratic conception of virtue as knowledge is still being discussed in the *Laws* (731c, 860-4).[11] A myth appears in the middle of the *Statesman*, as in the central speech of the *Phaedrus*.[12]

---

[9] F.H. Sandbach, in his excellent short survey in Easterling and Knox (ed.), *Cambridge Hist. of Classical Lit.* i (1985) 483.

[10] D. Bostock, *Plato's Theaetetus* 6-7 consequently argues for a post-*Republic* date for the *Cratylus*.

[11] Guthrie v. 376-8; see also his p. 329 for further parallels.

[12] For smaller-scale examples of myth adapted or deployed for didactic ends, see *Philebus* 16c-17a; *Laws* 713c-4b, 804e, 865d, 872de, 913bc, 944a. Cf. R. Wright in *Arktouros* ed. G. Bowersock and others (Berlin 1979) 364-71.

Yet it is difficult not to sense some change in the handling of the dialogues, which is surely related to the reduction in Socrates' role (though which is cause and which effect is unknowable).[13] There is a general increase in length, despite the curtailment of preliminaries and scene-setting. Long expositions become more common (apart from the *Timaeus*, the whole of book 5 of the *Laws* consists of a single speech by the Athenian), and respondents are willing and cooperative, rather than trying to resist or put opposite points of view. Aristoteles in the *Parmenides* sets the pattern, offering himself as interlocutor after Parmenides has said that the youngest of the company will suit him best, 'for he would make least trouble, and would be most likely to answer as he thinks' (137b). The second point is unexceptionable (cf. e.g. *Grg.* 487d, 492d), the first is startling. There is a parallel in the *Sophist*, where the visitor from Elea opts for question-and-answer rather than lecturing the company, as long as his interlocutor is not troublesome, and answers obediently (217d). It would seem that the *Republic* does mark something of a turning-point in one respect: from that dialogue onwards, Plato does not introduce characters who hold up the debate with trivia or personal preoccupations. Even major thinkers like Parmenides explain their ideas to Socrates and others, rather than showing off or playing coy like Protagoras. The arguments advance more sedately and with greater dignity, but there is some loss in variety.[14] In one or two places we may suspect that the author is teasing his readers with a sly reference to the more monotonal progress of argument: in particular, when the Eleatic guest counters a 'yes' from Theaetetus with the response: 'you assent, but do you recognise the category I mean, or has the flow of the argument carried you along to agree so readily from force of habit?' (*Soph.* 236d).[15]

Methodology also has some influence on form. Whereas in the early-to-middle dialogues Plato makes Socrates practise the question-and-answer method in an elenchus (interrogation) of his interlocutors' ideas, and also has him lay much emphasis on the need to test hypotheses, looking ever upwards to the ultimate or primary hypotheses (*Meno, Phaedo, Republic*), in the dialogues from the *Sophist* onwards he seems to prefer a procedure referred to as 'collection and division'. (Modern scholars use the Greek word *diairesis*, 'division', as shorthand for the whole procedure.)[16] Already in the *Phaedrus*, the relation of which to the late group is unclear, Socrates

[13] See further L. Campbell, in his introduction to the *Sophist and Politicus* (Oxford 1867), esp. xix-xxxiii, xl-xli – despite its date, still a valuable discussion and collection of examples; J. Stenzel, *Plato's Method of Dialectic* (Eng. tr. by D.J. Allan) (Oxford 1940) 1-22 (an essay originally written in 1916; rather abstract); Jaeger, *Aristotle* (Eng. tr.) 13-16, 24-9 (but p. 26 is overstated); H. Thesleff, *Studies in the Styles of Plato* (Helsinki 1967) 169-71.

[14] There are still occasional jokes of the kind found e.g. at *Grg.* 505c, where the discussion in some way reflects the subject-matter: see e.g. *Philebus* 23a, on the idea of 'paining' pleasure.

[15] Is *Philebus* 54b a joke about the artificiality of the question-and-answer dialogue form? Differently, ibid. 42e.

[16] Cf. Guthrie v. 124-33.

protests himself 'a lover of these collections and divisions' (266b). The procedure, which is seen as part of the essence of philosophic argument, involves the gathering of like categories and the subdivision of a complex category or genus into its various species, so that the philosopher may eventually see the fine distinctions which separate one abstract concept from another (though the process need not be applied only to abstractions). This process, while obviously a useful definitional tool, seems to be given an odd importance by Plato: certainly it dictates much of the form of the *Sophist* and the *Statesman*. In these works the aim is to define the entities after which the dialogues are named, and in the former the process is demonstrated by the example of an angler (218e-221c). A love of classification and categorising, exhaustive if possible, seems to characterise Plato's later work. These two dialogues in particular seem to spend an excessive amount of time on subdivision and classification, and there are passages in which the speakers refer to the long-windedness of the proceedings, apologetically or self-mockingly (*Statesman* 283b, 286b (referring back to the *Sophist*), *Philebus* 23d1-3). Whimsical though some of this practice may be, it is hard not to feel that the author has allowed his interest in a new method to get out of hand.[17]

On the level of vocabulary and verbal style, readers can again sense a difference of pace and vigour. We have already mentioned the slightly mannered artificialities of prose rhythm and hiatus, a marked change from the more mimetic spontaneity of Plato's earlier works. As for vocabulary, Campbell long ago amassed impressive evidence for the increased use of technical terms and of unusual or invented words, and of more familiar words used in abnormal senses.[18] These points apply especially to the *Sophist, Statesman, Timaeus* and *Laws*, and above all to the last two. The more poetical and heightened style is still present, but 'is concentrated on a few great subjects (Dialectic, Being, the Philosopher, the creation and preservation of the universe by God), and is less ready to light up with a spontaneous glow every new world of imagination'.[19] With the eclipse of Socrates, the type of irony which we associate with him also becomes rarer. The new figures who dominate the late dialogues are not devoid of humour and irony: a pleasant example comes in the *Timaeus*, where the Locrian refers to the traditions about the Greek noble families being descended

---

[17] À propos of the length of their proceedings, the Eleatic thinker introduces a discussion of *kairos* ('proportion') in the abstract, with special reference to the proper length of discussions (*Statesman* 283c-5c); this too, it may be felt, goes on too long, and it is interesting to contrast the vividly characterised and dramatically motivated discussion of procedure in the *Protagoras* (334a-8e): see p. 133 above. For other comments on the length of the discussion see *Philebus* 50c-e, *Laws* 890e.

[18] See his comm. on the *Sophist* and *Statesman* intro. xxiv-xxxiii.

[19] Campbell op. cit. xxii. For examples of the type of passage he presumably has in mind see *Timaeus* 47a-d, 90a-d, *Laws* 716c-8c, 902e-5d. See also Thesleff, *Studies in the Styles of Plato* 77-80, on what he describes as 'legal style' and 'onkos' (inflated or pompous) style; from the *Laws* he cites 847bc for the former, 666d-7a for the latter.

from the gods: 'we must trust those who have declared it in former times; being, as they said, descendants of gods, they must, no doubt, have had certain knowledge of their own ancestors. We cannot, then, mistrust the children of gods, though they speak without probable and necessary proofs ...' (40d).[20] But the teasing ironies of the later works are not of the *ad hominem* type which we find everywhere in the Socratic dialogues. Irony is directed not so much at the respondent (in the case of the *Timaeus* we are at this point not dealing with dialogue but with continuous exposition) but at mankind in general, its follies and delusions.[21]

Within the more formal and dignified structures of the late works there is still scope for Plato's amazing range of imagery.[22] We can defer quotation from the *Timaeus*, itself unique in Plato's work as a colossal 'image' of the cosmos in all its variety and splendour. As for other dialogues, Parmenides compares himself to an old race horse recalled to the course (referring to a poem by Ibycus on falling in love once more), and immediately shifts to yet another metaphor, saying that his memories make him frightened of 'setting out, at my age, to traverse so vast and hazardous a sea' (*Parm.* 137a). The conflict between the materialists and the realists is described in the *Sophist* in terms which allude to the mythical war of the gods and the Giants (246a-c). In an amazingly detailed and technical passage, a daunting prospect for any translator, the art of kingship is elaborately compared with the art of weaving (*Statesman* 279a-83b, 287b, 305e, 308d sq., 310e).[23] The workings of democracy are satirically treated, as in the *Republic*, using the examples of doctor and ship-captain to reemphasise the necessity of rule by experts (*Statesman* 298a sqq.). The Eleatic visitor and the others are like gold-refiners in their sifting of the different categories of authority-figures in search for the statesman (ibid. 303de; cf. *Philebus* 55c on testing metal). Memory and sensation combine to 'write words in our souls', and there is a painter in our souls as well (*Philebus* 39a-c). Life itself, being a mixture of pleasure and pain, is a tragicomedy (*Philebus* 50b, with the preceding exchange). In the grave perspective of the *Laws*, a different metaphor is employed: 'we may imagine that each of us living creatures is a puppet made by gods, possibly as a plaything, or possibly with some more serious purpose. That, indeed, is more than we can tell, but one thing is certain. These interior states are, so to say, the cords, or strings, by which we are worked: they are opposed to one another, and pull us with opposite tensions in the direction of opposite actions, and therein

[20] Cf. Hdt. ii 143 on Hecataeus' genealogy. See also *IAlc.* 120e-1a, *Laws* 886cd.

[21] Campbell xxi. Examples: *Statesman* 291ab, picked up at 303c; 298a-d (satire on democracy, cf. and contrast *Rep.* vi. 488a-9a); *Laws* 731d-2d, 800b-e, 805d-6c.

[22] See P. Louis, *Les métaphores de Platon* (Paris 1945): the arrangement of his book by topic makes citation of specific pages impracticable. See also A. de Marignac, *Imagination et dialectique* (Paris 1951). V. Pöschl, *Bibliographie zur antiken Bildersprache* (Heidelberg 1964) 303-16 is especially useful for specific images discussed in articles, theses, etc.

[23] Cf. Aristophanes, *Lysistrata* 565ff.; also Arist. *Pol.* 1265b19-21, 1325b40-6a5.

lies the division of virtue from vice' (*Laws* i. 644de).[24] The way in which some of these metaphors are introduced and the length at which they are developed may sometimes seem artificial, but there is no diminution in Plato's capacity to make imaginative connections.

In different ways, the *Parmenides* and the *Theaetetus* (which are surely close in date whatever their actual order of composition) indicate something of a change of course in Plato's career as a writer of dialogue. (Obviously, they also indicate, if not a crisis, a new phase in his philosophical development, as is widely acknowledged.) Yet they offer contradictory solutions to his dilemmas. *Parmenides*, after the rather brief preliminaries, moves as far away from dialogue form as is possible without abandoning it altogether; certainly there is no interaction or exchange of ideas, still less additional colour or comment. The *Theaetetus*, on the other hand, is one of the liveliest and most delightful of the dialogues in both literary and argumentative terms – so much so that before the advent of stylometric studies it was often taken to be a dialogue of the early period.[25] We shall shortly consider a few aspects of the *Theaetetus*, but it is worth raising, in general terms, the question whether Plato was actually conscious of being at something of a crossroads in terms of his literary career. The new subjects he was confronting seemed to demand a vaster canvas and new methods; neither subjects nor methods, perhaps, seemed altogether appropriate to Socrates, now a dimmer figure in his memory; and if he was writing the *Theaetetus* after 369,[26] when he himself was over 50, he may no longer have felt that he could afford the time and the energy to give each dialogue such dramatic energy and stylistic life. Perhaps indeed his own powers may have been failing.[27] The *Theaetetus* opens a new phase in his writing by saying farewell to the old, reviving a Socrates rich in humour, eloquent yet modest, protesting his ignorance while sympathetically guiding his youthful disciple, ironically awed before the wisdom of older thinkers (Protagoras and Heraclitus), yet criticising and satirising them with a mischievous wit and acuteness which we have not seen before. There is a tempting parallel here with some of the ancient poets: Horace and Propertius, for example, are never more themselves than when they resolve to pass on to pastures new,[28] and the new fields on which they embark

---

[24] Cf. 804b, 903d, and Dodds, *The Greeks and the Irrational* 214f.

[25] See Thesleff, *St. in Pl. Chronology* 152n.128.

[26] This is generally thought the most likely date for the battle in which Theaetetus was fatally wounded. The situation is complicated by the existence of an alternative opening to the dialogue (Anon. Comm. on Pl. *Tht.*, ed. Diels-Schubart (Berlin 1905) 3. 28ff.; Guthrie v. 61-3). Partly on this basis, Thesleff, *St. in Pl. Chronology* 85, 152-7, argues for an earlier draft which was later re-worked; preferring a date in the 390s for the mathematician's death, he puts the later version c. 375.

[27] Hinted at by Sandbach, in the essay cited in n. 9, 483; also Ryle, *Plato's Progress* 27.

[28] I think particularly of Hor. *Epist.* i. 1, and of the closing poems of Propertius' first book (where, after a book which has presented the writer as above all a lover, he indicates two other

sometimes bear surprising resemblances, only gradually apparent, to their earlier oeuvre.

These speculations need not affect our appreciation of the *Theaetetus* itself, to which we now turn. As already indicated, it is a dialogue which combines old and new in Platonic technique: like the short early works (*Euthyphro*, *Laches*, etc.), it is 'aporetic', but on the chronology accepted here it is longer than any earlier dialogue apart from the *Republic*, and it is obvious that far more can be learned, and more avenues are explored, than in any of the comparable early works. The frame sets the date after Theatetus' death: in 369, two friends of Socrates, Eucleides and Terpsion, also known from the *Phaedo*, recall how well he foresaw the young Theaetetus' promise in a conversation back in 399, shortly before Socrates' own death (see 142c6, picked up and made more immediate at 210d). The work thus commemorates both men. The dramatic movement of the dialogue is mainly shaped by Socrates' role as a 'midwife' to others' ideas, a particularly rich and memorable metaphor developed at some length (148e-151d).[29]

> My art of midwifery is in general like theirs; the only difference is that my patients are men, not women, and my concern is not with the body but with the soul that is in travail of birth. And the highest point of my art is the power to prove by every test whether the offspring of a young man's thought is a false phantom or instinct with life and truth. I am so far like the midwife, that I cannot myself give birth to wisdom; and the common reproach is true, that though I question others, I can myself bring nothing to light because there is no wisdom in me. The reason is this: heaven constrains me to serve as a midwife, but has debarred me from giving birth. So for myself I have no sort of wisdom, nor has any discovery ever been born to me as the child of my soul. Those who frequent my company at first appear, some of them, quite unintelligent; but, as we go further with our discussions, all who are favoured by heaven make progress at a rate that seems surprising to others as well as to themselves, although it is clear that they have never learned anything from me; the many admirable truths they bring to birth have been discovered by themselves from within. But the delivery is heaven's work and mine.
>
> The proof of this is that many who have not been conscious of my assistance but have made light of me, thinking it was all their own doing, have left me sooner than they should, whether under others' influence or of their own motion, and thenceforward suffered miscarriage of their thoughts through falling into bad company; and they have lost the children of whom I had delivered them by bringing them up badly, caring more for false phantoms than for the true; and so at last their lack of understanding has become apparent to themselves and to everyone else. Such a one was Aristides, the

---

paths he might follow, or has already followed: the detached and amused narrator of neoteric epyllion, and the gloomy, disillusioned commentator on civil war; the next book fulfils neither of these promises).

[29] Developed at 157cd, 160e, 184ab, 210b. The midwife-image is the subject of a brilliantly suggestive paper by M. Burnyeat, *BICS* 24 (1977) 7-16 = *Essays on the Philosophy of Socrates*, ed. H.H. Benson (Oxford 1992) 54-65.

son of Lysimachus, and there have been many more. When they come back and beg for a renewal of our intercourse with extravagant protestations, sometimes the divine warning that comes to me forbids it; and with others it is permitted, and these begin again to make progress. In yet another way, those who seek my company have the same experience as a woman with child: they suffer the pangs of labour and, by night and day, are full of distress far greater than a woman's; and my art has power to bring on these pangs or allay them. (150b-151b1, tr. Cornford)

This midwifery is directed towards the young Theaetetus, and a particularly satisfying aspect of the dialogue is the way in which he does react to Socrates' ideas and make his own contributions (147c sq., 191b, 195e, 199e, etc.).[30] As a foil Plato introduces the older mathematician Theodorus, the young man's mentor; his participation after initial reluctance is motivated by his obligation to defend the theories of his old friend Protagoras (160d-2a, 168d-183d; see esp. 183c): now that the latter is dead, his 'orphans' must be supported (164de).[31]

The subject of the dialogue is a particularly perplexing one, the definition of knowledge. Three definitions are considered: knowledge = sense-perception (this involves extended consideration of theories which Socrates sees as lying behind it, those of Protagoras and of Heraclitus); knowledge = true opinion (including a separate consideration of how false opinion can be possible); and knowledge = true opinion supported by a *logos* ('argument'? several senses of the word are considered). All three are rejected. It is surely appropriate that the concept of Socratic ignorance, and the associated midwife-talk, should be so prominent in a dialogue which explores the nature of knowledge; appropriate too that Theaetetus, who develops from an able youth into one of the most famous mathematicians of his day,[32] should be involved in the dialogue. Theaetetus does (later) possess knowledge (unlike the deluded interlocutors of the early aporetic works); moreover, his mathematical knowledge is of a kind which particularly interests Plato, being non-physical, demonstrable, and in a sense absolute.

The dialogue also, like the *Protagoras* and *Gorgias*, shows a concern with dialectical manners and method: comments by Socrates repeatedly refer to the danger of treating serious issues too lightly (168d; cf. 200d, 203e8-9), of arguing in an 'antilogical' or eristic manner (146a, 154de, 164c, 165de, 167de; cf. Theodorus at 179e-180d), of fastening on to the words or verbal slips of one's opponent rather than trying to do justice to the sense of his

---

[30] It may be suggested that this consistent responsiveness on Theaetetus' part is more convincing and effective than the single 'bolt-from-the-blue' insight of Cleinias in the *Euthydemus*, of which so much is made, even divine intervention being offered as a possible explanation (290b-91a, cf. p. 113 above).

[31] Note how the metaphor here picks up the actual situation of Theaetetus, whose guardians have defrauded their ward and deprived him of some of his patrimony (144d). As often, a small detail in the scene-setting is echoed in the main discussion.

[32] See, in brief, Ostwald in *CAH* v² 350; further, Burnyeat, *Isis* 69 (1978) 489-513.

argument (167bc). Socrates foresees such objections and finds fault with himself on Protagoras' behalf (162de, and context); this seems a fairer and more attractive proceeding than what happens in some of the earlier dialogues, where the inept or aggressive interlocutors illustrate these errors, and Socrates himself is not immune. At a late stage of the dialogue Socrates rebukes himself for garrulity and self-satisfaction (195b9 sq.); again, his mannerisms and personality are as individual as ever, but because of his positive attitude he seems less irritating than in a work like the *Ion* or even the first book of the *Republic*. Here his relations with his interlocutors are cheerful and good-natured: he jokingly appeals to Theodorus on professional grounds, pressing him to take part (169a) (similarly he invokes Protagoras' professional expertise in rhetoric, 178e), but Theodorus does not take his insistence badly (168e-9c, 177c, 181a). It will be better for Theaetetus to make his own responses rather than for Socrates to be a busybody on his behalf (184e). There may still be weaknesses in the argument of the dialogue, and most readers will be able to spot places where a different response might have had more fruitful results, but the discussion is being conducted in a suitably thoughtful and self-aware fashion.

To the reader familiar with the *Gorgias* and the *Republic* one of the most immediately striking passages in this dialogue is the famous digression at 172c-177b, which was much quoted and had enormous influence in antiquity.[33] This passage contrasts the man of affairs and the philosopher, the public speaker and the private thinker, the active and the contemplative; behind the vivid portraits lies the further contrast of two opposed value systems, the self-interested and pragmatic life of the ambitious man and the life of the man who believes in absolute moral truths. It has been described as 'philosophically quite pointless',[34] to which the natural answer may seem to be 'so much the worse for philosophy'. Although the passage is explicitly described as a digression (173b, 177b), it is well known that such interludes, while structurally subordinate, may include material which is thematically central (as in Virgil's *Georgics*).[35] One telling point is that Theodorus replies to Socrates that they have plenty of leisure time ('don't we?', 172c2). The idea of leisure as necessary for philosophy is again an influential one. But in the context of the dialogue it turns out that Socrates has only limited leisure available; at the end he must depart to keep an appointment at the stoa of the Archon basileus, to deal with the indictment lodged by Meletus.[36] The digression is further integrated by its

---

[33] Some examples in Burnyeat's introduction, 34-5 (his suggestions concerning the function of the digression, on pp. 32-9, are full of interest). On the passage's influence see W. Jaeger, *Aristotle* 426-61 (and for the earlier background to these ideas J.M. Carter, *The Quiet Athenian* (Oxford 1986)). For a much fuller account of this passage than is possible here, see now R. Rue, *OSAP* 11 (1993) 71-100.

[34] Ryle, *Plato's Progress* 158.

[35] For a different view see M. Heath, *Unity in Greek Poetics* (Oxford 1989), esp. chs. 1-2.

[36] Burnyeat, introd. loc. cit.

concentration on what the philosopher knows that the moral relativist does not (esp. 173b2-3, de, 174b); play with the vocabulary of knowledge and false opinion provides a thematic connection with the central enquiry of the dialogue. This is not to deny, however, that the passage raises wider questions and opens doors which would lead to other enquiries: some of these, indeed, point the way forward to the mystical metaphysics of the *Timaeus*. Although the passage is much too long to give as a whole, some quotation is essential to convey its extraordinary quality.

> The orator is always talking against time, hurried on by the clock; there is no space to enlarge upon any subject he chooses, but the adversary stands over him ready to recite a schedule of the points to which he must confine himself. He is a slave disputing about a fellow-slave before a master sitting in judgement ... hence he acquires a tense and bitter shrewdness; he knows how to flatter his master and earn his good graces, but his mind is narrow and crooked. His apprenticeship in slavery has dwarfed and twisted his growth and robbed him of his free spirit, driving him into devious ways, threatening him with fears and dangers which the tenderness of youth could not face with truth and honesty; so, turning from the first to lies and the requital of wrong with wrong, warped and stunted, he passes from youth to manhood with no soundness in him and turns out, in the end, a man of formidable intellect – as he imagines. (172d-3b)

> From their youth up they [the philosophers] have never known the way to marketplace or council chamber or any other place of public assembly; they never hear a decree read out or look at the text of a law; to take any interest in the rivalries of political cliques, in meetings, dinners and merrymakings with flute-girls, never occurs to them even in dreams. Whether any fellow-citizen is well or ill born or has inherited some defect from his ancestors on either side, the philosopher knows no more than how many pints there are in the sea. He is not even aware that he knows nothing of all this; for if he holds aloof, it is not for reputation's sake, but because it is really only his body that sojourns in the city, while his thought, disdaining all such things as worthless, takes wings, as Pindar says, 'beyond the sky, beneath the earth', searching the heavens and measuring the plains, everywhere seeking the true nature of everything as a whole, never sinking to what lies close at hand. (173c-4a)

> Evils, Theodorus, can never be done away with, for the good must always have its contrary; nor have they any place in the divine world; but they must needs haunt this region of our mortal nature. That is why we should make all speed to take flight from this world to the other; and that means becoming like the divine so far as we can, and that again is to become righteous with the help of wisdom ... In the divine there is no shadow of unrighteousness, only the perfection of righteousness; and nothing is more like the divine than any one of us who becomes as righteous as possible. It is here that a man shows his true spirit and power or lack of spirit and nothingness. For to know this is wisdom and excellence of the genuine sort; not to know it is to be manifestly blind and base. (176a-c) (Transl. Cornford)

Obviously, as in the *Gorgias*, this opposition not only sets out a contrast between different goals in life, but also anticipates the condemnation of Socrates in the courts of men of this world; but here the antithesis is presented in a series of speeches by Socrates, not in dramatic conflict with a Calliclean opponent. We see foreshadowed another feature of the later Platonic corpus, a sombre and austere moralising. The characterisation of the philosopher as lost in a world of higher thought, and the description of his task as becoming like god, and removing himself from the corruption of this world, make this ideal more remote from the historical Socrates. The incessant chatterbox of the agora becomes an almost mystical contemplative, a man apart.[37] The antagonism to worldly pleasures sounds a note unheard except in the *Phaedo*; the religious commitment, though anticipated in certain passages of the *Republic*,[38] points the way to the profound theism of the *Timaeus* (where the ideal of assimilation to god reappears, 90cd) and of the tenth book of the *Laws*. The mordant satire in the portrait of the orator, and the intensity of the contrasting praise of the philosopher, give this digression a tone quite different from that of the dialogue which surrounds it. For all the parallels and verbal echoes which remind us of other uses of these themes, this is a Socrates with whom we are not familiar. It perhaps becomes clearer, to us as to Plato, why Socrates could not be the central figure of the dialogues to follow.

The *Timaeus*

Few even among classicists are now familiar with the *Timaeus*, and still fewer would give it a special place in the list of their favourite dialogues (though C.S. Lewis thought it Plato's greatest achievement).[39] Yet for many centuries it was the most important and influential of all Plato's works, far better known than the *Republic* or the short Socratic dialogues. There are external historical reasons for this (particularly the fact that most of the Platonic corpus was lost to the West during the Dark Ages), but in a sense that only puts the question a stage further back: why did the *Timaeus* have the special status to survive in Latin translations, and why, having survived, did it have such influence? We shall return to the question of the work's historical importance at the end of this section, but we must also consider what intrinsic interest this dialogue retains for us today. In what

---

[37] Rue, art. cit., in a subtle and suggestive discussion, sees that the philosopher in the digression cannot be equated with Socrates, but interprets this as showing that Socrates is superior to both the orator and the philosopher whom he describes. This is a tempting reading as regards the *Theaetetus*, but perhaps does not take enough account of the general shifting of emphasis in Plato's later oeuvre.

[38] Particularly *Rep.* vi. 500b-d.

[39] See his *The Allegory of Love* (Oxford 1936) 95: 'Plato's most sublime and suggestive work.'

follows I shall concentrate on questions of form, conception and style, in keeping with the general approach adopted in earlier chapters.[40]

The *Timaeus* falls into three main parts, the first two of which are continuous. The first is an introductory exchange in which Socrates greets three friends – Timaeus, Critias and Hermocrates – and recalls how they met the previous day and considered in theoretical terms the social and economic structure of an ideal society: there are clear reminiscences of the *Republic*, but it is also obvious that much that was essential to that society is ignored. Socrates expresses the desire to see this ideal state in action, and the second part of the dialogue consists of a speech by Critias in which he declares that such a society can in fact be exemplified in early Athenian history, known from records of a forgotten age which were found by his ancestor Solon in Egypt. He whets the appetite of the company with the beginnings of his narrative, which will narrate the great war between Athens and the lost island of Atlantis; this topic, however, is deferred to the *Critias*, already anticipated as the second work of a trilogy. Today Timaeus, represented as a Pythagorean from Italian Locri, will give an exposition of something still older and perhaps more magnificent – an account of the creation of the universe. Timaeus' speech occupies the third and by far the longest part of the work, and can be further divided into sections. In brief, it describes the shape and structure of the cosmos, narrates in 'mythical' form the deliberate designing of it and all that it contains by a divine 'demiurge' (craftsman), and proceeds to describe in some detail its motion, its elements, the stars and planets (conceived as divine), and the living creatures, above all man, which have been created to inhabit the earth, placed at its centre. Part myth, part cosmology, part astronomy and rich in the vocabulary of medical science, it is both a hymn of praise to the creator and an analysis of the sources of human happiness and misery – in particular, the closing pages emphasise the ethical implications of this account of creation.

The interpretative problems are legion. One of the most substantial is also the most frustrating: Plato did not finish the *Critias* and as far as we know never embarked upon the third part of the trilogy.[41] We are therefore dealing with a truncated work, and this particularly inhibits our under-

---

[40] A.E. Taylor, *A Commentary on Plato's Timaeus* (Oxford 1928) remains a standard, though somewhat impenetrable, commentary on the Greek text. His view that Plato reproduces authentic 5th-century Pythagoreanism will be ignored here. Also essential is F.M. Cornford, *Plato's Cosmology* (London 1937), including translation. See also F. Solmsen, *Plato's Theology* (Ithaca, N.Y. 1942); G.E.R. Lloyd, 'Plato as a natural scientist', *JHS* 88 (1968) 78-92; G. Vlastos, *Plato's Universe* (Oxford 1975); F. Solmsen, 'Plato and Science', in *Interpretations of Plato*, ed. H. North (*Mnem.* Suppl. 50, 1977) 86-105. On the question of date see n. 2 above.

[41] The idea that the *Critias* is complete as it stands (W. Welliver, *Character, Plot and Thought in Plato's Timaeus-Critias* (Leiden 1977)) is as absurd as the hypothesis that Thucydides deliberately abandoned his History in mid-year and mid-sentence (a view apparently adopted by some of the ancient critics whom Dionysius criticises in *On Thucydides* 10).

standing of the Atlantis myth and its significance. In effect we are thrown back upon the *Timaeus*, where it is at least possible to consider the relation of the parts to one another. Why is the Atlantis-theme initiated in the *Timaeus*, rather than being reserved for the *Critias*? And what relevance does the speech of Critias in the first dialogue have to the larger portion of that work, the account of the cosmos? What kind of truth value does either the Atlantis story or the account of the cosmos have? How far is the latter scientific theology, how far fantasy? These questions should be asked, if not answered; but the general tendency of scholarship has been to consider the Atlantis myth and the speech of Timaeus in separate studies.

Socrates' reference to their conversation of the previous day is a typical case of blurred or elusive cross-reference: it tempts us to think of the *Republic*, in which the matters referred to were discussed, but the summary leaves out so much that we must hesitate. In any case, the completely different 'cast list' in this dialogue, and the incompatibility of the dates of the festivals mentioned (Bendis at the opening of the *Republic*, Athena in the *Timaeus*, 21a), must be intended to distance the present discussion from the conversation recalled in the *Republic*. Socrates' summary, which covers only the social structure of the ideal state and the reorganisation of family life (broadly, the material of books iii, iv and v of the *Republic*, but without the psychological analysis), must be interpreted from the *Timaeus* itself. It would seem that Socrates' perspective is being shown as limited to setting out a prescription for society: metaphysics and 'history' are beyond his powers. He himself refers to his own inability to do justice to his imagined citizens (19d), and looks forward to what the others, men who have combined political activity and philosophy, will be able to achieve. This might be seen as Plato's signal that Socrates has reached his limits, or that other spokesmen are now required, were it not that Socrates has been given so much larger a sphere of expertise in the past. Rather, the whole scope of the Platonic dialogue seems to be enlarged: non-Athenians will be involved (Timaeus himself and, we assume, Hermocrates, who in the *Timaeus* is silent but who makes one comment in the *Critias*), and the limitations of Greek conceptions of the past are stressed by the words of the Egyptian priest, who rebukes Solon for assuming that he and his people know anything worth mentioning about their history. As for subject matter, the first speech, that of Critias, though only anticipating his later exposition, already shows a new fascination with historical reconstruction, while Timaeus' speech also breaks new ground by examining cosmology. Restricting our view to the *Timaeus*, we can perhaps see analogies with the *Gorgias* and with book i of the *Republic*, in which each exchange goes deeper: here, we begin with 'conventional' social theory (perhaps recalling sophistic thought as well as the *Republic*), proceed to an account of unprecedentedly ancient history, and then to something still vaster and more ancient, the 'history' of the universe itself.

That Athens should have been the exemplar of the ideal state, even in the remote past, is a strange conception; stranger still that the wise Solon should have learned this tale of her days of greatness from an Egyptian priest who also emphasises Athens' former links with and similarities to his own society, which normally appeared to Greeks a world of alien and opposite customs.[42] The *Timaeus* concentrates on Athens, and makes only general reference to the lost civilisation of Atlantis which that ancient Athenian society had been able to resist with bravery and dedication (hints of the Persian wars here, it would seem). In the *Critias* we hear much more about Atlantis, its foundation, civic design and structure, constitution and so forth, but before that there is a briefer account of Athens (109-12) which includes some explicit contrasts with her condition in modern times (that is, in the late fifth or early fourth centuries?). Some of these contrasts concern the fertility of the land, or the quantity of soil on the Acropolis then and now; but others refer to the piety and morality of old Athens (112b-d), and presumably there is a didactic thrust to this passage, a message for the Athenians of a later and more decadent age. The portrait of Atlantis is of a far more exotic and wealthier society, a monarchy, perhaps with a suggestion of Persia or other eastern empires. Yet it too has some resemblance to classical Athens, particularly in its preeminence as a sea power. The relationship between Atlantis and modern Athens, ancient Athens and modern, has been the subject of much discussion,[43] but it seems clear at least that both Atlantis and Athens decline, the former eventually being destroyed, but the latter surviving and perhaps capable of learning from 'history' and turning to better political paths. Further than that, perhaps, we are unlikely to find firm ground for speculation, given the unfinished state of the trilogy. It is tempting to suppose that the presence of Hermocrates (and perhaps that of Critias, if the latter is the tyrant) may imply that later parts would have involved allusion to or foreshadowing of the Peloponnesian war and its conflicts, just as there seem to be hints of the Persian wars in the sections which we have.

Plato would surely have been amazed at the hold that Atlantis has gained on the imagination of centuries of readers: literally thousands of books have been published examining his myth and what might underlie it, and the name has become familiar to many who have never heard of the *Timaeus* through science fiction and popular archaeology.[44] That it is

[42] Plato is drawing upon various passages of Herodotus, esp. i. 30.1 on Solon's visit to Egypt, ii. 143 on Hecataeus' discomfiture when he boasted of his long genealogy. But literary history can only explain some of the elements used, not how they are combined. On the Greek perception of Egypt see further A.B. Lloyd, *Herodotus Book ii* (Introduction) (Leiden 1975).

[43] Notably by P. Vidal-Naquet in a well-known paper in *REG* 77 (1964) 420-44, tr. in *Myth, Religion and Society* ed. R.L. Gordon (Cambridge 1981) 201-14, and in a series of essays by C. Gill, of which 'The Genre of the Atlantis Story', *CPh* 72 (1977) 287-304 seems to me the most helpful: see also his Bristol Classical Press volume, *Plato: the Atlantis Story* (1980).

[44] Cf. H.D.P. Lee's appendix to his Penguin translation of both dialogues; T.H. Martin, *Études sur le Timée de Platon* (Paris 1841) i. 257-332; P.Y. Forsyth, *Atlantis: The Myth in the Making* (London 1980), etc. etc.

anything but a Platonic invention seems to me, I confess, totally implausible; but this does raise some problems which affect the interpretation of the dialogue as a whole. The story is presented as if passed down through an authentic tradition, and Critias lays stress on how eagerly he questioned and attended to his grandfather's narrative (26bc); moreover, Socrates himself says that it is a special bonus that the tale they will hear 'is not a fictional myth but a true story' (26e). As we have seen before, however, Plato often frames his narratives with elaborate explanations of how the detailed account has come down to the present occasion, but this does not generally persuade readers of the complete authenticity of dialogues such as the *Symposium* and the *Theaetetus*. Secondly, the same sort of question arises with the speech of Timaeus: is it to be considered a true account or a symbolic myth, not to be taken literally? There are a number of passages which highlight this uncertainty. In his preamble, Timaeus declares that the eternal and unchanging world of the Forms (or something very like them) must be distinguished from the physical universe, which merely imitates the forms: being must be distinguished from becoming, and different accounts are possible about each. Irrefutable and absolute statements are only possible about the world of being, whereas the world of becoming – the world we know – allows only a 'likely' or 'plausible' account (29, esp. cd). Elsewhere he says that his account is second to none in probability (44cd, 48d, 68d). Other passages defer or decline a fuller discussion, in a manner familiar from earlier dialogues: some aspects would delay them too long (38de, 54ab), others would be beyond their powers, even beyond any human being's (68b-d).[45] Most striking is 59cd: here Timaeus interrupts his description of the compounds of elements to say: 'it would be a simple task to make a list of other similar substances, following our principle of likelihood. And if, for relaxation, one gives up discussing eternal things, it is reasonable and sensible to occupy one's leisure in a way that brings pleasure and no regrets, by considering likely accounts of the world of change. So let us now indulge ourselves and proceed with an account of the probabilities in order.' The language here recalls the passage of the *Phaedrus* in which the philosopher is described as indulging in writing down his ideas as a mere recreation: that sort of pursuit is hardly serious work (*Phdr.* 276d, and context). Again, at the opening of the sequel Critias makes an elaborate comparison of their present activities to those of artists producing likenesses of material familiar to or remote from their audience's experience: obviously the audience will be in a better position to judge the former. So too with their different subjects: Timaeus has been concerned with the divine creation, and 'we are content with faint likenesses when their subjects are celestial and divine, but we criticise narrowly when they are mortal and human' (*Crit.* 107d). Both the analogy of the artist and the repeated references to likeness, probability and myth-making cast doubt

---

[45] Cf. *Rep.* 504bc, 533a; *Phdr.* 246a.

on the truth-value of both Timaeus' and Critias' speeches.[46] The fact that Plato's own pupils seems to have disagreed about the factual content, and many of the details, of the dialogue should also give us pause.[47] The speaker's qualifications may remind the reader of the terms in which Socrates concludes the myth of the afterlife in the *Phaedo*: 'now to make a firm assertion that these things are just as I have recounted would not befit a sensible man. But to suppose that either this, or some such thing is the case about our souls and their habitation, given that the soul is evidently immortal – this, it seems to me, is both fitting and worth the risk' (114d).

If, then, the narrative of Atlantis and the account of the birth of the world are both fabulous or mythical compositions, we must next consider what truths or implications they may convey in their mythical form. On one level, as has already been suggested, the Athens-Atlantis story may carry a political message for fourth-century Athens. Perhaps more significant is the fact that the version of that story in the *Timaeus* anticipates the principal theme of Timaeus' speech, God's foresight and deliberate planning for man. The Egyptian is said to have told Solon that the laws which govern both Egypt and primeval Athens pay close attention to learning, 'deriving from the divine principles of cosmology everything needed for human life down to divination and medicine for our health, and acquiring all other related branches of knowledge' (24bc). Athena founded this whole order and system, she chose the place and climate for Athens (d). According to the *Critias*, the gods look after mankind not by physical force but 'using persuasion as a steersman uses the helm to direct the mind as they saw fit and thus to guide the whole mortal creature' (109c); this passage takes up the important motif of persuasion from the cosmology of the *Timaeus* (48a).[48]

The speech of Timaeus can best be seen against the background of a number of passages elsewhere in Plato in which earlier thinkers are criticised for their inadequate explanations of the cosmos, explanations which are couched in materialist terms, or which describe the 'how' without considering the 'why'.[49] Particularly relevant is the criticism of Anaxagoras in the *Phaedo* (97b-99c).[50] There Socrates describes how excited he was to

---

[46] The passages cited are mostly discussed from a rather different viewpoint by Lloyd, *JHS* 88 (1968) 81-5. The question of the literal truth of the *Timaeus* was tackled in an influential essay by Vlastos, in Allen (ed.) *Studies in Plato's Metaphysics* 401-19. Cf. L. Tarán, in *Essays in Ancient Greek Philosophy* i, ed. J.P. Anton-G.L. Kustas (Albany N.Y. 1971) 372-407; Solmsen ap. North 93. As will by now be clear, I doubt if these discussions lay sufficient weight on the qualifications and undercutting-devices with which Plato habitually surrounds his visionary myths.

[47] Cf. the evidence cited in ch. 1, Appendix B, n. 94.

[48] Cf. Morrow, in Allen, op. cit.

[49] For earlier cosmologies see KRS; D. Furley, *The Greek Cosmologists* i (Cambridge 1987) and *Cosmic Problems* (Cambridge 1989).

[50] Cf. *Soph.* 265c, *Phileb.* 28d, *Laws* 888e-92c; Hamilton-Cairns, *Plato: the collected dialogues* index s.v. universe. Friedlaender iii. 362, 365f. also emphasises the *Phaedo* passage.

learn that Anaxagoras had written a book in which he made Mind or Intelligence the guiding force behind the world, for 'I supposed that in assigning the reason for each individual thing, and for things in general, he'd go on to expound what was best for the individual, and what was the common good for all ...'; but when he actually got hold of this book, he was downcast.

> My wonderful expectation was sadly disappointed, my friend; for when I went and read his book I observed a man who made no use of his 'Intelligence', nor did he attribute to it any responsibility for the organisation of the physical world, but gave that all to airs and ethers and waters and many other strange conceptions. It seemed to me that it was exactly the same with him as if somebody said that Socrates does all he does with his intelligence, and then tried to explain the reasons for everything I do, saying first that I am sitting here now because my body is composed of bones and sinews, and the bones are tough and have natural joints separating them from one another, whereas the sinews are capable of extending and contracting, and they surround the bones together with flesh and skin that holds them all together; so when the bones are lifted up at their own proper junctures, the relaxation and tensing of the sinews makes it somehow possible for me to bend my limbs, and it's for this reason that I am sitting here with my knees bent. And again he would tell a similar tale about the different 'causes' of my talking with you now, ascribing it all to vocal noises and air and hearing-processes and countless other things, failing to mention what are genuinely the causes – namely, that once the Athenians resolved that the preferable course was to vote against me, for that very reason I have resolved in turn that it's better for me to sit here and that my remaining to undergo whatever punishment they may decree is more in accord with justice. For by the dog! in my opinion, these sinews and bones of mine would long since have got as far as Megara or Boeotia, impelled on their way by my judgement of the best course, if I had not thought it more honourable and just to submit to whatever punishment the state might decide, rather than escaping and running away. But to call things like bones and sinews 'causes' is really too absurd. (*Phaedo* 98b-e)

The essential principle of the *Timaeus* is that physical explanations on their own are facile, without the further step of explanation on moral and theological grounds. The universe is an artist's creation, planned with an eye on a perfect model, planned, moreover, with purpose, and designed to fulfil its proper end. The sources and detail of Timaeus' exposition are often complex and obscure, but these fundamental points emerge clearly: the world is good, it is ordered and designed, it is prepared for the good of mankind. Cosmology merges into ethics. Man is a part of a divine and divinely-governed scheme. Moreover, the cosmos itself is a living being, with a 'world soul' (30ab, 34-6), forming a perfect sphere (33b); the heavenly bodies, describing their mathematical patterns, are visible gods moving in accordance with reason. The universe itself also moves, rotating on its axis, circular motion being conceived as the most 'rational' or perfect movement, appropriate to a rational organism (30ab, 34a). Thus the heavens declare the goodness of the universe, the intelligent design of god.[51] The very word 'cosmos' has come to mean 'order', a point already developed with considerable energy by Socrates in the *Gorgias* (508a).[52]

The *Timaeus* looks less freakish, less of an anomaly amongst Plato's works, when seen in the light of his constant preoccupation with finding a proper conception of the gods.[53] As early as the *Euthyphro* Socrates was casting doubt on the traditional myths about immoral and all-too-human gods; in the *Republic* the epic and tragic poets were stripped of their blasphemous utterances and had their most horrifying plots strictly censored; in works such as the *Phaedo* and the *Symposium* an other-worldly, almost mystical form of philosophic religion, much influenced by Orphism and Pythagoreanism, asserts the divinity of the soul and links it with the absolute world of the non-physical and transcendent Forms of beauty, justice, goodness and the rest. In the *Laws* Plato returns to the world as it is, and lays down terrifyingly harsh legislation for the correction and punishment of atheists (book x).[54] The *Timaeus* too seeks to inspire its readers with a more august vision of god: the references to the conventional deities of myth are mostly cursory or tinged with irony (see esp. 40d). Even the attempt to paint a partial picture of so great a subject is fraught with difficulty: in perhaps the most famous sentence in the dialogue, Plato makes Timaeus remark, with superb understatement, that 'it is difficult to find out the father and creator of the universe, and to explain him once found to the multitude is an impossibility' (*Tim.* 28c).[55]

The dialogue does not, however, present a simple picture of all-powerful providence and beneficent determinism. The physical world is a mirror or imperfect copy of the 'real' universe – as good as it can be, but not perfect, for the material which the demiurge used was not perfect. This means that not everything in the universe is wholly subject to reason: there are areas in which reason must come to terms with ('persuade') Necessity (47e-8e). Even the heavens share in this imperfection: while the creator, the demiurge, is immortal, the 'visible and generated gods' who inhabit the earth and heavenly bodies are not: they are potentially perishable, but the will of the demiurge preserves them (41b). Reason and necessity meet in the battleground of man. Man has freedom of will: he may turn his soul towards

---

[51] On the history of this conception see A.S. Pease, 'Caeli enarrant', *HTR* 34 (1941) 163-200. See also R. Parker, in *Apodosis* (Essays ... W. W. Cruickshank) (1992) 84-94, on its pre-Platonic history.

[52] Cf. Vlastos, *Plato's Universe* ch. 1.

[53] Here Solmsen's book *Plato's Theology* remains indispensable; see also V. Goldschmidt, *La religion de Platon* (Paris 1949); D. Babut, *La religion des philosophes grecs* (Paris 1974); Burkert, *Greek Religion* ch. 7, esp. 311-17, 321-9, 332-7. (More bibl. in Burkert 468-9.)

[54] Guthrie v. 256 aptly calls *Laws* 10 'the *logos* to Timaeus's *mythos*'.

[55] On the difficulty of saying anything definite about god cf. Xenophanes B34, Prt. B4, Hdt. ii. 3. 2, Antisth. fr. 40 Caizzi. But see J. Gould in *Greek Historiography* ed. S. Hornblower (Oxford 1994) 93-5, who emphasises that this is the normal Greek attitude: man cannot determine the nature or the will of the gods.

the contemplation of the heavens, through astronomy or the study of musical harmonies; but the appetites and the pleasures of the senses will draw him back to earthly things (as already in the anti-physical outlook of the *Phaedo*).[56] As so often in Plato, proper education is the key.

> Now if a man is engrossed in appetites and ambitions and spends all his pains upon these, all his thoughts must needs be mortal and, so far as that is possible, he cannot fall short of becoming mortal altogether, since he has nourished the growth of his mortality. But if his heart has been set on the love of learning and true wisdom, and he has exercised that part of himself above all, he is surely bound to have thoughts immortal and divine, if he shall lay hold upon truth, nor can he fail to possess immortality in the fullest measure that human nature admits; and because he is always devoutly cherishing the divine part and maintaining the guardian genius that dwells with him in good estate, he must needs be happy above all. Now there is but one way of caring for anything, namely to give it the nourishment and motions proper to it. The motions akin to the divine part in us are the thoughts and revolutions of the universe; these, therefore, every man should follow, and correcting those circuits in the head that were deranged at birth, by learning to know the harmonies and revolutions of the world, he should bring the intelligent part, according to its pristine nature, into the likeness of that which intelligence discerns, and thereby win the fulfilment of the best life set by the gods before mankind both for the present time and for the time to come. (90b-d, tr. Cornford)

The main speech in the *Timaeus* embraces an extraordinary range of subject matter and style, ranging from macrocosm to microcosm, from the cosmically great to the clinically minute: an example of the former might be the passage describing Time as the likeness or mirror-image of Eternity (37c-8c), of the latter the bizarrely technical discussion of the process of taste (e.g. 65b-6c). In this speech Plato draws on many fields which were evolving their own specialised vocabularies: mathematical astronomy, medicine, music, physical chemistry, metallurgy, to name but a few.[57] This is one reason that the *Timaeus* is one of the hardest of all Greek texts to translate; another is the way in which Plato is constantly trying to express in words what would be more easily conveyed by diagrams. Indeed, Timaeus himself remarks that it would be pointless to explore one question (the movement of the planetary bodies) any further without the assistance of visible models (i.e. an orrery), and most readers will already have lost his drift before that point (40d).[58] Given that the work, though of no great

---

[56] *Tim.* 42ab, 44bc, 69cd, 86b-7b; cf. e.g. *Phaedo* 66b-7b, 81-4b.

[57] Cf. Campbell's edition of *Soph.* and *Polit.*, already cited, xxxi: in the 91 pages of *Timaeus* and *Critias* there are 427 words which occur in no other dialogue. Further details in the adjacent pages. See also Thesleff, *Studies in the Style of Plato* 124-5. The view of P. Shorey, *CPh* 23 (1928) 343, that the *Timaeus* is not at all obscure, and contains few passages about which a competent Hellenist would be in doubt, fills me with envy.

[58] For intricate diagrammatic expositions see Cornford, passim; Vlastos, op. cit. 54-7.

length (Timaeus' speech itself is only about 70 pages, shorter than any three books of the *Republic*), is extraordinarily hard to follow in detail, readers who are well aware that the astronomy is outdated, the science bizarre in its wide-ranging inaccuracy, the theology at best founded on some important but unexamined premises, may well feel inclined to set the dialogue on one side.[59]

Such a decision, however understandable, would be profoundly unhistorical. A huge number of ideas basic to the history of European thought were given, if not their first, often their canonical and supremely influential form in Plato's mythical cosmology. We have already mentioned the relation of Time and Eternity (37c-8c), which stimulated lengthy comment from Augustine (*City of God* book 11).[60] Amongst others we may cite: the hierarchy of the heavenly bodies (36b sqq., 38b-e); the music of the spheres (35b sq.); the theory of humours (86e sq.); the sphere as the perfect form (33b-4a);[61] the four primary bodies or elements (fire, air, earth and water) (31b-2c); the structure of the human body as a coherent design, with the head in a justly superior position (so differentiating man from the beasts) (44d-5b, al.); and the concept of a *daimon* or spirit which accompanies us as a guide and protector through life (90a-c). All of these, and the overarching concept of a divinely-shaped universe, coherent and purposeful, have given inspiration and imaginative impetus to countless poets, theorists and thinkers.

The *Timaeus* itself swiftly gained a special place in ancient study of Plato's thought, and in the development of that thought through the Middle Academy and Neoplatonism to the early Christian Platonists and after them the Middle Ages.[62] Aristotle frequently tackles questions Plato had raised (especially in his *de caelo* and *de anima*). Major figures such as Crantor, Posidonius and Plutarch wrote commentaries and studies on the *Timaeus*, as did the Neoplatonist Proclus and many others; Epicurus tried

---

[59] As regards the science of the *Timaeus*, I am unqualified to speak. While I admire the determination with which enthusiastic critics sometimes try to show that Plato's ideas 'anticipated' or are confirmed by modern physics (e.g. Friedlaender i, ch. 11, and esp. P. Shorey, *Proc. Am. Philos. Soc.* 66 (1927) 161ff.), I regard this kind of approach as misconceived. The contrary argument, put forward in an extreme form by B. Farrington, *Greek Science* (1944) and in a modified version by Lloyd and Vlastos, argues that Plato's influence held back the development of science for centuries. On this I agree with Solmsen ap. North 104-5 (who cites some stimulating pages by C.S. Lewis in the epilogue to his splendid book *The Discarded Image* (Cambridge 1964) 216-23).

[60] See further R. Sorabji, *Time, Creation and the Continuum* (London and Ithaca, N.Y. 1983).

[61] Cf. Pease on Cic. *On the nature of the gods* i. 18, ii. 46-9.

[62] It is an intriguing contrast with modern interests that so much effort was devoted to the explication of Timaeus' speech, so little to Critias' account of Atlantis. Even Calcidius translates the earlier part but has no comment to make on it. For the legacy of the story in quite different genres see E. Rohde, *Der Griechische Roman* (ed. 3, 1914) 269-92; E. Gabba, *JRS* 71 (1981) 50-62; J.S. Romm, *The Edges of the Earth in Ancient Thought* (Princeton 1992) esp. ch. 4; F. Graf, *Greek Mythology* (Eng. tr. 1994) 192, on Euhemerus and Dionysius Scytobrachion.

to refute it; Cicero translated it, and a substantial part of his version survives (from 27d to 47b with some breaks); it provides much of the backbone for many 'introductions' to or epitomes of Plato's philosophy composed in later antiquity (e.g. those of Albinus[63] and Apuleius (the whole of book 1, on *Physics*)[64] and the account in Diog. Laert. iii. 69-77).[65] Fame provokes fakes: the central figure of the dialogue, Timaeus of Locri, was given the dubious honour of having an independent work forged in his name some time in the first century AD, which is an inferior paraphrase of the dialogue.[66] At times we may suspect that the very difficulty and obscurity of the dialogue offered a special challenge or a particularly prestigious platform from which to expound one's own thoughts: *omne ignotum pro magnifico*.

The *Timaeus* retained a place among the central Platonic dialogues throughout antiquity; it no doubt helped that rhetorical theory gave a particularly prestigious rank to works treating 'the divine things'.[67] The narrative of creation also enabled readers with Christian leanings to assimilate it to the version in Genesis: in the second century AD the Pythagorean Numenius provocatively asked 'what is Plato but Moses writing in Attic Greek?'[68] Probably in the fifth century AD, Calcidius produced a Latin translation of the first half of the work which, with his vast exegetical commentary, ensured its continuing fame over the next centuries, during which most of Plato's Greek text was unknown in the western world.[69] Directly or indirectly, the dialogue had immense influence on Plotinus, Augustine, Dionysius the Areopagite and Boethius, all of them crucial figures in the intellectual tradition.[70] The highest compliment of all was still in store: in Raphael's *School of Athens*, which at its centre has Plato pointing upwards to the heavens and Aristotle urging the claims of this world, each figure holds one of his own books: in Aristotle's hand is held the *Ethics* (still probably the most widely read of his works), in Plato's

---

[63] J. Dillon, *The Middle Platonists* (London 1977) 267-307. Ed. by P. Louis (Paris 1945); Eng. tr. J. Reedy with intr. by J.P. Hershbell (Grand Rapids, Phanes Press 1992).

[64] Dillon 306-38; cf. new Teubner edn. by C. Moreschini (Stuttgart 1991).

[65] Dillon 408-10.

[66] Edited by W. Marg in H. Thesleff, *The Pythagorean Texts of the Hellenistic Period* (1965) 203ff.

[67] D.C. Innes, *CQ* 29 (1979) 165-71; P. Hardie, *Virgil's Aeneid: Cosmos and Imperium* (Oxford 1986) ch. 1.

[68] Fr. 8 des Places, quoted by Clement and Eusebius; see further H. Chadwick, *Early Christian Thought and the Classical Tradition* (Oxford 1966) ch. 1.

[69] For Calcidius see J. Waszink's massive edition (London and Leiden 1962). See further the fascinating sketch by R. Klibansky, *The Continuity of the Platonic Tradition* (London 1939), one of the few works cited in this book which one might wish longer.

[70] See further R.T. Wallis, *Neoplatonism* (London 1972); A.H. Armstrong (ed.) *Cambridge Hist. of Later Greek and Early Medieval Philosophy* (1967) (note index 1 s.v. Plato, *Timaeus*). Both works have extensive bibliographies. See also P. Shorey, *Platonism Ancient and Modern* (Berkeley 1938); *Platonism and the English Imagination*, ed. A. Baldwin and S. Hutton (Cambridge 1994).

the *Timaeus*. The master artist pays tribute to what was seen as the master work of the great philosopher.[71]

The emphasis of this book has been more on Plato as a writer concerned with people and ideas in this world, and on the ways in which he makes those ideas come to light in the discussions of his characters. But it would be utterly misleading to leave out the side which the *Timaeus* most clearly illustrates: the imaginative vision of a thinker reaching for the heavens, seeking a proper conception of god and man and their relation in the universe. There are signs of this elsewhere, even in the most Socratic works. We have seen the detachment of Socrates from bodily desires in the *Symposium*, mentioned the otherworldliness of the *Phaedo*, and may recall the cosmography which figures in the myth there, as also in the *Republic*'s myth of Er. Other works suggest the attraction Plato found in the Pythagoreans' study of mathematics and music: though at times he makes fun of numerology, as in the calculation that the tyrant is 729 times worse off than the good ruler (*Rep.* 587e), he obviously found the order and regularity of mathematics fascinating, and surely took his lead from them in hypothesising moral absolutes which would be as perfect and permanent.[72] Although in a sense the *Timaeus* does show Plato allowing more importance to the physical world and to man's bodily constitution than in other works, the essential priority of soul over body, moral health over physical, being over becoming, is unaltered. The speech of Timaeus issues a clarion call to mankind: in such a universe, surrounded by such beauty and magnificence, can you fail to follow the path that God has laid out for you? Scientific speculation, religious faith and moral exhortation have seldom been so ambitiously combined.

The *Laws*

Plato's last and longest work cannot easily be summarised: its content is too diverse, its detailed expositions often seem long-winded to the point of obsession, its overall structure and design are hard to fathom. Monumental, obviously important, yet seeming to many unreadable, it stands like a massive testament at the close of Plato's literary career, impossible to ignore yet hard to read with sympathy. In modern times it has largely been abandoned by the philosophers, becoming the province of experts on historical institutions and Greek law. The following discussion does not

---

[71] The fresco, which is to be found in the Vatican, is often reproduced: e.g. by R. Jones and N. Penny, *Raphael* (Yale 1983), pl. 87. The detail showing the titles is shown on the cover of the Penguin Classics translation of *Timaeus* and *Critias*; also in Klibansky, op. cit. pl. 5.

[72] On the Pythagoreans see esp. KRS 214-38, with bibl.; for their influence on Plato see esp. *Rep.* vii. 530d, which actually cites them with reference to celestial music. Full discussion in W. Burkert, *Lore and Science in Ancient Pythagoreanism* (Eng. tr. Cambridge Mass. 1972; originally 1962) esp. 15, 83-96. See also Riginos no. 127, for the biographical dimension.

constitute a serious rehabilitation. All that can be done here is to relate some aspects of this vast work to the rest of Plato's oeuvre, and to suggest some ways of approaching it in literary terms.[73]

The absence of Socrates has already been mentioned; the location of the dialogue in a non-Athenian context must surely be related. Instead, an Athenian, a Spartan and a Cretan are introduced in mid-journey, as they proceed across Crete from Cnossos to the Cave where Zeus was said to have been born. Sparta and Crete were famous in antiquity for their law-codes and law-abiding practice, and Crete itself was said to have produced great lawgivers, notably Minos, himself son of Zeus and according to mythology a Moses-like figure who communed with his father and brought back his pronouncements to become Cretan law (Homer, *Odyssey* 19. 178f., cited on the first page of the *Laws*). The situation is propitious for a discussion of the principles of law and their execution in practice. Later a more specific motive emerges: at the end of book iii we learn that the Cretan, Cleinias, is a member of a commission involved in the establishment of a new foundation, a city to be founded in central Crete, not far from Gortyn, and to be named Magnesia. Although doubtless a fiction, this is not historically absurd: new colonies and settlements were often preferred to allowing a *polis*, of its nature a small community, to become over-large.[74] With this project in view, the proposals and arguments of the Athenian gain in relevance. The earlier books have included preliminaries on (principally) the nature of education, and the rise and decline of historical societies, with particularly interesting passages on the course of Athenian and Persian history.[75] From book iv onward the concern with legal detail markedly increases: after substantial prolegomena we are given prescriptions for the size and organisation of the citizen body, the institutions of government, and minute legislation on marriage, procreation, education (including literature and music, suitably selected), military training, economic organisation, the penal code, religious law, property and the family, restrictions on foreign travel, and much else. The work is far more, however, than a catalogue of crimes and penalties. Theoretical examination of the subject matter is common (notably in the discussion of the

---

[73] The commentary by England (1921) is very dated, and mainly concerned with interpreting the Greek. The French Budé edition (1951-6) has quite full introduction and notes. Saunders' Penguin tr. is invaluable, and is only the most obvious example of the huge contribution this scholar has made to the study of the dialogue over a period of more than thirty years. See further Morrow, Stalley and (in German) Görgemanns; Friedlaender iii. ch. 31. Guthrie v. 321-82 is particularly helpful for lucid orientation; older surveys by Grote ch. 37 (largely summary) and Zeller ch. 13. A very full bibliography has been separately published by Saunders (revised edn. New York 1979).

[74] See e.g. A.J. Graham, *Colony and Mother City in Ancient Greece* (1964, 2nd edn. Chicago 1983).

[75] R. Weil, *L'Archéologie de Platon* (Paris 1959).

theory of punishment in book ix),[76] and extended moral disquisition of a rather austerely didactic kind is prominent throughout – above all in book v, which is almost wholly devoted to an uplifting 'address' imagined as being delivered to the newly selected colonists as they begin the foundation of this brave new state. Individual laws are to be prefaced with preambles or 'proems', that is, explanatory passages which explain to the citizens why the regulations which follow are necessary and just: anything else, according to the Athenian, is unworthy of a real legislator, who should be seen as comparable with a good doctor who makes sure that his patients are fully aware of what his treatment involves, rather than keeping them in the dark (719e-24b).

Although the *Laws* falls into the category of political theory, such divisions are as artificial as elsewhere in Plato's works. Book x is largely theology,[77] and can be seen as continuing the projects of the *Timaeus*, while the lessons drawn from historical states in book iii can be compared with the analysis of constitutions in *Republic* viii and ix, with the broad pseudo-history of the Atlantis passages, and (very much *mutatis mutandis*) with the account of Athenian history in the *Menexenus*. But it is natural that most readers of the work have compared it with the *Republic* and with an intervening dialogue on political subjects, the *Statesman*.[78] Here the issue of Plato's development resurfaces: do the later political writings represent the same views as lay behind the *Republic*, or has the author changed his stand? And if the latter, what stage does the *Statesman* occupy in this process? The dialogues are very different in scale and scope: the *Republic*, to oversimplify, creates a distinctly unusual state as an illustrative analogy for the workings of the human soul, and to show philosophic rule in practice; the *Statesman* uses the elaborate method of subdivision to define a true ruler and a good constitution; the *Laws* envisages the actual foundation of a community and the drawing-up of a detailed law-code on sound moral principles. Hence there are distinct differences of emphasis: *Republic* examines the authority of rulers, *Statesman* of ruler, *Laws* of law. There is some overlap. In *Laws* 708e-12a, the Athenian suspects that a benevolent dictator will be required in order to put the state on a footing which will enable it to function properly; and the ranking of constitutions in 710-11 recalls the discussion in the *Statesman*, though the details differ.[79] But for

---

[76] For the definitive study of this side of the *Laws* see Saunders, *Plato's Penal Code* (Oxford 1991); see also M.M. Mackenzie, *Plato on Punishment* (Berkeley, Los Angeles and London 1981).

[77] See esp. Solmsen, *Plato's Theology*; also n. 53 above.

[78] On the *Statesman* see Skemp's introduction and running comm.; Guthrie v. 163-96. More generally see G. Klosko, *The Development of Plato's Political Theory* (New York and London 1986).

[79] For fuller discussions which compare the *Laws* with earlier works see G. R. Morrow, *Proc. of Americ. Philosoph. Ass.* 27 (1953-4) 5-23; A. Laks, *CAntiq* 9 (1990) 209-29; T.J. Saunders in Kraut (ed.) *Cambridge Companion to Plato* (1992) 464-92.

all the similarities and parallels, the gulf between *Republic* and *Laws* is vast, and whether or not we ascribe the change of heart to Plato's Sicilian experiences (p. 19), it seems clear from the text that the *Laws* enshrines a more realistic, less ambitious project than the vision of the *Republic*. The *Laws* does not begin from a paradox (the philosopher as king), but builds much more on Greek institutions as they are. One passage in particular emphasises that this project is 'second best', and the reader must surely be intended to think of the *Republic*. Magnesia is no Kallipolis.

> You will find the ideal society and state, and the best code of laws, where the old saying 'friends' property is genuinely shared' is put into practice as widely as possible throughout the entire state. Now I don't know whether in fact this situation – a community of wives, children and all property – exists anywhere today, or will ever exist, but at any rate in such a state the notion of 'private property' will have been by hook or crook completely eliminated from life. Everything possible will have been done to throw into a common pool even what is by nature 'my own', like eyes and ears and hands, in the sense that to judge by appearances they all see and hear and act in concert. Everybody feels pleasure and pain at the same things, so that they all praise and blame with complete unanimity. To sum up, the laws in force impose the greatest possible unity upon the state – and you will never produce a better or truer criterion of an absolutely perfect law than that. It may be that gods or a number of the children of gods inhabit this kind of state: if so, the life they live there, observing these rules, is a happy one indeed. And so men need look no further for their ideal: they should keep this state in view and try to find the one that most nearly resembles it. This is what we have put our hand to, and if in some way it could be realised, it would come very near immortality and be second only to the ideal. Later, God willing, we'll describe a third best. But for the moment, what description should we give of this second-best state? (739b8-e, tr. Saunders)[80]

The gap between *Republic* and *Laws* is still more palpable when we consider the dialogues as philosophic or imaginative constructions. The later work is far less challenging in its ideas, and mostly proceeds at a more prosaic and repetitive level of exposition. To the modern eye there is a lack of 'hard' philosophy: the Athenian is not stretching the Spartan and Cretan to their somewhat limited capacities, and the reader will often proceed for pages without meeting anything which looks like a sustained argument. Instead there is much moral high-mindedness, combined with exhortation and ethical assertion – well-exemplified in the imaginary 'speech' to the colonists, already referred to. We find no metaphysical dimension; book x, with its arguments against impiety and atheism, stands out, but is not a full-scale defence of religion (and indeed the arguments for the existence of god in that section, while enormously influential, have provoked bitter

[80] Cf. 807b, 841b, 875b-d.

disappointment among many thinkers). Hence it has been cogently argued that the *Laws* is, in a sense, not a philosophic work at all – at least, not in the way that the *Republic* or the *Parmenides* are. Rather, it is a 'popular' presentation of ethical and political thinking, intended to be read more widely than many of the late dialogues, and perhaps to enlighten, certainly to inspire, both legislators and citizens. This account of the work will explain the prominence of practical detail and the repeated emphasis on fairly straightforward points; it also helps us understand the relative absence of certain features of Platonic 'doctrine' – the Forms, for example.[81] It may even offer a further explanation for the disappearance of Socrates (though, as we saw, this is also part of a general tendency in later Plato): the teachings of the *Laws* are not tied to the principles of a single thinker, and it is appropriate that none of the three speakers should be a practising philosopher.[82] It may seem a paradox that the dialogue which many modern readers have found most repulsive and least readable should be considered a 'popular' work (though as always in dealing with the classical world we must remember that the reading public would have been a fortunate minority of the populace as a whole); but we are of course considering what Plato may have hoped of the book, not the audience that it could genuinely have reached. It must also be remembered that some of the difficulties which we find, particularly of organisation, would probably have been diminished through further revision had Plato lived long enough to apply himself to this. The work as we have it has surely not received the author's final attentions, even if Wilamowitz went too far in describing it as 'an astonishing Chaos'.[83]

The fact that the *Laws* may have been conceived as a more realistic treatment of the political themes of the *Republic* naturally raises the question whether it was also intended to affect real-life politics more directly and with more success. The issue is a delicate one. Generations of scholars have assumed with regard to both works that Plato was sketching serious plans for large-scale political and social reform, and that these were utilised as blueprints by those members of the Academy who were called upon to advise rulers or to draw up constitutions (as Protagoras may have done at Thurii). In a previous chapter it was argued that the project outlined in the *Republic* is sufficiently paradoxical, and its realisation confessedly so remote, that it is unwise to assume that Plato saw himself or any follower as translating these ideas into practical politics. Is the situation different in the *Laws*? Perhaps, since many of the more fantastic aspects of the *Republic* are now abandoned, and many of the institutions

---

[81] Cf. Wilamowitz, *Platon* i. 655, quoted by Guthrie v. 375. That the Forms still lie in the background seems established: see Cherniss, *Riddle* 60, 82f., and *Gnomon* 25 (1953) 375, Görgemanns 218ff.; Friedlaender iii. 442f., 570: Guthrie v. 378-81.

[82] For a detailed account of the Laws along these lines see Görgemanns (cf. Ostwald's review in *Gnomon* 34 (1962) 231-41).

[83] For evidence of incompleteness see Morrow, *Plato's Cretan City*, index s.v. 'Laws, composition of ...; irregularities in'.

and regulations expounded bear a recognisable relation to those known to the Greeks of Plato's own time, and not least to those of Athens.[84] Yet even with the *Laws*, there are qualifications. It is unsafe to identify the Athenian entirely with Plato (although the ancient scholia, and Cicero, *de legibus* i. 15, already assumed this identification). The fact that the project is envisaged as happening in Crete, with Cleinias actively involved, points one way; the fact that no detail is given about the reasons for the foundation, and precious little about its location and other essentials (the opening of book iv is extremely vague), points the other way. The idea of their building 'castles in the air' is implicit in the characteristically Platonic references to their efforts as 'old men's play' (iii. 685a, cf. iv. 712b, vi. 769a1, vii. 820c). The criticism of unreal and idealistic dreaming is half-accepted by the Athenian himself (746), particularly with reference to the limitations on wealth and property, and the geometrical layout of the city.[85] It is also asserted, and repeated in several places, that what they are drafting can only be selective (for all its seeming exhaustiveness), and that their successors as lawmakers will have much to add and amend (745e-6d, 768c-771a, 772ab, 779c; cf. *Statesman* 294e-7b). This might be seen as realistic, although it stands in tension with the detail and minuteness with which certain points are treated. More striking is the way that practical difficulties are ignored, and complex structures imposed on the new community for reasons partly administrative, partly the product of academic ingenuity. For example, the population is to be rigidly fixed at the bizarre number of 5,040 adult males, because that figure can be divided without fractions by every number from two to ten, an advantage for military and organisational purposes. How the citizenry is to be held at that level is far from clear.[86] Other ideas are perhaps only aired *exempli gratia* or undeveloped. We need not overstate the case. It is plain that the proposals in the *Laws* are in many respects applicable to new or existing constitutions, far more so, and much fuller in detail, than those of the *Republic*. But equally important is the assertion of the moral and educational principles on the basis of which detailed legislation should be drafted. Law should be coherent and consistent, not created piecemeal. The legislator is given a short speech in reply to the criticism of fantasy-building in book v.

> My friends, in these talks we're having, don't think it has escaped me either that the point of view you are urging has some truth in it. But I believe that in every project for future action, when you are displaying the ideal plan that ought to be put into effect, the most satisfactory procedure is to spare no detail of absolute truth and beauty. But if you find that one of these details is

---

[84] Morrow documents this in exhaustive detail; for contrary arguments see Brunt, *Studies* 245-81. See also D. Clay, 'Plato's Magnesia', in *Nomodeiktes*, Fest. M. Ostwald, ed. R.M. Rosen and J. Farrell (Ann Arbor, Michigan) 435-46.

[85] For the latter cf. Friedlaender i, ch. 17 on Atlantis.

[86] For many other criticisms and sceptical comments see Brunt, art. cit.

impossible in practice, you ought to put it on one side and not attempt it: you should see which of the remaining alternatives comes closest to it and is most nearly akin to your policy, and arrange to have that done instead. But you must let the legislator finish describing what he really wants to do, and only then join him in considering which of his proposals are feasible, and which are too difficult. You see, even the maker of the most trivial object must make it internally consistent if he is going to get any sort of reputation. (746 b-d, tr. Saunders).

This principle surely applies to the *Laws* as a whole.

We must now turn to the literary texture of the dialogue.[87] Notoriously, the *Laws* offers much less scope to the critic who looks for the flexibility of style, the cut-and-thrust of humorous argumentative exchange, which charms so many readers of Plato's earlier works. The relationship between the three speakers does not change: throughout, the Athenian is the authoritative figure, and the other two follow his lead, with only occasional dissent or surprise (much more often, enthusiastic approval). There are no sudden interventions by others, and the environment makes little impact on their lengthy stroll. There is considerable evidence that the dialogue structure itself is weakening:[88] long expositions are common, with the exchange of speeches suspended. Apart from the last two lines of the book, book v is entirely a lecture by the Athenian, and there are other speeches by him which go uninterrupted for almost as long. There are a few touches of characterisation which enliven the Spartan's and the Cretan's reactions, but these tend to be rather obvious, usually expressions of patriotic loyalty to their own ways, or references to national characteristics such as Laconian brevity.[89] Similarly, the ethics of dialectic and mutual criticism are not forgotten, despite the absence of Socrates; but again the references to these topics often seem perfunctory,[90] and the conversation as a whole involves little intellectual input from anyone but the Athenian. The humour of the dialogue is incidental (though there is a good deal of etymologising wordplay),[91] and has been described even by a sympathetic reader as 'elephantine'.[92]

What can be said in a more positive strain? Although we miss the memorable set-pieces which were typical of Plato at the peak of his powers – episodes such as the violent speech by Callicles on the superman, the parable of the prisoners in the cave, or the dazzling and thought-provoking

---

[87] There is little in the secondary literature, and I can attempt only a broad sketch here. See further Saunders, bibl. pp. 10-12; Thesleff, *Studies in the Styles of Plato* and *Arktos* 7 (1972) 219-27. The recent paper by A. Nightingale, *CPh* 88 (1993) 279-300 breaks fresh ground.

[88] For passages which comment on or otherwise relate to the structure and design of the work see 673d, 674c, 682e, 722cd, 732e, 734e, 832b, 858a, 890e, 907c.

[89] 638a, 641e-2e, 667a, 673b, 680c, 721e, 806c, 818e, 819d, 892e-3a.

[90] E.g. 633a, 635a, 667a9-10, 963d.

[91] E.g. 654a, 713e-4a, 957c, cf. 836e.

[92] Saunders, Penguin tr., intr. p. 39.

images of the charioteer in the *Phaedrus*, and the aviary in the *Theaetetus* – there is nevertheless much eloquence in the *Laws*. The modern reader finds it hard to respond to sermonising, however high-minded and lofty in style. But we should at least recognise that the style of the *Laws* is not homogeneous. The detailed exposition of legal provisions is one thing, the persuasive rhetoric of the preambles another;[93] on a still higher plane are the large-scale exhortations in book v, the passionate efforts to convert the atheist to true beliefs in book x, and other passages where the Athenian's emotions seem to be fully engaged and where fundamental choices between good and bad states of mind or conditions of society are involved. We need not (and are unlikely to) endorse the values of the Athenian wholesale, and it is obvious that few moderns would willingly accept an offer of citizenship in his supposed Utopia. But in literary terms there are many passages in the work which show us more clearly than elsewhere in the corpus the deep seriousness of Plato's discontent with Greek society and its priorities. The task of the lawgiver must be to contain mortal weakness and passion:

> If you neglect the rule of proportion and fit excessively large sails to small ships, or give too much food to a small body, or too high authority to a soul that doesn't measure up to it, the result is always disastrous. Body and soul become puffed up: disease breaks out in the one, and in the other arrogance quickly leads to injustice ... The mortal soul simply does not exist, my friends, which by dint of its natural qualities will ever make a success of supreme authority among men while it is still young and responsible to no one. Full of folly, the worst of diseases, it inevitably has its judgement corrupted, and incurs the enmity of its closest friends; and once that happens, its total ruin and the loss of all its power soon follow. A first class lawgiver's job is to have a sense of proportion and to guard against this danger. (691cd, tr. Saunders)

Other instances might be cited: for example, 716 (response to Protagoras: not man but God is the measure of all things),[94] 782-3 (basic human drives), 903b sq. (arguments directed to the young unbeliever), and 948b sq., on the importance of oaths and the enormity of perjury. The keynote of the dialogue is struck by this mixture of severity and deep concern for the consequences of popular error. Such themes are too serious, for a Plato now in his seventies, to be handled with the whimsy and light-heartedness of the early to middle dialogues.

A countering tone may nevertheless be detected, which seems more sympathetic, though still remote, to the modern reader suspicious of state omnipotence and official ideologies. This may loosely be described as religious pessimism. We have just seen that Plato re-emphasises a point implicit throughout his literary career, that God, not man, is the measure of all things. That proposition might lead to various consequences: exultant

---

[93] Cf. Cic. *Leg*. ii. 6, who refers to these preambles as encomia of the laws concerned.
[94] Cf. *Cratyl*. 386a sq., and the discussion of Prt. B1 in the *Theaetetus* (152a sq., 160d sq. etc.).

confidence in divine providence, reverential awe, devout submission. In several passages Plato makes the Athenian dwell not only on human weakness, but on man's smallness and triviality in comparison with god. A famous image captures this: 'let us imagine that each of us living beings is a puppet of the gods. Whether we have been constructed to serve as their plaything, or for some serious reason, is something beyond our ken, but what we certainly know is this: we have these emotions in us, which act like cords or strings and tug us about; they work in opposition, and tug against each other ...' (644de). Again, in a later passage, the image recurs ('men are puppets mainly, and have in them only a very little of reality'), and the Spartan complains 'you are making out that the human race is very small', to which the Athenian replies: 'Don't be surprised, Megillos, but pardon me. You see, I was looking to God, and that was why I was moved to say what I just did. All right then, if you wish, let this human race of ours be not small, but deserving of a little seriousness' (804b).[95] A further passage expresses pessimism about human nature even in the hypothetical law-abiding state (ix. 853b sq.) 'unlike the ancient legislators, we are not framing laws for heroes and sons of gods. The lawgivers of that age, according to the story told nowadays, were descended from gods and legislated for men of similar stock. But we are human beings, legislating in the world of today for the children of humankind ... powerful as our laws are, they may not be able to tame such people, just as heat has no effect on tough beans. For their dismal sake, the first law I will produce will deal with robbery from temples, in case anyone dares to commit this crime ...' We are reminded of the passage in book viii of the *Republic* which follows on the crowning vision of the philosopher's ascent to apprehension of the Good, and which introduces the gloomy tale of the inevitable decline of the perfect society (*Rep.* 546a sq.). Alongside the passion for systematic legislation goes a melancholy realisation that all such achievements seem to be imperfect and inadequate, doomed to be overthrown in time. Similarly, we learn from the historical sections of the early books that successful armies are defeated, great states enter a decline, and in the long perspective of world history civilisations are ruined by natural catastrophe, again and again.[96] Whatever the weaknesses of the *Laws*, the work is not based on facile optimism.

The *Laws* has an enormous amount to offer to the student of Greek society, culture, institutions, attitudes, religion, even economics. The greatest living authority on the dialogue has claimed in a recent essay that 'all human life is in it'.[97] While this may seem exaggerated, it is on the right lines; but the very inclusiveness of the work makes it hard to sum up or

---

[95] Rightly stressed by Dodds, *Greeks and the Irrational* 214f. On the puppet image see H.D. Rankin, *Eranos* 60 (1962) 127-31.

[96] 638a, 676bc, and esp. 677-9; cf. *Statesman* 273a, *Timaeus* 22c-e, *Critias* 109de, and Guthrie, *In the Beginning* (London 1957) 65-9.

[97] Saunders in Kraut, *Companion* 486n.26.

view as a whole. In some ways it is more accessible to a reader pursuing a particular theme through its tortuous and digressive structure – the importance of motive in crime, for example, or the role of the festival in Greek civic life. Its importance for the understanding of the ubiquitous role of religion in the classical city-state has recently been brought out in authoritative works, and need not be retailed here.[98] In the remaining pages four topics which are clearly germane to this book's themes will be briefly treated. Two of them (symposia and homosexuality) show a narrowing or rigidifying of attitude in Plato in his old age, while the other two (the arts and myth) perhaps present a more complex relationship between the *Laws* and what has gone before.

1. The first two books of the *Laws* are preliminary, and the third moves on to an entirely different topic; we may suspect that some connecting material had still to be written, for a promised discussion of gymnastics is lacking. While some of the material in these two books is of obvious importance as preliminary ground-clearing (particularly the exposure of Spartan-Cretan law as inadequate), it is much harder to see why the Athenian makes so much of the symposium and its potential educational role (a notion greeted by the others with incredulity).[99] Drinking-parties dominate two longish sections of the conversation, and the Athenian more than once half-apologises for the time spent on this apparently trivial subject (645c, 890e). At the end of book ii some justification is offered: the symposium is one case which stands as a paradigm of the need for the state to organise the pleasures of its citizens, and impose habits of moderation, and so the drinking party is to be regulated by an older supervising figure in the role of symposiarch. We may see this as paradigmatic in another way: it exemplifies the way in which Plato here adapts the institutions of everyday life rather than rejecting them. A firmer structure is imposed, but the Athenian legislates by building on what is there.

The contrast between the hypothesised symposium of the *Laws* and the occasion commemorated in the *Symposium* is very marked. We hear nothing here of competition or stylish oratory, still less of philosophy. The legislator's concern will be to restrain the appetites of the young while also observing their weaknesses and moral tendencies in their cups – *in vino veritas*, as Alcibiades observed and as his conduct illustrated (649d-50b, cf. *Smp.* 217e). Medical and psychological theories are also invoked, in book i to analyse the reduction of inhibitions and shame when wine is imbibed, in book ii to assist analysis of the benefit which will be gained from reducing the embarrassment of the elderly and encouraging them to sing and dance

[98] See Burkert, *Greek Religion* 332-7, and C. Sourvinou-Inwood, in O. Murray and S.R.F. Price (ed.) *The Greek City* (Oxford 1990) 295-322, and *Annali Ist. orientale di Napoli: Archeologia e storia antica* 10 (1988). See also Morrow ch. 8; O. Reverdin, *La Religion de la cité platonicienne* (Paris 1945).
[99] Unpublished work by M. Tecusan sheds much light on these sections of the *Laws*; see also her paper in *Sympotica*, ed. O. Murray (Oxford 1990) 238-60. I abstain from giving larger bibliography here, in view of the lavish lists in Murray's collection.

in honour of Dionysus at festive occasions – a grotesque picture which amuses most readers and may be partly composed tongue in cheek.[100] The essential point in both books is that symposia, in classical Athens traditionally a private form of male interaction and entertainment (sometimes a focus for conspiracy), are to be harnessed for the good of the state, institutionalised and controlled. Traditional aristocratic ideals of older friends or lovers instructing and improving the young (e.g. Theognis and Cyrnus) are updated and transformed, being combined with a more disturbing system whereby young men will be watched for their potential flaws – effectively, spied on – while intoxicated and off-guard.

2. Even before the discussion turns to symposia, the Athenian raises objections to the similar institution of the common mess or *syssition*, found among Spartans and Cretans.[101] These, along with gymnastic training, not only encourage association for revolutionary conspiracy, but also promote homosexuality, which the Athenian describes as unnatural and corrupt. This critical and negative attitude, astonishing to a reader fresh from the *Symposium* and the *Phaedrus*, recurs in a later and longer discussion in book viii, where the Athenian's objections are supported by a series of would-be arguments from what is 'natural'. Our knowledge of Plato's biography and psychology is insufficient to justify speculation on the reasons for his change of attitude, but the force of this passage seems too great to be explained only by a concern for orderly upbringing or for the need to promote marital stability and procreation. The vigour – one might almost say viciousness – of the passage is as startling as the counter-measures are extreme.

> You would argue that a man may have sexual intercourse with a woman but not with men or boys. As evidence for your view, you'd point to the animal world, where the males do not have intercourse with one another, because such a thing is unnatural. (836cd)

> [The lawgiver must take steps to surround this action with the kind of taboos which currently attach to incest:] ... the doctrine that 'these acts are absolutely unholy, an abomination in the sight of the gods and that nothing is more revolting'. We refrain from them because we never hear them spoken of in any other way. From the day of our birth each of us encounters a complete unanimity of opinion wherever we go; we find it not only in comedies but often in the high seriousness of tragedy too, when we see a Thyestes on the stage, or an Oedipus or a Macareus, the secret lover of his sister. We watch these characters dying promptly ... I said I knew of a way to put into effect this law of ours which permits the sexual act only for its natural purpose, procreation, and forbids not only homosexual relations, in which the human race is deliberately murdered, but also the sowing of seed on rocks and stone ... (838bc, e; cf. 841bc)

[100] For a standard reaction see Guthrie v. 328-9; on 382 he cites Saunders as detecting humour in this section.
[101] See further E. David, *AJP* 99 (1978) 486-95.

Some concession is made in the area of male-female relations, in that the Athenian allows that it will almost certainly be impossible to eradicate adultery completely; but if it is to be practised, it must be done in private and secretly, hidden from any other man and woman, and exposure will lead to deprivation of civic rights. But 'unnatural' love, in his opinion, should be eliminated entirely. The authority of Plato has made this text a sadly influential justification of repressive legislation in more recent times.[102]

3. In the *Republic* Socrates spoke of the ancient quarrel between poetry and philosophy (x. 607b sq.; cf. *Laws* xii. 967c).[103] There, the chief emphasis lay on censorship and on the potential dangers of the poet's influence; we heard little of any positive role for him in the ideal state beyond the specification of his chief tasks: hymns to the gods and encomia of good men (607a; cf. *Laws* 801-2). In the *Laws*, in line with the general tendency to greater practicality and greater attention to the social community, we hear a good deal more about the precise ways in which poetry, along with music, dancing and choral performance, can make a contribution to society. Poets are now permitted to exist, but rigidly controlled. The identity of justice and happiness is to be embodied in the words, rhythms and harmonies that they prepare for public performance (ii. 661c, 662b). They will be allowed to compose nothing that conflicts with the ethical standards laid down by the authorities, and no work may be published without the approval of the Guardians of the Laws and the appointed assessors (801b sq.). The conventional receptiveness of the general public to all the supposedly great poetry of old is unacceptable (810e-12a). Censorship must be imposed, or both the poets and their audiences will be corrupted (ii. 655-6, 659c). The poet must feed the audience good medicine; if the lawgiver cannot persuade him, he will use compulsion (659e-60a). Nor can just anyone become a poet: the singers for specific occasions will be selected from a specified age range (829cd). Comedy, perhaps the moralist's most frequent bugbear, will be regulated with special care: 'no composer of comedies, or of songs or iambic verse, must ever be allowed to ridicule either by description or impersonation any citizen whatever, with or without rancour' (xi. 935e). Illustrative and ornamental quotations are not infrequent in the *Laws*,[104] but there is a strong tendency to challenge the author quoted, and imagined exchanges with poets, insisting that they accept criticism and listen to reason, are not infrequent (i. 629b sq., with Tyrtaeus; see further 858e). Yet the familiar names are still favoured: Homer and Hesiod are said to appeal to older men,

---

[102] See further Dover, *Greek Homosexuality* 165-70, also treating Aristotle. A forthcoming paper by G. de Ste. Croix further documents Plato's importance in the history of sexual prejudice.

[103] For bibliogr. on Plato and the arts see ch. 8. iii above. For the *Laws* there is much of relevance in Morrow ch. 7.

[104] See further an unpublished paper by S. Halliwell, 'The subjection of muthos to logos: Plato's citations of the poets'.

and Homer is the most profound genius amongst the poets (658d, 776e). The achievements of the poets are recognised but devalued: pleasure is not admissible as the criterion for judging literature, and the poets have little else. Certainly they must not expect to be treated seriously as 'teachers' or moralists on the same plane as the legislator (858c-e, 957d; cf. *Rep.* x. 599c-600e).

Although the poetic flame may now burn low in Plato's imagination, the relation of his own work to poetry still seems to bother him. Throughout the *Laws*, whenever the Athenian returns to the subject, we seem to catch a glimpse of the author's deep distrust of, yet fascination with, the power of the poet. In a sense he presents the lawgiver as his rival – not so much because the 'creation' of the new state has a fantastic element about it which puts it in a similar epistemological category to poetry (though there are passages which suggest that this is intermittently in his mind)[105] – but still more because he is claiming the didactic authority which had tradi- tionally belonged to the poet.[106] The laws make men good, as the Greeks generally believed.[107] Plato also holds that the *Laws* itself, the legal code and perhaps the work before us, will be an education to men.

> But what about our 'serious' poets, as they're called, the tragedians? Suppose some of them were to come forward and ask us some such question as this: 'Gentlemen, may we enter your state and country or not? And may we bring our work with us? Or what's your policy on this point?' What would be the right reply for us to make to these inspired geniuses? This, I think: 'Most honoured guests, we are ourselves the authors of a tragedy, and that the finest and best which we can create. At any rate, our entire state has been con- structed so as to be a "representation" of the finest and noblest life, the very thing we maintain is most genuinely a tragedy. So we are poets like your- selves, composing in the same genre, and your competitors as artists and actors in the finest drama, which true law alone has the power to produce to perfection – of that, we are quite confident. So do not run away with the notion that we shall ever allow you to set up stage in the market-place and bring on your actors whose fine voices will carry further than ours. Do not think that we shall let you declaim to women and children and the general public, and talk about the same practices as we do but treat them differently – indeed, more often than not, so as virtually to contradict us. We should be altogether insane, and so would any state as a whole, to let you go ahead as we have described before the authorities had decided whether your work was fit to be recited and suitable for public performance or not.' (817a-d; cf. further 811c-12a, 964c)

No other passage brings home so paradoxically the philosopher's conviction that imaginative power is nothing unless backed up by knowledge of morality.

[105] Cf. p. 301 above. See also 769a-c for the analogy between the legislator and the painter.
[106] E.g. 858c-9b, 957c-e.
[107] See e.g. Macleod, *Collected Essays* 28n.39.

4. Finally, myth. The *Laws* includes no full-scale myth like those of the *Gorgias* and *Republic* x, although Plato had used such a passage in the middle of a dialogue as lately as the *Statesman*. The historical material in book iii, which naturally includes some unhistorical elaboration, heightening the moral, perhaps serves some of the purposes of a myth: the *Statesman* again anticipates that development, in that it offers a narrative about the remote past rather than of another world or afterlife. But myth of a more traditional type figures in the *Laws* as well. We can discern Plato's continued preoccupation with how myth can or should be used, how it can be subordinated to (or tamed by) rational thought. Least interesting are cases where stories from epic and tragedy are used casually to illustrate a point (e.g. Theseus and Hippolytus, 687e; Patroclus, 944a). Some routine censorship still appears, in the manner of books ii and iii of the *Republic*. It is quite wrong to suppose that the gods take things by deception and force: no one should assume, because of the lies of poets and storytellers, that he has *carte blanche* to be a thief or a mugger (941b).[108] Or again, it is wrong to suppose that Bacchus ever went mad because of Hera and that this is why he inflicted drink on mankind: 'this sort of story I leave to those who see no danger in speaking of the gods in such terms' (672b). Another approach utilises myth for salutary purposes. It is amazing, remarks the Athenian, what men can be led to believe, as the common acceptance of the tale of Cadmus sowing the dragon's teeth which then sprang up as armed men will show (663d sq.). In view of this, the legislator should not shrink from telling a lie which is in the interest of the young (we remember the 'noble lie' justifying the class divisions in the *Republic*). The passage which recommends shrouding homosexuality in the same cloak of guilt as incest falls into this category (838c, quoted above). Elsewhere we may feel less sure whether the Athenian or his creator is to be seen as accepting an ancient tradition because it is expedient or because it is true: on some topics, such as the guilt of the murderer, the power of the parent to curse a son who insults him, or the punishment which will come upon the temple-robber or the oath-breaker, we may suspect that Greek feeling was so strong that Plato might be prepared to accept traditional belief on his own behalf and not just for the good of the majority. Certainly he dwells on the 'myth' of vengeance exacted by the gods from a killer with remarkable emphasis (865d, 870de, 872d-3a).

Within the vast span of the *Laws* the most extensive account of what must rank for us as 'myth', though for Plato it was supported by reason, comes in the tenth book, which defends the principles that the gods exist, that they care for this world and for mankind, and that they have designed the world, which is therefore not the product of chance or accident. We at once recognise continuity with the ideas of the *Timaeus*. Here we have

---

[108] For the type of argument (gods do it, so why can't I?) see Eur. *Hipp.* 451ff., Ar. *Clouds* 1079-82; rather differently, *Heracles* 1318ff.; Dover, *GPM* 76.

argument rather than mythic exposition, and the implied audience is the 'heretic', the impious man who questions the existence or the impartiality of the gods. Much in Plato's treatment here is directed not at the ordinary unbeliever but at particular schools of thought, and the polemical slant diminishes its effect for later readers. But there are also passages in which, however much we may question the arguments, something of the imaginative grandeur of his cosmic deism comes through even to the modern sceptic. Here the philosopher both longs for the innocence of myth and draws upon its rich poetic roots.

> You see, one inevitably gets irritable and annoyed with these people who have put us to the trouble, and continue to put us to the trouble, of composing these explanations. If only they believed the stories which they had as babes and sucklings from their nurses and mothers![109] These almost literally 'enchanting' stories were told partly for amusement, partly in full earnest; the children heard them related in prayer at sacrifices, and saw acted representations of them – a part of the ceremony a child always loves to see and hear; and they saw their own parents praying with the utmost seriousness for themselves and their families in the firm conviction that their prayers and supplications were addressed to gods who really did exist. At the rising and setting of the sun and moon the children saw and heard Greeks and foreigners, in happiness and misery alike, all prostrate at their devotions; far from supposing gods to be a myth, the worshippers believed their existence to be so sure as to be beyond suspicion. (x. 887c-e)

> Seeing all this he [God] contrived a place for each constituent where it would most easily and effectively ensure the triumph of virtue and the defeat of vice throughout the universe. With this grand purpose in view he has worked out what sort of position, in what regions, should be assigned to a soul to match its changes of character; but he left it to the individual's acts of will to determine the direction of those changes. You see, the way we react to particular circumstances is almost invariably determined by our desires and our psychological state ... So all things that contain soul change, the cause of their change lying within themselves, and as they change they move according to the ordinance and law of destiny. Small changes in unimportant aspects of character entail small horizontal changes of position in space, while a substantial decline into injustice sets the soul on the path to the depths of the so-called 'under' world which men call Hades and similar names, and which haunts and terrifies them both during their lives and when they have been sundered from their bodies ... And in spite of your belief that the gods neglect you, my lad, or rather young man, 'This is the sentence of the gods that dwell upon Olympus'[110] – to go to join worse souls as you grow worse and better souls as you grow better, and alike in life and all the deaths you suffer to do and be done by according to the standards applied by like to like. Neither you

[109] Cf. the 'old-wives' tales' approved by Socrates in *Grg.* 512e, 527a (cf. M. Massaro, *Stud. Ital. Filol. Class.* 49 (1977) 104-35); more complex than these is the revisionist myth-making of *Statesman* 268d-70a.
[110] This is a quotation from Homer (*Od.* 19. 43), but with the sense changed, the tone made more solemn.

nor anyone else who has got into trouble will ever be able to run fast enough
to boast that he has escaped this sentence ... Make yourself ever so small and
hide in the depths of the earth, or soar high into the sky: this sentence will
be ever at your heels, and either while you're still alive on earth or after you've
descended into Hades or been taken to some even more remote place, you will
pay the proper penalty for your crimes ... (904b-5b, with omissions)

Myth is moralised, combined with physics, astronomy and psychology. The
results do not convince: the assumptions which the reader is required to
make are too large and significant, and the shadow of many centuries of
religious persecution makes us shudder at the ruthlessness with which the
Athenian establishes the judges and lays down the penalties for the impiety
trials of his new state. The *Timaeus*, though still resting on an archaic
science and an outmoded astronomy, appeals to us more because it is set
apart from historical events or potential victims: Timaeus' hearers, unlike
the imagined heretic, are willing listeners with the freedom to disagree if
they chose. But the *Laws* here shows us in its final form the results of
Plato's prolonged wrestlings with the mythical vision of the universe,
perhaps first glimpsed in the *Euthyphro*'s mischievous puzzling over the
relation between moral action and action which is approved by the gods. It
would be saddening to end this study on such a sombre note. One last
quotation may remind us that, even quite late in his career, he could leaven
solemnity with subtlety, myth with mirth:

Such, then, is the life of the gods. As for the other souls, the one which follows
a god most closely and resembles him raises its charioteer's head up into the
region beyond, and is carried round in the cycle, bewildered by the violent
movements of the horses and hardly able to perceive reality. At one moment
it is up, at another down, and as the horses struggle along it sees some things
but misses others. The other souls which are following in its wake, eager to
see the realm above but unable to do so, are carried along below the surface,
trampling and bumping into their neighbours, each trying to get ahead of the
other. There is confusion and competition and terrible sweat, and in the
course of this many souls are lamed through the bad horsemanship of their
drivers, and many damage their wings. But all of them depart, after much
hardship, without being fully admitted to behold reality, and once they depart
they resort to feeding on fancy. And it is for this reason they feel a tremendous
eagerness to discern where lies the plain of truth: it is from that meadow that
the proper sustenance comes for the best part of the soul, and the natural
strength of the wings, which give lightness to the soul, are fostered on that
fodder. And this is the edict of Necessity: whatsoever soul while in the
company of god has seen anything of true being, shall go unscathed until the
next cycle, and if it can continue always in that condition, it will be forever
free from harm. But whenever a soul which has been unable to follow and did
not see truth, then encounters some mishap and is weighed down, being filled
with forgetfulness and evil, and because of that weight loses its wings and
plummets earthwards – the law for a soul in that condition is that it does not
grown into any bestial state on its first rebirth, but rather, the soul which saw
most shall be reborn in a man who is to become a lover of wisdom or a lover

of beauty or an artistic and erotic type; the second in rank shall be born as a law-abiding king or a warlike and commanding character, the third shall become a statesman or an estate manager or a business-man ... (*Phaedrus* 248a-d)

Most readers of Plato today, at least in the West, do not believe in reincarnation; nor is astral religion part of our consciousness, any more than a divine geometrician and watchmaker. But there are imaginative truths as well as doctrinal, and throughout his career Plato shows his ability to move between the presentation, often humorous, sometimes saddening, occasionally despairing, of what man is, and the prospect of what he could aspire to be. Different works, and different parts of the same works, present the boldest and most creative vision of human potential, together with crushing pessimism about the likelihood of this potential ever being fully developed, human nature and human society being what they are. This tension between the ideal and the real, utopia and anarchy, philosophical revelation and worldly blindness, may well be what remains most vividly in the reader's memory after study of some of his greatest works. Fundamental to Plato's thought, this conflict is ceaselessly explored and illuminated by his art.

Appendix: the plan of the *Laws*

For a fuller analysis see the contents-page to T.J. Saunders's Penguin translation, or the introductions to the French Budé edition.

Book i. After some preliminaries, analysis of the objects aimed at by Spartan and Cretan laws; the limits of courage as a goal; drinking parties and their uses; purposes of education, and how symposia can help.

Book ii. The arts and their role in education; need for censorship and control. More discussion of symposia.

Book iii. What can be learned from history; early societies and their failures; Persia and Athens, and how they have been corrupted. Cleinias reveals his involvement in the establishment of a new colony in Crete.

Book iv. The new colony described; the colonists and foundation; the need for supremacy of law; the legislator's procedure must involve preambles explaining the rationale behind each law.

Book v (no dialogue; continuous exposition by the Athenian). General preamble to the code of laws as a whole. Importance of the soul; other moral duties. The founding of the new state: practical considerations, including size of population, size of property, property-classes.

Book vi. The administration. Guardians of the Laws; military officials; Council; other officials; country-wardens, city-wardens, minister of education. Law-courts. Marriage, procreation, etc.

Book vii. Education of the young, from the womb to adulthood. Prescriptions include rules on music and literature, dancing, sport and mathematical training.

Book viii. Sport and military training. Rules on sexual conduct (including discouragement of 'unnatural' conduct). Self-control. Farming, supplies and trade.

Book ix. Penalties incurring the death-penalty (sacrilege, subversion, treason). Theory of punishment. Law on homicide and assault.

Book x. Religion and impiety. Arguments against atheism.

Book xi. Law of property. Commercial law. Families (wills, inheritance, orphans, divorce, etc.). Various other legislation.

Book xii. Further miscellaneous legislation. The 'scrutineers'. Relations with abroad; limitations on foreign travel. The composition and duties of the Nocturnal Council; course of training for its members.

Bibliography

A. Editions, commentaries and translations

The standard edition of the Greek text of Plato has long been the five-volume Oxford Classical Text edited by J. Burnet; a completely new edition by several hands is underway, but as of 1994 only the first volume is even advertised. Other complete editions include the Loeb Classical Library, with facing translations; the French Budé edition consists of parallel Greek and French versions, with long introductions, many of them valuable.

There are Penguin Classics translations of almost all of Plato's works; many are also translated with useful notes in the Hackett Library (Indianapolis). The one-volume anthology *Plato: the collected dialogues* ed. E. Hamilton and H. Cairns (Princeton, Bollingen series 1961) is invaluable (omitting only a few works which are probably spurious), and has a helpful thematic index.

What follows is a list of commentaries, annotated translations, and special studies on particular works (usually keyed to a Greek text unless otherwise stated), arranged in the traditional order devised by ancient scholars and followed, despite its defiance of chronology, in modern complete editions. Where no other edition is cited, students should consult the Loeb or Budé editions; also useful for bibliography are the relevant parts of Guthrie *HGP* vols. iv-v, Friedlaender ii-iii. Since there are so many translations of Plato's most popular works, I have generally cited only those which offer especially full notes and/or introductory matter.

Euthyphro J. Burnet (with *Apology* and *Crito*, Oxford 1924)
Apology J. Riddell (Oxford 1867); J. Burnet, see *Euthyphro*; E. de Strycker and S.R. Slings (Leiden 1994). A commentary by M.C. Stokes is expected
Crito J. Burnet, see *Euthyphro*. See also R. Kraut 1984 [for references in this form consult Section C below]
Phaedo J. Burnet (Oxford 1911); C.J. Rowe (Cambridge 1993). See also running commentaries on translations by R. Hackforth (Cambridge 1955) and R. S. Bluck (London 1955); D. Gallop (transl. and philosophical comm., Oxford, Clarendon Plato series 1975)
Cratylus J.C. Rijlaarsdam (Utrecht 1978). For further bibl. see Baxter 1992
Theaetetus L. Campbell (2nd edn., Oxford 1883); F.M. Cornford, *Plato's Theory of Knowledge* (tr. and running comm. on both *Tht.* and *Sophist*, London 1935). The 'introduction' by M. Burnyeat to Levett's tr. in the Hackett library (Indianapolis 1990) runs to more than 200 pages and is a running commentary in itself
Sophist See above on *Tht.*; also L. Campbell (with *Statesman*, Oxford 1867). A commentary by L. Brown is eagerly anticipated
Statesman ('Politicus') Campbell (see above on *Sophist*); J.B. Skemp (intr., tr., running comm., London 1952)

Parmenides F.M. Cornford, *Plato and Parmenides* (tr. and running comm. London 1939)

Philebus R.G. Bury (Cambridge 1897); R. Hackforth, *Plato's examination of pleasure* (tr. with running comm. Cambridge 1945); J.C.B. Gosling (tr. and philosophical comm., Oxford, Clarendon Plato series, 1975)

Symposium R.G. Bury (Cambridge 1932); K.J. Dover (Cambridge 1980). The World's Classics translation by R. Waterfield (Oxford 1993) has a good intr. and bibl.

Phaedrus W.H. Thompson (London 1868); G.J. de Vries (Amsterdam 1969); C.J. Rowe (Aris and Phillips 1986). Less satisfactory is the running comm. on translation by R. Hackforth (Cambridge 1952)

Alcibiades I No modern commentary, but a useful study, with bibl., by J. Annas, in O'Meara 1985

Alcibiades II No modern comm.

Hipparchus No modern comm.

Lovers (Amatores, Erastai; also sometimes called 'The Rivals') (almost certainly spurious) No modern comm.

Theages (probably spurious) No modern comm. See Tarrant 1958

Charmides No modern comm.

Laches No modern comm., but see Stokes 1986

Lysis No modern comm. See D. Bolotin, *Plato's dialogue on friendship* (London 1979), incl. translation; D.B. Robinson, *ICS* 11 (1986) 63-84; Price 1989, ch. 1

Euthydemus E.W. Gifford (Oxford 1905); R.S.W. Hawtrey (intr. and notes only; Philadelphia 1981)

Protagoras A.M. and J. Adam (Cambridge 1921). Translations with notes by M. Ostwald (intr. by G. Vlastos) (New York 1956); B. Hubbard and E.S. Karnofsky (London 1982: an unusual work, with 'Socratic commentary' consisting wholly of questions); C.C.W. Taylor (tr., comm., Oxford, Clarendon Plato series, 1976, rev. 1991)

Gorgias E.R. Dodds (Oxford 1959), with outstanding comm. See also T. Irwin (intr., tr., comm., Oxford, Clarendon Plato series, 1979)

Meno E.S. Thompson (Macmillan, London 1901); R.S. Bluck (Cambridge 1964); R.W. Sharples (text, tr., notes, Aris and Phillips 1985). J. Klein, *A Commentary on Plato, Meno* (Chapel Hill 1965) is not really a commentary but a set of essays, some of them relating to the dialogue

Hippias Major D. Tarrant (Cambridge 1928); P. Woodruff (tr. and comm., Blackwell, Oxford 1982); I. Ludlam, *Hippias Major, an interpretation* (Palingenesia 37, Stuttgart 1991)

Hippias Minor J. Jantzen (Weinheim 1989; German); in English see Whitlock Blundell 1992

Ion No good commentary (J.M. McGregor, Cambridge 1912, is no more than a school book), but see Flashar 1958, Tigerstedt 1969, 13-29. See also the forthcoming volume *Plato on Poetry*, ed. P. Murray (Cambridge Greek and Latin Classics)

Menexenus No good commentary, but see Loraux 1986, Henderson 1975, Coventry 1989

Clitopho S.R. Slings (Amsterdam 1981)

Republic complete comm. by J. Adam, 2 vols. (Cambridge 1920-1, lightly revised by D.A. Rees, 1963); also note B. Jowett and L. Campbell (3 vols., Oxford 1894:

text, notes, essays). Separate editions of books 5 and 10 (text, tr., notes) by S. Halliwell (Aris and Phillips 1993, 1988 respectively)

Timaeus A.E. Taylor (Oxford 1928: intr. and comm. only); F.M. Cornford, *Plato's Cosmology* (London 1937) has tr. and detailed notes

Critias C. Gill, with Atlantis section of *Timaeus*, as *Plato: the Atlantis story* (Bristol 1980)

Minos No comm.; surely spurious

Laws E.B. England (2 vols., Manchester 1921). See also the Budé edition by E. des Places and A. Diès, with contributions from one of the great authorities on Greek law, L. Gernet). The Penguin tr. by T.J. Saunders is valuable. See also works cited in the notes to ch. 10 iii; T.J. Saunders, *Notes on the Laws of Plato* (*BICS* Suppl. 28, 1972)

Epinomis ['After the Laws'] F. Novotny (Prague 1960, in Latin); see also Tarán 1975

Letters (some certainly, and perhaps all, spurious) Translation of all, with essays, by G.R. Morrow, *Plato's Epistles* (Indianapolis 1962); L. Brisson (Flammarion, Paris 1987). See also Edelstein 1966 on the Seventh Letter

Major subsidia:

Ast, D.F. ('Astius') *Lexicon Platonicum* (Leipzig 1835) Selective, with quotations and Latin renderings of words

Brandwood, L. *A Word Index to Plato* (Compendia 8, Leeds 1976). Complete computerised index, but references only

Gigon, O.A. *Platon: Lexikon der Namen und Begriffe* (Zürich 1975)

Perls, H. *Lexikon der platonischen Begriffe* (Bern 1973)

B. Bibliographies and surveys of modern work

Brisson, L., *Lustrum* 20 (1977) 5-304 and, with H. Ioannidi, ibid. 25 (1983) 31-120, 30 (1988) 11-294

Cherniss, H., *Lustrum* 4 (1960) 1-316 and 5 (1961) 321-648

de Magalhaes-Vilhena, V. de, *Le problème de Socrate* (Paris 1952) 475-566

McKirahan Jr., R.D., *Plato and Socrates: A Comprehensive Bibliography* 1958-73 (New York and London 1978)

Morrison, D.R., *Bibliography of Editions, Translations and Commentary on Xenophon's Socratic Writings, 1600-present* (Mathesis Publications, Pittsburgh, Pa., 1988)

Skemp, J.B., *Plato* (Greece and Rome New Surveys 10, Oxford 1976)

For a bibliography of bibliographies (!) see Y. Lafrance, 'L'avenir de la recherche platonicienne' *REG* 99 (1986) 271-92

See also the extensive bibliographies in Kraut's *Companion*, in Laborderie 1978, and in Thesleff's two books (1967 and 1982) (see C below)

C. Modern works

To list every work cited in this book would be pointless. The following list consists of works which seem to me important or regularly useful; it therefore omits many items which appear in the footnotes only rarely or tangentially, and includes some items which are not cited at all. Subjectivity is implicit in the selection, and consequently I have also offered a few comments to help those unfamiliar with some of the authors.

Allen, R.E. (ed.) *Studies in Plato's Metaphysics* (London 1963)

Allen, R.E. *Plato's Euthyphro and the Earlier Theory of Forms* (London 1970)

Amory, F. 'Eiron and eironeia' *C&M* 33 (1981-2) 49-80

Amory, F. 'Socrates the legend' *C&M* 35 (1984) 19-56

Andersson, T. *Polis and Psyche* (Göteborg 1971)

Andrieu, J. *Le dialogue antique: structure et présentation* (Paris 1954). Disappointingly brief on Plato

Annas, J. *An Introduction to Plato's Republic* (Oxford 1981)

Annas, J. 'Plato's myths of judgement' *Phronesis* 27 (1982) 119-43

Annas, J. 'Plato on the triviality of literature', in Moravcsik-Temko 1982, 1-28.

Asmis, E. 'Psychagogia in Plato's *Phaedrus*' *ICS* 11 (1986) 153-72.

Babut, D. *La religion des philosophes grecs* (Paris 1974)

Bambrough, R. (ed.) *Plato, Popper and Politics* (Cambridge 1967)

Barker, A. and Warner, M. (edd.) *The Language of the Cave* (= *Apeiron* 25. 4, Edmonton, Alberta 1992)

Baxter, T.M.S. *The Cratylus: Plato's Critique of Naming* (Leiden 1992)

Benson, H.H. (ed.) *Essays on the Philosophy of Socrates* (Oxford 1992). Anthology of useful essays published since Vlastos's similar 1971 selection

Berg, G.O. *Metaphor and Comparison in the Dialogues of Plato* (Berlin 1904). Not seen

Blank, D. 'The Arousal of Emotion in Plato's Dialogues' *CQ* 43 (1993) 428-39

Bloedow, E.F. 'Aspasia and the mystery of the *Menexenus*' *WS* 8 (1975) 32-48

Blundell: see Whitlock Blundell

Boder, W. *Die Sokratische Ironie in den platonischen Frühdialogen* (Amsterdam 1973)

Booth, Wayne C. *A Rhetoric of Irony* (Chicago and London 1974)

Brandwood, L. *The Chronology of Plato's Dialogues* (Cambridge 1990)

Breitenbach, H.R. 'Xenophon' *RE* ix.A2 (1967) 1569-1928

Brickhouse, T.C. and Smith, N.D. *Socrates on Trial* (Oxford 1989)

Brickhouse, T.C. and Smith, N.D. *Plato's Socrates* (Oxford 1994)

Brisson, L. *Platon, les mots et les mythes* (Paris 1982)

Brock, R. 'Plato and comedy' *Owls to Athens* (Fest. K.J. Dover), ed. E. Craik (Oxford 1990) 39-49

Brunt, P.A. *Studies in Greek History and Thought* (Oxford 1993). Includes challenging essays on 'Plato's Academy and politics' and 'The model city of Plato's *Laws*'

Burkert, W. *Lore and Science in Ancient Pythagoreanism* (orig. 1962, Eng. tr. Cambridge Mass. 1972)

Burkert, W. *Greek Religion* (Eng. tr. Blackwell, Oxford 1985). A masterpiece

Burnyeat, M. 'Socratic midwifery, Platonic inspiration' *BICS* 24 (1977) 7-16, repr. in Benson, *Essays* ... 53-65. Very stimulating

Burnyeat, M. 'Sphinx without a secret' (review of L. Strauss's work) *New York Review of Books* 32 (May 30, 1985) 30-6. Highly entertaining and completely convincing

Carter, L.B. *The Quiet Athenian* (Oxford 1986)

Chadwick, H. *Early Christian Thought and the Classical Tradition* (Oxford 1966)
Chance, T.H. *Plato's Euthydemus: Analysis of What Is and Is Not Philosophy* (Berkeley and L.A. 1992)
Cherniss, H. *The Riddle of the Early Academy* (Berkeley 1945)
Cherniss, H. 'Ancient forms of philosophic discourse', in his *Selected Papers* 14-35
Cherniss, H. *Selected Papers* ed. L. Tarán (Leiden 1977)
Chroust, A.H. *Socrates, Man and Myth: The Two Apologies of Xenophon* (London 1957). Interesting material, but extremely speculative reconstructions of lost works
Classen, C.J. (ed.) *Sophistik* (Wege der Forschung Bd. 187, Darmstadt 1976)
Clavaud, R. *Le Ménexène de Platon et la rhétorique de son temps* (Paris 1980)
Clay, D. 'The tragic and comic poet of the *Symposium*' *Arion* n.s. 2 (1975) 238-61, repr. in J.P. Anton and A. Preus (edd.) *Essays in Ancient Greek Philosophy* ii (Albany, N.Y. 1983) 186-202
Clay, D. 'Plato's first words' *YCS* 29 (1992) (= *Beginnings in Classical Literature* ed. F.M. Dunn and T. Cole) 113-30
Cole, T. *The Origins of Rhetoric in Ancient Greece* (Baltimore and London 1991) Heretical
Collard, C. 'On stichomythia' *LCM* 5 (1980) 77-85
Connor, W.R. 'The other 399: religion and the trial of Socrates' in *Georgica: Greek Studies in Honour of George Cawkwell* (= *BICS* Suppl. 58 (1991)), ed. M. Flowers and M. Toher, 49-56
Cornford, F.M. *Plato's Cosmology* (London 1937)
Coulter, J.A. 'The relation of the *Apology* of Socrates to Gorgias' defence of Palamedes ...' *HSCP* 68 (1964) 269-303
Coulter, J.A. '*Phaedrus* 279a: the praise of Isocrates' *GRBS* 8 (1967) 225-36
Coventry, L.J. 'Philosophy and rhetoric in the *Menexenus*' *JHS* 109 (1989) 1-15
Coventry, L.J. 'The role of the interlocutor in Plato's dialogues: theory and practice' in Pelling 1990, 174-96
Crossman, R. *Plato Today* (London 1937)
Davies, J.K. *Athenian Propertied Families 600-300 BC* (Oxford 1971)
Davies, J.K. *Democracy and Classical Greece* (Glasgow, Fontana, 1978, rev. 1993)
Deman, T. *Le témoignage d'Aristote sur Socrate* (Paris 1942)
Dodds, E.R. *The Greeks and the Irrational* (Berkeley and L.A. 1951). Though one-sided on Plato, still essential reading
Dodds, E.R. *The Ancient Concept of Progress and Other Essays* ... (Oxford 1973)
Dover, K.J. *Lysias and the Corpus Lysiacum* (Berkeley and L.A. 1968)
Dover, K.J. (ed.) *Aristophanes, Clouds* (Oxford 1968)
Dover, K.J. *Greek Popular Morality in the Time of Plato and Aristotle* (Oxford 1974)
Dover, K.J. 'The freedom of the intellectual in Greek society' *Talanta* 7 (1975) 24-54, repr. in Dover, *The Greeks and their Legacy* 135-58. A seminal paper
Dover, K.J. *Greek Homosexuality* (London 1978, rev. 1979)
Dover, K.J. 'Ion of Chios: His Place in the History of Greek Literature' in *Chios*, ed. J. Boardman and C. Vaphopoulou-Richardson (Oxford 1986) 27-37 repr. in Dover, *The Greeks and their Legacy* 1-12
Dover, K.J. *Greek and the Greeks: Collected Papers I* (Oxford 1987)
Dover, K.J. *The Greeks and their Legacy: Collected Papers II* (Oxford 1988)
Edelstein, L. 'The function of the myth in Plato's philosophy' *JHI* 10 (1949) 463-81
Edelstein, L. 'Platonic anonymity' *AJP* 83 (1962) 1-22
Edelstein, L. *Plato's Seventh Letter* (Leiden 1966)
Ehrenberg, V. *The People of Aristophanes* (2nd edn., Oxford 1951)
Ellis, W.M. *Alcibiades* (London and N.Y. 1989)
Enright, D.J. *The Alluring Problem: An Essay on Irony* (Oxford 1986)

Erickson, K.V. (ed.) *Plato: True and Sophistic Rhetoric* (Amsterdam 1979)

Farrar, C. *The Origins of Democratic Thinking* (Cambridge 1988)

Fears, J.R. (ed.) *Aspects of Athenian Democracy* (= *Classica et Medievalia* 40, Copenhagen 1989)

Ferrari, G.R.F. *Listening to the Cicadas: A Study of Plato's Phaedrus* (Cambridge 1987)

Ferrari, G.R.F. see also Winnington-Ingram

Field, G.F. *Plato and his Contemporaries* (London 1930)

Fisher, N. *Social Values in Classical Athens* (London 1976)

Flashar, H. *Der Dialog 'Ion' als Zeugnis platonischer Philosophie* (Berlin 1958)

Frede, M. 'Plato's arguments and the dialogue form' *OSAP* Suppl. 1992, ed. Klagge and Smith, 201-19

Friedlaender, P. *Plato* (Eng. tr. by H. Meyerhoff) (New York 1958-69)

Fritz, K. von. *Platon in Sizilien und das Problem der Philosophenherrschaft* (Berlin 1968)

Furley, W.D. 'The figure of Euthyphro' *Phronesis* 30 (1985) 201-8

Gaiser, K. *Protreptik und Paränese bei Platon* (Stuttgart 1959)

Gaiser, K. *Platons Ungeschriebene Lehre* (Stuttgart 1963)

Gera, D. *Xenophon's Cyropaedia* (Oxford 1993)

Gill, C. 'The death of Socrates' *CQ* 23 (1973) 25-8

Gill, C. 'The genre of the Atlantis story' *CPh* 72 (1977) 287-304

Gill, C. 'Plato and politics: the *Critias* and the *Politicus*' *Phronesis* 24 (1979) 148-67

Gill, C. 'Plato's Atlantis story and the birth of fiction' *Philos. and Lit.* 3 (1979) 64-78

Gill, C. *Plato: the Atlantis Story* (Bristol 1980)

Gill, C. 'Plato on falsehood – not fiction' *Lies and Fiction in the Ancient World* ed. T.P. Wiseman and C. Gill (Exeter 1993) 38-87

Glucker, J. *Antiochus and the Late Academy* (Göttingen 1978)

Görgemanns, H. *Beiträge zur Interpretation von Platons Nomoi* (Zetemata 25, Munich 1960)

Gosling, J.R. *Plato*. Arguments of the Philosophers (London 1973)

Gould, J. *The Development of Plato's Ethics* (Cambridge 1955)

Gower, B. and Stokes, M.C. (edd.) *Socratic Questions* (London and N.Y. 1992)

Graf, F. *Greek Mythology* (orig. Munich-Zurich 1987; Eng. tr. Johns Hopkins 1993)

Grene, D. *Man in his Pride: A Study in the Political Philosophy of Thucydides and Plato* (Chicago 1950, later retitled *Greek Political Theory: The Image of Man in Thucydides and Plato*)

Griswold, C.L. *Platonic Writings, Platonic Readings* (London 1988)

Grote, G. *Plato and the Other Companions of Socrates* (3 vols, London 1865). Though over-long and one-sided (Plato seen as very much a liberal thinker and a man of this world), this is still a remarkable and stimulating interpretation

Grube, G.M.A. *Plato's Thought* (London 1935)

Grube, G.M.A. *The Greek and Roman Critics* (London 1965)

Gundert, H. *Dialog und Dialektik: zur Struktur des platonischen Dialog* (Amsterdam 1971)

Gundert, H. *Platonstudien* ed. K. Döring and F. Preishofen (Amsterdam 1977)

Guthrie, W.K.C. *In the Beginning* (London 1957)

Guthrie, W.K.C. *History of Greek Philosophy* i-vi (Cambridge 1962-81)

Hackforth, R. *The Composition of Plato's Apology* (Cambridge 1933)

Halliwell, S. 'Plato and Aristotle on the denial of tragedy' *PCPS* n.s. 30 (1984) 49-71

Halliwell, S. *Aristotle's Poetics* (London 1986)

Halliwell, S. 'Plato and the psychology of drama' in B. Zimmermann (ed.) *Antike Dramentheorien und ihre Rezeption* (Drama: Beitr. zum antiken Drama und seiner Rezeption, Bd. 1, Stuttgart 1992)

Hansen, M.H. *The Athenian Democracy in the Age of Demosthenes* (Cambridge 1991). Now the standard study

Haslam, M. 'Plato, Sophron and the dramatic dialogue' *BICS* 19 (1972) 17-38

Heath, M. *The Poetics of Greek Tragedy* (London 1987)

Heath, M. 'The unity of Plato's *Phaedrus*' *OSAP* 7 (1989) 151-73, with sequel 'The unity of the *Phaedrus*: a postscript' ibid. 189-91. Cf. reply by Rowe 1989, below.

Heinimann, F. *Nomos und Physis* (Basel 1945)

Henderson, M.M. 'Plato's *Menexenus* and the distortion of history' *Acta Classica* 18 (1975) 25-46.

Hirzel, R. *Der Dialog* (Leipzig-Berlin 1895)

Hornblower, S. *The Greek World 479-323 BC* (London 1983, rev. 1991)

Howland, J. 'Re-reading Plato: the problem of Platonic chronology' *Phoenix* 45 (1991) 189-214

Humbert, J. *Socrate et les petits socratiques* (Paris 1967)

Irwin, T. *Classical Thought* (History of Western Philosophy vol. 1) (Oxford 1989)

Jacoby, F. 'Some remarks on Ion of Chios' *CQ* 41 (1947) 1-17 (repr. in Jacoby 1956, 144-68)

Jacoby, F. *Abhandlungen zur griechischen Geschichtschreibung* ed. H. Bloch. (Leiden 1956)

Jaeger, W. *Aristotle: Fundamentals of the History of his Development* (orig. Berlin 1923, Eng. tr. Oxford 1934, 2nd edn. 1948)

Jones, A.H.M. *Athenian Democracy* (Oxford 1957)

Kahn, C.H. 'Did Plato write Socratic dialogues?' *CQ* 31 (1981) 305-20

Kahn, C.H. 'Drama and dialectic in Plato's *Gorgias*' *OSAP* 1 (1983) 75ff.

Kahn, C.H. 'Plato's methodology in the *Laches*' *Rev. Internat. de Phil.* 40 (1986) 7-21

Kahn, C.H. 'Plato's *Charmides* and the proleptic reading of Socratic dialogues' *JHPh* 85 (1988) 541-9

Kahn, C.H. 'Proleptic composition in the *Republic*, or Why Book 1 was never a separate dialogue' *CQ* 43 (1993) 131-42.

Kerferd, G.B. *The Sophistic Movement* (Cambridge 1981)

Kerferd, G.B. (ed.) *The Sophists and their Legacy* (*Hermes* Einzelschr. 44, Wiesbaden 1981)

Kennedy, G. *The Art of Persuasion in Greece* (Princeton 1963)

Kirk, G.S., Raven, J.E., and Schofield, M. *The Presocratic Philosophers* (2nd edn., Cambridge 1983)

Klagge, J.C., and Smith, N.D. (edd.) *Methods of Interpreting Plato and his Dialogues* (= *OSAP* Supplement, Oxford 1992). One of the better collections

Klibansky, R. *The Continuity of the Platonic Tradition* (London 1939)

Klosko, G. 'Criteria of fallacy and sophistry for use in the analysis of Platonic dialogues' *CQ* 33 (1983) 363-74

Klosko, G. *The Development of Plato's Political Theory* (N.Y. and London 1986)

Kraut, R. *Socrates and the State* (Princeton 1984)

Kraut, R. (ed.) *The Cambridge Companion to Plato* (Cambridge 1992)

Laborderie, J. *Le dialogue platonicien de la maturité* (Paris 1978)

Laks, A. 'Legislation and demiurgy: on the relation between Plato's *Republic* and *Laws*' *CAntiq* 9 (1990) 209-29

Lebeck, A. 'The central myth of Plato's *Phaedrus*' *GRBS* 13 (1972) 267-90

Ledger, G.R. *Re-counting Plato: a computer analysis of Plato's style* (Oxford 1989)

Leisegang, H. 'Platon (1)' *RE* xx (1950) 2342-2537

Lesky, A. *History of Greek Literature* (Eng. tr. by J. Willis and C de Heer) (London and N.Y. 1966)

Lewis, C.S. *The Discarded Image* (Cambridge 1964)

Lintott, A.W. *Violence, Civil Strife and Revolution in the Classical City* (London 1982)

Lloyd, G.E.R. 'Plato as a natural scientist' *JHS* 88 (1968) 78-92

Lloyd, G.E.R. *Magic, Reason and Experience* (Cambridge 1979). Many insights into central issues of Greek thought and society

Loraux, N. *L'invention d'Athènes: histoire de l'oraison funèbre dans la cité classique* (Paris 1981); Eng. tr. *The Invention of Athens: The Funeral Oration in the Classical City* (Cambridge Mass. and London 1986)

Louis, P. *Les métaphores de Platon* (Paris 1949). Arranged by subject matter of the image or comparison, but useful to consult

Ludwig, W. 'Plato's love epigrams' *GRBS* 4 (1963) 59-82

McCabe, M.M. 'Myth, allegory and argument in Plato' in *The Language of the Cave* ed. A. Barker and M. Warner (= *Apeiron* 25.4) (Edmonton, Alberta 1992) 47-68

MacDowell, D.M. (ed. and tr.) *Gorgias, Helen* (Bristol 1982)

Mackenzie, M.M. 'Paradox in Plato's *Phaedrus*' *PCPS* n.s. 28 (1982) 64-76

Mackenzie, M.M. 'The virtues of Socratic ignorance' *CQ* 38 (1988) 331-50

Macleod, C.W. *Collected Essays* (Oxford 1983)

Martin, Josef. *Symposion: Die Geschichte einer literarischer Form* (Stud. zur Geschichte und Kultur des Altertums, 17. 1 and 2, Paderborn 1931)

Meijer, P.A. 'Philosophers, intellectuals and religion in Hellas' in *Faith, Hope and Worship* ed. H.S. Versnel (Leiden 1981) 216-62

Meister, K. 'Stesimbrotus' Schrift über die athenischen Staatsmänner ...' *Historia* 27 (1978) 274-94

Melling, D.J. *Understanding Plato* (Oxford 1987)

Momigliano, A. *The Development of Greek Biography* (Cambridge Mass. 1971, revised 1993). Attractive lectures with wide implications, lavish bibliography

Montuori, M. *Socrates: Physiology of a Myth* (Eng. tr.) (Amsterdam 1981)

Moravcsik, J. and Temko, P. (edd.) *Plato on Beauty, Wisdom and the Arts* (Totowa, N.J. 1982)

Morgan, M. *Platonic Piety: Philosophy and Ritual in Fourth-Century Athens* (New Haven 1990)

Murdoch, I. *The Fire and the Sun: Why Plato Banished the Artists* (Oxford 1977)

Morrow, G.R. 'The demiurge in politics: the *Timaeus* and the *Laws*' *Proc. of Amer. Philos. Assoc.* 27 (1953-4) 5-23

Morrow, G.R. *Plato's Cretan City* (Princeton 1960)

Nock, A.D. *Conversion* (Oxford 1933)

Nightingale, A. Wilson 'Plato's *Gorgias* and Euripides' *Antiope*: a study in generic transformation' *CAntiq* 11 (1992) 121-41

Nightingale, A. Wilson 'Writing/reading a sacred text: a literary interpretation of Plato's *Laws*' *CPh* 88 (1993) 279-300

Nightingale, A. Wilson 'The folly of praise: Plato's critique of encomiastic discourse in the *Lysis* and *Symposium*' *CQ* 43 (1993) 112-30

Nussbaum, M.C. 'Aristophanes and Socrates on learning practical wisdom' *YCS* 26 (= *Aristophanes, Essays in interpretation*, ed. J. Henderson, 1980) 43-97

Nussbaum, M.C. *The Fragility of Goodness* (Cambridge 1986)

Oldfather, W. 'The date of Plato's *Laws*' *AJP* 44 (1923) 275-6

O'Brien, M.J. *The Socratic Paradoxes and the Greek Mind* (Chapel Hill 1967)

O'Meara, D. (ed.) *Platonic Investigations* (Washington DC 1985)

Osborne, C. 'The repudiation of representation in Plato's *Republic* and its repercussions' *PCPS* 33 (1987) 53-73

Osborne, C. 'Topography in the *Timaeus*: Plato and Augustine on mankind's place in the natural world' *PCPS* 34 (1988) 104-15

Ostwald, M., review of Görgemanns 1960, in *Gnomon* 34 (1962) 231-41

Ostwald, M. *From Popular Sovereignty to the Sovereignty of Law* (Berkeley and L.A. 1986)

Parker, R.C.T. 'The origins of Pronoia: a mystery' *Apodosis* (Essays presented to W.W. Cruickshank, London 1992) 84-94

Pease, A.S. 'Caeli enarrant' *Harvard Theological Review* 34 (1941) 163-200

Pelling, C.B.R. (ed.) *Characterization and Individuality in Greek Literature* (Oxford 1990)

Pfeiffer, R. *History of Classical Scholarship from the Beginnings to the Hellenistic Age* (Oxford 1968)

Pohlenz, M. 'Die Anfänge der griechischen Poetik' *Nachrichten von der Gesellschaft der Wissenschaften zu Göttingen*, Phil.-hist. Klasse (1920) 142-78 = Pohlenz, *Kleine Schriften* ii (Hildesheim 1965) 436ff.

Popper, K.R. *The Open Society and its Enemies* (1945; 5th edn. 1966). Of lasting importance

Price, A.W. *Love and Friendship in Plato and Aristotle* (Oxford 1989)

Radermacher, L. (ed.) *Artium Scriptores* (Vienna 1951). Collection of rhetorical and sophistic material

Reeve, C.D.C. *Socrates in the Apology* (Indianapolis 1989)

Riginos, A.S. *Platonica: The Anecdotes Concerning the Life and Writings of Plato* (Leiden 1976). Invaluable and meticulous, though tends to be sceptical of everything on principle

Robinson, R. *Plato's Earlier Dialectic* (Oxford 1941, 2nd edn. 1953)

Robinson, R. *Essays in Greek Philosophy* (Oxford 1969)

Romilly, J. de. *Magic and Rhetoric in Ancient Greece* (Cambridge Mass. 1964)

Rowe, C.J. *Plato* (Brighton 1984)

Rowe, C.J. 'The argument and structure of Plato's *Phaedrus*' *PCPS* n.s. 32 (1986) 106-25

Rowe, C.J. 'Platonic irony' *Nova Tellus* 5 (1987) 83-101

Rowe, C.J. 'The unity of the *Phaedrus*: a reply to Heath' *OSAP* 7 (1989) 175-88

Russell, D.A. *Criticism in Antiquity* (London 1981)

Rutherford, R.B. 'Plato and Lit Crit (review-discussion of Ferrari)' *Phronesis* 33 (1988) 216-24

Rutherford, R.B. *The Meditations of Marcus Aurelius: A Study* (Oxford 1989)

Ryle, G. *Plato's Progress* (Cambridge 1966). Enjoyably written, but full of wild and implausible speculations

Ste. Croix, G.E.M. de *The Origins of the Peloponnesian War* (London 1972)

Saunders, T.J. ' "The RAND Corporation of antiquity"? Plato's Academy and Greek politics' in *Studies in Honour of T.B.L. Webster* ed. J.H. Betts, J.T. Hooker, J.R. Green (Bristol 1986) i. 200-10

Saunders, T.J. *Plato's Penal Code* (Oxford 1991)

Scodel, H.R. *Diairesis and Myth in Plato's Statesman* (*Hypomnemata* 85, Göttingen 1987)

Seeskin, K. *Dialogue and Discovery: A Study in Socratic Method* (Albany, N.Y. 1987)

Segal, C. 'Gorgias and the psychology of the logos' *HSCP* 66 (1962) 99-155

Segal, C. 'The myth was saved: reflections on Homer and the mythology of Plato's *Republic*' *Hermes* 106 (1978) 315-36

Shorey, P. 'Plato's *Laws* and the unity of Plato's thought, i' *CPh* 9 (1914) 345-69

Shorey, P. *What Plato Said* (Chicago 1933). Mostly long paraphrases, of some use

Shorey, P. *Platonism Ancient and Modern* (Berkeley and L.A. 1938)

Sinclair, R.K. *Democracy and Participation in Athens* (Cambridge 1988). Covers a great deal more than the title might suggest; an excellent handbook

Solmsen, F. *Plato's Theology* (Ithaca, N.Y. 1942) Dated in some details, but still unreplaced

Solmsen, F. review of Edelstein 1966, in *Gnomon* 41 (1969) 29-34 = *Kl. Schriften* iii (Hildesheim 1982) 211-16

Solmsen, F. 'Plato on Science' in *Interpretations of Plato: a Swarthmore Symposium* ed. H. North (*Mnem.* Suppl. 50, Leiden 1977) 86-105 = *Kl. Schriften* iii (Hildesheim 1982) 217-36

Sorabji, R. *Time, Creation and the Continuum* (London and Ithaca, N.Y. 1983)

Sprague, R.K. *Plato's Use of Fallacy* (New York 1962)

Sprague, R.K. (ed.) *The Older Sophists* (Univ. of S. Carolina Press 1972)

Stadter, P.A. *A Commentary on Plutarch's Pericles* (Chapel Hill 1990)

Stadter, P.A. 'Pericles among the intellectuals' *ICS* 16 (1991) 111-24

Stalley, R.F. *An Introduction to Plato's Laws* (Oxford 1983)

Stone, I.F. *The Trial of Socrates* (London 1988)

Stokes, M.C. *Plato's Socratic Conversations* (London and Baltimore 1986)

Sullivan, J.P. 'The hedonism in Plato's *Protagoras*' *Phronesis* 6 (1967) 10-28.

Szlezak, T.A. 'The acquiring of philosophical knowledge according to Plato's Seventh Letter' in *Arktouros: Hellenic Studies presented to B.M.W. Knox* ed. G. W. Bowersock, W. Burkert and M.C.J. Putnam (Berlin 1979) 354-63

Szlezak, T.A. *Platon und die Schriftlichkeit der Philosophie* (Berlin 1985; Italian tr. 1989)

Tarán, L. *Academica: Plato, Philip of Opis and the Epinomis* (Philadelphia 1972)

Tarrant, D. 'Imagery in Plato's *Republic*' *CQ* 40 (1946) 27-34. Like her other articles, careful and interesting within its chosen limits

Tarrant, D. 'Colloquialisms, semi-proverbs and word-play in Plato' *CQ* 40 (1946) 109-17

Tarrant, D. 'Style and thought in Plato's dialogues' *CQ* 42 (1948) 28-34

Tarrant, D. 'Plato's use of quotations and other illustrative material' *CQ* n.s. 1 (1951) 59-67

Tarrant, D. 'Plato as dramatist' *JHS* 75 (1955) 82ff.

Tarrant, D. 'The touch of Socrates' *CQ* 8 (1958) 95-8

Taylor, A.E. *Plato, The Man and his Work* (London 1926, often reprinted with minor amendments). Now rather dated; mostly summaries and selective comment

Thesleff, H. *Studies in the Styles of Plato* (Helsinki 1967)

Thesleff, H. *Studies in Platonic Chronology* (Helsinki 1982)

Thesleff, H. 'Platonic chronology' *Phronesis* 34 (1989) 1-26. Afterthoughts to the previous item

Tigerstedt, E.N. *Plato's Idea of Poetical Inspiration* (Helsinki 1969)

Tigerstedt, E.N. *Interpreting Plato* (Stockholm 1977)

Tigner, S.S. 'Plato's philosophical uses of the dream metaphor' *AJP* 91 (1970) 204-12

Turner, F.M. *The Greek Heritage in Victorian Britain* (New Haven and London 1981)

Vickers, B. *In Defence of Rhetoric* (Oxford 1988). Anti-Plato, but valuable for its broad range and independence of mind

Vidal-Naquet, 'Athènes et Atlantide' *REG* 78 (1964) 420-44, revised Eng. tr. as 'Athens and Atlantis: structure and meaning of a Platonic myth' in R.L. Gordon (ed.) *Myth, Religion and Society* (Cambridge 1981) 201-14

Vlastos, G. (ed.) *The Philosophy of Socrates* (N.Y. 1971), reissued as *Socrates*

Vlastos, G. 'The individual as an object of love in Plato' in Vlastos, *Platonic Studies* 1-34

Vlastos, G. *Platonic Studies* (1973; 2nd edn., Princeton 1981)

Vlastos, G. *Plato's Universe* (Oxford 1975)

Vlastos, G. 'Socrates' *Proc. of the Brit. Academy* 74 (1988) 89-111

Vlastos, G. *Socrates: Ironist and Philosopher* (Cambridge 1991). In a class of its own

Vlastos, G. *Socratic Studies*, ed. M. Burnyeat (Cambridge 1994)

Vries, G.J. de. 'Laughter in Plato's writings' *Mnemosyne* ser. iv 38 (1985) 378-81

Walsdorff, F. *Die antiken Urteile über Platons Stil* (Leipzig 1927)

Weil, R. *L'archéologie de Platon* (Paris 1959)

West, M.L. 'Ion of Chios' *BICS* 32 (1985) 71-8

White, N. *A Companion to Plato's Republic* (Indianapolis 1979)

Whitlock Blundell, M. 'Character and meaning in Plato's *Hippias Minor*' *OSAP* Suppl. (1992) ed. Klagge and Smith 131-72. A model study

Wilamowitz-Moellendorff, U. von. *Platon* (2nd edn., Berlin 1920)

Winnington-Ingram, R.P. 'The unity of Plato's *Phaedrus*' *Dialogos: Hellenic Studies Review* 1 (1994) 7-20 (orig. inaugural lecture delivered in 1953), with response by G.R.F. Ferrari, ibid. 21-5

Worthington, I. (ed.) *Persuasion: Greek Rhetoric in Action* (London and N.Y. 1994)

Wright, R. 'How credible are Plato's myths?' in *Arktouros: Hellenic Studies Presented to B.M.W.* Knox ed. G.W. Bowersock, W. Burkert and M.C.J. Putnam (Berlin 1979) 364-71

Zaidman, L.B. and Schmitt Pantel, P. *Religion in the Ancient Greek City* (orig. Paris 1989; transl. and heavily revised by P. Cartledge, Cambridge 1992)

Zeller, E. *Die philosophie der Griechen in ihrer geschichtlichen Entwicklung* i (7th edn. Berlin 1923) and ii. 1 (5th edn. Berlin 1922). Cf. Italian translation with further revision by R. Mondolfo, Florence 1932-

Zeller, E. *Socrates and the Socratic Schools* (Eng. tr. by O.J. Reichel) (London 1868)

Zeller, E. *Plato and the Older Academy* (Eng. tr. by S.F. Alleyne and A. Goodwin) (London 1888)

Zeyl, D.J. 'Socrates and hedonism: *Protagoras* 351b-358d' *Phronesis* 25 (1980) 250-69 = J.P. Anton and A. Preus (edd.) *Essays in Ancient Greek Philosophy* iii (Albany, N.Y. 1989) 5-25

Index

Names of modern scholars are listed only when some substantial comment on their views is made. Otherwise, proper names in the text have been indexed generously, but not exhaustively; items in the notes are only listed when they cannot be traced in the text. Major discussions are listed in **bold** type.

psogos ('denunciation') 236 (*see also* encomium)

psychological criticism of effects of literature, 231-2, 307-8

psychologising, 20, 23

punishment, theory of, 128, 298

puns, *see* wordplay

Pythagoras, 103

Pythagoreans, 17, 38, 90n.54, 152n.17, 171, 191, 216, 273, 286, 292, 296

quibbling, 80

quietism: *see apragmones*

quotations, 75, 307

Raphael, 295

recollection, 4, 117, 257-8

reincarnation, 24, 216, 257-8, 311-12

religion, debates about (*see also* gods), 106

religious dogma and creed, absent in ancient Greece, 228

revolution, political (411 and 404 BC), 106, 151

rhapsodes, 228, 229

rhetoric, rhetorical techniques

  appeal to pity, 32-3

  art of self-preservation, 156-7, 165, 168

  'clever speakers', 32, 267

  contrasted with dialectic, 73, 133, 148, 150, 156-7, 158, 176, 260, 283-5

  defended by Gorgias, 147-8

  handbooks, 264

  its pretensions punctured, 80-1, 164, 170, 183

  listing of services to city, 32

  possibility of a 'purified rhetoric', 67, 156-7, 243, 260

  powers and limits of the art, 67-8, 147

  praise of, 145n.6

  professional speech-writers, 267

  techniques taught by sophists, 104-6

  'unaccustomed as I am', 32

  used by Socrates in the *Apology*, 29-35

'right of the stronger', 106, 160-1, 163-6, 207

Right versus Wrong (in Aristophanes, *Clouds*), 40, 91n.56, 162

Sacred Band of lovers, 185

salt, praise of, 182-3

satire, 81n.27, 205

satyr-plays, 205

science, Plato and, 294

self-knowledge, 124, 174

setting of dialogues 27-8 (*see also* Dialogues, setting)

Seven Wise Men, 136n.34

shame (theme in the *Gorgias*), 148, 149-50, 164, 170

Sicily, Sicilian expedition, 86, 248-9

similes: *see* comparison; imagery

Simmias, 44

Simon the cobbler, 44n.15, 69

Simonides, 14n.28, 75, 126, 212

  his poem discussed in the *Protagoras*, 121, **135-6**, 137

slaves, 219

Slings, S.R. (on *Clitopho*), 99-100

snobbishness, 81, 94, 163, 164, 166

'social contract' theory, 162, 207

SOCRATES

  and Arginusae trial, 33, 60, 109n.28

  appearance of, 58, 184, 199

  as lover (*see also* love), 54, 87, 158-9, 243-8, 254-57, 259-60, 262

  as midwife, 281-2

  as philosophic martyr, 35, 157, 167, 171

  as summed up by Aristotle, 57

  attitude to laws of Athens, 61-2

  attributes knowledge to others, 90, 177, 191

  campaigns, 32, 43, 83, 88, 200

  central figure in dialogues, 7

  compared with a satyr, 201-2

  compared with stingray, 82

  concerned with individuals, 9, 54, 109

  conversation not exposition, 58, 73, 110-11

  criticised by others, 28, 79-80, 81, 82, 96-101, 118-20 (cf. 223)

  daimonion, (divine voice) 43, 53, **59-60**, 89, 255-6

  defended by followers, 43-6, 49

  described as 'sophist', 80, 108

  eclipsed in some later works, 8, 274-6, 277, 300

  emotions of, 87-9, 192-3

  humour and irony, 53-4, 114-15, 265

  ignorance, 74, 90, 265, 282

  importance of his presence, 100, 120, 184-5

  intellectual development, 42n.12

  in Xenophon, 47-56

  makes long speeches, 23, 143, 146-7, 168

  'method', 53, 84-5, 112-15, 125, 132-5, 143, 148-9

  mixes with all sorts of people, 61n.61, 70

  morality of, 48n.25, 54, 63-4, 154, 155-6

  never gets drunk, 197

  no written works by, 2, 9, 58n.51

  not a traveller, 61-2, 109, 256, 275, 297

  objects to rhetoric, 31-3, 73, 74, 84, 140-71 passim, 241-71 passim, 283-5

  personality, 8, 58-9, 282-3